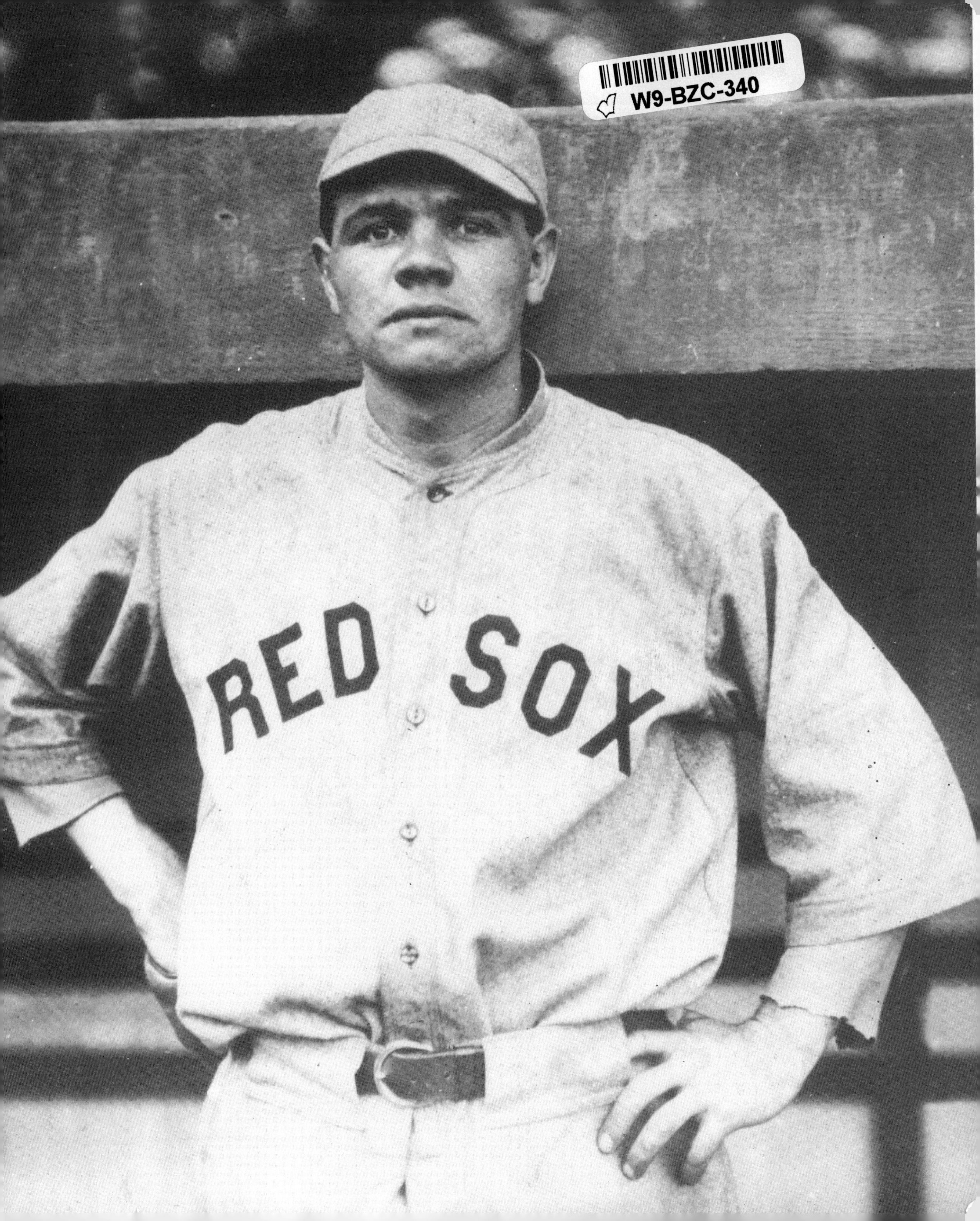
RED SOX

RED SOX CENTURY

RED SOX

THE DEFINITIVE HISTORY OF BASEBALL'S MOST STORIED FRANCHISE

CENTURY

GLENN STOUT and RICHARD A. JOHNSON

HOUGHTON MIFFLIN COMPANY   Boston • New York

First Houghton Mifflin Paperback edition 2004

Copyright © 2000, 2004 by Glenn Stout and Richard A. Johnson

For information about permission to reproduce selections from this book, write to Permissions, Houghton Mifflin Company, 215 Park Avenue South, New York, New York 10003.

Visit our Web site: www.houghtonmifflinbooks.com.

Library of Congress Cataloging-in-Publication Data
    Stout, Glenn.
    Red Sox century : the definitive history of baseball's most storied franchise / Glenn Stout and Richard A. Johnson.
      p. cm.
      Includes bibliographical references (p.) and index.
      ISBN 0-395-88417-9
      ISBN 0-618-42319-2 (pbk.)
      1. Boston Red Sox (Baseball team) — History.
    I. Johnson, Dick, 1955– II. Title.
    GV875.B62 S76 2000
    796.357'64'0977461—dc21   00-026729

Book design by Melodie Wertelet

Printed in the United States of America

KPT 10 9 8 7 6 5 4 3 2 1

Grateful acknowledgment is made to the *Washington Post* for the permission to reprint "Destiny Gets Big Assist from Little" by Thomas Boswell. Copyright © 2003, the *Washington Post*.

To my family, including my parents, Dr. Robert Johnson and Minna Flynn Johnson, my brother Robert, sister Amy, and finally to my home team of Mary, Bobby, and Lizzie, who were brave and loyal during the trying times in which this book was created, and for an unforgettable Saturday afternoon in April together at Fenway Park.

— **RJ**

For Siobhan and Saorla, who make me smile and understand. And for the "Knights of the Keyboard," the good men and women of the Boston press, whose words across a century have made a book like this possible.

— **GS**

CONTENTS

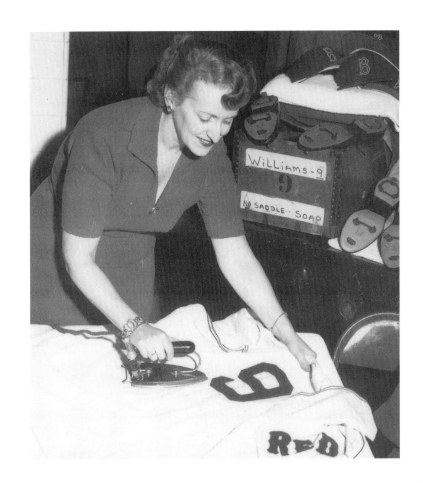

ACKNOWLEDGMENTS

The authors are particularly grateful to the following individuals, some of whom are no longer with us, whose generosity graces these pages. Thanks go to George Altison, Mike Andersen, Mike Andrews, Matt Batts, Dennis Bennett, the staff of the Boston Public Library, Scott Bortzfield, John Bradley, Dennis and Susan Brearley of the Brearley Collection of Rare Negatives, Dick Bresciani and Debbie Matson of the Boston Red Sox, John Brooks, Howard Bryant, Steve Buckley, the members of the Cambridge Cardinals, Bill Campbell, our wonderful editor Susan Canavan, Bernie Carbo, Dick Casey, Mrs. William (Carrigan) Crosby, Scott Chait, Bill Chapman, Marnie Cochran, Meg Cowe, Christine Corcoran Cox, John Cronin and Mark Torpey of the *Boston Herald*, Lib Dooley, John Dorsey, the members of the Douglas Pikes, Jim Dow, Rick Dunfey, Harry Frazee III, Max Frazee, Dan Friedell, Denny Galehouse, Peter Gammons, Julia Yawkey Gaston, Bill Gavin, George Gibson, Russ Gibson, David Halberstam, Kevin Hanover, Sean Heaney, Billy Hitchcock, Sinclair Hitchings, John Hooper, Tim Horgan, Thor Jourgenson, Pat Kelly of the National Baseball Hall of Fame, Alan Kimenker of Baseball Antiquities, Ethel Koneman, Mabrey "Doc" Kountze, Jack Kramer, the staff of the Lamont Library of Harvard University, Jack Lang, Steven Laski, Bill Lee, Bill Littlefield, Al Lizotte, Charles Longley, Ron Marshall, Hugh McGovern, Al McPheely, Catfish Metkovich, the staff of the Milford Public Library, Rick Miller, the members of the Milton/Hyde Park/Braintree A's, Jan Murphy, Karen Murphy and the family of Dick Thompson, the late Jerry Nason, the staff of the National Baseball Hall of Fame Library, David Nevard of the Buffalo Head Society, the staff of the New York Library of the Performing Arts, Dick O'Connell, Dave O'Hara, Mel Parnell, Johnny Pesky, Stephanie

Peters, Rico Petrocelli, Charles P. Pierce, Shel Pierce, Dick Radatz, Vic Raschi, Pat Remington, Bill Rohr, Mark Rucker, Mike Rutstein and everyone with *Boston Baseball*, Luke Salisbury, Henry Scannell, Aaron Schmidt, Dan Shaughnessy, the staff of the Sports Museum of New England — including Brian Codagnone, Tina Anderson, and Gene Valentine — Clifford Stoltze, George Sullivan, Birdie Tebbetts, the Thayer Memorial Library of Uxbridge, Massachusetts, Mrs. Fred Thomas, Dick Thompson, Vera Vaughn, Patrick Warner, Melodie Wertelet, Lisa White, Ted Williams, Saul Wisnia, Bob Wood, and Carl Yastrzemski.

1967 BOSTON RED SOX

INTRODUCTION

For more than one hundred years, the Boston Red Sox have been the most interesting team in baseball. Not the best team, and not the worst, and neither the team most worthy of success nor most deserving of defeat, but by far the most interesting franchise in the history of the game.

Other adjectives also apply. Aggravating. Thrilling. Frustrating. Electrifying. Baffling. They have been all this and more — often at the same time — for a century.

They are a gift to any historian, for in their dramatic history one also finds the story of baseball in the twentieth century. From their birth in 1901 to the present day the great issues of the game — from syndicate baseball and gambling, to the lively ball and the color line, to free agency, wild cards, and more — have all been played out in the continuing story of the franchise. In this story one also discovers a great part of the history of Boston and its people, for Red Sox fans are among the most loyal, passionate — even obsessive — in all sport.

Then there are the players, many of the game's greatest, like Cy Young, Jimmy Collins, Babe Ruth, Jimmie Foxx, Ted Williams, Carl Yastrzemski, Roger Clemens, Pedro Martinez, and Nomar Garciaparra. The Red Sox have participated in some of baseball's greatest games: the first World Series in 1903, the eight-game World Series in 1912, the first American League playoff in 1948, the 1967 World Series, the first divisional playoff in 1978, and game six in both the 1975 and 1986 World Series.

Before this volume, a thorough narrative history of the club has never been compiled. Red Sox history has been told in pieces. The early years of the franchise have never been fully explicated and neither have enormously significant events and personalities in their history, such as the 1918 World Series, Harry Frazee, Tom Yawkey, and the building and rebuilding of Fenway Park. These stories have long been glossed over or told incompletely. Unintentionally, some inaccuracies have ossified into fact and some facts inadvertently swept aside or ignored. Too often, legend has replaced reality.

The best reason one ever has to write a book is to fill a need in the literature of a subject — and to write what one wants to read oneself. The authors first met in 1986 and discovered in the other another who felt the existing written history of the Red Sox was lacking. We discussed the need for this volume and almost immediately began the work that has led to its publication. Over the next fifteen years, while sometimes pursuing other careers and writing hun-

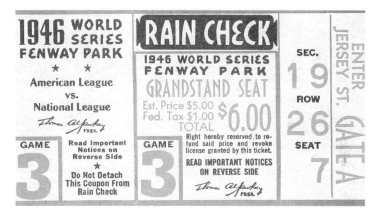

dreds of articles on the Red Sox and other sports topics in sources ranging from official Red Sox publications to national magazines, this project has remained foremost in our minds. While pursuing related subjects over the years, we have collected material and conducted interviews with this book in mind. The narrative we have compiled represents the culmination of thousands of hours of research in primary historical sources — old newspapers and microfilm, interviews with dozens of players, Red Sox personnel, and others — and untold hours of conversation with colleagues and each other. Our goal has always been to decode the events of one hundred years and present it in a coherent and intelligible form.

There is no mystery or riddle to the history of the Boston Red Sox. If there is one point above all others we have tried to address in this book it is that there are reasons they have won when they have, reasons they have lost when they did, and reasons why Red Sox fans have always reacted so strongly to both occurrences. One cannot write of the Red Sox without writing about their fans. But the Sox occupy the unique place they do in the hearts of their followers because of events that have actually happened, not those that have been imagined or corrupted into myth. One won't find discussions of New England's Calvinist sense of loss herein (although we admit to a measure of the Irish tendency to exalt loss, for neither of us is wholly capable of denying our own genealogy). We have tried to stick with the details of history and steered away from drawing too many conclusions apart from fact, extrapolating meaning where there is none, or indulging in intellectual exercises that conceal more than they reveal about the Red Sox. The truth told us more and, in the end, tells a better story.

We asked a number of other writers — those we knew and admired — to lend us their words in regard to the Red Sox, to write whatever they wished to give the reader the advantage of their disparate voices and perspectives. They demonstrate clearly, we believe, that just as the Red Sox are the most in-

SEVENTH GAME = LOST SERIES 4-3

BOSTON RED SOX VS. ST. LOUIS CARDINALS AT SPORTSMAN PARK DATE OCTOBER 15, 1946

PO	A	E	PLAYER	POS. & NO.	1	2	3	4	5	6	7	8	9	10	11	12	AB	R	H	BB	RBI	SB	
			MOSES	9			F.5			3A		K											2 base hits _____
			PESKY	6			4.3		5		9												3 base hits _____
			DiMAGGIO	8	F.9	K		BB		=												Home runs _____
			CULBERSON-R	8																		
			WILLIAMS	7	F.8		F.7	F.9	F.9													Double plays _____
			YORK	3	F.4	K		K													Bases on balls off _____
			CAMPBELL-R ⑨																		
			DOERR	4	E5	F.9		F.8	54												Struck out by _____
			HIGGINS	5	4.3	F.8	6.3	EC SH													Innings pitched by _____
			WAGNER	2	F.7	F.5		F.3			2	0	0							Earned runs off _____
			AB-RUSSELL ⑧ PARTEE	2																	Opponents' hits off _____
			FERRISS	1	F.7	1.3														
			DOBSON ⑤	1			=													Wild pitches _____
			AB-METGOVITCH ⑧																	Balks _____
			KLINGER ⑧	1																Passed balls _____
			JOHNSON ⑧	1							4.3								Winning pitcher _____
			AB-McBRIDE ⑨																	Losing pitcher _____
																						Umpires _____
			TOTALS	R / H	1 / 2	0 / 1	0 / 0	0 / 0	0 / 0	0 / 0	0 / 0	2 / 3	0 / 2					8			Scorer _____
				E/L/OB																	Time of game _____

teresting team in baseball, they are also the most interesting to write about. Were they not, a book of this kind would be impossible, for it is very much built with the words and impressions of hundreds of writers and observers that have preceded us and shared their eloquence.

The photographs and other illustrative material in this book have primarily been selected for their ability to enhance this story, to illuminate our conclusions, and to provide the reader with the faces of history. The photographic record of no other team in baseball has been so adequately recorded and preserved, and the several hundred photographs reproduced in this volume — many of which have never appeared previously in book form — represent the best of many thousands of images considered for inclusion.

For more than a hundred seasons of the Red Sox Century the Red Sox have played baseball in the city of Boston. And for more than one hundred seasons they have alternately frustrated, fascinated, and occasionally completely exasperated their followers. But they have rarely engendered indifference, a not unremarkable accomplishment. It is our hope that this book finds a similar reception among its readers.

Glenn Stout and Richard Johnson
January 2004

THE AMERICANS

1901 | 1902

Boston player-manager Jimmy Collins *(left)* is shown in a posed
action shot at the Huntington Avenue Grounds, circa 1901.
Collins lent the fledgling team instant credibility when he jumped
from the Boston Nationals to the American League franchise.

There were rumors everywhere.

At 'Nuf 'Ced McGreevey's Roxbury saloon — known as "Third Base" because it was "the last stop on the way home" — baseball reigned. Photographs of ballplayers adorned the walls and a mustachioed, life-size mannequin in a baseball uniform greeted guests from above the front door. After every game at the nearby South End Grounds, fans and players gathered at Third Base to discuss the afternoon's activities.

In the winter of 1900 those heated discussions were fueled by rumors of a great change about to take place in the baseball world. The "Hot Stove League" — where baseball was discussed through a long gray winter — was in full swing.

Standing before the carved wooden bar, smoking cigars and quaffing shots of rye and pints of beer, this disparate group of gamblers, working-class Irish, newspapermen, and local politicians included everyone from eventual mayor John "Honey Fitz" Fitzgerald to Sport Sullivan, the man who would later arrange the fix of the 1919 World Series, and Darkhue White, an African-American veteran of the recently completed Spanish American War.

This winter they ignored the burning public issues of the day, such as Carrie Nation's bottle-smashing sobriety crusade and the Philippine insurrection. These baseball kranks, known as the Royal Rooters, talked baseball, although any two men rarely came to agreement on the subject. Arguments and disputes were stopped by McGreevey himself, the ultimate arbiter of this off-season pastime. He'd render his decision by pounding his fist on the bar and calling out, "'Nuf 'Ced!"

Now those good-natured disputes didn't concern the team that played at the South End Grounds — the Bostons. Neither were they about seasons past or the hitting prowess of opposing players.

They talked only of a new league, a new team for Boston, and the one man who was promising to make it happen — Ban Johnson. Baseball in Boston would never be the same.

As much as any other place, the Boston area can lay claim to being the birthplace of baseball. In precolonial New England the earliest forms of the game, adapted from various English ballgames, were such a distraction that Plymouth colony governor William Bradford banned colonists from playing.

But there was no stopping "base ball." The game was played throughout the Northeast but became most popular in New England, where a distinct version known as "the Massachusetts game" emerged. As opposed to the New York version, in the Massachusetts game the batter stood apart from home base and ran around four other bases arranged in an open-sided square. Yet by the Civil War this regional variation gave way to the more popular New York form, from which today's modern game evolved.

In 1871 the Cincinnati Red Stockings, baseball's first professional team, returned to amateur status. But manager Harry Wright, his brother George, and several other players still wanted to play for a living. They moved to Boston and joined the National Association, a confederation of professional teams. When the Association disbanded and the National League was organized in 1876, the Bostons, who dropped the moniker "Red Stockings," joined.

The team was a terror. Over the next twenty-five seasons they won twelve pennants and the allegiance of every baseball fan in the city. In the late 1890s their battles with Baltimore created the game's first great rivalry. In 1897 the Bostons finished first but lost the postseason "Temple Cup" to second-place Baltimore. But their spirited play won the hearts of the men who gathered at McGreevey's. They began calling themselves the Royal Rooters.

They followed the team with obsessive passion, but their blind devotion was soon shaken. In 1899 Brook-lyn Superba manager and part-owner Ned Hanlon created a powerhouse by supplementing the Superbas with former Orioles, a team Hanlon had once managed and still owned a piece of. The new team won the pennant, knocking Boston into second place.

So-called "syndicate baseball" allowed one team to serve the interests of another and undermined the integrity of the game. Yet the National League didn't discourage the practice. Most owners owned shares in the competition. Even the Bostons' president, Arthur Soden, had a piece of the New York team. Although Boston and New York operated independently, the Rooters judged Soden guilty by his association with the concept.

Boston fans felt they'd been cheated out of a championship. They had paid dearly for that privilege and now felt taken for granted. A seat at the South End Grounds cost an outrageous fifty cents. In most other league cities, admission was half that.

The Rooters knew the money wasn't going to Boston's players, many of whom were regulars at McGreevey's, where they made their complaints well known. The National League, after surviving challenges from other competitive organizations like the Union Association, the American Association, and the Player's League, was a monopoly.

Exterior of Third Base, 940 Columbus Avenue. This was the second of McGreevey's Roxbury drinking establishments. The first had been located at 17 Linden Park, with the second opening at the time that both Boston major league teams played in the South End. It is shown here decorated in celebration of the Americans' triumph in the first world series in 1903.

No player earned more than twenty-four hundred dollars a season, a good wage but less than what many could command on the open market. They had no rights. Injured players were cut loose to fend for themselves. The "reserve clause," a standard part of every contract, bound a player to a team for life. If he didn't sign for what he was offered, he didn't play.

Boston players had it even worse. Soden was one of the architects of the reserve clause, and, like most of his kind, he was also a major league skinflint. He not only underpaid his players, he even made them pay for their uniforms and other incidentals. His players held no allegiance to the Boston Base Ball Club.

The Rooters were sympathetic. A spirit of reform was in the air and trade unionism was on the rise. They shared the players' immigrant, working-class roots, and the National League's refusal to recognize the Ballplayer's Protective Association or even listen to their complaints touched a nerve. The boys at McGreevey's were such staunch unionists they even sponsored benefit ballgames to help striking steelworkers.

The National League didn't even realize it was in trouble. Syndicate ball was a real concern. With twelve teams competing for a tainted title, most clubs were out of the race by June, which hurt attendance, affecting everyone. The owners constantly bickered with one another over the smallest issues, such as the hiring of umpires, and were unable and unwilling to work together on anything beyond keeping the players under their collective thumb.

An afternoon at the ballpark was gaining an unsavory reputation. Games were often marred by fights, rough play and obvious cheating. Umpires were regularly attacked by players and fans alike, many of whom only went to the game in the first place to gamble and drink to excess. Ballparks weren't considered appropriate places for respectable women. Even longtime supporters were becoming disenchanted. One of Boston's more influential fans, Arthur "Hi Hi" Dixwell, had become so dismayed that he hadn't attended a game in two seasons.

As the twentieth century approached, the National League was sinking under its own weight, a bloated, twelve-headed dinosaur that was surviving, not be-

Byron Bancroft Johnson, circa 1900. Under the direction of the former sportswriter the minor league Western League became the second major league, the American League. Johnson selected Boston as one of the "beachheads" in his assault on the National League. In time the Boston franchise would become the flagship of his fledgling league.

cause of any cunning on its part, but because it had no predators. Head down in a swamp of problems, the NL was virtually oblivious to its own precarious condition. But now a new animal was sniffing the air.

A tide of red ink during the 1899 season finally got the owners' attention, but it was too late. The four weakest franchises — Cleveland, Washington, Baltimore, and Louisville — were bought out, and the most obvious excesses of syndicate ball done away with.

But that was a poultice on a sport that needed a tourniquet. The surviving clubs went into debt to finance the buyout, then lost more money when attendance plummeted the following year. By the end of the season almost every team in the league was bleeding money.

The Bostons' slide continued as well. They lost twelve of their last fourteen games and played even worse than that. The heart of the one-time championship club was growing old. There was talk of change in what was beginning to be known as "the national pastime."

At McGreevey's, that talk centered around the aspirations of one man.

Byron Bancroft "Ban" Johnson knew baseball from

the ground up. Like most other American boys, he learned the game on the sandlots. While attending college in his native Ohio he played catcher in the days before the chest protector, glove, or mask, when pitchers still threw underhanded from a box. After one year in law school he became a reporter for the *Cincinnati Commercial Gazette*, becoming "sporting editor" in 1887. Baseball was part of his beat, and he gained a reputation as a cogent observer of the professional game's ever-changing landscape.

Johnson soon knew everybody connected with baseball in the Midwest, like Charles Comiskey, manager of Cincinnati's National League team, and owner John Brush. In 1894, at their recommendation, he was named president of a struggling Midwestern minor league, the Western League.

Johnson soon proved he had a facility for organization in a sport that desperately needed just that. He also realized that the men who owned professional baseball teams were, by and large, a vain, inglorious lot who, despite their personal wealth, were easily cowed. Most didn't know baseball and had no vision of its future. All they cared about were profits.

But Johnson was another species entirely, a man ahead of his time, fueled by moral bombast and backed by an uncanny sense of timing. He had a vision for the future of baseball. He seemed to know instinctively that if he made the Western League profitable, the owners would blindly consent to his authority over all other pertinent matters. His office allowed him to influence the game he loved and to wield the kind of power he had so often written about in others for the sports page.

Johnson demanded that the game be played with decorum. Fights and rough play were out. So, too, were franchises in small cities. He became a virtual dictator, ruling his small kingdom just as the boy who owns the bat and ball rules a sandlot game.

Fans responded to the more refined play of the Western League. Attendance soared. As the league became more profitable Johnson's power increased. Individual magnates owned the teams, but Johnson owned the magnates. In the name of profit, they acquiesced to his will.

He turned the league around and it soon became the most lucrative and competitive minor league in the country. It flourished in growing cities like Milwaukee, Detroit, and Indianapolis that the NL ignored.

That wasn't enough for Johnson. He had spent several seasons circling the National League from afar, watching it slip further and further into the mire. Now, he smelled blood. For the National League, his appearance marked the end of an era.

After a successful 1899 season Johnson made his move. He renamed his circuit the American League, a name that shook off the regionalism of the previous moniker and took direct aim at the NL.

Johnson convinced the NL to allow his St. Paul franchise to relocate to the South Side of Chicago, far across town from where the NL Cubs played. He moved another club to Cleveland, which the NL had recently abandoned.

The new American League thrived in 1900. On October 14, 1900, Johnson went in for the kill.

He shook the baseball world by moving Western League franchises in Indianapolis and Kansas City to Baltimore and Washington, two other cities formerly in the fold of the NL, and moving Minneapolis to Philadelphia, where the club would go head-to-head with an existing National League team. His American League was going major league.

In effect, Johnson owned every team in the league, as all eight clubs gave him an option on a majority in the franchise. Such an arrangement, argued Johnson, spread the risk among all and freed him to take action for the collective good. He ran the league and every team in it. The American League became the ultimate syndicate.

He hoped his ambitious moves would force the NL to accept the American League as a coequal. At the NL's annual meeting in November, Johnson asked for an audience to plead the logic of his case.

True to form, the National League underestimated both Johnson's resolve and his finances. They turned him down cold and told him he could go to hell. They then compounded their problem by telling the players, who were trying to organize and wanted some minor reforms in the standard player contracts, to go to hell, too.

Johnson took advantage. He moved quickly, securing land leases for ballparks in the new cities, then spreading the word that his league wasn't going to

The 1900 Boston Nationals led by Hall of Fame manager Frank Selee included many players, such as Collins, Stahl, Freeman, and Dinneen, who jumped to the Americans the following season.

Top row l–r: second baseman Bobby Lowe, unidentified player, outfielder Chick Stahl, outfielder Hugh Duffy, unidentified player.

Middle row l–r: Fred Mitchell, Buck Freeman, unidentified player, pitcher Bill Dinneen, pitcher Ted Lewis, unidentified player.
Bottom row l–r: unidentified player, outfielder Billy Hamilton, pitcher Kid Nichols, manager Frank Selee, shortstop Herman Long, first baseman Fred Tenney, third baseman Jimmy Collins.

recognize the NL's reserve clause and would sign any player not under contract for 1901. That was virtually everyone, for as a monopoly the NL had no incentive to sign any player for more than one season.

At first, the National League didn't take his threat seriously. They naively believed the players would remain loyal. They decided the best way to fend off Johnson was to support a third league designed to go head-to-head against the AL in most American League cities. They thought the new American Association would scare Johnson off and spook his investors.

But Johnson wasn't intimidated. He reacted to the rumored American Association in sporting terms,

saying, "We have the inside rail and no one can pass us," adding, "I do not believe for a minute that any of the [A.A.] clubs have money behind them." The press concurred, soon referring to the paper league as the "Hot Air," "Dream," or "Vapor League."

All Johnson needed to make his grand plan fly were some deep pockets, for he expected his fledgling league to lose money for at least several seasons. One year earlier he had convinced a Cleveland man named Charles Somers, who had made a small fortune in coal, lumber, and shipping on the Great Lakes, to finance the Cleveland franchise. Now Johnson made him his angel.

He gave Somers the meaningless title of league

vice president in exchange for access to his millions. At Johnson's behest, Somers advanced ten thousand dollars to Johnson's old friend Charles Comiskey to start the Chicago White Sox, then similarly backed the Philadelphia franchise until baseball manufacturer Ben Shibe bought him out.

This was just the beginning. Johnson eventually tapped Somers for as much as five million dollars.

Johnson was the talk of the baseball world in the fall of 1900 and 1901. At McGreevey's he was a savior. His David versus Goliath challenge to the NL dominated conversation.

There was as yet no serious talk about a Boston franchise in Johnson's league. He originally planned to stay out of Boston as a show of good faith toward the NL. But when the American Association announced its intention to place a team in the city and secured a lease on some land at Charles River Park for a ballpark, Johnson's plans changed.

As he later told the press, "The hostile attitude of the National League [toward Johnson] is responsible for us adding Boston." He learned that the welcome mat was out and Boston was ripe for an American League takeover. After all, the city was the best baseball town in the country. The rumor mill started cranking, turning talk into reality.

Day in and day out the Royal Rooters and the boys at McGreevey's represented as much as 10 or 15 percent of the crowd at the South End Grounds. No matter how bad the weather was or how poor the team was playing, there was always their second-favorite pastime.

Gambling filled the stands. They bet on everything, from spare change on whether or not the next pitch would be a strike or a ball to thousands of dollars on individual games and series. Without the support of gamblers, the Bostons would have had a hard time filling the stands.

There was little malice in the activity. Gambling was a part of the cultural legacy the primarily Irish group brought to America and as much a part of baseball then as it is to horseracing today.

Few worried about the impact of gambling on the integrity of the game, and politicians aligned with the Rooters had no fear of repercussions. The occasional fix was expected and recognized as one of the few ways players could get even with the owners and add to their income. As long as it didn't become too obvious, gambling was tolerated with a nod and a wink. Besides, over the course of a season a few fixed contests tended to even out. Really big games were usually played on the square.

The Rooters' support was important, for they set the tone for the rest of Boston fandom. Local newspapers spent nearly as much ink reporting on the Rooters as they did on the Bostons. In fact, most of the newspapermen *were* Rooters. 'Nuf 'Ced McGreevey was a celebrity, better known than most players. If the Rooters decided to support the new team, its success was virtually assured.

All this filtered back to Johnson, and he set his sights on Boston. He sent a popular emissary to pave the way. Connie Mack, a former player turned manager and part-owner of the league's proposed Philadelphia franchise, came to Boston in mid-January looking for a place to build a ballpark. If he succeeded, Johnson planned to drop plans for a Buffalo franchise in favor of one in Boston.

Over the course of a long catching career for Washington and Philadelphia of the NL, the East Brookfield, Massachusetts, native had remained popular in his home state. Although Mack now lived in Philadelphia he had been careful not to cut his local ties. In a tragic incident in January of 1900, popular Boston catcher and fellow Brookfield resident Martin Bergen went insane and axed to death his wife and two young children before slitting his own throat. Mack, not Arthur Soden, spearheaded a drive to erect a monument to the former ballplayer.

The Rooters fell all over themselves welcoming Mack to town. In less then two days he found the perfect place for a new ballpark.

The existing South End Grounds sat on the north side of Columbus Avenue, on approximately the same site now occupied by a parking garage near the Ruggles Street MBTA station. The park was bound on the west by Walpole Street, on the north by the New Haven Railroad repair yard and roundhouse, and on the east by Carter Field, an amateur diamond.

Built in 1888 on the site of the original home of the Red Stockings, the park was a palace that featured a double-decked grandstand adorned with six spires. But after it burned in 1894, a much smaller, less comfortable, and less distinctive single-decked park was rebuilt in its place.

The surrounding neighborhood was known as "the Village," a working-class community of Irish immigrants who worked in the many nearby factories, the railroad, and in the summer, the ballpark. On the edge of the neighborhood, almost directly opposite the South End Grounds across the tracks on the south side of Huntington Avenue, was an open tract of land leased by the Boston Elevated Railroad. The site had been used in the past by traveling carnivals and Buffalo Bill's Wild West Show.

Boston Elevated had subleased the land for use as a Victorian-era water park known as "the Chutes." Patrons rode down a wooden slide that shot them into the waters of an artificial pond. In the winter, the pond was used for ice skating. Today, it is occupied by Northeastern University's athletic facility.

Mack had found the perfect location. The land wasn't prime real estate — its proximity to the rail yard precluded many other uses — so the price was right. And it was within hitting distance of the South End Grounds, sending a none-too-subtle message to the Bostons and satisfying Johnson's ego. The old

park was certain to suffer in comparison to the planned new facility.

The Rooters were delighted and may have had a role in steering Mack to the site. Locating the new team in the neighborhood meant they could continue to use McGreevey's as their base of operations.

The only glitch was money. No local investor was willing to risk the several hundred thousand dollars required to build the new ballpark and get a new club up and running. Although Johnson was bullish on the league's prospects, even he had to admit that most clubs would lose money for the first several seasons.

So Johnson turned back to his angel, Charles Somers, and offered him a controlling interest in the new Boston team to go along with his piece of the Cleveland franchise. Somers bit and agreed to finance the new team.

Plans quickly proceeded from rumor to reality. On January 18, a *Boston Post* headline read "Rival Baseball Nine for Boston."

Soden wasn't impressed. "I can see only one termination of this state of things," he sniffed to a reporter the next day, "the newcomers will have to surrender . . . Baseball is not the attractive investment it was."

Somers and Johnson thought otherwise, and on January 28, 1901, Johnson made it official. At a league

Groundbreaking ceremony for the construction of the Huntington Avenue Grounds, circa 1901. Note that this photograph has been frequently misidentified as the groundbreaking for Fenway Park. Rooter Hi Hi Dixwell is holding the shovel. 'Nuf 'Ced McGreevey is sixth from left.

meeting in Chicago, he formally dropped the Buffalo franchise in favor of a new team in Boston. On that date, the team that would eventually become the Boston Red Sox was born.

Meanwhile, plans for the new ballpark at an estimated cost of thirty-five thousand dollars proceeded apace. According to the press, the new park, soon to be dubbed the "Huntington Avenue Grounds," would be a wood-frame facility whose main grandstand would be faced with concrete, making it appear far more substantial. Bleachers down each foul line complemented a single-tiered, roofed, three-section grandstand, which included a covered lobby underneath it to protect fans during rain delays. Although the original design called for the remaining stands to be covered by a canvas awning, as one newspaper reported, "doing away with the necessity of umbrellas," this innovative feature was not added for some time.

The players would have both a dressing room and a locker room, as well as "shower baths," a plumbing innovation just coming into vogue. Apartments were placed under the grandstand for the comfort of team management, and the press was accommodated by their own room with lockers, a feature the *Post* called "an innovation in Boston that will be appreciated."

With less than three months remaining until Opening Day, plans were quickly drawn up, submitted to the city, and approved. The tight schedule necessitated only one small change. Initially, the grandstand was supposed to be placed on the corner of Huntington Avenue and Rogers Avenue, with the left-field line running parallel to Huntington Avenue. But the pond on that corner needed to be drained, filled, and graded. Afraid that bad weather might stall the process, the orientation of the park was turned so the left-field line ran perpendicular to Huntington Avenue, allowing work on the grandstand to proceed simultaneously with any site work.

Now all the new team needed were ballplayers. Johnson knew exactly where to find them.

The National League's arrogance toward their own players made Johnson seem like some kind of reformer. Since the AL recognized neither the reserve clause nor the NL's twenty-four-hundred-dollar salary ceiling, every player in the league was, in theory anyway, available.

But Johnson didn't underestimate the ignorance of his own owners. To make sure they wouldn't bid against each other and drive salaries too high, Johnson distributed the rights to the best veteran talent.

He didn't even try to be fair. For the AL to survive, franchises in Chicago, Philadelphia, and Boston had to win immediately. They received the rights to the best players. Collegians, minor leaguers, and holdovers from the existing American League would fill the rest of the league roster.

The AL Boston team received the rights to most of NL Boston's veteran players. Yet one man stood out above all others. No one would be more important to the success of the new team than the acknowledged star of the Bostons and the best player in the city, third baseman Jimmy Collins.

The new American League club knew that if they could sign Collins, many of his teammates would follow suit. On Boston's behalf, Mack offered him four thousand dollars to play third and manage the new team, a role that then also included signing subsequent players to contracts, much like today's general manager.

The NL Bostons realized too late that Collins was prepared to jump teams and he turned down their last-minute offer. Charles Somers had guaranteed Collins's salary even if the new league failed.

On February 11, 1901, Collins became the first player under contract for the brand-new team. "I like to play baseball," he told reporters, "but this is a business with me . . . I look out for James J. Collins."

Other signings followed quickly. Collins focused his efforts on his close friends, center fielder Chick Stahl and slugger Buck Freeman.

Like Collins, Stahl came up by way of Buffalo, and in four major league seasons possessed a batting average of more than .300. He was a fine fielder and, like Collins, was particularly popular with female fans. Freeman, who could play both outfield and first base, was one of the game's great sluggers. With Washington in 1899, he took advantage of a short porch in right field to crack a then-remarkable twenty-five home runs.

Collins also wanted pitcher Bill Dinneen. Although Kid Nichols, at age thirty-one and already the winner of more than three hundred games, was the ace of the Bostons, Dinneen, six years younger, appeared ready to blossom.

Another factor may have influenced Collins's choices about whom he offered a contract. A 1902 article in *The Sporting News* stated that in the late 1890s the Bostons' clubhouse, much like the city, had been split along religious lines. With the Irish-Catholic Collins at the helm of the new team, he targeted fellow Catholics, tolerant non-Catholics, or those players for whom baseball was the only pertinent religion.

In early March Dinneen announced he had signed with the new team, then backed off when the Bostons sweetened their offer and advanced him part of his salary. For the next several weeks he waffled back and forth.

On March 9, 1901, the new team broke ground for the new ballpark. Honored guests at the ceremony included Boston's rooting royalty. While the champagne flowed, Rooter "Hi Hi" Dixwell, so named for his signature cheer, was given the honor of turning over the first spade of earth.

THE FIRST THIRD BASEMAN

After playing two seasons with Buffalo of the Eastern League, in 1895 Niagara Falls native Jimmy Collins joined the NL Bostons as an outfielder. In the opening weeks of the season he didn't hit and by mid-May was riding the bench. Rather than release him, in the kind of deal that made many question the integrity of the league, Boston loaned him to Louisville's National League team, subject to recall at the end of the year.

Collins flourished with the last-place club. And in midseason, he changed the way the game was played forever.

One day that season the old Baltimore Orioles — masters of strategic, "scientific" inside baseball — decided to test young Louisville third baseman Walter Preston with the bunt. He missed the first and came unglued, erring on the next three as the Orioles circled the bases. In desperation, Preston was banished to the outfield and Collins called in to play third.

Until that moment, third base was played much like first base. The fielder hung back close to the bag, guarding the line, leaving the shortstop to catch all but those balls hit directly down the line or popped foul. Batters took advantage of such stationary play with the bunt — at the time, perhaps the game's most dangerous offensive weapon. Unless the batsman bunted the ball too hard, he had a good chance of reaching base.

Collins was unfamiliar with the position, but as he said later, "I came to the conclusion there was only one solution to this bunting game. A third baseman had to give himself a chance against those fast guys . . . So I played them at the edge of the grass."

The first Oriole hitter, John McGraw, squared to bunt and Collins reacted. He charged hell-bent toward the plate, fielded the ball with his bare hand, and then threw to first while on the run. Out.

The Orioles refused to believe what they had just seen. No one had ever done that before.

The next batter tried another bunt. Collins swooped in once more and nailed the runner. As Collins later recalled, "I had to throw out four bunters in a row before the Orioles quit bunting that afternoon."

He never played the outfield again, nor did Preston return to third. For the remainder of the season Collins was a fielding wizard, as he played in or out, on the line or away from the base according to the situation. Other players took notice, and Collins's revolutionary style soon became the standard. A measure of his talent is that he still holds the NL record for most chances accepted by a third baseman in a single season, a remarkable 601, set in 1899.

Boston traded away veteran third baseman Billy Nash and recalled Collins in 1896 and discovered he was nearly as good a hitter as he was a fielder. Collins became the biggest star since Michael "King" Kelly thrilled fans in the 1880s. Boston fans naturally loved his tough Irish demeanor, smart play, clutch hitting, and daring baserunning. So did his teammates. On the championship clubs of 1897 and 1898, Collins was the best player on the field and the acknowledged team leader.

After he jumped to the Americans, his stature only increased. As player-manager he led the club to five straight winning seasons, two pennants, and one world championship while still playing the best third base in all baseball. Until Pittsburgh Pirate star Pie Traynor emerged in the late 1920s to set a new standard for fielding and hitting at third base, Collins was considered, without question, the best third baseman in the history of the game. ⚾

THE ROOTERS' VIEW

Boston fans are different. They believe they can accomplish the impossible, for in their hearts, Sox fans *always* expect their team to win. Yet over time they have simultaneously learned to *expect* them to lose. And the Red Sox, in an apparent contradiction that is both unique and endearing, have somehow managed to become a team that fulfills both prophecies.

To Red Sox fans, the prospect of winning a championship, that glorious carrot that has hung so tantalizingly close for generations, has always seemed the logical result of their determined and unyielding support. Historically, they grew accustomed to winning from the outset and passed that sense of entitlement down like an inexhaustible family inheritance. The right to win is damn near a birthright, a Boston rooter's promised homeland, one that with each passing year the imagination makes ever more magnificent. "Wait 'til next year" isn't a plea in Boston, but a promise they demand be fulfilled.

That's what makes baseball in Boston different than baseball in other cities. Baseball's not just a game in Boston; it's something more. Fans of most other teams expect to lose much of the time, which makes winning an enjoyable, happy accident.

But in Boston, it's quite the opposite. Since fans here believe they deserve to win, losing, particularly in more recent seasons, means more than just the loss of a simple game. Here, losing isn't a transient event. It's a permanent affront, a challenge, an insult and a slur. It is truly a loss, for losing deprives Boston fans of something they feel they've already earned.

Losing — particularly the way Boston has lost, which always seems to be in the most excruciating fashion and always when victory has appeared most certain — poses a moral question that challenges a way of thinking and leads fans into self-doubt. *What have we possibly done to deserve this?* Losing threatens an entire system of beliefs that at its worst reveals the potential breakdown of the moral universe. *It's just not fair.* Losing keeps you awake and makes you crazy. In Boston, losing *hurts*.

And that's why in Boston, in a funny way, any victory that doesn't result in a world championship isn't really winning at all but just another form of loss, which makes the experience of rooting for the Red Sox a peculiarly devout experience. That's what makes Boston fans special; they are different, and they know it. ⊘

Interior of 'Nuf 'Ced Mc-Greevey's saloon Third Base, circa 1906. Located at 940 Columbus Avenue in Boston, Third Base was as much a salon as a saloon. A generation of Bostonians drank under light fixtures made from the bats of stars such as Hugh Duffy and Napoleon Lajoie while discussing politics and baseball. Proprietor McGreevey would end all arguments by pounding on the bar and shouting "'Nuf 'Ced."

He was a wise choice. Nabbing the influential Rooter was nearly as important as securing Collins. His appearance at the ceremony, and the accompanying photograph in the *Boston Herald*, indicated that the Rooters were in the new club's corner.

A few days later a local sportswriter conceded as much, writing, "the adherents of the American League team outnumber the supporters of the National by four to one, and I think if I had said eight to one I would not have been making it too strong." For as Dixwell dropped that first shovel of dirt back to the ground, the fortunes of Boston's National League team were similarly buried. For the next fifty years they would be the second choice of Boston fans.

A few days later Somers sold his interest in the Cleveland club to focus on Boston and deflect obvious charges that the new league was simply syndicate baseball of a different order. The club signed new players almost every day, primarily minor leaguers, like shortstop Fred Parent and second baseman Hobe Ferris, who were procured from teams in Norwich and New Haven, Connecticut, and outfielder Charley Hemphill, from Kansas City.

The team still needed a pitcher. While Dinneen flip-flopped, Collins looked to the west, to veteran pitcher Denton True "Cy" Young of St. Louis, one of the game's great, though aging, pitchers.

Young disliked St. Louis and signed with Boston for thirty-five hundred dollars on March 19. One local writer still enamored of Dinneen commented that Young would make "a great second string."

As soon as Young signed so did both St. Louis catchers. Lou Criger served as Young's personal catcher in St. Louis and would do the same in Boston. A defensive wizard known for his incessant chatter, Criger was chronically out of the lineup because of one malady or another and couldn't handle the role alone. So the club also signed Ossee Schreckengost, a better hitter and one of the game's great characters. He later served as the catcher and roommate of the eccentric star pitcher Rube Waddell of the Philadelphia A's. The two shared a bed, leading Schreckengost to insert a clause in his contract banning Waddell from eating crackers in bed.

Dinneen finally decided to stay in the NL, concluding that the Bostons retained "some moral right to my services," although he commented that "I like the chances of the American League. They will win out for sure." So the upstarts signed yet another pitcher from the Bostons' roster, veteran George "Nig" Cuppy, who earlier had teamed with Young in Cleveland.

On March 21, the American League announced a 140-game schedule to begin on April 24, one week after the National League. If the National League had yet to regard the new circuit as a threat, they did now. In Boston, Chicago, and Philadelphia, the three cities that now sported teams in each league, the AL planned to go head-to-head against the incumbents, often playing in the same city on the same day.

Those plans made obvious what had long been rumored — Johnson was in a war and didn't plan to lose. His clubs in Boston, Philadelphia, and Chicago had to win immediately. At least for the first season, the entire league would be Johnson's syndicate.

That didn't bother Boston's Rooters. As long as *they* benefited, syndicate ball was fine. More than anything else, they wanted, and even demanded, a championship team. Nothing less would be satisfactory. Ever.

Away from the ballpark, the early rooters, royal and otherwise, were distinguished by where they were from or what they did. But that didn't matter much at the ballpark. There were few other places in the city where working men and those more powerful and important shared equal footing and the same goal.

The Bostons' performance in 1899 and 1900 precipitated a crisis. What had once made being a Boston fan so special — winning — became remote. The Rooters felt robbed and missed the attention. They looked to the new team as a source of salvation.

On March 28, those players signed by Collins in and around Boston boarded a train at South Station and headed south for spring training at the University of Virginia in Charlottesville. In a curious coincidence, the Bostons embarked at nearly the same time, heading for Norfolk, and the two teams actually shared the same train from New York to Washington.

Neither team had a nickname, nor would they for several more seasons. Both were simply called "the Bostons," although to differentiate between the two clubs, fans, sportswriters, and players commonly began referring to the NL entry as "the Nationals," and their American League counterparts as "the Americans." Other nicknames, such as the Pilgrims, Puritans, Plymouth Rocks, Somersets (so named after owner Charles Somers), or Collinsmen (after manager Collins) for the AL team and the Beaneaters, Triumvirs, or Seleemen (after manager Frank Selee) for the Nationals, were convenient inventions of the press. Their subsequent use by many historians is misleading. None of these nicknames was ever widely used by either fans or players.

When the Americans arrived in Virginia, they followed the standard training regimen of the day. Players worked practicing fielding and hitting in the morning and went on long hikes through the countryside in the afternoon.

They played their first game on April 5, shutting out the University of Virginia 13-0. Then the rains came and it was nearly a week before they were able to resume practice outside. Although Collins's day-to-day lineup was virtually set, there were still questions concerning the pitching staff and the one or two substitutes that would make the final fifteen-man roster.

The big news at camp was an ungainly young giant from Cambridge, rookie Larry McLean. At 6-foot-4, McLean towered over most of his teammates, most of whom were 6 or 8 inches shorter. A catcher and first baseman, McLean wowed his teammates with his long hitting and strong arm. He was the Americans' first phenom.

In mid-April, as the Americans prepared to break camp and head north, the club made a few final roster changes. Dissatisfied with the pitching staff apart from Young, the club inked pitcher Ed "Parson" Lewis, who had twice won over twenty games for the Nationals but had fallen out of favor with the team. Nig Cuppy, Cambridge rookie Fred Mitchell, and the

THE GAME IN 1901

When the Red Sox first started playing baseball, it was a different game. Although the rules were much the same as they are now, conditions under which the game was played were radically different.

The field itself was often little more than just that — roughly cut, uneven, and often pockmarked with holes and strewn with gravel. Wet and soft in the spring, after baking under the summer sun it turned as hard as concrete, then became a dust bowl as the sparse grass turned to straw.

Fielding baseballs on such a surface was a challenge. Players wore gloves barely the size of their hands, designed more for protection than to help with catching, making every hit and catch an adventure and demanding that players used both hands. Outfielders played so shallow that if a player didn't run hard to first or second on a hit, he risked being forced out by a quick throw.

Until after World War I, the same ball was used inning after inning and often not replaced until it was belted into the stands and not returned, or lost. Each inning it turned darker and softer, becoming a little more difficult to hit. The thick, heavy bats made of hickory, maple, or ash were not so much swung at the ball as maneuvered. A fly ball that traveled 300 feet was a deep drive, 350 feet truly prodigious, and 400 feet almost unheard of. Players wore heavy, wool flannel uniforms that were washed perhaps once a week and usually rank with sweat and dirt. Players wore white so-called "sanitary" socks beneath their colorful wool outer socks because the dye could infect open spike wounds and blisters.

Scientific "inside baseball" ruled. The bunt, the hit and run, and the stolen base were major offensive weapons. Home runs hit over the fence were rare, seeming more an accident. Strikeouts were a sign of selfishness. A single umpire, or sometimes two, tried to keep order.

Starting pitchers were expected to pitch the entire game regardless of the score, then pitch again two or three days later. They spit on the ball, slathered it with slippery elm, cut it on belt buckles and spikes, and aimed at heads without helmets.

Injuries hardly mattered. Spike wounds were rubbed in the dust, abrasions left to seep through uniforms, and sore arms ignored until they disrupted sleep. A staph infection could mean a death sentence. But if you couldn't play, you didn't get paid. So you played.

Ah, but it was the major leagues. ⌀

optimistically named Win Kellum, late of Indianapolis, rounded out the staff.

In the outfield, Stahl was flanked in right by Charlie Hemphill, another former member of the Cleveland/St. Louis syndicate, and Holyoke's Thomas "Buttermilk Tommy" Dowd, who had played the previous ten seasons without distinction for seven teams in two leagues.

The Nationals got a jump on the start of the season, opening at home on April 19 against New York. Kid Nichols threw a shutout before more than six thousand fans on a cold gray afternoon and they won, 7-0, thus giving Soden cause to celebrate. With the Americans several weeks away from their home debut since their ballpark was still under construction, the old club hoped to steal the headlines, and the crowd, with their quick start.

But rain washed out most of the NL schedule over the first week. In New York, Opening Day was put off every day for a week. Whatever edge the early start gave to the senior circuit was lost.

The Americans were supposed to open in Baltimore on April 24. Yet they too were soaked by the weather. Finally, on April 26, the skies cleared and Boston's Americans took the field for the first time.

Baltimore welcomed both teams as if the game were a Temple Cup rematch. Many of the players, like the Orioles' John McGraw, Steve Brodie, and Wil Robinson, and Collins, Stahl, Freeman, and Cuppy of Boston, were, in fact, veterans of the postseason war between the two old clubs. Ten thousand fans turned out at the park and thousands more lined the streets to watch a parade of ballplayers from the Eutaw House hotel (near today's Camden Yards) to Oriole Park, which had been spiffed up for the new team.

During a pre-game ceremony McGraw and Collins were given elaborate floral presentations, and Ban

The first Boston Americans team, 1901, as identified in the *Boston Post.* *Top row l–r:* Fred Mitchell, Harry Kane, Tommy Dowd. *Middle row l–r:* Charlie Hemphill, Fred Parent, Kit McKenna, Hobe Ferris, Win Kellum, Nig Cuppy, Buck Freeman. *Front row l–r:* Ossee Schreckengost, Lou Criger, Larry McLean, Jimmy Collins, Cy Young, Chick Stahl. (Note: McKenna never appeared in the regular season.)

The Boston Americans catching corps, circa 1901. *(l–r)*: Ossee Schreckengost, Larry McLean, and Lou Criger. In the inaugural season of 1901 Schreckengost and Criger mostly split the catching duties, with Criger serving as Cy Young's personal catcher. Cambridge, Massachusetts, native McLean played sparingly in reserve duty.

Johnson, in attendance with Charles Somers, threw out the first pitch.

But for Boston fans the fun soon stopped. Tommy Dowd led off against Oriole ace Joe "Iron Man" McGinnity, who, despite suffering from the final stages of malaria, induced him to ground back to the box and quickly retired the Americans.

Win Kellum was Boston's surprise starter. Collins preferred Cy Young, but on his way north the pitcher took a side trip to St. Louis to take care of personal business and contracted tonsillitis.

McGraw led off for Baltimore and brought the crowd to its feet as he banged a double off the right-field fence. Baltimore led 4-0 in the fourth before Jimmy Collins banged out Boston's first-ever hit, a double down the left-field line. He scored the Americans' first run a moment later when Buck Freeman singled him home.

Baltimore won going away, 10-6. Young took the mound the next day but in his weakened condition didn't make it out of the sixth inning and lost 12-6.

The Americans next traveled to Philadelphia, and Connie Mack's Athletics sent them to their third consecutive defeat. In the fourth game of the season, Cy Young took the mound still searching for Boston's first victory.

The Athletics jumped ahead 6-1, and another loss seemed likely. But as Young settled down the Americans chipped away at the lead. Entering the ninth inning, Philadelphia still led 6-4.

With Stahl on first and two out, Buck Freeman got a pitch he liked and turned on the ball, driving it long and deep to right field. It carried over the fence and, as one paper reported, "when last seen was headed south in the clutches of an urchin who failed to leave a card." The home run, Boston's first ever, tied the game.

The game entered extra innings, and in the tenth Hemphill knocked in one run with a single, and Stahl drove in another with a sacrifice fly. Young remained strong in the tenth, and he and Boston collected their first victory, 8-6.

Unfortunately, not even the venerable Young could pitch every day. Kellum was blasted in his second start, and it became clear that unless Young was on the mound for Boston or the Americans scored runs in bunches — a franchise trait still true today — victory would be hard to come by.

The team muddled its way toward Boston, usually winning under Young and losing under anyone else. Fortunately, the Boston Nationals were doing no better. By the time the Americans opened their home season on May 8 at the Huntington Avenue Grounds, both teams had identical 5-5 records.

Thousands of fans arrived early only to find long lines, as speculators took control of the gate and purchased most tickets in huge blocks, which they then resold at five or ten times the original price to the anxious crowd.

The park impressed everyone. As the *Post* remarked, "Everything inside the high fence was as new as a spring tulip."

The playing field was huge. The diamond was fully 90 feet from the surrounding stands, giving players plenty of room to snare foul balls. The fence in center was 530 feet from home plate and 320 feet down the foul lines, leading the *Post* to sniff that the new park would do away with any "'fake' home runs."

Although the stands seated only about nine thousand fans, thousands more could easily be accommodated on the field itself, standing behind ropes in the outfield and in foul territory. At the turn of the century, a drive of more than 350 feet was still considered monumental. A few thousand fans in the nether reaches of the field were of no consequence, and on this day, several thousand spectators stood and considered themselves lucky.

The new park had been built from scratch in only three months. The infield was already green with new sod. The only signs of construction were the bare, compacted earth of the outfield and some debris piled up in distant corners.

No matter, there was celebration in the air. As soon as the team appeared on the field, the festivities began.

As the Boston cadet band played a selection of popular tunes, two carriages bearing famous players from Boston's baseball past rolled from center field to home plate. The crowd greeted the old-timers by waving thousands of small American flags distributed by the club. The Americans quickly got loose, then took the field. As Charles Somers and his wife watched from seats behind the Boston bench, Jimmy Collins received the obligatory floral wreath, courtesy of the Rooters, which one paper gushed "slightly expressed the great regard lovers of baseball both in the profession and out have for the lad from Buffalo, the greatest third baseman of this or any other age, as unassuming as the sprig of maidenhead fern that trailed from the flowery horseshoe." Whoo.

"Hi Hi" Dixwell threw out the first ball as the Americans continued to court fans of the old Nationals. The strategy worked, for one paper reported "People were there from Bangor Me. to Newport R.I. and about every city between those points . . . In the crowd were clergymen, business men, professional people, ex ballplayers, old time fans, new recruits and many who had not seen a game in years." There were also hundreds of women, who the *Post* reported "warmed up the interior of the grandstand and seemed to rob the east wind of its chill."

Cy Young stood on the mound. As he prepared to throw the first real pitch for the new team in their new ballpark, a man with a megaphone stood behind home plate and announced the hitter. Some found the innovation distracting, as Walter Barnes of the *Boston Post* later complained that "his attempts to be witty were cheap . . . The crowd had the good sense

enough not to laugh." As the crowd roared, Young wound up and threw the ball home. The first Philadelphia hitter grounded to Collins, and Young quickly made short work of the rest. Boston rolled to a 12-4 win behind five triples and Freeman's inside-the-park home run.

After the game, the players settled into the city they would call home. Most boarded for the season only a few blocks up Huntington Avenue from the ballpark at the Putnam Hotel, known to everyone as "Put's." They soon became familiar figures in the neighborhood, greeted by young boys and "Baseball Annies" — female admirers — whenever they stepped outside.

There were plenty of other distractions. For those of a more refined nature, the Opera House and Symphony Hall were but a short walk away. For the ballplayers, nearby saloons provided the necessary libations.

Those seeking pleasures of a different sort were likewise accommodated. The collection of brownstones stuck between the Fens and Massachusetts Avenue housed Boston's most notorious red-light district, as nearly every street sported one or more brothels, a situation that had been tolerated by the local authorities with a nod and a wink for years, despite reform efforts.

Boston fans were thrilled with the team's first home win. The next day, another three thousand fans turned out as the club won again, 9-3, behind Cuppy.

Ban Johnson's venture was off to a good start. Meanwhile, attendance in the National League lagged, particularly in those cities with a club in each league.

Detroit was the surprise of the new league, as they jumped out fast and left the expected contenders behind. Boston, in particular, struggled. After winning the first two at home, they dropped five in a row to Washington and Baltimore before winning again.

Cy Young arrived in Boston in 1901 with 285 career victories, an average of 25.9 wins per season. In 1901 he led the American League in victories with a 33-10 won-lost record while contributing mightily to the second-place finish by Boston, who finished the season just four games behind Chicago.

In fifth place with a record of 8-10 in late May, the team embarked on a long road trip and continued to labor. They fielded well but hit inconsistently. Every pitcher other than Young caused manager Collins to hold his breath. He was already trying out new recruits.

Collins recalled a young pitcher he had seen earlier in the spring in York, Pennsylvania, where the Americans had defeated a YMCA team 5-0. YMCA pitcher George Winter, culled from the squad of nearby Gettysburg College, had been impressive. Collins sent him a wire inviting him to try out, and Winter met the team when they returned to Boston. Collins gave him a start against Detroit a few days later.

He proved to be a wonder, at least for a while. With a curve ball the equal of any in the league, he won his first start easily. His performance sparked the club to their best stretch of ball all season long. The club soon gained third place behind Detroit and Chicago, which had surged into the lead.

Chicago came into town on June 17, Bunker Hill Day, for a split-admission, morning and afternoon doubleheader. The day also marked the first time the Americans and Nationals both played in Boston on the same day.

The Americans won on both counts. Cambridge pitcher Fred Mitchell, who returned to the squad to take the place of the recently departed Win Kellum, hurled the team to an 11-1 win before five thousand fans in the morning contest. Then Young cruised to a 10-4 victory in the afternoon before another ten thousand, moving the club into a virtual tie for second place.

On the other side of the tracks, the seventh-place Nationals won too, although they clearly lost the larger battle of the box office, drawing only fifteen hundred fans.

The next day the Nationals cut the price of a grandstand seat from 50 cents to the American League standard of a quarter. It hardly mattered, for when the Americans won the next three from Chicago, including another win by Winter to move into first place, the Nationals became an afterthought to most Boston fans.

Winter captured his third straight on June 21, an 8-1 defeat of Cleveland, the club's fifteenth win in the

last sixteen games. But the Americans ended the spectacular homestand on a slide, dropping the next four games to Cleveland, allowing Chicago to move back into first place.

Boston's slump continued, and Chicago again pulled ahead in the pennant race. Much to the delight of Ban Johnson the two clubs shared first place for most of the remainder of the season. So far, everything was working out just as he had planned.

Yet the team that would one day be known as the Red Sox was already displaying the same nerve-racking personality that has characterized the club for most of this century and makes being a Red Sox fan a unique, thrilling, but often disheartening and frustrating experience. For Sox fans, unrequited love is the only kind offered. These first Americans teased their fans with the idea of a pennant for most of the year, particularly at home, only to fall short at the end. The usual suspect, even then, was pitching.

Boston nudged into first place in early July and stayed there until midmonth as they continued their remarkable record at Huntington Avenue, closing the homestand with an incredible twenty-three wins in their last twenty-six games in Boston. Unfortunately, on July 15 the club embarked on an exhausting twenty-four-game road trip. In an attempt to stay close to Chicago, Collins turned to a three-man pitching rotation of Young, Lewis, and Winter.

By the time the club returned to Boston, on August 15, they trailed the White Sox by two games with a record of 56-40. They had no time to rest, however, as Chicago followed them into town for a two-game showdown series. Boston needed to win both.

Young took the opener, 6-2, then Boston moved to within one game of first place with a 4-2 win as Parson Lewis bested Chicago ace Clark Griffith.

For most of the next week, Collins looked like a genius, as the Americans took three straight from Milwaukee, including a gutsy, thirteen-inning pitching performance by Winter and two in a row from Cleveland, drawing to within one-half game of Chicago.

But this was Boston, where the pressure of a pennant race has always put everyone on edge. After a 4-2 loss to Cleveland on August 25, umpire Joe Cantillion was accosted by a mob of fifty kranks still an-

The first Boston Americans team in uniform, 1901, as identified in the *Boston Post*.

Top row l–r: McKenna, first baseman Buck Freeman, pitcher George Winter. *Middle row l–r:* shortstop Fred Parent, pitcher Fred Mitchell, pitcher Cy Young, pitcher Ted Lewis, outfielder Tommy Dowd, outfielder Chick Stahl. *Bottom row l–r:* second baseman Hobe Ferris, catcher Lou Criger, manager and third baseman Jimmy Collins, catcher Ossee Schreckengost, outfielder Charlie Hemphill, and posed prone in front, first baseman Larry McLean.

gry over an earlier call at the plate. Chick Stahl saved the umpire from a serious beating by holding several fans at bay while the losing pitcher, Parson Lewis, magnanimously ushered the ump into his quarters under the grandstand.

The loss was the beginning of the end for Boston. While Young adjusted to the "one day on, two days off" schedule, Lewis and Winter wore down and Chicago began to pull away.

A September road trip ended Boston's pennant hopes for good, the first, but certainly not the last time their fans would witness a late-season fade. The club dropped four of six to Detroit in a home-and-home series, then went into Chicago and collapsed.

The club that couldn't lose to the White Sox in Boston was awful in Chicago.

The season ended as Boston took a doubleheader from Milwaukee to finish with a record of 79-57, four and a half games ahead of Detroit but four behind Chicago.

In every way but the final standings, the inaugural season of the Boston Americans had been a rousing success. From the first game, the team had won the hearts, minds, and wallets of Boston baseball fans. Attendance for the first season totaled some three hundred twenty-two thousand fans (although some later estimates conclude they actually drew only two hundred eighty-nine thousand). They had outdrawn

Former Red Sox shortstops Fred Parent (l) and Joe Cronin at the opener of the 1967 World Series at Fenway Park. At the time, Parent was ninety-one years old and was the last surviving member of the first world champions of 1903. The native of Biddeford, Maine, batted .281, including three triples in the 1903 world series. Standing behind Parent and Cronin are Boston Symphony conductor Erich Leinsdorf and former senator Leverett Saltonstall.

the Nationals by somewhere around a two-to-one margin and even turned a tidy profit.

The Americans had played exciting, winning baseball, particularly at home. Every regular stole at least ten bases, and the team combined for a .278 batting average. Buck Freeman hit .339 with twelve home runs and 114 RBIs, while Collins hit .332 and was fifth in the league in slugging. Cy Young, easily the best pitcher in the league, emerged as a crowd favorite the equal of Collins.

Over on Columbus Avenue, the Nationals, with their anemic offense, were old, slow, undistinguished, and scored 200 fewer runs than the Americans. They were never in the pennant race and finished a lackluster 69-69, twenty and a half games behind champion Pittsburgh, a .500 ballclub in every way.

Even though the National League narrowly outdrew the upstarts (because of the larger size of some NL cities) Johnson's league was a success. Of the three cities with franchises in each league, the AL enjoyed a huge advantage in Chicago and Boston and had kept pace in Philadelphia, where the Phillies had provided the only challenge to the Pirates.

That was enough to fuel the baseball war for another season. Johnson remained on the offensive and was already looking to replace franchises in small markets Milwaukee and Baltimore with teams in St. Louis and New York, and he continued to raid the NL of talent. After all, he still had several of Somers's millions left to play with.

In the off-season the Boston Americans quickly re-signed most of the roster and made a few deals to strengthen the club. Dissatisfied with Freeman's glove work at first, the club traded Ossee Schreckengost to Cleveland for dapper veteran first baseman Candy LaChance, opening up a spot in the outfield for Freeman. They then picked up a promising rookie outfielder, fleet Patsy Dougherty, and NL veteran Charley "Piano Legs" Hickman, dumping both Tommy Dowd and Charlie Hemphill.

But the club recognized that the difference between a pennant and second place was pitching. Young and Winter, despite slumping to a final record of 16-12, were set, but Lewis, Mitchell, and Cuppy were deemed expendable. Besides, Bill Dinneen's contract was up.

The Triumvirs offered him another bonus, but Dinneen used their offer as leverage, met with Collins, and signed with the Americans for about thirty-five hundred dollars. The Nats were hurt again when Nichols jumped ship, becoming player/manager for minor league Kansas City in exchange for a piece of the team.

Hoping for better weather, the Americans moved spring training farther south to the YMCA in Augusta, Georgia. Cy Young was excused from the first few weeks of training to tutor the pitching staff at Harvard.

The big news that spring was Charles Somers. He wanted out, or, more likely, Johnson wanted to use his money elsewhere. He had already moved Milwaukee to St. Louis and was looking to move the Orioles to New York.

But Johnson still couldn't find a local investor. Somers stayed on, although it was common knowledge that Milwaukee lawyer Henry Killilea had acquired a sizable portion of Somers's stock in the team.

While the team trained in Georgia, the Huntington Avenue Grounds were upgraded. Part of the grandstand had been damaged by a winter storm and needed repair, and the canvas awnings over the bleachers were finally put in place, although they wouldn't last long before the stiff ocean breezes. A second entrance to the stands was built off Rogers Avenue, but people still had to enter the park through the main gate on Huntington Avenue. For the comfort and convenience of fans, a paved walkway was built from the gate around the grandstand, so people wouldn't have to step through the mud.

The major league season opened in Boston on Patriots' Day, April 19, as the Nationals drew 13,000 fans to the South End Grounds. It was their biggest crowd in years, but they lost to Brooklyn in thirteen innings, 3-1. But the real story took place across the tracks.

The Americans weren't scheduled to open the season for another four days, but they didn't give the competition a holiday. They played an exhibition game with Baltimore.

The club drew a mob to Huntington Avenue. Fans set siege on the ticket office outside the grounds and spilled out onto the street, as those with tickets found it almost impossible to push their way back through the throng to the single turnstile. When they did, they discovered their tickets were useless. Ushers were asking for cash, some of which may have even found its way into club coffers.

Thousands eventually spilled over to the South End Grounds. But thousands more took matters into their own hands.

They pressed against a service gate in the centerfield fence until it gave way, then surged so close to the diamond that neither team could warm up properly. The only clear ground was that between home plate and the pitcher's mound.

It was a dangerous situation, and the *Post* reported that "Clothing was torn in some instances and several fainted in the crush . . . Nothing but the chivalrous gallantry on the part of the men around such unfortunates prevented these weaker ones from being hopelessly crushed."

At length, the players and police cleared the field. Still, the start of the game was delayed an hour. Boston won the meaningless contest, 7-6, in what the *Post* later called "one of the most remarkable contests ever waged on a local diamond."

Michael T. 'Nuf 'Ced McGreevey was the Boston Americans' biggest fan and leader of the Royal Rooters, a loyal cadre of fans who first cheered the Boston Nationals in their glory days of the 1890s before adopting the new team. McGreevey owned a tavern in Boston's South End named Third Base, "the Last Stop on the Way Home."

Yet those who had hoped the victory would prove a portent for the upcoming season were disappointed. Boston opened in Washington on April 23 behind Bill Dinneen and lost, 7-3. They got off slow and spent all season trying to recover.

Nothing went quite as planned. Winter pitched well when he pitched, but was in and out of the rotation with malaria and made only twenty starts. Dinneen ate up innings, but pitched in hard luck all year long, winning twenty-one but also losing the same number, the highest total in the league. Young again led the league with thirty-two wins, but for the second consecutive season, Boston's fourth starting slot was too often filled by whomever someone recommended to Collins for a tryout.

Boston's offense should have been able to make up the difference, but injuries took Collins, Stahl, and Patsy Dougherty, who hit .342 for the season, out of the lineup for extended periods of time. Collins and Ferris also lost time when they were suspended for harassing umpires. Charley Hickman could have made up the difference, but he was dumped after failing to crack the starting lineup. He surfaced in Cleveland, where all he did was lead the league in hits and bat .378.

By midseason the pennant race was an afterthought. For the first time, there was a real question as to whether the American League would remain in business.

In late June, Ban Johnson indefinitely suspended Baltimore player-manager, part-owner, and Boston nemesis John McGraw for harassing umpires. Once Johnson's staunchest ally in the creation of the new league, now McGraw turned against him.

The feisty Irishman believed that Johnson was selling him out in his negotiations to move the Orioles to New York for 1903. His suspension confirmed those fears. So McGraw decided that one way or another, he was going to get to New York.

First, he secretly accepted the job as manager of the Giants. But in order to do so, he had to liquidate his controlling interest in Baltimore, which he was only allowed to have because of his allegiance to Johnson. In so doing, he hoodwinked Johnson.

In a complicated deal, he sold the Orioles to a syndicate controlled by John Brush, chairman of the National League Executive Committee, and Arthur Freedman, owner of the NL Giants of New York. They summarily transferred the Orioles' best players to the National League, crippling the Baltimore franchise.

When Baltimore was unable to field a team on July 17, Johnson revoked the franchise, took it over, and restocked the team with players from other American League clubs. Baltimore finished in last place, but the integrity of the league was preserved.

It was a week of wild speculation, one that for a few days appeared to threaten the very survival of Johnson's enterprise. In Boston, events took an odd turn. As Johnson wrestled with the Baltimore situation, the Americans dropped four in a row to Cleveland at the Huntington Avenue Grounds. *The Sporting News* reported that there was "talk of a little joker about these games," meaning they may well have been fixed. The correspondent went on to complain about the number and audacity of the gamblers who regularly occupied the third-base stands and even walked onto the field between innings "calling odds for the scoring of the inning and the result of the game." Furthermore, wrote Dixwell, the "head of the gambling trust is friendly with the players" and "bet on Cleveland all he could in each and every of the four games."

At the time, gambling was as much a part of baseball as the stolen base. One can easily imagine that with the entire league in an uproar, certain players and sporting men may well have taken matters into their own hands for a few days, earning their own insurance against the possibility of any league-wide collapse.

As the season played out, no fewer than five clubs — Boston, Philadelphia, St. Louis, Detroit, and Cleveland — all had a realistic chance to win the pennant. This time, Boston shored up its pitching staff, acquiring Long Tom Hughes from Baltimore and Tully Sparks from NL New York, which had released him. While neither was the equivalent of Young, Dinneen, or Winter, they at least gave Collins an option.

Yet the chief obstacle to Boston's pennant chances that season proved to be Collins himself. A sore knee knocked him from the lineup in August and kept him there. Boston kept pace with Philadelphia until mid-September, then met the A's in a key doubleheader on September 15, trailing the Philadelphians by three games.

More than sixteen thousand fans squeezed their way into the Huntington Avenue Grounds, causing a delay as police and players fought to remove fans from the field. Boston dropped the first game 6-4 as Plank beat Dinneen when Hobe Ferris made three rare but critical errors. Boston was swamped in game two, 9-2, and the pennant was all but lost.

Although the team drew 348,567 fans for the season, three times as many as the Nationals and nearly 5,000 a game, only a few hundred fans turned out for the last game of the season against Baltimore. A number of players had already bolted. Boston ended the season with a 9-5 win with pitcher Long Tom Hughes filling space in the outfield and rookie Gary Wilson staking claim to a major league career at second base. Everyone played, as the *Post* reported, as if "anxious to finish up and get away." The Americans finished third, six and a half games behind the A's.

The next day at McGreevey's, however, was Opening Day for the Hot Stove League. They were already looking forward to next April. For if the first chapter in the history of the team had begun with whispered asides between the men at McGreevey's, so too did the second. A great change was in the air.

THE FIRST CHAMPIONS

1903

Player-manager Jimmy Collins (holding rope) prepares
to hoist the first world championship banner over the
Huntington Avenue Grounds on Opening Day 1904.

In one of his first spring training appearances in March of 1903, Cy Young had huffed and puffed his way through an early workout. By the end of the month, the pitcher would turn thirty-six years old, almost ancient in baseball terms. In his baggy wool sweater the ruddy-faced, portly Young looked like the farmer he was in the off-season. Nothing about him indicated he was one of baseball's great pitchers.

At the end of the practice session, young reporter Frederic O'Connell of the *Boston Post* approached manager Jimmy Collins and asked, "How long do you think he will last?"

Collins responded with a knowing smile. "The old fellow is O.K.," he said. "Like whiskey, he improves with age . . . Give me Cy Young for any five pitchers now in the game." By the end of the 1903 season Collins's vote of confidence would appear conservative.

The climate surrounding major league baseball had changed dramatically since the previous fall. For even as the Boston Americans played out the string in 1902, Ban Johnson moved out of the trenches. He now struck at the heart of the National League.

The Pittsburgh Pirates romped toward their second consecutive National League pennant, immune to the player raids that had decimated the rest of the league. For Johnson, always with an ulterior motive in hand, had declared the Pirates off-limits. He knew Pittsburgh owner Barney Dreyfuss was still miffed with the NL for cutting loose his Louisville franchise in 1900 and hoped Dreyfuss might eventually bring his entire team under Johnson's umbrella.

Johnson's policy regarding the Pirates created an unintended but welcome result. Their roster intact, the Pirates dominated the NL in 1901 and 1902, eventually winning the 1902 pennant by a staggering twenty-seven and a half games. Their success created an imbalance that hurt the gate of every other team in the league. In the last half of 1902 Johnson's league outdrew the NL by a wide margin.

Now Johnson discreetly asked Dreyfuss to switch leagues in 1903. When the Pittsburgh magnate politely refused, Johnson decided it was time to sneak behind enemy lines.

Johnson and Charles Somers traveled to Pittsburgh and met in secret with the heart of the Pittsburgh team, save star shortstop Honus Wagner. They left with catcher Jack O'Connor, pitchers Jesse Tannehill and Jack Chesbro, third baseman Tommy Leach, shortstop Wid Conroy, and outfielder Lefty Davis all under contract to the American League. Johnson was in the process of moving the decimated Baltimore franchise into New York, and the new club needed players.

The secret signings eventually brought the National League to its knees. Just after the first of the year, Johnson, Somers, and Henry Killilea represented the American League at a peace conference with their National League counterparts in Cincinnati, Johnson's old hometown.

On January 19, 1903, the two leagues ratified a peace agreement that essentially made each circuit separate but equal. They agreed to play by the same rules and respect each other's rights regarding players, which helped owners in both circuits deflate player salaries. The great baseball war was over.

The news was greeted with both delight and disappointment by Boston American fans. While they were thrilled that the city would remain a two-team town, they were disappointed to learn that the club's most recent acquisition, Boston Nationals star hurler Vic Willis, would be returned to the NL as part of the peace agreement, as would Leach and a few other recent signees. Willis, a twenty-seven-game winner in 1902, had made the Americans look like a sure bet

for the pennant. Without him the team was still a pitcher short.

Peace enabled Somers to get out from under the Americans. Johnson arranged for him to sell the club to his trusted crony Henry Killilea.

Apart from the abortive signing of Willis, the Americans made few changes in the off-season, earning the club a temporary nickname — "the Stand-Pats." But when backup catcher Jack Warner jumped the team, the Americans signed veteran catcher Charley "Duke" Farrell, a native of Marlborough, Massachusetts, to share catching duties with Criger, who had injured his back in a carriage accident in the off-season. Collins replaced Willis with Cincinnati's Nick Altrock.

The club left for training camp in Macon, Georgia, in mid-March. But they got little work done, for the players seemed more enamored of the local racetrack and the bar at the Hotel Lanier than the ballfield. Buck Freeman, Lou Criger, Bill Dinneen, and Altrock even left camp for about a week to gamble and drink their way into condition. Dinneen was feeling particularly garrulous, for he had earned a reported twenty thousand dollars in the off-season speculating on Indiana oil fields.

After a few weeks the club worked its way north playing a series of exhibitions in the Midwest. They impressed no one and lost as often as they won against minor league competition.

Meanwhile, new owner Killilea spent some coin to upgrade the Huntington Avenue Grounds. He raised and resodded the field, which had settled since initial construction and took forever to dry out. At the players' request, he also removed advertising from the 12-foot-tall center-field fence and painted it dark green to improve the background for hitters, unintentionally giving Boston fans a glimpse of the future by creating a far more distant and demure Green Monster, although no one thought to call it that.

The Americans opened the season with a separate-admission doubleheader on Monday, April 20, celebrating Patriots' Day, for Sunday baseball was still banned in Boston. George Winter started for Collins against the defending champion Philadelphia Athletics.

With the A's leading 1-0 entering the fourth inning,

Royal Rooter playing a bass drum at the 1903 world series. The Royal Rooters almost always traveled with a brass band to help amplify their boisterous support of the Americans. Most followed the team to Pittsburgh to cheer them on in the first world series.

Jimmy Collins earned his money. A's starter Rube Waddell had a well-deserved reputation as an eccentric whose odd behavior was often fueled by alcohol. He'd been spotted dead drunk the night before, and Collins decided to take advantage of his indiscretion.

The Americans ruthlessly attacked Waddell utilizing the weapon that had made Collins a star — the bunt. Batter after batter dropped bunts back to the fireballer, who was in no condition to deal with the onslaught. When he got to the ball at all, he got there late, then either bobbled it or threw it away. Boston scored five runs in the inning, and Waddell's disgusted teammates responded to the pitcher's lackadaisical effort with some lackluster play of their own, committing five errors in addition to the two

charged to Waddell. Boston won, 9-4, but dropped the second game 10-7, when an unknown rookie in his first major league appearance, nineteen-year-old Native American Albert "Chief" Bender, stopped Boston in relief.

The Americans and the A's met seven more times that month, with Philadelphia taking five of the nine contests as Boston got off to their now-traditional slow start. Barely a week into the season, Charley Farrell, batting .400, broke his leg. Criger was forced to do the bulk of the catching for the remainder of the season.

On May 7 one of the most contentious rivalries in all sport got its start. On that day, for the first time, Boston faced an American League team from the city

World series crowd at the Huntington Avenue Grounds, October 3, 1903. Fans are shown sneaking into the first world series via the helping hands of fellow fans.

of New York, the Highlanders. The club, also referred to as the Invaders because of their unwelcome migration from Baltimore, would later become the New York Yankees.

The five thousand Boston fans in attendance that day were not disappointed. For even then, there was more at stake when Boston met New York than a baseball game. Anyone who believes the rivalry between the two clubs did not begin until much later is badly misinformed.

From the very first game, several factors combined to transform a simple sporting contest into something more. Throughout the nineteenth century, Boston was considered the Hub of American culture, her most sophisticated and refined city. But the future

was New York. The city had grown exponentially since the Civil War. It had taken over as the nation's commercial center and was quickly usurping Boston's cultural advantage. The two cities were already in pitched competition.

In baseball terms, New York had already forged ahead. The old Massachusetts game had fallen before the New York version, and now, if one included Brooklyn, New York had three major league teams, more than any other city.

The fact that the Highlanders' lineage could be traced back through Baltimore only added to the drama, for the old Orioles had previously served as Boston's biggest baseball rival. Even now New York's roster included old Baltimore nemesis Wee Willie

Keeler. Their squad also included former Chicago ace pitcher-manager Clark Griffith, whom Johnson had transferred to New York to give the club instant credibility, and shortstop Herman Long, once the Boston Nationals' most popular player. Chesbro, Tannehill, O'Connor, Davis, and Conroy, all late of Pittsburgh, were also on the club, adding to the significance of the meeting. Before the first pitch was ever thrown, the two clubs eyed each other warily.

Dinneen beat Snake Wiltse 6-2 in the first game of the three-game set, as Boston took third place in the league and pushed New York into fourth. When Chesbro faced Winter the next afternoon, the rivalry ensued in earnest.

With the outcome of the game still undecided, New York outfielder Dave Fultz hit a groundball to LaChance at first. Winter raced over to cover the bag and as he reached for the throw and felt for the base with his foot, Fultz ran him down.

The pitcher was knocked nearly senseless. Although he finished the game, he was clearly shaken. New York pulled away to win 6-1 and regain third place. From that moment on, there was little affection between the two clubs.

Young opposed Tannehill in the series finale. Through four innings he shut Boston out, and when the game entered the bottom of the fifth, he led Young and Boston 2-0.

As the *Post* reported, then "It took about three minutes to change the whole aspect of the game."

With Patsy Dougherty on second and one out, Chick Stahl hit for Boston. When umpire Bob Carruthers called the pitch a ball, Tannehill was visibly upset.

Stahl then banged the next pitch past Conroy at third, scoring Dougherty. Tannehill dashed behind home to back up a possible play at the plate, then stayed around after Dougherty scored to argue with Carruthers over the previous pitch.

His teammates joined him. The angry arbiter tossed Tannehill from the game.

The New Yorkers went wild. Second baseman Jimmy Williams grabbed Carruthers by the collar of his shirt, pulled him close, and screamed in his face. Carruthers then tossed him from the game and ordered both Tannehill and Williams off the field.

They refused and continued to toss insults from the bench. The umpire calmly took a watch from his pocket and set a deadline for their departure. Only when Jack O'Connor pleaded with both men to leave did the game resume. Harry Howell took the mound in Tannehill's stead without the benefit of warming up. He was clocked and Boston cruised to a 12-5 win.

The tone was set. No New York–Boston game would ever be meaningless, despite what the standings sometimes said.

Boston then went on the road, where they continued to play so-so baseball, never winning two in a row, and unable to gain any momentum. By the time they reached Chicago in late May, Boston was fifth in the pennant race behind the first-place White Sox.

Despite Jimmy Collins's earlier proclamation, Cy Young's 5-3 record had thus far matched Boston's level of mediocrity. There were whispers that Young's age was finally beginning to catch up with him, as one Boston paper recently referred to him as "somewhat ancient but in a good state of repair." The club needed Young to turn back the clock.

He did that and more, pitching the best baseball of his career. Not Joe Wood in 1912, Jim Lonborg in 1967, Roger Clemens in 1986, nor Pedro Martinez in 1999 played the game the way Young did in 1903. Although there was no Most Valuable Player Award in 1903 and the word "clutch" was not yet used as a baseball adjective, Young provided the definitive definition for each.

In back-to-back performances, Young "kalsomined," or shut out, the White Sox and Senators to lift Boston into second place. They soon moved into first.

Cy Young once told a reporter that "Pitchers, like poets, are born, not made." Young may indeed have been born a pitcher, but he made himself a great one. When he first started playing baseball as a boy on the farm, the pitcher threw underhanded from a box 50 feet from home plate. As the game changed, so did Cy. Across nearly two decades of amateur and professional play, there was little he hadn't seen. With more than five hundred major league appearances under his more than ample belt, he knew more about pitching than any man alive.

Young knew how to pace himself. As he told a reporter long after he had retired, "I figured the old arm had just so many throws in it and there wasn't any use wasting them."

Of spring training, he said, "I would never touch a ball for the first three weeks, just do a lot of walking and running." Only after his legs were in shape would he throw, and even then "I never warmed up ten or fifteen minutes like most pitchers do, I loosened up for maybe three, four minutes."

On the mound, Young cut an odd figure. He was much bigger than most players of his generation, but not particularly menacing. He began his windup rocking his arms like a pendulum, then instead of lifting both arms over his head, as is customary, he simply raised both hands above his right shoulder as if hoisting a sack of laundry, pivoted, and strode toward the plate with little wasted motion.

His best pitch was his fastball, but he also changed speeds, threw a curve, a drop, and by the time he reached the Americans, a spitter. Equally comfortable throwing either straight overhand or from three-quarters or the side, a batter could face Young half a dozen times and never see the same pitch twice.

In the early innings, when the outcome was undecided, Young bore down. When he wanted to, he could throw harder than most pitchers in the game, and if the score remained close, he could keep it up for as many innings as he had to. Yet he didn't care about strikeouts; they required too many pitches. "I aimed to make the batter hit the ball," he claimed. "That's why I was able to work every other day."

But once he got a lead, Young changed strategy. He took something off the ball, varied his delivery, and worked the corners, saving his fastball for more important battles ahead. Anxious opponents found themselves swinging at the air or topping the ball as they desperately tried to adjust to his off-speed offerings. If they connected, he could still turn the faucet back on and pour on the heat.

By matching his style to the situation, Young became, in essence, his own relief pitcher in an era when complete games were required. The stuff he threw at the end of the game often bore little resemblance to the pitches delivered by the man who'd started it, yet he was one and the same, and still the best in the game. In 815 career starts, Young completed 749, and he pitched in relief on 91 occasions.

In the late innings, he often gave up a run or two or three, but he rarely allowed himself to get in real trouble. If the Americans scored two, Young might give up one. If they scored ten, he might give up five or six. He cared only about winning, and he won more than any man who has ever played the game, or ever will.

During an eleven-game Boston win streak, during which he made five appearances, either starting or coming on in relief, he earned the nickname "EmergenCy" from the *Boston Post*. Then Boston stumbled, losing when Young didn't pitch, as the Americans and the Philadelphia A's traded first place back and forth by percentage points. The Americans then lost two before winning the second game of a Bunker Hill Day doubleheader behind Long Tom Hughes in a game marked by the dangerous behavior of the holiday crowd at Huntington Avenue. Dozens of fans celebrated the holiday by shooting guns into the air.

Young then left the team to attend his mother-in-law's funeral. In his absence, Philadelphia took a slim lead in the pennant race. All the good work of the past month seemed about to come undone.

Then Boston's other pitchers suddenly rose to the occasion. When Young rejoined the club in Detroit on June 23 the well-rested Cy — it had been ten days since he last pitched — pitched the club to its fourth consecutive win by twirling a 1-0 shutout.

Five days later, following a shutout by Winter, he fashioned a second 1-0 victory, this time over St. Louis. As if inspired, Long Tom Hughes followed with a shutout of his own in the second game of the doubleheader. The Americans were on a roll.

Pitching again on two days' rest on July 1, Young did the remarkable. As Frederic O'Connell described it, "For nine innings the territory around second base was like a desert, and few traversed the ground around first," as Young and Chicago's Patsy Flaherty — who would lead the league with twenty-five losses in 1903 — each shut out the opposition through nine innings.

Then, in the Boston tenth, Ferris singled and was sacrificed to second by Criger. Up came Young. In a later era he would certainly have been lifted for a pinch hitter, but in 1903 a pitcher was still a ballplayer and expected to produce at the plate. Wrote O'Connell, "The mighty Cy came to the plate and sent a screaming liner just inside the foul line and almost over the third bag . . . Young went for two bases and Ferris came home." He then retired the side in the bottom of the inning to record his fourth consecutive shutout, third in a row by a 1-0 score.

It is difficult in any league, at any time, to record a shutout, but to do so by a score of 1-0 is doubly difficult, for there is little margin for errors of any kind. It was no easier in Young's era, for although the ball was "dead" and offense at a premium (the league hit only .255 in 1903), defenses were porous because of the size of the fielder's glove and field conditions. The Americans, considered one of the best defensive teams in the league that year, averaged two errors per game. Yet Young threw seven of the league's ninety-nine shutouts in 1903. The reason? He hardly ever walked a hitter. In forty appearances and 342 innings that season, he walked only thirty-seven batters.

With the Americans now leading the American League by several games, Young continued to demonstrate his remarkable versatility. In a July 4 doubleheader in Boston, the game was delayed when the umpire failed to show up on time. Young umpired behind the plate until the arbiter arrived, then coached first.

His duties expanded one week and one win later. As Boston baked under a massive heat wave that killed dozens and sent more than a hundred thousand to Revere Beach, Young stood outside the gate at the Huntington Avenue Grounds before the game with Chicago and handed out free passes to kids. Then, in the scorching heat, the old man won 8-5.

In his next start, on July 15 against Cleveland, Young proved that his game-winning hit two weeks before was no fluke. He and youthful Cleveland ace Addie Joss battled over nine innings to a 3-3 tie. In the tenth, Young showed Joss how it was done.

SOUVENIR CARD 10 CENTS

McGREEVY
On the Avenue
Nuff said . . . .

3rd Base

1903

..SOUVENIR CARD..

OF THE

World's Championship Games
Boston vs. Pittsburg

With Lou Criger on first Young sent a bullet just fair past first base. Criger scored easily and old Cy kept running as the ball bounced into the right-field corner, finally sliding into third with a triple to put Boston up, 4-3. He was left stranded, then dusted himself off, caught his breath, and retired Cleveland easily in the bottom of the inning to record the win.

Pope Leo XIII died on July 20, but even in Catholic Boston the pontiff's death had to compete with baseball in Boston's daily press. Pennant fever was gripping the Hub.

Yet they just couldn't shake the Philadelphia Athletics, who trailed by only a few games. With a showdown with the A's on the horizon, Boston traveled to New York for four games, then followed with a like number in Boston against the Highlanders.

Young beat Jack Chesbro 6-1, then defeated Tannehill four days later as Boston took five of the first six games. In the thirty-four days since he rejoined the club, Young had pitched and won nine games. In fact, if one ignored an earlier relief stint, he had won his last fourteen decisions dating back to May 20. For the season, he was a stellar 19-3.

Perhaps he finally tired. Or maybe he was looking ahead to the big Philadelphia series only a week away. At any rate, it all caught up with him on July 29 when he was matched with Chesbro in what one Boston paper called "easily the most remarkable game played here this season." It was also one of the most inartistic on record.

The New Yorkers jumped on Young, scoring three runs in each of the first two innings, as nearly every hit was compounded by a Boston error. But Chesbro was no better. Boston pounded him in the middle innings as Young continued to labor. Entering the seventh, the game was tied at 10-10.

Chesbro got relief, but Young stayed in the game,

Scorecard, 1903 world series. Notice that the term "world series" was not used on the Boston scorecard and that 'Nuf 'Ced McGreevey secured the prime advertising place for his saloon above the pictures of managers Jimmy Collins (l) and Fred Clarke (r). While "McGreevey" is the official spelling, "McGreevy" often appeared in print.

BORN TO PITCH

No pitcher in the history of baseball has ever approached Denton True Young's record 511 wins, and no pitcher ever will. Neither did any pitcher ever match his success while adapting to the radical rule changes that took place over the course of his career. When Young started playing sandlot ball, pitchers threw underhanded from a box only 50 feet from home plate. When Young's professional career began in 1890, overhand deliveries had been legal for only six seasons. The distance from the pitcher's plate to home wasn't increased to the now-familiar 60 feet 6 inches until 1893.

None of this ever seemed to matter to Young, who best illustrated his own adage that "Pitchers, like poets, are born, not made." He was a pitcher, period. Over the course of his first eleven seasons, first with Cleveland and then St. Louis, Young had won more than twenty games ten times, including three seasons of thirty or more wins.

The story behind his nickname "Cy" is uncertain. According to some historians he earned the moniker after several of his pitches damaged a wood fence in the manner of a cyclone. More likely is that Young, who was raised on a farm and farmed in the off-season, was dubbed Cy because of his off-season vocation. At the time, players from the farm were routinely called "Cyrus," considered a fitting name for such rubes.

But Cy Young was unquestionably one of the game's great pitchers. By the time he reached Boston he had already won 265 games. At 6-foot-2 and over 200 pounds, Young was a giant in an era when most players were at least 6 inches shorter. A good-natured man who liked his whiskey (despite advice he gave to others warning against it), Young could and did throw almost every day. He worked quickly, didn't warm up between innings, and could throw hard when he had to, but was particularly adept at keeping hitters off balance. Hitters knew they could expect strikes, but from exactly what angle or at what speed was another question. Young threw overhand and from both the side and three-quarters, could make the ball dip or curve both directions, and supplemented his repertoire with a spitball. He had masterful control and rarely fell behind or walked hitters, and he fully exploited the fact that the same ball was often used the entire game, getting darker, softer, and harder to hit with each inning. There could be no better choice for the award that now bears his name.

In 1899 Young was transferred from Cleveland to St. Louis as part of the syndicate deal between the two teams. Young didn't approve of the arrangement. He detested the weather in St. Louis and wanted to stay close to his farm in his native Ohio, but he was powerless to stop the transfer.

He pitched well for St. Louis, winning forty-six games in two seasons, but he also lost thirty-three with the .500 ballclub. In 1901, at age thirty-three, Cy was thought by some to be over the hill. His name was often preceded in the newspaper by the adjective "aged."

But Young aged like good whiskey. In only eight seasons in Boston, Young won 192. Nearly one hundred years later, no Red Sox pitcher has ever won more — Young is still tied with Roger Clemens for the club record. ⏀

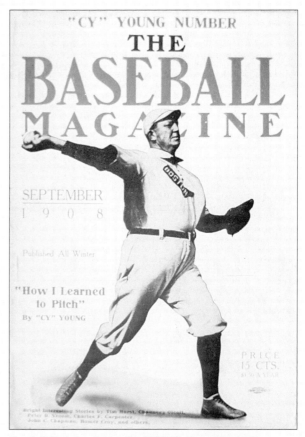

Baseball Magazine, September 1908 "Cy Young Number."
The burly Ohio farmer was the Boston Americans' first superstar, winning 192 games in just eight seasons with the franchise for an average of twenty-four victories per season.

saving the staff. He was clubbed for five more runs before the game mercifully ended after Boston scored four in the bottom of the ninth before finally going out with the tying and winning runs on base. New York won 15-14. Young went the distance.

In that single appearance Young gave up nearly 8 percent of all the runs that would be scored off him all year. Baseball scholars have since concluded that his earned run average for the season was a sparkling 2.08 (ERA was not an official statistic in the AL until 1913). If not for that singularly awful performance on July 29, his ERA would have been nearly a half run better.

The loss sent Boston reeling. The losing streak was three when Young pitched in another 1-0 shutout.

But this time Cy lost. Senator pitcher Howard "Highball" Wilson (a moniker that had nothing to do with the location of his pitches) threw the game of his life and pitched the only shutout of his career to beat the Americans in sixty-five minutes.

On the precipice of the most important series of games in the history of the franchise, Boston was playing its worst baseball of the season. Beginning on August 5 in Philadelphia, Boston and the A's played six consecutive games. The 55-33 Boston club led the 53-36 Athletics by two and a half games. The series seemed likely to decide the pennant.

Bill Dinneen, something of a disappointment thus far, drew the starting assignment for Boston opposite Waddell. In the first inning it became apparent just how important the series was to Boston.

Patsy Dougherty led off with a single, but was forced at second on a groundball by Collins. When Stahl struck out, Collins broke for second base on a delayed steal.

A's catcher Ossee Schreckengost wasn't fooled. His throw beat Collins to second and shortstop Monte Cross applied the tag with the force of a sucker punch.

Collins leapt to his feet screaming in complaint at the umpire. When the ump retreated, Collins grabbed him by the arm and was tossed from the game. Dinneen was in a hole before throwing his first pitch.

But Dinneen and shortstop Freddy Parent wouldn't let Philadelphia take advantage. In the second, Parent's relay throw nailed a runner at the plate and in the seventh, with a man on third, knocked down a soft fly with his glove hand, then plucked it out of the air with his bare hand, turned, and doubled a runner off third. Boston squeezed in three runs off Waddell, and Dinneen's three-hitter shut out Philadelphia. After the game the headline in the *Post* accurately stated, "Dinneen and Parent Covered Themselves in Glory."

But perhaps the biggest play for Boston that day was made by Cy Young, coaching third. With Boston leading 1-0 and Ferris on second, Criger bunted to Waddell. As Waddell bobbled the ball, Young bellowed, "Throw to third!" Waddell fell for the ploy and did so, but Ferris was already at the bag. He scored a moment later when Dougherty flied to the outfield.

Philadelphia recovered the next day, hitting Young hard and taking a 4-0 lead before Boston scored two in the seventh to make it close off Bender. Then, with a storm on the horizon, the umpires called the game because of darkness. Collins kicked at the decision, but he got no sympathy from the umpires. Boston's lead was back to two and a half games.

In the third game of the series, Boston took command. They battered Eddie Plank for seven early runs and rolled to an 11-3 win behind Long Tom Hughes. As the series continued in Boston, the A's were desperate. Waddell went AWOL, and as the *Globe* wryly noted, "from the reports of his doings it looked as if the champions would play in Boston without the famous 'Reuben.'" He was on a bender from which no one could predict his return.

The A's emergency starter Weldon Henley never got untracked and gave up eight second-inning runs. Meanwhile, as veteran scribe Tim Murnane wrote in the *Globe*, Dinneen "made the visitors look like a cluster of open chestnut burrs with the nuts all gone," pitching shutout ball until the ninth, when he allowed six meaningless runs in an 11-6 Boston win. The A's now trailed Boston by four and a half.

The following day Young fashioned one of his best all-around performances of the year. For the first seven innings he was perfect, as the *Boston Herald* reported the "feat was accomplished without the turning of a hair, and Cy worked all styles of delivery, and had perfect command." And that wasn't the half of it.

Nursing a 3-0 lead in the fifth, Young singled to center with one out. Patsy Dougherty then hit a groundball to second that Murphy let go through his legs, and Young raced toward third. As he approached the base, he read the eyes of Philadelphia third baseman Lave Cross tracking the throw. According to O'Connell in the *Post*, "Twenty feet from the base Young ran in a zigzag manner, and succeeded in his object for [center fielder] Pickering's throw hit the big pitcher in the leg." He was safe, and Dougherty raced to second while Cross chased down the ball. Then Collins grounded to Murphy, who threw home to try to get Young. But A's catcher Mike Powers dropped the throw and according to O'Connell "Young, either intentionally or unintentionally, kicked the ball, and this allowed Dougherty to score also."

The 7-3 loss all but killed Philadelphia. Over the next month, Boston surged as Philadelphia fell to third. By early September, Boston led second-place Cleveland by ten games. A Boston pennant was certain.

Over in the National League, Pittsburgh was in a similar position. Fans everywhere began to debate the relative merits of the two teams.

Talk turned to the possibility of a postseason meeting, what the press termed a "world's series" between the two clubs. Although there was no arrangement between the two leagues for such a contest, owners Dreyfuss of Pittsburgh and Killilea of Boston picked up on the idea. Sensing the opportunity to make money, they decided to make their own plans.

They ultimately agreed to meet in a postseason, best-of-nine exhibition slate beginning on October 1. The first three games would be played in Boston, followed by four in Pittsburgh, then, if needed, two more in Boston. Any player not on the roster of either team on September 1 was not eligible to play, and each league would supply an umpire. The winning owner would receive 75 percent of the basic admission charge for the series, although each would retain any income generated by grandstand and box seats in their own ballpark. When Boston clinched the pennant on September 17 and Pittsburgh did so the following day, the first world's series seemed certain to be played.

The players were as excited about the series as

anyone, but as with their two owners, the real attraction was profit. Occasional midseason exhibitions against semipro teams usually netted players several hundred extra dollars each; they expected to make much more in the series. But thus far, the negotiations had left the players holding an empty purse.

Dreyfuss already had the Pirate players under his thumb — their contracts ran through October 15. But Boston's contracts ended on September 30. Killilea was in Chicago when the players got wind of the financial arrangement for the series and demanded their share.

They wanted an additional two weeks' pay, amounting to perhaps a couple of hundred dollars each, plus Killilea's 75 percent share of the receipts, which they wanted to divide equally among themselves, with one extra share reserved for the owner.

Paying the players extra and sharing his windfall was a situation Killilea neither anticipated nor desired. He scoffed at their proposal.

In response, Criger and Young led an insurrection, leaving Collins, in an awkward position as both manager and player, as the agent to deliver their demands. Without pay, they simply wouldn't play.

The players put pressure on Killilea by organizing a postseason barnstorming trip through New England also scheduled to start on October 1. A few, like Criger, were prepared to skip out early and return home. He was already packed.

Desperate to save his money roll, Killilea finally countered with a proposal to split his 75 percent with the players. The Americans turned him down cold.

"So deep is the feeling [among the players]," wrote Fred O'Connell, "that a meeting was held at McGreerey's [sic] on Columbus Avenue to consider some means of bringing the two teams together." The players now attempted to make their own arrangements to play the series without any involvement by their owner and were negotiating for the use of the South End Grounds as home field.

The press reported that "fans are taking sides . . . the big majority with the players." Dreyfuss was becoming impatient and gave Killilea until September 25 to bring his players on board. Otherwise, the series was off.

Thus far, communication between Killilea and his

players had been by letter and telegraph. But with the entire series at stake, the team gathered in the Hotel Langham on Huntington Avenue, and a long-distance telephone connection with Killilea was secured.

Club business manager Joe Smart translated the demands of the players to Killilea and vice versa. Just before midnight, as Dreyfuss's deadline approached, they made a deal. The players agreed to the fifty-fifty split, and Killilea agreed to pay the players a flat sum for an extra two weeks of work. The series was saved, although the Boston players were still bitter over having to fight to be paid a fair wage. Their discontent would soon impact the series in the worst of all possible ways.

But at 'Nuf 'Ced McGreevey's there was jubilation. Not since the Bostons and Baltimore had met in the old Temple Cup series in 1898 had there been such

an opportunity to mix their three favorite pastimes: booze, baseball, and betting. The touts in the crowd got right to work.

Within two days there was so much speculation over the gambling angle of the series that owners of both teams found it necessary to deny that any of the games would be "fixed" to assure the series was played to its full nine games and allow for the largest possible gate. But day by day, the Boston press reported that gambling on the series was growing exponentially. On September 29, a story in the *Post* was headlined "Big Bets on Pittsburg [sic] American Series, with Locals Favorites." The report stated, "The amount of money wagered yesterday will easily

Outfield spectators, 1903 world series. The dimensions of the Huntington Avenue Grounds allowed for fans to purchase standing-room tickets that let them view the game behind a rope that separated them from the action. This photograph depicts the crowd relaxing prior to one of the first world series games.

Huntington Avenue Grounds, circa 1903. An overflow crowd fills the park for what most likely is a world series game.

amount to $25,000. The biggest single bet was made during the afternoon when Sport Sullivan bet $2500 that Boston will win." And Pittsburgh's well-heeled supporters hadn't even arrived in town yet.

Players on both teams, meanwhile, had a season to finish. Yet, unlike today, no one was rested, not even the pitchers. Pitching rotations and lineups remained intact. Any other approach, thought both clubs, might cause the players to lose their edge.

The two teams appeared evenly matched. Paced by Young, Boston's pitching staff was the best in the American League in 1903, as Young, Hughes, and Dinneen all won twenty or more games, topped by Young's league-best twenty-eight, and Gibson and Winter had chipped in with thirteen and nine, respectively. On offense, leadoff hitter Patsy Dougherty hit .331 and led the league in runs scored and hits, while Buck Freeman captured the home run and RBIs title. The club led the league in batting average, slugging, hits, and runs.

Pittsburgh was led by shortstop Honus Wagner, then considered the greatest player in the game.

Bowlegged and stocky, Wagner looked nothing like a ballplayer until he stepped on the field, where his huge hands caught everything and his legs carried him around the bases faster than any man in baseball. No less an expert than John McGraw once said he had the "natural ability to do most anything better than most players." In 1903, he led the NL with a .355 batting average.

But he wasn't Pittsburgh's only weapon. Player-manager Fred Clarke hit .351 and center fielder Ginger Beaumont .341. Little third baseman Tommy Leach, who hit a solid .298 with 87 RBIs, was considered Collins's equivalent in the field.

The pitching staff had more than made up for the loss of Chesbro and Tannehill. Sam Leever and Deacon Phillippe stepped up and won twenty-five and twenty-four games respectively, the best two marks in the league, while Massachusetts native Ed Doheny added another sixteen. Although Boston appeared to have the edge in pitching, the National League was still considered stronger. The early betting line installed Pittsburgh as a 2-1 favorite.

The impending series spawned the widespread development of a "sporting section" in Boston newspapers. Prior to the series, sports coverage usually came and went according to the significance of the event, often sharing space with theatrical and other "entertainment" news. But interest in the series sent circulation soaring and sparked a grand competition between the half-dozen major Boston dailies (the *Post, Globe, Herald, Journal, Transcript,* and *News*), each of which tried to outdo the other. The rivalry continued after the series as even the stodgy *Transcript*, essentially a financial paper, added a daily dose of sports news.

Most reports focused not on the relative merits of the two teams, but on the amount of money being wagered. Rumors about the health of the Pirates swung the odds to Boston's favor. Fred Clarke had a bad leg, Tommy Leach a bad finger, and pitcher Sam Leever had a sore arm. Another hurler, Ed Doheny, had become paranoid and left the club. When he tried to rejoin them he imagined he was pursued by detectives and was sent to his home in Andover, Massachusetts.

A few days before the series the *Boston Journal*

touted the prevailing odds on the front page as 10 to 8 for Boston, even listing the largest wagers to date. One man, J. J. McNamara of Roxbury, was reported to have $10,000 available to bet on Boston. There were dozens of reports of bets for $2,000 or more.

The potential result of such activity did not go unnoticed. On September 30, the *Post* felt compelled to discuss the potential for a fix, commenting that "there is too much at stake to risk having the series prolonged" by fixed games. Then the writer naively continued, "Baseball is too open to be crooked . . . Ask any great ballplayer if he could make an error on purpose and he would answer that he could, but that everyone would be 'on to him.'"

Wagering intensified once the Pirates and their backers arrived in town and set up shop in the Vendome Hotel just off Kenmore Square. The lobby was mobbed by gamblers and became an impromptu betting parlor. Boston's backers were forced to give even money in order to get a bet down with their more penurious counterparts from Pittsburgh. Action was particularly heavy on the outcome of game one, as the Boston men, smugly confident with the knowledge that Young would be pitching for the Americans, gave long odds to those who favored Pittsburgh and Phillippe. Reports that fifty thousand dollars were wagered in the hotel lobby in a single day were, if anything, conservative by several degrees.

The players all knew what was going on. They consorted openly with the gamblers and fans both at the hotel and in local taverns. In Boston, the two groups were one and the same.

At the time, there was little dishonorable about the relationship between gambling and professional baseball. While the magnates and players occasionally gave lip service to the evils of gambling (Johnson had banned the practice in American League ballparks on August 17, a ruling completely ignored in Boston), they were just as likely to place bets themselves. Barney Dreyfuss, in fact, bet thousands on his Pirates, promising his players he'd share his winnings with them. Gambling was as much a part of the game as was the spitball.

Yet even those who didn't gamble were swept up in

the excitement of the biggest series in the history of the sport. As one reporter noted, "Interest all over the city and by all classes is at fever heat. In the downtown hotels and sporting resorts last evening nothing else was talked of." The Americans wisely cashed in on the interest, raising ticket prices across the board. The era of twenty-five-cent baseball ended in Boston.

Hours before game one was scheduled to begin, foot traffic around the park picked up. Trolleys heading down Huntington Avenue were jammed and the stands quickly filled. The overflow crowd was once again routed onto the field, surrounding the diamond and ringing the nether reaches of the outfield. This time, the team was prepared for the onslaught — ropes were already in place and a small army of police manned the temporary barrier. The crowd stretched down each foul line to the fence, while in center field a constant stream of ticketless kranks scaled the center-field fence and either dropped down into the park or fought to preserve a seat atop the 12-foot wall.

At game time, Jimmy Collins and Fred Clarke met with the umpires Hank O'Day and Tommy Connelly at home plate to go over the ground rules. They agreed that any ball that rolled into the outfield crowds would be scored a ground-rule triple. Connelly yelled, "Play ball!" and the Boston Americans ran out onto the field and took their positions as the partisan crowd let out a roar of approval.

Cy Young took the mound and stared in at Criger as Ginger Beaumont of Pittsburgh dug in. The Pirates weren't strangers to Young — he had faced many of them in the National League and had even pitched against Pittsburgh the previous fall in an unauthorized exhibition.

The big pitcher wound up and threw a fastball. Beaumont watched it pass, and O'Day called out strike one. Beaumont worked him to a full count before flying out to Chick Stahl in center field. Fred Clarke then lofted a soft foul behind the plate that Criger caught easily for out number two. For Boston fans, that was the highlight of the day.

As the *Post* reported the following morning, "It was all over in ten minutes." For in the next few moments, the Boston Americans, the pride of the Amer-

ican League, played the absolute worst baseball of their three-year existence, handing the game to Pittsburgh in a manner that seemed suspicious then and seems even more so now. The very first game of the very first "world's series" was, in all likelihood, thrown by Boston.

Young, with two strikes on Pittsburgh's number-three hitter Tommy Leach, was one pitch away from getting out of the inning when he left a third fastball over the plate. Leach bounced it down the first-base line past Candy LaChance. When the ball rolled into the crowd, Leach loped to third with a ground-rule triple.

Next up was Pittsburgh's cleanup batter, Honus Wagner. Young tried a curveball but Wagner wasn't fooled. He pulled a soft liner to left between Collins and Parent. Leach scored the game's first run.

Things got strange fast. Wagner, one of the greatest base stealers in baseball history, did as expected and took off for second on Young's first pitch to Pirate first baseman and Worcester, Massachusetts, native Kit Bransfield. But Criger, easily the best defensive catcher in the game at the time, made a poor throw and Wagner was safe.

Bransfield then knocked a routine grounder to Ferris at second. He first bobbled the ball, then fell down, then threw late to first as Wagner went to third.

With second baseman Claude Ritchey due up next, sound baseball strategy called for Bransfield to stay put. Wagner was already at third, and with two outs there was too much risk and not enough advantage to have Bransfield test Criger's arm. Besides, Bransfield, at 5-foot-11 and 210 pounds, was no great base thief. For the entire season, he stole only thirteen bases.

But he lit out for second as Wagner held at third. Criger hesitated, then lofted the ball into center field. Wagner scored easily. Bransfield still had time to get up, dust himself off, and make it to third ahead of Stahl's throw.

Then Young, he of unparalleled control, walked Ritchey. Jimmy Sebring took the bat, and for the second time that inning the Pirates defied convention. Now Ritchey, with fifteen stolen bases to his credit in 1903, decided he, too, was Wagner's equal. He took off for second.

View of the Huntington Avenue Grounds, October 3, 1903. This photograph depicts an overflow crowd spilling onto the field prior to game three of the 1903 world series. Police wielded rubber hoses and bats to move the crowd back sufficiently for the game to be played. In this game flyballs hit a mere 250 feet, which normally would have resulted in outs, were scored as ground-rule triples.

Criger didn't even throw the ball. He bluffed a peg to third, but Bransfield hadn't moved. Sebring singled to left and both baserunners scored.

Criger wasn't quite finished. Pittsburgh's number-eight hitter, catcher Eddie Phelps, struck out as Young bore down, but Criger suffered his fourth defensive lapse of the inning and let strike three pass by. Phelps made first easily. Finally, Pittsburgh pitcher Deacon Phillippe struck out to end the inning as Criger finally held the ball. Pittsburgh led 4-0. The crowd was stunned.

Boston barely fought back. In the bottom of the inning, Phillippe, a curveball pitcher and no great strikeout artist, fanned Dougherty and Collins. Then Stahl hit a weak fly to end the inning. In the second, Pittsburgh threatened again but player-manager Fred Clarke thought his drive to right field had made the crowd and started to jog for third. It didn't, and he

was thrown out at second. But in the Boston half, the Americans suspiciously went down again, as Freeman, Parent, and LaChance all struck out. The Boston crowd began to catch on and started to boo.

Their scorn grew louder in the third, as Boston's poor play continued. Collins staggered under a fly by Wagner before finally catching it for the first out, then Bransfield looped a hit to right, which Freeman promptly overran and turned into a triple. Bransfield later scored, and now Pittsburgh led 5-0.

The game was essentially over, but that didn't stop Boston's poor play. In the fifth, Ferris blew another groundball leading to another Pittsburgh run, and in the seventh Freeman decided a ball had rolled into the crowd when it hadn't. As he strolled over to pick it up, Sebring tore around the bases for the first home run in series history.

It was 7-0 before Boston finally decided it was safe to play real baseball. In the bottom of the seventh Freeman and Parent hit back-to-back triples, leading to two runs, and Freeman scored another in the ninth after reaching home on an error by Wagner. Young sailed through the late innings, but Boston lost 7-3.

One may be tempted to blame Boston's poor play on nerves or chance, but Boston made at least eight questionable plays in the field during the game, four by Criger and two each by Freeman and Ferris. Early in the game, Boston's hitters swung the bat as if they had never before seen a curveball. And Cy Young's performance was entirely out of character. The likelihood of this all happening at the same time by coincidence is remote.

Although Freeman was no great defender, his miscues were so inept they were laughable. Criger was one of the best catchers of his era and probably the best defensive catcher in Red Sox history. In a career that spanned 984 games over sixteen seasons, he made only 170 errors, an extraordinarily small number for the time. He was so well thought of that in the inaugural balloting for the Hall of Fame in 1936, Criger received more votes than a number of eventual enshrinees, including such luminaries as Frank "Home Run" Baker, Joe McGinnity, Addie Joss, and Harry Heilmann. Yet in one single inning, he made two blatant errors, allowed a steal through indifference, and had a passed ball on a third strike. The game's best catcher played more like a rank amateur.

Ferris was also considered an excellent fielder. Yet he, too, made two critical errors at the worst possible time. And Young, in the midst of perhaps the greatest season of his career, was suspiciously wild, walking three — a season high — and reaching three balls on a number of other hitters. Most postgame reports noted that while he appeared to have his usual hard fastball at the beginning of the first inning, he soon appeared to lose something.

The performances of Boston's hitters were also suspect. Phillippe averaged only four strikeouts per game during the regular season, yet he struck out ten for the game and five of the first six.

Why would the players fix the contest? For the money, but not necessarily because they had bets on the game themselves or were doing the work of gamblers. Players on both sides were unhappy with their financial arrangements. The Pirates had only a vague promise from Dreyfuss that they'd receive a portion of his receipts. Although the Americans had reached a more secure arrangement, they had had to threaten to strike to get that and were still ticked off. Players from both teams had plenty of motivation to make the series go eight or nine games to ensure the largest possible take.

The venture carried no risk, for the men who ran each team cared only about making money themselves and stood to benefit from any extension of the series. And even if the fix was exposed, there was little stigma attached to it or danger of punitive action. The public wasn't naive. Arranged games took place all the time. The outcome of the old Temple Cup championship had been routinely manipulated for exactly the same reason.

Game one was an obvious choice for a fix. With Young on the mound, Boston was a heavy favorite. Arranging a Pittsburgh win allowed players on both teams either to bet against Boston themselves and make a killing, or have friends make the bets for them.

It didn't even necessarily undermine those Rooters who had bet on Boston to win the whole series. If anything, it helped their cause. For a game-one loss by Boston resulted in better odds for Boston bettors over the remainder of the series. Anyone who knew that game one was in the bag was in a great position to either "lay off" on the first game and reap a handsome profit, or take a loss knowing they could make up the difference in subsequent contests. Besides, if both squads agreed to fix a game or two and then play the remainder of the series on the square, the eventual outcome would not be affected. The players wanted to win. But they also wanted to be fairly compensated. The fix was the only way to ensure that.

Without screaming it in the headlines, the press later admitted that at least game one, and perhaps games two and three as well, hadn't been played quite "on the level." In postgame reports, some commentators excused Boston's poor play in the opener

The Boston Americans and Pittsburgh Pirates pose together in front of the grandstand prior to what would be the final game of the 1903 world series on October 13, 1903.

The Pirates are, *top row (l–r):* second baseman Claude Ritchey, catcher Harry Smith, catcher Eddie Phelps, outfielder Ginger Beaumont, pitcher Deacon Phillippe, pitcher Sam Leever, pitcher Bucky Veil, pitcher Gus Thompson, outfielder Tommy Leach, outfielder Jimmy Sebring, pitcher Brickyard Kennedy, catcher Fred Carisch, and shortstop Honus Wagner. *Middle row (l–r):* Pirate manager-outfielder Fred Clarke; Boston players: third baseman-manager Jimmy Collins, outfielder Chick Stahl, pitcher Bill Dinneen, outfielder Buck Freeman, pitcher Cy Young, first baseman Candy LaChance, outfielder Patsy Dougherty, pitcher George Winter, catcher Duke Farrell, outfielder John O'Brien, pitcher Long Tom Hughes. *Bottom row (l–r):* shortstop Fred Parent, catcher Lou Criger, second baseman Hobe Ferris.

as simply "nervous" baseball. But the *Post* reported that "many around town last evening asked if Boston lost on purpose." The *Globe*'s Tim Murnane wryly suggested that Ferris wear "toe weights for the rest of the series," a subtle reference to the intimation that he had "laid down" in the first game. He also noted that Criger's inept play in the first inning stood out to such a degree that it made him look like "a fur overcoat in July."

Within a few days, the *Post* was reporting that "Boston sports today are wondering if they got their money's worth — if Boston really played their best to win" and "wholesale charges of throwing the games have been making the rounds of the city since Saturday evening."

At any rate, Boston turned to Dinneen for game two on Friday, October 2. Poor weather and disgust with Boston's play the previous day held the crowd down to only ten thousand fans. A couple of thousand still had to stand on the field, but special ground rules had no impact on play.

Dinneen began by throwing three consecutive balls to Beaumont, then recovered to strike him out. Clarke then walked, but Leach struck out and Clarke was picked off first.

Patsy Dougherty led off for Boston in the bottom of the first. He turned on the first pitch thrown by Pirate pitcher Sam Leever and drove it to the fence in right field, then raced around the bases for a home run.

Collins flied out, but Stahl followed with a double and scored on Freeman's single. Boston led 2-0.

That was all for Leever. His arm was just too sore. After Pittsburgh went out in order against Dinneen

Royal Rooters show their support in Pittsburgh at game six of the 1903 world series. Outfielder Chick Stahl is shown about to wipe his face with a towel as a Royal Rooter grabs his glass of beer from atop the Americans' dugout. 'Nuf 'Ced McGreevey, middle of frame holding a towel, surveys the action from atop the dugout.

in the top of the second, he was pulled from the game.

Yet curiously, manager Fred Clarke didn't turn to either of the two veteran hurlers on his staff, Brickyard Kennedy or Kaiser Wilhelm. Instead, as if not expecting to win and giving credence to those who later thought the game was fixed, he chose twenty-one-year-old rookie Bucky Veil to relieve Leever. The youngster had made only twelve appearances all year long. After the series he played only one more game in the major leagues.

The remainder of the game went quickly. Dinneen was in command and struck out eleven while Pittsburgh managed only three hits. Veil struggled with his control, but apart from Dougherty's second home run, a long slicing drive over the left-field fence in the fifth, he mesmerized Boston. The Americans won handily, 3-0, conveniently evening the series at one game apiece and ensuring it would last at least four more games.

Improving weather and the weekend combined to make game three, on Saturday, October 3, one of the most memorable in Boston baseball history. Emboldened by Boston's success in game two, virtually every baseball fan in the city tried to squeeze into the Huntington Avenue Grounds.

Four hours before the game, fans were already clamoring for admission. When the gates finally opened at noon, speculators started buying tickets from the cooperative sellers in huge blocks, which they then resold to impatient fans waiting in line. One-dollar grandstand seats went for five bucks, while dollar-fifty boxes sold for as much as ten dollars.

By 1:15, the stands were already full and the field encircled by fans. Enterprising boys sold old chairs, tonic cases, and cartons so that standing-room fans could see above the heads of those in front. In center field, men threw ropes over the fence and stormed the park, climbing over the wall in an unbroken stream.

At 2:00 fans started ducking under the ropes in the outfield and racing toward the infield. In a flash, thousands were on stampede. The *Journal* later noted that the few police on hand "were tossed about like shuttlecocks."

The players, already on the field loosening up, stopped. Fans were suddenly everywhere, overrunning the skinned infield and dashing between fungoes to gain a foothold in front of the bleachers or behind the plate.

The situation was dangerous. A small fire erupted under the bleachers, but fortunately was put out by observant fans. Pirate outfielder Ginger Beaumont and Chick Stahl rescued two women, crushed and screaming for their lives in front of the first-base bleachers. Cy Young was even recruited to help take tickets and plead with fans to maintain order.

Police tried in vain to clear the field, clubbing fans with players' bats, but as soon as they cleared one area and turned their attention to another, the throng poured back in.

Reinforcements were called in and players from both teams grabbed more bats and joined the men in blue in their task. Someone grabbed a 30-foot rubber hose and used it as a whip. The cops and players slowly pushed the crowd from the field of play.

In twenty minutes, they succeeded in moving the crowd all of 40 feet. In the next half-hour, they doubled that amount, eventually succeeding in pushing the throng back into the outfield, but only 250 feet or so from home plate. In foul territory, fans straddled each baseline, allowing the players only a yard or two of foul ground and only 25 or 30 feet of open space behind home.

At 3:10, the umpires decided to let foul balls take care of the fans along the baselines and decided the field was clear enough to play. At least twenty-five thousand people, over half of them standing, had pushed their way into a ballpark that seated only nine thousand fans semicomfortably. Only a few more than eighteen thousand had paid to get in. No major league game this century has ever been played under more extraordinary conditions.

Collins and Clarke met the umpires at home plate and agreed that any fair ball hit into the close crowd would be a ground-rule double. Long Tom Hughes took the mound for Boston. Pittsburgh countered with Phillippe.

Neither team scored in the first inning. Then in the second, with two outs, Claude Ritchey lifted an ordinary flyball to shallow center field. Chick Stahl, playing 100 feet behind second base, watched it drop into the crowd for a double. On any other day, he would have had to come in to make the catch.

The cheap hit unnerved Hughes, and he walked Sebring. Phelps worked him to a full count, then lofted a fly to left. This time Dougherty watched the hit land amid the humanity for a double. The Pirates led 1-0.

After Phillippe retired Boston again, in the third Hughes gave up a leadoff walk to Beaumont. Clarke followed with what the *Post* called "another dumpy, illegal hit" to left field for a double. Jimmy Collins called time and yelled to the Boston bench for Young, but he was in the dressing room under the stands. While they waited for him to make his way to the field, Hughes was forced to pitch to Leach. He singled to score one, then stole second as Criger again let a strike pass by.

Young finally pushed through the crowd and Collins pulled Hughes. But Young struggled again. After going ahead of Wagner 0-2, he hit him to load the bases.

But Bransfield followed with a popup, and then Collins got a groundball force at home. Young needed one more out to escape the inning.

Sebring grounded to Parent, but he muffed the play and Leach scored, although Wagner made a wide turn at second and was caught off base and retired for the third out. Boston trailed 3-0.

That was all Pittsburgh needed, for when Boston came to bat in the bottom of the fourth, things got strange again. The police suddenly succeeded in pushing the crowd in the outfield back another hundred feet, creating more reasonable dimensions in the outfield. Had they done so before the game, none of Pittsburgh's doubles would have counted as hits. They'd have been easy outs and the Pirates would not have scored.

Conversely, in the early innings the Americans had been unable to take advantage of the close crowd. Now they started hitting the ball to the outfield, but the drives that an inning or two before would have fallen for doubles became outs.

The 4-2 final in favor of Pittsburgh disgusted the press. Most blamed the close crowd for the defeat and wondered about the timing of the police work in the outfield. And they once again puzzled over Boston's poor play during the game's most critical juncture.

But the Royal Rooters didn't pay much attention. They were already looking west to Pittsburgh, where there was money to be made and a grand time to be had by all.

Several hundred Rooters traveled together to Pittsburgh by train and set up shop in the same hotel as the Boston players, the Monongehela. The scene in the lobby soon echoed the spectacle that had taken place at the Vendome a few days earlier. Everyone was looking for some action.

The Rooters brought plenty of cash. With the Pirates needing only three wins to take the series, they hoped for more favorable odds.

But Pittsburgh backers, aware that the Pirates were short on pitching, refused to give in. The Rooters put their money down anyway.

Twenty years later, an affidavit surfaced in which Lou Criger claimed he was approached in the hotel lobby and offered $12,000 to throw the series. Ban Johnson used the statement against John McGraw, for Criger claimed that McGraw had introduced the gambler to him. Incredibly, Johnson then awarded Criger, a man who likely helped fix the first games of the series, a lifetime pension for his "honesty." More likely, it was a reward for providing Johnson with some damaging evidence against his old enemy.

Rain delayed game four a day, allowing one Rooter to scour a local music store in search of appropriate theme music. The Rooters traditionally sang and cheered as a group during the games and had even hired a band to accompany them to the ballpark.

The Rooter selected a popular little ditty called "Tessie," from the musical *The Silver Slipper*. Back at the hotel, 'Nuf 'Ced and his cronies laughed themselves hoarse writing parodies of the lyrics to annoy certain Pirate players. They printed the words on cards and distributed them among the Rooters.

The weather cleared and seventy-six hundred fans packed Exposition Park for game four. Collins gave the ball to Dinneen, while Clarke turned once more to Phillippe.

The tenor of the series changed. The unsavory play that marked the first three games in Boston magically disappeared in Pittsburgh, lending credence to the conjecture that one or more of the first three games in Boston had been arranged. The desired effect had taken place. Interest in the games in Pittsburgh was high, and reasonable crowds assured. Now Boston could play to win.

But Boston hadn't figured on the performance of Phillippe. The rainout gave him some needed rest, and for the third time in six days he baffled Boston's hitters. But Dinneen was almost as good. Entering the bottom of the seventh, Pittsburgh led 2-1.

Phillippe led off and lined a single down the left-field line, taking second when Dougherty bobbled the ball. Then Beaumont pushed the ball to LaChance, who fielded it cleanly but had no play at first when Dinneen was slow in getting to the bag. Phillippe moved to third.

Clarke flied out, and Beaumont raced to second. Then Leach tripled and Wagner singled. Suddenly Pittsburgh led 5-1.

The score held until the ninth. Then the Rooters, who had precious little to cheer for so far, got into the act.

Collins stepped to the plate with Boston three outs away from defeat. As he did, the Rooters gave him three loud cheers, then, for the first time, started singing "Tessie" as the band played in accompaniment. The captain ripped a single to center field.

The din continued when Stahl took his place in the batter's box. He pulled a single to left.

Now the Pittsburgh crowd turned silent. The only sounds in Exposition Park were the frantic cheers of the Rooters. Freeman singled to score Collins, and Parent followed with a groundball that forced Freeman at second, but Stahl scored. The tying run was at the plate in the form of Candy LaChance.

So far, the big first baseman had done little in the series. But now, as if boosted by the Rooters, he bounced a groundball over Phillippe's reach and into center field. Parent made third easily.

Collins had Farrell hit for Criger. He knocked a flyball to left, and Parent tagged up and scored. John O'Brien, batting for Dinneen, stepped up to the plate with the game on the line.

'Nuf 'Ced McGreevey, red-faced and aflame, stood atop the Boston dugout waving a multicolored parasol and singing "Tessie" with all his might. The band played and a big bass drum thundered across the field.

Then O'Brien swung. The ball went high into the sky, but came down in the hands of Claude Ritchey at second base. The Pirates had won, 5-4, and now led the series three games to one.

Yet the Rooters and the Boston Americans were strangely confident. Phillippe's spell had been broken. With Young scheduled to pitch the following day against anybody's guess for Pittsburgh, they liked their chances.

The Rooters' unrestrained enthusiasm had changed the character of the series. The Boston newspapers lauded the Rooters, giving them credit for inspiring the near-miracle comeback. They hardly needed any encouragement.

On the morning of October 7, the Rooters started singing and cheering at the hotel, paraded to the ballpark, and didn't stop until the game ended. For

1903 Pittsburgh Pirates in their dugout at the Huntington Avenue Grounds during the world series. They are (l–r): utility player Joe Marshall, infielder Otto Krueger, outfielder Jimmy Sebring, shortstop Honus Wagner, unidentified player, catcher Eddie Phelps, bat boy, pitcher Gus Thompson, pitcher Deacon Phillippe, first baseman Kit Bransfield, outfielder Ginger Beaumont, pitcher Sam Leever, second baseman Claude Ritchey, and pitcher Brickyard Kennedy.

five innings Brickyard Kennedy and Cy Young provided their accompaniment as each held the other team scoreless. In the sixth, Boston finally broke through.

Chick Stahl hit a short fly to left. With the Rooters creating a racket, neither Clarke nor Wagner heard the other call for the catch. They collided, Clarke dropped the ball, and Stahl made first. Freeman then singled and Parent bunted to Leach at third.

But the Pirates were rattled. Decades later, Leach admitted to Lawrence Ritter, "I think those Boston fans won the Series . . . We beat them three out of the first four games, and then they started sing-ing that damn Tessie song . . . Sort of got on your nerves after a while." Wagner raced to cover third, but couldn't handle Leach's throw. The bases were loaded.

The play sent McGreevey back atop the Boston dugout, and worried Pittsburgh officials, afraid that the stands would burst, propped up the fence before the Boston fans. But it was Brickyard Kennedy and the Pirates who truly needed help.

They came completely unglued. LaChance walked, Wagner made a bad throw on a grounder by Ferris, and then, after Criger sacrificed, Cy Young cracked the defining blow, driving a ground-rule double into the crowd. When Dougherty followed with a triple, Boston suddenly led 6-0.

According to the *Post*, now Boston's loyal Rooters "acted more like escaped patients from an insane asylum." But it was the Pirates who were driven nuts.

Throughout the remainder of the game the Rooters hooted and hollered Boston to victory, taunting Honus Wagner with a parody of Tessie that went

> *"Honus, why do you hit so badly,*
> *Take a back seat and sit down*
> *Honus, at bat you look so sadly.*
> *Hey, why don't you get out of town?"*

Souvenir card with lyrics to "Tessie" distributed by 'Nuf 'Ced McGreevey to members of the Royal Rooters. The Rooters serenaded the Americans with the song while altering the lyrics in a derisive manner directed toward the Pirates. Among the players chided was the great Honus Wagner, who was greeted with the lyric, "Honus, why do you hit so badly?"

Rooter's Souvenir
BOSTON · PITTSBURG
Oct., 1903. M. T. McGreevy

TESSIE,
You Are The Only, Only, Only.

CHORUS.

Tessie, you make me feel so badly;
Why don't you turn around.
Tessie, you know I love you madly;
Babe, my heart weighs about a pound.
Don't blame me if I ever doubt you,
You know, I wouldn't live without you;
Tessie, you are the only, only, only, -ly.

3d Base.   Nuf Ced.
Who Kidnapped the Pittsburg Band
Nuf Ced—McGreevy.

The Americans won 11-2, and the Rooters took to the streets afterward, parading through Pittsburgh in celebration. Pirate fans tried to match their Boston counterparts in enthusiasm, but they just didn't have it. When Bill Dinneen took the mound for Boston in game six, they showered the field with confetti, hoping to distract the hurler. Sniffed Tim Murnane in the *Globe*, "Boston rooters are educated in the fine points of their art and never root to bother an opposing pitcher. Not so with the local enthusiasts."

All the prank did was make Dinneen mad. He took it out on the Pirates, shutting them out for six innings before being touched for three runs in the seventh. But by then, it was too late, for Boston had already roughed up sore-armed Sam Leever for six runs. Boston won, 6-3, to tie the series at three games apiece.

Game seven would be the last in Pittsburgh. When scheduled starter Deacon Phillippe arrived at the ballpark, he complained to Pittsburgh owner Barney Dreyfuss of a sore arm, adding, "It's awful cold out there . . . I'm not fond of working under such conditions." With that, he swung his arm back and forth as if trying to crank-start a balky engine.

That gave Dreyfuss an idea. He conferred with Fred Clarke, decided that it was too cold to play, and postponed the game to Saturday.

Collins howled when he found out — it was windy, but nearly 60 degrees. But under the terms of the series, the home team had the right to cancel any game because of the weather. Dreyfuss's thermometer said it was too cold to play.

Of course, there was much more to it than that. Now Phillippe had an extra day of rest, and the crowd on a Saturday was certain to be larger. The Rooters were also supposed to leave for Boston at midnight. The Pirates were sick to death of "Tessie" and thought they'd be rid of it. But the Rooters weren't going anywhere.

With the weather little improved on Saturday,

Flag raising was a common sight in the club's early years. Here the players help hoist the flag to celebrate a patriotic holiday, probably Patriots' Day.

more than seventeen thousand fans packed the ballpark. Just like in Boston, special ground rules had to be put in place making any ball hit into the crowd a triple.

When Patsy Dougherty stepped in to face Phillippe in the top of the first, the scene turned ghostly. Heavy black smoke from nearby steel mills floated over the field and blocked the sun. Clarke called time and raced in to confer with the umpire. But Collins, fearing another delay, would have none of it. He raced out and jawed with Clarke, and the umpire soon sent both men back to their places and motioned for Phillippe to throw the ball.

Dougherty grounded out on the first pitch, but an angry Collins smacked the ball into the crowd for a triple. Stahl followed with another three-bagger and later scored on an error to put Boston ahead, 2-0.

That was about all Young needed. He shut down the Pirates until Boston scored two more in the fourth. He then allowed a single run, gave up another in the sixth, and eventually won 7-3. Boston now led the series four games to three.

With the last out, the Rooters raced from the stands and surrounded their heroes. McGreevey led everyone on a parade around the field and, with the

players in tow, down the streets of Pittsburgh to the hotel, then on to the train station. When the entourage arrived at South Station Sunday afternoon, they were met by hundreds of fans. Boys and men together rushed the platform, and Cy Young was carried from the train and passed into the station on the shoulders of his admirers.

The Pittsburgh players received no such greeting. On Monday morning, they awoke to some horrible news. A headline in the *Post* screamed "Pitcher Doheny a Raving Maniac." On Sunday, their former teammate Ed Doheny had attacked a private nurse with a stove poker at his home in Andover, nearly killing him, then held dozens of neighbors and local police at bay for over an hour before he was overpowered. Doheny was immediately committed to an insane asylum in Danvers, Massachusetts, and never recovered.

Rain postponed the game until Tuesday. The Rooters were given seats of honor in four rows of highbacked chairs placed in front of the grandstand. Accompanied by the Letter Carriers Band, they arrived early.

But poor weather combined, perhaps, with some fatigue on everyone's part kept the crowd down to just over seven thousand zealots. For the finale, Boston turned to Dinneen, while Pittsburgh trotted out Deacon Phillippe for the fifth time in thirteen days.

Dinneen was right from the start, striking out Beaumont to begin the game and retiring Clarke and Leach easily. But Phillippe proved he still had enough, as Boston was no more successful.

In the third, Sebring ripped a line drive back to the box. Dinneen reached for the ball with his bare hand and knocked it down, then threw Sebring out at first.

But the drive split open a finger on his pitching hand. It bled for the rest of the game, staining the ball red. Collins, taking no chances, immediately ordered Cy Young to get ready. For much of the rest of the game Young played catch behind the grandstand, following the game by listening to the crowd.

He heard Boston break through in the fourth. Freeman tripled, then Parent reached base with an infield hit and moved to second on a forceout. Ferris plated both men with a single, and Boston led 2-0.

Dinneen was not to be denied. Every time Pittsburgh put a man on, he seemed to find the pitch he needed. By the seventh inning, with Boston up 3-0, the Letter Carriers Band was playing a never-ending version of "Tessie" for a chorus of 7,455.

In the ninth, still bleeding, Dinneen retired Clarke and Leach before Honus Wagner came to the plate.

The great player had had a terrible series, making as many errors as hits — six — and stealing only one base.

Dinneen didn't let up. Wagner worked him to a full count.

For the first time in a week, the Rooters turned silent. Dinneen wound up and threw a chest-high fastball.

Wagner swung through the pitch. Criger threw the ball high into the air.

The band started playing. A roar went through the crowd. The Rooters jumped from their seats and raced onto the field.

Boston had won.

The crowd swarmed around the Boston players. A desolate Phillippe trudged from the mound, dodging fans, and offered Jimmy Collins a quick handshake. The captain was soon swept up by the crowd and lifted on their shoulders, as were Dinneen, Parent, Stahl, and Ferris. They were carried to the grandstand and then to the clubhouse for a brief private celebration.

Meanwhile, McGreevey, the Rooters, and the band started parading around the field, joined by hundreds of delirious fans. McGreevey led the parade out of the ballpark and down the street to his saloon, where the drinks were plentiful, but not complimentary.

RED STOCKINGS AND RED FACES

1904 | 1911

Cy Young prepares for action on the sidelines. Known as the "King of Pitchers," Young pitched a perfect game at the age of thirty-seven on May 5, 1904, at the Huntington Avenue Grounds while besting Athletics ace Rube Waddell. In 1908 at the age of forty-one Young pitched a no-hitter against the New York Highlanders and was just one walk shy of another perfect effort.

Everybody loves a winner, but in Boston that aphorism is usually followed by another. Next to honoring its champions, the town's favorite pastime is knocking them off their pedestals. The tradition began in 1903.

Less than twenty-four hours after the Boston Americans became world champions, the shine began to wear off the triumph. While the Rooters were delighted and enriched by the outcome (Sport Sullivan alone reportedly made more than $20,000 on the series), the joy of the Boston players soon soured. Most received their first batch of bad news while still nursing hangovers from the previous night at McGreevey's.

One day after the series, each man received a check for $1,182.34 from team owner Henry Killilea, precisely the distribution agreed upon. But Pittsburgh's Barney Dreyfuss turned over his entire share of receipts to his players, netting each $1,316.00. The Pirates earned more for losing than the Americans did by winning.

The press continued to raise questions about the first three games. When asked by the *Post* to sum up his feelings the day after the series, Jimmy Collins defensively snapped, "We won . . . The games have been cleanly played, and no one can say otherwise . . . Our victory should make those 'knockers' ashamed of themselves. It is impossible for baseball to be played dishonestly."

Even the Rooters were criticized. *The Sporting News* blamed McGreevey for the lack of a suitable public celebration following the victory, complaining that "some of the head people worked it [the victory] for all it was worth and one cheap guy who runs a cheap barroom near the ballgrounds schemed it out for a big ad and a big drinkfest at his saloon. He had the band and some of the rooters headed over toward his gin mill before the rooters were wise." But the series made newspaper publishers smile. They'd learned that baseball sold papers. The Boston Americans remained big news.

Goaded on by the Rooters and disgruntled players, the Boston press carped all winter about the absentee owner. They characterized Killilea as a greedy cheat who had swindled the players out of their fair share of the receipts and gouged fans by selling tickets to speculators. The Americans had won in spite of their owner. He received no credit for their victory.

Killilea didn't help matters. In December he sent right-handed pitcher Long Tom Hughes, who won twenty games in 1903, to New York in exchange for lefty Jesse Tannehill.

On its face, the deal didn't look bad. Tannehill, age twenty-nine, had won twenty games or more four times for Pittsburgh before jumping to New York in 1903, where he slumped to 15-15. Hughes, only twenty-five, had been a mediocre performer before breaking out in 1903.

The problem was perception. Ban Johnson needed the New York franchise to succeed. Killilea served as his willing puppet, allowing the Americans to be used to benefit New York.

The critics argued that Tannehill was in decline, while Hughes was on the upswing. Even though Hughes had disappointed Collins in the series and the manager wanted a left-handed pitcher, he was lukewarm about the trade. He liked his pitchers big, like Young, Dinneen, and Hughes, all of whom stood over 6 feet tall. Tannehill was only 5-foot-8.

By the spring of 1904, Killilea was fed up. With the club's popularity at its peak, he decided to cash in and sell out.

Johnson was delighted. He wanted a local owner to provide the press a more convenient target for their assaults.

Killilea was inundated with offers. Most weren't serious. In three years the team had proven to be a cash cow, probably the most lucrative in baseball. In 1903 alone, Killilea cleared an easy fifty thousand dollars.

A number of Rooters believed they were perfect candidates to run the ballclub, but most lacked the capital. Rooter Mike Sullivan, the former Nationals pitcher turned state senator, made an offer, but he was only the front man for a syndicate of fans.

Johnson and Killilea ignored the bid. Syndicates were hard to control. Johnson wanted one man, preferably someone who would still be willing to allow Johnson to run the show.

The most serious suitor was John "Honey Fitz" Fitzgerald. But Fitzgerald was too much his own man for Johnson and too likely to act independently. Fitzgerald thought he had a deal to buy the team, but Johnson nixed the deal. He wanted a patsy.

While the first act of this political melodrama was being played out in the press, the Americans, still cocky from their world series, opened the regular season with three games in New York. The Invaders won the opener, 8-2, as Jack Chesbro defeated Cy Young. But the Americans rebounded to win the next two games, battering former teammate Tom Hughes in the process, and returned to Boston for their home opener on Patriots' Day, April 18.

Ten thousand fans cheered as Collins hoisted two 30-foot pennants up the flagpole in center field. The first said simply "American League Champions." The second emphatically added "World Champions."

Tannehill squashed any doubts over the trade by shutting down Washington on only two hits while the Americans scored five. Boston fans left the park certain they were witnessing the beginning of another march toward the pennant.

Most were surprised to learn the next morning that the team had finally been sold. The new owner was not Fitzgerald, who had been spotted the previous day at the game in animated conversation with Johnson and Killilea, but another newspaperman, John I. Taylor, son of *Boston Globe* publisher General Charles Taylor.

In reality, the General's money changed hands. The son, referred to by one and all simply as "John I," was simply the beneficiary of his father's indulgence. The price was one hundred forty-five thousand dollars, five thousand more than Fitzgerald's bid.

Since the club's inception, John I. had been a familiar face in the stands. Little else interested him.

He'd briefly given the newspaper business a try, working in the advertising and editorial departments of the *Globe*, but had retired to live on his father's money. Since then he had gained a reputation as an empty suit and good-natured layabout and playboy who liked his cocktails. Since the son was wasting his life at the ballpark anyway, the father decided that he might as well give him a stake in the matter and named him club president.

A firebrand he was not. His tenure at the helm of the team was easily the most unsuccessful of any Boston owner — no small accomplishment considering the competition. Yet history has treated Taylor kindly, for he gave the team its nickname and its ballpark, which have obliterated the fact that he ran a championship team into the ground through pure incompetence.

The young scion easily met Johnson's criteria for ownership: the check cleared and he was easy to control. The new owner readily agreed to retain Green as business manager and offered no objection to the schedule.

The next day, Fitzgerald and Johnson attacked one another in open letters each released to the press.

Johnson stated that "I had no personal feeling against Fitzgerald . . . My reasons for refusing the sale were purely because of the political strife I feared would follow." Fitzgerald countered by writing, "Mr. Johnson does not tell the truth," and hinted at the more sinister reasons behind his refusal. But ever the politician, Fitzgerald took care to add that "Whatever turn my relations may take with Mr. Johnson and Mr. Killilea, the principle which actuated me in going after the franchise — that the club be owned in Boston — is carried out and this gives me the greatest satisfaction. This is what the public destined, and I am proud that it was due to my initiative that this action has been brought about."

The gracious Fitzgerald then curried favor by publishing a puff piece in the *Republic* extolling the virtues of General Taylor as a progressive employer. In return, the ballclub wisely started advertising in Fitzgerald's paper.

The sale had little impact on the field. Within a week the club surged into first place and looked like a lock for their second consecutive pennant.

That seemed even more likely after the Philadelphia A's came into Boston in early May. Many considered them the only team capable of stopping Boston. On the afternoon of Thursday, May 5, they sent Rube Waddell out to the mound hoping to slow the champions' march. But Boston had Cy Young.

Ten thousand fans turned out for the matchup, the largest regular-season weekday crowd in club history at the time. The last time the two pitchers had faced each other Waddell had thrown a one-hit shutout.

For the first four innings, Waddell and Young kept the game scoreless. Although Boston threatened, Waddell's marvelous fastball, which he used to strike out a record 349 batters that season, got him out of trouble.

Meanwhile, Young had it easy. The A's hardly got the bat on the ball, and when they did, they hardly got the ball out of the infield. At the start of the fifth, a few fanatics paying close attention stood and cheered. In less than a minute, their enthusiasm spread throughout the park. For Young had retired all twelve men he had faced. Apart from a fine running catch by Buck Freeman in short right field in the third, no A's player had come close to getting a hit.

Boston American owner John I. Taylor was handed the reins of power by his father, General Charles H. Taylor, who saw the team as a diversion for his wayward son. John I. Taylor broke up the pennant-winning team of 1904 and also named the team the Red Sox in 1907. It was General Taylor who selected the site for Fenway Park in 1911 and began construction before selling the team to James McAleer.

Young was throwing a perfect game, a feat considered impossible at the time.

His mastery continued in the fifth, as did Waddell's good fortune. In the sixth, with the crowd roaring with each pitch, Young set down the A's again, fanning Waddell to retire his eighteenth consecutive batter.

In the bottom of the inning Boston finally broke through when Chick Stahl and Buck Freeman hit back-to-back ground-rule triples into the crowd in right. Boston led 1-0, and with Young pitching on this day one run was as good as ten.

Leading off the seventh, A's outfielder Danny Hoffman hit a high curving foul fly deep to left field. Patsy Dougherty gave chase and, with his back against the fence, jumped and caught the ball. Young then induced Charlie Pickering to ground out to Parent at short and closed the inning by striking out Harry Davis for the second time.

Boston then scored twice in the bottom of the inning to give Young a cushion. At the beginning of the eighth Candy LaChance called out to Young from

THE BOSTON FITZGERALDS

When he learned that the Red Sox were for sale in 1904, Honey Fitz stepped out from the crowd.

In the past decade the Boston native had deftly parlayed his Irish roots and personal charm through the snakepit of Boston ward politics to become one of the most powerful Democratic politicians in the state. In 1892 he won election to the state senate, and in 1894 he moved to the United States House of Representatives, representing the Tenth District.

But Fitzgerald had higher aspirations. In Massachusetts, the real political power lay in Boston politics. Fitzgerald wanted to be mayor, and in 1900 he gave up his congressional seat to make a bid for the mayor's office.

But he miscalculated. Another Irishman, Patrick A. Collins, won the support of Boston's ward politicians and became mayor. Fitzgerald was left on the outside.

He bided his time and continued to build his political base, jumping on the bandwagon of the new baseball team and assuming a role as a leader of the Royal Rooters to keep his visibility high. He also purchased a small financially struggling Catholic weekly newspaper, the *Republic,* for five hundred dollars.

Publishing a clever mix of Irish-Catholic political reportage, social news, and serialized moral parables, Fitzgerald made the *Republic* required reading for Boston's Irish-Catholics, which at the time numbered over one hundred thousand households. Advertisers wisely followed. By 1903, the newspaper, which sold for five cents or a dollar fifty per year, was earning Fitzgerald an annual profit of more than twenty-five thousand dollars.

To Fitzgerald's political supporters, being a baseball fan was nearly as important as being Irish-Catholic or a Democrat. Flush with cash from the *Republic,* Honey Fitz viewed the opportunity to buy the team as a chance to solidify his political base and expand his profile by keeping his name in the paper until the next mayoral election in 1905. He hoped to ride the coattails of the championship team into office.

When current owner Henry Killilea heard of his interest, he told Honey Fitz the price of the franchise was one hundred forty thousand dollars, an opening bid calculated to gauge his interest. Fitzgerald didn't blanch at the figure or even try to negotiate. He just said yes. With the hook so deeply set, Killilea quickly passed the good news on to Ban Johnson.

At first, Johnson shared Killilea's enthusiasm for the deal. Fitzgerald was local, had the money, and as a former congress-

man possessed an impeccable reputation, at least as far as Johnson cared. Fitzgerald's ties to machine politics and his social proximity to gamblers were of no consequence.

The three men met several times in early March in both Chicago and Boston to iron out the details of the sale. At the end of the month, Fitzgerald thought he had a deal.

Then one of the team's attorneys, Joseph Pelletier, found out about the impending sale. He tipped off a crony, Massachusetts congressman William McNary, and a political enemy of Fitzgerald.

McNary viewed Fitzgerald's purchase in purely political terms, reasoning that if Honey Fitz owned the Americans, his election to the mayor's office in 1905 would be a mere formality. He didn't want that to happen.

McNary expressed his opposition to Johnson and issued a vague warning that hinted of political consequences. Then he sent Pelletier and Charley Green, the team's business manager and a Johnson appointee, to meet with Johnson in person in Chicago. They intimated to Johnson that Fitzgerald's ties to New York's Tammany Hall political machine could put the team at risk. Fitzgerald, they whispered, might really be just a front man for National League interests still bitter over the recently negotiated peace. As evidence, they offered Fitzgerald's stated intention to replace Charley Green with his own man.

That got Johnson's attention. He remembered how John McGraw had nearly destroyed the league by selling out the Orioles and how hard Tammany Hall had worked to prevent Johnson from moving into New York.

Besides, Johnson, a Presbyterian, was wary of Irish-Catholics. The more he pondered a Fitzgerald-run Boston franchise the more he disliked the idea. Fitzgerald didn't even own the team yet and was already complaining about the 1904 schedule, which sent Boston to Washington on both Bunker Hill Day and the Fourth of July, two lucrative holidays. Fitzgerald wanted those games to be played in Boston so Boston's working class — all potential Fitzgerald voters — could attend on the holidays.

Johnson disliked such interference and realized that Fitzgerald's ego matched his own. Honey Fitz was a man Johnson would never be able to control. Pelletier had given him an excuse to say no.

When Fitzgerald met with Johnson and Killilea to sign the final papers and take control of the club, Johnson pulled the deal

Often misidentified as the opening of the 1912 World Series in Boston, this photo shows politician John F. Fitzgerald, who served as both mayor of Boston and congressman from East Boston, throwing out the first ball of a game at the Huntington Avenue Grounds. His daughter Rose, later to marry Joseph P. Kennedy, is seated third from the right above the dugout. Fitzgerald, a longtime member of the Royal Rooters, thought he had purchased the team from Henry Killilea in 1904 only to have the deal voided by league president Ban Johnson.

off the table. Just as his own enemies had once complained that the only problem was "too much Johnson," Johnson now told Fitzgerald he was "too much Boston."

Fitzgerald was incensed and went public, hinting that Johnson was anti-Catholic and anti-Irish. He recruited Frederic O'Connell of the *Post* to deliver his charges, and O'Connell readily complied. After all, his two elder brothers were solidly in Fitzgerald's camp. Brother Joseph won election to Congress in 1908, while Daniel later served as Honey Fitz's personal secretary.

The potential consequences of a Fitzgerald-owned team is fascinating to consider and may well have changed the course of Boston baseball history. And because of the Byzantine nature of Boston politics, so too may have political history been irrevocably altered. For in 1907, after Fitzgerald finally won election to the mayor's office, he angered Pelletier by leaving Michael Mitchell, one of Pelletier's friends, out to dry in a corruption scandal.

Pelletier, who later became district attorney, eventually got even. In 1913 Daniel Coackley, the one-time sports editor of the *Boston Herald* turned lawyer and the unsuccessful defender of Mitchell, went after Fitzgerald, who was again running for mayor. With Pelletier's assistance, they exposed Honey Fitz's unseemly relationship with a cigarette girl in the so-called "Toodles" scandal, leading him to withdraw as a candidate and delivering the election to James Michael Curley. The exposé effectively ended Fitzgerald's political career. Those unfulfilled aspirations would be left to a later generation, represented by his grandson John Fitzgerald Kennedy. Had Fitzgerald's attempt to purchase the ballclub been successful, his legacy may well have been based in baseball rather than politics. ⚾

first base, "No one's been by here yet." Young knew what was at stake and didn't relax. The A's were quickly set down.

The game was barely an hour old when Boston went out quickly in the bottom of the inning. Young took the mound at the top of the ninth as ten thousand voices called out his name.

Shortstop Monte Cross led off, desperate to make contact. Young struck him out.

Next was Ossee Schreckengost, the former Boston catcher. While Young's pitching was no secret to "Schreck," that gave him little advantage. Young jammed him, and he bounced a groundball to Parent. Two down. Young was one batter — Rube Waddell — away from making history.

A's manager Connie Mack chose not to pinch hit. The eccentric hurler was a fair batsman and there was no one better on the bench.

Waddell swung at the first pitch and lifted the ball high to center field.

As it soared through the air, silence engulfed the Huntington Avenue Grounds. Young spun, tilted his head back, and followed the flight of the ball. As he said later, "Never did a ball seem so slow in dropping."

In center, Chick Stahl took a few steps and raised both hands before his face. "As it dropped into Stahl's glove," wrote Frederic O'Connell, "a roar as if a hundred cannon [sic] had belched forth rocked the stands and bleachers." Cy Young had accomplished the impossible. He had pitched the first of only fifteen perfect games (through 1999) in modern major league history.

His teammates and several hundred fans swarmed around the mound, and the big pitcher grinned and waved at the crowd. Stahl handed him the ball and a fan pressed a five-dollar bill in his right hand. Young fought his way through the crowd to the clubhouse, shaking the hand of every fan he could reach.

"Happy?" he said in response to a question from the press, "I should say I was. It's hard for me to tell how I did it. I never felt better in my life.

"I kept mixing the balls. Criger says I didn't throw two balls alike and I guess I'll take his word for it.

"I would throw a curve, then a slow straight one, then a fast straight one. I knew the batters pretty well

and tried to throw them where they couldn't hit them."

Then, for the only time in his long career, he talked at length about the game that had brought him fame. As he spoke, Denton True Young shared the kernels of homespun wisdom that made him great, saying, "I like the sound of base hits better than grand opera, if my team is making them," "Don't let your head turn because the crowd cheers you," and "Dissipation of any sort will shorten your baseball career."

The A's were magnanimous in defeat. Connie Mack said, "I am proud to be defeated by such pitching." Even Waddell didn't mind, saying, "I wouldn't have missed it for a hundred dollars."

Young's accomplishment was so shocking that a day later the *Post* ran an illustration favorably comparing Young's right arm to that of heavyweight champion boxer Jim Jeffries. Doctor Roland Brayton analyzed Young's "pitching apparatus," his right arm, noting that Young's shoulder musculature was "thick and heavy," his pectorals "deep and firm," and his right side "unusually soft and pliable." He finally concluded, "Careful husbanding of his strength has made him the pitcher he is today."

The victory gave the Americans a record of 13-3. Boston, at the beginning of a long homestand, appeared nearly unbeatable. Then New York came into town.

The two clubs didn't get along, and Jimmy Collins and New York manager Clark Griffith goaded each other in the press, Collins boasting that "We hate to be hoggish, but we need all the games we can win," to which Griffith replied, "We are not afraid of the world champions."

After losing the first game when pitcher Tom Hughes booted several bunts, the New Yorkers spanked the Americans twice, winning 6-3 and 2-1. The wins vaulted New York over the .500 mark and exposed a subtle crack in the champions' armor.

While Boston continued to play well, New York settled into the first division. Soon they were battling Philadelphia and Chicago for second place.

But Ban Johnson feared a Boston runaway would hurt attendance throughout the league. And in New York, the Invaders were in a pitched battle over the baseball dollar of New York fans with the National

League Giants of John McGraw. They needed a little help.

The New Yorkers were already upset with the outcome of the Hughes-Tannehill trade. Hughes had been a failure and would soon be traded again. Johnson decided to make things right.

On June 17, he arranged the trade of popular Boston outfielder Patsy Dougherty to New York in exchange for utility player Bob Unglaub. A cooperative John I. Taylor, who thought Dougherty was ungrateful for a recent raise, quietly acquiesced to the deal.

It was one of the worst trades in team history and precipitated a decline on the field far worse than that which was later blamed on the sale of Babe Ruth sixteen years later. Collins and his players were stunned and lost all respect for their new owner who, as Freddy Parent described in a 1968 interview, "was drunk half the time" and Johnson's pawn even when

sober. Collins barred Taylor from the clubhouse, where he had been making regular appearances after games, sometimes delivering praise, but more often barbed criticism. For the rest of Collins's tenure Taylor took up residence in a chair outside the clubhouse door where he could snipe at players on their way in and out.

Dougherty was one of the most popular men on the team and one of the best young players in the game. Although he was hitting only .273, he had entered the season with a .336 career batting average.

Unglaub had originally been Boston property, signed under a curious arrangement that had Ban Johnson's fingerprints all over it, for New York had the right to claim him on demand, without compensation. After the 1903 season, they had done just that.

But after playing only six games, he got blood poi-

Main grandstand of the Huntington Avenue Grounds, circa 1904. Note the small upper deck, spacious foul territory, and almost universal presence of bowler hats on fans.

soning and was now unable to play. When New York squawked, the trade was made to rectify the Tannehill transaction and Unglaub's inconvenient illness.

Dougherty left a gaping hole in the Boston outfield. He went on to lead the league in runs scored and specialize in embarrassing Boston almost every time the two clubs played each other. Unglaub, meanwhile, played a grand total of nine games for the Americans in 1904.

The Boston press and the Royal Rooters saw through the deal. "Anything to strengthen New York," was the consensus opinion, although most still felt good about Boston's pennant chances.

Their confidence was soon shaken. New York came into Boston a week later and Dougherty made a triumphant return by banging the ball all over the lot. Boston lost two out of three. Suddenly there was a pennant race.

The two clubs battled for the remainder of the year, but neither was able to gain advantage over the other. In mid-September, in a virtual tie for first place, they squared off in Boston to play three doubleheaders on three consecutive days. Each team won two and lost two, with the other two games end-

Boston players relax prior to a game around 1906–07. Star pitcher Bill Dinneen (center, holding glove) sits among teammates and a Chicago opponent.

ing in ties because of inclement weather and encroaching darkness. Nothing was decided.

The season proceeded as if the baseball gods were determined to push the concept of a pennant race to its most implausible and anxiety-ridden conclusion. Over the season's last weekend the two teams played each other in a five-game series in which the balance of power swung back and forth with every pitch.

Coming into New York on Friday, October 7, Boston, with a record of 92-57, led 90-56 New York by one-half game and had momentum. But New York had Jack Chesbro. For that one single season no other pitcher in modern major league history has ever been his equal.

He was already a star, having led the NL with twenty-eight wins for the champion Pirates in 1902. In 1903 the North Adams, Massachusetts, native jumped to New York. In 1904, he pitched as if he had made a pact with the devil.

Although the press called him "Happy Jack," he was anything but. His suspicious, scowling, sour countenance led some to question his sanity. Like his one-time teammate Ed Doheny, Chesbro was paranoid and often imagined he was being persecuted and pursued by detectives.

But on the mound his peculiarities served him well. An early master of the spitball, Chesbro pitched as if possessed by the furies.

In 1904, after starting the season 4-3, he reeled off fourteen straight wins. Over the course of the season he started — and finished — nearly one-third of New York's games and made several more relief appearances. For the year, he started an amazing fifty-one contests, completing forty-eight and hurling a remarkable 454.1 innings.

He faced Boston on October 7 with forty wins in fifty decisions. With Tannehill unavailable because of a pulled groin muscle, Collins sent Norwood Gibson to the mound.

Both teams showed their nerves, and the game was marred by errors and nervous play. Patsy Dougherty took advantage of two Boston errors to score twice, and despite an eighth-inning rally, Boston fell to New York, 3-2. Chesbro was carried off the field on the shoulders of the delirious New York crowd.

The two teams were supposed to play a doubleheader in New York on the following day, Saturday, October 8. But earlier in the year, when it appeared as if Boston would win the pennant going away, New York owner Frank Ferrell had rented his field to Columbia for a football game. So as soon as the game ended, players on both clubs boarded a train and headed to Boston.

New York manager Clark Griffith ordered Chesbro to stay behind and rest for the return engagement on October 10, but he showed up on the platform at Grand Central Station and challenged his manager, asking him bluntly, "Do you want to win the pennant?" Griffith waved him aboard.

The next day, thirty thousand partisan fans poured into the Huntington Avenue Grounds and onto the field. Chesbro took the ball for the second consecutive day. Collins chose Dinneen to pitch for Boston.

For three innings Chesbro was nearly perfect, giving up only a third-inning walk and nursing a 1-0 lead. But in the fourth, in his 445th inning of the season, Boston broke him, romping to a 13-2 victory to pull back into first place.

Boston remained on the field as Dinneen walked off and Cy Young took his place. In less than a minute, game two was under way.

Young shut out New York on six hits. Yet New York's Jake Powell was better and gave Boston only four.

But one was an infield hit to Hobe Ferris in the sixth inning. Criger sacrificed him to second. Young flied out to John Anderson in center field, but Ferris tagged and scored. Boston held on to win 1-0. With two games remaining, Boston led New York by a game and a half. The Invaders needed to sweep a doubleheader on Monday in New York to win the pennant.

Chesbro faced Dinneen in the opener. With the game scoreless and one out in the third, Chesbro stepped to the plate. The game was halted and New York fans presented him with a fur coat in appreciation for his accomplishments. He responded by knocking a triple, but Dinneen struck out Dougherty and Keeler to end the threat.

Then in the fifth, with two out, Kleinow and Chesbro both singled. Dougherty galled Boston fans by singling Kleinow home.

Dinneen walked the next two batters, forcing in Chesbro, before he escaped. With four innings left, New York led 2-0.

But not even Chesbro could do everything. In the seventh his defense fell apart and Boston scored twice. The two teams entered the ninth inning still tied.

For Boston, Johnny Pesky allegedly held the ball and Bill Buckner let it go between his legs, two events fans seem unable to forget. Long ago in the city of New York, a single pitch thrown by Jack Chesbro once resided in a similar Hall of Infamy.

Criger opened the inning by beating out a slow roller to short. Dinneen sacrificed him to second. But with the game on the line, Chesbro induced Kip Selbach to tap back to the mound. Criger took third as Chesbro got the out at first base.

Freddy Parent stepped in for Boston. Twice before

Happy Jack Chesbro came by his nickname in much the manner an overweight person would be called "Slim." His superb season of 1904, which saw the righthander win a league-leading forty-one games, was marred by his wild pitch in the first game of a season-ending doubleheader that allowed Boston to break a 2-2 tie and win their second league championship.

Chesbro had sent Parent back to the bench with a strikeout. Now he threw two pitches and Parent swung through each to go down two strikes.

Chesbro was one pitch away from the third out, but after 454 innings, one pitch was one too many. He threw a spitball. Just as Boston fans would later debate whether Bob Stanley's pitch to Mookie Wilson in the ninth inning of game six of the 1986 World Series should have been caught by catcher Rich Gedman, New York fans in the early part of the twentieth century debated Chesbro's next toss.

The pitch slipped from his saliva-grip and sailed high. Kleinow reached up and jumped for the ball — perhaps, as some argued, a half-beat slower than usual, while others insisted later that it was uncatchable — and the pitch sailed past, hitting the backstop on the fly and dropping to the ground. Criger trotted home and Boston led 3-2.

Chesbro escaped the inning without further damage, but one run was all Boston required. New York threatened in the ninth and with two out had a man on first base.

Patsy Dougherty was up. But Bill Dinneen, ever the money pitcher, reared back and gave his former teammate all he had. For what seemed the first time all year, Dougherty failed to come up big against his former team and struck out on three pitches. The pennant was Boston's.

Apart from the usual histrionics in the stands by the Royal Rooters, there was no further celebration. With little delay, the two teams played out the string in game two, which New York won, 1-0, in ten innings. Only then did the Collinsmen cheer their good fortune.

But there would be no world series in 1904, although just about everyone — the Americans, the players of the NL champion New York Giants, the press, and baseball fans all over the country — pleaded for one. For two months before, Giant owner John T. Brush had painted himself into a corner and now refused to admit his error.

By midsummer, his Giants had the National League pennant locked up, eventually winning by thirteen games over second-place Chicago. Fans were already comparing his club with Boston and looking ahead to a second world series.

But when the Invaders pulled ahead in early August, Brush got nervous. He was still angry at the American League and didn't want to risk playing his crosstown rivals and giving them credence. He summarily announced that his team was "content to rest on its laurels" and had no intention of playing any postseason series — against anyone.

When Boston won, Brush held firm. Ironically, in the off-season he then headed up a commission that in 1905 made the World Series an annual event. By default, Boston retained the title of world champion.

It was just as well, for by the end of the 1904 season the Americans were not quite the same team that had started the year. They'd have been hard-pressed to beat the Giants, for after losing Dougherty, they'd been outplayed by both New York and Chicago and had barely out-stepped Cleveland and Philadelphia.

Their quick start and the players' good health won Boston the pennant. Only five pitchers saw duty all year, with a cumulative ERA of 2.12, while six of the eight regulars started more than 150 games, an example of stamina that has never been seen since in the annals of major league baseball.

Their astounding fortitude concealed the truth. The defending world champions were at the beginning of a precipitous decline. The team had absolutely no depth and few prospects on the horizon. The champions were getting old.

Virtually the entire lineup had been together for four seasons. And the heart of the club — Criger, Young, Freeman, Stahl, and Collins — were all over thirty years old in an era when life expectancy was only fifty.

John I. Taylor didn't get it, a fact revealed by his continued meddling in the off-season. In January, he traded their best prospect, twenty-six-year-old George Stone, to St. Louis for aging Jesse Burkett, a lifetime .340 hitter who had won three batting titles in the 1890s. But his average had dropped each of the last three seasons and he'd failed to hit .300 in either 1903 or 1904. His decline would continue in 1905, while Stone, like Dougherty the year before, went on to lead the American League in hits.

The 1905 Americans started spring training in Macon, Georgia, fat and out of shape. Several players were sent to Hot Springs, Arkansas, to soak off the pounds in the warm medicinal baths.

No one was too concerned until the team opened the season. They lost their first six games and seven out of nine.

Taylor panicked. He forced Collins to cut Candy LaChance, who had only six hits in forty-one at bats, a dismal performance but not much worse than that of several others. He wasn't adequately replaced, forcing Collins to bring back Freeman from the outfield and sending Selbach, forced to the bench by Burkett, back into the lineup.

Offense was on the decline throughout the league as pitchers became ever more adept at doctoring the baseball, but nowhere was the problem more obvious than in Boston. The team hit only .233. The league's second-best offense in 1904 was now sixth, and dropping fast.

Their paltry attack wasted another string of fine performances from the pitching staff. Young, despite a minuscule ERA of only 1.82, went 18-19. Tannehill got all the good luck and finished 22-9, but no other starting pitcher was above .500.

The Americans were out of the pennant race by May, as first Cleveland and then Chicago and Philadelphia took command. Only a strong finish and an utter collapse by Cleveland allowed the Americans a veneer of respectability, as they ended the season in fourth place at 78-74, sixteen games behind the A's.

The fans were surprisingly patient. Attendance dropped, but held firm at an average of nearly six thousand fans per game. Most observers took comfort in the team's September performance and expected the club to rebound in 1906. But such optimism merely masked a serious state of decay.

In January, there was speculation that Johnson, upset by how Taylor had allowed the club to deteriorate, might force a sale. But the General intervened. Johnson didn't want to alienate the most powerful newspaper publisher in the city and backed off.

An uneasy truce held through spring training. The fantasy of a comeback was still alive as Stahl and

The 1905 Boston Americans, still holding on to their claim as "world champions." *Clockwise from upper left:* John I. Taylor, Bill Dinneen, Lou Criger, Cy Young, Charley Green, Bob Unglaub, Duke Farrell, Fred Parent, Jesse Burkett, Candy LaChance, Chick Stahl, Buck Freeman, Moose Grimshaw, George Winter, Hobe Ferris, Jesse Tannehill, Norwood Gibson. *Center:* Jimmy Collins.

most other veterans showed up at camp reasonably trim and apparently eager to prove that their 1905 performance was an anomaly.

Jimmy Collins knew better. He wanted to break up the veteran club while it still had some value and acquire younger talent, but he and John I. Taylor were no longer speaking. Collins's criticism had so angered Taylor that he all but took his ball and went home. Just to spite Collins he refused to make any deals at all. The team went an incredible two and a half years, from January of 1905 until June of 1907, without making a single, genuine, player-for-player trade.

Despite the estrangement, Taylor had neither the

authority nor the nerve to fire Collins. He was a favorite of Ban Johnson's, a god to the men at McGreevey's, and one of the game's all-time greats. He also had an ironclad contract guaranteeing him $10,000 a year plus 10 percent of any profits above $25,000. He wasn't going anywhere.

As young Taylor pouted and whined, the General began taking a larger role in the business activities of the team. But while John I. was inept and ill-tempered, the General was disinterested and distracted by his publishing business. The ballclub was adrift.

Publicly, optimism reigned over the prospects of the club. Privately, Collins didn't know what to expect. He knew that the loss of 20 pounds here or there couldn't stave off the advance of time. It didn't make him feel any better when Bill Dinneen held out in a salary dispute with Taylor. Burkett and Duke Farrell both retired, and Lou Criger was incapacitated with back trouble.

Boston outfielder Kip Selbach is shown in a rare action shot taken at the Huntington Avenue Grounds in 1906. Note the tiny fielder's glove and unmanicured outfield grass.

Unable to make a deal, Collins did what he could with rookies and veterans no one else wanted. To make up for the loss of Dinneen, he picked up pitcher Joe Harris. A native of nearby Melrose, Massachusetts, Harris had won twenty-five games for minor league Fall River and been impressive in three late-season appearances for the Americans in 1905. Collins filled the remaining breaches in the roster with several warm bodies of no particular distinction.

The season started badly as Boston dropped their first three games to New York. Then the club won five of nine and Dinneen returned. Optimism blossomed with the spring.

At the end of the month they faced New York and Jack Chesbro again. They knocked him out of the game in the fifth inning, took a 4-2 lead into the ninth, then pounded out ten hits in nine minutes to score nine runs and cruise to a 13-4 win. Perhaps, noted observers, there was still some life left in the body after all. If the team could keep hitting, Young, Tannehill, and Dinneen could still pitch.

That notion soon appeared absurd. Only two years removed from a world championship, over the next twenty-three days the Boston Americans lost twenty consecutive games, losing at least once to every team in the league.

There was no end to what went wrong. They stopped hitting and wasted several outstanding pitching performances. When they did hit, so did the opposition. Even the weather conspired against them. On May 5 they were beating Washington when a rainstorm wiped out the game.

By May 12, with a record of 6-17 and the losing streak at ten, they began to give up. Merely inept play was now supplemented by the indifferent. The small nagging injuries that plague every ballclub turned huge, for as the losses added up, so did the wounded. Moose Grimshaw broke his wrist. Jesse Tannehill turned an ankle. George Winter's malaria flared up. Utilityman John Goodwin got a charley horse. Jimmy Collins had a bum knee. Hobe Ferris just got plain sick.

Those afflictions paled compared to the condition of Lou Criger. The delicate catcher, who had battled ill health for years, had a bad back that stemmed from a carriage accident several years before. The old injury had flared up during the off-season, forcing him into a New York hospital. He found relief in morphine.

The medication, at the time available over the counter in a variety of forms, eased his pain. Although in no condition to play, he remained with the club. But as the Americans drifted toward the cellar, Criger began wasting away.

By mid-May he stopped eating and was dosing himself six times a day, even waking at night to keep the drug coursing through his system. There was nothing clandestine about his use. The use of morphine by ballplayers at the time, while rarely acknowledged, was relatively common. The drug was widely available and its use carried little social stigma. Many iron-man exploits common at the time, particularly

Boston Americans on Saint Patrick's Day 1903, Macon, Georgia. Children surround a group of stylishly dressed players as they hope for both a kind word and possibly a tip for running an errand. *Players (l–r):* Long Tom Hughes, Patsy Dougherty, Jimmy Collins, Chick Stahl, Jake Stahl (?), Hobe Ferris, Norwood Gibson (?), unidentified, Lou Criger, John O'Brien (?). Candy LaChance is the mustachioed player at the top right.

by pitchers, may well have been due in part to the use of the drug.

As Criger deteriorated, so did Boston's play on the field. Ban Johnson dropped in for a visit on May 13 and announced, "There is no doubt the Collins team needs strengthening." After a 14-1 loss to Cleveland on May 18, the club's fifteenth loss in a row, the *Post*'s headline read "Slaughter of the Innocents Goes On." Following another loss, an anonymous poet in the same paper wrote, "Last night I dreamed a sweet, sweet dream / I thought that we had won a game / Someone had doped the other team / Their infield and their outfield both were lame . . ."

But even that wouldn't have helped the Americans. As the streak approached twenty games the players appeared to be running into outs on purpose. Dinneen blew a win by swinging at a pitch on a double steal, then not running out his groundball, giving Detroit an easy double play and costing his team a run in a game they lost 3-2.

On May 24, following a 7-5 loss to Chicago, the *Post* announced "All Hope Seems Lost for Former Champs." Then a miracle happened. They won.

On May 25 Jesse Tannehill discovered the only way to win. He threw a shutout and beat Chicago 3-0, to give Boston a 7-27 record, already sixteen games out of first place.

That same day, General Taylor placed Lou Criger under a doctor's care. But there was no similar cure for Boston's ills.

Tannehill's victory was followed by another round of defeats, and the players began sniping at each other. Collins didn't want to go to the ballpark anymore. He hadn't been able to play because of a bad knee since May 22, and after attempting to play only to have his leg collapse beneath him, he gave up. He even started managing in his street clothes. John I. was hanging him out to dry. Collins knew it, but there was little he could do.

The General was no happier about the situation. He'd bought the team to give his son something to do. Getting involved himself wasn't part of the plan. Tired of his son's sniveling, he shipped him off to Europe for the rest of the season and took command.

It was too late, although he did give the okay to acquire star Holy Cross catcher Bill Carrigan, an inexperienced but promising improvement over the pretenders who had thus far filled in for Criger. But nothing could help this team.

On July 6, New York held Boston scoreless and swept a doubleheader, 4-0 and 8-0. The next day, Chicago shut out Boston 12-0 as the former champions made nine errors.

The Boston *American* called it "a dismal exhibition for the fans who were thunderstruck at the woeful play . . . and were unable to comprehend the slip-ups which came as a continual thing." The *Post* concurred. O'Connell quipped, "It was a case of Worse and more of it. The Boston team is absolutely demoralized. Harris pitched poor ball and showed no headwork at all. Freeman did the best he could at first, Goodwin again showed he is too light to hold down third, Hayden was a frost at the bat, Hoey fumbled one hit in left field and Ferris dropped an easy throw . . . even Chick Stahl, the only man on the Collins team who has played his real game this season, made two errors . . . The fans can't be expected to tolerate such play."

Collins apparently agreed with the fans. After the game he disappeared and no one heard from him for a week. Chick Stahl took over as acting manager.

Ban Johnson ordered Taylor to suspend Collins, then came to town and tracked him down himself. After meeting with the General, Johnson ordered Collins to the sidelines and extracted a promise from Taylor to spend some money to help the club.

Collins did as he was told. Some speculated that Detroit, a decent team but thus far a financial drain on owner William Yawkey, would be sacrificed to benefit Boston, with the Americans receiving several promising players, including a young outfielder named Cobb. But Yawkey wanted one more year to make it in Detroit. Since attendance at Huntington Avenue was holding steady, and Boston's National League representatives were playing just as poorly, Johnson allowed Boston to wallow into 1907.

Nothing changed except the number of games between Boston and first place. Even Criger's return from the living dead made no difference. By late August, Collins was beside himself.

On Sunday, August 26, he went for a carriage ride with several friends. A passing automobile frightened the horses and they bolted. Collins ended up face-down on the highway, his face and hands scraped raw.

The next day, he failed to show at the ballpark or give notice of his absence. After missing another game he was suspended once again.

If it bothered him, he didn't show it. Collins was reported to be at Nantasket Beach, partying and frolicking with friends. The team was unaffected. They lost for Stahl just as they had for Collins.

The season's nadir came three days later, on September 1, as the Huntington Avenue Grounds hosted one of the most remarkable games in Boston baseball history. It was as if the frustrations of the entire season were distilled and compressed into a single game.

A surprisingly large crowd of more than thirteen thousand turned out to see the Americans host the third-place A's, who were still in the thick of the pennant race. Colby College's Jack Coombs took the mound against local-boy-made-bad Joe Harris.

Despite allowing the fewest hits per inning of any pitcher on the team, Harris had pitched just well enough to lose. When Boston scored runs, he gave up more; when he pitched well, he brought out the best in the opposing pitcher. He had already been on the wrong end of eight shutouts.

Harris had won only two games and lost nearly twenty, including fourteen in a row. But those bad memories were about to be erased by one even worse.

With the game scoreless in the third and one out, Coombs bounced the ball back to Harris. He fielded the ball, turned to throw to first, and fell down. Coombs made the base uncontested and later scored when Harris was slow to cover first on a groundball. The single run, caused by Harris's own ineptitude, would come back to haunt him.

Boston tied the score in the sixth, then Coombs and Harris both settled into a groove. Although each team threatened in the eighth and ninth, neither scored and the game entered extra innings.

Time then seemed to stop, as the boy running the scoreboard marked the passage of each inning in chalk while the score stubbornly remained the same. It looked like a baseball game, as players from both teams got on base with regularity, but it was as if a coda had been installed at third, allowing no one to continue past.

Neither Coombs nor Harris gave in to either fatigue or common sense, as both kept pitching. After more than four hours of play the boy working the scoreboard wrote out "23" in the innings column and in a light moment added the word "skidoo" just below.

It didn't help. Both pitchers completed inning twenty-three as they had twenty-one others, scoreless. Both had pitched magnificently. Only one flyball to the outfield had been recorded the entire game.

At the beginning of inning twenty-four the umpires decided enough light remained to play only one inning more. So Joe Harris trudged out to the mound for the twenty-fourth time, hoping to pitch his twentieth consecutive scoreless inning.

With one out, Harris gave up a single to Topsy Hartsell, the A's thirteenth hit of the day. If Harris were superstitious, he should have known what to expect next.

Lord struck out in the diminishing light, but Hartsell stole second. Then Ossee Schreckengost stepped up.

Harris quickly got two strikes on him. But Schreck smashed the third pitch back through the box.

Earlier in the game, Harris might have stabbed the drive between his knees, but in the fading light his tired reflexes were a fraction too slow. The ball scooted into center field. Hartsell scored and the A's led, 2-1.

Time resumed its passage. Harris's magical performance was over, and the nightmare of the 1906 season resumed. The next two batters tripled, and the A's led 4-1 before Harris could record the seventy-second out of the game.

There was no Boston comeback. After twenty-four innings and four hours and forty-seven minutes of play, the A's won what was then the longest game in major league history, 4-1.

Only months after succeeding Jimmy Collins as Red Sox player-manager, Chick Stahl committed suicide in West Baden Springs, Indiana. Stahl, a near Hall of Fame caliber player, had married in the off-season and was driven to end his life by the threat of blackmail by a woman who allegedly bore his child out of wedlock.

The Americans finished the year 49-105, the worst record in baseball. Harris ended a dismal 2-21 and in the last week caught typhoid fever.

John I. Taylor returned to Boston in November and his father again handed him the reins of the club. Taylor decided to retain Chick Stahl as manager.

Stahl wasn't so sure. He was close to Collins and wanted to make sure the ex-manager was taken care of before he took over. On November 14, Stahl married a local girl, Julia Harmon, who grew up just around the corner from the ballpark. They went to Buffalo on their honeymoon to visit Collins.

Several events coincided with the visit. Collins's lawyer looked at his contract and informed the team he couldn't be sold or traded. Collins told Stahl his knee was feeling better and he'd be happy to return as a player but he'd had enough of Taylor. He urged his friend to stay on as player-manager. And the new Mrs. Stahl abruptly left her new husband and returned to Boston. Stahl continued on to Fort Wayne and spent the rest of the winter living apart from his new wife.

It wasn't the first time Stahl had had trouble with women. Darkly handsome, he was often pursued and

1910 Red Sox and various anonymous prospects at spring training in Hot Springs, Arkansas.

Top row (l–r): unidentified, unidentified, unidentified, outfielder Harry Hooper, pitcher Charley Hall, pitcher Joe Wood, pitcher Ray Collins, pitcher Frank Arellanes, third baseman Harry Lord, pitcher Ed Karger, unidentified, pitcher Ed Cicotte, unidentified. *Middle row (l–r):* outfielder Harry Niles, outfielder Jack Thoney, unidenti-fied, utilityman Clyde Engle, infielder Charles Wagner, unidenti-fied, unidentified, second baseman Amby McConnell, catcher Bill Carrigan. *Front row (l–r):* unidentified, unidentified, unidentified, first baseman Jake Stahl, manager Patsy Donovan, unidentified, outfielder Duffy Lewis, infielder Larry Gardner, outfielder Tris Speaker. The little girl may be Joe Wood's sister.

did little to discourage the attention. But he apparently strung his suitors along. A Fort Wayne woman had once tried to stab him and a Boston woman had tried to shoot him. Stahl escaped serious injury each time. If he hoped marriage would end his troubles, he was mistaken.

Yet he appeared to be the perfect choice as manager. While not quite as popular as either Cy Young or Collins, Stahl was highly respected by both his teammates and the Boston fans. He had played hard throughout the previous season. While he was showing his age, at the end of the 1906 season he held most of the team records and no fewer than sixteen American League career marks, among them batting average, slugging percentage, home runs, runs, runs batted in, total bases, and extra base hits. Had there been a Hall of Fame at the time, Stahl would have been a shoo-in.

In mid-March, after training for a few weeks in Lit-tle Rock, the team broke camp and began to barn-storm their way north, playing exhibitions, winning more often than not against sub-par competition. Stahl was reportedly adjusting well to the rigors of management.

But on March 25 in Louisville, Kentucky, all that changed. Stahl resigned, saying only that the job was "too big" and he had neither eaten nor slept for five days. Now the press reported that Stahl had looked troubled for weeks.

The next day, Stahl reluctantly agreed to stay on until a replacement could be hired. The Americans boarded a train for their next game in West Baden Springs, Indiana, a popular resort community adjacent to French Lick.

It was raining when the team arrived on the evening of March 27. The club checked into their ho-tel, then the manager went to the lobby and sent a cryptic telegram to his wife that read, "Cheer up little girl and be happy. I am all right now and able to play the game of my life."

The next morning, Stahl awoke in the suite he shared with Jimmy Collins, ate breakfast, checked the condition of the local field, and then stopped at a drugstore. He purchased a small vial of carbolic acid, which was often used as an antiseptic or muscle rub.

He returned to the suite, and Collins heard him shuffling about. Then Collins heard Stahl begin to gag and retch.

He saw his teammate collapse on the bed, the empty bottle of acid in his hand. Stahl sputtered and gasped, "I couldn't help it. I did it Jim. It was killing me and I couldn't stand it."

Collins ran for help, but it was too late. The acid caused massive internal hemorrhaging. In minutes, Chick Stahl was dead.

Boston papers scrambled to get the news out, and several published extra editions and devoted nearly the entire front page to his death. Reporters covering the team expressed shock and speculated that the pressures of managing had been too much for the popular outfielder. But within a few days, most, like Tim Murnane of the *Globe*, hinted that "baseball affairs were only incidental" to Stahl's death. Frederic O'Connell stated bluntly that domestic troubles were the cause.

The truth was a little more revealing. As first reported by Glenn Stout in 1986, Stahl was driven to his death, not by baseball, but by the baseball life. The previous year, a casual affair with a woman in Chicago resulted in a pregnancy, which Stahl didn't learn about until after his marriage. The anonymous Chicago woman, reputedly a groupie, or in the parlance of the day, a "Baseball Sadie," was blackmailing Stahl. Apparently overwhelmed by guilt and fear, Stahl took his own life.

The team was stunned. Collins was too upset to attend the funeral, which was the biggest in the history of Stahl's hometown, Fort Wayne, Indiana. Within a couple of weeks, the club was rocked again by the death of *Post* reporter Fred O'Connell, who contracted pneumonia in West Baden and died. His stories about Stahl's death were the last he ever wrote.

If the 1906 season had been a comic debacle, 1907 was becoming a tragedy. All that was required was the continuing intrusion of John I. Taylor.

He decided to make himself manager, but when Ban Johnson found out, Taylor sheepishly backtracked. Then he rashly named Cy Young to the position before asking the pitcher, who refused to accept. Young finally agreed to take the job temporarily until Taylor found a permanent replacement. Seven games into the season, Taylor made his pick.

He chose George Huff, the athletic director at the University of Illinois and a part-time scout for the Cubs.

The team was shocked. They didn't think Huff, who they disdainfully called "the Professor," was remotely qualified for the job, a perception he reinforced by his first act, the release of Buck Freeman.

Huff soon put his education to use. After thirteen days he got on a train and went back to the University of Illinois. Taylor kept him on the payroll as a scout.

Now Taylor had to select his fourth manager in less than six months. His pick? Twenty-five-year-old Bob Unglaub!

Although Unglaub had won the first-base job and been named captain by Huff, he was hardly managerial material. The Rooters, still chafing over the Dougherty trade, howled at the selection. Veteran players were utterly dismayed.

Taylor responded by dumping the disgruntled, shipping Bill Dinneen to St. Louis for a failed pitcher named Beany Jacobson, and trading Collins to Philadelphia for a twenty-nine-year-old rookie infielder named Jack Knight. Unglaub didn't have the guts to stop him. With the club wallowing near last place with a record of 14-27 in mid-June, 1907 was already looking a lot like 1906.

Enter Ban Johnson. After he met with John I., Taylor suddenly stopped making stupid trades, Unglaub became a first baseman again, and Jim "Deacon" McGuire, a veteran catcher most recently with New York, became Boston's manager.

The club went from pitiful to vaguely promising. Since no one could hit, McGuire had them steal, and the club played above .500 until September when they slumped to finish seventh, thirty-two and a half games behind first-place Detroit, but ten wins better than the 1906 club.

In September, fans got a glimpse of the future. George Huff, who'd agreed to do some scouting for the team, signed two young Texas League outfielders at $750 apiece, and each made a brief if undistinguished appearance. Tris Speaker and George Whiteman appeared in seven and four games respectively. In the future, both would figure prominently in the team's return to glory.

At age forty, Cy Young rebounded to win twenty games. In fact, the pitching staff had been a pleasant surprise. Except for Joe Harris. He went 0-7 and was released with a miserable 3-30 career record.

But Taylor wasn't satisfied with a ten-game improvement and resumed his yard sale of players. On the rare occasion when he didn't take cash, he took broken-down ballplayers or nonprospects instead. By comparison, Harry Frazee's infamous talent auction from 1919 to 1923 appears conservative. At least Frazee's sale was precipitated by a crisis. Taylor's

was the result of his own meddlesome delusions of grandeur.

Yet, to his credit, he did use some of the money to scout and sign younger players, particularly from the West, an area few major league teams paid much attention to at the time. But any success Taylor enjoyed was not the end result of either a grand design or his own savvy judgment. He ran enough talent through the club's roster that some of it, eventually, had to stick. Not even John I. could be wrong all the time.

On December 18, 1907, he proved so. For on that date he made the best decision of his life.

Just before leaving to winter in California, Taylor met with representatives of Wright and Dixon, a local sporting goods supplier, to order uniforms for the upcoming season.

The previous season the Boston Nationals had abandoned their traditional red stockings in favor of blue. Taylor took note and decided to take the color scheme for his team. While on the road his team

Spring training at Hot Springs, Arkansas, included long hikes in the Ozarks to keep players fit. This group of unidentified Boston players hikes the wooded trails in full uniforms, including baseball spikes.

would wear gray uniforms trimmed in red with pale blue stockings, at home the club would wear white uniforms with bright red stockings. And they would be called the "Red Sox."

The decision was something of an experiment and a little controversial. The Nationals' red stockings had been a dark, deep red. Taylor, on the other hand, selected a bright, fire-engine red.

As the *Boston Journal* noted, "It will be an aggressive, blazing color scheme that will be heard farther than the chortle of the fan when the home team wins out in the fifteenth inning." In fact, club officials were concerned that the new stockings would be too garish. They worried that they might "interfere with fans' vision or . . . incite the crowds to riot."

In *The Sporting News* Tim Murnane wrote, "Well, what do you think of that? The Boston Americans have a new name . . . the 'Red Sox.' Ever since Boston became identified with the American League an effort has been made to give the team an appropriate nickname which would sound good in print . . . but no two writers will agree on any one name. It was consequently up to John I. Taylor to re-christen his bunch and he has done so effectively."

But the change was primarily cosmetic. The club may have been all dressed up, but there was still nowhere for them to go, as Taylor soon resumed his destruction of the team. In January Hobe Ferris was sold to St. Louis, and in April the White Sox purchased Freddy Parent. Two youngsters who had played the previous season for Providence, Amby McConnell and Harry Lord, took their places and played well.

When the season opened Taylor kept the signs up in the yard. In midseason he dumped George Winter, Tannehill, and Unglaub. Then in August he sold promising slugger Gavvy Cravath and fired manager McGuire and sold him to Cleveland. Fred Lake, a former player who now made Boston his home, became the manager.

Because no one else was left, he was forced to play the younger players. Most failed, as thirty-nine different players appeared for Boston in 1908. But some talent began to show. Twenty-four-year-old pitcher Ed Cicotte won eleven games and eighteen-year-old

Tris Speaker, circa 1908. Encouraged by the coaching of Cy Young, who hit him endless fungoes, Tris Speaker emerged as the most complete player in Red Sox history. His .344 lifetime batting average ties him with Ted Williams at the top of the team list.

pitcher Joe Wood was impressive in six late-season appearances.

Tris Speaker, despite nearly being lost after Taylor forgot about him and failed to send him a contract in the spring, returned after a stint in the minors and started to play the best center field in baseball. Charles "Heinie" Wagner was a steady performer at short, and Maine's Amby McConnell took over at second. The youngsters could run and Taylor was soon referring to the Sox as his "Speed Boys," a nickname that proved more popular than "Red Sox" for the next year or so. The retooled team won sixteen games more than in 1907 and finished fifth at 75-79.

Had Taylor known when to stop, Boston may well have won a pennant in 1909, but with veteran players

John I. was like a drunk in a bar with a hole in his pocket dropping money on the floor.

In December, after promising Lou Criger he'd finish his career in Boston, Taylor traded him to St. Louis for cash and Tubby Spencer, a catcher in name only. Criger was crushed. Then in February, while at the league meeting in Chicago, Taylor did the unthinkable. He traded Cy Young to Cleveland.

In exchange for perhaps the greatest pitcher in the history of the game, not to mention a man who had won twenty games with a career low 1.26 ERA in 1908, Taylor received twelve thousand five hundred dollars and two throwing arms belonging to the unremarkable Charlie Chech and Jack Ryan. It was beyond belief.

The rumor mill spread two stories about the deal. The first blamed it on a late-night drinking binge at the annual league meeting between Taylor and Charles Somers, who now owned Cleveland. The second blamed Ban Johnson, concluding the deal's one-sided nature bore his inimitable stamp. Many assumed he had arranged the deal to help out his former "'angel" after the Indians missed the 1908 pennant by one-half game.

No matter. Chech and Ryan combined for eleven wins for Boston in 1909, while Young, at age forty-two the oldest man in baseball, won nineteen for a Cleveland squad that finished nine games below .500. The deal cost the Red Sox a pennant, as Boston finished only nine and a half games behind first-place Detroit despite spending most of the season trying to find a replacement for Young, eventually using eighteen different starting pitchers.

Yet Boston drew nearly seven hundred thousand fans to the ballpark, a club record that wouldn't be broken for more than thirty years.

With three emerging stars in center fielder Tris Speaker, left fielder Duffy Lewis, and right fielder Harry Hooper, and second-year third baseman Harry Lord already considered by many to be the best in the game, Taylor expected his team to contend in 1910. But when manager Fred Lake had the temerity to ask for a salary increase, he was sacked.

Taylor named Irish-born former NL star Patsy Donovan, who'd already managed Pittsburgh, St. Louis (NL), and Brooklyn into mediocrity, his new manager. A Boston scout in 1909, he got on Taylor's good side, which was enough to estrange the remaining veterans on the team and ensure failure.

Injuries and illness didn't help. McConnell was out for most of the year with a sore arm and a sick belly, Speaker battled a sprained ankle, and team captain Harry Lord reportedly had "malaria," an affliction often used by the press as a euphemism for a variety of social ailments. In late August, he argued with Donovan and was stripped of his captaincy. After Taylor first announced he wouldn't think of trading Lord for anyone but Cleveland star Napoleon Lajoie, the owner's usual lesser judgment took over. True to form, he sent Lord and McConnell to Chicago for two players who made no difference.

Red Sox fans howled. The press called Taylor "Phineas Taylor Barnum," but he paid no attention to the criticism. He never had. The deal virtually completed his three-year dismantling of the club, during which time he'd traded, sold, or simply released fourteen regulars and twelve others. In exchange, the Sox didn't receive and retain a single bonafide major leaguer of value.

In second place at the time of the deal with a fine record of 60-44, the Red Sox players quit after the trade and won only twenty-one of their remaining forty-nine games to finish fourth, twenty-two and a half games behind champion Philadelphia. In the off-season, Taylor once more proved his stripes by proposing that Tris Speaker, the best center fielder in baseball, be moved to first base. This was a suggestion even Donovan could ignore.

The 1911 season brought no improvement, as injuries disabled the team, although Joe Wood emerged as a big star, winning twenty-three games and striking out 231, second-best in the league. But the season's real significance stemmed from the two best decisions John I. Taylor and his father ever made as baseball magnates. The first was to build a new ballpark. The second was to sell the team.

To Taylor, timing was everything. The lease for the Huntington Avenue Grounds was expiring, and the club needed a new ballpark. But while Taylor had the money for a new park, he didn't expect to spend it. He wanted to sell the team to raise the money for the park, which he would retain and rent out to the new owners. Not only would he make an immediate profit, he would make money on rent for years. It was an ingenious plan.

Early in the year, Washington Senators manager James McAleer indicated his interest. He'd been trying to buy into a club for several seasons and had his eye on Boston once before, only to back out when Taylor insisted on staying on in some capacity.

But in early September, Taylor had second thoughts. With Ban Johnson serving as mediator, Taylor and McAleer began negotiations. It was no secret that McAleer was only the front man in the deal. Most of the money was Johnson's. Despite their play, Boston was the most lucrative franchise in the league and he wanted in on it.

On September 15, Taylor agreed to sell half the club to McAleer and Ban Johnson's secretary, Robert McRoy. McAleer would become team president. John I. Taylor would serve as vice president and oversee the physical plant, but have no role in the baseball end of the team.

Now Taylor could do what he really wanted to, which was to become a landlord. He'd had plans for a new park drawn up a year before, and after considering a site in Charlestown, he selected another site of just over 330,000 square feet in the Fenway.

A new facility was needed. A spate of disastrous fires had destroyed many of the old wooden parks, which increased insurance costs and sparked some design innovations. New, safer and larger concrete and steel parks had recently been built in most other major league cities.

In fact, Taylor had been thinking of a new park since 1909, when he signed Harry Hooper. When Taylor learned that Hooper had a civil engineering degree from St. Mary's College, he told him he might have him do some engineering work on his new ballpark.

But the final decision to build the new ballpark reached beyond baseball. General Taylor was a major shareholder in the Fenway Realty Company, which had invested heavily in reclaimed land in Boston's Fenway, a once unsightly and ill-smelling area of mud flats made more palatable by Frederick Law Olmsted's manipulations of the landscape in the 1880s. Nearby Kenmore Square was just beginning to be built up, and the Fenway was the logical choice for future development.

Still, the area had no identity and was inaccessible by trolley. Building a ballpark there would solve both those problems.

Armed with cash from the sale of the Red Sox, General Taylor and several partners bought the land for the ballpark for $300,000 from the Fenway Realty Company. Taylor then issued bonds for $275,000 to finance construction. The city agreed to extend trolley lines down Ipswich Street to service the park, at the same time dramatically improving access to Fenway Realty Company's other holdings.

John I. Taylor announced that he planned to call the new ballpark Fenway Park "because it's in the Fenway, isn't it?" thereby insuring that no one would forget the name of his dad's real estate company either. The cost of the ballpark would be more than offset by the increase in land values in the surrounding area. There was backslapping all around.

But it was already fall, and time was running out to build the new facility. Fortunately, architect James McLaughlin's plans were already virtually complete, but as originally conceived, Fenway Park was a much different place than was actually constructed.

McLaughlin's design had to fit the misshapen piece of property acquired by the Taylors. He could have easily created a more symmetrical park on only a portion of the parcel, but the Taylors were dumping the entire plot. McLaughlin was ordered to design a

"The King of Pitchers" trophy presented to Denton T. Young by the readers of the *Boston Post,* August 13, 1908. The trophy is part of the permanent display at the National Baseball Hall of Fame in Cooperstown, New York.

park that completely enclosed the site, resulting in the field of play being much larger than that required by the way the game was played at the time. He was further ordered to retain the orientation of the Huntington Avenue Grounds in relation to the sun, with the third-base line pointing almost due north. This placed the left-field fence hard against Lansdowne Street, barely 300 feet from home plate down the line.

But that distance was of no concern, for at the time no one hit the ball that far. Had it been an issue, the street could have easily been acquired. This is the only reason Fenway Park is so misshapen today.

Lack of time necessitated other changes. Although originally designed with a double deck, then standard in most new parks, Taylor wanted to make sure the park was ready for Opening Day. He decided to save some money and forgo the second deck, knowing it could be added later if needed. Instead, the new park would consist of a simple grandstand around

the infield (roughly from section 27 to 13 in today's park), a roofed pavilion down the right-field line (sections 12 to 6), and some simple bleachers standing alone deep in right field.

Construction began immediately. By November, the foundations were nearly complete and 6 inches of loam had already been spread and seeded. Tim Murnane noted that the field was already as "green as the flag of the Gael." By the new year, the grandstand was nearly complete and work had started on the roof.

As 1911 turned into 1912, McAleer, McRoy, and Taylor met as required under New Jersey corporate law and fully consummated their deal by electing each other to the expected positions. Jake Stahl, who'd manned first base for the club in 1909 and 1910 (and was no relation to the late Chick Stahl), was enticed out of retirement to return as player-manager.

Opening Day, and a brand-new era of Red Sox baseball, was only three months away.

INVINCIBLE SUMMER

1912

Tris Speaker batted .383 with a league-leading fifty-three doubles
to help lead the Red Sox to the 1912 world championship.
Speaker also captured the Chalmers Award as league MVP.

When he learned of the official change in ownership, catcher Bill Carrigan was managing his cigar store in Lewiston, Maine, staying in shape snowshoeing in the pine forests near his home. Pitching ace Joe Wood was on his poultry farm in Pennsylvania and sneaking off to go hunting whenever he could. And in Ventura, California, Mexican-American pitcher Carlos Clolo, known to fans by the adopted Anglo name Charley "Sea Lion" Hall, was on his honeymoon.

Hall wrote the *Boston Post* that he hoped to help "Old Jake [Stahl], pull off that rag [win the pennant]." The players were pleased with Stahl's appointment as manager and the prospect of playing in brand-new Fenway Park.

Stahl quit his job as a Chicago banker and wrote sportswriter Paul Shannon that "I expect to leave here about Feb. 20 putting in a good two or three weeks of good hard work at the Springs [Hot Springs, Arkansas] before the club arrives . . . I am very enthusiastic over our prospects and . . . am anxious to see those new grounds . . . I hope also that the fences will not be so far away but that a fellow will get a chance to put the ball over now and then."

The 1912 Red Sox were in transition, with a new owner, new park, and new manager, yet their roster was virtually unchanged from 1911. Neither the press nor the fans expected much of the team.

As workers scrambled to finish Fenway Park, the players made their usual trek to Hot Springs for spring training. Only center fielder Tris Speaker was absent. He remained in Texas while holding out for a better contract.

When Speaker came to terms, the lineup was set. Apart from Stahl taking over at first base, the only significant change took place in the middle infield where Stahl had second baseman Heinie Wagner and shortstop Steve Yerkes swap positions.

The Sox believed they were capable of challenging Connie Mack's Athletics for the pennant. The confident Mack, however, predicted his defending world champions would not only win their third title in a row, but set a league record in the process. He was nearly correct, for in 1912 his club would win more games than in either of their past two pennant-winning seasons. But neither Mack nor anyone else thought the Red Sox would render that performance moot and supersede his dynasty with another.

The Red Sox opened Fenway Park on April 9 with an exhibition against Harvard University. Just over three thousand fans endured snow flurries as a group of regulars defeated Harvard by a score of 2-0.

The new park was a blend of old and new. Its red brick facade in the "tapestry" style echoed the tidy brick and brownstone townhouses of the nearby Back Bay, while the main grandstand was similar to the new concrete and steel structures in vogue throughout the major leagues. Yet the wood bleachers, which stood alone in center field, harked back to an earlier era.

The park sported several new features that soon became standard in other parks, including a small parking area for automobiles just off right field, a wire screen in front of the stands behind home, and

Player-manager Jake Stahl with team owner James McAleer at Hot Springs, Arkansas, March 1912. Stahl left his job as a banker to rejoin the Red Sox as player-manager in 1912. McAleer was one of the first former major league players to serve as a team owner and chief executive.

an electric scoreboard. In all, the park contained fifteen thousand reserved grandstand seats and thirteen thousand unreserved and bleacher seats, nearly double the size of the Huntington Avenue Grounds.

While finish work on the park continued, Boston opened the season in New York, and Joe Wood scattered seven hits in a complete-game 5-3 triumph over the Highlanders. He went on to win five of his next seven starts, including a crucial 2-0 shutout over Hall of Famer Ed Walsh of the White Sox, the first-ever at Fenway Park.

Smoky Joe Wood was a product of the western plains, growing up in the frontier outposts of Ouray, Colorado, and Ness City, Kansas. He started playing baseball pitching for town teams, often playing against men four and five years his senior.

He turned pro for twenty dollars, playing infield for the barnstorming Bloomer Girls, an allegedly all-girl outfit, in which the boyish Wood was, in fact, one of four male players who appeared in drag.

Wood soon returned to the pitching mound, and within two years his blazing fastball earned him a spot with Kansas City of the American Association. Boston purchased his contract in August of 1908, and he soon became fast friends with another rookie, outfielder Tris Speaker.

Like Speaker, Wood wasn't an immediate success in the major leagues. In time, however, the young pitcher gained command of his fastball, and in 1911 he joined the pitching elite with a record of 23-17, including a no-hitter on July 29 versus the St. Louis Browns.

But in 1912 he was the best pitcher in baseball. Even Walter Johnson, the greatest pitcher of the generation, thought so, responding to a reporter's question by asking rhetorically, "Can I throw harder than Joe Wood? Listen, my friend, there's no man alive that can throw harder than 'Smoky' Joe Wood."

After Wood's Opening-Day victory, Boston won three of their next four. They were scheduled to open their home season and inaugurate Fenway Park on April 17, but that game and the next three, including the traditional Patriots' Day doubleheader, were rained out, costing the club thousands in admissions. All may have been avoided if the new infield tarp had arrived on time from the factory in Detroit.

When the field finally dried out, the Sox christened Fenway by playing the New York Highlanders on April 20. While the crowd buzzed with talk about the tragic sinking of the S.S. *Titanic* days before, the new park opened to little fanfare, for the delays caused most opening ceremonies to be canceled. Boston mayor John "Honey Fitz" Fitzgerald threw out the first pitch before twenty-four thousand enthusiastic fans.

Brockton native and spitball artist Buck O'Brien started for Boston and quickly fell behind by four runs. Yet Charley Hall shut down the New Yorkers in relief, and in the eleventh inning Tris Speaker drove a single through the left side to score Steve Yerkes and secure the 7-6 come-from-behind victory.

But *The Sporting News* soon reported that home attendance was down 25 percent. Correspondent Tim Murnane complained that "the new park is not as handy to reach and get away from as the old park has hurt some and will until people get accustomed to journeying in a new direction."

Murnane missed the old Huntington Avenue Grounds. He bemoaned the loss of the single common entrance, writing, "I find much of the old sociability gone. At the old grounds you were continually running into old friends as grandstand and bleacher patrons passed through one long runway to be distributed like a lot of mail at various stations."

In time, Murnane and countless others would warm to both the location and the configuration of Fenway, which drew far less comment then than it does today. In 1912 the outfield fences were considered to be so deep that their varying dimensions were of no consequence to the game on the field. From home plate to the far corner of center field, where the flagpole stood, was a whopping 550 feet, and it was over 300 feet down each foul line.

The one exception was the left-field fence. An oddity of ballpark architecture, it featured a 25-foot wooden wall fronting Lansdowne Street, built to prevent fans from climbing in without tickets or watching for free from the roof of the building across the street. Inside, fronting the scoreboard, a 10-foot slope of earth ran the length of the wall, designed so standing-room crowds could see the game over each other's heads. While Fenway Park was neither the first nor the last ballpark to include such a feature (most notably in Cincinnati's Crosley Field), nowhere else did it become so memorable.

The reason was the guardian of this unusual piece of real estate, left fielder George "Duffy" Lewis. As a member of what may have been baseball's best-ever defensive outfield, Lewis, also the team's cleanup hitter, was much admired for his unique ability to scamper up and down the mound in pursuit of flyballs. Sports cartoons of the period often depicted him as a mountain climber making catches amid sheep and snowcaps.

Superstars Joe Wood and Tris Speaker rented a house in Winthrop during the 1912 season. The lifelong friends played together on three world championship teams, two in Boston and one in Cleveland.

In a 1962 interview with John Gillooly of the *Boston Record-American* Lewis described how he played the cliff. "At the crack of the bat you'd turn and run up it," he said. "Then you had to pick up the ball and decide whether to jump, go right or left or rush down again. It took plenty of practice. They made a mountain goat out of me." The feature became known as "Duffy's Cliff" in honor of his unique prowess.

While the left-field wall and Duffy's Cliff were the most prominent physical features of the park, neither came into play very often in the park's early years, for in the Dead Ball Era hits to such distant realms were rare. On April 26, Red Sox backup first baseman Hugh Bradley became the first man to

homer over the left-field wall, but the blast, one of only two Bradley ever hit in the major leagues, was considered an aberration.

Compared to other parks of the era, Fenway Park was huge. In fact, its outfield was among the most spacious in baseball and perfect for a team, like the 1912 Red Sox, that featured speed, defense, and pitching.

Alongside Lewis in center field was Texas native Tris Speaker, known to many as "Spoke." Entering his fourth major league season, Speaker already played center field in spectacular fashion and was ready to emerge as an offensive star of similar merit. In 1912 he became perhaps the most complete player in baseball.

Paced by Speaker's all-around play and the pitching of Wood, the 1912 Red Sox moved into first place on June 18. From that point on, they were never seriously challenged, for the club avoided the string of injuries that had beset the team the previous three seasons. Manager Stahl had little more to do than write out the lineup card. He even hit .300 as he dismissed the effects of his year-long layoff. The Sox were on their way to the greatest season of any American League team to date.

The key was pitching, for the staff was even deeper than in the days of Young, Tannehill, and Dinneen. Wood led the way, and rookie Hugh Bedient and second-year starter Buck O'Brien both won exactly twenty games for the only time in their careers. Charley Hall and Ray Collins rounded out a staff that eventually led the league in the most important statistical categories. Future star Eddie Cicotte, a little-used righthanded spitballer and future Black Sox co-conspirator, was deemed expendable and sold off to Chicago.

As the 1912 season progressed Wood began fashioning one of the most amazing individual seasons in baseball history. Although he depended primarily on his fastball, he was a complete pitcher. On July 8,

September 6, 1912. Joe Wood warms up at Fenway Park for his duel with Walter Johnson. Wood captured his fourteenth consecutive victory on his way to winning sixteen consecutive games. An overflow crowd filled the park to the extent that fans sat within feet of the foul lines. Wood secured a 1-0 victory when Speaker and Lewis hit back-to-back doubles in the sixth inning.

when he defeated the St. Louis Browns by a score of 5-1, Tim Murnane described his repertoire as a mixture of "slow drops" and "dreamy curves." Wood, like Walter Johnson only five days before, had just embarked on a headline-grabbing win streak.

For the next seven weeks Wood and Johnson blazed through the league without losing a single game. With the pennant all but decided, fans began to look forward to a late-season matchup between the two best pitchers in the game. Senators manager Clark Griffith gave the game the atmosphere of a title fight by challenging Wood in the newspapers, saying, "We will consider him a coward if he doesn't pitch against Johnson . . . The race isn't over yet. Just wait until my team gets through wiping up the floor with the Red Sox and then you'll see we have a chance."

The Red Sox took note, and when Washington came into Boston in early September, they moved Wood up a day in the rotation to put his now thirteen-game winning streak on the line against Johnson. Although Johnson's streak had ended at sixteen games a week before, interest in the matchup was intense.

On September 6, all Boston seemed to converge on Fenway Park. Team treasurer Robert McRoy later called the throng the largest regular-season weekday crowd in the history of baseball. That may well have been true, for the Red Sox sold tickets oblivious to Fenway's capacity. Attendance was announced as twenty-nine thousand, but the true number of fans in Fenway Park that day likely approached forty thousand.

The overflow crowd filled the stands and the nether reaches of the outfield, including Duffy's Cliff. And for the first and only time in the history of Fenway Park, fans were allowed to stand along the perimeter of the infield. They pressed to within inches of both foul lines and surrounded home plate and the ground in front of each dugout. Remarkably, a young boy hit by a foul tip was the only recorded injury.

Both pitchers warmed up in foul ground surrounded on all sides by fans. As Wood took the mound to throw the first pitch, the atmosphere was unlike anything seen or heard in Boston since the world series of 1903. The crowd kept up an incessant racket, chanting and singing in unison as they

TRIS SPEAKER'S STRANGE TRIP

Born in Hubbard City, Texas, the son and nephew of Confederate Civil War veterans, Speaker grew up in what was still very much part of the American frontier. As a boy, he worked the family ranch while earning a reputation as a local football and baseball star. Childhood friends remembered him as a loner. After the death of his father when he was ten, he became socially withdrawn but increasingly wild and competitive on the playing field, reminding many of Ty Cobb.

Like fellow Red Sox greats Babe Ruth and Ted Williams, Speaker started his baseball career as a pitcher. At age ten he broke his right arm working on the ranch and, while recuperating, learned to throw lefthanded, becoming virtually ambidextrous. His pitching prowess and academic standing gained him admission to Fort Worth Polytechnic Institute in 1905, where he played for two years before being offered his first professional contract.

His baseball apprenticeship reads like a tale from American folklore. For the sum of a single dollar — train fare from Hubbard City to Cleburne, Texas — Speaker became a professional. He pocketed the dollar and hopped a freight train instead, arriving in Cleburne only moments before his first game. Manager Ben Shelton scowled at the rookie and informed him he was his starting pitcher.

Despite lack of rest, Speaker pitched well, but lost 2-1. He lived up to his reputation by chewing out his manager and picking a fight with his second baseman over a costly error.

Despite his combativeness, or perhaps because of it, Speaker soon made a name for himself. Impatient with his antics and spotty mound performance, Shelton irrevocably altered the course of Speaker's career and the history of the Red Sox by deciding to teach the brash lefthander a lesson. He left Speaker on the mound in a game in which he eventually yielded twenty-two runs. As Speaker later recalled, "That game convinced everybody, including me, that I was an outfielder." Thus began the career of the greatest all-around outfielder of the Dead Ball — and possibly any other — Era.

In the outfield Speaker blossomed. Over the remainder of the season he hit .268 and stole thirty-three bases. When the Cleburne team was absorbed by a Houston franchise in a merger of the North and South Texas Leagues, Speaker attracted the attention of major league scouts. Team president Doak Roberts offered to sell his contract to the St. Louis Browns for fifteen

hundred dollars, with a bonus of 200 acres of prime Texas cattle land if his young outfielder made the team. The Browns rejected this offer, as did the Pittsburgh Pirates, who cooled on Speaker when Pirate owner Barney Dreyfuss, who believed "No man who smokes cigarettes will ever be a big league ballplayer," learned Speaker smoked.

Roberts finally reduced his asking price to $750, at which point Red Sox scout and former manager George Huff became interested. But the transaction was jeopardized when Speaker's mother refused to sign for her minor son. She remarked, "I've never been so insulted in my life. I will not have my boy sold around like a slave for so many dollars." She eventually relented. Her son took his Texas League batting title and brimming self-confidence to Boston for the first time in September 1907.

Upon Speaker's arrival at the Huntington Avenue Grounds, Red Sox manager Jim McGuire greeted him by asking, "You're who?" In seven games at the end of that dismal season Speaker reinforced his anonymity by collecting only three hits, all singles.

Unimpressed, the following spring team owner John I. Taylor neglected to mail his young prospect a contract. Crushed, Speaker wrote to almost every other team in the major leagues begging for a tryout, but was spurned. Giant manager John McGraw dismissed Speaker with a telegraph that read, "I'm sorry kid, I've already got more players in camp than I know what to do with."

But Speaker showed up at spring training anyway. Boston allowed him to train with the team without a contract, then gave him to minor league Little Rock as payment for the use of their park during spring training.

The indignity only inspired the stubborn Texan. He dominated the Southern Association in 1908 with a combination of batting and fielding that suddenly had scouts ecstatic. But Little Rock owner Mickey Finn had agreed to a provision that allowed Boston to reacquire Speaker by paying their back rent on their ballpark — five hundred dollars. Boston paid and obtained their greatest player to date.

Although Speaker quickly became a crowd favorite, in thirty-one games by the end of the season he hit only .220. But now his potential was obvious.

Cy Young recognized the extraordinary defensive ability of the stocky outfielder and spent hours helping Speaker hone those skills, hitting him thousands of fungoes and running him back and forth across the expanse of the Huntington Avenue Grounds.

In time, fans paid just to see Speaker field and throw, for he played center field as if he were a fifth infielder. No one ever played a shallower center field than Speaker did.

Speaker later explained his approach. "I know it's easier," he told sportswriter Bob Broeg, "basically to come in on a ball than go back . . . I still see more games lost by singles that drop just over the infield than triples over the outfielder's head. I learned early that I could save more games by cutting off some of those singles than I could lose by having an occasional extra base hit go over my head."

His spectacular play became legend. He even made unassisted double plays, snaring line drives off his shoe-tops then sprinting to second to double off baserunners. When the opposi-tion bunted, Speaker played so shallow that he'd dash in to cover second base.

The combination of his cunning and his powerful arm made him deadly to baserunners. He threw out 449 runners in his career, including four seasons of thirty or more capped by an American League record total of thirty-five achieved in both 1909 and 1912.

At bat, only Ty Cobb and Shoeless Joe Jackson surpassed Speaker in his era. In nine seasons with the Red Sox he hit .337, and his .344 lifetime batting average ties him with the career mark achieved by fellow Red Sox legend Ted Williams. Nine decades after he last played he still appears near the top of many of the team's career offensive categories, a fact made more impressive considering his career took place entirely in the Dead Ball Era. ⚾

Tris Speaker riding an alligator at spring training, Hot Springs, Arkansas, circa 1912. The dapper outfielder was both a college man and a cowboy and was considered the most complete player of his era.

bobbed back and forth trying to keep their balance in the cramped stands.

Both pitchers were at the top of their game. For five innings the game was a scoreless stalemate. As the row of zeros on the left-field scoreboard lengthened, the tension only increased.

But in the sixth inning with two outs, Boston broke through. Tris Speaker, who would later be named league MVP, slapped a Johnson fastball down the third-base line into the close crowd for a ground-rule double. A mighty roar went out across the Fens.

Duffy Lewis followed him, and with the outfield inexplicably playing him to pull Johnson, he, too, went the other way and hit a flare to right field. Danny Moeller of Washington made a long run for the ball and reached out, and it trickled off his fingertips. Speaker dashed home.

Fortified with this single run, Wood blazed through the Senator lineup for the final nine outs of his fourteenth consecutive victory, allowing only six hits and striking out nine, while Johnson yielded but five safeties and struck out five. Wood then won his next two starts to tie Johnson's record at sixteen wins in a row before falling to the lowly Detroit Tigers on September 20. He finished the season with a club-record thirty-four wins.

The Red Sox had established a new won-lost record for the American League with a mark of 105-47. Included in that number were fourteen straight wins over New York, the team that would soon be known as the Yankees, a gaudy mark that inspires envy even today.

The pennant gave the Red Sox a chance to settle an old score, for the New York Giants won the National League flag and the right to play in the World Series. Few in Boston had forgotten the end of the 1904 season, when New York owner John Brush had refused to play Boston and branded the club "a bunch of bush leaguers." Giant manager McGraw was still a sworn enemy of Ban Johnson, and old-time Boston fans still held McGraw in disdain for his brutish style of play with the Baltimore Orioles two decades earlier.

The Red Sox were quietly confident. As both teams prepared for battle, the press hyped what was expected to be a "dream" Series. In hotel lobbies and taverns of both cities, as usual, the gamblers held sway. Tin Pan Alley composer and Giant fanatic George M. Cohan told Boston owner James McAleer, "I have $50,000 to wager on the Speed Boys [Red Sox]." Tim Murnane later commented "there was more money wagered on this series than ever before," in excess of one million dollars. Not surprisingly, Red Sox game-one starter Joe Wood received several death threats.

Despite Cohan's defection, most of the New York money remained loyal to the Giants. After all, McGraw's team had enjoyed a rather spectacular season of their own. Pitcher Rube Marquard had trumped both Wood and Johnson by winning 19 in a row, and the Giants had won 103 games to finish 10 games in front of the Pittsburgh Pirates.

The Giants were well balanced, combining a consistent hitting attack with aggressive baserunning that made their Boston counterparts look slow. They were led by second baseman Larry Doyle, the NL's MVP, supplemented by the pitching of Marquard and the great Christy Mathewson.

But before game one Giants fans were shocked to see rookie righthander Jeff Tesreau warming up. While Tesreau's superb control of his spitball had allowed him to lead the league with a 1.96 ERA (the first season the NL kept the statistic), most assumed that McGraw would pitch Mathewson opposite Wood. But as if conceding the first contest, McGraw saved Mathewson for game two, a tougher assignment at Fenway Park, to be followed by Marquard in game three.

As the crowd packed the Polo Grounds on the afternoon of October 8, a similar crowd formed in Boston on Washington Street's newspaper row. During the game, men on scaffolds moved wooden figures and numbers on a billboard, re-creating the action in New York. As children rode piggyback and workers rubbernecked from office windows, a man with a megaphone shouted out the play-by-play in dramatic bursts followed by long pauses as he waited for news of the next pitch relayed via a telegraph operator from the distant ballpark. He covered up momentary lapses in transmission by conjuring up imaginary foul balls and delivering sales pitches for the sponsors of the free spectacle.

As the man described each strike thrown by Joe Wood, the crowd roared. For over two hours the throng stood, listened, and alternately cried and celebrated.

For five innings McGraw's hunch paid off as Tesreau, bolstered by the home crowd, nursed a 2-0 lead over the best pitcher in baseball. But Speaker scored after tripling in the sixth, and in the seventh Boston broke through.

With one out, Wagner and Cady singled. Then Wood hit a double-play ball to Doyle.

The MVP bobbled it and was able to get only the force at second. Harry Hooper then tied the score with a hard double down the first-base line to the wall, and Steve Yerkes followed with a single to put the Red Sox up by a score of 4-2.

The score held into the bottom of the ninth. Then with one out, Wood tired and gave up successive singles to Fred Merkle and Buck Herzog. With the partisan crowd roaring, catcher Chief Meyers then singled to right. But Harry Hooper saved the game and perhaps the entire series by grabbing the ball on the run barehanded and throwing a blind strike to Red Sox catcher Hick Cady. Although one run scored, Hooper's astonishing throw forced McGraw to hold Herzog at third. Yet the Giants still had the tying and winning runs in scoring position as Meyers went to second on the throw.

Wood, bolstered by the great play, then reached back for whatever reserves remained in his 353rd inning of the season, striking out both Art Fletcher and Doc Crandall. Boston won 4-3. The Royal Rooters celebrated Boston's first Red Sox World Series win in nine years with a raucous party on the hometown's infield.

Both clubs immediately embarked by train for Boston for game two, and at first light on the morning of October 9 the streets around Fenway began to fill with people. As one fan described the scene in a letter to *The Sporting News*, "We hurried into the bleachers and our long vigil began. It was then about ten o'clock. Four hours to wait for the game to start and the worst of it was there wasn't a moment that we did not expect to hear that there would be no game [because of poor weather] . . . a small crowd of fellows gave an impromptu concert in which the

Joe Wood was a superior hitter, compiling a .283 lifetime batting average as both a pitcher and outfielder. In the 1912 World Series Wood batted .286 in addition to winning three games.

crowd joined in with a will . . . 'Tessie,' 'Sweet Adeline,' 'I Want to be Down in Dixie' were the favorites concluded with a 'Star Spangled Banner' and everybody stood up and cheered like mad . . . By 12 the stands were well filled and every woman who passed in front of the center field bleachers received an ovation."

The crowd was huge and filled stands that were erected for the Series down the left-field line and in right-center, fully enclosing Fenway Park for the first time. Ticket prices ranged from fifty cents in the center-field bleachers to five dollars for the three rows of temporary box seats that ringed the infield.

The usual suspects were all in attendance, from 'Nuf 'Ced McGreevey to Boston Mayor John Fitzgerald. As lefthander Ray Collins took his final warm-up tosses the skies looked as if they would burst. But the weather held, and it was the Red Sox who burst forth, taking advantage of poor fielding by Mathewson to score three runs while hitting only one ball out of the infield.

But as Mathewson steadied, the Giants chipped away at Collins, scoring single runs in the second and fourth innings to reduce the Boston lead to one run. Then in the fifth inning Boston countered with a single and subsequent steal of second by Hooper. He scored on a hit by Steve Yerkes to give Collins back his two-run cushion.

Play was surprisingly sloppy on both sides, a product of both the weather and the stakes. In the eighth inning Duffy Lewis dropped an easy flyball hit by Fred Snodgrass, leading to two New York runs to tie the game.

Jake Stahl pulled Collins and sent in Charley Hall. Buck Herzog greeted him with a double into the left-field stands to put the Giants ahead.

Now it was New York's turn to play with the baseball. With two outs and Mathewson seemingly in control, Duffy Lewis atoned for his error with a double. Larry Gardner then sent an easy grounder to shortstop — and through the legs of Art Fletcher, allowing Lewis to tie the score at 5-5.

The game entered extra innings. The Giants refused to die, and in the tenth Fred Merkle socked a triple and ultimately scored on a sacrifice fly by Harry McCormick. With New York leading, the encroaching darkness threatened to end what had been one of the most exciting World Series games ever played. Most believed the umpires would call the contest at the end of the inning.

With one down, Tris Speaker stepped to the plate. The crowd roared his name and all stood as he glared out at Mathewson for the fifth time that day.

He swung and connected solidly, driving the ball over Snodgrass's head in center field. From his first step, Speaker was determined to score.

He rounded third as the relay throw came into shortstop Tillie Shafer, who had replaced Fletcher. But Shafer dropped the throw and Giant third baseman Buck Herzog, taking a cue from McGraw's old Orioles, tried to slow Speaker by "accidentally" bumping him as he turned for home. But Speaker stayed on his feet and arrived at the plate at the same instant as Shafer's hurried toss.

Catcher Art Wilson couldn't hold it. The ball popped from his glove as Speaker slid over the plate. Then, as sportswriter Fred Lieb wrote, Speaker jumped up after his slide and "tagged the plate again to make the run doubly sure and then started up the third-base line after Herzog."

The two players stood toe-to-toe, barking and stalking one another like boxers until separated. Then the umpires waved the teams back onto the field for yet another inning.

Stahl called on rookie Hugh Bedient to pitch the top of the eleventh. His nerves showed as he first hit Snodgrass and walked Becker, sandwiched around a strikeout.

But McGraw was too anxious. As soon as each man reached first, he sent him to second where each was thrown out by Bill Carrigan, and the Giants failed to score.

But it was now too dark to see. After Mathewson set down the Sox in his half of the inning, umpire Silk O'Loughlin informed both managers, "It's too dark for any more baseball today," and players of both squads trudged off the diamond as the crowd stood in place, suddenly deflated by the 6-6 tie. Christy Mathewson later called the contest "the hardest ballgame I ever went through."

Action continued the following day, both on and off the field. In the morning, Giant manager John McGraw was confronted in his hotel room by a committee of Giants fans who demanded he replace error-prone shortstop Art Fletcher in the starting lineup with Shafer. He quickly sent them on their way.

In another hotel suite, representatives of the National Commission, Major League Baseball's ruling body, met with players from both teams to decide what to do with the proceeds of the tie game. All players of both squads were supposed to receive a share of the gate from the first four games of the Series, but a tie, an extra game, was unaccounted for.

National Commission chairman Garry Herrmann ultimately gave the money to the owners. The players were none too pleased, as they correctly concluded it gave the owners an unearned, one-game windfall.

In effect, the game would be replayed in its entirety, so both teams remained in Boston rather than return as scheduled to New York. Buck O'Brien faced Rube Marquard in a battle of twenty-game winners.

The game was every bit as nerve-racking as that of the previous afternoon. With New York leading 2-1, two runners on base, and two out in the bottom of the ninth, Boston catcher Hick Cady socked a drive to the deepest section of right-center field. As the ball sailed over right fielder Josh Devore's head, Boston fans rose to applaud what seemed to be the game-winning hit as both runners dashed for home. Instead, they saw Devore stretch out on the dead run, catch the ball, and run off the field, not breaking stride, thus saving the Giant victory.

At least, that's what some fans saw. Others thought Cady's drive had fallen safe and left Fenway thinking both Stahl and Wagner had scored to end the game. They didn't learn of the loss until the next day, when they read about it in the newspaper. The Giants' win knotted the Series.

Returning to the Polo Grounds, the next contest was a reprise of the Series opener. Joe Wood and Jeff Tesreau squared off for the second time, both men pitching with just two days' rest.

Despite allowing nine hits, Wood gave up only one run and helped his cause by smacking two of the eight hits in the 3-1 Red Sox win. He was saved by shortstop Heinie Wagner, a native New Yorker, who made several key plays. In his ghostwritten column the next day, Tris reportedly offered, "Wagner never played more brilliantly than today and he never will, because that would not be humanely [sic] possible."

But all wasn't well. Observers noted that Wood had abandoned his fastball for curves, leading to speculation that something was wrong with his arm.

It was back to Boston for game five. Following his spotty performance in game two, much was expected of Christy Mathewson in his second start. Hugh Bedient made his first Series start for Boston.

With a cold wind blowing in, both teams wore full-sleeve undershirts and sought the comfort of horse blankets and wool mackinaws on the bench. The conditions seemed to assure a low-scoring game.

In the third inning, Hooper led off with a triple and scored when Yerkes followed with his own three-bagger. Tris Speaker came up next.

In a play involving both league MVPs, Speaker topped a groundball that had as much to do with

Charles "Heinie" Wagner was the backbone of the 1912 world champions. The shortstop, a six-year veteran, was respected by all in a clubhouse often divided along social and religious lines.

the Series outcome as any tape-measure homer or dropped flyball. Giants second baseman Larry Doyle fielded the slow roller, glanced at Yerkes sprinting toward home, and then fumbled the ball.

The run was the game-winner as Bedient allowed only three hits, striking out four and allowing just one run. The great Mathewson lost.

With a commanding three-games-to-one advantage, the Red Sox were confident that their next appearance in Fenway Park would be as world champions. As they jogged off the field Red Sox players were overheard shouting, "That was it!" After all, they

Smoky Joe Wood *(l)* and Christy Mathewson *(r)* prior to the start of game eight of the 1912 World Series. Wood enjoyed the greatest season ever by a Red Sox pitcher as he spun a 34-5 won-lost record in the regular season followed by a 3-1 won-lost record in the World Series. He beat Mathewson in the clinching game of the Series in relief of starter Hugh Bedient.

thought Joe Wood would pitch game six against Rube Marquard. With Wood on the mound, the Red Sox felt invincible.

With Sunday baseball banned in both cities, the teams traveled to New York on the off day. The mood on the Red Sox train was almost euphoric. Sports-writers observed Boston players with pencils in hand calculating their soon-to-be-won winner's shares, which in many cases would be greater than their salaries for the entire season.

Manager Jake Stahl planned to watch Joe Wood work his magic in what he hoped would be his forty-first and final start of the season. Then James

McAleer paid a late-night visit to Stahl's New York hotel room.

McAleer asked Stahl to reconsider his decision to start Wood. He argued that twenty-game winner Buck O'Brien, a hard-luck loser to Marquard in game three, deserved the start and a chance for revenge. Furthermore, McAleer reasoned that Wood could use a third day's rest and should be held in reserve for a possible third and final rematch against Jeff Tes-reau in game seven.

But that's just what he told Stahl. McAleer was a shrewd businessman who knew the value of the gate he and his partners would collect if Wood were to start an additional game at Fenway Park. Although he wouldn't openly root against his team at the Polo Grounds, McAleer was both confident enough and greedy enough to gamble near-certain victory and a world championship for a chance at another lucrative Fenway payday.

McAleer's interference angered Stahl, yet pleased many of the gamblers and other sharpies that circled the Series like vultures. The possibility of one more game meant one more chance for a big score, and Red Sox watchers already knew it wouldn't be the first time a Series game involving Boston had been tampered with to extend the life of the Series.

Street logic now assumed the Red Sox would take the championship and that easy money could be made by extending the Series. The gamblers who had once made certain areas of the Huntington Avenue Grounds their private offices had done the same at Fenway.

Stahl tried to resist McAleer's "suggestion" and made a passionate counterargument that the Red Sox were ready to win now. Wood hadn't complained about his arm or asked for an extra day. But McAleer would hear none of it and told Stahl the team should and would be able to win behind O'Brien. He was the boss and O'Brien would pitch.

Word of the change spread fast among the players, and at breakfast the next morning the mood turned ugly as Wood and Speaker told their teammates in no uncertain terms what they thought of the idea. Wood, who had often pitched on two days' rest, was primed for battle, and the letdown was dramatic. By the time they reached the Polo Grounds the Red Sox were already a beaten ballclub.

The only positive note for the team was the robust support provided by the Royal Rooters. As the *Boston Post* reported, "Led by Johnny Keenan, 'Nuff Ced' McGreevey and Al Keating with their band playing tantalizing 'Tessie' the gallant 300 started from the Elks Club at noon and paraded along Broadway for 12 blocks. As the procession proceeded the people who lined the streets cheered the smiling invading rooters."

Other Boston fans weren't quite so giddy. Joe Wood's brother Paul seethed as he watched O'Brien warm up. Certain his brother would pitch, he'd already bet the Red Sox to win. He wasn't alone, and rumor had it that O'Brien, oblivious to his assignment, had been out late the night before drinking himself into a stupor. The timing of McAleer's intrusion and the ensuing outcome makes one wonder if the Red Sox owner might well have chosen to put his money on the Giants himself that day, or picked up O'Brien's tab.

Stahl's worst fears were soon realized. In the top of the first, following two scratch hits and a steal, O'Brien balked in the first run, then came completely unglued, allowing four hits sandwiched around an error and a double steal. Boston trailed 5-0 before they got out of the inning.

A wild throw by Marquard in the second started a Red Sox rally, which netted two runs, but Marquard held Boston at bay for the remainder of the day and New York won, 5-2. With a victory the next day, the Giants could tie the Series.

As the Red Sox left New York, the *Boston Post* published a cartoon featuring a large satchel of money marked "extra gate receipts" surrounded by two men identified generically as a club owner and a member of the National Commission, both shedding crocodile tears. McAleer wisely made himself unavailable following the game. Thus far, his ploy had backfired, demoralizing his team and allowing the Giants a stay of execution, while placing incredible pressure on Wood to win the next day.

On the train ride to Boston, tensions erupted. Paul Wood, enraged at losing one hundred dollars on the game, sought out O'Brien and blackened one of the pitcher's eyes in a wild fistfight. Although the incident was widely reported and later denied, the team was clearly in trouble.

But despite their record, there had been trouble all season. The team was split into two factions: one Catholic, led by Lewis, Carrigan, O'Brien, and Hooper, and the other Protestant, led by Speaker and Wood. The newspapers referred to the two cliques as the "knights" and "masons."

Such division wasn't anything new in Boston, which had elected its first Irish-Catholic mayor less than a decade before. Issues of class, religion, and race had defined the city since before the Civil War and do so to the present day. The Red Sox were, and still are, one of the most visible institutions in the city. Then, as now, their internal problems often only mirror those of the city at large.

Despite the simmering sectarian friction, the Sox

still faced the larger and more pressing problem of trying to win the Series. Then, as Stahl was preparing his men for what they still hoped would be a triumphant victory, management again created almost unimaginable turmoil.

Originally, the best-of-seven series included only three games in Boston. But the tie gave Boston an unscheduled contest, and the Royal Rooters' usual allotment of several hundred seats in the left-field stands had not been accounted for. The influential group of fans still assumed they would receive their usual seats. But in a huge miscalculation, team treasurer Robert McRoy made the Rooters' tickets available to the general public.

As was their custom, the Rooters and their entourage marched onto the field like a conquering army. Then they found strangers in their seats.

As R. E. McMullin, sports editor of the *Boston Herald*, wrote, "[The Rooters] made a flank movement toward their usual left field reservations . . . [and] found them occupied. There was some more parading and a lot of cheering for everyone but the Sox management. Finally the Rooters were corralled and placed in the left field bleachers, standing up just behind the fence. Here they remained docile until just before the game started. Then they jumped the barrier and began to make a raid on the grandstand. A quick charge of the mounted police choked this sally and pushed the McGreeveys back behind the barrier, whereat the R. R.s [Royal Rooters] pushed with great force against the fence and knocked it flat." At length, the Rooters were finally calmed — and convinced to hold up the barricade for the balance of the game.

As confusion reigned, the players tried to warm up. But the events of the previous day were still simmering. Joe Wood was livid.

Despite later serving as baseball coach at Yale, Wood was no milquetoast. He played for money, and after he retired he was implicated along with Ty Cobb and Tris Speaker in a betting scandal over games during the 1919 season. On this day he didn't hesitate to defend his brother's honor.

He verbally abused O'Brien in the runway leading from the clubhouse to the field, then assaulted him, reportedly beating him with a baseball bat. Team-mates pulled the two men apart as their season hung in the balance.

In the cold wind, after a fight, and with a sore arm, Wood had just started to throw when the Rooters took over the field and caused a delay. The pitcher and his teammates eventually retreated to the bench to wait out the battle before taking the field.

From Wood's first warm-up toss, it was apparent that he bore no resemblance to the man who had taken the mound on forty-two other occasions in 1912. He lobbed the ball, as Tim Murnane described it, in "a clear case of cutting the ball over the heart of the plate."

John McGraw took notice and reportedly told his team to swing early and often. It was almost as if they knew what was coming. They well might have.

Leadoff hitter Josh Devore swung at the first pitch and hit a roller to Wagner, who bobbled the ball. Then Doyle pasted a line drive into right field for a single.

With Snodgrass up, Wood inexplicably pitched from the full windup instead of the set position normally used with runners on base. Devore and Doyle noticed and executed a double steal, as a surprised Cady dropped the pitch.

On the next pitch — Wood's fourth of the game — Snodgrass smacked a line drive to right. Hooper caught it at his knees, then kicked it out as Snodgrass waltzed into second.

Murray bunted the next pitch to Jake Stahl at first, who became the first Boston player of the day to play the game as intended, fielding the ball cleanly for an out as Snodgrass made third. Then Fred Merkle lofted a simple fly to left that the wind turned into a single and Duffy Lewis turned into a double by making a wild throw. Snodgrass scored the Giants' third run.

When Herzog grounded back to the box, Merkle, on second, lit out for third. He was surprised when Wood made a play on him and was caught off base for the second out.

But the Giants weren't finished, although it was obvious Wood was. Chief Meyers singled home Herzog. Then Art Fletcher singled, and then Meyers scored as Jeff Tesreau singled off Wood's glove.

Then, on what was variously reported as either

Wood's thirteenth or fifteenth pitch of the inning, Tesreau executed the first half of a double steal. Boston catcher Hick Cady threw — too late — to second baseman Yerkes, who then held the ball too long to get the speedy Fletcher at home. Tesreau kept running and finally ran into the ball in someone's glove to end the inning. Six runs had scored in less than five minutes.

All told, Wood was reported to have thrown between thirteen and fifteen pitches. Seven were struck by New York hitters, six falling safely. In the field, Lewis, Hooper, Wagner, Wood, Cady, and Yerkes all made errors of one kind or another. Only manager Jake Stahl failed to avail himself of the opportunity to screw up. Boston fans, already upset by the rousting of the Royal Rooters, watched in a state of shock as the best pitcher and the best team in baseball unraveled in the most dubious fashion right before their eyes.

Wood was finished. Charley Hall mopped up, allowing another five runs in the ensuing eight innings. Boston scored four runs but squandered several other opportunities by making egregious baserunning errors rarely seen even on the sandlot. Those few fans who bothered to stay were rewarded with one spectacular moment when Speaker snared a ninth-inning drive by Art Fletcher and then outraced Giants catcher Art Wilson to second, recording the only unassisted double play by an outfielder in World Series history.

Boston fans had never before experienced such a singularly depressing series of events in one afternoon. The previous 108 victories of the season faded when compared with the windswept few minutes in which the team turned on itself and its fans.

While Wood's arm may well have been sore and stiffened because of the pre-game delay, it is equally true that, given the events of the previous day, neither Wood nor many of his teammates may have much cared what happened in game seven. Not since the opening game of the first World Series nine years earlier had a Boston team turned in a performance with such an unpalatable stench. It is not inconceivable to believe that the Red Sox, already upset with management, threw the game in order to recoup their losses by laying money on the Giants in game

Harry Hooper arrived in Boston with an engineering degree from St. Mary's College in 1909. He ended up playing on four Red Sox world champion teams and was a member of the famed Lewis-Speaker-Hooper outfield considered to be the best major league outfield trio of the Dead Ball Era.

seven at favorable odds. In the days that followed, Boston newspapers intimated precisely that, and Sox fans learned a valuable lesson: when it comes to the Olde Towne team, there is no such thing as a "sure thing."

The incredible defeat led to yet one more unbelievable spectacle. After the game, the Rooters made their usual commotion and paraded off the field. But once outside the park, they mobbed Jersey Street and sang their usual complement of songs — substituting lyrics that sang the praises of the Giants and skewered Boston's front office.

The Series was now tied. And no one yet knew where, or when, game eight would be played.

After the debacle, Baseball Commission member Garry Herrmann tossed a coin to decide the site of game eight. Most commission members and many loyal Red Sox fans were hoping the game would be played in New York. They'd had it with the hometown.

Herrmann tossed the coin skyward and John McGraw called "Heads." The coin landed tail-up.

The odds still favored New York, for McGraw had Christy Mathewson available, and the chances of Mathewson starting three games without securing a win seemed impossible. Although Stahl knew that Joe Wood would be ready to pitch after throwing barely a dozen pitches, he couldn't trust him to start the game. The circumstances had been just too questionable. He picked Hugh Bedient instead.

On October 16, 1912, Fenway Park was barely half full for what many would later describe as the greatest World Series game of the Dead Ball Era. The events of the previous day kept the crowd sparse, and more than a few writers observed that the empty seats were ample evidence of a profound lack of faith on the part of the Boston fans.

But despite their low numbers, those who did attend were enthusiastic. Thousands of wooden rattles were distributed and, according to the *New York Times*, "when beaten together or on the backs of seats set up a chorus like that of giant crickets. At times the noise was weird in the extreme." Only slightly weirder was the boycott of the Royal Rooters, most of whom protested their shabby treatment of the previous afternoon by staying home. In the morning papers, the most "Royal" of all Rooters, Boston mayor John "Honey Fitz" Fitzgerald, called for the immediate removal of McRoy. Apart from the intermittent clicking of rattles, the Fenway crowd was strangely quiet for this most important game.

So was the Red Sox clubhouse. The players met privately before the game to air their differences and called an uneasy truce.

For the first two innings Bedient and Mathewson both held the opposition scoreless. In the third, Bedient gave up a run when Josh Devore scored from third on Red Murray's double over Speaker's head. But in the fifth, he showed signs of tiring.

With one out and none on, Larry Doyle socked a drive that everyone thought was headed for the new bleachers in deep right-center field. Boston right fielder Harry Hooper did not agree.

He got an excellent jump on the ball, tracked it back, and as it descended turned completely around on a dead run and reached for the ball with his bare hand. Then he tumbled over the outfield wall and into the arms of grateful fans. A moment later he emerged holding the drive in his hand.

Hooper could barely believe he had made the catch. The Giants didn't, protesting that Hooper had either left the playing field prior to making the grab, which would have rendered his catch meaningless, or had been handed the ball by a fan while out of view. The argument was futile.

Still down by one run in the seventh, Gardner led off with a fly out to center. Stahl then lofted a soft fly to left that dropped between fielders for a base hit. Mathewson walked Wagner on four straight pitches before Cady popped up to Fletcher for the second out.

Knowing that Boston might not get another opportunity to score off Mathewson, Stahl pinch-hit for Bedient, calling on outfielder Olaf Henriksen, who had come to bat only fifty-six times all year, and not once in the Series.

With two strikes, Mathewson threw a letter-high curve. Henriksen was fooled, but lunged at the pitch and hit it toward third base.

It hit the bag, just fair, then bounced crazily into foul territory. As the ball careened toward the Giants dugout, Stahl raced home with the tying run and Henriksen, running hard, made it to second. Hooper then flied out, but the score was tied.

Stahl had a decision to make. He called on Wood to start the eighth.

His decision tends to cast the events of the previous day in a more sinister light, for Wood was suddenly back to normal. Had a sore arm been the sole cause of his trouble in game seven, it wouldn't have gotten better in only twenty-four hours.

Mayor John "Honey Fitz" Fitzgerald (in light hat) leads the parade celebrating the 1912 world championship. Included in his car are *(top l–r)* player-manager Jake Stahl, pitcher Joe Wood, mascot Jerry McCarthy, catcher Hick Cady, and, to Fitzgerald's right, infielder Larry Gardner.

With a chance to lead his team to the world championship, restore his reputation, and win his third game of the Series, Wood retired the Giants in both the eighth and ninth innings, as Mathewson did the same for Boston. The game would continue.

In the top of the tenth, after Snodgrass fouled out, Murray doubled. Fred Merkle then sent a sinking line drive toward center.

As Speaker well knew, more games are lost on singles that fall before outfielders than on extra-base hits over their heads. But it is equally true that games are also lost on errors of judgment, and Speaker made just such an error. Instead of playing it safe, he tried to make a shoestring catch. The ball squirted past, and Murray scored while Merkle made second to put New York ahead, 2-1.

Wood was in trouble. But he bore down and then threw what he later claimed were his "hardest three pitches of the season." He struck out Buck Herzog for the second out.

But the effort exhausted him. Facing Chief Meyers,

Wood left a ball over the plate with nothing on it and the Giants catcher drove it back at Wood faster than it had come in.

Wood had little time to react. He threw his bare hand at the ball, knocked it down, picked it up, and threw out Meyers for the final out. By the time he reached the bench, the hand was already beginning to swell. He was done for the day, no matter what happened next. Boston had to win now.

Mathewson was only three outs away from winning the most important game of his distinguished career. He had pitched brilliantly, and now the odds were in his favor, for Wood, scheduled to lead off, was unable to bat. Stahl pinch-hit outfielder Clyde Engle, 0-2 thus far in the Series and only a .234 hitter for the season, for what would turn out to be one of the most noteworthy at bats in the history of baseball.

Engle lifted a routine fly, described by sportswriter Fred Lieb as the proverbial "can of corn," to Fred Snodgrass in center field. He dropped it. Engle, running hard, slid safely into second then stood up, grinning. Harry Hooper stepped in to face Mathewson.

He hit a liner to center, and now Snodgrass made a catch as spectacular as his previous effort had been awful. Engle tagged up and advanced to third.

Speaker was on deck as Mathewson faced Yerkes. Yerkes worked him for a walk, bringing up Boston's best hitter at precisely the time they needed him the most.

The two future members of baseball's Hall of Fame eyed each other warily for a moment, then got to the task at hand. Speaker hit a popup foul.

Mathewson, catcher Chief Meyers, and first baseman Fred Merkle formed a wide circle under the ball and Mathewson called for Meyers to catch it. But the big pitcher misjudged the popup. Merkle had the better angle but pulled up as Meyers lunged for the ball. It dropped untouched, giving the American League MVP another chance. As Mathewson walked back to the mound, Speaker reportedly grinned and called out in his rough Texas twang, "Well, you just called for the wrong man [Meyers]. It's gonna cost you the ballgame."

With that boast ringing in Mathewson's ears, he wound up and delivered. Speaker turned on the pitch and spanked it into right field for a long base hit. Engle scored the tying run as Yerkes slid into third and Speaker went to second on the throw.

McGraw ordered Mathewson to walk Duffy Lewis, setting up a force play at every base. Then Larry Gardner lifted a long fly to Josh Devore. He made the catch easily and threw home, but Steve Yerkes out-raced the ball to score the winning run of the Series.

The half-empty stands suddenly seemed full and erupted with shouts and songs. The Giants were stunned. Mathewson had been magnificent in defeat, and many in the crowd recognized the fact. As the big pitcher trudged off the field, he received a standing ovation.

Despite being outhit and outscored by the Giants over the course of the Series, the Red Sox prevailed — game seven notwithstanding — on the basis of superb pitching, consistent fielding, and solid clutch hitting. But questions surrounding game seven had left a bad taste in the mouths of many, and victory celebrations later that night were subdued. In the annals of baseball history, the defining moment of the Series became neither Speaker's nor Gardner's clutch hitting, Harry Hooper's catches, Joe Wood's three victories, nor Mathewson's critical miscall on the foul popup.

Instead, and somewhat inexplicably, Fred Snodgrass became the scapegoat. His dropped flyball became known as the "$30,000 Muff," a reference to the monetary difference between winning and losing. Good thing, for his error has since served to obscure the events surrounding game seven.

In the minds of most observers at the time, it was a tainted crown, one that Boston didn't so much win, as New York lost. With three pennants and two world championships in their first twelve seasons, the Red Sox were already facing the specter of high expectations. Even in 1912, in Boston, winning wasn't quite enough.

FROM "ROUGH" TO RUTH

1913 | 1916

George Herman Ruth arrived in Boston as a brash nineteen-year-old on July 11, 1914. On that day he met his first wife, Helen, then a waitress at Landers Coffee Shop. He also won his first major league game against the Indians.

Sports, politics, and revenge have long been considered Boston's three favorite pastimes. In the last years of baseball's Dead Ball Era all three converged as the Red Sox built a dynasty and the city played host to five world champion teams in only seven seasons. For one glorious decade the city was the center of the baseball universe.

Boston was booming, experiencing its last years of growth and prosperity before it would see decades dominated by war, Prohibition, and the Depression, leading to general and widespread decline. The new and controversial Custom House, Boston's first skyscraper, dominated the Boston skyline, and the incursion of the automobile and streetcar pushed the city's population into the suburbs. Immigrants filled triple-deckers and carved out a portion of the American dream. The ascendance of the Irish-American was highlighted by the election of both Honey Fitz Fitzgerald and the irrepressible James Michael Curley as mayor. In the midst of such optimism, the Red Sox and the Braves seemed to provide proof that Boston was on the rise.

But the defending world champion Red Sox faced lingering resentment from fans alienated during the 1912 World Series. Worse, the team was still divided against itself. They were champions, yet the Hot Stove League boiled over with talk of dissension. Throughout the long cold winter the press criticized owner McAleer and team secretary Bob McRoy unmercifully.

In such a negative climate, only a few players were able to cash in on their fleeting notoriety. Buck O'Brien and Hugh Bradley, joined by former teammate Marty McHale and Bill Lyons, hit the vaudeville circuit as "The Red Sox Quartette." They toured the far reaches of New England where the sight of a bonafide major leaguer enthralled unsophisticated fans, singing popular hits and novelty tunes like "The Ballad of Buck O'Brien, the Spit Ball Artist."

The 1913 Red Sox began spring training with the same players and problems of the previous season. The pundits were unconvinced by the victory over New York and already viewed the championship cup as half-empty. Connie Mack's Athletics were favored to win the pennant.

Spring training was uneventful except for one small item reported in several papers. On March 8, Joe Wood, playing third base in practice, sprained an ankle taking a throw wide of the bag.

The following day Tim Murnane reported, "Joe Wood is limping around with a strained ankle which may affect his pitching for months to come." Murnane was right. Already the Red Sox pitching staff made more than a few observers nervous, for virtually everyone had enjoyed a "career year" in 1912. The odds were against an encore, and one-year wonders would soon be a recognizable Red Sox trait.

But two rookies gave the staff a measure of protection. Dutch Leonard, like Hooper and Lewis an alumnus of St. Mary's College, had gone 29-9 with Denver in the Rocky Mountain League. Joining him was twenty-four-year-old Rube Foster, a 5-foot-7 right-hander who dazzled the Texas League in 1912 with a 24-7 record. Both made the team that spring, as did fellow rookie and Boston English infielder Hal Janvrin.

Boston began the season with one of the biggest payrolls in baseball and, despite lingering rumors of disharmony, full of confidence. But Opening Day provided a one-game synopsis of the season ahead.

With former Red Sox ace Bill Dinneen working as home plate umpire, Joe Wood received the honor of pitching the first game of the season. He struck out six in the first four innings, then faltered, giving up five runs in seven innings in a 10-9 loss to the Athletics before twenty thousand fans at chilly Fenway.

Wood, perhaps bothered by the ankle, continued to struggle, and the team got off to a slow start. Then, in a relief appearance at Tiger Stadium on May 12, he slipped fielding a bunt and injured his right thumb. He missed four starts before rejoining the rotation, but altered his motion slightly to compensate for the thumb injury and his still-weak ankle. As Wood told Lawrence Ritter years later, "I don't know whether I tried to pitch too soon after that, or whether maybe something happened to my shoulder at the same time. But whatever it was, I never pitched again without a terrific amount of pain in my right shoulder. Never again." Today, it seems likely that Wood was well on his way to tearing his rotator cuff, one of the worst injuries a pitcher can suffer.

As Wood fought to regain his form, the Red Sox never got untracked, and Boston fans lost enthusiasm. Even though Wood was pitching, only sixty-five hundred fans turned out on June 26 for the raising of the 1912 world championship banner. Mayor Fitzgerald and most of the Rooters were conspicuously absent.

Management needed a scapegoat. In early July, club president James McAleer called Jake Stahl into his office. McAleer heard a rumor that Stahl, a minor shareholder in the club and off-season bank executive, was about to succeed him as president. Stahl denied the story and indicated that his hands were full running his underachieving team, telling the press, "There's nothing to it — someone is working a fake. Mack [McAleer] and I have no differences." But McAleer was unconvinced and feared the manager was playing politics behind his back. On July 14 he fired Stahl and replaced him with catcher Bill Carrigan.

The move was popular with the largely Irish-American press contingent that covered the team. In "Rough" Carrigan, they saw a self-made man, someone who embodied their own aspirations.

When McAleer offered him the manager's job, Carrigan was initially stunned, but they agreed to terms almost immediately. Yet he knew the club well and was aware that his task would not be easy.

After only a few days on the job, it became even more difficult. Joe Wood tried to chase down future Hall of Famer Sam Crawford in a rundown, slipped again, and broke his thumb. He missed the rest of the season, and his blazing fastball was gone for good. Over the remainder of his career, he won only twenty-four more games.

Carrigan spent the rest of the season trying to rebuild. As many had feared, most of his pitchers slumped. Vaudevillian Buck O'Brien started the season out of shape, and the opposition soon solved the mystery of his spitball. He won only four games before being traded to the White Sox. Twenty-game-winner Hugh Bedient slipped to 15-14. Dutch Leonard, despite leading the team in ERA, struggled with his control and finished 14-16. Only veteran Ray Collins, who won nineteen, approached his 1912 performance. The Red Sox simply couldn't make up for the loss of Wood and finished a disappointing fourth, 79-71, fifteen and a half games behind the Athletics.

Of the regulars, only Speaker, Lewis, and Hooper played to their usual standard. In 1913 they formed perhaps the best defensive outfield in the history of the game. Tris Speaker hit .365, stole forty-six bases, and threw out an astounding thirty baserunners. Lewis nailed another twenty-nine and Hooper shot down twenty-five more, giving the three the all-time standard for assists by an outfield with eighty-four.

THE MAN THEY CALLED "ROUGH"

Bill Carrigan is the only manager in major league history to win back-to-back world championships and not be enshrined in the Hall of Fame. Despite this oversight, there is little question he is the greatest Red Sox manager of them all.

Carrigan's father owned a grocery store and sponsored a sports club in Lewiston, Maine, providing equipment, playing fields, and coaches for local boys. The son worked for the father while earning a reputation as a standout football tackle and baseball captain at Lewiston High. While playing college football at Holy Cross, he was injured in his sophomore season and thereafter concentrated on baseball. After starring in his junior year, he left school several credits shy of receiving his degree to sign with Boston. After a brief stop with Toronto of the Eastern League, he made it to the majors for Boston in 1906.

In 1909 he supplanted Lou Criger behind the plate and quickly became a fan favorite. Respected by everyone, he was particularly close to fellow Catholics Duffy Lewis, Harry Hooper, and Heinie Wagner, who often joined him in the occasional card game and postseason hunting trip to his Maine camp.

Carrigan earned the nickname "Rough," considered a badge of honor in the often brutal world of dead-ball baseball. In an era in which the home run was rare, teams had to scratch out a run at a time. Carrigan set the tone for Boston, earning a reputation as a master handler of pitchers, while his powerful arm and sentry-like ability to block the plate kept opposing baserunners at bay.

He feared no one on the field, not even the mighty Ty Cobb, earning the grudging respect of baseball's greatest and most infamous competitor. According to legend, Carrigan once tagged the hard-charging Tiger on the mouth as Cobb attempted to spike Carrigan on a slide at home.

When the situation called for it Carrigan was even known to invite physical confrontation with his own teammates, once even taking care of Tris Speaker in a clubhouse fistfight. Yet Carrigan was as fair as he was tough. Although he and Speaker were barely civil to each other, Carrigan never played favorites or allowed his personal feelings to get in the way of winning. As Red Sox manager, he commanded the respect and obedience of every man on the roster. No other manager has come close to matching his record. ⚾

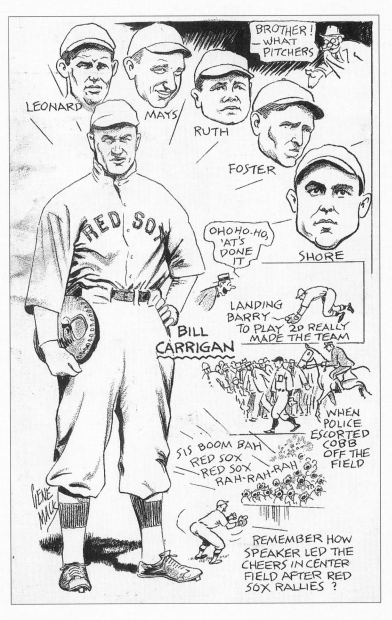

Player-manager Bill Carrigan provided the leadership that saw the Red Sox win consecutive world championships in 1915 and 1916. The rugged catcher was a superb handler of pitchers and was the manager whom Babe Ruth credited for much of his development on and off the field.

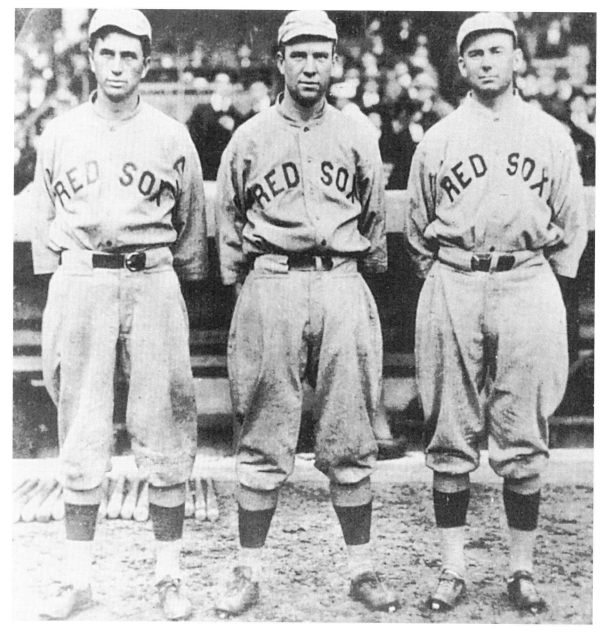

The unsung hero of the great Red Sox outfield of Hooper, Speaker, and Lewis was Duffy Lewis. Not only was he the master of the left-field embankment known as "Duffy's Cliff," but his clutch hitting and fielding helped the team to three world championships.

At the end of the season, as Carrigan returned to Maine to ponder his strategy for 1914, McAleer packed a steamer trunk and prepared to embark on Charles Comiskey and John McGraw's world baseball tour. The four-month, around-the-world voyage was designed to spread the "gospel" of the national pastime across the globe. Tris Speaker was among the many all-stars on board. But McAleer never suspected what AL president Ban Johnson had in mind during his absence.

Johnson had soured on McAleer, and Jake Stahl was his close friend (Johnson served as a pallbearer at Stahl's funeral in 1922). Continuing resentment over the mismanagement of World Series tickets had hurt attendance and cost him money. Even more important was the fact that the Midwestern Federal League, a minor league, announced that in 1914 it would become a third major league. Just as the American League had done, the Feds began to raid the rosters of both the American and National League clubs, driving up salaries dramatically. McAleer had once served Johnson's purpose, but he'd quickly become too independent and didn't have enough money to compete with the Feds. So as McAleer enjoyed the good life cruising the world, Johnson plotted his removal as owner of the Red Sox and began looking for another candidate. It was politics as usual.

In typical fashion, Johnson spoon-fed his supporters in the press word of McAleer's impending retirement — which McAleer as yet knew nothing about — so that his eventual ouster would not come as a complete surprise.

Johnson selected real estate magnate Joseph L. Lannin to become the new owner. Lannin, a native of Quebec who had immigrated to Boston as a teenager, had worked his way up the ladder in Horatio Alger fashion. Starting as a bellhop, he became a real estate magnate whose holdings included apartment houses, golf courses, and at least one of the hotels where he had formerly carried bags.

Lannin was a competitive golfer, lacrosse player, and tournament checker champion (a game more similar to chess than the more familiar parlor version). He was also a rabid baseball fan and owned a minority interest in the Boston Braves. But he really wanted to own a club outright. When Johnson first approached him, he was trying to buy the Philadelphia Phillies.

He fit Johnson's desired profile for a club owner to a tee: he was wealthy, loved baseball, and could be easily controlled. With Johnson's ever-important blessing, Lannin divested himself of his interest in the Braves and paid two hundred thousand dollars for the controlling shares of the Red Sox. The team changed hands for the fifth time in thirteen seasons.

Lannin gave Carrigan full control of baseball operations, and Carrigan got to work, reviewing all player contracts and even choosing the new team uniforms. When spring training began in March, he ran it his way.

He reduced the exhibition schedule to only twelve games and conducted one long daily workout — from 10 A.M. to 3 P.M. — as opposed to the customary two, saving the team from providing lunch. He eliminated the mountain hikes of previous years and required all players to either run or walk the two miles from their hotel to the practice diamond and back.

On March 6, 1914, the most important drama of the spring unfolded dockside in New York City. Joe Lannin and team vice president John I. Taylor met the Cunard liner *Lusitania*, which carried the members of the world baseball tour, including Tris Speaker. Their mission: to re-sign Tris Speaker before agents of the Federal League, also in town to greet the liner, could obtain his signature on a contract. Lannin knew Speaker could command baseball's biggest salary, and he was eager to avoid a bidding war.

The stakes were enormous. Short of Ty Cobb, there was no more electrifying performer or greater all-around player than Speaker. For the Feds, signing him meant instant credibility. For Lannin, keeping him meant preserving his investment. Losing Speaker would cost the team both on the field and at the gate.

On their way to the Hudson River piers, Lannin and Taylor spotted several Federal League rivals. The street-smart Lannin then saw an opportunity to gain advantage. He spied the local revenue cutter (a customs vessel) about to embark for the *Lusitania* and used a combination of charm, connections, and, in all likelihood, cash, to talk Taylor and himself onto the boat. The Feds were left on the dock as the Red Sox brain trust sped toward a rendezvous with their center fielder.

When Lannin and Taylor scrambled aboard the liner, Speaker was surprised to see his new boss alongside the man who had signed him to his first Red Sox contract nearly a decade earlier. According to news accounts, Lannin remarked, "I have a signed contract in my pocket and you can fill in your own terms, provided, of course, that they are within reason. I would like to settle this matter at once." But Speaker was aware of his situation and politely informed Lannin that he intended to listen to the Feds. But he did promise to talk with Lannin again after meeting with Federal League president James A. Gilmore and other league officials at the Knickerbocker Hotel.

At the Knickerbocker, Speaker's suitors placed a signing bonus of fifteen thousand dollars cash on a table before him and offered him a three-year contract for another fifteen thousand per season. Despite what must have been an enormous temptation,

Speaker knew how badly the Red Sox wanted to retain his services. As he departed the meeting he thanked the Federal League officials for their generous offer but indicated his desire to remain in Boston.

He joined Lannin and Taylor for dinner and signed a two-year, thirty-six-thousand-dollar contract, the biggest in baseball history. Afterward, the Texan told the press, "I'm glad to be back in the USA and delighted to be on the Boston payroll again. President Lannin and Vice President Taylor have treated me with great generosity and I would be ungrateful had I not decided to meet them halfway. The Red Sox are a great team, Boston is a great ball town, and it goes without saying that Manager Carrigan will surely have the best that is in me at all times." Speaker had doubled his salary and couldn't conceal a smile.

The Feds were less pleased. They had failed in their attempt to sign the game's acknowledged superstars — Speaker, Cobb, and pitcher Walter Johnson. They made do with the services of lesser luminaries like Hugh Bedient and Cub second baseman Johnnie Evers.

Still, the Fed threat forced Lannin to increase salaries across the board. Before he had seen his team play a single inning, the owner had already laid out more money than he could have ever imagined. Johnson had chosen his patsy well.

But there was a silver lining within the storm clouds the new league had caused. Baseball press coverage during the off-season increased drastically and interest in the 1914 season was high. When tickets for the new season first went on sale in Boston, fans stood six deep at the ticket windows at Fenway Park. Advance sales set a club record.

The big question at Hot Springs that March was whether or not Joe Wood would return to form. In addition to his ankle, arm, and thumb trouble, he'd also had an appendectomy. Carrigan told the righthander to pace himself rather than rush back and further jeopardize his career.

After the disappointment of 1913, Carrigan brought more players to camp than any previous Red Sox manager. He wanted competition and players who followed his combative lead. On the eve of the season Carrigan remarked, "I will make no predictions . . . [But] I am leading a team of game determined fighters, men who will go after every game as though the championship depended on it. We will be heard from all through the season . . . We will start this season at least even with any other club in the American league, the champion Athletics not excepted. I need hardly say any more."

The Red Sox started slowly, losing to Walter Johnson on Opening Day. Then Carrigan's young pitching staff began to come around. Although second-year lefthander Dutch Leonard lost twice in April, both defeats were by scores of 1-0. And rookie righthander Rankin Johnson looked like a find after he beat Walter Johnson in his major league debut, then faced the star twice more and split, losing only a 1-0 game at Fenway Park.

Rookie shortstop Everett Scott, who arrived from St. Paul to anchor the Red Sox infield, was a steady performer and was soon considered among the best defensive shortstops of his era. He ultimately set the consecutive games played record until Lou Gehrig broke it.

Boston fans warmed to Carrigan's team and their new owner. Lannin was equally pleased, and on May 13 he bought out John I. Taylor and took complete control.

Two days later Joe Wood made his season debut at Fenway Park in a ninth-inning relief appearance against the St. Louis Browns. As Murnane wrote, "As the spectators realized that it was Wood they commenced cheering, first in the bleachers back of third base then along through to the grandstand and around the field to the bleacherites in center field, all cheering madly as soon as they saw who the player was . . . It was a reception fit for some great general returning home from a campaign of glorious victories." Wood rewarded the crowd by striking out the first hitter he faced and pitching a scoreless inning in the 9-3 Boston loss.

But by June the Philadelphia Athletics were in command of the American League. The Red Sox lingered in the middle of the pack, a .500 ballclub. The pennant was out of reach.

Lannin and Carrigan reached a consensus, deciding to build for 1915 by preserving the nucleus of the present team. Lannin was both planning for the future and responding to pressure from Ban Johnson to counter any Federal League attempt to break up his team. It was no secret that Federal League agents had approached several Red Sox players, including Lewis.

Unlike in St. Louis, Chicago, and Brooklyn, where the Feds went head-to-head against established major league franchises, in Boston the new league was little more than a costly nuisance. But the Feds soon factored into one of the greatest transactions in team history.

In Baltimore, the fledgling Terrapins of the Federal League were making life difficult for the International League Orioles, building a ballpark right across the street from the long-established club. Even though owner Jack Dunn's Orioles were in first place, attendance plummeted because of the Terrapins. Dunn tried unsuccessfully to move his franchise, then was forced to do what owners have hated to do since the professional game began — sell prized players to keep from going out of business.

Over a three-day period he peddled the guts of his ballclub. Fortunately for Boston fans, the Red Sox were in nearby Washington when Lannin heard about the sale. He immediately traveled to Baltimore, met with Dunn, and acquired nineteen-year-old Oriole lefthander George Herman Ruth, who currently sported a record of 14-6; righthanded pitcher Ernie Shore; and catcher Ben Egan for what was variously reported as between twenty and twenty-five thousand dollars.

Lannin had no idea he had just acquired the man who would become the greatest player in the history of baseball. No one did. Dunn had already offered Ruth to Connie Mack and been turned down cold. Ruth was just another prospect — a good one, but just a prospect.

Carrigan had heard of Ruth and told Lannin that both Ruth and Shore were worth pursuing. But it was difficult to gauge the competition in the International League that year — many of the best players had jumped to the Feds, and the league's level of play had suffered. Ruth was a risk, but Lannin, new to the league and flush with cash, could afford to gamble. Besides, he was afraid he might still lose some regulars to the Feds, and he needed as many players as

Tris Speaker resisted the advances of the fledgling Federal League after team owner Joe Lannin signed him to a two-year contract in 1914 worth eighteen thousand dollars per season. On the eve of the 1916 season Lannin shipped his superstar to Cleveland in one of the most controversial deals in franchise history.

possible under contract. Although Boston felt Ruth had the most potential and was the key player in the deal, Shore was ready to contribute immediately. Egan was a throw-in.

Ruth arrived in his new hometown on the morning of Saturday, July 11. He met his future bride at Landers Coffee Shop, where Helen Woodford served him eggs and bacon. He also started that afternoon's game against the last-place Cleveland Indians.

Ruth held the Naps to five hits in six innings, with one strikeout, but was hit hard in the seventh, when the visitors tied the score on three singles and a sacrifice. Tim Murnane reported, "The giant left-hander, who proved a natural ballplayer and went through his act like a veteran of many wars. He has a natural delivery, fine control, and a curveball that bothers the batsmen, but has room for improvement and will undoubtedly become a fine pitcher under the care of manager Carrigan . . . He looked weak only in comparison with Dutch Leonard, who pitched the last two innings, putting six men out in order, four of them on strikes."

Bill Carrigan *(l)* and Tris Speaker *(r)* at the 1915 World Series in Philadelphia. Carrigan and Speaker allegedly led the two major cliques on the Red Sox, one composed of Catholic players (known in the press as the "KCs," aka Knights of Columbus) and the other composed of Protestant players ("Masons"). Both men put aside their differences as the Red Sox captured their third World Series title against the Phillies in 1915.

As Ruth adjusted to major league life, Carrigan tutored the young southpaw. He was careful and used Ruth sparingly as the summer progressed. In his first month with the Red Sox Ruth pitched only ten major league innings, although Carrigan did use him on the mound in lucrative Sunday exhibition games against Lawrence and Manchester of the New England League (Sunday baseball was still banned in Boston). By contrast, Shore immediately started taking a turn in the regular rotation.

The brash, young prospect immediately began to rub certain veterans on the team the wrong way. Like Ted Williams some twenty-four years later, Ruth was fresh, unaffected, and supremely confident of his own abilities, the happiest nineteen-year-old in baseball and almost oblivious to anything but his own desires.

Tris Speaker and Joe Wood routinely led the hazing of newcomers, and both had words with Ruth. He demanded to take batting practice, unheard-of for a rookie pitcher. That, and his carefree manner, ticked off many veterans. Ernie Shore even complained to Carrigan that when he informed Ruth he was using Shore's toothbrush, Ruth had replied, "That's OK, I'm not that particular."

At the same time, Ruth wasted little time exploring his new home. He soon discovered the red-light district in the nearby Fens (where he'd later rent an apartment) and spent many evenings in the company of women not named Helen Woodford. Hangers-on, gamblers, Royal Rooters, and other fans soon discovered that Ruth was just a big kid and agreeable to just about anything. They took advantage of him, and days were few that Ruth awoke with any money left in his pocket. The team eventually put him on a daily stipend to help preserve his salary and Carrigan, for a time, became Ruth's roommate.

As Ruth learned the ways of the world, Carrigan, ever the astute handler of pitchers, discovered a flaw in Ruth's delivery. When throwing the curve, Ruth stuck the tip of his tongue out of the corner of his mouth and tipped off the pitch. The manager convinced Ruth to keep his mouth shut, at least while pitching.

Boston surged briefly in July, but then fell out of contention just as more optimistic fans began talking about the possibility of a streetcar series, for the Braves were streaking their way to the National League title. Ruth was sent down to Lannin's minor league team, International League Providence, for the balance of the season. He won six consecutive games and smacked his only minor league home run as he helped the Grays win the International League pennant as Dunn's decimated Orioles fell back. Despite spending seven weeks with Boston, Ruth still won twenty-two games in the IL.

Ruth returned to Boston for the final week of the American League season and held New York to six hits in an 11-5 victory, the second and final win of his rookie season. He also stroked his first major league hit, a double off Leonard "King" Cole, and later scored his first run.

Harry Hooper probably described the young Ruth best when he told Lawrence Ritter that "Ruth joined us in the middle of 1914, a 19 year old kid. He was a left-handed pitcher then, and a good one. He had never been anywhere, didn't know anything about manners or how to behave among people — just a big overgrown ape . . . You know I saw it all happen, from beginning to end. But sometimes I can't believe what I saw . . . a man transformed from a human being into something pretty close to a god. If somebody had predicted that back on the Boston Red Sox in 1914, he would have been thrown in a lunatic asylum."

Most fans and reporters were more excited by the exploits of Ernie Shore, who went 10-5 after joining the team. The young pitching staff being assembled by Carrigan was on its way to becoming one of the greatest in baseball history. Foster won fourteen, Leonard nineteen, and Collins twenty. Their 2.35 ERA led the league, paced by Dutch Leonard's all-time best of 1.01, later recalculated as 0.96, as did their twenty-six shutouts. They couldn't catch the A's, but the club won eight of its last ten to finish second, eight and a half games back, at 91-62.

But the Braves overshadowed the Sox by winning fifty-two of sixty-six games from July to early September, rising from last place to first in less than two months and earning the appellation "Miracle." Lannin agreed to lease Fenway Park to the Braves for the last month and a half of the regular season as well as during the World Series, where they stunned the baseball world by sweeping the Athletics. Their own park, the South End Grounds, was hopelessly obsolete. The Braves remained Lannin's tenant until the newly constructed Braves Field was finally completed in the summer of 1915. The unexpected windfall helped offset the salary hikes caused by the Feds and earned Lannin a healthy profit.

As the Braves were toasted in every tavern from Bangor to New London, Lannin and Carrigan were determined to regain both their position in 1915 as the top team in Boston as well as a berth in the World Series. With the best outfield and best young pitching staff in baseball, Carrigan returned to Maine expecting the 1915 season to be the best in franchise history.

Talk that spring centered around the dozen or so candidates for what the press termed "the million dollar pitching staff." Ruth, Collins, Shore, Foster, Leonard, former twenty-game-winner Vean Gregg, and rookie Carl Mays all vied for spots on the staff, as did Joe Wood. But it didn't look promising for the former star. In the off-season he had sought the advice of doctors for his sore shoulder. One quack advised him to cure his arm by throwing as hard as he could until the pain became unbearable. Now Wood could barely lift his arm to brush his teeth, much less pitch.

In an innovative attempt to lure fans to Fenway Park, Lannin undertook one of the first media campaigns in sports history. During spring training he hired George Murray to take photographs and motion pictures. The film was later screened for free across New England to help promote the club.

Newspaper accounts lauded both the technical quality of the film as well as the unprecedented inside look at the workings of a major league ballclub. Unfortunately, this important visual record has since disappeared.

Carrigan nurtured his team in intra-squad games between the "Yannigans" — rookies and substitutes — and the regulars. He gave Ruth particular attention, making the husky pitcher work off extra weight by shagging flyballs.

Off the field, Carrigan tried to breach the divisions on his team by organizing group activities like fishing, golfing, and riding parties. Most players relished the warm weather and country-club atmosphere of the resort town. Lannin's Providence club shared the facilities and provided the Sox with springtime competition.

On Opening Day the Sox were greeted in Boston by a crowd of 10,937. Ernie Shore beat Bob Shawkey and the Philadelphia Athletics 7-6.

Many early-season games were canceled because of poor weather, causing a number of doubleheaders to be scheduled later in the season. This would prove to be an advantage to the Sox, for they already boasted six legitimate starting pitchers and added another on May 29 — a future Hall of Famer at that

geo Foster geo Dauss "Dutch" Leonard Chester Thoma
Cooper "Babe" Ruth Pat Haley "Germany" Schaeffe
Scott HAGERMAN Carl Mays Jean Gregg
FOREST CADY Ernie Shore
Brownie

A

Jim McDonough Joe Lannin CARRIGAN Joe Burns
Flanagan Bill Sweeney

The 1915 Red Sox pose on a steamroller at spring training at Hot Springs, Arkansas. They were the second of the four dissimilar world championship teams the franchise developed in the decade.

— twenty-one-year-old Herb Pennock, acquired on waivers from the Athletics.

Over the first two months of the season Boston trailed the streaking White Sox and Tigers, but soon Boston began to close the gap. And with the onset of warm weather, Joe Wood, still only twenty-five, tried to pitch again.

On June 1 at the Polo Grounds against the Yankees, the same site of his World Series triumph in 1912, he began one of the most heroic comebacks in baseball history. To the first three New York batters, he surrendered a home run, a double, and a single. But despite excruciating pain, Wood eventually settled down.

He didn't have a fastball or much of anything else anymore. All he had was heart and courage and guts. He sometimes paused so long between pitches waiting for the pain to diminish that the crowd would begin an impromptu countdown. Yet on that day he somehow hung on for thirteen remarkable innings and emerged with a 4-3 win. For the rest of the season, throwing when he could stand the pain, he proved a valuable addition to the staff.

Wood wasn't the only player battling injuries. Speaker was beaned, Ty Cobb spiked Everett Scott, and Heinie Wagner had a sore arm. Nevertheless, by late June Boston drew even with Detroit and was within eight and a half games of the first-place White

Sox. To bolster their pennant chances, Lannin sent Connie Mack eight thousand dollars for Philadelphia shortstop Jack Barry.

Barry, who along with Eddie Collins, Frank Baker, and Stuffy McInnis made up Mack's famed "One hundred thousand dollar infield," was a local favorite who had starred in both baseball and basketball at Holy Cross. He was also one of the smartest and most versatile players in the game. Carrigan asked him to play second base, replacing Heinie Wagner. The team responded by going on a winning streak in July that included a sweep of three straight double-headers — six wins in three days.

On July 18 streaking Boston went into Chicago for a four-game series with first place at stake. Joe Wood asked Carrigan for the ball in the first game of the series against future Hall of Fame pitcher Red Faber.

Wood was no less than dazzling. Relying on guile and a changeup rather than a fastball and fear, no Chicago runner made it past first base after the first inning. Wood even stroked two hits and scored a run in Boston's biggest victory of the season to that point. The win was an inspiration to Wood's teammates, who saw him appear to reclaim a career that many had feared was lost. Boston went on to win three of four games at Comiskey Park and take command in the pennant race.

On July 21 Babe Ruth treated St. Louis fans to a glimpse of the future. In four at bats the twenty-year-old phenom socked a single, two doubles, and a remarkable home run that cleared the bleachers at Sportsman's Park and landed on Grand Avenue. With relief help from Wood, he also pitched the team to a 4-2 win. Boston won thirteen of twenty on the road trip and returned to Boston hailed as conquering heroes.

In their first home game in nearly a month Joe Wood won his tenth game of the season, scattering four hits in a 3-1 victory over the White Sox. Not only did the fans give Wood a standing ovation, but they also roared when the public address announcer, megaphone in hand, announced that the defending world champion Braves, in the middle of the pennant race again, had captured a ninth-inning win over the Dodgers in Brooklyn. Fans left the park talking of a

Harry Hooper not only saved the 1912 World Series with his sixth-inning game-saving catch in game eight but also gained fame as the first player to hit two homers in a World Series while leading Boston to victory over the Phillies in 1915. In twenty-four World Series games for the Red Sox Hooper batted .293 while helping lead the team to four world titles.

streetcar World Series. Boston was the undisputed capital of the baseball world.

But Wood's arm was hanging by a thread. It hurt so badly he had to lift his right arm with his left hand to change his shirt. He was soon shut down and wouldn't pitch again until September.

Boston's deep and talented staff made up for his loss. By the end of August the White Sox had slipped back and the Tigers provided Boston's only competition. On August 24 Ernie Shore faced Detroit in another critical contest.

Ty Cobb's Tigers did everything in their power to distract Shore, repeatedly asking the umpire to inspect the baseball. Cobb himself nearly incited a riot when he erupted in fury after being tagged out at home. Later, after being thrown out on the bases, he rushed the Red Sox dugout and tried to provoke a fight. Carrigan stood his ground and ordered Cobb to leave as players and umpires watched in silence. Boston faced down the greatest competitor in baseball history in one of the most important games of Cobb's career and beat him, 3-1.

The following day Cobb provided more of the same, leading the hostile crowd in anti-Boston chants. He even stationed a young boy directly behind home plate and instructed the lad to wave a straw boater in an effort to distract Red Sox pitchers. Nevertheless, Ruth and Leonard beat Detroit 2-1 in thirteen innings.

There was no stopping Boston, which won twenty-four of twenty-nine to increase their lead over Detroit. Pitching and defense were the key, for Detroit scored nearly one hundred more runs than the Red Sox.

Ruth's emergence as a star was key to the team's success, and no one was more responsible for his success than Carrigan. Carrigan served Ruth as a combination father confessor, drill sergeant, psychologist, and Dutch uncle. He tested his progress by inserting the young star into pressure situations.

With two outs in the ninth inning and the bases loaded on September 8 in an important game against the Athletics at Fenway Park, Carrigan pinch-hit Ruth for himself. Facing righthander Tom Sheehan, the overanxious slugger-to-be swung at three bad pitches in a foolish attempt to win the 1-0 game with a home run. Reporter Edward F. Martin commented that "Ruth's attempt to deliver was pathetic. Every ball he swung at was poor and had he not attempted to hit any of the three balls that were strikes he would have walked, tying the score."

Two days later Carrigan called upon the lefthander to pitch against the Athletics. He viewed Ruth's failure as a learning experience. This time, Ruth retained his composure and held the defending champions to five hits in a 7-2 victory. He was growing up, getting better, and on his way to eighteen wins for the season.

Boston fans were apoplectic over the Red Sox. On September 20, some 37,528 fans crammed each and every one of Fenway's many nooks and crannies and saw Ernie Shore scatter six hits in twelve innings while shutting out the Tigers. But Tiger pitcher Harry Coveleskie was just as stingy.

Detroit rallied in the final inning to load the bases, but Shore wriggled free when Tiger first baseman Marty Kavanagh made the third out by passing teammate Sam Crawford on the basepaths.

Boston made the most of their good fortune in the bottom of the inning. With Lewis in scoring position, Carrigan pinch-hit for Shore, singled, and plated the winning run. Newspaper accounts called it "the greatest game of ball ever played in this city."

The win gave Boston a three-and-a-half-game lead over the Tigers with only ten days left in the season. On the next-to-the-last day of the season, Joe Wood pitched three innings to record his fifteenth win, one of five Boston pitchers to reach that figure. The victory would be his last in the major leagues and his last appearance in a Boston uniform.

The Red Sox finished 101-50, two and a half games ahead of the Tigers. And just as the Red Sox had allowed the Braves to use Fenway in 1914, the Braves now returned the favor for the World Series against the National League champion Philadelphia Phillies. New Braves Field was not only the largest in the major leagues in terms of crowd capacity, but its mammoth field dimensions favored a Red Sox team built on pitching, defense, and speed.

It also helped negate the power of Phillie slugger Gavvy Cravath, whose twenty-four home runs in Philadelphia's cozy Baker Bowl set a modern standard. In contrast, the Red Sox hit fourteen home runs for the entire season.

The series featured the same two cities as the 1914 classic, which had matched the Braves and the A's. The similarities between the two clubs didn't stop there. Each club was managed by a New England–born catcher known for his handling of pitchers, with Pat Moran of Fitchburg, Massachusetts, managing opposite Carrigan. Each team was also known for its superior pitching. Grover Cleveland Alexander led the Phillies with a record of 31-10 and a 1.22 ERA, while Boston's big three of Leonard, Shore, and Foster crafted a combined won-lost record of 52-23 with a 2.03 ERA.

On the eve of the opener, the smart money was on Alexander to win at least one game, but for the Red Sox to capture their third World Series in as many tries. But Carrigan, remembering how the Braves

1915 world champion Red Sox.

Back row (l–r): Del Gainor, Dutch Leonard, Duffy Lewis, Forest Cady, Vean Gregg, Bill Carrigan, Ernie Shore, Ray Collins, Tris Speaker, Babe Ruth. *Middle row (l–r):* Larry Gardner, George Foster, Joe Wood, Chet Thomas, Dick Hoblitzell, Harry Hooper, Heinie Wagner. *Front row (l–r):* Jack Barry, Hal Janvrin, Carl Mays, Olaf Henriksen, Jerry "Red" McCarthy, Everett Scott, Herb Pennock.

had thrashed the A's the year before, was keenly aware of the danger inherent in being the favorite. He was particularly worried that his club might have to face Alexander three times. He told his pitchers that they couldn't give up more than one run and still hope to beat the future Hall of Famer.

After rain caused a delay of several days, Phillies manager Pat Moran chose Alexander to start the opener at Philadelphia's Baker Bowl on October 8. Shore started for Boston.

Interest in the series was high. As fans converged on the Baker Bowl on the eve of the first game, scalpers sold three-dollar tickets for forty bucks.

On the morning of October 8, the grounds crew arrived early. To dry the field they spread gasoline over the turf and set it afire. The rank smell of smoke still hung in the air as the capacity crowd pushed their way in, filling first the main stand, then temporary stands in left and center fields.

The temporary bleachers played a critical role in the Series. Under normal circumstances it was already less than 300 feet to the fence in right field (hence Cravath's record number of home runs), while dimensions in center and left were more spacious, at 408 and 335 feet respectively. But the addition of temporary seats in both areas cut the dimensions dramatically. Then, in what would prove to be a critical decision, both teams agreed to generous ground rules that turned any ball that *bounced* into the stands into a home run.

In game one, the Phillies scored first. In the third inning Dode Paskert lofted a Texas Leaguer toward Hooper which plopped in the mud for a hit. He moved to second when Cravath bunted as Moran played for a single run, then to third on an infield out. He finally scored when Possum Whitted barely beat out a slow roller to Jack Barry.

Boston didn't break through on Alexander until the eighth, when Speaker walked, moved up on an error, and scored on a two-strike single by Duffy Lewis. But further damage was prevented by a sensational running catch made by Paskert on a drive by Larry Gardner.

The game was tied, but not for long. In the Phillies' half of the eighth, with one out, Shore walked Milt Stock. Rookie and future Hall of Famer Dave "Beauty" Bancroft then bounced a groundball up the middle. Barry made a backhand grab, but Scott missed the pivot at second and everyone was safe. Paskert then walked to load the bases.

Gavvy Cravath stepped in as the Philadelphia crowd cheered for him to sock a home run. He lined the ball up the middle, and Stock scored as Scott threw to first for the out. Shore then mishandled Luderus's infield hit and watched Bancroft cross home with the Phillies' third run.

That was the game. Boston threatened with one out in the ninth, but Ruth, pinch-hitting in his first Series appearance, lined out and Hooper flied out to end the game. A headline in the *Boston Globe* summed it up succinctly, if not efficiently: "Luck-Freaks and a Bit of Brain Fog Beat Red Sox 3-1."

History was made in game two. Woodrow Wilson became the first president to attend the Series, arriving in the company of his baseball-loving fiancée, Edith Galt, and the 350 Rooters in attendance led the crowd in singing "The Star-Spangled Banner." Ruth begged Carrigan for the start, but the manager told him he was being saved to pitch in Boston. Carrigan selected Rube Foster to face fellow righthander Erskine Mayer.

Boston struck first. Hooper worked a leadoff walk then streaked to third on Speaker's single. The two vets then worked a double steal and Hooper scored.

Foster held Philadelphia scoreless into the fifth, when Cravath led off the inning with a double to left and scored on Luderus's double to right-center. But that was all. For the remainder of the game Foster gave up only one more hit.

He was just as effective with the bat, making three hits, all struck with two outs, including a double and two singles. His single to center in the top of the ninth scored Larry Gardner with what proved to be the game-winning run. Tris Speaker supported the stocky righthander with two superb running catches, including a dazzling snare to end the game.

Game three at Braves Field featured a duel between Dutch Leonard and Grover Cleveland Alexander, who was pitching on just two days' rest. Manager Bill Carrigan chose to start behind the plate himself, not trusting anyone else to work with the pitcher he had transformed from a wild phenom into one of the best in baseball.

Philadelphia scratched out their only run in the third when Dave Bancroft singled home Ed Burns. He was the last Phillie hitter to get a hit, as Leonard retired the next twenty batters. Included in those outs was a catch by Duffy Lewis of a 400-foot drive by Cravath. In the Baker Bowl, it was a home run. In Braves Field, it was just a loud out.

The Red Sox tied the game in the fourth inning on Tris Speaker's triple and Hoblitzell's sacrifice fly. The game then remained deadlocked as Leonard and Alexander battled to the bottom of the ninth.

After Harry Hooper led off with a single, Scott sacrificed, and Alexander intentionally walked Speaker.

Duffy Lewis stepped in brimming with confidence. He had already touched Alexander for four hits in the Series. His fifth, a drive to center, won the game. As he recalled years later, "The crowd came out of the stands, over the fences and they carried me off. They were so excited that they almost broke my back." The win gave Boston a 2-1 edge in the Series.

Lewis was also the difference in game four. He knocked in the game-winner with a double as Shore held the Phillies to a single run.

Game five was played the following afternoon in Philadelphia. But Rube Foster, who'd been nearly unhittable in game two, wasn't as sharp the second time around. In the first, the Phillies loaded the bases for Cravath, but Moran, in one of the most inexplicable moves in Series history, tried to get cute and ordered the slugger to try a swinging bunt. The result was a rally-killing, home-to-first double play. Although Luderus later drove in Bancroft and Paskert with a double, the Phillies missed a chance to put the game away.

Thus far, the close confines of the Baker Bowl had had little effect on play. But in the third inning, with the Phillies leading 2-1, Harry Hooper lifted a routine fly to center field. It landed in the temporary seats for a home run.

But Luderus returned Hooper's favor with a home run of his own, and the Phillies scored again to go ahead 4-2.

Relief pitcher Eppa Rixey had shut Boston down since coming on in relief. But in the eighth, Del Gainor, who had replaced Hoblitzell at first, beat out a groundball to third. The Phillies anticipated a steal and Moran called for a pitchout.

Rixey's toss floated too close to the plate and Lewis jumped at it, driving the pitch into the bleachers in left-center. The drive tied the score.

With one out, Hooper stepped in. Once again he drove a liner to center field. This time the ball skipped into the stands for a home run, Hooper's second of the day and Boston's third, fully 21 percent of their regular-season total.

The run proved to be the difference. Boston won 5-4 and captured the Series in five games.

Afterward, Carrigan stated what had become obvious. "We have heard a lot about those short field fences," he said, "and how things were going to be to the disadvantage of the Red Sox . . . Today we showed that we had some men who could knock the ball over those short fences as often as anyone else did, and a little oftener."

But Boston pitchers had held the Phillies to a .182 batting average. While the Sox offense was little better, the clutch hitting of Lewis and Hooper combined with the flawless fielding of Jack Barry tipped the scales. Boston won the world championship despite not using either Babe Ruth or Joe Wood in the Series.

The champions returned to Boston the following morning to little fanfare, as most fans had expected their arrival later that afternoon. The players hardly even bothered to celebrate the win themselves, for Carrigan made it clear that the championship was simply what he had expected. Besides, he'd decided to quit. He owned a bank in Maine and was anxious to focus on his fiduciary responsibilities.

Lannin made it his off-season mission to make the manager change his mind. At length, and with a lu-

Lanky righthander Ernie Shore arrived in Boston as part of the same transaction that sent Babe Ruth to Boston from the minor-league Baltimore Orioles. In four seasons with Boston he won fifty-eight games with a superb 2.10 ERA. He also won one game in the 1915 World Series and two in the 1916 Series with a combined 1.82 ERA in both. His most noteworthy effort was a perfect game pitched in relief of Babe Ruth on June 23, 1917, when he picked off the one baserunner allowed by Ruth while retiring the next twenty-six batters.

crative new contract, he convinced him to return for another season. Little did the thirty-three-year-old banker know what challenges lay ahead.

As the team gathered for spring training in 1916, the club looked even stronger. The young pitching staff had been tested. Carrigan planned few changes.

But he did have a few concerns. The Federal League had collapsed, and now Lannin and other owners were playing hardball in contract talks with their stars, most of whom had seen their salaries rise dramatically over the past two seasons.

Both Tris Speaker and Joe Wood held out. With no competition from the Feds, Lannin offered Speaker a new contract worth only half of the eighteen thousand dollars he had earned in 1915. Since Speaker's batting average had fallen annually since 1912, from .383 to .365, .338, and .322, he argued that the cut was justified.

Wood received a similar offer. The sore-armed pitcher responded that he wouldn't play ball "for such a measly salary." Lannin callously replied that he was only paying for "Wood's measly victories in 1914 and 1915." While Speaker worked out with the club hoping to come to an agreement, Wood stayed home in Pennsylvania for the entire year. It was just as well. He couldn't pitch anyway.

Conflicting reports in the press indicated Speaker was on the verge of signing, while others claimed he'd be traded. On the eve of Opening Day, Red Sox fans awoke to banner headlines announcing the latter was true.

Tris Speaker was sold to the Cleveland Indians for fifty thousand dollars and two players, pitching prospect Sad Sam Jones and infielder Fred Thomas. The greatest Red Sox player of them all was gone.

The deal was the most lucrative in baseball history at the time and stunned observers, for despite his holdout, no one truly expected Speaker to leave Boston, at least not for cash. Lannin was doing well and hardly needed the money. But as usual in the American League, when something smelled, Ban Johnson was often in the vicinity.

His crony Jim Dunn had recently purchased the Indians from Charles Somers when Johnson's angel began to run out of money. Johnson had even loaned Dunn part of the purchase price and retained a portion of the club for himself.

When Lannin balked at paying Speaker, Johnson put together the deal before any other club knew Speaker was available, much to the dismay of teams like the Yankees, who lusted after Speaker themselves. The value of Johnson's investment had just gone up.

The entire affair enraged Boston fans, and there is some evidence Lannin was coerced by Johnson into making the trade, for soon relations between the two cooled dramatically. It was a huge loss for the club, at least as significant as the losses of players like Ruth, Clemens, and Vaughn in later years. Carrigan's dynasty appeared to be in jeopardy.

But Boston still had pitching, and in the Dead Ball Era that was enough. While the Sox had a hard time scoring, the opposition had it even worse against Boston's pitching staff. Ruth and Carl Mays emerged as stars, while Leonard, Shore, and Foster continued their usual good work. Veteran outfielder Tilly Walker, acquired from the Browns, took Speaker's place. While he wasn't quite the Texan's peer, he was still a valuable player who provided just enough punch to help mask his loss.

Boston fans watched in horror as Speaker's previously inept Indians pulled into first place in early May. Boston stumbled along in fourth place, behind both the Senators and the Yankees.

But Carrigan didn't let his team give up. Once the club adjusted to Speaker's absence, they began to respond to Carrigan, a master motivator. At team meetings he allowed all players, stars and subs alike, to voice their views, an unheard-of proposition with Speaker and Wood on board. The cliques that had once characterized the club became a thing of the past.

To motivate his pitchers he refused to name his starters for crucial games in advance. Then, on the day of the game, he'd stand before the entire team and ask, "Who wants the ball?"

His pitchers responded with a number of remarkable performances, highlighted by two no-hitters at Fenway Park. The first, by righthander Rube Foster on June 21, was a 2-0 victory over the Yankees that took only an hour and a half. Similarly, lefty Dutch Leonard no-hit the St. Louis Browns in an hour and thirty-five minutes on August 30. These two games, coupled with Babe Ruth's domination of the great Walter Johnson, whom he beat four times over the course of the year, characterized the season.

No team in the league could match Boston's pitching. As summer turned to fall the Indians and Yankees fell back and Boston pulled into first place. The club then escaped a late charge by both the rapidly improving White Sox and the Tigers to win the pennant by two games. The Brooklyn Dodgers, another team built on pitching and defense, won the National League crown.

Lannin again abandoned Fenway for Braves Field in the World Series. The players were more than happy with the arrangement. Braves Field was good for an extra ten thousand fans per game.

Carrigan chose Ernie Shore to open the series against future Hall of Famer Rube Marquard. But Marquard, who had beaten the Red Sox twice in the 1912 World Series for the Giants, was victimized by terrible defense and left the game after giving up five runs. Shore, with relief help from Carl Mays, hung on to earn the win in the 6-5 victory.

Ruth finally got his chance to pitch in the Series in game two. His twenty-three wins had led the club, and his 1.75 ERA was the best in the league.

In the first inning, Brooklyn outfielder Hy Myers hit a fly to center field. The ball dropped in front of Tilly Walker, then bounced over his head. Myers scored on an inside-the-park home run as Walker tracked the ball down in the nether reaches of the outfield. Brooklyn led 1-0.

But Ruth helped even the score in the third. After Everett Scott tripled, the pitcher plated him with a groundball to tie the game.

Then Ruth and burly Dodger left-hander Sherry Smith settled down. Although both clubs threatened, neither pitcher broke and neither team could manage to score.

The stalemate reached the fourteenth inning. In the dwindling light, Boston finally got a break.

Smith committed the pitcher's sin by walking Hoblitzell to start the inning. Carrigan responded by ordering Duffy Lewis to sacrifice him to second. With Hoblitzell now in scoring position, Carrigan sent in speedy Mike McNally to pinch-run and had Del Gainor, a righthanded batter, pinch-hit for lefty Larry Gardner.

Gainor pulled Smith's third pitch on a line over the head of third baseman Mike Mowry. Brooklyn's Hall of Fame left fielder Zack Wheat started for the ball then slowed as he lost it in the backdrop of the stands and dwindling light. McNally never stopped running and crossed the plate with the winning run in the 2-1 contest. Braves Field exploded as the Red

Sox sprinted from the dugout to engulf McNally. Ruth put Carrigan in a bear hug and bellowed, "I told you I could take care of those National League sons of bitches!"

The Series moved to Brooklyn the next afternoon. Brooklyn owner Charlie Ebbets tried to cash in on the Series, charging an unheard-of five dollars per ticket, and alienated fans, a situation not helped by

Vermont native Larry Gardner manned third base for the Red Sox for ten seasons and was a key member of three world champion teams. The University of Vermont product was especially valuable during the 1916 season when, with the departure of Tris Speaker, he was the lone regular to bat .300 or better for the pitching-rich champions.

game-time temperatures just above the freezing point. Only 21,087 greeted the two teams in Ebbets Field.

Red Sox starter Carl Mays was less than effective in the cold, as Brooklyn peppered him with seven hits and three walks over five innings, good for four runs. Foster shut down the Dodgers the rest of the game, but the Red Sox could only scratch out three runs off Jack Coombs. Jeff Pfeffer retired the last eight men in order to preserve the win.

The crowd was more enthusiastic for game four, as Brooklyn opened the game against Dutch Leonard with two hits and a walk, good enough for two runs.

But their good cheer didn't last long as Boston belted Marquard for the second game in a row and Leonard settled down. The Sox rolled to a 6-2 win, only one victory shy of their second consecutive world championship.

Game five was played in Boston on Columbus Day, October 12, and for the fourth game in a row, Brooklyn scored first, touching Shore for a run in the second on catcher Hick Cady's passed ball. But just as they had done in game four, the Red Sox came right back when Lewis tripled and scored on Gardner's sacrifice fly to tie the score.

One inning later Boston went ahead for good, sandwiching two hits and a walk around some shoddy Dodger defense to score twice. Hooper added an insurance run in the fifth when he scored on Hal Janvrin's double, and Boston now led 4-1.

Shore was in total command. He tossed a three-hitter as Boston won 4-1 to again capture the Series in five games. The Red Sox were world champions for the second consecutive year, achieving something that only the Cubs and Athletics had done before them.

This time, there was a celebration, tempered only by the knowledge that Bill Carrigan was finally making good on his intention to retire. His wife was pregnant and insisted that baseball take a back seat to family life, championship or no championship.

Only thirty-three, Carrigan left the game and the ballclub that so respected him to enjoy the solitude of the Maine woods. No subsequent Red Sox manager has approached his level of success, and his delicate handling of the 1916 team stands as his singular achievement. Things just wouldn't be the same without the quiet, fiery leader. The *Boston Post* provided Carrigan's elegy:

> *Now Carrigan they say is done*
> *With baseball for all time*
> *But many honors he has won*
> *Shrewd Bill, who's not a lime*
> *So if he never does come back*
> *This statement makes it plain*
> *The game will lose a crackerjack*
> *Who hangs his hat in Maine.*

SOX WIN

THE LAST CHAMPIONS

1917 | 1918

Boston Evening Globe

(Trade-Mark Registered)

Evening Edition — 1c

VOL. XCIV—NO. 73   BOSTON, WEDNESDAY EVENING, SEPTEMBER 11, 1918—FOURTEEN PAGES   COPYRIGHT, 1918 BY THE GLOBE NEWSPAPER CO.   CLOSING MARKET PRICES

EVENING EDITION—7:30 LATEST

SOX WIN CHAMPIONSHIP

U. S. TROOPSHIP TORPEDOED, BUT ALL ON BOARD SAVED

LONDON, Tuesday, Sept 10—A troopship with 2800 American soldiers on board has been torpedoed. All hands were saved. The troopship was beached.

Transfer Made Quickly

GUIDE FOR MEN REGISTERING FOR THE DRAFT TOMORROW

ICE REPORTED IN MANY PLACES

7 A.M. to 9 P.M. the Time

REGISTRATION CARD

FRENCH CAPTURE TRAVECY VILLAGE

PARIS, Sept 11 (Havas)—

Full Score of the Game:

BOSTON	AB	R	BH	TB	PO	A	E
Hooper rf	4	0	0	0	3	0	0
Shean 2b	3	0	1	1	3	2	0
Strunk cf	3	0	0	0	2	0	0
Whiteman lf	3	1	1	1	1	0	0
Ruth lf	0	0	0	0	0	0	0
McInnis 1b	4	0	1	1	16	0	0
Scott ss	3	0	0	0	0	2	0
Thomas 3b	3	0	0	0	2	3	0
Schang c	3	1	1	1	0	1	0
Mays p	3	0	0	0	0	5	0
Totals	27	2	4	5	27	15	0

CHICAGO	AB	R	BH	TB	PO	A	E
Flack rf	3	1	1	1	1	0	0
Hollocher ss	3	0	0	0	1	5	0
Mann lf	4	0	2	2	1	0	0
Paskert cf	2	0	0	0	4	0	0
Merkle 1b	4	0	1	1	11	0	0
Pick 2b	4	0	1	1	2	3	0
Deal 3b	3	0	0	0	0	2	0
Zeider	1	0	0	0	0	0	0
Barber	1	0	0	0	0	0	0
Killifer c	2	0	0	0	3	0	0
Tyler p	2	0	0	0	0	1	0
Hendrix p	0	0	0	0	0	0	0
O'Farrell	1	0	0	0	0	0	0
McCabe	1	0	0	0	0	0	0
Totals	00	1	6	6	24	12	2

COLLECTOR MALLEY TO AID IN REGISTRATION

SCH GOV POWERS CREW LANDED

GERMANS USE NEW GAS PROJECTILE ABOUT THE SIZE OF ORANGES

SHORTAGE OF 1,000,000 BARRELS OF GASOLINE INDICATED

WASHINGTON, Sept 11—

PETROGRAD AFIRE, MANY PEOPLE SLAIN

WASHINGTON, Sept 11—

LATE CZAR NICHOLAS' MINISTERS EXECUTED

LONDON, Sept 11—

BROCKTON FAIR

The Show Wonderful

Oct. 1-2-3-4

Licensed Liquor Stores

Will please comply with the request of Governor McCall and Mayor Peters and be closed for the sale of liquors during the hours of registration tomorrow.

Hours of Closure from 7 A.M. to 9 P.M.

MATHEW CUMMINGS, President, Fourth-Class Dealers' Association

JAMES J. DOHERTY, President, Boston Liquor Dealers' Association

UNIFORMS ARMY AND NAVY Officers and Enlisted Men — STUDENT CAMPS EQUIPMENT — HARDING UNIFORM CO. 22 School St.

BELL-ANS FOR INDIGESTION

Winter Tops

NORRIS 161 TREMONT STREET

The 1918 Red Sox world championship garnered headlines that otherwise would have been devoted to news from the battlefields of Europe.

1918.

Any real baseball fan knows the significance of that date. That was the last year the Boston Red Sox won the World Series and right to hoist a pennant naming them world champions. They've been trying to do it again ever since.

For most Red Sox fans, mention of that season evokes emotions at once both profound and enigmatic. One recalls not the joy of victory but the heartache and despair of all the defeats and near-misses that have followed. Perhaps that is why the events of the 1918 season are among the most overlooked and ignored in the history of the franchise.

The 1918 season provided a pivotal moment in team history. Under the watch of new owner Harry Frazee, 1918 was the last time that the Red Sox organization did everything right. Not even a world war could stop them.

The story of the last champions begins like most events of that era, with the assassination of Austrian Archduke Ferdinand by a Serb in 1914, the event that sparked the Great War. The conflagration overspread the world and by the spring of 1917 had pulled the United States into the conflict. Over the next year, few aspects of American society proved immune to the effects of war. Life in America changed forever. So, too, did the game of baseball.

Less than a month after winning his second World Series, Joe Lannin decided to sell the Red Sox. In his three years as owner, he had reportedly made four hundred thousand dollars while most other owners had been strapped by their battle with the Federal League. Now, with a real war on the horizon, no one was quite sure what would happen next.

But in the Byzantine world of the American League, little happened that was unaffected by its internal politics. As usual, Ban Johnson played a central role.

Apart from his worry over the war, Lannin had tired of Johnson's constant interference. His intrusion during the sale of Tris Speaker had been the last straw. Lannin had since come to believe that Johnson had ordered umpires to mistreat his ballclub. When he complained, Johnson's many friends in the press mocked him.

Not even a world championship offset Lannin's growing dismay with the inner workings of Major League Baseball. He realized that the rules for doing business were different if your name was Mack or Comiskey. Besides, Lannin had heart trouble and admitted to the press "I'm too much of a fan." It was a good time for him to sell.

Johnson had always bullied his way into every franchise sale by either initiating the transaction or engineering it outright. But Lannin wanted to leave on his own terms and for the best price.

Although a handful of local investors tried to put together a deal, including one that involved Honey Fitz's son-in-law, Joseph Kennedy, Lannin ignored their proposals. He had already found a buyer, Harry Harrison Frazee.

Frazee was a man symbolic of the age, a pure product of America who started with nothing and built an empire. His improbable story reads like a plot line from the stage, the very place where he found his true calling and earned his fortune.

Yet he is remembered for only one act. Harry Frazee sold Babe Ruth, ultimately — and unfairly — finding tragic infamy and being blamed for the subsequent demise of the Boston Red Sox franchise. His grandson, Harry Frazee III, recalls learning when he was only four or five years old that his grandfather had sold Ruth. Now retired in Washington State after a career in advertising and journalism, Frazee follows baseball closely and considers himself a fan of "The Red Sox, Yankees, and, of course, the Mariners." He is rarely asked about his grandfather and is resigned to the fact that few people really care to know the truth about him. For if there is any kind of curse that haunts the Boston Red Sox, it's not one that has anything to do with the sale of Ruth. Rather, it is the way history has been misused to provide excuses for the real failures that have haunted the team.

Frazee was born in Peoria, Illinois, in 1880. In high school, he played third base on the school team and was a teammate of Harry Bay, who later played outfield for Cleveland. "Big Harry," as he is still referred to in the family, stomped out of the house following an altercation with his parents at age sixteen. Determined to seek his fortune, he found a job as assistant business manager at the Peoria Theater, which meant he took tickets, posted bills, and swept the floor.

The next year he worked as the advance agent for a traveling show and met former Boston Nationals manager Frank Selee. When the minor league Western Association disbanded on July 4, 1899, Frazee booked the Peoria club on a successful barnstorming tour.

Frazee returned to the theater that fall, but retained an intense interest in baseball, as enamored of the players and the notoriety they brought him as of the money the game could produce. Two years later, while managing a show entitled *Mahoney's Wedding*, he turned the light musical farce into a minor hit and made fourteen thousand dollars.

That return attracted investors and Harry Bay backed his next venture. In four months, Frazee earned Bay a 1,000 percent profit. Frazee was off.

Between 1904 and 1907 he produced a string of successful light comedies in the Midwest, turning other people's money into profit and creating a fortune of his own. He built the Cort Theater in Chicago, then set his sights on New York.

Frazee had an uncanny sense of what the public liked. In New York he was able to duplicate and expand on his earlier successes. His first New York hit was the musical *Madame Sherry*, which ran for 231 performances in 1910 and netted a quarter of a million dollars. A string of similar successes followed, including *Ready Money* in 1912, *A Pair of Sixes* in 1914 (which the *New York Times* called "one of the most successful farces of the decade"), *A Full House* in 1915, and *Nothing But the Truth* in 1916.

Frazee was a success, and his social circle included the most popular actors of the era, as well as those who sought their company, scions of finance and politics in the world's greatest city. His social register eventually included everyone from George M. Cohan and New York Mayor Jimmy Walker to Charles Lindbergh.

His theatrical genius was twofold. He focused on easy-to-produce and popular farces and light comedies. As soon as he sensed success, he put touring companies of the same production on the road, multiplying his New York success before the plays became stale, offering audiences in the hinterlands the opportunity to see the shows that were still hits in New York. Everything he touched turned to money.

He branched out, buying more theaters and earning money on both ends of the production. Yet he was still a stranger to the public, a little-known genius behind the scenes.

Sports appealed to his baser nature. Frazee knew the power of publicity and that owning a baseball team made a man a big shot. And a ballpark full of fans appeared at least as lucrative as the theater.

In 1909 he approached John I. Taylor about buying the Red Sox. Taylor said no. In 1911 he made a bid to buy the Braves and made subsequent overtures for the Cubs and the Giants.

A 1913 profile of Frazee in the *New York Times* claimed "Frazee's original idea concerning his future comprised no less a goal than the ownership of a baseball club." Although his initial efforts to buy a team failed, he still got into the sports business. He made what the *Times* called "a small fortune," sponsoring a tour by boxer Jim Jeffries; hired boxer James Corbett to appear in some of his productions; and made Corbett his partner, managing the successful fighter "Kid Chocolate." Frazee also promoted champion wrestler Frank Gotch. In 1915 he made a splash, if not a profit, when, after being rebuffed in the United States trying to match the white boxer Jess Willard with black champion Jack Johnson, Frazee put up the money behind their famous bout in Havana, Cuba.

By 1916 his empire had expanded to include real estate management and a stock brokerage business. He was already a millionaire, successful, connected, gregarious and flamboyant, a hard-drinking impresario of the first order. Frazee was a man who never let his marriage get in the way of his relationships with young actresses, one of whom he kept in a house on Long Island for a decade before his wife found out and divorced him. Lyricist Irving Caesar once described Frazee as a man who "made more sense drunk than most men do sober." Dark and stocky, dubbed "Handsome Harry" by the press, Frazee dressed sharply, talked fast, and didn't suffer fools. A lifetime of success gave him the confidence to speak his mind.

Although he loved baseball, he viewed it as just another production. "Baseball is essentially a show business," he told one interviewer. "If you have any kind of a production, be it a music show, or a wrestling bout, or a baseball game that people want to see enough to pay money for the privilege, then you are in show business and don't let anyone tell you any different."

To Frazee, buying the Red Sox was akin to investing in a show that had already opened to good reviews and, apart from the increasing threat of the war, showed no signs of ending its run. It had "can't miss" written all over it.

Nothing dampened Frazee's enthusiasm. To his mind, what he called "the amusement business, of which baseball is a part," seemed nearly immune to most economic pressures. War meant work, plenty of money to spend, and plenty of reasons to escape the front page. The future didn't scare him. For twenty years all he'd done was make money.

He knew Lannin, whom he later claimed had given him a "moral option to buy the team" several years before. Late in October of 1916, Frazee and partner Hugh Ward, who managed the Australian operations of a British theater company, offered $675,000 for the club, far more than anyone else.

The offer was too good for Lannin to refuse but, in retrospect, less than overwhelming. Although Frazee and Ward were using their profits from the stage to buy the team, they were unwilling to risk their entire fortune. They needed to maintain a healthy reserve to finance future theatrical productions. Frazee never allowed his baseball and stage interests to mix. They were kept separate and had to be self-supporting.

Rather than buy the team outright, Frazee offered half the sale amount in cash. He paid the balance with notes he expected to pay off with profits he would earn from the team.

The deal included Fenway Park, which the Taylor family and the Fenway Realty Company had finally divested themselves of. In fact, the ballpark may have been the key to the deal. Land in the Fens was becoming pricey. There was immediate speculation that Frazee would raze the park, move to Braves Field, sell the property, and reap a gigantic profit. He may well have been able to pay his notes on the value of Fenway Park alone.

But the deal still worked for Lannin. The Red Sox had always made money. The way the deal was structured gave Lannin a tidy profit and, in essence, allowed him a percentage of the proceeds over the next several years.

Although Frazee took Ward as a partner, Ward was rarely heard from. From the outset, there was no question that Harry Frazee owned the team.

On November 1, 1916, within only a few hours of passing papers, Frazee, ever the showman, bragged that he'd already offered sixty thousand dollars for Washington pitcher Walter Johnson, thereby ensuring a positive reception in the press. In the *Globe*, Tim Murnane predicted that "Messers. Frazee and Ward will no doubt win their way to the hearts of Boston fans."

They weren't so lucky with Ban Johnson. When he found out about the deal, he almost had a stroke.

After the war with the Feds and the prospect of a real war on the horizon, Johnson thought the last thing baseball needed was a spendthrift like Frazee to drive up costs when everybody else was trying to keep them down. Prices for everything in America were soaring. Even the cost of a major league baseball had jumped 20 percent since the end of the 1917 season, from $1.25 to $1.50.

Everything Frazee represented was an insult to Johnson, who Charles Somers once described as "someone who always remembers a friend, but he never forgets an enemy." By crashing Johnson's league without an invitation, Frazee became an enemy, and Johnson never forgave him. Frazee was the ultimate outsider — young, brash, and a New Yorker to boot, neither one of Johnson's longtime partners nor one of his toadies. From the moment Frazee took command of the Red Sox, Johnson did everything in his considerable power to drive him from the game.

One day after the sale he fired a warning shot, releasing a statement that read "As I do not know either of them (Frazee or Ward) I must withhold judgement [on the deal]." Then he scrambled behind the scenes to stop it.

A few weeks before, Lannin and National League president John Tener had had a spat. Johnson, ever the guardian against the National League, offered the incident as an excuse for the sale, saying that he believed evil John Tener's harsh words had intimidated poor Joe Lannin into leaving the game. If so, said Johnson, "Lannin will be given every opportunity to reconsider the deal."

But Lannin wouldn't cooperate. He enjoyed sticking it to Johnson, and Harry Frazee was in to stay.

Accustomed to running the show, Frazee quickly took command. He tried but failed to convince Bill Carrigan to return, then named second baseman Jack Barry as his replacement. He announced that he planned to turn his full attention to baseball and would "temporarily retire" from the theater. He sold his interest in the Longacre Theater and promised not to return to the stage for a year or more, a promise he kept until 1918 when he mounted *Ladies First*, the first production featuring songs written by the Gershwin brothers.

The Sox began the 1917 season with virtually the same team that won the World Series in 1916. Frazee remained in the background, at least as far as the public knew. But behind the scenes, he was already rankling some feathers.

He erroneously believed he would be judged wholly on the success of his production in Fenway Park. In ever-parochial Boston, that was a critical miscalculation.

Free passes to the ballpark for local politicians and others, like the more influential members of the Royal Rooters, were established Boston traditions. There were often more city workers at Fenway Park than at city hall. But Frazee, who had some experience with paying customers, cut back on the popular perk. The move alienated many longtime supporters, including the Royal Rooters, whose notoriety began to wane.

He similarly estranged the press, treating them like theater critics, with whom he'd had a volatile relationship that on at least one occasion had ended in fisticuffs. When they gave Frazee's team what he considered an unfair review, he made the perpetrator pay his way into the park, then threatened to ban him if coverage didn't improve.

Baseball writers weren't as easily cowed as theater critics, and they held grudges for a long time. Most writers who covered the Red Sox were openly supportive of Johnson — they'd known him since the founding of the league and credited him with its success. Johnson's scorn for Frazee led the local press to a similar conclusion. They yearned for a local owner and soon held Frazee in contempt.

Frazee's enemies were rapidly increasing in number, and the backlash soon started. The estranged writers began to focus on Frazee's theatrical background and New York residency and jumped to an erroneous conclusion they whispered about for years

Stuffy McInnis signs his contract for the 1918 season with owner Harry Frazee and former manager Jack Barry, who served in the navy during the war. Frazee's acquisition of McInnis and other key players enabled the Red Sox to steal a pennant and world championship in the war-torn 1918 season.

and occasionally alluded to in print, often referring cryptically to the "mystery" of his religion.

In other words, Frazee's enemies thought he was Jewish, which, in Hibernian Boston, was considered nearly a sin. The city's veiled anti-Semitism would poison the public perception of who he was and what he did to this day, long after the rumors of his religious orientation subsided. Frazee, even before the sale of Babe Ruth, became to some a vile caricature, a greedy, money-grubbing carpetbagger and con.

In truth, Frazee was Presbyterian, and a Mason, facts that he kept private. For in New York, which was approximately one-quarter Jewish, having people think he was Jewish probably worked to Frazee's advantage, lending him an aura of financial acumen according to the stereotype. But in regard to Frazee, the Boston press never bothered to unearth facts where falsehoods told a better story. For more than eighty years, the myths surrounding Harry Frazee have been erroneously taken as the truth.

The 1917 Red Sox nearly repeated their pennant-winning effort of the previous year, but in the end didn't have enough hitting to keep pace with Chicago. The White Sox pulled away over the last six weeks of the season and won the pennant by nine games over Boston.

Babe Ruth, as people were beginning to expect, provided most of the year's excitement. On June 23 he was intimately involved in what the *Post*'s Paul

Shannon called "the most remarkable twirling feat ever recorded at Fenway Park." And all he did was throw four pitches.

In the first game of a doubleheader against Washington, Ruth walked leadoff hitter Ray Morgan on four pitches. After each pitch Ruth complained ever more vigorously to umpire Brick Owens. As Morgan took first, the *Post* reported that Ruth yelled to Owens, "Keep your eyes open," to which the umpire responded, "You get back in there and pitch or I'll run you out of the ballpark!"

This set Ruth off. "If you run me out of the ballpark, I'll take a punch at you on my way!" he bellowed. The newspaper probably got everything right except the exact words, for Ruth's foul mouth was undoubtedly in full display.

Owens tossed him from the game and Ruth tried to make good on his promise, reaching around catcher Chet Thomas and throwing a couple of punches before the police escorted him from the field.

Without warming up, Ernie Shore came on in relief. Morgan was thrown out trying to steal, and Shore retired the next twenty-six batters, a feat that baseball allowed to be registered as a perfect game.

The following day, Ban Johnson told the press, "We will take care of Mr. Ruth." That he did. Ruth was eventually suspended for nine games and fined one hundred dollars.

When Ruth returned, his behavior was increasingly erratic — on and off the diamond — as fame and fortune created an ever-more-volatile mix. Ruth spent most of his time between starts drinking and whoring. He even maintained an apartment in the Fenway's red-light district while Mrs. Ruth remained at his farm in Sudbury.

Just after the end of the season, he was briefly in the news again after crashing one of his many automobiles into two trolley cars and sending a female passenger — not Mrs. Ruth — to the hospital. The Babe, who seemed superhuman, was unhurt.

While the 1917 season had proceeded as if oblivious to world events, after the World Series it became obvious the sport would not be unaffected by the war. The American military mobilized, and by the end of October the first American troops were in the trenches of France. The Selective Service Act had been passed the previous April and now threatened to eviscerate major league rosters. Scores of players either joined the reserves, got married, had children, or made the acquaintance of friendly doctors to avoid the draft. Meanwhile, the Eighteenth Amendment prohibiting the sale of alcohol had passed the Senate in August and was expected to pass the House of Representatives and soon become law. Change was in the air.

Although attendance had risen in 1917, many teams were still recovering from the financial damage caused by the war with the Federal League. Many were almost broke.

Connie Mack's Philadelphia Athletics were in particularly dire straits. Although Mack's club made it to the World Series in 1913 and 1914, competition from the Feds left him with the highest payroll in baseball. He lost sixty thousand dollars in 1917 and could no longer compete in a marketplace of inflated salaries.

To survive, Mack decided to sell off his best players, bide his time, and try to rebuild when conditions improved.

He held his sale and the A's became a last-place team. But Mack still feared the draft would strip his club of its remaining talent and leave the stands empty, perhaps putting the entire 1918 season at risk.

Mack hadn't endured in the game for more than three decades by being shortsighted. To ensure his financial survival and, he hoped, leave his team in the black and ready to spend money whenever the war ended, Mack put his few remaining players of value on the market.

First baseman Stuffy McInnis was a solid .300 hitter, Amos Strunk and Ping Bodie were both among the league's premier outfielders, and catcher Wally Schang was the best-hitting backstop in the league. And Joe Bush, despite an 11-17 record in 1917, was one of the best young pitchers in baseball.

In December, at the annual American League meeting in Chicago, Mack told Ban Johnson of his plans. Johnson knew who had money and who didn't. Most didn't. But Boston did, sort of.

Johnson thought of Frazee. Attendance at Fenway Park was off only slightly, which had allowed Frazee to meet his debt and still have cash to spare. But Frazee had made it clear that he thought Johnson was inept and shortsighted. He was already politicking for his removal.

So Johnson steered Mack to Frazee, purposely keeping New York, the other team with money, in the dark. Johnson wasn't being generous — he was helping Mack, not Frazee. It was the first of a series of moves made by Johnson calculated to try to undermine Frazee financially and force him out of the league, a scheme whose ramifications are still felt — and cursed over — in Boston today.

Frazee was in a gambling mood, eager to prove that he could be as successful in ballparks as he was in theaters. Where others saw disaster, he sensed opportunity. The war didn't concern him, while every other owner, except Huston and Ruppert in New York, was broke and paralyzed by the uncertainty. Harry Frazee may have just been lucky, but he was the only man in baseball who realized that baseball would survive the war and that the situation created a unique window of opportunity for the 1918 season.

He met with Mack on the evening of December 14. A few hours later, they had a deal.

Frazee sent a telegram to the Boston newspapers that read, "Just closed deal with Philadelphia and purchased the following players for Boston Red Sox. Outfielder Amos Strunk, Pitcher Joe Bush, and

Fenway Park, circa 1917. Note early version of the left-field wall fronted by the embankment of Duffy's Cliff and the wooden bleachers in right-center field.

Catcher Walter Schang; terms, $60,000 and players Gregg, Thomas and outfielder Kopp. This is the heaviest financial deal ever consummated at one time in the history of baseball."

It was. The deal was ten thousand dollars richer than the sale of Tris Speaker and was trumpeted on the front page of all the Boston papers the next morning. The three players he gave up were inconsequential. At the time, the trade was by far the best in club history.

When the Yankees found out, Huston and Ruppert howled. They also had plenty of cash and complained that they'd never been given the opportunity to make a bid, a complaint they had made after the sale of Speaker as well. As if to appease them, a deal that delivered Ping Bodie from the A's was eventually arranged. But significantly, the two Yankee owners now began to take a critical look at Johnson.

Frazee was just getting started. A few days later he announced, "I am going to give Boston a championship team before we start south." On January 10, he delivered.

All Mack had left was twenty-six-year-old Gloucester native Stuffy McInnis, a player Frazee had been trying to acquire for a year. Now he was so eager to make a deal he agreed to a terrible arrangement. McInnis was moved to Boston on January 10. In return Frazee handed over a substantial check and agreed to either acquire players Mack wanted or provide some off his own roster.

Frazee signed McInnis immediately, which gave him good press in Boston but stripped him of any leverage with Mack. The two owners haggled for months trying to conclude the open-ended deal.

Enter Ban Johnson. In early March he coerced Frazee into sending the A's three Boston players: Larry Gardner, outfielder Tilly Walker, and catcher Hick Cady.

On paper, Mack got the better of Frazee. While Cady was washed up, Gardner and Walker were both starters and remained productive for another five years.

But Frazee was either lucky or wise beyond his years, for McInnis played a role in 1918 that neither Gardner nor Walker could have performed. He played understudy to the entire roster, filling in wherever needed. And while the trade left Boston thin — third base would be a trouble spot all year — compared to other teams in that war-ravaged season, Boston was loaded. It was a one-sided deal that for a single season — 1918 — worked for Boston.

Only one more move remained. Frazee wanted to retain Jack Barry as player-manager and even petitioned his friends in high places to get Barry a military furlough until the fall, but got nowhere.

On January 22, when the Sox received official word that Barry and several others, including Lewis and Shore, would have to remain in the service, Frazee shifted gears. Even as the *Post* trumpeted his accomplishments in a headline that read "Harry Frazee Beat 'Em to It," he set his sights on a new manager.

Since December, he'd been regularly picking the brain of Ed Barrow, a longtime baseball man who, ironically enough, had once served as manager of the Detroit Tigers under William Yawkey. He was currently the president of the International League but on increasingly thin ice. At their annual meeting in early February his salary was cut by two-thirds, a move backed by former Red Sox owner Joseph Lannin who, after selling the Red Sox, had retained an interest in Buffalo's International League franchise and realigned himself under the good graces of Ban Johnson.

Barrow quit. Frazee, an old friend who referred to Barrow affectionately as "Simon Legre," asked him to serve as manager. Barrow, who already called Frazee "Boss," was so eager to show up Lannin and the others that he offered to do so for free. Frazee paid him anyway.

Barrow's background was invaluable. His vast experience in the game as both manager and magnate made him familiar with almost every player in baseball. He scoured the waiver wire and contacted minor league free agents in an effort to shore up the team. With the club roster changing almost daily as players learned of their draft classification, veterans with deferments became valuable properties.

His best pick-up was George Whiteman, who had originally been signed by the Sox along with Tris Speaker in 1907. But while Speaker had become a star, Whiteman had wandered the nether reaches of the minor leagues, looking for a break.

Like Frazee, he was a native of Peoria and may well have been acquainted with his boss. Athletic and strong, as a teenager Whiteman had toured the nation as part of a high-dive act, jumping off a tower into a barrel of water at carnivals. But when his partner died in an accident in Texas, Whiteman turned to baseball. He joined Waco of the Texas League in 1905 as a twenty-three-year-old rookie.

Since then, apart from his brief three-game tryout with Boston in 1907, he had been a star nearly everywhere he played, from Montgomery, Alabama, to Missoula, Montana, to Houston and Montreal. In 1913, he hit .344 in a late-season trial with the Yankees — hit .344, yet was released.

In 1917 the fleet outfielder popped up in Toronto of the International League. There he fashioned the greatest season of his minor league career, hitting .342.

When Barrow went looking for talent that winter,

he remembered Whiteman. With the loss of Lewis, the Red Sox needed another outfielder, and Whiteman, who had played on so many championship teams he was nicknamed "Lucky," was a safe choice.

Still, Frazee continued to explore further trades, as almost every day the newspapers carried word of impending deals for the likes of St. Louis first baseman George Sisler, veteran infielder Napoleon Lajoie, or Giant second baseman Del Pratt. But the Red Sox had grown too strong. Other teams were afraid Boston would run away with the pennant and shied away from further deals. Had they tried, Johnson likely would have blocked them anyway.

When the team embarked for spring training from South Station on March 9, Babe Ruth was the only player in tow. The war had disrupted everything. While the entourage was joined by a number of other players on the way to Hot Springs, Barrow wouldn't really know who he would have available until they walked onto the field.

Not that many people cared. In an enormous political miscalculation, the previous November Ban Johnson had proposed that each major league team be allowed to exempt eighteen players from the draft.

Neither the public nor the politicians found any redeeming qualities in the notion, and Johnson's arrogance put the entire 1918 season at risk. Any goodwill the game retained was gone. Government propaganda espoused a "Work or Fight" ethic, strongly suggesting that those who were ineligible for the draft, like ballplayers with children, find work in the war industries. By July of 1918, that edict would become law.

The public agreed. They concluded that most players were nothing more than a bunch of "slackers," the worst non-Germanic epithet of the era.

Boston began spring training with hardly enough players to hold a scrimmage. That is the only reason that Babe Ruth, at age twenty-three one of the best pitchers in baseball, ever had the chance to step to the plate and change the game forevermore. Because the Red Sox were short of players, Ruth played in the field and took a regular turn in the batting order. He soon demonstrated that while he could throw as well as anybody who had ever played the game, he could hit the ball like no one else.

In his ghostwritten autobiography, *My Fifty Years in Baseball*, Ed Barrow took full credit for Ruth's transformation. Team captain Harry Hooper, in Lawrence Ritter's oral history, *The Glory of Their Times*, made a similar claim.

One might as well credit Archduke Ferdinand. For it was the war, which changed everything in America, that turned Babe Ruth into the Bambino.

At the first Red Sox workout on March 13, Ruth played first base, an act that drew no comment from the press. It was common for players, particularly young players with ample energy, to work out at a variety of positions to help get in shape.

On March 17 Boston and Brooklyn, who also trained in Hot Springs, met in the first exhibition game of the spring. Ruth played right field because Harry Hooper had just arrived in camp and wasn't in condition to play.

Ruth walked in his first at bat, then came up for the second time against a pitcher whose name was listed in the newspapers as, appropriately enough, "Hittman" (likely an anglicized moniker for pitcher Harry Heitmann). Ruth hit a long drive to the gap in right-center and ran around the bases for a home run. In his next at bat, he did even better. The *Post* reported that he hit the ball "so far over the right field fence . . . even players of the Brooklyn team had to arise to the occasion and cheer."

A few days later, with first baseman Dick Hoblitzell still not in camp and Stuffy McInnis playing third, Ruth again filled in at first. Two days later a cartoon appeared in the *Post* that showed Ruth pestering Barrow to play the outfield. By all accounts he was in great shape that spring, and enthusiastic to a fault.

When an exhibition was rained out on March 23, Ruth entertained soldiers by taking batting practice. He wowed them by smacking five home runs described as "farther here by thirty feet than . . . the right field pavilion at the Polo Grounds," drives well in excess of 400 feet.

Yet even as Ruth's bat drew raves, with the season rapidly approaching he returned to the pitcher's mound. As the Sox barnstormed their way to Boston by way of Texas, Alabama, and Tennessee, Ruth took his regular turn in the starting rotation but didn't play elsewhere. His two weeks as a hitter seemed relegated to agate type of old newspapers.

By Opening Day much had changed, or was about to. All across America men were marching to the local draft board and then either boarding ship for Europe or trying desperately to find a job in the war industries. American women, empowered for the first time through their status performing "essential" war work, were marching in the streets and demanding the right to vote. Czarist Russia was collapsing under the pressure of the proletariat. The Allied Army, buoyed by fresh American troops, had the Hun on the run all along the 150-mile Somme front in France. The biplane heralded a new era in warfare and transportation. Daylight-saving time went into effect for the first time, and airmail service was inaugurated between Chicago and New York. The Jazz Age was just around the corner. But the war would change everything. The world would never be the same.

Neither would baseball, for a similar transition was about to take place on the diamond. In 1918 the game was the sporting equivalent of trench warfare. The upcoming season was the last gasp of "scientific" hit-and-run baseball, where the perfect run scored on a walk, a stolen base, a groundball, and a sacrifice fly. The ideal game was a pitchers' duel, preferably extending into extra innings, which ended with a score of 1-0. But the home run would soon change everything.

The Red Sox opened fast and never looked back, as Ruth, pitching and batting ninth, won the opener

versus Philadelphia 7-1. The club went on to a 12-3 start, their best ever to that time.

The American League eventually lost 124 players to the war that year. As a result, talent was the weakest it had been since 1901. But Boston, with its pitching staff intact and its lineup bolstered by Frazee's trades, was easily the most gifted team in the league.

Not that they were unbeatable. Barrow and Harry Hooper, who made most game decisions, got the most from what they had. They went with the "hot hand" and juggled players in and out of the lineup all year, cutting and pasting as necessary. First baseman McInnis began the year at third, one of seven players to appear there during the season. Schang, a catcher, ended up playing almost everywhere. Forty-year-old has-been Dave Shean played second. In any other year, they'd have been lucky to be a .500 ballclub. In 1918, they were a powerhouse.

No player was more affected by the dilution of talent and Barrow and Hooper's strategy than Babe Ruth. For when slumping first baseman Dick Hoblitzell injured his hand, Barrow didn't want to move McInnis off third. So on May 6, 1918, Ruth, who in the previous game had homered into the upper deck in right field of the Polo Grounds in a 5-4 loss, his second defeat of the season, played first. He repeated his performance, driving another home run, again to the upper deck, although the Sox were routed 10-5.

The Yankees were impressed. No one could do what Ruth did, either on the mound or at the plate. In 1918 that kind of versatility was priceless. New York was desperate for a drawing card and offered Frazee one hundred fifty thousand dollars in cash for Ruth.

Frazee didn't need the money and turned down the offer. After all, the show had just opened and the reviews weren't in yet. He sensed he had another hit on his hands. He filed away New York's level of interest.

The next day, in Washington, Ruth played first and homered again, this time off the great Walter Johnson, thrilling fans, sportswriters, and, just as significantly, himself. But Boston lost again, 7-2.

Ruth was becoming as enamored of his hitting as the fans were. Between May 4 and May 11 he went fourteen for twenty-nine, with three home runs. He was leading the league in hitting and was the only positive note in an otherwise dreary season.

Babe Ruth increased his string of consecutive scoreless innings pitched in World Series competition to twenty-nine and two-thirds before the Cubs scored twice in a 3-2 Boston win in game four of the 1918 World Series. Ruth's record stood until Whitey Ford of the Yankees broke it six decades later.

But on May 18, Provost Marshal General Enoch B. Crowder ruled that baseball was a nonessential activity. All players were supposed to either join the service or find work in the defense industries. The so-called "Work or Fight" order threw the rest of the season into jeopardy.

Ban Johnson went into overdrive, pulling every string and calling in every chit he had to try to save the season. But when Johnson went to Washington to talk politics, he was in over his head. Instead of convincing the authorities to extend the season, after they met with Johnson they seemed more determined to end it.

Johnson and the rest of the National Commission meekly prepared to cease operations. Johnson announced that "except for the cremation ceremonies," the season was dead. But Harry Frazee didn't agree. He had too much invested in the game.

Frazee wasn't alone, and he formed a coalition with several other disgruntled American League owners and those of the National League. They went behind Johnson's back and petitioned the government themselves. Frazee even paid a personal visit to Secretary of War Newton Baker and convinced him that baseball was good for the nation's morale. The National Commission belatedly adopted the same argument, and in late July the government agreed not to enforce the work or fight order for ballplayers until October, as long as the baseball season ended by September 1. Johnson readily agreed and made plans to close shop by August 20 so that the World Series could be concluded by the September 1 deadline.

Frazee took the initiative again and successfully argued that the World Series was not part of the season. Because of his efforts players in the World Series received an exemption from the order until September 15, allowing the regular season to last another ten days, giving every owner in the league the opportunity to make a little more money. But just as significantly, for the second time that season Frazee caused Johnson to lose face.

Johnson, of course, tried to take full credit for saving the season. Frazee already blamed Johnson's awkward lobbying efforts for ruining attendance and nearly costing the season. Now, he thought even less of him. Johnson privately fumed that Frazee had usurped his authority and openly consorted with the National League. The enmity between the two men was palpable.

In the interim, as Johnson bobbled the ball, a number of players simply said the hell with it and went to work — sort of — in the shipyards. Their labor was usually put to good use playing baseball in fast, new industrial leagues. They were paid well to play ball and not expected to do much more.

Meanwhile, Ruth resumed his sensational play and homered in four consecutive games, one of which he pitched, while playing center field for an injured Amos Strunk in the others.

But before his next scheduled start, Ruth complained of a sore arm and told Barrow he wanted no more of pitching. Barrow didn't believe him, but caved in. Crowds were down, Ruth was a definite drawing card, and besides, Sad Sam Jones had pitched well in Ruth's stead, while George Whiteman was proving to be a defensive liability in the outfield. Ruth took Whiteman's place. For the next few weeks he was a sensation as he feasted on sub-par pitching.

But in midseason Ruth slumped badly. Lefthanded pitchers, even poor ones, gave him trouble. Boston's opponents took note, and suddenly every lefty in the league was pitching against Boston.

Barrow sat Ruth down, and George Whiteman started seeing more time in the outfield. Most of Ruth's spectacular slugging that year had come in two brief streaks. Otherwise, he'd hit just a bit above average, hardly worth turning a team upside down over. The Red Sox, in fact, had a better record before Ruth started appearing in the field.

What Boston needed was pitching. Mays and Jones were doing fine, but Joe Bush was struggling and Dutch Leonard was in the service. Barrow asked Ruth to return to the rotation. Ruth refused. He just wanted to hit.

Ruth grew increasingly uncooperative. On July 1, Barrow fined him for ignoring a "take" sign while at bat. Ruth pouted, then took his ball and ran away from home, contacting the Chester Shipyards team in Chester, Pennsylvania, and offering to join up.

On July 3, he jumped the club.

When Frazee found out, he threatened the shipyard with legal action. Then Ruth discovered that the shipyard team also expected him to pitch. He sheepishly agreed to return to the Sox, meekly acquiescing to Barrow, and finally stopped trying to pull left-handed pitching. For most of July Ruth's bat led the Sox on a midseason surge, although he failed to hit the ball out of the park.

The Sox led the league by four and a half games in late July when Barrow again asked Ruth to pitch. Ruth agreed to do so for the good of the club. For the rest of the season he pitched every fourth day and occasionally spelled Whiteman in the outfield.

With their pitching woes behind them, the Sox cruised to the pennant. They finished 75-51, two and a half games ahead of second-place Cleveland. Ruth won nine of his last eleven decisions to finish 13-7 and hit an even .300 in seventy-two appearances in the field, fifty-nine in the outfield. He clubbed eleven home runs, while the rest of the league hit eighty-seven.

No one quite knew what to think about Ruth's performance at the plate. The fact that he had hit so well against pitching made second-rate because of players lost to the service made his slugging suspect. No one was looking then to Ruth's 50-ounce black bat to see the future of the game.

In Boston, the immediate future was of more concern. The Chicago Cubs waltzed to the National League pennant in that ragtime year by ten and a half games over second-place New York. They were led by the pitching of lefthanders James "Hippo" Vaughn, "Lefty" Tyler, and righthander Claude Hendrix, each of whom won nineteen games or more as the staff recorded a stellar 2.18 ERA.

The war affected the Series just as it had the regular season. Wartime travel restrictions forced baseball to schedule the first three games in Chicago and the remainder in Boston. Even in Chicago and Boston, war news relegated coverage of the Series to secondary status on the front page, often below the fold, and for the first time in Series history, tickets were widely available.

Outside of the two participating cities, interest in the Series was almost nonexistent. Johnson's groveling had turned off fans. Moreover, every day brought news of more casualties. For many, the sight of apparently healthy ballplayers playing a game in the sunshine while so many lay dying in the trenches was too much to bear. Most fans considered the remaining players "slackers."

Red Sox third baseman Fred Thomas's experience was typical. As his wife, Constance, recalled in 1993, "Everybody was pointing a finger at him because he was a professional ballplayer, being a draft dodger. [They didn't know] He was a born diabetic and he was drafted and he didn't pass because he was diabetic. He went back to baseball and everybody pointed their finger at him. He couldn't stand it, so he dieted real, real strong and got in. But he wasn't in long. They found out he did have diabetes." Typically, Thomas spent most of his time in the service playing ball for the navy at the Great Lakes Training Center. He received a furlough to play in the Series.

While those who were paying attention considered the Cubs, with their superior pitching, to be narrow favorites, owner William Weeghman and manager Fred Mitchell, who'd pitched for Boston in 1901 and 1902, weren't quite so confident. Ruth's bat scared them. Instead of playing at their home park, cozy Wrigley Field (then called "Cubs Park"), the club made arrangements to play in the much more spacious home of the White Sox, Comiskey Park.

Ruth was lefthanded, and the right-field fence at Comiskey Park was, on average, 50 or 75 feet farther from home plate than its counterpart in Wrigley. Surely even Ruth, they believed, would have a hard time hitting one out. Ruth even caused Mitchell to go with an all-lefthanded pitching rotation, dropping Claude Hendrix despite his 20-7 record.

Most observers expected Ruth to play a larger role in the Series at the plate than on the mound. H. W. Lanigan of the *Boston American* wrote that Joe Bush would pitch the opener because "Barrow wants to keep Battering Babe Ruth on duty in the left pasture in all the games." Chicago was expected to counter with either Lefty Tyler or Hippo Vaughn.

When the Red Sox took the field for batting practice early on the afternoon of September 5 to open the Series, the sparse crowd of only 19,274 woke up when Ruth stepped in to take his cuts. With a strong wind blowing across the diamond toward first, he didn't disappoint, knocking the first pitch deep into

the right-field stands. So much for Fred Mitchell's strategy.

Both managers tried to keep their pitcher a secret. Mitchell had Tyler and Vaughn warm up in tandem, while Barrow did the same with Ruth and Bush. But when the batteries were announced before the game, Barrow pulled the big surprise, choosing Ruth to oppose Hippo Vaughn, even batting him ninth in the order, just like any other pitcher. George Whiteman played left and hit cleanup.

Whiteman made Barrow look like a genius. For while Ruth received credit for throwing a shutout, Whiteman paced the Sox at bat and in the field.

Both pitchers struggled early. Chicago loaded the bases in the first, but with two out Whiteman made a fine running catch of a dying line drive to bail Ruth out.

Entering the fourth inning the game was scoreless. Then Vaughn walked Dave Shean, and with one out Whiteman, who had already singled in the second, came to bat.

He fought off what Burt Whitman of the *Herald* described as a "dinky curve" and lifted it just to left of second base. Shortstop Charlie Hollocher leapt for the soft drive but missed. Shean held at second.

Stuffy McInnis was up next. Boston decided to gamble on a hit-and-run play, and McInnis smacked a hard drive that fell just in front of Leslie Mann in left. Shean scored easily to put Boston ahead 1-0.

The run gave Ruth a lift, and he set Chicago down easily in the fourth and fifth. But in the sixth Chicago threatened when Paskert and Merkle singled with one out.

Once more it fell to Whiteman to squelch the rally. He again made a fine catch, his glove showing white as he barely retained control of the ball.

Before Chicago came up in the bottom of the seventh, the game was halted as the band played "The

World War I veterans sell cigarettes in front of Fenway Park during the 1918 season to benefit the dependent families of soldiers on the front. Note the fifty-cent pavilion seat entrance and the twenty-five-cent bleacher entrance.

Crowds gather outside Fenway Park prior to game four of the 1918 World Series, the first Series game to be played at Fenway Park since the 1914 Braves met the Athletics.

Star-Spangled Banner." Although some have later claimed that this was the beginning of what is now a baseball tradition, in truth the tune had first been played before a game in Boston eighteen years earlier and on several subsequent occasions.

Boston hung on for the 1-0 win. Although the victory ran Ruth's string of scoreless innings in a World Series to twenty-two and two-thirds innings with his six-hit shutout, Whiteman was the hero of the moment, for Ruth had scuffled on the mound and gone hitless.

As Paul Shannon wrote in the *Post*, "Three times this afternoon Boston's chances would have gone a glimmering had Whiteman not been the experienced veteran that he is and had he not been able to play the garden as no one but Hooper could have played it. Three of his five catches were sensational." In the *Herald*, Burt Whitman added that his performance meant "Barrow will keep Whitey in left field so long as manager Mitchell continues to throw left-handed pitchers . . . This means that Ruth will be out of the game."

That was precisely the case in game two, as "Bullet" Joe Bush of the Sox faced the Cubs' Lefty Tyler. Ruth stayed on the bench as Whiteman again got the start in left and hit cleanup.

He led off the second, singled, moved up when Tyler and Killefer collided going after McInnis's sacrifice, then was sacrificed by Scott to third. When Thomas grounded to second, Whiteman broke for home but was nabbed by Charlie Pick's throw.

At the end of the inning, another game took over. The day before, Cubs coach Otto Knabe had ridden Ruth so mercilessly and with such foul language that Ruth had gone looking for him after the game. On this day, Knabe aimed his barbs at Boston coach Heinie Wagner.

Wagner was less patient. Instead of returning to the Boston bench from his place in the coach's box after Whiteman was thrown out, he stormed into the Cubs' dugout throwing punches at Knabe, and the two men tumbled to the ground.

When the Red Sox realized what was happening, they poured into the enemy dugout and in a few moments emerged with Wagner. As *Baseball Magazine* later reported, "Fans who could see it declared that when they heard two Germans were fighting, they merely encouraged them to beat each other up."

The rest of the game was marked by rough play. Every tag was hard, every slide meant to cause harm, and every opportunity to push or shove the opponent taken advantage of.

The Cubs scored three in the third, and apart from back-to-back triples by Strunk and Whiteman in the ninth, the Sox couldn't touch Tyler. Chicago won 3-1.

After the histrionics of game two, everyone expected more in game three, but it drizzled on and off all day and cooler heads prevailed. Mitchell kept Ruth on the bench by bringing back Hippo Vaughn on only one day's rest to face Carl Mays of the Red Sox. If not for George Whiteman, the strategy might have earned the Cubs a win.

For with the game scoreless in the fourth and one out, Whiteman took an errant toss in the ribs and made first. McInnis singled him to second and Schang brought him home with another hit. When Everett Scott dumped a grounder in front of the plate, Vaughn bobbled it and McInnis scored to put Boston up 2-0.

In the fourth, Whiteman robbed Paskert of a home run by grabbing his drive out of the front row of the bleachers in left. Mays gave up only a single run in the fifth, and the Red Sox collected a tidy 2-1 win, to take the Series lead, two games to one.

At eight o'clock that evening the two clubs boarded the same train for the twenty-seven-hour trip to Boston for game four. The long journey gave them the opportunity to wade through some legal documents they had received from the National Commission just before game one. They didn't like what they contained.

World Series receipts had been climbing, but before the start of the 1918 season, the National Commission, acting on behalf of the owners in both leagues, changed the distribution of the money. Although the changes had been announced in the press, the players were otherwise not notified. By the fall of 1918 they had forgotten all about it.

In previous years, players had shared 60 percent of the receipts of the first four games, resulting in payments to each player of between three and four thousand dollars. The commission and owners shared the remaining receipts.

But the new plan called for the players to receive only 55.25 percent of the receipts of the first four games. Yet of that sum, only 60 percent would be awarded to the players of the two World Series clubs. The remainder would go to the players of the teams that finished in second, third, and fourth place in each league.

The ingenious plan was wholly in favor of the owners, who gave up nothing while the players on the two pennant winners coughed up over half their share, which was then distributed to other players. In those penurious times, the plan, in turn, allowed the club owners to scale down salaries, for they could argue that half the players in the league stood to receive a "bonus" of at least several hundred dollars after the season. Everybody won — except the players in the Series.

Ban Johnson had made the deal even worse. He ordered each player in the Series to "donate" 10 percent of his take to war charities. Low attendance and reduced ticket prices only made the problem worse.

Although the players had no union protection, they weren't stupid. They soon figured out that win or lose, they'd be lucky to earn a thousand dollars apiece. Members of the two teams started talking.

While they were enemies on the field, they were united on this issue against the owners. On the way to Boston, Harry Hooper and Dave Shean of the Sox plotted strategy with Leslie Mann and Bill Killefer of the Cubs.

At least one player was disinterested. Babe Ruth spent most of the trip indulging in high jinks of one kind or another, which included punching out the top of every straw hat worn by passengers on the train.

But as the train chugged into Massachusetts on the afternoon of Sunday, September 8, Ruth either ran out of straw hats or met a man who chose not to donate his chapeau willingly. He either punched through a hat and into the steel wall of the train, took a wild swing at teammate Walt Kinney while shadow-boxing after running out of hats, or got into a scuffle with an unwilling participant. The end result was the same. The middle finger on his pitching hand swelled to twice its normal size.

Barrow found out and was furious. He wanted Ruth to pitch game four. But he didn't know that game four was no longer a certainty.

The players had come to a consensus. Unless the commission backed down, there would be no game four.

Early Monday morning, the players' reps went together to the Copley Plaza Hotel, informed the three commissioners of their decision, and requested a formal meeting.

The commissioners were surprised and feigned ignorance. They lied and told the players that without consulting all sixteen owners in both leagues, they were powerless. The players scoffed at that, but when the commission assented to a more formal meeting later, they agreed to play game four.

The Series resumed at Fenway Park on the afternoon of September 9. Ruth's finger was still swollen and had been drained to reduce the swelling. He arrived at the park with it stained by iodine. He convinced Barrow that he could still pitch, although the manager again had both Ruth and Bush warm up before the game. The Cubs stuck with Lefty Tyler.

But once the game started, Ruth was in trouble nearly every inning. His finger made it difficult for him to grip the ball.

Boston's defense bailed him out and kept him in the game. A first-inning rally died when catcher Sam Agnew picked a runner off first. In the third inning, Ruth did the same. In the fourth, Everett Scott robbed Paskert of a hit, and after Ruth walked two in the sixth, a double play snuffed out another rally. His performance was hardly Ruthian, but the Cubs couldn't score.

At the plate it was a different story. With the game scoreless in the fourth, Shean and Whiteman walked before Shean was erased on McInnis's fielder's choice. Ruth stepped to the plate with Whiteman and McInnis on base.

Tyler pitched carefully and gave Ruth three straight balls.

He should have walked him. Everett Scott, on deck, had only one hit for the entire Series.

Ruth took two pitches for strikes, and then Tyler threw again.

As Paul Shannon of the *Boston Post* wrote, "A report like a rifle shot rang through the park. Twenty-five thousand rose as one man, and while the bleachers shrieked in ecstasy. The Cubs right fielder [Flack], taken unawares, dashed madly for the center field stands while two red-legged runners scampered around the bases." Ruth slid into third ahead of the relay as both runners scored easily to give him a 2-0 lead.

Then Tyler settled down. When Ruth came up again in the seventh with McInnis on first and no outs, Barrow had him bunt. Boston didn't score.

It was still 2-0 in the eighth when Ruth came apart. He walked Bill Killefer, then gave up a single to Cub pitcher Claude Hendrix, who pinch-hit for Tyler. A wild pitch moved the runners up and Killefer scored on a force play. Mann then singled to tie the game.

Ruth's record World Series scoreless streak was over at twenty-nine and two-thirds innings. But in 1918, no one cared about obscure records. It was barely noticed.

With Tyler gone, "Shufflin'" Phil Douglas, one of the game's notorious drunks but a fine pitcher, came in for Chicago. The end came quickly.

Schang pinch-hit a single, went to second on a passed ball, and scored when Douglas botched Hooper's sacrifice bunt and threw the ball away. Now Boston led 3-2.

In the ninth, a fading Ruth gave up a single and a walk to the first two hitters. That was enough. Barrow brought in Joe Bush and pulled George Whiteman, sending Ruth to left, either for defensive purposes or to make a point with the undisciplined star.

Bush squelched the rally and Boston won. They were one victory away from their sixth world championship in eighteen seasons.

But the players hadn't forgotten about the promised meeting. Early that evening Hooper, Wagner, Mann, and Killefer went to the Copley Plaza.

For the second time in two days, chairman August Hermann, National League president John Heydler, and American League president Ban Johnson told the players where to go. They repeated their argument that the ruling was a league matter, releasing a statement that read, "We are powerless to change the situation. This legislation has been enacted by the American and National Leagues, and the other teams figuring in the split could bring suit against the National Commission and beat the suit if we were to make any change."

As far as the commission was concerned, that was the end of it. But after the meeting the players decided that if the commission didn't change their tune, they'd refuse to play game five.

The next morning Hooper and several others made one last attempt to meet with the three commissioners, but the commission refused to back down. Ban Johnson ordered them to the park and pledged to hold another meeting after game five.

It was a hollow promise. Players on both teams knew that if Boston won the Series was over. Another meeting would be pointless.

The commissioners stalked off. Confident they had stymied a rebellion, Johnson, Hermann, and Heydler retired to the bar at the Copley Plaza Hotel to celebrate their ability to get the players to do their bidding.

But the players weren't through. They returned to Fenway, but by 2:00, with more than twenty thousand fans swarming into Fenway Park for the scheduled 2:30 start, the players remained in their clubhouses. They were on strike.

Word traveled fast. As soon as Messrs. Heydler, Hermann, and Johnson learned what was happening,

Submarine pitcher Carl Mays was the ace of the Red Sox pitching staff in 1918 when he went 21-13. In the World Series he won twice more, including the clincher, a 2-1 complete-game victory at Fenway Park.

they rushed to the ballpark, miffed at having to cut pre-game libations short.

As rumors of the strike swept over the stands, the crowd grew anxious. Extra police were called in. The band, which had been playing nonstop for more than an hour, stopped to rest and threatened to go on strike themselves. The only uniforms in sight were those on the soldiers in the crowd and that of the Red Sox batboy.

At 2:45 the commissioners met with Hooper, Shean, Mann, and Bill Killefer in the umpires' room beneath the grandstand. Hermann and Heydler were only half in the bag, but Johnson was smashed.

Before the players had a chance to speak, Hermann assumed powers he had not admitted to two days before and threatened to cancel the Series and not pay anybody anything. Hooper countered that money wasn't the issue. As far as the players were concerned, the money could all go to charity. They asked only that the commission restore the traditional split of receipts. It was purely a matter of principle.

The commission would have none of it. Giving money away for no good reason made no sense to them, but at this point, little did. It was obvious to the players and the handful of writers in attendance that none of the three commissioners was in any condition to have a serious discussion about anything.

The standoff pushed Johnson to tears, and he pulled out all the maudlin stops, doing everything but claiming that the bat and ball were his and running home. "*I* did it, Harry," he pleaded to Hooper. "*I* went to Washington and had the stamp of approval put on this Series, *I* did it, Harry, *I* did it."

Hooper tried to interject several times but was cut off by Johnson's glazed soliloquy. Then Johnson seized on his trump card. The players had to play, he said, for they owed it "to the soldiers in the stands," a number of which were now on the field keeping the crowd in their seats.

As Nick Flately of the *Boston American* described it, Hermann interjected, "'Let's arbitrary [sic] this matter, Mister Johnson,' then he launched forth into a brilliant exposition of the history of baseball's governing board. Expert reporters took note for a while and then quit, befuddled."

Hooper gave up, too. He couldn't argue with three men who could hardly stand up. After Hooper extracted a promise that the players would face no retribution for their actions, Boston Mayor John Fitzgerald took the field and announced that although the players felt they were receiving a raw deal, they

RIGHTING THE WRONG

A few weeks after the end of the World Series, members of the world championship 1918 Red Sox received a letter from John Heydler. Because of the strike, stated Heydler, the World Series emblems given to every other winning team to date — medallions equivalent to today's rings — would be withheld.

That was a direct contradiction of what the players had been told when they agreed to end their strike and play, but the National Commission didn't care — it was payback time. But the players never forgot they had been denied the symbol of the championship they won.

George Whiteman, among others, wrote the commission repeatedly to request his emblem, writing "I have never asked baseball for anything in my life," and even submitting a canceled check to prove he'd donated 10 percent of his Series share to war charities. But the commission passed the buck and never responded to his request.

Harry Hooper was most adamant about getting the emblems. Until his death in 1974, he petitioned every baseball commissioner for his medallion, and every commissioner turned him down. His son John continued the campaign and was similarly rebuffed by Bowie Kuhn, Peter Uebberoth, and A. Bartlett Giamatti.

But in 1993 Glenn Stout wrote about the controversy in a story entitled "The Last Champions" for *New England Sport* magazine, the official publication of the Sports Museum of New England. Publisher John McGrath and editor Fred Kirsch then approached the Red Sox about getting the medallions awarded as part of a seventy-fifth anniversary celebration of the 1918 world championship. The Red Sox agreed.

The Red Sox asked and after seventy-five years of saying "no," this time baseball agreed to award the medallions. The reason? Since there was no baseball commissioner, neither was there a final authority to refuse. Stout and the Red Sox tracked down the descendants of team members, ranging from Fred Thomas's widow to George Whiteman's ninety-five-year-old sister-in-law, and the club arranged for the families to come to Boston. On September 4, 1993, the seventy-fifth anniversary of the scheduled start of the 1918 World Series, the medallions were awarded during a pre-game ceremony and a 1918 world championship banner was unfurled at Fenway Park.

About time. ⚾

"have agreed to play for the sake of the public and the wounded soldiers in the stands."

The announcement was answered with jeers. Little had appeared in the press about the controversy, and most of the crowd blamed the players for the delay. When they finally took the field, they were greeted with calls of "Bolsheviki!" "Slackers!" and, presumably, less delicate epithets.

When the game finally began before 24,694 disgruntled fans, Boston played as if unsure whether or not they were still on strike. Big Hippo Vaughn shut the Sox out on only five hits while Sad Sam Jones was nicked for three runs. Only George Whiteman kept the game from getting out of hand, as he again made several stellar plays in the outfield.

Disgust was the emotion of the day before game six as only 15,238 fans filed into Fenway Park to witness what would be, for at least another eight decades, the last world championship for the Red Sox. Barrow selected Carl Mays to throw opposite Tyler.

In the third inning, with no score, George Whiteman came to the plate with two on. He hit the ball on a line to right field. Cubs outfielder Max Flack raced in, but as he reached for the ball it glanced off his hands. Shean and Mays scored to put Boston ahead.

In the press box, someone scrawled the news on a scrap of paper and tucked it into a small metal canister bound to the leg of a carrier pigeon. The bird was thrown from the box, and it wheeled over the field, then headed toward Fort Devens, carrying the score to the soldiers in camp.

The Cubs got a run back in the fourth as Flack atoned for this error with a single, took second on a hit batter, stole third, and then scored on a hit by Merkle.

Still, Boston clung to its narrow lead. In the eighth the Cubs' Turner Barber smacked a vicious, sinking line drive toward Whiteman. The thirty-five-year-old outfielder tore in at full speed, stuck out his glove,

THE BOSTON RED SOX 1918
LAWLER MILLER JONES THOMAS RUTH HOOPER MAYS SHEAN KINNEY STRUNK McINNIS BARROW
SCOTT DUBUC BUSH WHITEMAN SCHANG MAYER WAGNER AGNEW COFFEY

The 1918 world champion Red Sox. The 1918 champions not only received the lowest winning share in Series history ($1,102.51) but were also forced to wait seventy-five years before the families of the champions finally received the World Series winners' emblems due their deceased relatives. The gold emblem was the early equivalent of today's championship ring.

dove, and somehow caught the ball before turning a complete somersault.

For three full minutes the crowd stood and cheered for George Whiteman as he stood, bent over, and twisted back and forth, trying to shake off the effects of his tumble. Observers at the time called it the greatest catch in Series history. For that brief moment the problems of the strike and the war seemed irrelevant. He remained in the game for another batter, then waved to Barrow and called for a replacement.

The crowd rose again and their cheers escorted him off the field. Almost unnoticed, Babe Ruth trotted out to take Whiteman's place in the outfield, completely upstaged for one of the few times in his career.

Carl Mays bore down. One inning later, when second baseman Dave Shean fielded Leslie Mann's grounder and tossed it to Stuffy McInnis at first, the Red Sox were again world champions.

No wild parades or spontaneous public celebrations followed the victory. The next day, the players met and the Sox distributed fifteen full shares of $1,102.51, while each Cub received $671.09; each was the smallest in Series history. In the Series' six games, the Cubs scored a total of ten runs, the Red Sox only nine, yet somehow the Red Sox were still able to win.

With receipts so slim, Frazee wanted to take the Cubs and Red Sox to Europe and make some money playing another Series for the troops, but Ban Johnson and the government blocked the plan. Then, two weeks later, the National Commission reneged on their promise not to take any punitive action and withheld the Red Sox players' World Series emblems, golden medallions that are the equivalent of today's championship rings. One cannot help but wonder whether the fact that it was Frazee's team that won the championship played a role in Johnson's decision.

Yet the players' strike and war-shortened season may have helped avert a larger tragedy. For in late August, soldiers returning from Europe to Fort Devens started to become sick. They began dying in the first week of September, and Boston became the first American city to experience an outbreak of the so-called Spanish flu. In a little more than three months, nearly 500,000 Americans, including 6,508 Bostonians, succumbed to the disease. Had the Series been better attended or taken place at its usual time in early October, when the outbreak was in full swing in Boston, the postseason classic may well have hastened the spread of the pandemic and been responsible for the unintentional deaths of thousands more. As it was, the disease killed *Globe* sportswriter Edward Martin and *Record* sports editor Harry Casey. The rapid spread of the epidemic to Chicago may well have been initiated by fans and players who had been in Boston for the contests.

On November 11, the war ended. A nation turned from the past and looked for a return to normalcy, changed in ways no one could yet imagine. In Boston, the tainted 1918 world championship was quickly forgotten as the city simultaneously celebrated the Armistice and mourned her dead. After winning their sixth title in eighteen years, Red Sox fans fully expected they would soon have another, more satisfying world championship to savor.

HARRY FRAZEE AND THE TRUTH ABOUT RUTH

1919 | 1922

Babe Ruth emerged as the game's greatest offensive force in 1919 with a record-shattering twenty-nine home runs. But he balked at pitching and created problems in the clubhouse, winning only nine games on the mound as the Red Sox failed to repeat as world champions. His subsequent sale to the Yankees in January 1920 is still the most talked-about transaction in sports history.

Harry Frazee was in his glory. Boston's World Series victory confirmed his wisdom. Of all the major league owners, only Frazee had correctly read the unique circumstances caused by the war and won. "Handsome Harry" had yet another hit. Even though attendance had dropped in half in 1918, for which Frazee rightly held Ban Johnson partially responsible, he now looked forward to the economic benefits of an extended run.

The accepted account of the remainder of Frazee's reign holds that after 1918 a string of theatrical failures put him in financial difficulty. Then, to stay afloat, he crassly sold the human assets of the Red Sox to prop up his stage interests, resulting in the nefarious sale of Babe Ruth and others to the New York Yankees for far less than they were worth. *Boston Herald* writer Burt Whitman termed it "the Rape of the Red Sox." This legend has since been used as a convenient excuse to explain all things Red Sox in Boston.

Yet this popular account is almost pure fiction, an incomplete story that leaves an entirely false impression and ignores ample evidence to the contrary. Frazee never had a run of theatrical failures and was never in serious financial trouble. And his many deals with the New York Yankees were neither one-sided nor part of some fiendish conspiracy.

While Frazee did sell Ruth and eventually broke up his ballclub, his reasons had nothing to do with personal finances. They had everything to do with Ban Johnson and Frazee's increasing political problems with baseball's establishment. When observers blamed Frazee alone for the loss of Ruth and the demise of the franchise in the 1920s, they got the wrong guy.

Not that Frazee didn't make mistakes. He did, but not with any malice. His only real error was misinterpreting what winning the World Series meant both for himself and his ballclub. Convinced of Johnson's incompetence and emboldened by victory, Frazee attempted to lead Major League Baseball into a new era. He naively believed that being right qualified one for leadership.

Frazee's success and daring offended many of his fellow magnates, who already viewed him suspiciously as an interloper in their exclusive club. No one was more offended than Ban Johnson.

Johnson had never wanted Frazee in his league, and that was never more true than after Frazee and the Red Sox came out on top in 1918. For as the Red Sox had surged to the championship, the outspoken Frazee had freely criticized Johnson's mismanagement of the war-shortened season. Before the World Series he even complained about umpire assignments and scheduling arrangements. The players' threatened strike increased the discord and distrust between the two men.

After the Series, they became even more estranged. Frazee complained bitterly when the Series emblems were withheld, but he was ignored. *The Sporting News*, which served as Johnson's mouthpiece and gave him full support, then reported that in 1918, Frazee, with entertainer George M. Cohan and fellow stage impresario Sam Harris, had tried to buy the New York Giants.

Frazee could not have conceived of a greater affront to Johnson, who still detested the National League in general and the Giants in particular. *The Sporting News* warned that "some who are not kindly disposed to him [Frazee] say that he will be displaced or eliminated," and that "he [Frazee] senses an effort . . . of 'getting' him as a magnate."

Frazee didn't back down. Any publicity was good publicity. He reveled in the growing controversy. When one of his theater partners passed away, Frazee responded to rumors that he would sell the team by toying with the press. "I was thinking about disposing of the Red Sox," he said, "but only for a minimum of one million dollars." But he decided to keep the club and even announced that he was considering a move to Braves Field. His production was a hit on any stage. Fenway Park real estate was becoming far too valuable for just a ballpark.

Nothing came of those plans, but as they receded from the headlines they were replaced by others. In late November, Frazee and New York Giants owner Harry Hempstead announced they had asked former president William Howard Taft to consider serving as a one-man commissioner of baseball, replacing the three-man National Commission headed by Johnson.

Although Taft turned them down, the entreaty was a frontal attack on Johnson's authority and front-page news in the *New York Times*. The baseball world awaited Johnson's reaction.

Publicly, there was none. Privately, Johnson twisted arms, and no other owners openly lent Frazee their support. In a story headlined "Looks Like He's Playing Lone Hand," *The Sporting News* reported that Frazee's coup had failed. But neither Frazee nor Johnson was finished.

Frazee knew that taking on Johnson was risky. As he left for the league meeting in Chicago on December 10, he admitted to the *Times* that he and Johnson were on a collision course, confessing, "I would rather lose the World Champion Red Sox than be downed by Johnson."

On the surface, the league meeting was uneventful. Johnson pruned the 1919 schedule to 140 games and cut rosters to save money. Frazee disagreed, but went along. He wanted to pay players during spring training, a plan the tight-fisted Johnson loathed. It failed.

But behind the scenes, Frazee was gaining support. White Sox owner Charles Comiskey had a falling out with Johnson over the assignment of a player and backed Frazee's idea of a one-man commission.

So did Yankee owners Colonel Tillinghurst l'Hommedieu Huston and beer baron Colonel Jacob Ruppert. Huston and Frazee were close and moved in the same social circles. The Yankees were still angry with Johnson for not being allowed to bid on Tris Speaker in 1916 and for the A's players Frazee had acquired in 1918. All three clubs were also miffed when they learned Johnson had recently propped up the Cleveland franchise with fifty-eight thousand dollars of his own money. They wanted Johnson gone.

Johnson and Frazee avoided confrontation and never spoke at the meeting. The armistice lasted only until Frazee boarded a train to return to New York.

Now Johnson cut loose and promptly told the *Times* he had "certified information . . . that gambling existed at Fenway Park, and under the league constitution membership in the American League could be terminated."

Johnson's sudden Puritanical conversion was akin to the logic of Claude Rains's character in the film *Casablanca* who, upon closing down Humphrey Bogart's Café Americain, announces, "I am shobked, *shocked*, to find that gambling is going on in here." Johnson had given lip service to the gambling problem for years, but had taken little action. The problem was no worse in Boston than it was elsewhere.

Frazee was greeted in New York with a banner headline in the *Times* that stated "Johnson's Declaration of War on Frazee Threatens Eruption of League." The article speculated that "Frazee will not allow

Johnson to oust him from the league without a struggle."

Frazee responded in a story headlined "Boston Club Owner Defies Johnson to Force Him Out of the American League," saying he'd done all he could to oust gamblers from Fenway. "It has seemed a war of extermination on the part of Mr. Johnson," lamented Frazee, "since I bought the Boston American League club . . . Mr. Johnson seems to pick me out as his particular target."

Johnson hoped Frazee would simply get mad and sell out, but he underestimated Frazee's resolve and knowledge of legal issues. Frazee knew the courts would overrule any attempt by Johnson to revoke his franchise. When Frazee refused to be cowed, Johnson made a tactical retreat.

Like their counterparts in the recent war, Johnson and Frazee dug in and prepared for an extended siege. Neither was prepared to give ground. Johnson wanted Frazee out — someday, some way — while Frazee was determined to stick around until either Johnson was ousted or he could leave on his own terms, for a fair price.

The first few months of the standoff passed quietly as plans for the 1919 season occupied both men. With the impending return of people like Jack Barry and Duffy Lewis, Frazee had players to spare.

The Yankees didn't, but unlike most other clubs, they had money, for the two colonels were filthy rich. So on December 18, 1918, Frazee sold some of his surplus, shipping Duffy Lewis, Ernie Shore, and Dutch Leonard to New York for some minor talent and between fifteen and fifty thousand dollars. It was just the first of many deals the two clubs would make over the next several seasons strengthening their alliance against Johnson.

The deal served Frazee on several levels: clearing Boston's roster, providing him with ready cash were he to fall into a protracted legal battle with Johnson, and, perhaps most significantly, ensuring the continued allegiance of Ruppert and Huston to his cause.

It didn't hurt the Red Sox, for only Leonard had made a contribution in 1918. The acquisition of Bush and Strunk and the emergence of Ruth as an outfielder made Shore and Lewis expendable. Leonard refused to report, so he was eventually sold to Cleveland for another seventy-five hundred dollars. Before spring training, Fred Thomas and Sam Agnew were similarly sold for cash.

Still, the 1919 Red Sox looked strong. They retained their top four starters from 1918 — Ruth, Mays, Bush, and Jones — and in Strunk, Hooper, Schang, McInnis, and Scott, their best position players. Frazee even traded for veteran Ossie Vitt of Detroit to patch the hole at third. The club was so well stocked that George Whiteman, hero of the Series, was quietly released. Although he played professional baseball for another decade, he never made another appearance in a major league uniform.

The Sox were no worse off than before the war, and with Ruth's emergence as a hitter, they were probably better. Ed Barrow looked forward to Ruth returning to the pitching rotation, pinch-hitting, and taking the occasional turn in the outfield.

But Babe had other ideas. After doing double duty in 1918 he felt underpaid. Advisor Johnny Igoe, who owned a Boston drugstore and later dealt in bootleg liquor, convinced him to hold out for a better contract, despite the fact that he was already signed for seven thousand dollars for the 1919 season.

In January Ruth outlined his demands, telling Frazee he wanted either a one-year contract for fifteen thousand dollars or a three-year deal for thirty thousand dollars. And he didn't want to pitch anymore. Frazee laughed him out of the office.

Every player wanted more money, and Frazee played hardball with them all. Harry Hooper said he was making more on his ranch than in baseball and threatened to retire.

Over the next few weeks, Frazee and Ruth continued to snipe at each other. When Ruth threatened to retire and become a boxer or an actor, Frazee warned, "If Ruth doesn't want to work for the Red Sox . . . we can make an advantageous trade."

Spring training began in mid-March, with the abbreviated season slated to begin on April 23. The delay gave both parties extra time to talk contract. Frazee and McGraw's Giants had agreed to train together in Tampa, Florida, to take advantage of Ruth's drawing power in exhibition games, but without Ruth, the pairing didn't make much sense.

With Frazee's lucrative spring plans at risk, and

Ruth worried about the trade rumors, both men got antsy. They agreed to the three-year, thirty-thousand-dollar deal.

Ruth arrived in Tampa and made his customary first appearances in the field as he slowly got his arm into shape. He wowed observers with his hitting, indicating that his 1918 performance, although made against sub-par pitching in a war year, was the real thing.

He pitched a few innings in a scrimmage, but when the exhibition season began on April 4, Ruth played left field and continued his prodigious clouting. He smacked one of his longest home runs ever, a blast variously estimated at between 500 and 600 feet, still marked today by a plaque on the campus of the University of Tampa.

As the Sox barnstormed north, crowds turned out in droves to see Ruth hit. Boston's pitching continued to impress and gave Barrow no reason to send Ruth to the mound.

Yet Barrow was not yet convinced that Ruth's hitting was genuine. Neither were some other longtime baseball men, like John McGraw, who predicted that if Ruth "plays every day the bum will hit into a hundred double plays." That spring Ruth had done most of his damage against second-line pitching and those still working their way into shape. But as Opening Day approached, Hooper and Everett Scott lobbied Barrow to keep Ruth in the outfield. He reluctantly agreed, but cautioned that if Ruth slumped, he would have to pitch.

Barrow hadn't forgotten that much of Ruth's hitting in 1918 had come in streaks, that he'd struggled against lefties, that Fenway's spacious right field robbed him of much of his home run power (only eleven of Ruth's eventual forty-nine home runs in a Boston uniform were hit at Fenway Park), and that Boston had won a World Series in which Ruth had starred, not with his bat, but with his left arm. Besides, there was simply no standard with which to compare Ruth's work at the plate, which tested the borders of belief. No one had ever hit home runs as long and far as Ruth. To expect him to continue to do so was rank speculation.

That wasn't Barrow's only worry. Ruth's off-field behavior and effect on team chemistry was of equal or greater concern. He'd proven undependable, jumping the club twice in 1918 then hurting his finger during the Series. Relying on Ruth appeared increasingly risky.

Still, when the Red Sox opened the season at the Polo Grounds in New York against the Yankees, they were favored to win the pennant. They made that prediction look conservative, as Ruth, batting fourth and playing left field, hit a ball over Duffy Lewis's head for a home run, and Carl Mays shut down the New Yorkers for a 10-0 Boston win.

Boston won their second game 8-0 in another shutout, and Ruth blasted a triple. His hot hitting continued the next day as he doubled and tripled off Washington's Walter Johnson, and Mays won for his second time, 6-5.

But Ruth's ceaseless merrymaking still concerned Barrow. He sat in the hotel lobby one night and waited for him until 4:00 A.M. before he gave up. Barrow didn't mention his stakeout to Ruth, and that afternoon Ruth went hitless as the club suffered its first loss, 4-3.

The next evening, Barrow paid a hotel porter to play detective and tell him when Ruth came in. The porter knocked on Barrow's door at 6:00 A.M.

Barrow went to Ruth's room and found the slugger in bed, but fully dressed, smoking a pipe and in his cups. Disgusted, he told Ruth he'd see him at the ballpark.

Ruth arrived at the park in a fighting mood. In the clubhouse he confronted his manager, telling him, "If you ever come to my room again, you son of a bitch, I'll punch you right in the nose."

Barrow and Ruth spent a few uneasy moments fuming nose-to-nose before being separated. Barrow suspended him and Boston won anyway, 6-1.

The celebrated incident cooled later that day, and when Ruth apologized, manager and player reached an understanding. Barrow promised to stop the bed checks if Ruth simply left him a note each night telling him when he got in. The arrangement worked. Neither man confronted the other on the issue again.

Ruth was reinstated just in time for Boston's home opener on May 1. Although Babe doubled in his first at bat, he played poorly in the outfield and Boston lost 7-3. The next day, he went hitless and again

Boston lost. Barrow and Frazee announced he would return to the pitching rotation and play the outfield only occasionally.

The move paid off as Ruth, despite pitching only once all spring, beat New York 3-2 and helped his own cause by doubling in a run. But Ruth was back in left field a few days later and didn't pitch another game for nearly two weeks.

He also didn't hit, and neither did anyone else on the team. The Sox went into an extended slump. Joe Bush had arm trouble and only Carl Mays was pitching very well. By the end of the month, the Red Sox were in sixth place, below .500, far behind the first-place White Sox, out of the pennant race altogether.

No single player was more responsible than Ruth. He was barely hitting .200 with only a couple of home runs, numbers either Whiteman or Lewis could easily have matched. His defense was equally poor. Although he won when he pitched, he wasn't throwing well, and his resistance to regular use forced the Red Sox to use pitchers who were clearly inferior. Ruth's slide from being one of baseball's best pitchers to one of average ability in 1919 was as precipitous as his rise as an offensive player had been the year before.

Ruth was also causing trouble in the clubhouse, lobbying to have Jack Barry resume his managerial duties. Harry Hooper also wanted the job and, accustomed to being the club's offensive star, was jealous of Ruth's special treatment.

Frazee and Barrow tried to get some help before the season slipped away, buying outfielder Bill Lamar from the Yankees, and over the remainder of the year he hit nearly .300. In late June, they shipped Barry and Amos Strunk to the A's for twenty-six-year-old Braggo Roth and twenty-two-year-old second baseman Red Shannon. Moving Barry helped quell the dissension, but he refused to report and retired. Frazee made up the difference with cash. When the trade was made, Roth was hitting .323 for the last-place A's and outslugging Ruth.

Ruth finally emerged from his slump, raising his

In 1923, his final season as Red Sox owner, Harry Frazee confers with manager Frank Chance at Yankee Stadium.

average above .300 by the end of June while cracking home runs at a record pace. But it made no difference in the won-loss column, for Braggo Roth immediately got hurt and the Red Sox slipped further below .500, finishing the month a pitiful 12-16.

Ruth became the entire story. He was the only reason fans were coming out to Fenway Park and he knew it, demanding to play the outfield exclusively. Barrow caved in as Frazee concluded it was time to give the people some of what they wanted. The pennant was already lost.

On July 5 against Philadelphia, Ruth cracked two home runs in a single game for the first time in his career, including his first over the left-field wall at Fenway, serving notice that for the remainder of the month he would hit home runs as no man had ever done before. But Ruth couldn't stem the team's slide.

Pitcher Carl Mays was the only Boston player performing to his usual standard. But Mays had pitched in hard luck all year long. From May 13 through June 16, Mays gave up only twelve runs in five starts yet lost all five times because of Boston's atrocious defense and failure to score a single run.

The temperamental pitcher grew increasingly frustrated and in Philadelphia threw a ball at a heckler. Ban Johnson fined him one hundred dollars, but Mays refused to pay.

Mays's life was a shambles. His mother's house had burned and Mays thought it was arson. He'd recently married and there were reports of trouble at home. A 3-0 loss to St. Louis on July 9 dropped his record to 5-11 despite the fact that he sported the fourth-lowest ERA in the league.

The last straw came on July 13 in Chicago. In the first inning, with one out and a man on, second baseman Red Shannon fielded a double-play ball, swiped at the runner, missed him, and then had no time to get the runner at first. Mays lost his composure and gave up three consecutive hits and four runs.

In the second inning, Eddie Collins tried to steal and Wally Schang's throw to second hit Mays in the head. In the bottom of the inning, the pitcher led off for Boston and singled, but was left stranded. Instead of returning to the mound he stalked off into the clubhouse, showered, took a cab back to the hotel, gathered his belongings, and was on a train before the game was over. Boston lost 14-9.

Back in Boston Mays told reporter Burt Whitman, "I'll never pitch another game for the Red Sox . . . I have pitched better ball than ever before. The entire team is up in the air and things have gone from bad to worse . . . so I am getting out . . . I believe the team ought to be fighting for the lead right now, but there is not a chance of this with the way things are being handled." Mays left town and went fishing.

He never directly addressed the reasons he left the club, although years later he admitted, "I was young, impetuous, hot-tempered, discouraged, frustrated and in debt . . . At that moment my whole world was tumbling down." The special treatment accorded Ruth was likely the cause of his discontent.

As Mays baited hooks, Frazee was deluged with trade offers. Half the teams in the league put in bids for the star hurler, including an offer of fifty thousand dollars cash from the White Sox.

Ban Johnson took great umbrage to Mays's walk-out, told the bidders there would be no deal until Boston had dealt with Mays. In Johnson's mind that meant a suspension and healthy fine.

Frazee disagreed. Once it became obvious Mays wasn't going to come back, Frazee concluded a suspension or fine would only postpone the inevitable. So he sat back and waited for the price to rise.

On July 29, just before the August 1 trading deadline, Frazee weighed all offers and sent Mays to New York for forty thousand dollars, pitcher Allan Russell, and sore-armed prospect Bob McGraw. He explained that he had accepted New York's offer because they were the only team that offered both players and cash.

Although the trade has since been cited as an early example of the "rape" of the team, it wasn't. Mays went 9-3 over the remainder of the year for the Yankees, but Russell was 9-4 for the lackluster Sox. Frazee didn't pocket all the money, either. He outbid several other clubs for the contract of Joe Wilhoit, who had hit .422 for Wichita of the Western League.

But when Ban Johnson heard about the sale, he went ballistic, believing the two clubs had conspired to challenge his authority. He called the deal off, ordered Frazee to return the money, and suspended Mays indefinitely.

The two clubs ignored him. "This action of Johnson's is a joke," said Frazee bluntly. "Evidently he is still trying to run the Boston ball club and make things unpleasant for its management . . . the New York owners must thrash it out with Mr. Johnson." The simmering conflict between Frazee and Johnson flared up again. The eventual fallout would claim several victims, eventually toppling Johnson and ruining Frazee's reputation in Boston forever. The once-proud Boston franchise would serve as their battleground.

The league president ordered the Yankees not to pitch Mays. The outraged Yankees appealed the suspension, a motion Johnson summarily denied. So the two colonels went to court and secured an injunction restraining Johnson from interfering. Mays entered New York's rotation and all parties involved called their lawyers.

All the while Babe Ruth continued his assault on the record books, despite being forced to pitch occasionally to make up for the loss of Mays. As July turned to August the Red Sox were 39-48. Ruth, however, was hitting .321, among the league leaders, and had cracked sixteen home runs, tying the American

League record held by Socks Seybold. The existing modern major league mark of twenty-four, set by the Phillies' Gavvy Cravath in 1915, was within reach, as was the all-time mark of twenty-seven set by Ned Williamson of the Cubs in 1884, who had taken advantage of a right-field porch only 215 feet from home.

Fans relished following Ruth's record chase over the final two months of the season. Although he slumped in early August when the Red Sox played at home, as soon as the team went on the road Babe took advantage of the smaller ballparks to go on another tear, hitting seven home runs in twelve days. In some previous years, seven home runs in a season had led the league.

Frazee milked Ruth's popularity for all it was worth. On September 1, Labor Day, the Sox announced that Ruth would pitch the first game of a doubleheader against Washington, and thirty thousand fans turned out.

Ruth knew how to work a crowd. In the first game he threw what would be the last great game of his major league career and beat Washington 2-1. He also tripled to drive in one run and scored the other. In game two he hit his twenty-fourth home run to tie Cravath.

Meanwhile the Yankees and Johnson pled their case over Mays's sale to a legal referee. Johnson testified for over two hours, failing to impress the New York state attorney who referred to him as a "czar" and "unmolested despot." The attorney found that Johnson was unable to dispense equitable justice because of his investment in Cleveland, describing him as "curiously slothful" in this regard. The first round went to the Yankees, and the case was passed on to the New York Supreme Court for final disposition.

The suit caused a split in the entire league. For as Comiskey and the White Sox reinforced their alliance with the Yankees and Frazee, the other five league owners remained cowed and backed Johnson.

But there was still baseball to be played. After two more home runs Ruth went into another drought as fans rooted for a new record.

On September 19, the Chicago White Sox arrived in Boston on the verge of clinching the American League pennant. After a single game on September 19, the two clubs were scheduled to play a double-header the following day, which Frazee promoted as "Babe Ruth Day," ensuring another good crowd.

Boston dropped the first game of the series, yet the most notable event of the day took place not in Fenway Park, but in the Buckminster Hotel in Kenmore Square. After the game, notorious Boston gambler and Royal Rooter Sport Sullivan, who knew everybody in baseball, accepted an invitation to meet with White Sox first baseman Chick Gandil.

Gandil knew exactly who he was dealing with and got to the point quickly. As Sullivan fished for tips on the World Series, Gandil said, "I think we can put it in the bag." He wasn't referring to winning — he was referring to throwing the Series.

Sullivan was intrigued. Although he has since been mischaracterized as a minor figure, Sullivan was both wealthy and well connected, friends with guys like George M. Cohan, and he lived in a mansion with servants in nearby Sharon. He knew that Gandil was proposing something much more than the occasional single-game fixes that had become almost standard in the postseason classic.

Sullivan agreed to help out, and the greatest scandal in the history of baseball was in the works. The fallout would eventually help topple Johnson and turn Babe Ruth into baseball's savior.

On his day Ruth received cash and gifts from fans worth several thousand dollars. Although he later complained that all Frazee gave him that day was "a cigar," the *Boston Herald* reported that Frazee gave Ruth a bonus of five thousand dollars to make up for his inability to earn several pitching-related contract incentives. Ruth started game one on the mound, and although he pitched poorly and finished the game in left field, his ninth-inning home run won the game and tied Williamson's record. Then in game two he scored the winning run as the Red Sox swept Chicago.

Boston finished the season on the road, and Ruth hit two more home runs, including number twenty-nine in Washington on September 27 to set a new record. But Ruth angered both his teammates and Boston management by skipping the last game to play in a lucrative exhibition game in Baltimore.

He hadn't asked permission, he'd simply left. Boston lost, 8-7, landing the club in sixth place, twenty and a half games back of the White Sox. Had they won, they'd have finished fifth. Nevertheless, Ruth ended the season as the most popular and most talked-about player in the game, sporting a .322 batting average to go with his league-leading 114 RBIs and 103 runs scored.

Yet even as league attendance more than doubled in 1919, crowds in Boston, even with Ruth, lagged behind. They fell from third to fifth in league attendance. The Sox drew just over four hundred seventeen thousand fans, only one hundred seventy thousand more than in 1918 and far fewer than in their championship seasons of 1912, 1915, and 1916. Despite his home-run record, Ruth wasn't worth as much at the gate in Boston as a winning team.

The Cincinnati Reds stumped the experts by dumping the White Sox in the World Series, and the usual rumors of a fix spread, but few paid attention at the time. Sport Sullivan, who'd done his job and made all the arrangements, cleared fifty thousand dollars — which he promptly lost at a Maryland racetrack.

The court battle between Johnson and the Yankees was the big baseball news of the fall of 1919. New York Supreme Court Justice Robert Wagner presided over the hearing.

Johnson didn't stand a chance. He was the visiting team in the New York court and the colonels and Frazee were all close to Wagner. In fact, the future United States senator later served as Frazee's divorce attorney. On October 25, Wagner issued a permanent injunction restraining Johnson from interfering with Mays's use by the Yankees, finding that Johnson did not "evince a desire to do equity to all parties concerned."

It was a crushing defeat for Johnson, one that noted baseball historian David Voigt has since referred to as "a blow from which he would never fully recover." Yet it would take several years for Johnson to fall. On his way down, he was determined to bring others with him. The battle lines were now clearly drawn, with Frazee, Comiskey, and the two colonels on one side — dubbed "the Insurrectos" by the press — and Johnson and the rest of the American League owners on the other. The political standoff exerted a heavy influence over the events of the next several months and would leave a lasting and indelible mark upon the Red Sox franchise. In the process, unfairly and for all time, Harry Frazee was demonized.

The legal victory emboldened the Insurrectos, who, by chance, were all serving rotating terms on the league's three-member board of directors. They called for Johnson to resign, contending that according to the league constitution Johnson, who'd rammed through a motion in 1910 giving him a twenty-year contract, was holding his post illegally.

They also threatened to withdraw from the American League and form a new league, taking with them some National League clubs, who were ecstatic as they watched Johnson twitch in the wind. Incredulous reporters referred to the new circuit as the "Hot Air," or "Pipe Dream League."

But Johnson, although wounded, still had leverage. Five votes were needed in the eight-team league to take action. He still had the allegiance of what the press termed "the Loyal Five" franchises and was prepared to fight it out at the league meeting in December.

The meeting was as contentious as any in baseball history. Over the course of several days, buoyed by lawyers, the Insurrectos and Johnson battled. But Johnson had the votes, which no number of lawyers could change. He ousted the Insurrectos from the board and suspended the remainder of the meeting until February. In response, the Insurrectos filed a laundry list of lawsuits.

Over the next two months, both sides maneuvered to gain the upper hand, calling in every available chit and marker. Frazee soon discovered that Johnson again held the advantage.

Ruth had capitalized on his sudden fame, barnstorming around the country hitting home runs before landing in Los Angeles, where he was testing the waters of the film industry. He earned ten thousand dollars on his sojourn, which, combined with his baseball salary, bonus, and other income, pushed his annual take toward thirty thousand dollars for the year.

That wasn't enough. Ruth still felt underpaid and told the press he wanted a twenty-thousand-dollar contract for 1920 or he might not play at all. At the time, Ty Cobb and Eddie Collins, who each earned fifteen thousand dollars annually, topped the scale.

Frazee laughed. Ruth was under contract. If he didn't want to play in 1920, fine.

Frazee had never shown any patience in the theater with those who failed to live up to their contracts or tried to squeeze him. The show must go on — the players were interchangeable and secondary to the larger production. He had fired performers and writers who had failed to live up to their contracts. To Frazee, ballplayers were no different. Besides, in the post–Federal league era, salaries were dropping. If he caved in to Ruth again, every player on the team would want more.

In the larger scheme of things, Ruth wasn't even Frazee's most pressing problem. His war with Johnson and his determination to retain his team were paramount. Ruth was a worry Frazee simply couldn't afford.

The usual bickering between club owner and star commenced. Frazee announced he'd trade anyone on the team except Harry Hooper.

In late December, the Boston press weighed in on the issue, publishing a series of puff pieces that touted Ruth's batting achievements. Yet at the same time, they recognized his potential for disruption. On December 21, the *Post*'s Paul Shannon allowed that Ruth "has hurt morale considerably," and speculated that he might be traded. On December 30 he added that many Boston veterans were "following Big Babe's example," and wanted to renegotiate. "If Ruth makes good on his threat and retires from the game he will be badly missed," he continued. "But even as big a figure as Ruth is, the public would soon forget all about him . . . a contract is a contract. Right is right in baseball as in anything else. In no other business in the world would a man sign an agreement then hope to evade the terms later on."

Neither Shannon nor anyone else in Boston knew that Ruth was already the property of the Yankees.

Four days earlier, on December 26, Frazee had agreed to sell Ruth to New York for a total of one hundred thousand dollars — twenty-five thousand dollars in cash and three twenty-five-thousand-dollar notes, payable at one-year intervals, at 6 percent interest. The deal, the most lucrative in baseball his-

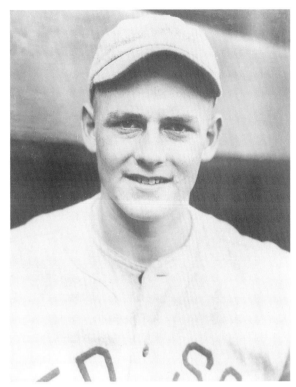

Righthanded pitcher Waite Hoyt won only ten games in two seasons with the Red Sox in 1919 and 1920. He was one of several future Hall of Famers eventually dealt to the New York Yankees.

tory at the time, was conditional on New York getting Ruth under contract. Frazee and Ruppert also reached another agreement, upon which — significantly — the Ruth sale was not contingent. Ruppert agreed to either help Frazee obtain a loan or loan him outright three hundred thousand dollars, with Fenway Park as the security.

Had Frazee put Ruth on the open market, he likely could have received more, for the St. Louis Cardinals had recently turned down an offer of seventy thousand dollars plus four players for star infielder Rogers Hornsby. But Frazee's war with Johnson limited his market. He accepted the Yankee offer of cash and notes only after Ed Barrow told him there were no players on the New York roster he wanted.

The deal still worked for Frazee on several fronts. It rid him of a problem, strengthened his coalition with New York in the war with Johnson, and gave him the cash he knew he'd need to rebuild his ballclub.

Yet it wasn't one-sided on Frazee's behalf. Apart from the risk of taking on Ruth, the Yankees didn't want to pay Frazee the full amount in cash — they, too, were worried about their legal problems with Johnson and concerned that the New York Giants, from which they rented the Polo Grounds, might give them the boot. They paid on the installment plan in case they had to build a new ballpark.

The loan was another matter entirely. That agreement wasn't between the two ballclubs, but between Ruppert and Frazee. And according to a notation in the notebooks of Harold Kaese, longtime baseball writer for the *Boston Globe*, Frazee already had negotiated a two-hundred-fifty-thousand-dollar loan using Fenway as security from another party, which he canceled when Ruppert offered more money at better terms.

Like Frazee, Ruppert didn't have all his eggs in one basket. Prohibition was due to go in effect in just a few days, but the brewer had already made his fortune. The loan, secured by Fenway Park, was virtually risk-free — the land on which Fenway sat was worth more than the loan amount. Frazee was eyeing the purchase of a New York theater, and Ruppert was simply offering him more flexible terms than a bank would. Besides, in case of disaster, having Fenway Park in Ruppert's hands was far better for Frazee than the alternative. If Frazee defaulted, he could always rent the park back from Ruppert. A bank would sell it off, and Johnson and his cronies would surely be waiting in the wings.

Three days later, while Ruth's sale was still a secret, Frazee began rebuilding his club, trading Roth and Shannon, both of whom had been disappointments, to Washington for veteran infielder Eddie Foster, outfielder Mike Menosky, and lefthanded pitcher Harry Harper.

Harper was the key to the deal. Only twenty-four, he was considered one of the best young pitchers in the league. He'd pitched in hard luck for the seventh-place Senators in 1919, going 6-21, but his ERA was a respectable 3.72, and he helped offset the loss of Mays. Frazee didn't mind that the trade added to his contractual obligations, for Ruth's sale gave him some maneuverability. The press reacted favorably. Paul Shannon even called Harper "the biggest find we have acquired since Babe Ruth."

New York manager Miller Huggins traveled to California, met with Ruth, and got him to agree to fulfill his existing contract and accept a twenty-thousand-dollar bonus. The deal was announced on January 5, 1920.

The news hit Boston hard, but none were hit harder than Boston sportswriters, who cherished Ruth as good copy. The deal was the front-page news.

Two cartoons best illustrated the reaction. One from the *Boston Herald* showed "For Sale" signs placed before cherished Boston institutions like Faneuil Hall and the Boston Public Library. But the *Post*, despite running an editorial that bemoaned the sale, published a cartoon that illustrated the logic of the deal. Entitled "The Bull in Frazee's China Shop," it showed Frazee holding the tail of the out-of-control bull (Ruth) amidst shattered glassware labeled "team morale," "disgruntled players," and "discipline." Jacob Ruppert held the shop's door open, waving a bag of money and saying, "This way out Harry."

The deal was not greeted with the explosion of utter outrage characterized in most subsequent accounts. For the record, the *Herald* and *Evening American* were most critical of the deal, the *Post* relatively neutral, while the *Globe* and *Evening Transcript* backed Frazee.

Frazee was prepared to be criticized and released a fifteen-hundred-word statement that outlined his thinking. Ruth, said Frazee,

. . . had become impossible and the Boston club could no longer put up with his eccentricities. While Ruth without question is the greatest hitter that the game has seen, he is likewise one of the most inconsiderate men that ever wore a baseball uniform . . . Twice before he has jumped the club and revolted. He refused to obey orders of the manager and he became so arrogant that discipline in his case was ruined. He would not pitch . . . had no regard for anyone but himself . . . was a bad influence upon other and still younger players on the team. He left us in the lurch many times . . . two or three times [in 1919] . . . Ruth was given permission to run to another town where he got four or five hundred dollars for playing, and at the same time the club was paying him for his services . . . A team of players working harmoniously together is always to be preferred to that possessing one star who hugs the limelight to himself. And that is what I'm after.

Frazee's grandson recalls that these were the reasons for the sale he heard about while growing up in the 1930s. "He [Ruth] had jumped the club," he recalls. "He was making demands. He was just hard to get along with. After he signed contracts, he wouldn't live up to them. This just infuriated Big Harry. In the theater, he was used to people living up to their contracts."

Frazee's statement continued.

Ruth is taking on weight tremendously . . . He doesn't care to keep himself in shape, . . . He has a floating cartilage in his knee [which] may make him a cripple at any time . . . New York is the only outfit in baseball that could have bought Ruth. Had they been willing to trade players, I would have preferred the exchange [but] Huggins would have had to wreck his ball club . . . I am willing to accept the verdict of baseballdom and I think that fair-minded parties of the sport will agree with me that Ruth could not remain in Boston under existing conditions.

Local baseball figures like Hugh Duffy, Bill Carrigan, and Fred Tenney all agreed with Frazee. And Ruth's Boston teammates stayed suspiciously quiet, giving their tacit support to the transaction.

But the transaction provided fuel for those writers already predisposed against Frazee. Longtime friends of Ban Johnson gave plenty of ink to disgruntled Boston fans, primarily former Royal Rooters still miffed at Frazee for pulling the plug on their perks. Charley Lavis said, "I figure the Red Sox are ruined," and 'Nuf 'Ced McGreevey added, "The Babe and I have been friends for years. I think every Boston fan will regret his departing."

There were even more subtle, political reasons why the deal made sense to Frazee. It bolstered the alliance of the Insurrectos and provided him with operating capital and a reserve were Johnson to try to mount a legal challenge to his right to operate the franchise. Significantly, the only other proposition he had received for Ruth that off-season was from fellow Insurrecto Charlie Comiskey, who offered Joe Jackson.

In hindsight, there were plenty of baseball reasons for Frazee to deal Ruth. Although the Babe went on to crack another 665 home runs, at the time of the sale he still represented a significant risk and was clearly worth more to the Yankees than he was to Boston. New York needed a draw, and in the Polo Grounds Ruth hit like nowhere else.

Apart from his behavioral problems, Ruth's lifestyle didn't suggest he would have a long career. At a time when many players were washed up at age thirty, Ruth, almost twenty-five and growing heavier and more out of shape each year, was a profound physical risk.

Neither was his continued stardom a sure bet. Most observers thought his pitching career was over, and continued improvement at the plate was no certainty. Lefthanded pitching still gave him trouble, he was prone to prolonged slumps, and his power wasn't as obvious at Fenway Park with its distant right-field fence. Never in his career did he hit a ball into the bleachers there.

Had Ruth stayed in Boston, he may have still become the greatest home run hitter of his era, but he never would have approached the marks he set with the Yankees, either in an individual season or for his career. Of additional significance is the fact that the lively ball, which later inflated his power, had yet to be introduced. There was simply no way to predict what Ruth would become. The Yankees were taking a huge and expensive gamble.

Frazee told the press that he planned to use the proceeds of the sale to help strengthen the club, which, in fact, he had already done with the Harper deal. Indeed, he almost immediately moved to sell the notes at a discount in order to receive the full amount up front.

The long-accepted interpretation of the sale of Ruth and others to New York contends that Frazee was in financial trouble and used the proceeds to finance his stage interests, which eventually paid off in the success of *No, No, Nanette*. As a result, Boston was left with a cursed, second-rate franchise. Frazee has been described as everything from a simple fool and selfish buffoon to a con man and the devil incarnate. Yet this version of history, like a third-rate melodrama that supplies an obvious villain, is spurious on its face and virtually unsupported by any factual evidence apart from a series of misconceptions and distortions. The truth is a more complicated story.

Significantly, in light of the events of the next few months and the way history has judged Harry Frazee, at the time of the sale there was no mention anywhere that Frazee was in any kind of financial trouble whatsoever.

That's because he wasn't. All evidence indicates otherwise. Stories that put him in the poorhouse were created out of whole cloth years later by Boston writers who hated him from the very beginning because of his background and alleged Jewish genealogy.

Frazee never bothered to correct the perception because, on the one hand, he really didn't care what the press said about him, and on the other, it was and still is sound business practice for baseball owners to have their wealth underestimated. Crying "poor mouth" — or not correcting others who do — helps hold down salaries. It served Frazee well for some in Boston to believe that he was broke just as it helped him in New York for some to believe he was Jewish.

The press reported that Frazee turned a profit on the Red Sox in 1919. And Harry Frazee's grandson recalls that no financial trouble was ever mentioned by his father when he was growing up, nor has he ever

uncovered any evidence of it in family papers. "Harry had so much going on [financially]," he recalls. "He had several balls in the air. He had a theater chain, three Schubert theaters [which he leased], his [own] two theaters, a real estate management firm, a real estate investment company, another kind of management company, and a stock brokerage company."

If anything, Frazee's stock was rising. On December 3, 1919, his new play, *My Lady Friends*, opened to rave reviews, eventually running for 228 performances. According to the *Boston Post*, at the time of Ruth's sale the show was earning Frazee three thousand dollars a week. He put it on the road, and a Boston engagement was similarly successful. Frazee was looking to expand — he had his eye on the purchase of a New York theater. But potential trouble was lurking nearby. Ban Johnson hadn't forgotten about Harry Frazee.

In May of 1919 Frazee stopped making interest payments to Joseph Lannin. Then on November 1, 1919, Frazee purposely missed payment on a note for one hundred twenty-five thousand dollars.

He had been assessed Boston's thirty-thousand-dollar share of the AL's legal settlement with the Federal League, but Frazee thought the fee was Lannin's responsibility. He had the money, or at least much of it. He simply wanted Lannin to pay settlement costs.

Lannin kept demanding payment and Frazee kept ignoring him. But when Ruth was sold, the dynamic changed.

After the sale, the Boston papers spread rumors of impending deals to make up for Ruth's loss. Other teams knew Boston was in the market for players, and Frazee and Barrow entertained a number of offers.

But Boston wasn't anxious to make a deal. The longer they waited, the more leverage they had.

Meanwhile, on February 1, the Yankees filed suit against Ban Johnson for five hundred thousand dollars over the Mays deal, for Johnson had withheld New York's third-place money and failed to recognize any game in which Mays pitched for New York. When

Waite Hoyt was known as "the Schoolboy" during his two seasons in Boston. During his stint he pitched with two future Hall of Famers named Pennock and Ruth who eventually became his teammates on the New York Yankees.

the suspended league meeting resumed in Chicago a week later, the war heated up again.

Wary of the cost of litigation, Johnson's "Loyal Five" temporarily broke ranks. They reinstated Mays, gave the Yankees their third-place money, and forced Johnson to cede much of his authority. In return, the Yankees dropped their lawsuits.

But Johnson didn't surrender. There was still revenge to consider. Getting Frazee now became his goal, much as Frazee himself had speculated years before when he charged that Johnson had made him "his particular target." That he was.

Just before the annual AL meeting, Johnson had attended the minor league meeting in Kansas City. Lannin, as owner of International League Buffalo, was also there. The two men, once at odds, now discovered they had a common enemy — Harry Frazee — and Lannin disliked Barrow as well. They apparently ironed out their earlier difficulties and hatched a plan.

For on February 9, as Frazee helped undermine Johnson in Chicago, Lannin did the same to Frazee in Boston. He slapped a lien on Fenway Park. Unless Lannin was paid off by March 3, he'd sell Fenway at auction. Although the *Post*'s Paul Shannon initially reported that "This action has nothing to do with the trouble between Frazee and Ban Johnson," he soon backed off, admitting that the timing of events suggested that "Johnson may have put something over" on Frazee.

Frazee was caught off-guard. He returned to Boston amid more rumors that he would sell. When Lannin heard this, he got another injunction that barred Frazee from "disposing of any more of the playing assets pending an accounting of affairs." On the precipice of spring training, with Ruth in New York and no one to replace him, Frazee was legally restrained from making any trades.

Johnson thought he had Frazee cornered and returned to the fray. He came to Boston intent on putting together a group to buy the Sox on the cheap and get rid of Frazee for good.

But Frazee showed amazing resilience. Under no circumstances was he going to allow Johnson the satisfaction of showing him the door. He spurned offers for the team, made some legal maneuvers against Lannin to gain some time, and started making plans for the 1920 season. Johnson returned to Chicago empty-handed.

The Red Sox began spring training in disarray. As Frazee had feared, catcher Wally Schang and third baseman Oscar Vitt had followed Ruth's lead and were holdouts. In the press, expectations were low. Joe Lannin even bragged to *The Sporting News*, "I have a better club than Frazee."

But a funny thing happened on the way to last place. The Sox played well in the South. Joe Bush's arm felt better, and holdovers Herb Pennock, Sam Jones, and Waite Hoyt, supplemented by Russell and Harry Harper, gave Boston the deepest pitching staff in the league. While the offense wasn't particularly potent, the team knew how to manufacture runs and the defense was superb. Even *The Sporting News* was forced to admit that the "team may not be such a wreck after all."

The Red Sox opened the season with two wins. On Patriots' Day, April 19, the Yankees came into Boston for a doubleheader.

Before ten thousand fans in the opener Waite Hoyt shut out New York, 4-0. Ruth received a huge ovation but did little damage against the twenty-year-old pitcher.

In game two, twenty-eight thousand more fans filled Fenway to hoot Yankee starter Carl Mays, who was "roasted unmercifully" by the crowd. Joe Bush downed the New Yorkers 8-3, and Boston took the final game of the series the next day. After twelve games, the Ruthless Red Sox were a surprising 10-2, and the Yankees were in the second division. Maybe Frazee had been right all along.

While the quick start relieved Frazee of one worry, he still had to foist off Lannin. Because of the lien, he had to allow his loan agreement with Ruppert to expire and was temporarily in no position to deal with banks. He asked Ruppert and Huston for an extension to May 15, ending a letter saying, "I need this agreement signed by you very badly to complete the balance of my negotiations."

The negotiations he was referring to were twofold. He needed both to settle his account with Lannin and to conclude a deal he'd agreed to on March 27 to buy the Harris Theater on 42nd Street in New York. Ruppert agreed to the extension.

Frazee knew Lannin had pushed too hard and a court case would hurt both parties. Besides, the "putsch" Lannin and Johnson had hoped to inspire had failed. Now Lannin just wanted to settle.

On May 10, *The Sporting News* reported that "the matter was compromised and settled to the satisfaction of both parties," as Lannin and Frazee settled out of court. Frazee had one less problem.

Another disappeared soon after. Suddenly optimistic about the season, Frazee signed Vitt and Schang for what *The Sporting News* reported as "pretty near what they asked for," hardly a move by an owner strapped for cash. The team suddenly looked like a sure-fire pennant contender. Babe who?

With the legal decks clear, the three-hundred-thousand-dollar loan from Ruppert went through on May 25. Six weeks later the *New York Times* reported that Frazee completed his purchase of the Harris Theater, which he renamed the Frazee. It was a savvy buy. Broadway was booming in the 1920s and theaters were in short supply. Frazee's purchase began earning money immediately.

Meanwhile the Red Sox continued to play better than expected, ending May at 22-14, just ahead of the 23-15 Yankees. Tim Hendryx, a journeyman who replaced Ruth in the lineup and from whom nothing was expected, was leading the league with a .397 batting average. Attendance at Fenway was holding steady, and in their first eight meetings the Ruthless Red Sox beat the Bambino's Yankees five times. Frazee looked like a genius.

Frazee might have been off the hook had not a streak of bad luck and a spate of injuries large and small exposed the club's weakness — depth — particularly for position players. Hendryx went down with a bad leg so Schang was moved to the outfield, but his replacement behind the plate, Roxy Walters, didn't hit. Then Hoyt pulled a groin muscle so badly he had surgery and missed thirteen weeks. Allan Russell collapsed from a cerebral hemorrhage and Harry Hooper was hospitalized with an abscess after he fouled a ball off his shin. The team's defense suffered, and now Boston lost the close games they had won during the first two months of the season. In June and July they were 18-38.

Barrow and Frazee tried to fill the holes, but were

unable to make any trades. They weren't dealing from strength to begin with, but there was another factor — Ban Johnson.

Although Johnson had been stripped of much of his power, he was still league president and wielded considerable influence over the Loyal Five. The three Insurrectos were virtually unable to make significant deals with the other five clubs in the league, all of whom knew they risked Johnson's wrath if they dealt with New York, Chicago, or Boston. Indeed, from 1920 through the end of Frazee's reign in 1923, Chicago made only one trade (with Boston), New York made seven deals (six with Boston and one with Washington), while of the eleven Red Sox trades, only three involved the Loyal Five, and one of those was for a player on the suspended list. Frazee's only

THE DEMONIZATION OF HARRY FRAZEE

History has judged Harry Frazee harshly as a figure of lasting contempt. That is no accident. For Frazee's lasting reputation is the only remnant of the war he waged with Ban Johnson. The victors write history, and although the battle between Johnson and Frazee was a virtual standoff, Johnson won the war in the press. Frazee paid the price.

Most Boston sportswriters of the era — notably the *Herald*'s Burt Whitman, Nick Flately of the *Evening American,* and Paul Shannon of the *Post* — were Ban Johnson partisans from the start. They disliked Frazee from the instant he bought the club because of his attitude, age, background, business, alleged Jewish background, and his suspension of perks for themselves and their friends. Most of the inaccuracies concerning Frazee begin with these men. They consistently cast Frazee in the worst possible light, without regard to fact, in some cases even recasting their own initially positive stories into revisionist accounts that completely disregarded the truth. Through *The Sporting News,* these impressions gained a national distribution.

Frazee never disputed their claims — he didn't care what people thought of him — and after he sold the Red Sox, neither did anyone else. But not until Frazee's death 1929 did the assassinations on his character expand and begin to supplant the truth.

Paul Shannon's obituary of Frazee in the *Post* is most notorious for its inaccuracies, and he again raised questions over Frazee's religion. Those distributed by the Associated Press and the *New York Times* are little better. The *Times* made a particularly egregious error, reporting that Frazee died nearly broke. A few days later, they corrected that inaccuracy, but subsequent Frazee chroniclers have overlooked the error. The value of his estate was eventually reported to be approximately 1.3 million dollars.

Noted baseball writer Fred Lieb then expanded on these misconceptions. A sportswriter and columnist for several New York papers from 1911 through 1934, a frequent contributor to *Baseball Magazine,* and a correspondent and columnist for *The Sporting News,* Lieb was the ultimate insider, a man who valued his contacts with figures like Ban Johnson and Judge Landis. His work reveals that he saw himself not just as an observer, but as part of the game he covered. His efforts were rewarded by recognition in the Baseball Hall of Fame.

After publishing his first book on spiritualism, in the 1940s and 1950s he wrote an influential series of team histories, including the first substantial history of the club, *The Boston Red Sox,* published in 1947. For years, Lieb's accounts served as sort of unofficial "official" histories. While they were easily the best such books of their kind at the time of publication, today they appear unscholarly and anachronistic. They are full of fanciful anecdotes, secondhand reporting, and inaccuracies.

In *The Boston Red Sox,* Lieb devotes several chapters to the Frazee years. Apart from two paraphrased references to conversations he claims to have had with Frazee, Lieb apparently uses Burt Whitman as his major source in regard to Frazee, including his notorious phrase, "the Rape of the Red Sox." Lieb miscasts Frazee as a failure in the theater and creates a caricature of Frazee as a greedy, self-centered fool who maliciously ran the franchise into the ground.

Subsequent accounts appear to have been written almost entirely from Frazee's obituaries and the fictions spouted in Lieb's book, ignoring the primary historical resources, such as newspaper accounts and standard theatrical reference works, that tell a different tale. With each retelling of his story, Frazee has become more a character of fiction and less a man of history. He became the ultimate scapegoat for devoted fans who have found the failures of the franchise increasingly hard to swallow, and for a franchise that has never been eager to admit to its own failures. ⊘

options in 1920, Chicago and New York, were battling for a pennant and couldn't risk a deal. The Red Sox were effectively excluded from the trade market.

But in June they did pick up Cleveland pitcher Elmer Myers on waivers. He was the league's best hurler for the rest of the year, winning nine of ten, but it wasn't enough.

Johnson didn't hide his enmity toward Boston. Earlier that year Barrow had loaned third baseman prospect Harold "Pie" Traynor to Portsmouth, Virginia, making a standard "gentleman's agreement" that Traynor belonged to Boston. But a few months later, Portsmouth sold Traynor to Pittsburgh for ten thousand dollars. Barrow appealed to Johnson, but the league president delighted in taking no action. Traynor soon manned third for Pittsburgh and became an all-time great.

Frazee and Johnson continued sniping at one another whenever they had a chance. When Boston's injured players returned to the lineup in August, the club started winning again and finished fifth with a record of 72-81, only a few percentage points worse than the year before. New York finished third, three games behind Chicago and the pennant-winning Indians. Ruth had been incredible, hitting fifty-four home runs, batting .376, driving in 137, and scoring 158.

Frazee was, however briefly, vindicated. For without Ruth Boston had finished in virtually the same position as the 1919 club (with an even better record at home) and had even scored more runs per game. Attendance held steady and *The Sporting News* reported that "Frazee the past season began to see velvet [i.e., a profit] in his baseball venture and has also prospered in other enterprises."

But when the season ended other battles ensued. The Black Sox scandal came to light, which eventually led baseball to ban Joe Jackson and several other White Sox players for life. When Sport Sullivan's role became public in September, the man who knew everybody suddenly became a stranger. After Sullivan was indicted, he disappeared, allegedly either moving to Mexico or being killed by gambling associates.

The scandal provided additional fuel for Frazee, who still wanted to do away with the National Com-

mission and appoint a single commissioner of baseball. The Insurrectos again joined with the National League and threatened to form their own league and leave the Loyal Five out in the cold unless the single-commissioner plan was adopted. In a contentious set of meetings that began in mid-October, the single-commissioner proponents finally won out. In mid-November Kenesaw Mountain Landis was named the first commissioner of baseball. Johnson remained AL president, but lost his title as the most influential man in baseball. Revenge was all that remained.

Frazee remained Johnson's nemesis. Through Johnson's friends in the press, the trashing of Harry Frazee began in earnest.

Frazee continued to run his franchise his way. When the Yankees made a pitch for Ed Barrow, Frazee let him go and hired Hugh Duffy in his stead. Then, on December 15, he made another deal with the Yankees. With the White Sox paralyzed by the emerging scandal, New York became Frazee's only market.

Frazee sent Waite Hoyt, Harry Harper, Wally Schang, and Mike McNally to New York for catcher Muddy Ruel, infielder Del Pratt, veteran outfielder Sammy Vick, and pitcher Hank Thormahlen. From Frazee's perspective, he was dumping one injury-prone, problematic pitching prospect who was threatening to jump the club (Hoyt), another who just couldn't win (Harper), a poor defensive catcher who was a regular holdout (Schang), and a backup infielder (McNally). In return, he received the game's best young catcher (Ruel), the league's second-best second baseman (Pratt had hit .314 with 97 RBIs for NY in 1920), a young pitcher with at least as much promise as Hoyt (Thormahlen), and a solid veteran outfielder (Vick). It was a good deal for Boston, and no money was involved.

Paul Shannon of the *Post* described it as "equitable" and already the cause of "caustic criticism in New York." The *Globe* reported, "It looks as if the Boston people got the better of the deal," and stated the trade had been in the works for over two months — before New York hired Barrow. Burt Whitman called the deal so one-sided in Boston's favor it "almost makes one think that Frazee is getting a conscience payment from the Yankee owners over Ruth . . . all Boston fans must applaud the move."

Others weren't so even-handed. *The Evening American*'s front-page headline read "Red Sox Team Wrecked in One-Sided Trade with Yankees," and writer Nick Flately — who detested Frazee — tried to organize a fan boycott for 1921. The most honest appraisal appeared in the *Boston Traveller*, where W. C. Spargo wrote, "Since the Yanks got Ruth and since the news of Jacob Ruppert's loan of $300,000 to Frazee became known, everything with a New York flavor as regards Red Sox doings has had a disagreeable taste."

The national press wasn't so understanding. In the wake of Johnson's ouster and the trade, *The Sporting News* embarked on a none-too-subtle campaign of character assassination. On January 3, it reported "the rival factions in the AL are filled to overflowing with thoughts of assassination" in regard to Frazee, and begged Commissioner Landis to end it by "grasping one H. Frazee by the neck and tossing him into eternal discard . . . Frazee is baseball's stormy petrel. He has the faculty of making more enemies in a single year than any human can accumulate in a lifetime." The house organ went on to report that Frazee's theater business was failing and that he had received twenty-five thousand dollars in the recent deal with New York. Both were utter fiction, but later accepted as gospel.

The tide against Frazee turned for good in the spring of 1921. Hooper, upset at not being named manager, was once again grousing for more money and threatening to retire. On March 1 he was traded to the Chicago White Sox for two starters, outfielder–first baseman Shano Collins, a Charlestown native, and outfielder Nemo Leibold. While neither man was Hooper's equal, together they more than made up for his loss.

The Boston press, while admitting that Leibold and Collins were valuable players, didn't see it that way. Hooper was a longtime favorite, a veteran of four world championships, and an old friend.

Red Sox manager Frank Chance greets Yankee manager Miller Huggins at Fenway Park prior to a game in 1923. Chance led the team to their second consecutive last-place finish with a won-lost record of 61-91. Huggins's Yankees, led by former Red Sox stars such as Ruth, Sad Sam Jones, Waite Hoyt, Joe Dugan, Herb Pennock, Joe Bush, and Everett Scott, finished first, a full thirty-seven games ahead of the Red Sox.

Frazee was skewered, and although all parties denied it the press charged he had accepted an unknown payment from the White Sox to make the deal. Feelings were so hard that most Boston papers cut back dramatically on their coverage of the Sox that spring. Several papers hardly bothered to cover the team at all.

Yet for the second year in a row the Red Sox surprised. The club got off to a decent start, paced by Ruel and Pratt, both of whom hit well over .300 for the first month of the season. The Sox even led the Yankees, for whom Wally Schang opened the season a miserable zero for twenty-five.

But the team was hounded by bad weather and lousy press, a situation not helped by the dismal performance of the Braves who, since winning the NL pennant in 1914, had become annual residents of the second division. Attendance slumped badly. All Boston soured on baseball, at least of the major league variety. Semipro "Twilight League" baseball, which was more convenient for workers than the usual 3:00 P.M. start at Fenway Park or Braves Field, provided an attractive alternative. Twilight contests routinely drew more fans than Major League Baseball in Boston during this time period, with some crowds approaching twenty thousand.

The Sox slumped badly during a western road trip in May, but recovered in June to pull back over .500. Then, for the second year in a row, the club was decimated by injuries as first Pratt, then Collins, Vick, and Menosky all went down. Although the pitching held up, paced by Sad Sam Jones and the miraculous return of Allan Russell, Boston went a dismal 9-20 in July. In an era of increasing offense, they simply couldn't score any runs.

When everyone got healthy they started winning again. Boston was ten games over .500 in August and September and challenged for third place before finishing in fifth again with a record of 75-79, twenty-three and a half games behind New York, which won its first pennant behind Ruth.

For the first time, as rumors that Frazee was preparing to sell swirled anew, his frustration began to show. "Let those who want the club show me the money and they can have it," he snapped at a questioner. Yet even though the Sox drew only two hundred seventy-nine thousand fans, the press reported that for the fourth time in Frazee's five-year tenure, the club turned a profit.

The rumored sale never took place, and in the off-season Frazee was active in the trade market once more. The Loyal Five continued to freeze him out, and the Yankees remained virtually his only option.

On December 20 he traded longtime shortstop Everett Scott, twenty-three-game winner Sam Jones, and Joe Bush to New York. In return, he received shortstop Roger Peckinpaugh, two years older than Scott but considered his superior by far, and three pitchers: veteran Jack Quinn and youngsters Rip Collins and Bill Piercy.

Frazee took the heat again as the *Post* screamed "Frazee Junks His Ball Club," while the *Herald* printed an above-the-fold page-one cartoon showing Frazee setting off an explosion labeled "Red Sox." Burt Whitman's campaign of misinformation continued, as he made a ridiculous claim that Frazee had also received seventy-five thousand dollars from New York, a figure absurd on its face.

But the *Globe* averred that Jones and Bush were "as good as they were ever going to be," and even Nick Flately in the *American* thought the acquisition of Peckinpaugh made sense. The *New York Tribune* concurred and thought Boston got the better end of the deal.

Frazee then pulled a surprise. Slugging Cleveland first baseman Joe Harris was on the suspended list after jumping the club in 1920. The Indians were anxious to get something for him, and Frazee was willing to gamble, so on December 21 Cleveland broke the ice with Boston and acquired Stuffy McInnis for Harris, hard-hitting George Burns, and Elmer Smith.

Once more, Boston's parochial press took personal offense at the loss of local boy McInnis, ignoring that in exchange Boston had received three quality players who could hit. Smith had hit .290 in 1921 and led the Indians with sixteen home runs, Burns had rapped righthanded pitching for a .361 average in part-time duty, and in his last big league season, 1919, Harris had hit .375. It was a one-sided deal — for Boston — but no one chose to see it that way.

Predictably — and against all logic — the Boston press derided the trade. Burt Whitman even telegraphed Ban Johnson for his reaction, and Johnson responded by calling Frazee "the champion wrecker of the baseball age."

Such venom didn't deter Frazee. His grandson recalls being told as a boy that Big Harry took special delight in jumping into Boston cabs, pulling his hat down over his face, and asking the cab driver, "What do you think of Harry Frazee?" chuckling at the string of expletives that usually followed.

A month later, he guaranteed that response. In a three-way deal with the A's and Senators he sent Peckinpaugh to Washington for shortstop Frank O'Rourke and Philadelphia third baseman and Holy Cross alum "Jumpin'" Joe Dugan — so named because of his tendency to jump contracts, which made him expendable to Connie Mack.

Burt Whitman once again led the charge against Frazee, slandering him by making another unfounded charge — that stuck — that the financially desperate magnate had received as much as fifty thousand dollars in the transaction. He claimed Dugan had been acquired only at the behest of New York and would be sold to them for another fifty thousand dollars before ever appearing in a Boston uniform.

But Frazee still wasn't in financial trouble. His latest production, starring Lynn Fontanne, was the George S. Kaufman comedy *Dulcy*. The show had been running since August in the Frazee Theater and eventually racked up 246 performances.

Frazee gave yet another indication of his solvency in March, when he offered to put up three hundred fifty thousand dollars for a fight between heavyweight champion Jack Dempsey and the black champion Sam Wills, which he planned to stage either at Fenway Park, in New York, or in Jersey City. But in less than twenty-four hours — without being asked — the Massachusetts Boxing Commission nixed the proposed bout, frowning on the prospect of a black champion being crowned in Massachusetts. New York and New Jersey soon followed suit and the bout was never held.

For the third year in a row the Red Sox pulled a spring surprise and opened the season playing better than expected, even earning Frazee grudging praise in *The Sporting News*, which headlined a report "Quick Start Has Fans Praising Frazee." But Boston's success was short-lived. While they had plenty of offense, they missed Bush and Jones, and Dugan balked at playing shortstop. On Memorial Day, the Sox dropped a doubleheader and fell into last place, then pitchers Herb Pennock and Allan Russell got hurt and the Red Sox nose-dived.

By midseason, even Frazee had to admit he was "disgusted" by his team in general and with Joe Dugan in particular. He made Burt Whitman look like a prophet when he traded Dugan and Elmer Smith to the Yankees for a couple of backup outfielders, shortstop Johnny Mitchell, pitcher Lefty O'Doul, and — finally — fifty thousand dollars. Dugan plugged a hole in New York, and none of the players Boston received in return did much. It was the first really bad deal he'd made since dumping Duffy Lewis in 1918, and a sign that Frazee was finally preparing to sell out.

But to the Boston press, it was the last straw. Whitman called the deal "disgusting," then let Ban Johnson do his typing, praising Johnson's "splendid efforts to keep the game on a high plane" and deriding Frazee again in Johnson's phrase as "the champion wrecker of baseball." The few writers with any objectivity observed that Dugan had proven to be a liability and, as one accurately observed, "if the trade would have been with any club but New York there would not have been much noise."

But Frazee wasn't yet prepared to abandon his team. He announced he still planned to rebuild, then dropped nearly twenty thousand dollars on three minor league prospects to make good on his claim.

It was too late for 1922. The Red Sox were in free fall and landed in last place. The Yankees were on their way to their second consecutive pennant.

A celebrated incident on the next-to-the-last-day of the season graphically illustrates the way facts have since been twisted to cast Frazee in the worst possible light.

New York came into Boston in the next-to-the-last series of the year needing to win only one of three games to clinch the pennant over the St. Louis Browns. In the first game, former Yankee Rip Collins, acquired in the Everett Scott trade, won his team-leading fourteenth game of the season as Boston won 3-1. The next day Jack Quinn, acquired at the same time, beat New York 1-0. The Yankees nevertheless clinched a tie.

According to legend, on the final day of the season Frazee vetoed manager Hugh Duffy's plan to pitch future Hall of Famer Herb Pennock in favor of Alex Ferguson, a journeyman whom Boston had acquired the previous February on waivers from the Yankees. Ferguson gave up singles to the first four hitters he faced (including a bunt by Ruth) before being relieved by Pennock, who shut down New York the rest of the way. New York won, 3-1, and captured the pennant. The intimation is that Frazee essentially threw the game to the Yankees to ensure a New York pennant.

But like so many tales concerning Frazee, the accepted account is full of omissions. For one, had Frazee wished to hand the pennant to New York, it would have been safer and made more sense to do so early in the series, allowing the New Yorkers to rest before the World Series. Yet Boston's best two pitchers in 1922 started and won. Another omission is that entering the third game, Pennock was 10-17 and in the midst of his worst big league season. Ferguson was 9-15, yet his ERA was nearly half a run better. And in their most recent starts, Ferguson had given up ten hits in seven innings to Detroit in a 5-3 loss on September 22, while two days later Pennock had been horrific, giving up eight hits and ten walks in seven innings. Furthermore, the Yankees had just lost twice to righthanded pitchers, and using a lefthander in Fenway, even then, was considered risky. Righthanders, particularly Collins, Quinn, and Ferguson, who had played for New York and were familiar with their hitters, appeared to have the Yankees' number.

Ignored completely is that in the ninth inning, as Boston threatened, pitcher Bennie Karr, in relief of Pennock, snuffed out what could have been a winning rally. He fouled a bunt into catcher Wally Schang's mitt, enabling Schang to pick off Johnny Mitchell at second to quash the threat. And even if the Red Sox had won, New York would have finished in no worse than in a tie with the Browns. The Yankees still had one game left to play, a makeup against the Senators, and would have needed only a victory themselves or a loss by the Browns to win the pennant outright.

Frazee's alleged role in the selection of the pitcher isn't mentioned in any account of the game. On the contrary, most reporters supported Duffy's choice of Ferguson and used glowing terms to describe Boston's effort in the season-ending contests. Even Frazee-hater Nick Flately commented that New York had been forced to "put everything they had into winning one of three from a club that has been a league football."

No matter. Given the blame already foisted on Frazee and that still to come, one more slur of history hardly matters. The Red Sox finished the season 61-93, thirty-three games behind New York, despite finishing the year with a 13-9 mark against the pennant winners, including eight victories in their last ten meetings. Some fix.

At long last, Ban Johnson's campaign to be rid of Harry Frazee appeared to be working. The relentless anti-Frazee campaign in the Boston press, combined with the even worse performance by the Braves and the option of Twilight League baseball, so soured fans that attendance plummeted to two hundred fifty-nine thousand, the lowest in club history at the time, apart from the war-shortened 1918 season.

Frazee began looking for a way out and turned his attention back to the theater. He announced the team was for sale and even announced he would accept less than one million dollars, as long as it was in cash. On October 2 he sold Del Pratt and Rip Collins to Detroit for fifteen thousand dollars. On October 5 he bought the Arlington Theater in Boston. On the stage, anyway, at least he knew who the bad actors were.

EMBERS IN THE OUTFIELD

1923 | 1932

Baseball clowns Nick Altrock *(l)* and Al Schacht *(r)* escort an
unsettled-looking Bob Quinn as the Red Sox owner takes part in
an on-field ceremony before the all-too-familiar empty grandstand
at Fenway Park during the not-so-roaring twenties.

The pending sale of the Red Sox rapidly became a fait accompli. It was no longer a question of whether Frazee would sell, but to whom, for how much, and precisely when.

Only in the final months of his reign did Frazee ever resemble the figure of contempt he has become known as today. Once he made the final decision to sell he did, indeed, milk the dwindling production for as much as he could get before leaving town. He had good reason: he knew the new owner would likely be someone either selected or approved by Johnson, and Frazee had little incentive to preserve the resources he had for one of Johnson's pawns. Given his treatment by Johnson and the Boston press, few could blame him, although everybody has.

Frazee was moving on, already in the midst of repackaging his successful play *My Lady Friends* into the musical *No, No, Nanette*. It opened in the spring of 1923 to mixed reviews in Detroit, then was retooled and ran for a year. Frazee himself took over as director and in the fall of 1925 opened the show on Broadway. It became the most successful musical comedy of the era, touring the world and netting him upward of four million dollars. It is important to note that in the time between the sale of Ruth and the opening of *No, No, Nanette* Frazee mounted several successful productions. Any claims that Ruth was sold to finance *Nanette* are entirely without foundation.

Although Boston papers carried rumors every week of a new buyer for the club, no one in Boston with any money wanted the team. Frazee let Hugh Duffy go, then hired former Cub first baseman and manager Frank Chance out of retirement. But Chance, who had won four pennants with Chicago and was known as the "Peerless Leader," had little to lead.

On January 11, 1923, Frazee traded young pitcher George Pipgras and another player to the Yankees for backup catcher Al De Vormer. The deal was cautiously praised in Boston, for Pipgras hadn't won a game in the major leagues. Naturally, he won twenty for New York. Then the final sell-off began.

Lefthanded pitchers have always been in short supply, making Herb Pennock, despite a poor record, a valuable commodity. He went to New York on January 30 for fifty thousand dollars and three nobodies.

After learning of the deal, catcher Muddy Ruel threatened to retire unless he was dealt, too. Frazee got what he could for the league's best catcher, packaging him with Allan Russell and receiving three backup players and some cash from the Senators.

Chance told Frazee at the start of the season that the team had absolutely no chance to win — they had a little pitching, but couldn't hit, field, or run. This time no quick start masked reality, and the team went straight to the cellar.

Business manager Bob Quinn of the St. Louis Browns asked Frazee to name his price. Frazee said he wanted 1.15 million dollars. Quinn started putting together a syndicate to meet Frazee's price.

Quinn, who'd formerly worked for the Columbus, Ohio, franchise in the American Association, tapped his connections in the Midwest and rounded up four investors — the most important of which was Indiana glass bottle baron Palmer Winslow. The group trusted Quinn and agreed to name him club president if he could put together a deal.

Ban Johnson loved the idea of Bob Quinn owning the Red Sox. Quinn was everything Harry Frazee wasn't — a *baseball* man, accustomed to playing by the rules and kowtowing to authority. Even better, he wasn't playing with his own money, and Johnson knew from experience that the best owners — from his perspective — were rich guys who lived out of town and let others fritter away their bankroll on ballplayers.

Browns owner Phil Ball, Johnson's closest friend in the game, initially held up the deal, for the Browns had improved each season under Quinn's stewardship. But Johnson's friendship with Ball eventually secured Quinn's release.

On July 1 Quinn began negotiations with Frazee, and his lawyers began auditing Frazee's books. Frazee tried to jack up the price and stiff Quinn with some bills and then demanded 25 percent of the sale price in cash. The complicated negotiations proceeded more or less smoothly, but Quinn and his backers had a hard time getting the cash together, the first inkling that the new regime would be no fiscal improvement on Frazee. On July 12 they came to an agreement.

Johnson was ecstatic. On July 19 a headline in *The Sporting News* blared "Johnson Elated That Frazee Is Finally Out of Baseball," quoting Johnson as saying that "as a sportsman he [Frazee] was a total failure, as a trouble maker he was a huge success." Johnson must not have been counting the 1918 world championship.

But Frazee couldn't resist getting in a few shots on his way out. On July 16 a story broke that Frazee planned to take his money and buy into the Yankees, buying out Huston. Although Jacob Ruppert personally disliked Frazee and denied the story, it sent shudders through Johnson. He immediately returned to Boston, in his words, "to aid in the riddance of Frazee."

Frazee wasn't done. He held up the final sale until August 1, allegedly over a bill due Harry Stevens, the hot dog vendor. While that has since been held up as a sign of Frazee's financial desperation, it was, in reality, an example of his shrewdness. The July 31 trading deadline had been created because of Frazee. Now, by holding up the deal until August 1, Frazee made it impossible for Johnson or Quinn to make any trades of consequence to help the 1923 Red Sox, who were in last place and looking for somewhere to hide. Take that.

On the evening of August 1, 1923, the Boston Red Sox officially passed from the singular possession of Harry Frazee to the syndicate headed by Quinn.

With that, Frazee washed his hands of baseball and returned to Broadway. Although he'd won only

Somerville High standout Danny MacFayden joined the Red Sox in 1926 and in seven seasons won 52 games while losing 78. He later pitched for the Yankees, Reds, Pirates, Senators, and Braves. In this cartoon, artist Gene Mack refers to his outstanding 17-13 record for the 1936 Boston Bees (Braves).

one world championship in nearly seven seasons — fewer than what Boston fans had come to expect — if that is the standard of success, no subsequent Red Sox owner has proven to be his equal. And none has ever approached his impact and influence on the game. Only in Boston could that make a man a pariah.

Boston sportswriters could hardly contain their glee at his departure. Quinn made them feel comfortable, bought them lunch and picked up the tab. He was lauded as a hero and Frazee bid good riddance.

Quinn said, "Our big idea is to go out and get ballplayers." Over the next seven weeks he spent two hundred fifty thousand dollars acquiring no fewer than seventeen minor league stars in a buying frenzy. Shortstop Dud Lee cost fifty thousand dollars.

But Quinn wasn't the judge of talent he thought he was. "Dud" would aptly describe most of his acquisitions. Over the next few years he would prove far guiltier of the crimes against the franchise assigned to Frazee than the theater owner ever was. Yet because of his baseball pedigree, each of Quinn's indiscretions was forgiven as he turned the once-proud franchise into a running joke.

The 1923 Sox were in free fall, although pitcher Howard Ehmke, somehow on his way to twenty wins, tossed a no-hitter on September 7. In his next start, he twirled a one-hitter, the single controversial safety being a groundball that outfielder Howard Shanks, playing third, stopped with his chest instead of his glove. Three days later, first baseman George Burns turned a rare unassisted triple play against the Indians. With runners on first and second moving on a hit-and-run, he snagged a line drive, tagged one runner, and outraced the other to second base. But the

Pitching for the awful Red Sox from 1924 to 1930, Red Ruffing's record was a horrific 39-96. Traded to the Yankees, he flourished and ended a twenty-two-year career with 273 victories. He was elected to the Hall of Fame in 1967.

Red Sox still finished last, 61-91, thirty-seven games behind the Yankees.

Quinn canned Chance and brought in ex-Browns manager Lee Fohl. Then he engineered a massive trade with Cleveland, acquiring second baseman Bill Wambsganns, catcher Steve O'Neill, and others for George Burns, Chick Fewster, and catcher Al Walters. Although the deal was essentially a wash, the Boston press reacted as if Quinn had reacquired Ruth.

Quinn appeared to be a success, for in 1924 the Sox won seventeen of twenty-four in May to reach second place behind the Yankees. On both June 4 and June 9 they even nudged into first.

Pennant fever swept the Hub. Even 'Nuf 'Ced Mc-Greevey, who'd disappeared from the scene after Prohibition closed his saloon, resurfaced and talked about bringing back the Royal Rooters. Everybody started humming "Tessie."

Then reality set in. The 1924 Red Sox had just had a hot month. Wambsganns and O'Neill were essen-

tially through, while Fewster and Burns far outplayed both men for Cleveland. They fell to seventh place, and only a similar collapse by the White Sox saved them from finishing last. But backed by good press, attendance nearly doubled to 448,556, the most since 1916 and probably enough to ensure a modest profit.

Quinn looked forward to spending more of the syndicate's money, but it was not to be. Palmer Winslow became ill and withdrew his promise of support, and the other investors didn't have any real money of their own. When Winslow passed away in 1926, the key to the vault, and any chance for the resurgence of the Red Sox, went with him to his grave.

Quinn and his partners should have sold out, cut their losses, and repaid the widowed Mrs. Winslow as best they could — lots of people had money in 1926. But Quinn genuinely wanted to repay Winslow's widow the full four hundred twenty-five thousand dollars her late husband had invested in the team. And he still held to the dim hope that he was the genius they once thought he was in St. Louis. Besides, owning a major league ballclub means membership in one of the most exclusive men's clubs in America. He chose to stay on.

His decision directly resulted in the most unsuccessful era in Red Sox history. The franchise paid the price, and the Red Sox soon became one of the worst teams in the history of baseball.

All Quinn's high-priced phenoms proved to be fakes. Attendance soon dropped, and without Winslow's money Quinn could hardly make payroll. Babe Ruth earned more in one season than did the entire Red Sox roster.

Quinn was in a dilemma. Without players, there were no fans. Without fans, there was no money to acquire players, no money to maintain Fenway Park, and no money to retain the few good players Quinn had. The team started out 2-10 in 1925 and dug fast.

What little talent Quinn had should have been playing in the minors, but Quinn rushed everyone to the big leagues. Eventually, infielders Jack Rothrock, Bill Rogell, and pitcher Red Ruffing would become stars — for other teams — and Ruffing even gained admittance to Baseball's Hall of Fame. But in 1925 they were all overmatched. Boston finished a dismal 47-

Red Sox notables Smead Jolley, Rabbit Warstler, and Dale Alexander joke before a game at Fenway Park in 1932. During a historic season Alexander captured the league batting crown with a .372 batting average as the team slumped to a dreadful 43-111 won-lost record and played before fewer than two hundred thousand fans for the entire season.

Green Light, Green Monster
by Luke Salisbury

Every team has a spirit, an essence, a *zeitgeist*. To survive a lifetime of rooting, especially for a club with as difficult a history as the Red Sox, this essence must be reckoned with, even loved. What is the spirit of this team that allows, even compels, us to love them in spite of the agony? Who are they and who are we?

I have loved the Boston Red Sox since I was a ten-year-old on Long Island and chose, of my own free will, to be a Red Sox fan. Everyone else had the smug perfection of the Yankees, the colorful Dodgers, or Willie Mays and the Giants, but I chose Ted Williams and the ineffable magic of the syllables "Boston Red Sox." It wasn't the mystique of Fenway Park. I wouldn't actually get to Fenway until much later. In 1957, on black and white television, the "lyric little band-box" looked like a dump.

I was the only Red Sox fan I knew. They were mine, all mine, but soon I learned their wonderful and sad history. Yankee fans instructed me. I learned fate had not been on Boston's side. The Red Sox sold Tris Speaker and Babe Ruth. They won the first World Series, but had lost their last because a Boston player hesitated, and a man with the perfect baseball name, Enos Slaughter, killed their dream. I discovered the Red Sox lost the first American League playoff and the very next year came into New York needing one win in two games for the

pennant and lost them both. This was my first experience of loving something that hurts and may keep hurting, but it made me love them more. I felt noble, like Davy Crockett at the Alamo.

Boston hadn't won a pennant since the year before I was born, and they certainly weren't going to win in 1957, but the Red Sox had the last man to hit .400, and he'd been a combat fighter pilot. Sixty years later Ted Williams is still the last man to do both. Ted's wars were important. Almost everyone's dad, including my own, had been in World War II. Mickey Mantle could run faster; he hadn't been in a war. In '57 Williams outhit Mantle .388 to .365.

I fell in love with a team that had a past, a style, a poetry before I had a past and long before I knew what style or poetry were. I fell victim all the same. T. S. Eliot said poetry communicates before it's understood. The Red Sox spoke to me long before I understood their past and poetry, but I felt it.

Since I didn't live in Boston, the Red Sox were largely my own creation. They weren't on TV often, and I saw them in person only once. I knew them through box scores, baseball cards, and imagination. The night I saw the Red Sox at Yankee Stadium — my first game — Ted Williams didn't start, but hit a pinch-hit homer off Whitey Ford in the ninth, making the score 7 to 1. The Red Sox then rallied for three more and lost. It was their history in miniature. A bright shining moment — Ted Williams did something marvelous — followed by a loss. It was yet another failure in New York,

another rally that fell short. Another loss with style. It was also magic. I saw Ted Williams hit a home run in the only at bat I ever saw him in person. I wanted that more than I wanted anything. I didn't know it in 1957, but I'd fallen in love with a dream of loss, magic, and unrepeatable perfection.

Maybe it was Ted's life average that made it so special — on the back of Topps' cards it ran .348, .350 after '57, and finally .344. No one else challenged history like that. No one else was close to Babe Ruth and Tris Speaker and Lou Gehrig's life number. No one else batted with the all-time greats. Musial dropped out of the .340s; DiMaggio finished at .325. Williams was different. Ted walked where Cobb and Hornsby and Sisler walked. His numbers had a seriousness that made winning a World Series or MVP or batting title ephemeral. Ted Williams played against the immortals. Mickey Mantle, good as he was, played against Al Kaline and Roy Sievers.

I don't know exactly how a team, or hero, shapes us at the age when rooting is prayer, God exists, and hearing your father talk about war is history itself, but I know I learned and changed.

Williams and the Red Sox also taught me about yearning, longing, and wanting the past because it was perfect. They had a past I'd never seen (Five World Championships! Babe Ruth a Red Sox! Williams in '41!) and I wanted it. You can study the past; you can read and dream, see photographs and remember numbers, but you can't have that time back. This sounds like love, which you think will kill you when it goes away, but it instructs — in pain, survival, nostalgia — because love, first love anyway, is a trance, and if waking teaches pain, it also teaches memory and the hard sweetness of lost things.

The Red Sox also taught me about imagination. I learned if you can't have the past, you create a dream of the past. It's not the past exactly but an image, a memory of things you never saw. This narrative — this imagined, created past — is another country, and it's yours. I needed something imagined and secret and mine in 1957.

Ted Williams taught me another lesson. Perhaps the deepest. Baseball is a team game about winning, but Williams was not a team player and his greatness was not winning. Joe DiMaggio, Mickey Mantle, Yogi Berra, and the Yankees were about winning. Ted Williams and his numbers challenged the past. He challenged the world I was conjuring from Joe Reichler's *First Complete Book of Baseball Records*, *Who's Who in Baseball*, and *Sport* magazine. Williams played now but he also played against then — the Yankees played the American League. Ted was everything that wasn't winning — the beauty of his swing, the beauty of his numbers, the beauty of his place in time. He hit for a high average when no one, not even on the Yankees or the whole National League, could sustain that day-to-day excellence. Williams played a game within a game. He showed me other worlds and how to win alone. Winning alone takes cour-

age too. Ted didn't sit on .3995 in '41. He didn't sit during Korea.

By fifth grade, I knew I was never going to be the star of any team, but believed I had some vague but inevitable encounter with fate. Would it be in a war, like my father? I was pretty sure it wouldn't be in some distant batter's box, but being in the batter's box, alone, watched by everyone, facing a hardball, was the most public yet inward experience. For the first time

---

I have loved the Boston Red Sox since I was a ten-year-old on Long Island and chose, of my own free will, to be a Red Sox fan.

---

in my life, I was in a magic circle with fear and desire. Tested. Finding out who I was. I was facing God.

This was what my hero did better than anyone alive. He mastered the crucial solitude in the white box facing the white ball. He mastered fear. He mastered himself. It didn't matter if Ted's teammates were mediocre, or what people said, or how many times they walked him and robbed him of batting titles or didn't give him the MVP. When Ted batted, it was history. When I batted, I was alive.

I spent seven years trying to recapture the thrill of the batter's box. Seven years wondering if I'd admire anyone as much as I admired Ted Williams.

In the spring of 1965 I read *The Great Gatsby* and my life changed. It was wonderful and devastating.

I didn't think a book could explain the way I felt about so many things. I didn't know language could be so precise and gorgeous — didn't know language was so important or that a book could be perfect. How could one book conjure and explain so completely the world I saw growing up on Long Island? I didn't know anyone else was quite so "enchanted and repelled" by the rich, or felt such elegant longing for the promises of lost evenings and lost love. Reading *Gatsby* was like watching Ted Williams in the batter's box again — it didn't matter what sort of person, husband, or father Scott Fitzgerald was, or what a mess he made of his life, just as it didn't matter how angry or bitter Ted Williams was; in the batter's box, in that book, talent was focused into the effortless perfection of genius. There's divinity in perfection. A whisper of worlds in worlds. Love that can't be lost.

When I was ten I dreamed of playing baseball. At seventeen I dreamed of being a writer. In a way I was ruined. All I wanted to do for the rest of my life was try to capture a world with the precision and elegance Fitzgerald had. At ten, I knew I couldn't hit a fastball, let alone a curve. At seventeen, I wasn't sure I could sit still long enough to write anything, let alone a novel, but knew I would spend the rest of my life trying. Nothing else seemed serious. Nothing was as important. Nothing else was facing God.

Thirty-five years later, I still love the Red Sox and *The Great Gatsby*. It's ironic one should be so imperfect —

who in 1957, who in his right mind, could have imagined Jim Burton in the seventh game of the World Series, the mind of Don Zimmer, Bucky Dent, Bill B***ner — while the other remains perfect, not a word out of place, not a phrase that isn't both surprising and right, nothing wasted: a little book that

Yearning for Ruth or Joe Wood or Ted Williams is like Jay Gatsby yearning for Daisy Buchanan.

has all the beauty and ugliness of America, all the wonder and cruelty of worshipping a woman or the past. All the danger of yearning for perfection when perfection doesn't exist — except in imagination. Except in art.

Perhaps the Red Sox and the book aren't so different. The Red Sox have had moments of impossible luck, moments that must have seemed as perfect to those who saw them as the first and last pages of *Gatsby*. The 1912 Series victory was as wild and unlikely as the '86 loss to the Mets — the bottom of the tenth inning of the final game had not one but two B***ner-type misplays by the Giants. Babe Ruth later pitched twenty-nine and two-thirds consecutive scoreless World Series innings for the Red Sox. Ted Williams went into the last day of the '41 season hitting .3995 and went 6-for-8 to finish at .406. We've had our perfect innings.

Yearning for Ruth or Joe Wood or Ted Williams is like Jay Gatsby yearn-

ing for Daisy Buchanan: yearning for love as it was the first time and won't and can't and shouldn't be again. When Fenway Park is gone, we'll feel like Nick Carraway sprawled on Gatsby's beach, summer over, imagining Long Island as it "flowered once for Dutch sailors' eyes — a fresh green breast of the new world." Something "transitory" and "enchanted" lost forever but redeemed by Nick's remembering and F. Scott Fitzgerald's words.

Then there's 1967. I was twenty in 1967 and feel sorry for anyone who wasn't. The whole year was an eruption of marvelous rebellious energy, and baseball followed the track of that energy. The hundred-to-one Red Sox won the American League pennant when winning the pennant meant beating every other club over 162 games. This was inconceivable. Since the retirement of Ted Williams the Red Sox stank. There was no other word for it. Carl Yastrzemski's two batting titles had made him more like Pete Runnels than Ted Williams. Then Yaz had arguably the greatest year anyone has ever had — if greatness is to be judged by winning in an impossible situation. For once, the Red Sox didn't choke. No shortstop looked at the wrong base, no manager sent a retread out to pitch a playoff game, no right fielder couldn't get to a pop fly. This wasn't '46, '48, or '49. This was 1967 and the world was upside down for one beautiful summer. It was love. It was the Red Sox and a feeling of change and newness and liberation that wasn't invented by the media or

politicians. It all came crashing down a year later with assassinations, Vietnam, and harder drugs, but for one season, it happened. Rules were broken. The Red Sox won. It was like seeing Ted Williams or reading *Gatsby*. We were visited by the miraculous.

Thinking of '67 makes me feel like Gatsby wanting to repeat the past, but I know that even if, like Gatsby's dream, "it was already behind him, somewhere back there in that vast obscurity beyond the city, where the dark fields of the republic rolled on under the night," I've seen it; I saw the Red Sox at their best. I imagine and remember and dream '67 and that changes me. Now I make my own books and family and redream my memories, but I don't judge success by obvious standards. I don't want to be a New York Yankee. What started as a child's need to tell his own base-

The long Red Sox seasons are like the long seasons of marriage: wins and losses, wonder and disappointment.

ball story and embryonic appreciation of genius with Ted Williams has become a vocation, a way to see life, a way to live. Hitting became writing. Telling a baseball story became making books. The long, sweet, painful love affair with the Boston Red Sox illuminates and sustains my life. I root for my books — some falter after good starts; some are defeated by the world. I root for my marriage. The long Red

Sox seasons are like the long seasons of marriage: wins and losses, wonder and disappointment. I root for my son. I rethink and reimagine the baseball I've seen and dreamed and rethink and try to know my wife, my son, myself.

Someday Fenway Park will be gone, and like Ted Williams's swing and Yaz's magic, we will have to conjure it with memory and video tape and great words like Updike's. Fenway will be gone like the romance of Daisy and Gatsby, Gatsby and the past, Nick and the East, Nick and the past — and we will be left, like Nick at the amazing ending of that amazing book, dreaming an incommunicable dream of the Red Sox and ourselves. It's lost but it's here. It's here if we can conjure it and know beauty and sadness. This is the Red Sox essence, the spirit and *zeitgeist*. Incommunicable loss redeemed by dreaming of Williams's swing, Yaz in '67, ourselves once, because winning isn't obvious and we don't live only in this world but in as many worlds as we can make. Even if the Red Sox drive us crazy, it's all right if we know who we are. It's all right to be Gatsby looking at the green light on Daisy's dock. It's all right to hunger for Babe Ruth, Ted Williams, and the perfect summer of 1967. It's right to mourn and conjure because we're lovers, yearning and dreaming.

The Red Sox and *The Great Gatsby* are, as the years go by, the same.

Luke Salisbury is the author of *The Answer Is Baseball, The Cleveland Indian,* and *Blue Eden.* He teaches English and film at Bunker Hill Community College in Boston.

105, forty-nine and a half games behind the pennant-winning Senators. They were last in the league in runs scored and first in runs allowed, and the pitching staff, paced by Ted Wingfield's twenty defeats, Ehmke's nineteen, and Ruffing's eighteen, was the worst in the league, as was their defense.

Quinn's vain attempts to keep the team sent his club ever deeper into the league cellar. Promising players were usually sold or traded as quickly as possible, usually for players much older and, in the long run, cheaper. His deals, none of which worked, made those of Harry Frazee seem the work of genius. All Quinn ever really received in exchange for his prospects was time, the ability to meet his payroll for a few weeks or months, and players whom other clubs considered has-beens, cast-offs, or problems not worth holding on to. He spent all his energy trying to get ahead, but instead only played catchup.

Many of the players Quinn acquired were indistinguishable from one another. If they could hit, they couldn't field, run, or throw. If they could field, batting was a mystery. And no one could pitch.

Nothing about the entire operation was major league. Most clubs were beginning to make agreements with minor league teams that guaranteed them an option on their players, while free-market prospects were being sold for as much as one hundred thousand dollars. Quinn couldn't afford to participate in either arrangement. His scouts scoured the lower minors for overlooked gems. They found mostly coal.

Fenway Park looked like an abandoned warehouse, for it sat beside a dump and Quinn couldn't afford any but the most necessary upkeep. Attendance over the next few seasons averaged barely three thousand fans per game, a figure that was, in fact, only rarely reached for holiday games, and the occasional appearance of Ruth and the Yankees skewed the figures. Without them, the Sox wouldn't have drawn one hundred thousand fans a year.

The 1926 season brought Quinn no deliverance from his slow torture. The club briefly battled the Browns for last place before sinking to new lows and rapidly outdistancing the competition. The highlight of the year was the day Fenway Park nearly burned to the ground.

AFTER A LONG CROSS COUNTRY SPRINT, FLAGGY GRABBED ONE LIKE THIS ON BABE RUTH

The best everyday player on the Red Sox during the dreadful decade of the twenties was center fielder Ira "Pete" Flagstead. In seven seasons in Boston he batted .294 and thrilled fans with his fielding.

During a game on May 7, several small fires broke out in the papers and refuse strewn beneath the wood-frame bleachers that ran down the left-field line from the grandstand to Lansdowne Street, represented in Fenway Park today by sections 29 to 33. Alert fans extinguished each blaze before any damage was done.

But the club didn't clear the area of trash, and it may have sparked an idea. The next evening the night watchman smelled smoke and spotted another fire beneath the bleachers. He called the fire department, then fought the blaze by fire extinguisher with the help of manager Lee Fohl and a handful of park employees.

Their efforts failed to contain the flames. A brisk wind fed the blaze, and soon embers were flying onto the roof of the grandstand and into the open dump that ran on both sides of Jersey Street (now Yawkey

Way) all the way to Boylston Street. Employees of the S.S. Pierce Company, across Brookline Avenue, saw what was happening and rushed to the ballpark. They manned the groundskeeper's hoses until the fire department arrived. By then the three-alarm fire had spread to both the grandstand roof and the dump.

Firemen chopped holes through the fence behind the bleachers to run water into the park and cut holes in the grandstand roof to allow the trapped heat to escape before the fire spread to the entire park. It took nearly an hour to extinguish the blaze.

Newspapers reported that the fire caused twenty-five thousand dollars' damage to Fenway Park, much of it covered by insurance. The fire department said the fire was accidental, but given that it was the fourth fire in the same place in less than thirty-six hours, the circumstances appear suspicious.

Quinn was glad to collect the twenty-five thousand dollars but would have been better off had the entire park burned. He didn't rebuild but used the windfall to make payroll and gain a few months of breathing room.

While the big charred timbers were hauled away and the grandstand roof and fencing were repaired, the area that once held the bleachers was left as is — a cinder-strewn vacant lot, inadvertently creating, for a time, one of Fenway Park's most unique features.

For the rest of Quinn's tenure, the ground beyond the grandstand along the left-field line was the most expansive area of foul territory in the major leagues. Foul balls hit past the stands down the left-field line remained in play all the way to the fence paralleling Brookline Avenue. While chasing after such balls the left fielder or shortstop sometimes disappeared from sight, sending the base umpire after him and leaving baserunners unsure whether to tag up or not.

In midseason, Quinn traded his only player of value, sending Howard Ehmke to the A's for pitchers Slim Harriss and Fred Heimach. Like most of Quinn's trades, it looked good — Ehmke was 3-10 while Harriss and Heimach had both pitched well in limited duty with Philadelphia. Of course, once the deal was done Ehmke resumed pitching like a twenty-game winner, leading the A's in victories for the balance of the season, while Heimach and Harriss went a collective 8-19 for Boston.

Desperate for good publicity, Quinn fired Fohl and lured Bill Carrigan, only forty-six years old, away from his business interests in Maine.

Such was the respect for Carrigan that the Boston press reacted as if a pennant were in the offing in 1927. But the game had changed since he'd managed the Red Sox to a world championship and, unfortunately, so had the players. While Carrigan had a well-deserved reputation as a teacher, even he could do little with the Red Sox pupils. The 1927 Red Sox, once more, were miserable from the outset.

Their best player was center fielder Ira Flagstead, a slick fielder who, though he lacked power, was one of the few decent hitters on the club. He'd been considered a phenom when he hit .331 with Detroit as a rookie in 1919, but had never fulfilled his promise and had later run afoul of Tigers manager Ty Cobb.

The Sox picked him up after Detroit released him early in the 1923 season, and he passed for a fixture at Fenway Park for much of the remainder of the decade, the best defensive center fielder Boston had between Tris Speaker and Dom DiMaggio. Had it not been for Flagstead providing consistent offense and catching flyballs between left and right fielders who generally lacked the collective speed to cover one-third of the outfield, much less two-thirds, the Red Sox may well have collapsed into oblivion.

Quinn was near the end. He wanted to sell the land beneath Fenway Park, but in order to do so, he'd have to pay rent to play at Braves Field. But the Braves balked at the deal, and Quinn worried what would happen to his team if he couldn't meet his obligations to the Braves.

From the playing field at either Braves Field or Fenway Park, baseball looked all but dead in Boston. Together, the two clubs were barely drawing a half million fans per season.

The only interest in the game was in the semipro Twilight League, where big games at places like Hoyt Field in Cambridge sometimes drew twenty thou-

In 1931 right fielder Earl Webb made baseball history as he socked a single-season major league record sixty-seven doubles while batting .333. The Red Sox traded Webb the following season for eventual league batting champion Dale Alexander.

sand. And the skill level of the players was often on par — or even better — with Boston's big league imposters, for in the 1920s and 1930s it was often possible for players to earn more playing semipro ball than in either the major or minor leagues, with the added benefit of being able to stay at home and have a job in the off-season.

Year after year big league baseball in Boston became a "more of the same" situation, as Quinn stubbornly held on. Under Carrigan, the team finished last in 1927, fifty-nine games out of first, last in 1928, forty-three and a half games out, and last again in 1929, forty-eight games out.

On June 4, 1929, Harry Frazee died of Bright's disease, a kidney ailment. At his side was New York mayor Jimmy Walker. Frazee had been sick for a year and had sold his Greenwich, Connecticut, estate, "Freestone Castle," to spend much of the remainder of his time in the south of France.

No, No, Nanette had been his last big score. A follow-up, based on Nothing But the Truth and not so inventively titled Yes, Yes, Yvette, had failed on Broadway in 1927 despite good reviews.

He left an estate of well over a million dollars, although at the time of his death Boston papers aped an erroneous report in the New York Times that stated he was almost broke. The Times corrected their report a few days later, but the Boston press wasn't so conscientious. He predeceased his nemesis, Ban Johnson, who'd retired as American League president at the end of the 1927 season after seeing most of his power stripped away, by nearly two years.

The stock market crash in 1929 doomed any chance Quinn had to sell the ballclub at a profit. Carrigan tired of finishing in last place with no hope of improvement and was replaced in 1930 by coach and former Red Sox shortstop Heinie Wagner.

He proved no more adept at extracting victory from Boston's sorry collection of players. They finished last again, 52-102, a full fifty games behind Philadelphia.

Quinn shuffled the deck once more at the end of the season, hiring popular Charlestown native Shano Collins, who had more or less played outfield for the team from 1921 to 1925, as manager. But not even John McGraw could have led this Red Sox team to the title, for although the 1931 team finished sixth, they were still forty-five games out of first place.

The highlight of the season and, in fact, of Quinn's tenure as owner, was the single remarkable record by an otherwise undistinguished outfielder named Earl Webb. Absolutely out of nowhere, he smacked an incredible sixty-seven doubles, still the all-time record, bettering the old record of sixty-four set by former Red Sox first baseman George Burns with Cleveland in 1926.

But what is most interesting about the

In 1932 the Red Sox lost a team record 111 games despite the fact that league batting champion Dale Alexander (.372) and left fielder Smead Jolley (.309) proved a formidable duo in the Boston batting order. Fielding, however, was a problem.

mark is not the number of doubles struck. Rather, it is the man who did it. For Webb's performance was a pure anomaly. He had never before hit more than thirty doubles, never again hit more than twenty-eight, and, in fact, was out of the major leagues for good by 1934.

The former coal miner started his professional career as a pitcher before finding some success as a good-hitting, poor-fielding outfielder, once admitting, "I've seen some mighty bad outfielders, but none of them had anything on me." But as a hitter, he was pretty good. That made him perfect for Quinn's Red Sox, who acquired him in 1930 to play right field, and he led the team in batting. On the dreary Sox, he was a star.

As a lefthanded hitter who often hit to the opposite field, he took advantage of all of Fenway's quirks, which gave him plenty of room to drop base hits. Since he couldn't run, and the Red Sox were so often behind, the outfielders played him far back and spread out. So whenever Webb managed to hit a line drive between them, over their heads, or down the left-field line into the open space where the left-field bleachers once stood, even Webb could make it as far as second.

But he couldn't make it any farther. Had Webb been able to run he may well have set a record for triples that season, but his lack of speed held him to only three for the year. And once he became aware that he had a shot at setting a new mark, he started stopping at second base — making it to third wasn't going to change Boston's season. He ended his pursuit of history on September 17, 1931, tying and breaking Burns's mark by doubling off the left-field wall once in each game of a double-header.

But although his .331 average, ninety-six runs, and one hundred three RBIs all led the club that year, the Boston press was not particularly impressed with his record sixty-seven doubles. The *Globe* called it a "stunt" and sniffed, "Webb has been shooting for the record all season." True, but Webb's mark stood for the remainder of the century. And of all baseball's major single-season records, only Dutch Leonard's 1914 ERA of 0.96 and Webb's sixty-seven doubles were set by players in a Red Sox uniform.

Red Sox owner Bob Quinn meets with Thomas Austin Yawkey in 1933. When Yawkey turned thirty in February 1933 he took control of the Yawkey fortune and bought the Red Sox from the cash-starved Quinn.

As if the club needed it, the 1932 season started off with a bad omen. Hard-drinking pitcher Ed Morris, who'd won nineteen games in 1928 before hurting his arm in a fight with two Detroit cops, attended a going-away fish fry just before spring training. He got in a fight with another man, was stabbed, jumped into the Perdido River, and swam from Florida to Alabama to escape his attacker. He survived the initial assault, but the murky river water caused an infection that killed him.

Boston had become a dumping ground for players

who possessed only one or at most two of the five necessary baseball tools (run, throw, hit, hit with power, and field), and over the course of the 1932 season Quinn acquired several players who fit that description perfectly. In fact, after fifty-two games he traded Earl Webb, who returned to mortality by hitting only nine doubles, to Detroit for two such players, first baseman Dale Alexander and outfielder Roy Johnson, and he traded Jack Rothrock and catcher Charlie Berry for a third, outfielder Smead Jolley.

All three players acquired weighed well over 200 pounds and looked it. They could hit, but could do little else. Jolley was installed in left field, where he turned every excursion up Duffy's Cliff into an adventure, once missing a ball between his legs in front of the wall, only to turn around and miss it again when it rolled back between his legs on the way down. Although Alexander led the league with a .372 average, Johnson hit .299, and Jolley knocked in ninety-nine runs, the 1932 team was easily the worst Red Sox team of all time. Only one of their eighteen pitchers, Ivy Andrews, finished above .500. The club led the league in most of the categories they'd have preferred not to.

After an 11-46 start, Shano Collins wisely walked away. Quinn tapped infielder Marty McManus to replace him, and the team made nominal improvement — they lost only two of every three games the rest of the way as opposed to four of five.

The club had reached its nadir. Quinn had borrowed and bargained the franchise nearly into oblivion and now had little choice but to sell. The Boston Red Sox, once the flagship franchise of the American League, were now the sorriest team in baseball. The near future looked even bleaker than the recent dark past.

The Red Sox needed some kind of savior. What they got was someone quite different, a young man with a seemingly endless supply of money who thought that money would be enough to perform a miracle and transform the Red Sox into world champions. While both he and Red Sox fans alike would eventually learn the folly of that belief, at least the new owner wasn't afraid to spend a fortune finding out. In Boston, in 1933, that counted for something.

THE RICHEST BOY IN THE WORLD

1933 | 1935

SOUVENIR SCORE CARD

Opening Day

New

Fenway Park

APRIL 17, 1934

HOME OF THE

BOSTON AMERICANS

PRICE 10 CENTS

Opening Day program from the opening of the newly renovated Fenway Park, April 17, 1934. In the off-season between the 1933 and 1934 seasons Tom Yawkey undertook the largest private contracting project in Boston during the Depression, the renovating and rebuilding of Fenway Park. Nearly two thousand union workers were employed in the winter of 1933–34 to turn his dream into a reality.

As bad as it already was for Bob Quinn and the Red Sox, it was getting worse by the moment.

The forty-three wins by the 1932 Red Sox were the fewest in team history, as were the 182,150 fans that bothered to pass by the body of the once-proud franchise in shabby Fenway Park. Deteriorating economic conditions in Boston made no one optimistic about the future.

The Depression had hit Boston hard. That winter the city stopped using mechanized plows to remove snow, instead hiring men with shovels to provide a few days' employment. Quinn was similarly buried under the increasing drifts of debt. Like everyone else, he lived day-to-day and prayed for a miracle. In the off-season he even borrowed against his personal insurance policy to meet payroll and secure a spring training site for the club. At the same time, he entertained any and all offers to sell the club.

He'd abandoned any notion of turning a profit. He just hoped to break even and get out of his personal indebtedness.

In late February he announced, "I have been dickering with several partners, three to be exact," to which Jack Malaney of the *Post* cynically responded, "It [the Red Sox] has been 'sold' so often in the past few years that little attention is paid to new rumors." But Malaney identified the main suitor as a "New York millionaire," a description that led many to recall, without much fondness, Harry Frazee. Yet it was hard to imagine why anyone, anywhere, would want to buy the Red Sox. During the Depression even millionaires were short on cash and not disposed to send good money after bad.

Even as newsboys on the street were distributing Malaney's remarks, Quinn invited the press to one of his famous luncheons, where he curried their favor in advance of another desultory season. Most thought he'd refute rumors that Babe Ruth would be named manager, announce the retention of manager McManus, and open the bar.

But something was up. At the head table sat several strangers, including a wide-browed, husky young man who was mistaken by most as a secretary. Quinn then surprised the press corps by saying, "I haven't got the money to continue. I have been carrying a load that very few men could have suffered without jumping out a window." He announced he had reached a handshake agreement to sell the team and Fenway Park for 1.2 million dollars.

Despite their recent performance, the club was a bargain. Even in the Depression the Fenway Park real estate was worth more than that. Then Quinn introduced the new owner of the Red Sox. Flanked by his lawyers, the purchaser was the husky young man of means just four days past his thirtieth birthday. His name was Thomas Austin Yawkey.

No one had ever heard of him. Yet for the next forty-five years it would be impossible to think of the Red Sox apart from their owner, for the ballclub soon became an extension of his self, subject to his own peculiar tastes and shortcomings.

Few ever realized how much this very private man shaped the personality of his team, traits still recognizable today. For despite the length of his tenure and public profile, Yawkey relished his own privacy. He was a complex man whose life was full of contradictions.

To the public, he appeared as the beneficent, paternal Mr. Yawkey, who liked to hunt and fish and play catch with his players, take batting practice, and picnic in the outfield of Fenway Park with his wife. He paid his players generously, gave to charity, and fawned over the Red Sox like an expectant father.

But in private, Yawkey was driven by his need to make peace with his past. He was sometimes prone to alcohol-fueled outbursts of anger, paranoia, and petty acts of selfishness. He was a stranger to his own adoptive daughter and blocked the integration of baseball. He had many acquaintances but few friends. He idolized baseball people, yet felt insecure in their company and therefore hired a series of underlings whose primary qualification was their willingness to share his liquor and adopt his views. Cloistered in his New York apartment, his suite at the Ritz, or on his immense South Carolina estate, Yawkey lived vicariously through his ballclub, sharing in their limited successes, but more often identifying with their failure. His team reflected his own character, for good and bad, in victory and defeat, until long after his death.

While he would eventually be lionized as baseball's last gentleman-sportsman owner, Tom Yawkey was also the first of a new breed. With a zeal that makes George Steinbrenner appear frugal, he tried to buy a championship. A man-child playing with millions of real dollars, his personal indulgence, purely by accident, was rewarded with the blind faith and fanatic affection of the people of New England. Even now, when fans speak of the Red Sox or attend a game at Fenway Park, their allegiance is to the ballclub Tom

Yawkey created. He remains the franchise's central figure.

Yet his ultimate reward would be disappointment. The Red Sox he helped create were either talented yet flawed teams that failed to perform to expectations, or overpaid collections of pampered prima donnas.

All Tom Yawkey ever really wanted to do was win a world championship. He never did.

Yawkey spoke only briefly at the luncheon, saying he intended to "put the Red Sox back on the map. We are out to give the Boston fans the best break in the world . . . It will not change in a day, a month, or even a season, but we are going through to the end." He spent the rest of his life trying to fulfill that promise.

That day he gave the press the only few clues they would ever receive to his character. "I was born the year my father bought the Detroit club," he said. "I saw many games there and contributed my share of hero worship." A short time later he added, "I expect to get a great kick out of making something out of it [the Red Sox] . . . The big kick comes from taking something that's down and seeing if you can put it up and across. That's what my daddy did. *I want to see if I'm as good a man as he was.*" Few would ever realize precisely how true that statement was. Yawkey spent the rest of his life trying to emerge from his father's shadow.

The scion of a lumber and mining fortune whose adoptive father, William Yawkey, had once owned the Detroit Tigers, Yawkey grew up around ballplayers. He eventually inherited the family fortune worth between eight and twenty million dollars, controlled by a trust until his thirtieth birthday. He attended the Irving School, the same prep school attended by Philadelphia A's star Eddie Collins, whose name graced the school's athletic medal, an award Yawkey desperately wanted but never won. After graduating from Yale with a general science degree, he finally met Collins at the funeral of the prep school's principal. They shared a similar background and soon became close. Collins, like Ty Cobb before him, became Yawkey's surrogate father, a role he would retain for nearly a decade.

As Yawkey approached age thirty, he told Collins that he wanted to buy a baseball team. Collins promised to let him know if he heard of any opportunities.

Collins was perfectly positioned to act as Yawkey's broker. Highly respected throughout the game, he had Connie Mack's ear and Mack, who'd already owned and managed the A's for thirty years, knew everybody in the game. If anyone was looking to sell, Mack would know.

Collins spread the word. It was a buyer's market. Although baseball had been a moneymaker for decades, it was now experiencing hard times.

Yawkey had a chance to buy a minor league team, but turned it down. Bill Yawkey had owned a big league team and Tom Yawkey wanted nothing less. In 1932 he was offered a half-interest in the Brooklyn Dodgers, but Yawkey again refused, saying he had no interest in owning "half of anything."

After talking with Quinn at the 1932 World Series, Collins told the Red Sox owner about Yawkey. For the next few months Quinn quietly checked the young man out.

Yawkey had heard that the Red Sox might be available. With his thirtieth birthday only a few months away, he directed his attorneys to begin an examination of the team. By the first of the year Quinn and Yawkey were talking.

Quinn's only concern was Yawkey's inexperience. The franchise was on the brink of going under, and he worried that Yawkey, despite his millions, might not act decisively enough to save it. He told Yawkey he needed a baseball man to help him out.

Anxious to make a deal, Yawkey offered Quinn the role. If he'd stay and teach Yawkey the ins and outs of the operation, he could retain a small piece of the club.

But Quinn was worn out by the baseball wars and knew that Boston needed a new face. He wanted to make a clean break. He suggested that Yawkey ask Collins instead.

Yawkey jumped at the idea. While he hadn't been Collins's peer on the athletic field, his money could make him Collins's superior. That was better than winning any medal.

He offered to cut Collins in if he agreed to serve as vice president and general manager, a promotion from the role he held with the Athletics. While Yaw-

Thomas Austin Yawkey was the privileged nephew of William Yawkey, who once owned the Detroit Tigers. Note the inscription from Yawkey to Ty Cobb. Young Tom enjoyed playing catch with the Georgia Peach on the front lawn of his uncle's home and later invited the Tiger great to hunt with him at his South Carolina estate.

key learned the baseball business, Collins would run the team.

Collins was intrigued. While he was loyal to Mack he knew the A's president and manager was years away from stepping down. Yawkey's offer was a real opportunity. When he asked Mack's advice, Mack wished Collins well and told him if he were foolish enough to turn Yawkey down, Mack would fire him anyway.

Given the events that soon transpired between the two teams, Mack's benevolence appears somewhat disingenuous. Mack was also in financial trouble. He had found an angel in Sox owner Harry Frazee following the 1917 season when he decided to break up his ballclub. Once again, he was in the midst of breaking up a great ballclub.

Although the A's won the World Series in 1929 and 1930, Mack was in debt, and the banks had called in his loans. He'd already dealt slugger Al Simmons and several others to the White Sox for one hundred fifty thousand dollars.

Allowing Collins to work for Yawkey — who was young, impatient, impulsive, and solvent to the point of excess — gave Mack a real advantage when he was ready to sell more players. By then Collins, who knew Mack's players as well as he did, would be Yawkey's trusted confidant. Mack could rebuild courtesy of Yawkey's fortune, just as he had once done with Frazee's.

Collins told Yawkey he was in, and on February 21 Yawkey turned thirty and took control of his fortune. It would be over two months before he took legal possession of the club. Until then, he could only act like an owner.

The Sox opened spring training in Sarasota, Florida, on March 3. Collins arrived early to evaluate talent and plan for the future.

There wasn't much to evaluate. *Post* columnist Bill Cunningham accurately described the club as "a tattermedallion aggregation of cripples, has-beens and would-bes, playing in a poor folksey park in a poor folksey way."

They had a few hitters, but the pitching staff was baseball's worst. Rebuilding was a misnomer. The Sox would have to start from scratch. Franklin Roosevelt, who was sworn in as president on March 4 and declared a week-long bank holiday the next day as he began to implement the New Deal, faced a task different in scale but hardly more daunting than that which confronted Yawkey and Collins.

Yawkey arrived at camp by plane on March 9, drawing comment for his extravagance and having the pilot buzz the field. He sat in the stands with Collins for the next five days and scratched his head.

Observers soon realized he had no more understanding of baseball than the average fan. From the sidelines, Yawkey couldn't even tell the difference between a fastball and a curve. Then again, some Red Sox players had the same problem in the batter's box.

They performed poorly all spring, often losing to minor league competition. No one was optimistic about the club's chances in 1933. While the Yankees were 2-5 favorites to win the pennant, the Sox were the longest of long shots, 500-1.

On Opening Day, April 13, Boston lost to the Yankees 4-3. Over the ensuing decades of the Yawkey regime, losing to the Yankees would become a familiar refrain.

The Sox played spirited ball early before settling into the cellar on April 29. The press chided the club by referring to them as the "Yawkees," but it would take more than the change of a single letter to compete with the Yankees.

Yawkey officially took over the reins in early May, just in time for the annual American League spring meeting, held in Cleveland on May 9. His purchase was approved without opposition.

As the owners started to consider other more mundane league matters, Tom Yawkey took a page from Bill Yawkey's biography. He vaulted out of his chair and announced that he was there to buy ballplayers, didn't have time to mess around, and that "the money is on the table."

The other owners were shocked. Nothing like that had ever happened before. New members usually sat quiet, for it took several years to gain acceptance from their peers and several more to wield any real influence.

But tradition meant nothing to Yawkey. He knew the other owners were broke and saw no reason to wait or follow some dim protocol. Cash gave him instant credibility.

He immediately became one of the most powerful and influential owners in the game. For the next forty-five years that influence grew. On issues of player relations, finance and organization, and other matters, the other owners soon found themselves responding to the lead of their wealthiest and most powerful member.

Before Yawkey waved his checkbook in the air, the owners traditionally had dealt with one another by the same unspoken set of rules. No one had ever asked for players and offered the keys to the vault before.

While the players were property subject to purchase and sale, most money deals were for untested minor leaguers, role-playing veterans, and disgruntled stars. The Yankee dynasty had been built in just that fashion. But Ruppert and Huston had merely taken advantage of Harry Frazee's ill fortune to sup-

FROM JÄKY TO YAWKEY

The Yawkey legacy began with Tom Yawkey's great-great-great-grandfather, Johann Georg Jäky, who immigrated to Philadelphia from Germany in 1736. His grandson Georg anglicized the name to Yaky and moved first to New York and then to Ohio. Up to this time, the family was no different from millions of other American families. They farmed, worked hard, and died in anonymity.

Georg Yaky's son, John Hoover Yaky, gave the family its name, anglicizing Yaky even further, first to Yockey and, finally, Yawkey. He planted the seeds that by the end of the century made the Yawkey family one of the wealthiest in America.

He left the farm and worked as a clerk in a hardware store before opening a small sawmill in Millersport, Ohio. As the population in Ohio quadrupled from five hundred thousand in 1820 to nearly two million by 1850, the business thrived. By 1851, John H. Yawkey and Company was one of the largest lumber enterprises in the state, processing over 1.5 million board feet a year.

His son, William Clyman Yawkey, born in 1834, followed him into business and realized the real money in lumber was in raw timber. Ohio was logged out, so he looked north to Michigan and set up a mill just outside Flint, buying raw timber from Michigan's vast virgin pine forests in the Saginaw valley and reselling it to larger firms based in Chicago.

Yawkey realized what was taking place all around him: what would later be referred to as "the rape of Michigan." Supposedly inexhaustible stands of pine covering thousands of square miles in the central and northern parts of the state were virtually logged out in less than two decades.

He bought the few remaining uncut stands of timber, then watched as others exhausted their land before harvesting his own vast holdings at top dollar.

He then invested in timberlands in Minnesota, Wisconsin and Canada, and Alabama and Florida, moved his business to Detroit, and added mining operations in Minnesota's Mesaba iron range and the coal fields of West Virginia to his holdings.

By the 1880s he owned upward of 250,000 acres of timberlands, an area of nearly 400 square miles, or one-third the size of Rhode Island. By way of comparison, the largest private landowner in the United States today is reportedly media mogul Ted Turner, who owns a reported 1.25 million acres of land in Montana and other western states.

What Vanderbilt was to the railroad, and Carnegie to steel,

Yawkey was to lumber. At a time when 1 percent of the American population controlled 99 percent of the wealth, William Clyman Yawkey was a secure member of that select society. In 1900 he was the wealthiest man in Detroit, a stern, sometimes taciturn man known for his no-nonsense nature and work ethic. He had little time for what others would refer to as leisure.

William Yawkey had only two children, Augusta, born in 1871, and William Hoover, born in 1875. And just as William's brother Samuel groomed his own son Cyrus to take over their share of the business, so too did William Clyman attempt to do the same with his son, William Hoover.

But Samuel was the more successful father. Cyrus Yawkey continued to expand the Yawkey business empire in Wisconsin, the Pacific Northwest, Florida, California, and Canada, adding paper mills and lumber products to his end of the Yawkey empire. To this day, a number of corporations, among them the Monsanto Company, owe their existence to Cyrus Yawkey.

That drive was not passed down to the progeny of William Clyman Yawkey. They chose to reap the benefits of great wealth without great effort.

Augusta's job was to marry well, and she did, wedding Thomas J. Austin, a young insurance executive, in 1893. Their daughter, Emma Marie, was born a year later. Then Tom Austin was brought into the Yawkey fold. With his father-in-law he purchased Fitzwilliam Island in Ontario, 18,000 acres of untouched timber and mineral reserves at the mouth of Lake Huron's Georgian Bay, and moved into the Yawkeys' Detroit estate.

But the bulk of William Clyman Yawkey's fortune went to his son, William Hoover Yawkey. The younger Yawkey had little in common with his father. While the elder Yawkey was described in the press as a man of "scrupulous honesty and a retiring disposition," the son was later described by noted baseball historian Fred Lieb as "a man of few inhibitions [who] spent money like a drunken sailor and liked to be near the bright lights," someone with "playboy proclivities" who could "drink three men under the table." He developed an early taste for liquor and other fine things in life and eschewed the business end of things. Cousin Cyrus was the family's reigning entrepreneur. "Bill" Yawkey, or "Good Times," as the press called him, wanted to have fun.

When William Clyman retired in 1900, Bill Yawkey was off

and running, as likely to appear at the racetrack, the ballpark, a hunting lodge, or a tavern as he was at the family offices. When he cared to, he was reportedly a shrewd businessman who did a more than adequate job of maintaining the fortune. But Bill Yawkey did little to increase it. On his own for the first time in his life, he took full advantage of his father's absence.

On February 21, 1903, in Detroit, Augusta gave birth to her second child, a son she and her husband named Thomas Yawkey Austin. Born into massive wealth and privilege, the young boy who would one day own the Red Sox appeared destined to fulfill his family's legacy.

But seven months later, summering on Fitzwilliam Island, the boy's father fell ill and on September 18, 1903, Thomas Austin died of pneumonia.

After his son-in-law's death, William Clyman returned to Detroit and his grieving daughter, where he apparently lost patience with the antics of William Hoover. For just as General Charles Taylor had once purchased the Boston Americans for his son, John I., William Clyman began negotiating for the purchase of the Detroit Tigers to occupy his fun-loving son.

He died before those negotiations were consummated, but his estate, valued at perhaps as much as twenty million dollars in cash and property, primarily fell into the hands of Bill Yawkey, who bought the Tigers for fifty thousand dollars.

Yawkey wasn't satisfied to sit in the stands and watch his players from afar. He wanted to win and be in on the action himself. He opened up his wallet in 1904 and purchased ballplayers as much for their personality as for their ability to play ball, spending over fifty thousand dollars to stock the club with men who shared his approach to life and could play a little. Buying ballplayers was a way to buy friends, and a friend of Bill Yawkey's was anyone who could keep up with his prodigious appetites for alcohol, gambling, and women. He had little trouble finding ballplayers who qualified.

The team fueled Yawkey's zest for life. When they played well, he handed out cash bonuses and picked up bar tabs. When they lost, he still picked up the tab. The Tigers fed his need to gamble, and he would bet on anything at any time, at any place. He fancied himself an athlete, kept professional wrestlers under his employ, and volunteered his services as a training partner. He once wrestled another man for ten thousand dollars, lost, and laughed about it. It was all fun.

Apart from occasionally acquiring players regardless of the club's needs, Yawkey didn't interfere on the field. But as soon as the game ended, the players were often invited along to the party that followed him everywhere. Once, during a particularly brutal slump, Yawkey had the players ferried to a brothel and left instructions that they were not to return until morning. Thus rejuvenated, the team won five straight.

Although the club finished a poor seventh in 1904 and Barrow resigned in midseason, the Tigers were soon battling for the pennant. Paced by outfielders Sam Crawford, Davy Jones, and a brash young man from Georgia named Ty Cobb, the 1907 Tigers won the American League pennant by a game and a half over Philadelphia. Bill Yawkey's team was going to the World Series.

They played the Chicago Cubs, but the youthful Tigers were outmanned and managed only a first-game tie before dropping the next four games. Yawkey softened the blow by distributing his share of the Series money to the players, and they earned more than the victorious Cubs. That's the kind of guy Bill Yawkey was.

At that, Yawkey withdrew. He decided to move to New York where the big fun was, and there was no sense running the ballclub if he wasn't around to enjoy it. He loaned his business manager, Frank Navin, the money to buy half his interest in the team and thereafter treated the Tigers in true Yawkey fashion, as another investment, enjoying the return but leaving the headaches of management to someone else.

By now, young Tom Austin was calling him "Father." His relationship with Bill Yawkey would prove to be the most important of his life. He did little in his life that his uncle-turned-surrogate-father hadn't already done, or tried.

In 1906 Augusta Yawkey Austin turned her son and daughter over to brother Bill, and they grew up in a fantasy world in a posh apartment at 12 East 87th Street in New York catered to by maids, nannies, and servants. The boy lacked for nothing. From his uncle, he developed a genuine love for the game of baseball.

Bill Yawkey regularly entertained his friends from the baseball world at the family home. Dining on exotic meals of wild game and lubricating themselves with vast quantities of alcohol, Bill Yawkey and his friends talked baseball far into the night.

Young Tom Austin hung on every word as his uncle's friends, like Ty Cobb, regaled him. Tom thrilled at these stories of a world far removed from his genteel upbringing as a young gentleman.

Bill Yawkey purchased a 25,000-acre former rice plantation

on the South Carolina coast, and he and his companions made regular trips there to fish, shoot game, and indulge in other manly pursuits. Ty Cobb was the most famous and one of his most frequent companions. Bill Yawkey usually got the first call when Cobb got into trouble, and before Cobb became wealthy in his own right, Bill Yawkey's checkbook and political connections often got Cobb off the hook. The famous ballplayer became Tom Austin's favorite, whether he was talking about the run he stole, the woman he maligned, or the man he beat up just for the hell of it. Tom was mesmerized.

Yet at the same time, his early years were likely confusing and somewhat lonely. His mother, Augusta, played a diminishing role in his life, and Bill Yawkey, although he took the boy hunting in South Carolina and on tours of the families' timberlands, was still very much a single man and absent for extended periods of time. He didn't marry until 1910, when Tom Austin was seven years old, wedding Margaret Draper.

The only story Tom Yawkey ever told the press concerning his childhood was about his aunt Margaret. According to the apocryphal tale, one day the boy told his aunt that he must be the richest boy in the world. She marched him into the kitchen, filled several plates with beans, and told Tom that the beans represented the wealth of families like the Vanderbilts, Morgans, and Astors. Then she took a single bean, placed it in a bowl, and said the Yawkeys' fortune was the equivalent of that single solitary bean.

At age nine Tom was sent to the Irving School in Tarrytown, New York, a prestigious boarding school for young men of means where he would spend his formative years.

Of the Irving School's distinguished alumni, none was more important to Tom than Edward Trowbridge Collins, a standout multisport athlete who later found fame as the star second baseman of Connie Mack's Philadelphia A's. One of the greatest players ever, Collins was a fine hitter, daring baserunner, and superb fielder who served as Mack's on-field general, respected as much for his baseball savvy as for his skills. The school's annual medal awarded to the best student-athlete bore Collins's name, and every Irving boy hoped to equal his accomplishments. That was Tom Austin's dream.

On September 5, 1918, the same day the 1918 World Series began at Cubs Park in Chicago, Tom's mother, Augusta, died of influenza. The boy was now an orphan and also the sole heir of his mother's estate, worth some four million dollars, which was

Thomas Austin Yawkey was a "gentleman sportsman" who preferred to hunt, fish, and follow his baseball team rather than manage his fortune. When not living in New York or visiting Boston, Yawkey lived on an enormous seaside estate at South Island in South Carolina.

held in trust and managed for him until he reached the age of thirty.

Shortly after Augusta's death, Bill Yawkey and his wife formally adopted both Tom and his sister Emma. Thomas Yawkey Austin now became Thomas Austin Yawkey.

The following February, the Yawkeys went on an extended vacation, driving west from South Carolina to California. On the way they stopped in Augusta, Georgia, so Bill Yawkey could visit with Ty Cobb. While there Bill Yawkey caught pneumonia and died at the Plaza Hotel on March 5, 1919, Ty Cobb at his bedside.

Bill Yawkey's will was made public on March 18, 1919. That is certainly the most important date in Red Sox history, for a headline in the New York Times screamed "Schoolboy of 16 Inherits $20,000,000." According to the will, the bulk of the estate was to be split equally between his widow and adopted son, with Tom Yawkey's share to be administered by conservators until he reached the age of thirty.

It must have been a heady and somewhat awkward realization for the young man. The money was his, but yet not his. He was a Yawkey, but not a Yawkey. He was the titular head of a family of vast wealth and influence, but as yet he wielded no power. He was half.

When the will reached probate the size of the estate was appraised at only $9,422,460, as the value of Yawkey's land holdings were assessed in their raw state. After taxes and various charitable contributions were accounted for, Tom Yawkey's share came to $3,408,650. Combined with his earlier inheritance from his mother, he was now worth a minimum of seven and a half million dollars. That wasn't twenty million, but it still warranted another front-page story in the Times.

Included in the estate were 492 shares in the Detroit Tigers, appraised at a value of $113,013. But his conservators had no interest in the stock and soon sold it for five times that amount.

The deal taught Tom Yawkey two valuable lessons. Foremost was the fact that he as yet held no sway in the management of the estate, for the Tiger stock was the most attractive to him. But the lesson was clear. Wealth without control over it meant little. One day Tom Yawkey would have control and learn how to use it. The second lesson was that baseball could be profitable — Bill Yawkey's initial investment had paid off and increased in value by nearly 1,000 percent. In professional baseball, profit can never adequately be measured on a year-to-year, bottom-

line basis. Profit accumulates over time, through the increase of the club's overall value. As Tom Yawkey later admitted to Joe Williams of the New York World Telegram, "I bought it [the Red Sox] as a sporting gesture and a business investment. I am sure, in the end, it will pay dividends on both counts."

After Bill Yawkey's death, Tom Yawkey returned to Irving. He coveted the Collins award, and although he was a relatively talented athlete, he was not the best at any sport. His own roommate, Alan McMartin, won the award in both Tom's junior and senior years.

It was just as well, for Tom Yawkey was being groomed in business and had no chance of an athletic career. He applied and was accepted to the Sheffield Scientific School at Yale, where he studied chemistry, mining, and forestry. It was 1920, and Tom Yawkey was on his way to becoming a man.

There was perhaps no better time in American history to be young and wealthy. The nation was in the midst of great social change, and the giddy combination of youth and money allowed Yawkey to ride the crest of those changes. Of course, Prohibition took effect on January 16, 1920, but the ban on alcohol did little to dampen the enthusiasm of the era.

Instead, Prohibition fueled the indulgences of sex, song, and liquor that marked the era. The Jazz Age was in full swing, the Roaring Twenties were about to earn their name, and Tom Yawkey was eighteen years old and filthy rich.

Even at upper-crust Ivy League Yale, Yawkey stood out, for the Yawkey bean was bigger than that of most of his classmates. On his own for the first time and fueled by an educational allowance that enabled him to act almost as wealthy as he was, Yawkey spent the 1920s living life in the same style as his adoptive father had.

He was a fair student, but the classroom didn't mean much to Tom Yawkey. He played baseball and basketball for his class team after failing to make the varsity, but Yawkey later admitted, "I was a mediocre ballplayer, I didn't work too hard at it. I was mostly a second baseman [who] hit the ball pretty good but my fielding probably wasn't anything too sharp." Nevertheless, he later bragged about once making an unassisted triple play.

Yawkey's real education took place neither in the classroom nor on the baseball field. A classmate once told a reporter that Yawkey's years at Yale were "a life of fast cars, pretty girls, drinks and laughs." He spent freely, invited friends along for the ride, and showered them with money. Behind the wheel of a sleek

From 1933 through 1941 general manager Eddie Collins and owner Tom Yawkey spent millions on players. The result? An average fourth-place finish in the eight-team American League.

sedan with a slew of companions in tow, bolting from one speakeasy to another or nipping from a flask, Yawkey was the center of the party. He found it easy to attract women. He was clearly a catch.

But Yawkey didn't allow himself to be caught by any of the girls he found around New Haven. He did the choosing.

In 1924 Yawkey attended a performance by a traveling classical "terpsichore" or dance and choral troupe. A shapely dancer caught his eye, and he arranged to meet her after the show. That November, he and Elise Sparrow, often referred to as "Elsie" in the press, were engaged.

They appeared to have little in common. The daughter of a Birmingham, Alabama, fireman, after graduating from high school Sparrow went to work in an office. Then she entered and won a beauty contest sponsored by the local newspaper, earning her the title of "Miss Birmingham" and the right to appear as a contestant in the "Pageant of Beauty" at Atlantic City, the forerunner of the Miss America pageant. While there, she was spotted by graphic artist James Montgomery Flagg, best known for his creation of the famous World War I "Uncle Sam Wants You" army recruiting poster. The garrulous Flagg, as was his pattern, made Sparrow his model, protégée, and for a short time, probably his mistress.

Back in Birmingham, her run of good fortune with Flagg earned her the nickname of "the Cinderella Girl." When she met Yawkey, midnight was postponed indefinitely.

Just after Yawkey graduated from Yale, in June of 1925, Elise Sparrow became Mrs. Tom Yawkey. They moved to New York, where Tom Yawkey began to take a more active role in the management of the Yawkey bean.

But Yawkey found it no easier to settle down than his uncle had. He went hunting and fishing whenever he could, often with the same men who had accompanied Bill Yawkey years before, such as Ty Cobb, who in some ways became Yawkey's surrogate father and role model.

When he grew bored with the singular company of men, he went on full-blown expeditions lasting weeks, once renting a steamboat and inviting four hundred friends to tag along on a bear hunt in Alaska.

Under the conservative stewardship of his trustees, Yawkey Enterprises, which still consisted primarily of timber and mineral holdings, spiced with increasing chunks of blue chip stock, almost managed itself. Although Yawkey took on a larger role in the company, he was just marking time until he reached the age of thirty and would take full control.

While on a hunting trip with Cobb in 1926, the ballplayer told Tom he should buy a baseball team, just as Bill Yawkey had done, and offered to help in any such effort. But on a similar trip in 1927, Cobb took a shot out of turn, and Yawkey took offense. They fought, Cobb won, and the volatile former player never spoke to Yawkey again.

By then, however, Yawkey had given Cobb's suggestion some thought. The idea of buying a ballclub was intriguing. Tom Yawkey was almost thirty years old and about to meet his destiny. ⚾

plement what they already had, just as Frazee had once used Connie Mack. No one had ever been so brazen as to try to build an entire team from scratch through such a crass strategy.

Yawkey, on the other hand, created the market himself by opening his wallet and asking, "How much?"

He didn't have to ask twice. Within minutes, Yawkey was cornered by Phil Ball, owner of the only team with the ability to challenge the Yawkees for last place, the St. Louis Browns. After a few moments Yawkey took out his checkbook and gave the Browns a check for what Collins referred to as "a whale of a lot of the coin of the realm," believed to be fifty thousand dollars, and catcher Merv Shea. In return, the Yawkees received pitcher Lloyd Brown and catcher Rick Ferrell.

A new era in baseball had begun. Ferrell and Brown weren't big stars. While Ferrell was a very good player, Brown was a journeyman. The price Yawkey paid was stunning.

That first transaction was emblematic of many others Yawkey would make. Over and over again, he overpaid for talent past its prime or players whose personalities offset their on-field contributions. Then, once he had them, Yawkey paid the players more than they were worth. A disproportionate number were cut in the mold of Ty Cobb and were natives of the South (Brown was from Texas and Ferrell from North Carolina).

Still, for the 6-13 Sox, any deal was a plus and symbolic of Yawkey's commitment to the team. He told the press, "I am in the market for good players and will buy any that are available. I do not intend to stop until the Red Sox are strong enough to compete with any club in the league on even terms."

As visions of dollar signs danced in their heads the other owners soon recovered from their initial shock. After digesting Yawkey's deal with the Browns, they realized he wasn't just rich — he was naive, the equivalent of a novice poker player who'd just bought in to a game he didn't understand. They welcomed him to the table.

On May 12, the Yankees were the recipients of his philanthropy. With the May 15 trading and roster deadline approaching, New York was two players over the limit. It was common knowledge that they would have to release a pitcher and an infielder, two positions where the talent-laden club was overstocked.

Yawkey happily solved their quandary. He paid an astounding one hundred thousand dollars for pitcher George Pipgras, a former star on his way down, and rookie shortstop Billy Werber, two players he could have gotten for almost nothing a few days later.

The cost of doing business in baseball had just gone up. One day later Yawkey paid minor league Newark thirty thousand dollars for twenty-five-year-old North Carolina native Dusty Cooke, an outfielder. Had the trading deadline of May 15 not been in effect, he may never have stopped.

In only five days, at a time when people were begging in the streets for food, Tom Yawkey had spent approximately two hundred thirty thousand dollars on ballplayers, an amount that even Eddie Collins admitted was "a sum so vast as to shock the baseball world in these parious times."

But neither the press nor the public took offense at his profligacy. They took a vicarious thrill as Tom Yawkey acted as if hard times didn't exist and just kept getting richer. In July, his aunt died and he inherited another three million dollars. That more than paid for his new toys: the ballclub, Fenway Park, and his brand-new players.

Baseball had no desire to rebuke the young owner as everyone was concerned only about the bottom line and the short term. Money ruled. But Yawkey's approach inflated the value of ballplayers and sent baseball on an upward monetary spiral that led directly to the era of free agency in place today not only in baseball, but in other professional sports as well.

Although the new players helped the team, in 1933 the additions were more symbolic than substantive. The Sox were better, but still very bad. As the 1934 *Spalding Official Baseball Guide* later noted, "It is useless to review the work of the team in the 1933 season except in terms of reconstruction."

They finished the year 63-86, twenty games better than 1932, but still thirty-four and a half games behind Washington, who upset the Yankees to win the AL pennant. The highlight of the season was a five-game sweep of the Yankees by the Yawkees in mid-

June that permanently lifted the team from the basement to seventh place. In July they even won more than they lost, their first month over .500 since August of 1924. Attendance was even up.

Yawkey spent as much time as possible attending to his team, but his office and home were in New York. Day-to-day affairs were left to Eddie Collins.

Collins made some changes behind the scenes.

Many longtime employees who worked on the grounds or in concessions had been with the team since they played at the Huntington Avenue Grounds. He sacked almost everyone.

According to the late Bill Gavin, who worked for the club in the late 1920s, religion was the reason. Collins was Episcopalian, and most of the workers Irish-Catholic.

THE LEFTY

In an era dominated by hitting, Lefty Grove was one of the most dominant pitchers ever. The Baltimore Orioles' Jack Dunn, the same man who discovered Babe Ruth, also found Lefty Grove. Dunn knew what he had and kept Grove with Baltimore until he'd already won 109 games for him. He was finally sold to the Philadelphia Athletics in 1925 after Dunn demanded, and received, more than he had for Ruth.

Grove went on to win another 300 games in the majors. From 1927 to 1933 he never won fewer than twenty games a season, going a remarkable 79-15 from 1929 to 1931. Over his nine-year career in Philadelphia, he led the league in strikeouts seven times, ERA five times, and wins four times. In 1931 he went 31-4 for the pennant-winners, including a stretch in which he won seventeen straight.

Grove's fastball was the best in baseball, the near-equal of Walter Johnson's or Joe Wood's, and he had magnificent control. Moreover, the rough-hewn veteran from the hardscrabble hills of western Maryland hated to lose. Ill-tempered and hard to get along with even when he pitched well (he regularly grabbed scorecards from kids who wanted his autograph, tore them up, threw them in their faces, and laughed about it), when he lost he was even worse. He thought nothing of berating his infielders in the middle of a game for failing to make plays. His teammates knew to stay out of his way, but they also knew what he meant to a ballclub. With Grove on the mound, you won. It was that simple.

But Grove came with a price. The lefthander expected, and received, special treatment. In Philadelphia, he was the only player on the club who dared cross Mack, curse him, or address him as "Connie." He worked out and trained according to his own schedule and occasionally asked for and received brief midseason "vacations," during which he often pitched for semipro clubs at top dollar. At contract time, he was a tough negotia-

Robert Moses "Lefty" Grove was a particular favorite of owner Tom Yawkey, who loved to invite the temperamental star to his South Carolina estate to hunt during the off-season. At Fenway Park Grove crafted a phenomenal won-lost record of 54-17 while pitching for the Red Sox.

tor and, despite his eighth-grade education, a shrewd businessman who managed to keep his money during the market crash.

One of the great misfortunes of Red Sox history is that Boston acquired Grove at the precise time his arm went bad. Had he remained healthy, the Red Sox may well have won a pennant or World Series. Even with a bad arm, he still pitched well enough to remain in the top ten in many team pitching categories. And his 55-17 record is the best record of any left-handed pitcher in Fenway Park.

Yawkey wasn't bothered by such mundane matters. He was focused on his decaying ballpark, a fact no amount of paint could disguise.

No one had ever waxed rhapsodic about old Fenway Park or called for its preservation. It was just a place to watch the Red Sox, nothing more and, in recent years, even less.

Yawkey knew that unless he improved the park, fans wouldn't come to Fenway no matter who he brought in to play. He made plans to renovate.

At first, he simply intended to spruce up the old joint to the tune of five hundred thousand dollars, replacing old seats, adding covered stands in right, and making a few cosmetic changes. But after discussing his ideas with Osborn Engineering of Cleveland, he embarked on a near-total reconstruction.

He decided to rebuild the right-field bleachers in concrete and extend them into center field, integrating them with the rest of the park, and build new concrete grandstands in right field and left. The existing grandstand would be almost entirely rebuilt, the footings reinforced, and the steelwork supporting the roof enhanced to support a second deck, in case he ever decided to add the feature. Additional box seats would be added in front of the stands, and home plate pushed toward the outfield. Duffy's Cliff would be greatly diminished, and the left-field fence would be razed and rebuilt to accommodate a huge new scoreboard. The reconstruction would increase seating capacity from twenty-six thousand to thirty-eight thousand fans.

He also added a new press box and pressroom where the bar was always open and the food was always free. The most comfortable in the majors at the time, such creature comforts helped ensure that Yawkey would be treated kindly by local scribes.

The cost increased to one and a half million dollars, but Yawkey was unconcerned. "Renovate be damned," he told a reporter. "Let's build a new ballpark and have it right."

The project was even more significant to the public than was his purchase of ballplayers. For with the exception of the construction of the Mystic Bridge in Charlestown, it was the largest building project completed in Boston during the Depression. Building New Fenway Park employed approximately 750 skilled union workers, used 15,000 cubic yards of concrete, 550 tons of steel, 100,000 bricks, 8,000 cu-

General manager Eddie Collins gives Tom Yawkey and his first wife Elise (also referred to as Elsie by the press) a tour of the Fenway Park reconstruction in the winter of 1934. Yawkey and Collins sought nothing less than the complete overhaul of the organization in an effort to erase fifteen years of futility.

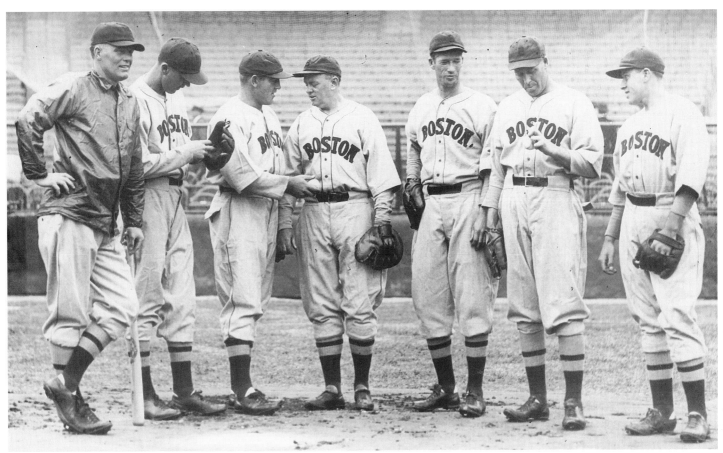

bic feet of sod, and 500,000 feet of lumber, some of it undoubtedly harvested from the Yawkey lands. It was like Yawkey's own private WPA project and turned hundreds of workers and their families into Red Sox fans.

His only problem was time. George Preston Marshall's National Football League Boston Redskins occupied Fenway Park until December. Most construction had to take place in the dead of winter.

Meanwhile Yawkey didn't ignore what was happening on the field. On October 2, he fired manager Marty McManus. He wanted his own guy and could have hired anyone. All of a sudden, the Red Sox manager's job was a plum.

But he already had someone in mind. Player-manager Bucky Harris had led Washington to pennants in 1924 and 1925 and earned the nickname "The Boy Manager." He moved on to Detroit in 1929 and had since retired as a player, but had been unable to duplicate his early success and had been sacked with two games left in the 1933 season.

But that wasn't why Yawkey wanted to hire him.

Harris was married to Elizabeth Sutherland, the daughter of a United States senator. Yawkey's wife was friendly with Mrs. Harris, and Harris was close friends with George Preston Marshall, who highly recommended him.

Yawkey impetuously hired him without consulting Eddie Collins. That was a mistake.

Collins and Harris had hated each other since their playing days. Collins was livid at Yawkey's decision, but had to accept it. Still, the hiring soon caused a schism between the field and the front office, for GM Collins acted without regard to manager Harris's wishes. Another Yawkey tradition was born.

After football season, work began at Fenway Park. Virtually the entire park was razed, leaving little more that the original structural steel supports in the grandstand.

The owner was still in a buying mood and in minor deals had already acquired several hot prospects. But at the winter meetings in Chicago he outdid himself.

In exchange for one hundred twenty-five thousand

Unidentified, pitcher Johnny Welch, second baseman Bill Cissell, catcher Gordon Hinkle, pitcher Lefty Grove, pitcher Rube Walberg, and Bill Werber gather at the Yankee Stadium backstop, circa 1934.

On January 5, 1934, fourteen years to the day after Babe Ruth had been sold to the Yankees, a fire broke out in the wooden framework under the centerfield bleachers. Insurance covered part of the quarter-million-dollar loss and necessitated the use of double shifts to complete park renovations by Opening Day.

dollars and two inept players from the Quinn era, Rabbit Warstler and Bob Kline, Connie Mack gave Yawkey star second baseman Max Bishop and veteran pitcher Rube Walberg, who despite going 9-13 in 1933 had won seventeen in 1932.

But that wasn't the half of it. For another one hundred twenty-five thousand dollars Yawkey also bought the best pitcher in baseball, Robert "Lefty" Grove.

When Grove first learned about the terms of the sale, he reportedly demanded and received 10 percent of the purchase price. Yawkey also raised his salary from twenty-five thousand dollars to thirty thousand dollars.

In Philadelphia, Connie Mack had Grove's respect and had been able to keep him in check. But in Boston the lines of authority were blurred. Grove

shared Collins's dislike for Bucky Harris and treated the manager with disdain. When he wanted something, he went straight to Yawkey, and the starstruck owner readily accommodated him. Grove came and went as he pleased, kept liquor in his locker, and regularly used Tom Yawkey's private office as his own, where he particularly enjoyed putting his feet up on the desk.

As surely as the club was improving, it was also being split in two camps, one of surly, high-priced veterans who did what they wanted, and the other of lesser-paid role players. Harris couldn't control either faction, Collins didn't want to, and Yawkey was too starry-eyed to try. A dangerous precedent was set, one that would plague the team for years.

Grove, Walberg, and Bishop had cost Yawkey two

How the Housewarming Will Look! By Coyne

Cartoonist Bob Coyne depicts both how the new Fenway Park will look and how much it will cost. The near-total reconstruction created a park that barely resembled its predecessor. However, as in the old park, the left-field wall was retained and was still covered with advertising.

hundred fifty thousand dollars. In only ten months, his total investment in the team and park was now over three million dollars and climbing.

After the Grove deal the *Boston Globe* announced, "Fenway Park Club in Race," and the *Post* echoed that sentiment with a headline that read "Means Boston Will Be Pennant Contender." Two days later Yawkey made even those lofty claims seem pessimistic when he traded three players for St. Louis Browns outfielder Carl Reynolds, a career .300 hitter with some power.

The team was changing as rapidly as Fenway Park, and the pace of rebuilding had quickened. In order to pour concrete during cold weather, engineers warmed forms under a temporary canvas roof heated by thirty-eight miniature furnaces called "salamanders." It was an expensive way to build, but Tom Yawkey wasn't concerned about the money. By the first of the year, the bleachers were almost finished as workers rushed to complete the job as quickly as possible. They even left the wooden formwork in place. Tom Yawkey was in a hurry.

But just after one o'clock on the afternoon of January 5, one of the men working in the center-field stands smelled smoke. The network of wooden forms and the canvas covering provided ample fuel and within minutes the bleachers were ablaze. In a few moments the wind-whipped canvas shredded and the fire jumped to buildings across the street. Dense smoke caused rail traffic on the Boston and Albany railroad to halt.

The five-alarm fire destroyed the new bleachers as the intense heat blasted holes in the concrete. The cause was never determined. Investigators speculated that the salamanders were somehow to blame but found no real evidence to back up their claims.

Yawkey, vacationing on his South Carolina estate, was informed immediately. Smoke still hung in the air when Eddie Collins announced that Yawkey had decided to rebuild and have the park ready by Open-

Lefty Grove arrived in Boston in 1934 with a sore arm. He eventually recovered to win 105 games with Boston, including a twenty-win season in 1935. Grove won his three hundredth and final game at Fenway Park in 1941.

The fire department concluded that the second fire was arson, as, they now surmised, the first had been as well. They speculated the fires had been set to cover up a planned payroll heist.

But there were other reasons to burn the park, namely one thousand men working in three shifts and collecting overtime who otherwise would have been out of work. Those jobs were highly valued. When the nephew of the city building commissioner was inadvertently laid off, for instance, the commissioner came down hard on the project, costing Yawkey thousands of dollars in delays and changes.

After the second fire Collins announced, "We are going to open this park on April 17 if we have to call out the state militia." Work proceeded under private armed guard.

With a new ballpark on the horizon and virtually a new team on the field, Red Sox fans and officials were optimistic as the team began spring training in Sarasota in early March. Lefty Grove gave the team its first stopper in years, and there appeared to be an abundance of talent at several positions.

But as Sox fans had long been accustomed, early optimism rarely lasted. Grove came to camp with a sore left shoulder, which team doctors concluded was due to several abscessed teeth. They were pulled, but his vaunted fastball was gone.

Nevertheless, the Sox were still picked by the Associated Press to finish third behind Washington and New York.

They opened the 1934 season in Boston at New Fenway Park. Club officials were stunned when 32,909 fans pushed through the turnstiles for their first look at the remade ballyard.

They weren't disappointed, at least in the new accommodations. Tom Yawkey's money turned the park into a virtual palace. It would look much the same for the next forty years.

New, wider seats and additional stands increased the park's capacity by more than eleven thousand. Apart from the bleachers, the stands were roofed and the entire park painted "Dartmouth green." New construction coupled with the relocation of home plate some 10 feet toward center field greatly diminished foul territory, and the new stands in right and

ing Day. "Fenway will be completed by April 1 and will be ready for the opening game in all its glory," he said.

Within the next few days, the workforce increased by three hundred. The blaze had caused two hundred fifty thousand dollars in damages and was only partially covered by insurance. But Yawkey was committed to the project and it was too late to turn back anyway. The bleachers were raised as work continued at a frantic pace.

But six weeks later, on February 19, workers in center field noticed a "curl of smoke and a tongue of flame" licking through the canvas at the precise spot where the earlier fire had begun. They attacked the small fire with chemical extinguishers and put it out before it caused more than superficial damage.

center fields greatly reduced the distance to those fences.

But the real change was in left field, where the fence supported a huge new electric scoreboard, the first to use the now-standard green and red lights to denote strikes and balls. Three large advertisements covered most of the rest of the green wall, which was still years away from being dubbed "the Green Monster."

But monstrous it would be, for good and ill. For although the wall at the left-field foul line was marked as 315 feet from home plate, that figure was a fantasy from the first day the new park was opened. Blueprints dating from the reconstruction place the wall at only 308 feet from home plate. For the first time, it assumed its now familiar dimensions, towering 36 feet above the subtle rise of a greatly diminished Duffy's Cliff that served as a warning track. The new lively baseball made the once-distant wall the park's dominant feature.

The Sox were upbeat about the future. But real fans couldn't have helped but notice that this brand-new team, which so many expected to be a contender, was still lacking. With Grove out, the Opening Day starter was Gordon "Dusty" Rhodes, a dismal 13-23 in 1932 and 1933. He was the best they had.

In the first inning, two walks, three hits, and three errors led to four Washington runs. Boston lost 6-5 as Senators pitcher Earl Whitehill later homered into the right-field stands for the first round-tripper in the new park. Boston still had a long way to go.

Inconsistent pitching and porous defense became a club trademark. Grove returned in relief on May 5 against St. Louis but couldn't get anyone out before leaving the mound in disgust. He tried again nine days later and did better as the Sox fell to 11-12 with an 8-2 loss to Chicago, but his return was premature. For much of the year he was either injured or sick as doctors removed still more teeth and even his tonsils. When he did pitch, he was maddeningly inconsistent. Once he put on a Boston uniform, the best pitcher in baseball became one of the worst.

Although attendance was up, Yawkey was impatient. On May 15 he gave New York twenty thousand dollars and an infielder for veteran shortstop Lyn Lary, whom Frank Crosetti made expendable. Lary

Brothers Wes (*l*) and Rick Ferrell (*r*) were Red Sox teammates for four seasons, during which time Wes won sixty-two games and hit .308 while Rick batted .302. The ever-volatile Wes earned a reputation as one of the most vocal players in the majors. He was, at times, his own worst enemy in a career that saw him play for a total of six teams over eighteen years.

became Boston's starter while Werber was moved to third.

The move made no difference. On May 25 Yawkey got antsy again.

As Boston pitchers were giving up twenty-four hits and forty-three total bases in an 18-3 rout by the Indians, Yawkey sent Collins to see Cleveland general manager Billy Evans. Four-time twenty-game winner Wes Ferrell, Rick Ferrell's brother, had held out and been suspended by Cleveland. He was playing semipro ball in his native North Carolina.

There was nothing wrong with his arm, although his head was another matter, for Ferrell had a well-deserved reputation for being a bad-tempered prima donna. Yawkey didn't care. He needed pitching.

Cleveland, glad to be rid of him, accepted Yawkey's offer of two players and twenty-five thousand dollars for Ferrell and outfielder Dick Porter.

Ferrell was quickly reinstated by Landis and given his raise by Yawkey. In his first appearance on June 4, he shut down the first-place Yankees and the Sox

Washington Senators player-manager Joe Cronin meets with Red Sox outfielder Mel Almada prior to the opening of the new Fenway Park on April 17, 1934. Within a year Cronin would be dealt by his father-in-law Clark Griffith to the Red Sox for two hundred fifty thousand dollars and Boston shortstop Lyn Lary.

Winning, however, was. Near the end of the season, Yawkey reportedly asked Collins, "Who's the best ballplayer in the league?" Collins replied, "Joe Cronin," the Washington Senators' shortstop and manager.

Although Cronin was in the midst of a storied career, few others in baseball at the time would have agreed. Originally signed by Pittsburgh off the San Francisco sandlots at age seventeen in 1925, he was eventually sold to Kansas City before Washington pried him away for fifty thousand dollars in 1928.

By 1930 he was a star, earning MVP honors while hitting .346. In 1933 he was named player-manager and was given credit for wresting the pennant from the Yankees.

But Cronin had since slipped. He had an off-year in 1934, hitting under .300 for the first time since 1929 and fielding poorly as the Senators finished seventh, twenty games under .500 — and ten games behind Boston. In early September he had broken the wrist on his throwing hand after colliding with Wes Ferrell on a play at first base.

He was still a very good ballplayer and had played particularly well against the Red Sox. But in a league that still included such luminaries as Charlie Gehringer, Hank Greenberg, Lou Gehrig, Jimmie Foxx, and Al Simmons, all of whom were in their prime, Collins's response was flawed. Nevertheless, Yawkey said, "Go get him."

Now Collins tried to talk him out of it. He told Yawkey that Cronin had just married Washington owner Clark Griffith's adopted daughter and niece and Griffith was unlikely to make the deal at any price. Besides, Lyn Lary was a fine shortstop. Boston needed pitching and a power hitter, not another infielder. Philadelphia slugger Jimmie Foxx was reportedly available.

But Tom Yawkey was still the kid who had learned the nuances of the game from Bill Yawkey and men like Cobb. As he earlier told Bill Cunningham, Yawkey believed that "baseball needs a lot more of the old time religion . . . I mean the game was better back then. Sluggers have changed baseball completely, and I'm not at all sure the change has been for the better." Cronin was more his kind of player. Besides, Yawkey was the boss and more than a little drunk

pulled to within a game of .500, only four and a half behind New York.

But Grove continued to get pounded and the Sox lost traction. They watched helplessly as Detroit, New York, and Cleveland pulled away in the second half. They finished fourth, 76-76, twenty-four long games behind pennant-winning Detroit. Attendance had doubled since 1933, to six hundred thousand fans, a level that would remain more or less constant for the next decade. Ferrell managed to go 14-5 but Grove finished 8-8 with an ERA of 6.50.

Connie Mack offered Yawkey his money back for the damaged star, but Yawkey turned him down. Money, as yet, was no object to Tom Yawkey.

with the power of his inheritance. If Collins thought Cronin was the best player, well, that's what Tom Yawkey wanted. Period.

Collins warmed to the idea when he realized that if the Sox got Cronin, Harris would have to go. That suited him just fine, for as the *Globe*'s Mel Webb later commented, it was "well known that during the later part of last season all was not just 'beer and skittles' between the clubhouse and the office upstairs."

Yawkey called Griffith personally and proposed a deal. Griffith, who had never sold a ballplayer, put him off at first, but Yawkey kept upping his offer until Griffith gave in and said yes. Like almost every other owner in the game, he was in the red and Yawkey's offer gave him a quick way to balance his books. So for a remarkable two hundred fifty thousand dollars,

plus Lyn Lary, Griffith sold off his son-in-law, leading one writer to quip, "I wish I could sell my son in law for $250,000. Any bidders?"

The Boston press was overjoyed as Cronin, who'd been tipped off about the impending deal, said all the right things from his San Francisco home. "Boston is one of the greatest sports towns in the world," he said. "A fellow with an Irish name like mine ought to get along well there." A five-year contract to serve as player-manager for thirty thousand dollars a year, a raise of ten thousand dollars, would help. The deposed Bucky Harris returned to Washington and took Cronin's place as manager.

Cronin was just the beginning of that off-season. But instead of going after Foxx, Yawkey sent Mack another big check for aging outfielder Bing Miller

Joe Cronin was welcomed by Boston fans after his purchase by Yawkey in 1935. They hoped the Washington "boy wonder," who led the Senators to a pennant in 1933, could duplicate his success in Boston. It took him eleven seasons.

and dumped another fifty thousand dollars plus for rookies Babe Dahlgren and Mel Almada from the Pacific Coast League.

The press expected Boston to challenge Detroit and New York for the pennant. In the spring Lefty Grove's arm showed signs of life, Ferrell and Fritz Ostermueller pitched well, and righthander Johnny Welch was the camp sensation. Dahlgren looked great at first, and the outfield of Roy Johnson, Reynolds, and Mel Almada appeared adequate.

On Opening Day in New York Wes Ferrell tossed a two-hitter and Billy Werber stole a run with some aggressive baserunning. For one day, anyway, the Red Sox were in first place.

They didn't stay there for long. The club soon began showing enough cracks to make the fans impatient, the press suspicious, and Tom Yawkey nervous. Joe Cronin started making unforgivable errors on routine groundballs.

His miscues gave his teammates pause. The veterans on the club, like Grove and Ferrell, were already distant to the new manager, whom they hadn't liked as a player for Washington. While they didn't go into open revolt, they didn't bother to hide their disdain.

In fact, the entire pitching staff mistrusted Cronin, who tried to call pitches and criticized them in the press. They thought he was overpaid and a defensive liability. He wasn't even hitting.

By May 1 the team's troubles were being aired in the press. Even *Post* columnist Bill Cunningham, a Cronin apologist, had to admit that Cronin appeared to be a victim of "nerves" and wondered whether his broken wrist had permanently diminished his level of play. "As a matter of fact," wrote Cunningham, "if first for the Sox were guarded by a less agile and spectacular fielder than young Babe Dahlgren, Marse Joe would stand charged with more errors than he has."

As the White Sox, Yankees, and Indians all got off to quick starts and pulled ahead, Yawkey kept his checkbook at the ready. Even as he traveled to Alaska with his wife and another couple to hunt bear, when Cronin complained that Max Bishop was slowing down at second base, Yawkey authorized another check and the Sox bought young A's infielder Dib Williams.

But when Williams failed to impress, Collins and Yawkey didn't waste time. Three weeks later they bought aging St. Louis Browns second baseman Oscar Melillo.

Yawkey had better luck going after bear, for his deals made no difference. Despite the return of Grove, who learned to depend on his other pitches and won twenty games while leading the league in ERA, and twenty-five wins from Wes Ferrell, the Red Sox sputtered through the season, a contender on paper only.

A single play epitomized the team's performance in general and Cronin's in particular. In the first game of a doubleheader against Cleveland in Fenway Park on September 7, the Red Sox, trailing 5-1, rallied in the ninth to score twice.

With the bases loaded and no outs, Cronin ripped a line drive toward third. The ball struck third baseman Odell Hall on the head and deflected toward shortstop Bill Knickerbocker. He grabbed the ball in the air to put out Cronin, then tossed to second baseman Roy Hughes to double off Billy Werber, then Hughes threw to first to catch Almada. The triple play ended the game.

The 1935 season ended a few weeks later. Despite the addition of Cronin and the expenditure of another three hundred thousand dollars plus on ballplayers, the team the press now sometimes called the "Gold Sox" or "Millionaires" finished only a game and a half better than their record in 1934, in fourth place at 78-75, sixteen games behind Detroit.

After three years as owner, Tom Yawkey still had one season remaining to match the record of his uncle Bill, who had won a pennant in his fourth season as owner of the Tigers. At the cost of three and a half million dollars, he had learned that it was indeed possible to buy a ballclub, a ballpark, and any ballplayer he wanted. But his larger goal still remained out of reach. Apparently, a world championship team couldn't be bought at any price.

YAWKEY'S WAYS

1936 | 1938

Joe Cronin was the most noteworthy of Tom Yawkey's Depression-era purchases. Upon his arrival in 1935 the ruddy-faced player-manager became an instant fan favorite in Irish-Catholic Boston.

Entering the 1936 season, the Red Sox' weaknesses were obvious. In an era that increasingly valued power, the Red Sox were lacking. In 1935 they had scored 201 fewer runs than the pennant-winning Detroit Tigers. They were also the worst defensive team in the league and had little pitching depth beyond Lefty Grove and Wes Ferrell.

Moreover, the combination of Yawkey's profligate spending, impatience, and lack of baseball savvy created a club increasingly divided against itself. The players were split into several camps: the younger role-players who supported Cronin, and the well-paid veteran stars who did not. Cronin and Collins also didn't see eye to eye. Each man regularly went over the head of the other to Yawkey, where they had to stand in line behind players who were doing the same thing.

Yawkey didn't know how to bring everyone together and reach a consensus, and he couldn't say no to anyone who had ever donned a major league uniform. He responded impulsively to most problems by throwing money in their direction. That had once been Bill Yawkey's way. Now, it was Tom's.

The Boston press and fans eagerly awaited the annual winter meetings scheduled for December. Everyone wondered who Yawkey would buy this time.

The Athletics still had Yawkey's eye. In November Mack offered the Red Sox the better half of his starting lineup, including slugging first baseman Jimmie Foxx, shortstop Eric McNair, promising third baseman Pinky Higgins, and outfielders Wally Moses and Doc Cramer, whom *Baseball Magazine* lauded as "one of the half dozen leading outfielders in the major leagues." All he wanted in exchange was Billy Werber, a holdout who was beginning to grate on the Boston front office; a few warm bodies; and a couple of hundred thousand dollars. Chicken feed.

The proposed deal illustrates the problems with the Red Sox front office, for it all but ignored the presence and wishes of Cronin, a player whom just one year earlier Collins and Yawkey had considered the best in the league. McNair was a shortstop, and a pretty good one. The press speculated that Cronin would move to first while Jimmie Foxx went to the outfield.

But Cronin had other ideas. He responded to rumors by telling the *Post,* "We can certainly use Foxx and Roger [Doc] Cramer would be a star in any man's ball club. But I don't know what in the world we would use McNair for. I plan to play shortstop myself."

Cronin's misgivings were ignored. Yawkey acquired Foxx and pitcher Johnny Marcum for two players and between one hundred fifty and two hundred thousand dollars. A second

Although he stood only 6 feet tall and weighed 190 pounds Jimmie Foxx was known throughout the American League as "the Beast" because of his talent as a pure hitter. Foxx belted 222 of his career total of 534 home runs for the Red Sox while becoming the first Red Sox player to sock fifty homers in his MVP season of 1938.

Originally signed by Mack at age sixteen as a catcher, Foxx sat on the A's bench for several seasons before taking over as regular first baseman at age twenty-one in 1928. The stocky, powerfully built Foxx, whose bulging forearms earned him the nickname "the Beast" from his teammates, soon became Philadelphia's answer to the Bambino.

His powerful bat helped lead the club to American League pennants in 1929, 1930, and 1931. In 1932 he nearly topped Ruth's home run record when he cracked 58 home runs and knocked in 169, narrowly missing the batting title but winning the AL's MVP award. Then, in 1933, he won the triple crown and repeated as MVP. In 1934 and 1935, despite the fact that Mack was selling off everyone else in the lineup, Foxx continued to knock the ball around the American League, striking for forty-four home runs in 1934 and a league-best thirty-six in 1935. Only twenty-eight years old, Foxx already had 303 career home runs.

He also had a strong arm and ran surprisingly well. Yet he never approached Ruth's popularity, for Foxx lacked the Yankees slugger's charisma. Even on the A's he'd been overshadowed by Simmons, Mickey Cochrane, and Grove.

Foxx was delighted by the trade, for he knew he'd get a raise from Yawkey and told the press his contract would have to be adjusted to make up for the income he'd lose from his business interests in Philadelphia. He then predicted that in 1936 he would be good for "no less than 200 hits, which will include fifty home runs, 150 RBIs and 125 runs scored."

But Yawkey wanted more. Hotheaded New York outfielder Ben Chapman, a .300 hitter and one of the best base stealers in the league, had worn out his welcome in New York after getting into an altercation with a Jewish fan and making some anti-Semitic remarks. He later became infamous as manager of the Phillies for his vile, racist bench-jockeying of Jackie Robinson in 1947. Although Chapman repented before passing away in 1996, his bigotry and ill temper marred an otherwise fine career.

But Chapman's baggage didn't matter in Boston. Yawkey made New York a generous offer, but New York manager Joe McCarthy squashed the deal,

deal was also cut, although it wasn't made official until January for tax purposes. For another seventy-five thousand dollars and two nonentities Yawkey would get Cramer and McNair. Higgins, Moses, and Werber, for the time being, stayed put.

But before the deals were made public, it took Yawkey and Collins two hours to convince Cronin to go along with the transactions. The Boston press ignored the rift and again predicted a pennant, as the *Globe*'s Gerry Moore giddily pronounced, "Boston today ascended to the position of No. 1 baseball city of the universe on the wings of Tom Yawkey's magic pocketbook."

On paper, such optimism appeared warranted. Marcum had just won seventeen games for Mack's 58-91 Athletics, and Jimmie Foxx was aptly described as "the right-handed Babe Ruth." Fenway's left-field wall would never be looked at quite the same way again.

knowing the longer he waited, the more Yawkey would pay. Besides, he didn't want Chapman to go to a rival.

Yawkey was still hungry, and on December 17 he shipped Carl Reynolds and Roy Johnson to Washington for outfielder Heinie Manush, a thirteen-year veteran with a career batting average of over .330. But he overlooked the fact that Manush was coming off his worst big league season and had hit just .273 in 1935. That kind of deal was becoming a Yawkey trademark.

Boston began spring training with one of the strongest lineups in baseball. But in an attempt to satisfy all parties, a number of players were shuffled into unfamiliar positions. Manush and Cramer played left and center, but Billy Werber was thrown into right field and McNair moved to third so Cronin could play short, with Melillo at second and Foxx at first. Ferrell, backed by the studious Moe Berg, was a stalwart behind the plate, and with Marcum to supplement Grove, Ferrell, and Ostermueller, it appeared that, for once, Boston had four solid starting pitchers.

But all was not well. Manush, Melillo, and Miller all showed their age, Cronin continued to struggle in the field, Marcum had a bad elbow, and Foxx wasn't hitting. Team chemistry was rotten. The club played poorly, and by the end of March the press was intimating there were deeper troubles.

On April 1, the *Post*'s Bill Cunningham aired a rumor that "Jimmy [sic] Foxx is drunk all the time," and that other players were running wild late at night. Werber held out for more money, blasted some of the other Sox infielders, then reluctantly signed, but became a problem in the clubhouse.

Alcohol abuse has always been baseball's dirty little secret and has probably ruined or cut short more careers than the combined effects of torn rotator cuffs and anterior cruciate ligaments. The Red Sox haven't been immune to the malady. In the first decade or so of Yawkey's ownership they earned a reputation as the hardest-drinking team in the game. It started at the top. For Tom Yawkey, taking another page from the life of his uncle, often led the parade.

Foxx, although in his prime, "liked his brew and broads" in the words of one scribe. Owner and player

Joe Cronin and Connie Mack meet at Fenway Park in 1938. Mack supplied much of the high-priced imported talent purchased by Yawkey during the thirties, including future Hall of Famers Lefty Grove and Jimmie Foxx. Most of the deals were engineered by his former second baseman and Red Sox general manager Eddie Collins.

spent many evenings carousing together, which caused the divisions on the team to deepen. Discipline was impossible to enforce. Everyone knew that Yawkey's favorites were allowed to play by a different set of rules.

The press finally began to take a critical look at Yawkey. He had now spent nearly four million dollars on the Sox, including more than a million dollars for players, with few results apart from a doubling of home attendance. There had to be an end somewhere, and they speculated he was finally running out of cash.

Yawkey scoffed and said he "wasn't very likely" to ever run out of cash. He wasn't being brash. He was still loaded.

The question of precisely how much Yawkey was worth when he came into the game of baseball and how much his fortune grew during his years in the game is difficult to answer with any certainty. For while his birthright had totaled only some nine million dollars, that doesn't take into account any increase in value over the years.

Contemporary accounts identified him as one of the ten or twelve wealthiest individuals in America, not insignificant at a time when John D. Rockefeller and Henry Ford still walked the earth.

Several incidents in the spring of 1936 strongly suggest that Yawkey hadn't underestimated his fortune. Rule changes in 1931 allowed teams to start building their own minor league farm systems. While most teams were slow to take advantage, others, most notably Branch Rickey's St. Louis Cardinals and the New York Yankees, were not. They both quickly developed extensive farm systems, signing and supplying players to teams they owned or controlled in order to ensure a constant influx of new talent while selling off the surplus to other teams.

In 1936, Yawkey and Collins decided to start doing the same. They hired former umpire and Cleveland general manager Billy Evans to run the operation, then spent fifty thousand dollars — a pittance to Yawkey — to build a network of working agreements with nine minor league teams from San Diego to Rocky Mount, North Carolina. Evans was given a lucrative twelve-thousand-five-hundred-dollar contract to run the operation.

It was also reported that Mrs. Yawkey lost and then recovered a million dollars' worth of jewelry in a hotel. At the same time Yawkey embarked on an ambitious set of improvements to his South Carolina estate: altering the landscape to provide additional cover for shore birds and game and building a virtual village to house his employees. According to local residents he even bankrolled a brothel, the Sunset Lodge, that catered to Yawkey, his well-heeled friends in the area, and his club as it barnstormed north every spring. Clearly, the Yawkey bean was still firmly planted and spreading like a weed.

The Red Sox opened the season crushing the A's 9-4 at Fenway as Jimmie Foxx slammed three hits, including a triple. Yet even in victory, there were al-

THE YAWKEY BEAN

Comparing wealth across eras is notoriously difficult and imprecise. Simple inflation, which measures the average price changes for a variety of consumer goods, doesn't really measure wealth. If one considers only inflation, a dollar in 1933, when Yawkey bought the Red Sox, was worth about thirteen dollars by 1999, so his purchase of the team in 1999 dollars would represent approximately fifteen million dollars.

Other, more complex, methods consider wealth on a relative basis and, in regard to Tom Yawkey, give a different and perhaps more accurate presentation of his wealth. If one compares Yawkey's inherited wealth in 1933 to that of the Gross National Product of the United States (another widely accepted method of comparing wealth across eras), his eight- or ten-million-dollar fortune in 1933 would be the equivalent of a fortune some 150 times greater in 1999, or well in excess of one billion dollars. The 1.2-million-dollar purchase price of the Red Sox would equal perhaps as much as two hundred fifty million dollars in 1999 (roughly the estimated value of the franchise in 1991 — by 1999 their value had increased to perhaps as much as four hundred million dollars), while the two hundred fifty thousand dollars he paid for Joe Cronin would represent a 1999 expenditure of thirty-seven and a half million dollars!

But exactly how much money did Yawkey have in 1933? For although he'd inherited some eight to ten million dollars, how much his fortune had grown by then is unknown, although the press estimated his total fortune at between thirty and fifty million dollars. If that figure is accurate, then according to the method of estimating wealth described above, the 1999 equivalent would be a fortune of four and a half to seven and a half billion dollars. To place that in perspective, in 1998 *Forbes Magazine* reported that there were only 189 billionaires in the entire country.

By whatever method one chooses, Yawkey was extraordinarily wealthy, and the Red Sox were never more than a minor portion of his financial portfolio. When Yawkey bought the Red Sox he was likely one of the wealthiest twenty-five or thirty individuals in the country. In Eddie Collins's words, that was, unquestionably, "A whale of a lot of the coin of the realm." ⚾

ready signs the "Millionaires" had a hole in their pocket.

In the second inning, Cronin booted an easy groundball and was jeered. Two batters later he was cut down at second on a force play, landed on his right hand, and broke his thumb in two places.

"What Price Victory?" wondered Bob Coyne's cartoon in the *Post*. But others saw a silver lining in the injury, which sent McNair back to shortstop and Werber back to third. "The cold truth of the matter," wrote Bill Cunningham in the *Post*, "is that his [Cronin's] short stopping is scarcely on a level with the rest of the infielding . . . Local baseball gamblers weren't betting on whether the Sox would win but whether Jimmie Foxx would hit a home run and Joe Cronin make an error." Those who bet Cronin ended the day in the black.

For two weeks the Sox made good, finishing April in first place at 11-5, their best start since 1920. Then the "Millionaires" began playing like paupers.

On their first big road trip in early May they stumbled and never recovered as the Yankees pulled away. Cronin ran a revolving door at second base, Manush broke a finger, and Marcum and Ostermueller pitched poorly. Foxx, as expected, provided plenty of offense, but his fielding at first base made no one comfortable.

Even those players who performed well caused problems. Grove returned to form but pitched in hard luck all year and on occasion had to baby his arm. Ferrell took up the slack, but was in open revolt against Cronin, complaining on several occasions after Cronin returned, "If we had a shortstop we'd win the pennant."

Yawkey and Collins just kept adding more players to the mix. They acquired pitchers Jack Russell and Mike Meola from the Senators and the Browns, brought in rookie hurler Ted Olson from Quincy, Massachusetts, and even signed high school phenom Frank Dasso of Chicago to the biggest bonus ever given to a high school player at the time. All disappointed.

In July, Yawkey momentarily turned his attention from the Red Sox to Mrs. Yawkey, who was increasingly becoming an afterthought. He had tried to interest her in his passions — baseball, hunting, and fish-

Elise Yawkey and adopted daughter Julia visit Tom Yawkey's Red Sox office in 1939. Following their 1944 divorce Elise married a wealthy businessman. Daughter Julia rarely saw her father afterward, and many longtime Red Sox employees thought he was childless.

ing — but the marriage was in trouble. She rarely came to Boston anymore, preferring their Fifth Avenue penthouse and plantation home in South Carolina, where she loved to throw lavish parties her husband hated.

Nevertheless, in July the childless couple traveled to Evanston, Illinois, to "the Cradle," a home where the rich and the famous sent their pregnant, single daughters and pregnant, secret mistresses to have babies and where the same constituency, such as former New York mayor Jimmy Walker and singer Al Jolson, came when looking to adopt.

The Yawkeys, apparently unable to have their own child, adopted a nine-week-old girl whom they named Julia Austin Yawkey.

At the courtroom hearing to finalize the adoption, Mrs. Yawkey drew chuckles when she quipped, "If it were a boy, I'd be in constant fear Tom might trade him." She needn't have worried — Yawkey never showed a sustained interest in the child. As soon as the adoption was finalized, he left for New York, leaving his wife and new daughter behind with a nurse. They followed him home a week later.

Meanwhile, the Sox continued to stumble as the

Pitcher Wes Ferrell is shown here shortly after having been fined one thousand dollars by the Red Sox following an incident at Yankee Stadium on August 21, 1936. The talented but testy righthander, disgusted by what he thought was poor fielding, stalked off the mound and deserted the team for the second time in five days.

Yankees pulled far ahead in the pennant race. By August, the Sox were in third place, barely over .500, and slipping fast.

Wes Ferrell had had it with Cronin's fielding and attempts to call pitches. Egged on by a number of veterans, the pitcher finally took a stand.

The problems started in a doubleheader in Chicago on August 3. In the first game, while the Sox were technically errorless, they fielded indifferently and lost. Ferrell pitched game two.

Boston jumped out to a 9-1 lead. But in the fifth inning Ferrell walked two hitters and began squawking at the umpire. Zeke Bonura then hit a scorcher to Cronin, but he fumbled the ball and a run scored. Ferrell lost his cool and threw a wild pitch, plating another. Two innings later, still leading 11-3, Ferrell fell apart, giving up five runs on five hits, several of which the pitcher thought were catchable. Wilson and Ostermueller failed in relief, and Boston lost in twelve innings, 12-11.

After the Yankees crushed any remaining hopes of a Boston pennant with a three-game sweep, Cronin took himself out of the lineup. Ferrell won his next start, then faced the Senators in the first game of a doubleheader on August 16.

With the game tied 3-3 in the eighth, Washington scored three runs on three cheap hits and a walk.

After every bleeder, Ferrell stomped around making it clear that he thought each hit was playable. When McNair missed the last one, a bouncer through the middle, Ferrell stormed off, cursing and waving his hands in the air. Cronin, who didn't have a pitcher warming up, was forced to put in Jack Russell cold. Washington won, 7-6.

In any other club in baseball, Ferrell's tantrum would have led to an immediate suspension. But on the Red Sox it was overlooked. Cronin, although livid, was powerless. Ferrell had the support of half the team.

In his next start in New York on August 20, the still-piqued pitcher upped the ante. After McNair made another critical error, Ferrell threw his hat and glove into the air and walked off before they could hit the ground. He went all the way back to the hotel. The Yankees won, 4-1.

Cronin exploded after the game. "I'm all through with him," he said. "He's gonna be fined $1000, suspended and sent home. I don't care if he goes to Boston, North Carolina or the Fiji Islands, I'm washed up with the guy." Eddie Collins concurred. "Anything Joe Cronin has done will be backed up by Tom Yawkey and myself to the limit."

Ferrell wasn't finished. Later that evening, after threatening to "punch Cronin in the nose," he offered a lame excuse that he thought Cronin had waved him off the mound, a spurious assertion that he said was backed up by a mysterious "woman in red," then trashed Cronin in every way possible. He told reporters, "You fellows know what's wrong with the ball club. I don't have to tell you. He's too damn easy with the club . . . There have been too many mistakes all season long. When fellows make repeated errors they aren't trying . . . I was starring before Cronin was allowed to go to bat. I know what has to be done on a ball club. Joe doesn't. If he does, he doesn't do anything about it," concluding snidely, "*Connie Mack* is a manager."

Although none of his teammates publicly backed him up, what went on behind closed doors was another matter. Ferrell had the tacit support of many of his teammates.

Then Tom Yawkey got into the act. He first dismissed the gravity of the incident, telling the press, "The next fifteen months will see such upheaval on this club that the whole matter will be completely obliterated," then cut the season-ending suspension handed down by Cronin to only ten days.

What was Yawkey thinking?

At first blush, Yawkey's decision to back Ferrell over favorite son Cronin appears totally perplexing. But 1936 was Yawkey's fourth year at the helm. Bill Yawkey's Tigers had made it to the World Series in his fourth year. Thus far, the adoptive son had failed to reach his goal.

He hadn't given up, but there were intimations that Yawkey was frustrated by his team and soured on Boston. Indeed, after the Ferrell incident Yawkey didn't return to Boston for six months. Meanwhile, Yankee owner Jacob Ruppert was ill and contemplating selling the Yankees. Yawkey was interested, for while he was only in Boston purely by circumstance, his ties to New York through school and business were genuine.

Selling the Red Sox and buying the Yankees — a stronger franchise in every way — would allow him to achieve his goal of winning the world championship and have the resources to remain competitive for years to come.

His pandering to the club's veteran players, resulting in Ferrell's reinstatement, fits this scenario, for the Red Sox were more valuable with Ferrell than without him. His twenty victories that season were third best in the league, and he led the circuit in innings and complete games. In contrast, as a player, Cronin was damaged goods and as manager was expendable to a degree Ferrell was not.

But Yawkey may also have been referring to a total change in his approach. For after buying ballplayers at every opportunity for four years, at a cost of over one million dollars, Yawkey suddenly closed his checkbook. His reinstatement of Ferrell and subsequent six-month exile from Boston may well have represented the impatient owner's figurative "the hell with it." It would be almost forty years before he chose to revisit his profligate past.

Yawkey caved in completely, reinstating Ferrell and even rescinding the thousand-dollar fine. The pitcher was all smiles afterward. He'd challenged his own manager and won on every count.

But his return made little difference to the sixth-place team, apart from the fact that Yawkey's intrusion stripped Cronin of whatever shred of respect and authority he retained. They finished sixth, 74-80, twenty-eight and a half games behind pennant-winning New York, and four and a half games worse than in 1935.

Yet in Fenway Park, the club was 47-29, almost invincible, exhibiting for the first time a trait that would become a Red Sox tradition. Foxx and Boston's predominantly righthanded lineup rattled the left-field wall at will, giving the club a huge advantage at home, particularly against lefthanded pitching, for the wall turned some players of average talent into all-stars and some all-stars into Hall of Famers. Based on their offensive success in 1936, the Sox began a decades-long strategy of stocking their lineup with righthanded sluggers.

But what the wall provideth it also taketh away, for it gave the club a false sense of success. And by overtly tailoring the club to Fenway Park and focusing on righthanded power at the expense of elements like pitching, speed, and defense, the club was lacking on the road, where they had finished a miserable 27-51 in 1936. The focus on power simply didn't travel well, a fact lost on the front office for years. While the Sox were often a pennant-winner in Boston, elsewhere those home runs and doubles were simple outs. On the road, the Red Sox were also-rans, a trait that drove their fans crazy.

It took years before the club realized a second, but even more important, impact Fenway Park had on the club's hitters. While righthanded batters found power, lefthanded batters found hits, for Fenway's

old pitcher and outfielder. The youngster was hardly playing but Collins saw him swing in practice, then hit in several games when he filled in for an injured regular.

That singular swing reminded Collins of the greatest players in the game, and Collins had seen them all. Although the young hitter appeared nervous and jittery, as the pitcher wound up, the batter's body became silent and his attention focused on the ball. Then he swung like a spring suddenly uncoiled, his bat sweeping across the plate in a swift blur. Although he was still easily fooled, and displayed little power, Collins knew greatness when he saw it.

Collins took an option on the player, but San Diego owner Bill Lane tried to talk him out of it. He couldn't see the kid's potential and didn't want his fledgling relationship with the Red Sox soured by a bad deal. Lane refused to take any money from the Red Sox until and if Boston actually took possession of their prize.

The young hitter was Ted Williams. No player would ever have a greater impact on the franchise.

For the first time since buying the team, Yawkey sat on his money during the off-season. He made only one significant trade, dumping Billy Werber on the A's for third baseman Pinky Higgins. He even sold players, peddling utilityman John Kroner to the Indians and Babe Dahlgren to the Yankees. Ferrell stayed put, and Yawkey even evinced public support for Cronin, saying, "I think the purchase of Cronin is the best deal I've made and I'd make the deal tomorrow at twice the figure." With all evidence to the contrary, it seems likely that Yawkey may well have been trying to pump up the value of his slumping franchise.

That winter, Eddie Collins gave a wide-ranging interview to *Baseball Magazine* and confirmed it

right field was the biggest in baseball, giving left-handed hitters plenty of room to plop basehits. It is no accident that most of the team's greatest hitters, like Williams, Yastrzemski, and Boggs — and all batting champions after 1938 except for Carney Lansford and Nomar Garciaparra — were lefthanded. But it took decades before the club recognized that fact.

All was not lost, however. In June, Eddie Collins traveled to the West Coast to scout players in the Pacific Coast League and check out the San Diego Padres, with whom the team had a working agreement. Although he passed on outfielder Vince DiMaggio, brother of the Yankees' young star Joe, he liked young second baseman Bobby Doerr, on whom the club already had an option, and pitcher George Myatt. He immediately bought their contracts from San Diego owner Bill Lane.

Only a few weeks before, the Padres had signed a local high school star, a tall skinny seventeen-year-was no longer business as usual at Fenway Park, announcing, "We have abandoned, definitely, the attempt to fight our way to a pennant by the purchase of ready-made stars." Instead, he said, the Sox planned to "develop players, preferably through minor league affiliations."

But Boston's decision to change course was ill-conceived. For a fraction of what he'd spent on players thus far, Yawkey could have acquired nearly every premier prospect in the country and created the most productive and extensive farm system in baseball. Yet he missed a remarkable opportunity.

Inexplicably, Yawkey went only halfway. His eight-club system wasn't nearly as deep as that of the Cardinals, which had twenty-eight teams, or the Yankees. Even Detroit and Cincinnati had more teams than Boston. Yawkey never caught up and never even tried to, for year after year the Sox' farm system remained one of the smallest in the majors. And by pre-

maturely deciding to stop "buying" before the under-sized farm system matured, the organization stalled. By the time Williams, Doerr, and other farm products began to shine, Cronin, Foxx, and Grove were all on the downside of their careers. Then World War II got in the way, and after the war every team got heavily involved in the minors. The ground-floor opportunity was gone, and later, when the color line fell, the Red Sox were again slow to react and fell further back. Had Yawkey either continued to buy for another year or two, committed fully to the farm system, or done both, he may well have reached his goal several times over.

Instead, his failure became institutionalized. Lack of depth became a trademark of Yawkey's teams. Year after year, the Red Sox always appeared to be just a player or two short. The Yankees, who often had twice the number of minor leaguers under contract, never were.

(l–r): Johnny Peacock, "Indian" Bob Johnson, and Bobby Doerr. Doerr, shown here in 1944, came up with the Red Sox in 1937 and within a season nailed down the second base job. A superb batter with a classic Fenway Park stroke, he served as captain of the great Red Sox teams of the late forties.

Cramer and rookies Buster Mills and Fabian Gaffke made the outfield. Grove and Ferrell propped up a mediocre staff.

No one was fooled in 1937. All the moves meant nothing. The Red Sox still had the same weaknesses of the 1936 club. The Yankees of Gehrig, DiMaggio, and Dickey were still one of the greatest teams in the game. The Red Sox were mere pretenders. Hardly a player in the Boston lineup was better than his New York counterpart. Collectively, they didn't have a chance. Then again, neither did any other team in baseball.

The Yankees jumped out quickly in April as the Red Sox floundered. Boston celebrated the beginning of June by dropping into fifth place. Doerr slumped badly after a fine start, then got homesick and was benched as McNair, who in six big league seasons had played a total of only fifty-nine games at second, took over.

Apart from the rejuvenated Cronin, no one was hitting, not even Foxx, who ended the season with a batting average of only .285. Other than Grove, no one was pitching well. Ferrell, who caused everyone to jump through hoops, had an ERA of over 7.00 and seemed finished.

The front office made one last-ditch effort to salvage the season. On June 10, as they languished nine games behind New York, they dumped the Ferrell brothers and Mel Almada on the Washington Senators. In exchange, they received two talented yet troublesome ballplayers, outfielder Ben Chapman and pitcher Bobo Newsom.

It was a typical Yawkey acquisition, for the club merely traded one set of problems for another. Though Newsom and Chapman were both supremely

Before spring training of 1937 Cronin announced that *he* planned to play third base and move Higgins to second, with McNair remaining at shortstop. It was the third time in as many seasons that Cronin had decided to move a player to an unfamiliar position to accommodate himself. But at camp, his wrist suddenly felt better and he decided to return to shortstop. Higgins remained at third, while nineteen-year-old second baseman Bobby Doerr, who had already played three seasons in the PCL, hitting .342 in 1936, became the starting second baseman and lead-off hitter. Foxx rounded out the infield, while Doc talented, Chapman didn't get along with anyone, but that reminded Yawkey of Cobb. And Newsom made even Ferrell appear even-tempered.

Chapman initially provided a much-needed offensive spark, Newsom was an improvement on Ferrell, and the catching duo of Gene Desautels and Moe Berg made up for the loss of their slumping predecessor. Although the Yankees forged ahead, the Red Sox were at least competitive.

During a few weeks in late July and early August, they seemed to be much more. For the first time since Yawkey purchased the club, the Sox appeared to play to their potential. They ripped off twelve victories in a row and reached second place. When the Yankees came to Boston for a four-game series on August 10, the Sox' record was 57-38. They trailed New York by only nine and a half. A sweep would create a pennant race.

For the first time in twenty years pennant fever gripped the Hub in August. Nearly forty thousand fans poured into Fenway Park for the opening doubleheader. Scalpers actually had some success working the crowd outside.

Their customers wasted their hard-earned cash. Boston lost the first game 8-5 in extra innings and was blown out 10-4 in the second. The two clubs split another doubleheader the next day, and the Yankees left town leading Boston by eleven and a half as the Sox dropped into third place behind Detroit.

They never recovered, and they played poorly for the remainder of the season, returning to fifth place with a record of 80-72, although they again had a stellar record at home, going 44-29. The Yankees won 102 games to win the pennant going away.

The best news for Boston was in San Diego. Ted Williams was maturing as a hitter.

At the end of the season, Boston moved to take possession of their prize, but Collins was under no illusion that Williams was ready for the major leagues. He was at least a year or two away from the majors, an indifferent and erratic fielder and baserunner, and didn't appear particularly interested in improving either skill. In the meantime, outfielder Joe Vosmik, who'd hit .325 with forty-seven doubles and ninety-three RBIs for last-place St. Louis Browns and worn out the left-field wall while visiting Boston, was available. The Browns took Newsom, Buster Mills, and a minor leaguer for Vosmik.

It took several months before Williams officially became the property of the Red Sox, for he was under the age of consent and they had to work out a deal with his mother as well as pay off Lane. Since they'd first taken out their option, other clubs had seen what Collins had and were pressuring the family. Finally, in December, the Sox gave Lane twenty-five thousand dollars and twenty-five thousand dollars' worth of ballplayers, allegedly paid his mother several thousand dollars for her signature, and signed Williams to a two-year contract. They told him to report to spring training in Sarasota on March 1, 1938.

He got off to a bad start, as heavy rains in California prevented him from leaving California on time, and the arduous cross-country automobile trek with Bobby Doerr and two other major leaguers took longer than expected. Williams finally arrived in Sarasota on March 8 and worked out for the first time the next day.

Club veterans were laying for him when he arrived at spring training. They'd heard all about the precocious prospect and weren't disappointed as Williams, who masked his insecurity with cockiness, was an easy mark.

When one veteran cautioned him that he ought to see Foxx hit, Williams snapped back, "Foxx ought to see me hit." That set the tone. He pushed his way into the batting cage without regard to the unspoken pecking order that gave veterans the right to hit first, spoke before he was spoken to, and inundated everyone with his opinions about everything. He preened for newsreel cameras, showed off his outfield arm while the regulars were still using caution, and challenged every man on the team to a footrace. He'd slap himself on the rear end with his glove while chasing flyballs, practice his swing in between pitches, and kibitz with the crowd. He called Joe Cronin "Sport," and catcher Moe Berg "Adge" as in "agitator." And he let Ben Chapman, Doc Cramer, and Joe Vosmik know that he was after their jobs.

Williams impressed everyone at the plate, even the veterans who hated him, and Cronin described his fielding as "much better than expected." But in intra-squad games and the first few exhibitions Williams couldn't back up his boasts and began pressing. Veteran pitchers turned it up a notch against him, took note of his eagerness, and threw him off-speed pitches off the plate. They soon had Williams lunging at pitches he didn't have a prayer of hitting.

Had Williams kept his mouth shut and just hit, he may well have made the team. But that wasn't Williams's way and never would be. Besides, the Sox didn't want him to sit on the bench — neither Ted nor the rest of the team could have survived that. He needed to play and grow up. The Sox had just entered into a working agreement with Minneapolis of the American Association, and the Miller's Nicollet Park, where the right-field fence was only 279 feet 10 inches from home plate, was ideally suited to Williams's swing. In Minneapolis, the Sox hoped Williams would gain both confidence and experience. On March 21 he was optioned out, news that delighted the Sox veterans.

"Where you going, California?" one of the Sox veteran outfielders taunted. Williams fired back, "I'll be back, and I'll be making more money than the three of you put together." As Sox fans would later learn, Williams was never better than when backed into a corner. He could hit himself out and soon would make good on his promise.

With Williams gone, camp was a lot less interesting, and a lot quieter. The remainder of the spring was uneventful, apart from the fact that the Sox' vaunted offense was virtually silent. Even minor league teams had little trouble shutting down Boston. In their final tuneup before facing the Braves in the annual city series, the Sox even lost 3-2 to Holy Cross.

Boston's one find that spring was pitcher Jim Bagby, Jr., son of former Cleveland pitcher Jim Bagby. Cronin was so impressed by the youngster, who had won twenty-one games and been named MVP in the New York–Pennsylvania League, he passed over everyone else and selected Bagby to start on Opening Day against the Yankees in Fenway on April 18.

After being burned in 1937, the prognosticators shied away from the Sox in 1938. The Yanks were

The Red Sox take time out from spring training to line up forty-five players to spell the word "Sox."

Red Sox manager Joe Cronin *(l)* and Boston Braves manager Casey Stengel *(r)* discuss a preseason city series game at Fenway Park in this photograph from the late thirties. Such meetings were a preseason staple.

heavy favorites, with Boston lumped together with Detroit, Chicago, and Cleveland to decide second through fifth place.

Opening Day proved the folly of trying to predict the outcome of any single game. Although Bagby struggled with control, he held the Yankees at bay long enough for the Red Sox hitting attack to get going. Trailing 4-2 entering the sixth, the Red Sox then blasted Red Ruffing, flexing every offensive muscle they had to win 8-4.

But by the second week in May they had fallen to fourth with an 11-8 record, although Foxx was off to a fabulous start. Grove and Marcum were undefeated, but the other pitchers, including Bagby, were struggling, as was the last half of the batting order.

Cronin celebrated the birth of his son against Cleveland on May 8 with a home run and a double as Jack Wilson struck out twelve to beat Cleveland, 5-0. The victory keyed a hot streak, and for the next week the Sox broke the league up, beating Denny Galehouse and the Indians 15-3 as Foxx cracked two home runs, then beating Ferrell and the Senators 10-0. Foxx was magnificent and hitting the ball better than ever, including an eleventh-inning blast into the

center-field bleachers for one of the longest home runs in Fenway history to beat the Senators, 10-9. By the end of the week they'd won eight straight in Fenway and pulled into first place.

Then the Red Sox went on the road. Their bats went dead in Chicago and stayed dead in Washington. They came to New York for a doubleheader on May 30 in free fall, but still in second place behind Cleveland. The Yankees were in fourth and also in trouble.

One of the largest crowds in baseball history, 83,533, turned out for the holiday doubleheader. In the fourth inning of the first game, trailing 3-0, the Sox lost their cool, lost the game, and took a great stride toward losing the season.

The Yankees' Jake Powell walked to the mound after being dusted off by McKain, and when Cronin came to the pitcher's defense, Powell baited him into a fight. Both players were tossed for the duration of the day, and the Yankees swept, 10-0 and 5-4. The Sox fell to fourth and New York vaulted into second place. Boston never got that close again and played out the remainder of the season in typical form, beating the hell out of everyone in Fenway

Park and getting the hell beaten out of them everywhere else.

No player typified the season better than Jimmie Foxx. He won the MVP award and set team records with fifty home runs and 175 RBIs. In Fenway he fashioned the greatest year a Red Sox hitter has ever had in Fenway Park, where he hit .405, cracked thirty-five home runs, and knocked in 104 for a Ruthian .887 slugging percentage. With Foxx knocking the wall into Lansdowne Street, Lefty Grove was 7-0 and Boston was 52-23.

Yet on the road, Foxx was only very good, hitting .296 and connecting for only fifteen home runs. Unfortunately, most of the rest of the team was well below average. They failed to play .500 baseball, wasting a league-best batting average of .299. Still, they finished second with their best record to date in the Yawkey era, 88-61. But the Yankees won ninety-nine.

Meanwhile in Minneapolis, Ted Williams was all he was advertised in every way possible. Rogers Hornsby, the game's greatest righthanded hitter, spent spring training with the club and impressed upon Williams the need for a hitter to "get a good ball to hit." Williams listened well to that lesson, but found others harder to learn.

He quickly got on the bad side of manager Donie Bush, who thirty years before had played shortstop for Bill Yawkey's Tigers. In an early-spring appearance, Williams failed to run out a groundball he thought was foul and dropped an easy flyball. But he was as spectacular at bat as he was indifferent in the rest of his game.

After opening the season hitless in his first three games, Williams threatened to quit and get a job with the railroad. But in his fourth game, he hit two long home runs and was off.

Williams's bat made up for everything, as he hit .366 with forty-two home runs and 142 RBIs. But his behavior drove Bush to distraction. In right field he still pantomimed his swing for the crowd. Sometimes he grew bored, sat down between batters, and watched routine flyballs hit his way drop for hits. On other occasions, he forced his own pitcher to wait as he held court with the fans.

Bush tried everything to get him to take the game seriously, but reaming him out, benching him, and long fatherly talks made little impression on Williams.

Despite his antics, Williams was oddly endearing. There was no malice in his behavior. He was an individual, gloriously himself to a fault. To an old baseball man like Bush, being around Williams was torture. Bush loved the way he hit, but his personality drove him batty.

In midseason, Bush even went to club owner Mike Kelly and told him that if Williams remained on the team, he was quitting. But Williams, not Bush, was hitting .360. Kelly explained that it was Williams whom the fans were coming out to the ballpark to see. Bush correctly came to the conclusion that he was more expendable to the franchise than the boy genius with the bat.

After all, it was becoming clear that Williams's time in the American Association would be brief. He was ready for Boston, or at least his bat was. The only question was whether or not Boston and the rest of the American League would be ready for him.

ENTER THE KID

1939 | 1941

Following a spectacular rookie season, Ted Williams was moved from right
to left field where he became a master at playing the odd bounces characteristic of the tin-covered structure. In this posed photograph he displays
the form that made him a master of the Wall's eccentricities.

Teddy Ballgame was coming to town.

As Eddie Collins said of Ted Williams in 1938, "All Ted lives for is his next turn at bat." For much of the next two decades, a similar statement — "All Boston lives for is Ted's next at bat" — would be equally true. The Red Sox organization and their fans were soon mesmerized by Williams's talent.

The promise contained in Williams's next at bat became a goal unto itself, often more significant than either victory or defeat. In time, his remarkable ability to hit would both reveal and obscure the deficiencies of the organization.

It wasn't Williams's fault, although he was often blamed. As all eyes focused on him, the team's performance went almost unnoticed at times as he took the heat off the front office and masked their real problems. Somehow, his presence became a convenient yet spectacular excuse that allowed the organization to founder. It began before he even stepped in the batter's box at Fenway Park.

The addition of Williams to a team that had just won eighty-eight games should have made the Red Sox a pennant contender, if not a winner, in 1939. Instead, and incredibly, it made no difference at all.

Cronin and Yawkey continued to be poor judges of talent. They remained active in the off-season, now concentrating on trades rather than purchases, but were still unable to secure a pennant.

Williams's pending arrival made right fielder Ben Chapman and his .340 batting average — third best in the league — expendable. He was traded to the Cleveland Indians for right-handed pitcher Denny Galehouse. The exchange was made only slightly more equitable by the subtraction of Chapman's abrasive personality. Galehouse, who would later figure prominently in the 1948 playoff, always looked better at a distance. In the bullpen or pitching against the Red Sox, he looked fabulous. But on the mound for the home team, he pitched just well enough to lose.

The club made another — even worse deal — trading pitcher Archie McKain and third baseman Pinky Higgins, who had hit .302 and .303 in Boston, to Detroit for submarine starting pitcher Elden Auker and two others. Higgins was dispensable because Cronin had fallen in love with rookie third baseman Jim Tabor and wanted him to start at third in 1939. It was a great deal — for the Tigers. Auker had won only eleven games with an ERA over 5.00 in 1938.

Cronin made the deals because he couldn't hit Auker or Galehouse and, despite evidence to the contrary, didn't think anyone else could either. Collins, who had already proven he was a poor judge of pitching, agreed, and Yawkey still put his faith in both men.

So Boston dumped two of their more productive offensive players for a couple of .500 pitchers. Although Tabor and Williams more than adequately replaced Chapman and Higgins, had the Red Sox received equal value for them the 1939 season may well have turned out differently.

The Sox' one bold move could have made up for the poor trades. Instead, it eventually became the most poignant example of Cronin's faulty judgment.

The previous summer, farm director Billy Evans scouted Louisville shortstop Harold "Pee Wee" Reese. Reese was easily the American Association's best fielder, blessed with great quickness and incredible range. He wasn't much of a hitter, but was only eighteen and holding his own. Cronin was getting older, and Evans thought Reese could solve Boston's problem at shortstop.

He asked Yawkey to get him, so in the off-season Yawkey helped Minneapolis manager Donie Bush and others purchase Louisville for nearly two hundred thousand dollars, taking one-third of the club for himself. Bush became manager, the Sox severed ties with Minneapolis, and Reese was theirs. All they had to do was wait.

Waiting was the theme in the spring of 1939. Ted Williams was late getting to spring training when he got the grippe driving from San Diego and had to be hospitalized in New Orleans for a few days.

The moment he got in, Cronin sent for him. After Williams took some hitting Cronin sat him down and said, "You've got a lot of ability and have had enough schooling. This is serious business and there's no place for clowning." He told Williams that no matter how he played that spring, he'd be in right field on Opening Day.

Although Cronin told the press, "Everybody who's seen him agrees he can't miss. If we're wrong about Williams, all baseball is wrong," in private he didn't think Williams could hit the ball low and away. He preferred to tout Tabor, whom he called "a courageous kid I'm not worried about at all," implying the opposite about Williams.

The press flocked to Williams. In contrast to the taciturn Collins, the company line of Cronin, and the arrogance of the club's stars, Williams was a verbal inspiration, a player whose personality equaled his talent. He had opinions on everything and wasn't yet wary of the printed word. Nearly every press report that spring featured Williams, and his picture was splashed across the Boston papers almost daily.

In another time, the club would have helped shield their young star, but there was already enough resentment over Williams that he was left to learn his own way around the press. Besides, when the writers wrote about Williams they left everybody else alone.

Williams didn't disappoint anyone that spring, with either his bat or his tongue. He hit the hell out of the ball while his mouth and attitude got him in trouble.

In an exhibition in Atlanta, Williams smacked a bases-loaded triple, but in the outfield let a ball roll between his legs. Later, after striking out and throwing his bat in disgust, he took off after a towering foul down the right-field line, pulled up short when he heard the crowd, and let it drop.

As the partisans laughed at him, Williams threw the ball over the roof of the right-field grandstand. Cronin pulled him from the game, fined him fifty bucks, and said, "I've got to take the busher out of him." Unimpressed, Williams told Cronin, "I'll pay you fifty dollars for everyone I throw out if you'll pay me fifty dollars for everyone I hit out." The next day, he homered, demonstrating his signature response. Whenever Ted was in trouble, his bat got him out of it. It happened far too often to be a coincidence. Turmoil drove Williams, and he was at his best when he had the most to prove.

On Opening Day in New York on April 20, he played right field and hit sixth, between Tabor and Bobby Doerr. Red Ruffing struck him out on a curve in his first appearance, but in his second at bat Williams doubled off the low wall in right for his first major league hit. But the Yankees beat Lefty Grove 2-0, a result more indicative of the immediate future than Williams's 1-for-4 was.

Ted Williams made his Boston debut in a city-series game against the Boston Braves on April 15, 1939. Hall of Fame catcher Al Lopez and umpire George Magerkurth observed Williams go hitless in four at bats.

He broke out for the first time on April 23 in Fenway. Against A's pitcher Luther Thomas, he hit his first home run, a long drive that landed in the right-field bleachers, only the sixth time anyone had homered to that part of Fenway Park. His next time up, he hit a ball off the wall in left center, then later singled twice. He even made a great catch in the field, and fans in right field greeted him like a hero.

Although the Sox finished April with a 5-3 record, tied with New York, and went on to win sixteen of twenty-five in May, the pennant race was soon over. The Yankees and Joe DiMaggio lost only four games all month and continued their fine play in June while the Sox tailed off.

Williams was soon providing Sox fans their only entertainment. No rookie ever enjoyed himself more. After a big hit he would pull his cap from his head by the button on top and wave it wildly to his adoring fans, a huge grin plastered on his face.

Yet Williams still suffered from periodic lapses of attention. In early August he loafed his way through an entire game, turning a certain triple into a double and not running out a flyball. Cronin yanked him and announced, "He was taken out because he did not hustle on the fly, because he had not been hustling all afternoon and because he had not been hustling for about a week." So, typically, Williams's ninth-inning double the next day won the game.

The Sox briefly resuscitated their pennant hopes just before the All-Star break, beating the Yankees five straight times in New York, but that was their last gasp. Grove was their only dependable pitcher, but he needed a week between starts. Everyone else was close to awful. Auker didn't win a game in Fenway all year.

But poor defense was the real culprit in 1939. Williams committed an astonishing nineteen errors,

Ted Williams enjoyed a youthful following in Boston to rival that enjoyed nationally by fellow teen idol Frank Sinatra. Williams devoted much of his free time to Boston charities such as the Jimmy Fund, visiting sick children on the condition that no press and photographers follow him.

while Tabor contributed forty, and Cronin chipped in with thirty-two.

The answer, or part of it, was playing short in Louisville. But that solution never made it to Boston.

In the spring the Sox had battered Louisville 24-2 in an exhibition game. Reese, who was ill, went hitless and made two errors. Cronin, who already felt threatened, abruptly decided he couldn't play.

According to an unpublished interview Billy Evans gave to *Globe* writer Harold Kaese in 1945, after the exhibition Cronin told Yawkey to sell Reese and Yawkey ordered Evans to wire every team in baseball and ask them to make an offer. None did, for Boston's sudden rejection of the shortstop made other clubs cautious.

But by midsummer Reese was everything that Evans had promised. Other teams now clamored for him. Evans begged Cronin to reconsider his evaluation, but he stubbornly refused. So in July Reese was sold to Brooklyn for seventy-five thousand dollars and five players, and Yawkey bought out Bush and his partners. Reese led Louisville to the Little World Series and beginning in 1940 became a star in Brooklyn, anchoring the Dodger infield, making ten All-Star teams, and leading the team to seven National League pennants.

Meanwhile, balls bounced through the left side of the Red Sox infield all summer long. The Yankees finished seventeen games ahead of second-place Boston and won their fourth world championship in a row.

Williams was the whole story. He finished at .327, with a league-best 145 RBIs and thirty-one home runs — including six more to the right-field bleachers. By midseason Cronin had moved him to cleanup. Foxx hit .360, but hit only thirty-five home runs. Doerr emerged as a star at second base, and Tabor hit well. With hitters like Foxx and Williams in the middle of the lineup, it was hard not to succeed. Everyone got pitches to hit.

In the off-season, the Sox appeared to admit that the Yankees weren't catchable anytime soon. With one notable exception, Yawkey and the Sox were more interested in selling rather than acquiring players.

Auker was sold to the Browns, and Joe Vosmik — a career .300 hitter — was shipped to the Brooklyn Dodgers for twenty-five thousand dollars. To replace him, Boston paid between seventy-five thousand and one hundred thousand dollars for Dominic DiMaggio, the younger and smaller brother of major leaguers Joe and Vince, and pitcher Larry Powell.

In three years with the San Francisco Seals of the PCL, DiMaggio had become a star, equal — in every way but power — to his brother Joe, who earlier had similarly starred for the Seals. He hit .360 in 1939. Yet Dom stood only 5-foot-9 and wore glasses, a factor that kept many talented ballplayers in semipro ball or the minor leagues for life.

But Boston had received good reports on DiMaggio, particularly for his defense. The Sox had plenty of power. All they needed him to do was get on base and catch the ball.

The Red Sox expected more from Williams in 1940. Yawkey even reconfigured Fenway Park to accommodate his swing, moving the bullpens from foul territory to in front of the bleachers in right. Construction pared the power alley from 402 to 380 feet and the distance down the line from 325 to 302 feet. The press thought the changes gave Williams a shot at breaking Ruth's home run record.

They also moved Williams to left field, penciling DiMaggio into right. Williams wasn't fast and had a hard time covering Fenway's spacious right field, the largest in baseball. In an era when most games started at 3:00 P.M., it was also a notorious sun field, and they worried that the sun might damage Williams's eyes. He also moved up to third in the batting order, bumping Foxx to fourth. Now Double-X was expected to provide protection for Williams, the reverse of the situation that developed in 1939.

But little went as planned in 1940. When Williams trotted out to left field for the first time in Fenway Park, he heard something new. He was booed.

The darling of 1939 was now held to a higher standard. The changes set him apart. Fans resented the fact that he received special treatment. Furthermore, the usual crowd in left field resented the Vosmik trade. It didn't matter that none of the changes were Williams's doing. He was on his way to becoming a scapegoat.

It didn't happen instantaneously, for although Williams got off slow, so too, for once, did the Yankees. In mid-May, the Red Sox were in first place.

But all was not well. DiMaggio hurt his ankle and Lou Finney had to play right. When Foxx slumped

Rookie Dom DiMaggio indicates the starting date of spring training as he visits Fenway Park for the first time in January 1940.

the opposition pitched around Williams, throwing him junk. He tried to pull everything, started pressing, and although he still got his hits, lost power. The harder he tried to reach the new bullpens the more he popped the ball up. The boo-birds discovered his rabbit ears and turned up the volume.

Even though the Sox led the league, Williams brooded. He complained that Fenway wasn't a good park for a lefthanded hitter and by hitting third he couldn't win the RBI title. Lou Finney was on fire and now received some of the cheers that had been Williams's alone in 1939.

His dissatisfaction showed up in indifferent play in the field, a pattern that dogged him throughout his career. After loafing after a ball one day, Lefty Grove threatened to punch him out. Later Doc Cramer and Williams came to blows in the runway between the Red Sox dugout and the clubhouse. But Williams didn't change.

In mid-May, as the Sox traveled to Cleveland, Cronin told Harold Kaese of the *Boston Transcript* that he was going to bench Williams. "I didn't want to do this," he admitted. "I don't want Williams to get this kind of reputation, but there's no other way." Yet

after venting his dissatisfaction, Cronin changed his mind.

To date, the Boston press had given Ted a pass, chalking up his eccentricities to immaturity and looking the other way. But now Kaese wrote a column on Williams's growing shortcomings. He cited his "extreme selfishness and egoism, somewhat along the Ferrell-Chapman lines, and a lack of courage." He concluded with a broadside. "Whatever it is," he wrote, "it is probably tied to his upbringing. Can you imagine a kid, a nice kid with a nimble brain, not visiting his father and mother all of last winter?"

Williams's strangely painful, lonely upbringing was always a sore spot, an area of his life he rarely spoke about, publicly or privately. He was the product of a loveless marriage between Sam Williams, an itinerant photographer and Spanish-American War veteran, and May Venzor, a holier-than-thou, half-Mexican foot soldier in the Salvation Army. The man who wanted people on the street to see him and say, "There goes the greatest hitter who ever lived," virtually raised himself in the parks, playgrounds, and canyons of San Diego. Solitary pursuits — hitting a baseball, hunting, and fishing — were all that ever mattered to him and just about all that ever would. He was the rarest talent, a prodigy with a work ethic to match, for Williams himself once said, "No one ever practiced hitting a baseball more than I did." He was blessed with remarkable ability and just as remarkable a blind spot to just about anything or anyone else. It made him a great hitter, but made the rest of his life more difficult than it should have been.

At heart, Williams has always seemed like someone for whom baseball somehow filled a void. And although neither he nor anyone else has ever seemed to know what he was striking against each time he stepped to the plate, Williams had that swing and took his frustrations out at the plate. Hitting made up for everything else. No matter what else he did or how he behaved, there was no disputing his swing.

Red Sox fans were the recipients of the resultant glory.

Kaese's comment about Williams's parents was a low blow that he immediately regretted and tried to have killed, but an editing error left it in his column. When the story broke, Boston's seven other daily papers scrambled to catch up. They learned that Ted Williams sold newspapers. It was open season on Williams for much of the rest of his career.

True to form, Williams soon went on a brief tear and homered into the bleachers in a 7-2 loss to New York on May 26. But the damage, both to the 1940 Red Sox and Williams's long-term reputation, was done.

The club slowly fell apart as the pitching staff self-destructed and Cronin panicked, making Foxx catch after DiMaggio returned so Finney could play first base. The Sox could hit with any team in the league, but pennants are won with defense and pitching. Boston had neither.

Had Yawkey only decided to make a deal for some pitching, the Sox might have had a chance to win, as the Yankees slumped. But he didn't, and neither did they.

Williams continued to mope, and in an otherwise lackluster season, everything he said made it into print. After he blurted out to a news service reporter, "Nuts to baseball — I'd rather be a fireman," the White Sox taunted him with bells, sirens, and fire hats.

He was the most miserable .340 hitter in the history of the game. Williams had little personal insight and couldn't understand how the press and public could turn on him so suddenly. He was about to explode.

By now he should have known better, but in mid-August he popped off to *Evening American* columnist Austen Lake, saying, "I've asked Yawkey and Cronin to trade me away from Boston many times this summer. I don't like the town, I don't like the people and the newspapermen have been on my

back all year long. You can print the whole rotten mess just as I said it."

Every writer in town felt the need to respond and most did. Jack Broudy of the *Traveller* summed up their attitude, writing, "Your author, for one, is weary of being frostbitten by his cold fury and stabbed by

Center fielder Roger "Doc" Cramer was one of the Red Sox regulars irritated by the cocky Williams. The two came to blows in the runway from the dugout to the clubhouse after words were spoken during practice. In five seasons with the Red Sox Cramer batted a solid .302.

his dirty looks. If Theodore is really looking for war, there is no sense in declaring him an open city and bombing him with nothing heavier than fluffy adjectives."

Had Williams been cautious around the press and spoken in platitudes, he might have avoided twenty years of trouble. But that wasn't Ted. He was himself to a fault.

Williams made the war certain by calling Lake a liar and saying he'd never asked to be traded. Although there would be the occasional truce, from then on Williams and the writers dug in and eyed each other warily from the batter's box to the press box and back, tossing the occasional salvo as if to make sure the other was truly paying attention.

Nearly a dozen papers covered the Red Sox. At any given time it was inevitable that at least one writer would be warring with Williams. And just as he heard the one raspberry in a chorus of cheers, Williams read everything and remembered the single unkind comment in a cacophony of praise. In truth, the press wasn't nearly as anti-Williams as Williams himself believed and has since led others to think. And although they got under his skin, they also did him a great service. Perhaps no athlete in American history had ever received so much ink. Williams was a legend before he turned twenty-five years old.

Ted Williams endeared himself to Red Sox fans for generations with an enthusiasm that was matched only by his mercurial temper and passion for hitting.

The most disturbing aspect of Williams's battle with the press was the role the Red Sox played. They neither protected him nor taught him how to respond. For they knew every story about Williams meant fewer stories about Cronin's managing, Collins's deals, or Yawkey's record of ownership. As long as Williams played for the Red Sox, there was little scrutiny of the organization as a whole.

Over the final month or so of the season, Williams finally began to make adjustments and hit for power, but it was too late to make a difference in the season. On the final day of the year in a doubleheader sweep of Philadelphia he went 5-for-8 with five RBIs to pull the Sox into a tie with Chicago for fourth place at 82-72, only eight games behind pennant-winning Detroit.

The Sox had missed a fabulous opportunity to steal a pennant. Williams hit .344 with twenty-three home runs, but only nine in Fenway Park, and 113 RBIs. Stung by criticism, he decided that he would never again tip his cap to the fans in Fenway Park. He held out for almost fifty years.

The one bright spot for Boston was second baseman Bobby Doerr. He emerged as a star in 1940, hitting .291 with sixty-nine extra-base hits, including twenty-two home runs, only one fewer than Williams.

As a person, Doerr was everything Williams wasn't. Quiet, unassuming, and unfailingly polite, he was the perfect counterpoint to Williams's volatility. On the field and in the clubhouse, he served a similar role. The only dependable glove in the infield, at bat Doerr was as steady as Williams was streaky. And while Ted often fumed, Doerr was dependable and courteous to the writers, if not particularly colorful. He was also a player whom Williams respected, a rare figure whose personal dignity and character made those around him display their better nature. He was about the only player on the club to whom Williams deferred, and in whom he would confide. In Williams's darkest hours, he often looked to Doerr for the support the Red Sox organization so often withheld.

Boston's finish fooled the club into thinking they were better than they were. In reality they needed lots of help, particularly on the pitcher's mound.

But that fall they dumped the few pitchers they had, selling Galehouse and Ostermueller. Then on December 12 they traded All-Star Doc Cramer, whose 200 hits had led the AL, to Washington, not for another pitcher, but for veteran outfielder Gee Walker. Then they packaged Walker with catcher Gene Desautels and Jim Bagby — whose ten wins were second on the club in 1940 — to Cleveland for two journeymen — catcher Frankie Pytlak and second baseman Odell Hale — and twenty-three-year-old pitching prospect Joe Dobson. They had dumped over 440 innings of admittedly mediocre pitching and one solid .300 hitter for a couple of backups and one unproven arm.

Had they made another trade for a front-line starter, the deals may have made sense. They were, in fact, pondering just such a blockbuster, one that would have eclipsed the sale of Ruth. The Chicago White Sox offered Boston twenty-six-year-old righthanded starting pitcher Johnny Rigney and outfielder Taft Wright. All they wanted in return was Ted Williams.

Boston was tempted. After his troubled sophomore season they weren't sold on Williams and wondered if he was worth the trouble. Rigney was one of the best young pitchers in the league. His 1940 ERA was a stellar 3.11, better than any Boston pitcher by nearly a run. And Wright was a pure hitter, albeit one with little power, who in three big league seasons had hit .350, .309, and .337.

Yet even in 1940 the sale of Ruth cast a long shadow in Boston, and a late-season surge had been promising. The club had already been burned by the Reese deal and couldn't risk dumping another player with so much potential.

But love may well have nixed the deal. Rigney was dating Charles Comiskey's daughter, whom he later married. Neither club could pull the trigger and the deal died.

The Sox still needed help, for in addition to weakness in pitching and defense, Cronin and Foxx were showing their age. But Boston had little left to offer.

Instead, they stood pat and cast their lot in 1941 with much the same team they had put on the field in 1940, albeit in different positions. DiMaggio went to center, Lou Finney returned to right field, and Foxx gratefully moved back to first. On the mound, untested rookies and shopworn veterans engaged in a contest of survival of the fittest.

Williams arrived at camp oozing confidence, asking the writers rhetorically, "How can they stop me

Ted Williams (l) and Bobby Doerr (r) were discovered by Red Sox general manager Eddie Collins on a scouting trip to view Pacific Coast League prospects in 1936. Never had a scouting trip proved so fruitful, as the former Hall of Fame second baseman signed two future Hall of Famers.

from hitting? They can't, that's all." Then he set out to prove it in a way no subsequent hitter ever has.

But in an exhibition game against Newark on March 19, Williams fell down, as one Boston writer quipped, "like an old cow." X-rays uncovered a bone chip in his ankle.

By the time the season opened, Williams could hit, but couldn't run, and Pete Fox started in left. That was fine with Williams, for he spent hours late that spring taking game-condition batting practice from Joe Dobson.

Opening Day revealed a sure sign that a championship flag was unlikely to fly above Fenway Park anytime soon. Jack Wilson, he of a 5.08 ERA in 1940, was Boston's Opening Day pitcher against the Senators.

He didn't last, but Williams's pinch-hit double in the ninth inning keyed a comeback to give the Sox a 7-6 win. He remained in that role before returning to the starting lineup for good on April 29. Williams was already hitting an even .400 and the Sox were 7-4. The Yankees were only 8-5. For what it was worth, Boston was in the race.

They stayed there the next few weeks as Williams went absolutely crazy at the plate, even cracking two home runs off Johnny Rigney, before taking the collar on May 14 to drop his average to .336. Boston was 13-9, three and a half games behind Cleveland, while the Yankees were stuck at .500.

On the following day, May 15, the AL pennant race became a historical footnote to a larger drama. For on that day Ted Williams and New York's Joe DiMaggio both embarked on the longest hitting streaks of their respective major league careers, streaks that carried each man to his most memorable season and coupled them to one another as the defining players of their generation. From 1941 onward, it wasn't just Boston versus New York. It was Boston against Joe DiMaggio and the Yankees, and New York against Ted Williams and the Red Sox.

The pairing served each man well, for their individual skills stood out in comparison with the other. The temperament of each even seemed better suited to the other's city. Fans in both places still wonder how the righthanded hitting DiMaggio would have fared playing full-time in Fenway Park, or how many home runs Williams would have hit aiming at Yankee Stadium's short right-field porch.

Williams was the supreme hitter and DiMaggio the consummate player, evaluations each man made of the other. Over much of the next decade the debate over their remarkable talents fired the imagination of millions of fans. The first spark was struck on May 15, 1941.

Both streaks began in defeat. Williams singled off the glove of Cleveland second baseman Ray Mack in the eighth inning of a 6-4 loss to the Indians. The loss — Boston's third in a row — dropped the club into third place. That same day DiMaggio singled and knocked in the Yankees' only run in their 13-1 drubbing at the hands of the White Sox as New York fell to 14-15.

But in one of the great ironies of that season — and representative of the destiny of each hitter — Williams's streak coincided with a disastrous slump by the Red Sox, while the Yankees followed in DiMaggio's wake, playing better as his streak grew. Boston lost seven in a row before they finally won again as Williams's streak reached a modest six games.

New York passed the slumping Sox three days later as they began their inexorable climb toward first place. No one was surprised, for as Dom DiMaggio later admitted about the Yankees, "We used to say 'They'll win the pennant by Labor Day.'" Boston's expectations — and their confidence — stopped at second place.

Meanwhile, Williams was crushing the ball, banging out two or three hits almost every game and hitting with more power than ever before. He helped the Sox stem the tide for a while. Cronin nearly kept pace with Ted, and Dom DiMaggio was hitting even better than his streaking brother was.

On June 1, Williams went 4-for-9 in a doubleheader sweep of Detroit, his nineteenth and twentieth consecutive games with at least one base hit. His gaudy .430 batting average led *Boston Herald* writer John Drohan to pronounce "Hugh Duffy beware!" in reference to the Red Sox coach's record .438 batting mark set in 1894.

Williams's streak lasted another three games, ending at twenty-three on June 8 when he went hitless in

The infamous "Williams shift" was first employed by White Sox manager Jimmy Dykes on July 23, 1941. Williams is shown slicing an opposite-field double in the seventh inning to foil Dykes's scheme. The shift would resurface five seasons later as Cleveland manager Lou Boudreau utilized it to greater effect.

a doubleheader in Chicago. He had hit .488 during the stretch. In an AP story the previous day, it was first noted that Williams had a great chance to be the first batter to hit .400 since Bill Terry hit .401 in 1930.

Now DiMaggio's continuing streak began to capture the attention of the press. And as June turned into July, the Sox, although playing well, fell behind the pace set by the Yankees. The club had plenty of offense, but the pitching was still spotty. Grove was throwing well, if not very often, in pursuit of his 300th win, and at age thirty-one rookie Dick Newsome was winning more than his share. But too many games were left to pitchers not up to the task.

DiMaggio broke George Sisler's modern hitting streak record of forty-one games on June 29, then broke Willie Keeler's all-time mark of forty-four

games on July 1 as the Yankees swept Boston in a doubleheader. The Sox fell seven games back.

At the All-Star Game in Detroit, Williams temporarily pushed DiMaggio from the headlines with one of the signature performances of his career. He hit cleanup behind the Yankee star, and both players squandered opportunities to be the hero in the early innings as the National League took a 5-3 lead into the ninth. Then the AL rallied. With the bases loaded, DiMaggio beat out a double-play ball to score one and bring Williams to the plate with two on and the American League trailing by only a run.

On the third pitch he saw from Cub pitcher Claude

Passeau, Williams turned on the ball and sent it high and deep down the right field, where it cut through a cross wind and cracked off the façade of the upper deck of Tiger Stadium. The towering blast gave the American League a 7-5 win.

As he half-ran, half-leapt around the bases, pinwheeling his arms in joy with a huge grin plastered across his face, Williams was, for a moment anyway, the same kid who'd endeared himself to the fans in 1939. The hit remains one of the highlights of his career.

In the second half of the season, as the Yankees continued to pull away, Boston fans focused on matters other than the standings. Williams was chasing .400 and Grove was after win number 300.

For a while it seemed as if both would fall short. In the first game after the break, Grove, although he pitched well, lost 2-0 and remained stuck on win number 299. Williams sprained his ankle in the game and went hitless to drop below .400.

He was still recovering when Grove gave it another try in Chicago on July 18. The pitcher should have gotten the win, but Boston's defense, as usual, was atrocious. As the *Herald* observed, "runs on each side were cheap, either undeserved, often unearned or seldom clean-cut . . . You just had to feel sorry for Grove."

Errors by Foxx and Cronin led to two Chicago runs. Then, in the seventh, with the Sox up 3-2, Grove himself erred on a bunt by Chicago third baseman Jimmy Webb. Grove moved to field the ball, but his forty-year-old legs no longer followed his commands. He got there late, then slipped, and Webb beat his throw. Disgusted, Grove forgot to hold him on and Webb stole second. Webb scored when Johnny Rigney bounced a ball past a lumbering Cronin to tie the game. At the end of the inning, Grove showed his frustration by throwing his glove into the air.

Lou Finney dropped a flyball in the tenth and lost the game. Three hundred wins would have to wait.

Williams returned to the lineup on July 22, and Cronin, oddly, doctored the batting order. He switched with Williams, moving to third as Ted hit cleanup. Foxx, on the decline as a power hitter but still hitting .300, remained fifth.

The change had a huge impact on Williams's pursuit of .400. When he'd hit third, with Cronin and Foxx behind him, the opposition had to give him pitches to hit. In the cleanup spot, with a less-than-menacing Foxx on deck, Williams was pitched around. His keen eye and patience led to an enormous number of walks in the second half, helping his task immeasurably. Meanwhile Cronin, with Williams behind him, got plenty of balls to hit himself.

On July 23 Williams's hot hitting inspired White Sox manager Jimmy Dykes to unveil a new strategy. Although Cleveland Indian manager Lou Boudreau has been credited with inventing a defensive shift in 1946 to stop Williams, Dykes was actually the first to use the strategy.

Although it was often used with the bases empty, when Williams came to bat Dykes moved his shortstop into shallow right center, moved his third baseman into the vacant hole at short, and put all three outfielders on the right side of the field. Since Williams usually pulled the ball, the strategy stacked the field with defenders on the right side.

But it didn't work. Williams went to the opposite field far more than he was given credit for. Facing the shift in the seventh inning he punched the ball to left field and loped into second base as the White Sox chased down the bounding ball. Dykes never used it again.

On July 26, on a hot and humid afternoon in Fenway Park, Grove trudged back onto the mound once more in search of win 300. Little remained in his storied left arm. The Cleveland lineup raked him for nine hits and four runs in the first four innings. Then, from somewhere, Grove drew upon twenty years of pitching savvy and settled down. The Red Sox scored ten runs, including a homer by Williams. Grove gamely hung on, outlasting three Indian pitchers and going the distance for a 10-6 win, his 300th. But he would not win another game in baseball.

Williams continued his singular pursuit of .400. Since DiMaggio's hitting streak had ended at fifty-six games on July 17, and the Yankees were running away with the pennant, the stage was Williams's alone. He performed like a marathoner, relentlessly maintaining his pace as the finish line drew closer. He refused to swing at bad pitches, walking more of-

Lefty Grove celebrates his three hundredth victory on July 26, 1941. Congratulating the forty-one-year-old on what would be his last major league victory are Johnny Peacock (l) and Jimmie Foxx. Foxx won the game with a tie-breaking eighth-inning triple.

ten than getting a base hit, but rarely missed when the ball came over the plate.

But no matter how well Ted Williams was hitting, Tom Yawkey wasn't happy. Grove was finished. Foxx, although only thirty-three, looked and played a decade older as hard living had taken its toll. And Cronin was in decline. Even with the addition of Williams, DiMaggio, Doerr, Tabor, and others, Yawkey's millions had still gone to waste.

As the Yankees made more obvious by the day, any thought that the Red Sox were close to a pennant was fraudulent. So Yawkey changed course again. Now he wanted to make some money.

While he'd lost a small fortune thus far, attendance was up and he was about to break even. Even his investments in the minors were making money. He began to question the wisdom of Collins and Cronin, particularly Collins.

Without consulting either man, Yawkey decided to take command. He convinced Bill Evans to relocate from his home in Cleveland to Louisville, home of Boston's Triple-A franchise. "This is just between

us," he told him over Lobster Newburg and champagne in his suite at Boston's Ritz Hotel. "Nobody knows anything about it — Collins, Cronin, anybody.

"I want you to move there," Yawkey continued. "Buy a house. We'll buy it for you. We'll give you a $5,000 raise. We've made money there every year and we'll give you ten percent of the profits each year."

Evans was ecstatic — he would finally get to run the system as he saw fit, without interference from Cronin, whom he'd recently told would lose his job in 1942 to rookie shortstop Johnny Pesky. Pesky was leading the league in hitting at Louisville.

The manager had been critical of Evans ever since their disagreement over Reese. Whenever a rookie failed, Cronin had blamed Evans. And when one succeeded, Cronin complained he had remained in the minors for too long.

Three days later, Yawkey met Cronin in New York, where the Sox played the Yankees. Cronin had gotten wind of Yawkey's plan and didn't like it. A few days later, a New York paper reported that Yawkey was going to break up the Red Sox in the off-season and start from scratch.

The Boston papers felt jilted and said so. In response, an irate Yawkey sent a long telegram to *Herald* writer Bill Cunningham, which Cunningham called "The longest I have received in my life . . . It's nice to know rich people. He didn't send it collect."

In the communiqué, which Cunningham published in its entirety, Yawkey was curiously caustic and

Hall of Fame umpire Billy Evans helped establish the Red Sox' minor league operations in the thirties. On September 6, 1941, less than a month after being hired to run the Red Sox Louisville farm team, Evans was fired over the telephone by owner Tom Yawkey.

paranoid. He first downplayed the story, which he termed both "made up" and released "without my authorization." Then he wrote cryptically, "Incidentally, of Boston's own hire and fire members of my organization such as Collins, Cronin Etc., do you suppose they ask for my ideas or intentions or thoughts about such matters first? The Answer is No." Yawkey was clearly perturbed.

As Williams chased history and kept everyone distracted, the front office was in turmoil. On September 4 New York clinched the pennant in Boston. Then the Sox followed the Yankees back to New York to play out the string.

According to Harold Kaese, after the game one night Boston coach Moe Berg, who had sat on the bench for Evans with Cleveland, accompanied Yawkey back to his Manhattan apartment. Yawkey started drinking. Precisely what they discussed is uncertain, but it led Yawkey to pick up the phone.

He called Evans in Cleveland and sounded drunk. "Billy," he said, "we think it's in the best interests of the Red Sox if you were to sever your connection with the club."

Evans was stunned. He'd turned his life upside down for Yawkey and was now being fired. But he didn't fight. "If you feel that way I'll resign," he said. "I've enjoyed my association with you very much and hate to leave." Yawkey then rambled on for a few moments, telling Evans that Cronin was the most important man in the organization and threatening to call Collins in Boston and fire him as well before finally hanging up.

The firing stood, although Evans thought that if he hadn't been home that night or had called Yawkey back when he had sobered up, he could have kept his job. He blamed Cronin, and it seems likely the manager got to Yawkey and presented an ultimatum. Evans lost.

If winning the World Series was really Yawkey's ultimate goal, dismissing Evans was one of his biggest mistakes. Coach Herb Pennock took over as farm director, but the system rapidly became far less productive than it had been under Evans, although it remained profitable. Since Yawkey wasn't buying players anymore, the club was chronically undermanned, a team of all-stars and also-rans, without any depth. The few players who did progress were nearly all signed under Evans's watch.

Evans's dismissal went virtually unnoticed, for in the final weeks of the 1941 season, particularly in Boston, all eyes were focused on the Splendid Splinter.

His pursuit of .400 served as the perfect counterpoint to the Yankees' inexorable drive to the pennant, an individual achievement that gave Boston something to cheer about in the face of New York's collective accomplishment. The Boston press made it a big story because they didn't have anything else. In 1940, hitting .400 shouldn't have been that big a deal.

Although the barrier had last been broken in 1930, when the Giants' Bill Terry hit .401, it had since been seriously challenged four times — by the A's Al Simmon's .390 in 1931, by Pittsburgh's Arky Vaughan's .385 in 1935, the White Sox' Luke Appling's .388 in 1936, and Joe DiMaggio's .381 in 1939. An occasional, brief drought between .400 hitters wasn't unique. No one had hit .400 from 1902 through 1910, or from 1913 through 1919 either.

Hitting .400 was no aberration; a player not hitting .400 was. What Williams was attempting to do was, at the time, not as uncommon as hitting fifty home runs, knocking in more than 170, or, over the previous three decades, pitching and winning thirty games on the mound.

This is not meant to diminish Williams's achievement, but to place it in perspective. The fact that no one has hit .400 since is what makes Williams's mark important. Had the Red Sox been in a pennant race in 1941 Williams's individual quest would have received far less attention than it did. But they weren't.

In fact, it wasn't until the Yankees clinched that Williams became the big story. On September 7 in New York he received a standing ovation after taking his 400th at bat, which qualified him for the batting title.

The opposition all but stopped pitching to Ted, and Williams felt no pressure to do anything but take the walks and focus on getting base hits. On September 12 and 13 in St. Louis, he came to bat nine times. He failed to get a hit, but he walked five times.

The next day, playing in front of Boston's largest crowd of the season against Chicago, Williams struck out for the first time in three weeks and smacked his thirty-fifth home run of the season, his sixth of the year off Johnny Rigney.

He stayed above .400 for the next week, but as the end of the season approached, he finally began to press. On September 23 against Washington, his only hit was a flyball his old teammate Doc Cramer

Upon arriving at his first spring training camp at Sarasota in 1938 Williams was approached by manager Joe Cronin, who exclaimed to the minor leaguer, "You should see [Jimmie] Foxx hit." Williams's reply was, "Foxx should see me hit." At 6-foot-3 and barely 175 pounds the young Williams earned the nickname the "Splendid Splinter."

Ted Williams possessed a charismatic personality to match his baseball talent. No Boston athlete and few major leaguers attracted the amount and depth of coverage given the temperamental slugger.

dropped. The press referred to the subsequent scoring decision as "tainted." In a doubleheader the next day, Williams went 1-for-7, dropping his average to .401, his lowest mark since July 25. Umpire Bill Grieve had been the only person in the ballpark who thought he beat out a groundball hit to second, only his third infield hit of the season. According to the *Herald*, the 7,500 umpires in the stands "hooted long and loud" after the call. They didn't mind if Williams

hit .400, but they did mind the fact that he appeared to be getting some help.

The Sox traveled to Philadelphia for the final three games of the season. Williams caught a break as the Sox enjoyed their last two of nine off-days for the month. He took advantage by taking hours of extra batting practice.

Joe Cronin admitted that Williams's chase of .400 was all that mattered in these last three games.

He tried to take the pressure off, telling the press, "I may yank him in the second game if he's got his hits."

The next day, Williams and the Sox faced an unfamiliar pitcher, rookie knuckleballer Roger Wolff, who'd shut down Washington on three hits in his first major league appearance a week before. Williams always said that pitchers with whom he was unfamiliar gave him the most trouble, and Wolff proved him correct.

After walking in the second, Williams doubled in the Sox' four-run fourth, but in three subsequent at bats, Wolff held him hitless in Boston's 6-1 win. His average dropped to .3995.

Much has since been made of the fact that if Williams had sat out the season-ending doubleheader, his .3995 average would have been rounded off to .400. His decision to play has often been described as courageous and emblematic of his character.

But, in fact, the *Boston Herald*'s headline — "Williams Dips Below .400" — told the truth. If Williams's average had been rounded to .400, no one would have given him credit for it. At best, the mark would have carried a sizable asterisk and been considered dubious, particularly in light of the fact that at least two of his hits during that last week had been tainted.

Besides, there were other reasons to play in the finale. Williams was leading the league in batting average and home runs and trailed DiMaggio by only a few RBIs. With a great day, he could snatch the Triple Crown and perhaps the MVP award. Dick Newsome was trying to collect win number twenty in game one, and Lefty Grove was scheduled to make his last major league appearance in game two. Had Williams sat out either game he'd never have been forgiven. He had enough problems with the press already. The notion of sitting out the doubleheader never went further than Cronin's statement two days before. Williams had to play.

But he was still nervous. The night before the game he walked the Philadelphia streets for hours with clubhouse attendant Johnny Orlando, working off nervous energy. The A's were playing out the string and planned to throw a couple of rookies, pitchers Williams knew nothing about.

A crowd of just over ten thousand fans turned out

John Michael Pesky enjoyed a superb rookie season in 1942, leading the American League with 205 hits while batting .331. Pesky would play shortstop and third base for Boston while batting .313 in eight seasons with the Red Sox.

to watch Williams and bid Grove goodbye, several thousand more than would normally have come to Shibe Park. When he came to bat for the first time in the second inning of game one, A's catcher Frankie Hayes told him, "Mr. Mack told us we let up on you he'll run us out of baseball. I wish you all the luck in the world but we're not giving you anything." But Mack had also told his pitchers to pitch to Williams, to give him a chance.

Umpire Bill McGowan was on Williams's side too. As Williams stepped in, McGowan muttered, "To hit .400 a batter has got to be loose."

Williams took two balls off pitcher Dick Fowler, then hit a hard groundball through the right side. His average nudged above .400.

He came up again in the fifth, feeling more at ease. This time he drove a pitch from Fowler over the right-field wall for a home run and bought himself some breathing room.

In the sixth he singled off relief pitcher Porter Vaughn, to all but secure a .400 average for the season. Another single in the seventh lifted his average to .405, then it dropped to .404 when he reached base on an error in the ninth. Boston won 12-11.

There was no reason at all to sit out the second game. Even if he went 0-for-4, he'd still hit .400, and with two RBIs in the first game, he still had an outside chance to catch DiMaggio.

Grove started the game and was awful, giving up four hits and three runs in the first inning, leading the *Herald*'s Burt Whitman to describe him indelicately as "a pathetic figure." Perhaps the greatest pitcher of all time, or at the very least one whose name belongs in that conversation, Grove's career came to an ignoble end, all but eclipsed by Williams's achievement. He ended his Boston career with a record of 105-62 in eight seasons, second at the time only to Cy Young.

Williams secured his place in the record book with a first-inning single. Then in the fourth, he topped off his day by driving a wicked line drive to right center, where it crashed through a loudspeaker high on the wall for a double. He flied out in his final at bat to finish at .4057, rounded off to .406. He missed the RBI title by five, with 120 to DiMaggio's 125.

Boston ended the season in second place with a record of 84-70, but closer to seventh place than first, for the Yankees won 101 games. But Williams had rendered Boston's finish almost immaterial. With attendance of more than seven hundred thousand, the fourth best in baseball, the Red Sox were making money and keeping their fans entertained, if not completely satisfied. Williams was entering his prime and seemed to be improving each season. Boston fans were already anticipating his next at bat and looked to the day when the Red Sox, with Williams, might finally topple the vaunted Yankees.

Then, on December 7, 1941, the Japanese bombed Pearl Harbor.

OF FRONT LINES AND COLOR LINES

1942 | 1945

Ted Williams departs 150 Causeway Street after enlisting
in the Naval Flight Training Program in Boston in 1942.

While baseball lost few players to the military in 1941, the war effort went into overdrive after the bombing of Pearl Harbor. On January 14, 1942, Commissioner Landis wrote President Roosevelt, asking, "Baseball is about to adopt schedules, sign players, make vast commitments, go to training camps. What do you want it to do? If you believe we ought to close down for the duration of the war, we are ready to do so immediately. If you feel we ought to continue, we would be delighted to do so. We await your order."

The cooperative tone of Landis's letter exemplifies baseball's attitude during the war. Everyone wanted to keep playing, but they were also willing to fight or do whatever their country asked of them.

The legacy of Harry Frazee, who'd successfully lobbied for the continuation of professional baseball during World War I, won out. Roosevelt, aware of the role baseball had played in the last great conflict, responded, "I honestly feel it would be best for the country to keep baseball going." And so it did, under restrictions and unique conditions, and without many of its finest players. Although the quality of play was major league in name only, baseball did its duty on and off the field.

Initially, the Red Sox, like most teams, were barely affected, losing only pitchers Mickey Harris and Earl Johnson and catcher Frankie Pytlak in the off-season. The American war machine took a while to get going, and in the early months, many players were exempt from the draft because of age, marital status, and other factors. Ted Williams was designated 3A because he supported his mother after his parents' divorce. Fathers over the age of twenty-five were given similar deferments at the beginning of the war.

But draft boards soon began to take a harder look at the list of potential draftees. In January of 1942 Williams's status was upgraded to 1A, making him subject to the draft at any time.

Williams didn't like it — he felt his deferment was justified. He hired an attorney, appealed, lost, then appealed again to the presidential draft board. The second time he won.

But he lost the public. They viewed him as a slacker getting special treatment. Criticism was so severe that the Sox tried to convince him to reconsider the appeal and not to go to spring training. But Williams was oblivious — at first. He signed a new contract and reported to Sarasota.

He wasn't the only member of the organization troubled by the war. Prior to the start of the season Tom Yawkey, now thirty-nine years old, put to rest a rumor he was entering the service as a commissioned officer.

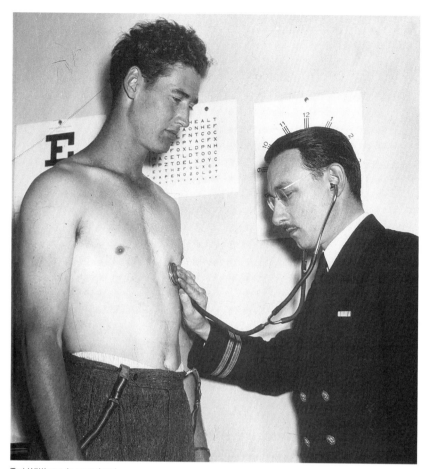

Ted Williams is examined by a navy physician upon enlisting in 1942. His eyesight was determined to be the best of any air cadet tested.

Yawkey and his wife had grown ever further apart. She wanted to live a life of high society, entertaining at lavish parties either in New York, their South Carolina estate, or Beverly Hills, while Yawkey wanted no more of the social whirl. When he was in New York he kept busy tracking his fortune, but his lawyers did the heavy lifting. In South Carolina he stayed outdoors, roaming the grounds with friends or employees, hunting for game. He spent thousands of dollars constructing dikes and remaking the coastline into an environment more friendly to his favored target, shore birds. His young daughter was becoming a stranger.

Julia Yawkey has never agreed to be interviewed about her father, apart from a single, curious comment to a reporter in the early 1970s when she offered only, "He's a strange man." When contacted recently for an interview, on or off the record, she politely refused, responding only with a brief note that explained, "As you know my parents separated shortly after I was born. I had very little contact with my father after that." Indeed, by 1941 the Yawkeys had parted ways.

Elise Yawkey may well have gotten wind of Yawkey's connection to a Georgetown woman named Hazel Weiss, who from 1934 to 1969 operated a well-known bordello in Georgetown known as the Sunset Lodge. Georgetown journalist Jack Leland once wrote that the place was regularly patronized by "an Eastern sports franchise," on annual stopover on the way to Florida for spring training. In 1989 the *Boston Globe* reported that Yawkey didn't just patronize the establishment, he financed it as well.

Alcohol may well have been another part of the problem with his marriage. For as Yawkey and his wife grew apart, his alcoholism increased and began to affect the way he ran the team. He'd always surrounded himself with front office toadies whose main qualification was their ability to nod in agreement and share a drink, but never more so than in the early war years, when he felt particularly frustrated and alone, and given the state of wartime baseball, unable to pursue his peculiar chimera.

Older than his players, he increasingly felt like a stranger in their midst. Now when Yawkey came to Boston he stayed in seclusion in a suite he kept at the

"No, I'm not going into service yet," he told the *Post*'s Gerry Moore. "My business interests outside of baseball are busy right now helping furnish tools and equipment for the armed forces. I consider that just as important a war effort as toting a gun." As a purveyor of raw materials, Yawkey was well positioned during the war. While the Red Sox were one of only six teams that lost money from 1942 through 1945, Yawkey made up the difference in private business. He never joined the military.

Yawkey was passing into middle age, and his level of involvement with the Red Sox began to change. Over the next decade he withdrew from the day-to-day activities of the team, entrusting Cronin to make most of the decisions. While Yawkey still wanted to win, a world championship eventually became less of an obsession. He took most of his pleasure in owning the team simply from the relationships it provided with ballplayers and baseball people.

Ritz. He even took meals in his room, usually venturing out only to go to Fenway Park. He'd arrive early in the morning, and instead of working out with the players as he once had, he now paid batboys and other employees to throw him batting practice. All he wanted to do was hit one over the left-field wall, even hitting juiced-up baseballs in an attempt to do so, yet according to Carl Yastrzemski, Yawkey admitted he never accomplished the feat, not even once.

When the players began arriving, Yawkey would retire to his office, and, as game time approached, he'd take his position in his special box alongside the press box, usually accompanied by Collins. He'd start to drink, particularly if the Red Sox played poorly, and after the game be chauffeured back to the Ritz. The pattern would then be repeated the next day, and his personal frustrations and the occasional hangover dissolved into sweat as Yawkey again would try to hit one over the wall. When the team was out of town, he sat in a chair on the infield, a radio at his side, a boy in a park with no playmates.

Then came Jean Hiller.

Born Jean Hollander in 1909, the future Mrs. Yawkey married Charles Hiller, her high school sweetheart. The marriage broke up in 1933, and the striking young divorcée worked as a saleswoman and model at Jay Thorpe, an exclusive women's clothing store in New York.

Hiller modeled clothing for her wealthy clients and their husbands, one of whom was Elise Sparrow Yawkey. Such women had notorious reputations as gold diggers — precisely why attractive young women took such low-paying positions. She met Tom during one of Elise's shopping sprees and found a man worth millions bored with his life and estranged from his wife.

As the Yawkeys drifted apart, Jean Hiller took on a discreet role in his life. Finally, in November of 1944, Elise and Tom divorced in Reno, Nevada. She, too, had taken a lover, and on December 2 married wealthy businessman Harry Dorsey Watts, eventually settling in the Hamptons on Long Island. In contrast, Yawkey turned away from that world. On Christmas Day, in a simple ceremony before a judge and two witnesses in Georgetown, Tom married Jean. She saved him, caring for him like a child and mak-

ing up for the normal family life he never had. She accompanied him into the field to hunt and fish, not because she had to, like the first Mrs. Yawkey, but because she enjoyed the outdoors. They moved out of the formal main house at South Island and lived in a cabin instead. Jean Yawkey stayed by her husband's side and grew to share his love of baseball.

Like their owner, the Red Sox also changed during the war years. Lefty Grove wisely retired after 1941. While barnstorming in the off-season, Jimmie Foxx was hit in the head by a pitch thrown by Negro League pitcher Chet Brewer and would never be the same player. And Joe Cronin finally relinquished his hold on shortstop. Yawkey's millions were slowly being replaced by Yawkey's minor leaguers. Yet the two clubs barely overlapped. Depending on one's perspective, Yawkey either stopped spending too early, or started building too late, and a team that featured five eventual Hall of Famers in its starting lineup (Foxx, Grove, Cronin, Williams, and Doerr) never even won a pennant.

Two new players made a huge impact in 1942. On the mound handsome University of Texas grad Cecil "Tex" Hughson made up for the loss of Grove and proved his five wins at the end of 1941 were no fluke. And Johnny Pesky beat out Eddie Pellagrini to win the job as shortstop. Both were a significant improvement on their fading predecessors.

Pesky, whose real surname is Paveskovich, was earmarked as a ballplayer at an early age. Growing up in Portland, Oregon, he played sandlot ball and was taken under the wing of former Sox pitcher Carl Mays, who ran a baseball camp. Then Pesky got a job working in the clubhouse of the Portland Beavers in the Pacific Coast League. While playing semipro ball for a lumber camp team in 1939, he was spotted by Sox pitcher Jack Wilson, who recommended that Boston sign him.

Pesky played one year of Class-A ball for Boston in Rocky Mount, North Carolina, and moved up to Triple-A Louisville in 1941. On Opening Day of the 1942 season, he was twenty-two years old, and for the first time since 1934 a man not named Cronin was the Red Sox shortstop.

Pesky gave the Sox something they'd lacked for several seasons: defense and speed. A place hitter, he was the perfect complement to hit behind Dom Di-Maggio and ahead of Doerr and Williams, working the hit-and-run or the sacrifice bunt to perfection while providing just enough line drive power to keep pitchers honest.

Boston's losses to the draft in 1942, though few, proved just enough to keep them from winning a pennant. While the starting lineup matched up well with the Yankees, the pitching staff, minus Harris and Johnson, was still thin. Dick Newsome tumbled out of the rotation, and after Hughson, Charley Wagner, and Joe Dobson, the other spots in the rotation were up for grabs. New York bolted ahead early, and while the Red Sox kept pace, they never really pressed New York.

Had Jimmie Foxx remained productive that season, the result might have been different. But after being beaned he started bailing out and in the spring broke a rib.

Cronin stuck with him for two months. But after only nine extra-base hits in 100 at bats, Tony Lupien was given the first base job and Foxx was waived out of the league, finally signing with the Chicago Cubs. He took his departure hard. He claimed Cronin had talked him out of retiring and felt misled. In Chicago, when a reporter asked him about the difference between A's manager Connie Mack and Cronin, he fired a parting shot, saying, "One manager knew what he was doing; the other didn't."

Foxx was the greatest righthanded hitter to ever play for the Red Sox in Fenway Park. His numbers over his first five seasons in Boston rival those of any Red Sox hitter, including Ted Williams. For it is Foxx, not Williams, who still holds the club single-season record for home runs, RBIs, and total bases, all set during his spectacular 1938 season. From 1936 through 1940 he *averaged* .325, with forty home runs and 133 RBIs and 123 runs scored.

The war made it impossible for the Red Sox to do anything to catch the Yankees, as the draft-inspired shortage of talent made trading difficult. Even Ted Williams got frustrated as the press continued to blast him over his draft appeal. He finally said the hell with it. After receiving assurances that he wouldn't be called into active duty until the fall, he enlisted in the Navy Air Corps.

Enlisting was the smart thing for most players to do, for it allowed a player at least some control over his future, and Williams wanted to learn how to fly. Before the end of the year, a number of other Red Sox players followed suit. Pesky also enlisted in the Navy Air Corps, and Dom DiMaggio joined the Coast Guard.

Williams followed his spectacular 1941 season with another nearly as impressive, winning the Triple Crown with a .356 average, thirty-six home runs, and 137 RBIs. Hughson led the league with twenty-two wins, and Pesky hit .331. But Boston, despite going 93-59, finished nine games behind the Yankees, and New York second baseman Joe Gordon edged out Williams for the MVP award, as Williams's enlistment failed to rehabilitate him in the eyes of the voting members of the fourth estate.

After the 1942 season the war had a dramatic effect on baseball. No team was hit harder by the draft and rash of enlistments than the Red Sox. From 1942 through 1945, twenty-two Red Sox players put in a total of fifty-three years in the service.

Between the end of the 1942 season and Opening Day of 1943, Boston lost virtually its entire starting team. Only Bobby Doerr, Tony Lupien, Jim Tabor, and Tex Hughson remained. By 1945, except for Lupien, they, too, would all be in the service. Baseball continued during the war, but it wasn't the same game.

The game's most important number during that time was not that of batting averages, wins and losses, or ERA, but the draft designation 4F. Scouts scoured the country for players too old, too young, or too risky, physically, for the service. Career minor leaguers became instant major leaguers, while recently retired players and others over the hill suddenly found their careers extended. Joe Cronin, for example, stayed active to play third base.

The best ball during much of the war was played in the service, as the various service branches and bases put together clubs of genuine major league and minor league talent to entertain the troops. Many players gladly accepted such stateside service roles, which were easily obtained. Others felt too guilty to play ball in uniform and demanded to be given active service.

The best team was that assembled at the Great

Opening Day 1943 with members of the Red Sox, Braves, and local players return-ing to Fenway Park in uniform. *Top row (l–r):* Ted Williams, Johnny Sain. *Bottom row (l–r):* Johnny Pesky, Lt. Commander E. S. Brewer, Buddy Gremp, Joe Coleman.

Lakes Naval Training Station in Chicago. A virtual all-star team, the Great Lakes squad went 48-2 in 1944 and defeated major league teams in exhibitions in eleven of twelve games, including the Red Sox twice. Dom DiMaggio and Charley Wagner played for the Norfolk, Virginia, Naval Training Station team, and both Ted Williams and Johnny Pesky briefly played baseball while stationed in North Carolina. Tex Hughson later told reporters, "I fought World War II with a bat and glove." But when a story broke in 1944 that revealed that nearly three hundred professional baseball players were still stateside, most of them playing ball, these powerhouses were broken up — only to re-form overseas.

In November of 1942 the government asked major league teams to save on travel and hold spring train-ing in the North. The Red Sox were the first club to agree, making arrangements to train at Tufts Univer-sity, six miles north of Fenway Park in Medford, for the next two seasons, before holding camp in New Jersey in 1945.

Conditions weren't bad, for Tufts had a large field house, enabling players to throw, hit, and take ground-balls. But it wasn't Florida. Whenever the weather al-lowed, the team practiced outside. For many, it was the first time they'd ever played baseball wearing long johns.

Training close to home meant a dearth of exhibi-tion games. The Sox scrimmaged local college teams, but they provided little competition. But every team in the majors faced the same difficulties.

Playing Major League Baseball during the war years was a humbling experience for many players. Teams were routinely bumped from trains in favor of

Ted Williams lights Babe Ruth's cigar prior to a war-charities game at Braves Field in 1943.

Ted Williams, on the other hand, spent three years stateside, eventually being stationed in Pensacola, Florida, where he became an officer and trained as a flight instructor. The best part of the war for Williams was that he was exposed to sport fishing and found an obsession that nearly rivaled hitting a baseball.

From 1943 through 1945 pennants were won by accident. Plugging holes in the roster as best they could, the Red Sox of this era were reasonably mediocre, not the best team in the American League, but neither were they the worst.

In 1943 the Yankees jumped into first place early and ran away from the field. Boston stayed around .500 into August, but ran out of gas and collapsed in September to finish seventh, twenty-nine games behind the Yankees but still twenty games better than last-place Philadelphia.

But in 1944, they appeared poised to steal a pennant. Yawkey still had money and in the off-season purchased aging slugger Bob Johnson from Washington. Johnson, whose brother Roy had played the Boston outfield a decade earlier, had been an all-star with the A's for a decade before slowing down. But he resurrected his career against wartime pitching and provided the power Boston desperately needed. Hughson was dominant, and entering the last week of August the Browns, Yankees, Red Sox, and Tigers were bunched in a pack atop the league, separated by only a handful of games.

Then the war got in the way. Over a two-week period Boston lost Hughson, Doerr, and catcher Hal Wagner to the draft — the club's best pitcher and two leading hitters. They went 8-16 in September and faded to fourth place. The St. Louis Browns stole the pennant.

Even as it became apparent by the spring of 1945 that the war would soon end, more players were still entering the service than were coming out. That spring Jim Tabor, the last man left from the pre-war Sox, got the call-up, just as Sox pitching prospect Dave "Boo" Ferriss was being mustered out because of asthma. He replaced Hughson as the staff ace, but Bob Johnson was a year older, and after Ferriss the best pitcher on the team was forty-two-year-old Mike Ryba. The Red Sox never had a chance.

The club ran a virtual tryout camp all year long.

servicemen, which sometimes turned even short trips into day-long excursions. Players were forced to bunk four or six to a room, and equipment was in short supply. In 1943 the Sox even went through spring training without caps, as the club donated their supply to soldiers.

But relatively few major leaguers saw combat, and no one on a major league roster at the time of the bombing of Pearl Harbor was killed. Those who did see action, however, performed with distinction. Boston's war hero was Earl Johnson, who won both the Bronze and Silver Stars in the Battle of the Bulge and received a field commission to lieutenant after braving German fire to save a jeep that carried needed electronic equipment.

Boston hung in for half the season again, then, for the third year in a row, collapsed, this time sinking to seventh place as MVP pitcher Hal Newhouser led Detroit to the pennant.

Yet the lasting impact of the war on baseball lay not in the heroics of its players in battle, or in its champions on the field. For the war changed baseball as it changed America. Nowhere was that made more visible than in the fact that the war forced organized baseball to confront the racial barriers it had erected over the years and the Jim Crow policies it had pursued in order to keep Major League Baseball white. Logic held that if a man was willing to die for his country, upon his return to civilian life in the United States he deserved equal treatment. Although there were no legal restrictions barring black players

like those instituted in the South after the Civil War, the result had been the same. In Boston, that self-examination would prove particularly distressing.

There had always been those who had spoken out against the racial injustice of organized baseball. In Boston, the local black press led the cause, particularly a young African-American journalist named Mabrey "Doc" Kountze. Kountze, who served as sports editor at one time or another for both the *Boston Chronicle* and the *Boston Guardian*, made the integration of Major League Baseball, in particular the Braves and the Red Sox, his special cause.

In the mid-1930s, Kountze and his colleagues in the black sporting press, such as Wendell Smith of the *Pittsburgh Courier* and Sam Lacy of the *Chicago Defender*, formed the National Negro Newspaper All-

During the war player-manager Joe Cronin filled in at third base. Note the advertising on the left-field wall as well as the Cities Service billboard, the predecessor of the Citgo sign, just next to the wall-mounted speakers.

American Association of Sports Editors with the express purpose of highlighting the achievements of the black athlete and bringing them to the attention of whites. As Kountze later described it, the NNNAASE began "feeding black sports data into the white daily press to drum up support." They attacked not so much the policies of Major League Baseball as the underlying argument baseball used to justify the course. Over time, they made it impossible for baseball to claim that no black players had major league ability.

In 1935, Kountze put the question to both Ed Cunningham, secretary of the Braves, and Phil Troy, who

Joe Cronin broke his leg early in the 1945 season, which was later offered as an excuse why the Red Sox didn't sign Jackie Robinson. The Hall of Famer continued to manage the team on crutches but drew a curtain on a playing career that saw him retire with a .301 batting average.

held a similar position with the Red Sox, asking simply if they were aware there were black ballplayers of major league ability and if they agreed with the color bar.

According to Kountze, both men admitted that they knew there were many black players with major league ability and that they personally disagreed with baseball's color bar. When Kountze asked Troy why the Red Sox didn't have any black players, ac-

cording to Kountze Troy "shrugged his shoulders and pointed toward the 'Front Office.'" Yawkey himself, however, would never meet with Kountze.

The Braves gave Kountze a slightly better reception. He met with both team owner Judge Fuchs and Bob Quinn, who served as Braves president after selling the Red Sox. In a 1938 meeting, Quinn told Kountze that while he personally disagreed with the color line, any effort at that time to break it would be "voted down" by the other owners. Nevertheless, Kountze's efforts in Boston eventually led first the Braves and then the Red Sox to open their ballparks to barnstorming Negro League teams, and Kountze became the first African-American to break the color barrier in the press box of both teams, doing so in Fenway Park in 1957.

Ever so slowly, the mainstream white press began to acknowledge the obvious injustice. In Boston, columnists Bill Cunningham of the *Post*, and later the *Herald*, and Dave Egan of the *Boston Record* both openly advocated the integration of baseball at a time when most of their peers stayed silent.

The war undercut any argument otherwise. There was increasing pressure from a number of groups to end Jim Crow practices everywhere in the workplace, a movement that was gaining political momentum and support.

During the war the integration of Major League Baseball began to appear inevitable. In 1944, Bill Veeck, owner of the Browns, made plans to buy the Phillies and stock the club with Negro League talent, but Judge Landis got wind of the plan and arranged a sale of the team to another party. Landis died shortly thereafter and was replaced by Happy Chandler, former United States senator from Kentucky, and a man more savvy to the possible implications of baseball's untenable racial position. Baseball enjoyed an antitrust exemption, and no one wanted any trouble with that.

In Boston, Jewish city councilman Isadore Muchnick took up the fight. In the spring of 1945 he threatened to block the annual renewal of the license issued to both the Braves and the Red Sox that allowed them to play baseball on Sunday. In a letter to both Yawkey and Quinn, he wrote, "I cannot understand how baseball, which claims to be the national sport and which in my opinion received special favors and dispensations from the Federal Government because of alleged moral value, can continue a pre–Civil War attitude toward American citizens because of the color of their skin."

Muchnick's threats received wide play in both the black and mainstream press. Eddie Collins wrote him back and said the Red Sox would be agreeable to trying out black players but "none have ever asked," and "none wanted to play in the major leagues" because they were better off financially in the Negro Leagues.

At the same time, Joe Bostic of the *New York Age* was pressuring Brooklyn's Branch Rickey over the same issue. Rickey, who had already decided to break the color line and was working on a plan to do so, resented the extra pressure. He held a cursory tryout of Terrence McDuffie, but resisted being put on the spot.

Jackie Robinson had been a member of the Negro League Kansas City Monarchs for only a few weeks, but was already well known to readers of the black press, where his career as an All-American football player at UCLA had received wide play. When he was still in college, the NNNAASE had identified him as an athlete who not only possessed the right physical abilities to break the color line, but, with his education and military record, the social and intellectual skills required to be acceptable to white America. After he signed with the Monarchs, the black press touted his abilities on the baseball diamond out of all proportion, for Robinson, who'd hit under .200 while playing for UCLA, was still an unproven commodity as a baseball player.

Muchnick decided to take the Red Sox at their word and find black players who wanted a tryout. He enlisted the help of Wendell Smith of the *Pittsburgh Courier*, and in early April Smith collected Robinson and two other Negro League players — Sam Jethroe of the Cleveland Buckeyes and Marvin Williams of the Philadelphia Stars — and brought them to Boston. Smith and Muchnick called Boston's bluff and said to both the Red Sox and the Braves, "Here are three men who want a tryout."

Reportedly refused lodging in a downtown hotel, Smith and the three ballplayers stayed in a private home while Muchnick tried to arrange the tryout. The Red Sox and Braves did everything they could to discourage him.

"They are not fooling me," Muchnick told Smith. "Collins and Quinn are giving us the run-around. They promised me they had no desire to bar Negro players and yet they 'run out' every time I try to pin them down. These boys came here to get a tryout and if they don't get one it will simply be another mark against the undemocratic practices of major league owners and officials. We are not going to stop fighting no matter how much they duck and try to evade the facts."

The mainstream press finally picked up on the story when the *Record*'s Dave Egan wrote that the three players were in town awaiting their promised tryout. Trapped by their own words, the Red Sox reluctantly agreed to hold a tryout. The players were told to report to Fenway Park at 10:30 A.M. on April 16, the day before the Red Sox opened the 1945 season in New York. What happened next still haunts the Red Sox.

Marvin Williams later recalled that "It was a beautiful day," a rare, fine early spring morning in Boston. Upon arriving at the park, Eddie Collins had the three players fill out a standard form of essential personal information, just as all prospects did. They were escorted to the Red Sox locker room and changed into the uniforms they brought with them to Boston.

Coach Hugh Duffy ran the tryout, and the three men were ushered onto the field. Scout Larry Woodard was already on the field, working out a half-dozen or so white players, part of the club's incessant search for players — as long as they were white — during the war.

Manager Joe Cronin sat stone-faced in the stands with Smith and Muchnick. A handful of reporters sat nearby and prepared to watch in earnest. But Eddie Collins, the man ultimately responsible for signing players, didn't watch the tryout. His disappearance is revealing.

The players weren't intimidated by being in Fenway Park — they'd played in major league ballparks as Negro Leaguers. Jethroe later recalled that he was surprised by the left-field wall which "was even closer than I thought. I remember speaking to myself 'I wouldn't mind playing in a ballpark like this.'"

But none of the three players was under any illusion about their chances of signing a contract. Jethroe later recalled, "To be honest, I never wondered if we were going to be offered contracts. All I knew was that I had been selected for this workout and we were going to be able to do what we do best and that was play baseball. I mean, I had a lot of fun playing in the Negro Leagues. I really didn't have a need to go. We all knew we were as good as the white boys."

Duffy began the tryout by hitting to the players. Jethroe shagged flies in the outfield while Williams, a second baseman, and Robinson, then a shortstop, took groundballs.

A short time later, the three players took batting practice, probably against one of the semipros trying out, although Williams said that he believed the other players were members of the Red Sox farm system.

Jackie Robinson later recalled, "I still remember how I hit the ball that day, good to all fields. What happened? Nothing!" Jethroe recalls that "All of us did all right. I hit a few off the wall and tried to show them my speed." Muchnick remembered that "You never saw anyone hit the wall the way Robinson did that day."

Duffy ended the hour and a half tryout and told the players, "You boys look like pretty good ballplayers. I hope you enjoyed the workout." He also gave them a vague promise that they'd hear from the club, "probably in the near future."

According to *Boston Globe* writer Clif Keane, who watched the tryout from the stands, as the players were leaving the field, a voice boomed out from the shadows in the back of the grandstand, "Get those niggers off the field!"

"I can't recall who yelled it," Keane said later. "People used to say it was Collins. But I really don't know." Interestingly enough, doorways in the upper grandstand lead directly to the club's offices.

Neither the three players, Muchnick, nor Smith ever confirmed the incident, and Smith later wrote that "at no time did they [the Red Sox] appear perturbed over the situation." But Jackie Robinson, significantly, reserved a particular and lasting enmity toward the Red Sox. Bill Gavin, who worked for the

Red Sox as a clubhouse boy in the late 1920s and early 1930s, once recalled that he had an opportunity to meet Robinson during spring training in the 1960s. Robinson, Gavin, and several other men were lounging on the grass around a spring diamond shooting the breeze when Gavin asked Robinson about the tryout. According to Gavin, "Robinson's demeanor changed completely. He jumped up and hissed — actually hissed — and said, 'I played in the National League!'" then stormed off. And in the final days of the 1967 season a United Press reporter asked Robinson who he favored in the close American League pennant race between Minnesota, Detroit, Chicago, and the Red Sox. Robinson told the reporter he was pulling for the Minnesota Twins, then added, "Anyway, because of Boston owner Tom Yawkey, I'd like to see them [the Red Sox] lose, because he is probably one of the most bigoted guys in baseball." That's a strong statement from a man who carefully measured every word he said, made even stronger by his close friendship with Sox manager Dick Williams dating back to their days together as teammates on the Dodgers.

Duffy supposedly recommended that the Sox sign Robinson, and Smith wrote that of the three players, Cronin was particularly impressed with Robinson and Williams, but expressed a wish that he could "see them under fire," in a game. But nothing happened.

The three players returned to the locker room and changed back into their street clothes. As they did, the Red Sox' new third baseman, Jack Tobin, entered the clubhouse and greeted Robinson. Tobin had played collegiate ball at St. Mary's College in California and played against Robinson many times. Typical of wartime ballplayers, Tobin, although talented, also carried a liability. He was a raging alcoholic, which then didn't disqualify him for the big leagues. In fact, Cronin even promised him five thousand dollars if he could stay sober for the season, but he failed to last the summer.

The two men talked for a few moments, then Tobin left to catch a train to New York for the Boston's season opener, a major leaguer. Robinson, Jethroe, and Williams figuratively headed for the back of the bus and the Negro Leagues.

Cronin broke his leg a few days later, and the Red Sox opened the season with six losses. He later cited the injury as his excuse why the club failed to sign any of the players, an absurd notion. If anything, Cronin's injury left Boston even more in need of players.

Cronin's story about that day changed with the times. In the 1950s he said, "They weren't ready for the majors," and that it would have been impossible for the Red Sox to sign the players and send them to Triple-A Louisville in segregated Kentucky. But even during the war, the Red Sox had other minor league teams, and loaning players to other clubs was common. Had the Red Sox really wanted to, they could have found room at the inn.

But by the late 1960s Cronin was telling a slightly different story, admitting the obvious by saying that the Red Sox had made a mistake by not signing Robinson, then adding, "I didn't do the hiring anyway. I was just the manager." He personally disliked Robinson, and when Robinson spoke at the 1972 All-Star Game just a few weeks before his death, Cronin, then AL president, found a convenient excuse to leave rather than appear publicly in his company.

The voice that boomed from the shadows of the grandstand, which others have since speculated belonged to Collins, or perhaps even Tom Yawkey, still echoes through Fenway Park, and its sting is still felt. Since that day the Red Sox have not been able to shake the reputation that they are a racist organization, nor worked as hard as many believe they should to shed that perception, for they have never really confronted it directly. In the end, that characterization has proven to be as much an impediment to the franchise's ability to win a world championship as any other factor.

Player-manager Joe Cronin meets with players at spring training camp at Pleasantville, New Jersey, in March 1945. The war decimated the Red Sox, although rookie phenom Dave "Boo" Ferriss won twenty-one games for the seventh-place finishers.

"It's [the team's racist reputation] almost an impossible thing to shake," said Red Sox Chief Executive Officer John Harrington to Leigh Montville of *Sports Illustrated* in 1991. "I don't know how you do it. I've been told it will take fifty years, generations before this thing is gone. I won't be around and you won't be around. It's impossible."

And it has already been more than fifty years. The Red Sox missed a remarkable opportunity.

Had the Red Sox signed Robinson in 1945, even to a minor league contract, he may eventually have made the difference on a club that would lose in the most heartbreaking fashion in the final game of the season in three of the next four years. Being the first club — or even one of the first — to sign an African-American ballplayer would have given the Red Sox a tremendous advantage, just as it did the Brooklyn Dodgers a few years later. The Red Sox may well have won another pennant or two, if not a world championship, or created a dynasty to supplant the Yankees.

Robinson did get to play in Boston in 1945. In mid-August the Monarchs appeared at Braves Field opposite a team of all-stars from the Charlestown Navy Yard. Despite the fact that Satchel Paige missed the game because of his arrest by a traffic cop after a minor transgression, Robinson led the Monarchs to an 11-1 win. Playing one of his best games of the year, Robinson put on a one-man show, wowing the crowd with two hits and steals of second, third, and home. Two weeks later, Branch Rickey sent word that he wanted to meet Robinson personally. Jethroe was eventually also signed by Rickey, then was sold to the Braves for one hundred fifty thousand dollars and five players. In 1950, he was named NL Rookie of the Year.

The Red Sox were not the only team slow to embrace integration. But they were among the first to reject it so conclusively and so publicly, and then, after Robinson donned a Dodger uniform and breached the color line in 1947, to resist it so staunchly. It is the single greatest error in the history of the franchise, far more significant and consequential than the sale of Ruth to the Yankees. For Boston's failure to sign Robinson left no imaginary curse upon the franchise, but a real one, with genuine and lasting consequences.

THREE-TIME LOSERS

1946 | 1949

Manager Joe Cronin enjoys the good news while it lasts.
His paper contains what could have been a standing
headline regarding the team for much of the late forties.

After the end of the war, the Red Sox, like the United States Armed Forces, looked invincible. The heart of the club — Pesky, Williams, Doerr, and DiMaggio — all returned from the service healthy and in their athletic prime. Tex Hughson's sore arm had healed, Joe Dobson and Mickey Harris were better-than-average major league pitchers, and Boo Ferriss was one of the few wartime finds with the talent to survive a return to normalcy. The American League would soon learn that no team was in better shape than the Red Sox.

But just as America soon learned that victory delivered no lasting guarantee of peace, Red Sox fans learned that the appearance of invincibility brought no guarantee of a world championship. Within a few years their seemingly inevitable march to a world championship would stall.

The postwar Red Sox were dramatically different from the pre-war version. Foxx, Cronin, and Grove were gone. Built from within, the postwar Sox represented the bounty of Billy Evans's careful tending of a farm system that, in his absence, was already in decline.

Optimism wasn't confined to the front office, either. Boston was beginning to boom as a generation looked confidently toward the future. The GI Bill made education accessible to everyone, and the American economy was the most powerful in the world. Fans viewed the upcoming baseball season as confirmation that America was not only back to normal, it was better than before. Attendance at Fenway Park would nearly triple from pre-war levels, to over one and a half million fans. For the first time since buying the club in 1933, Yawkey began turning a regular profit.

Almost by reflex, the press still picked the Yankees to win the pennant, with the defending-champion Tigers also likely to contend. But in January, anticipating the return of Hank Greenberg, Detroit swapped first baseman Rudy York to Boston for shortstop Eddie Lake, whom the return of Pesky made expendable. York's swing was built to pepper the left-field wall, and he plugged one of the few holes in the Boston lineup.

Williams resumed form immediately. On March 3 against the Braves he homered in his first exhibition game at bat and knocked in seven runs. His bravura performance set the tone for the remainder of the season.

Joe Cronin — a full-time manager at last — spent the spring sorting out the returning

The 1946 Red Sox bullpen included (l–r) Bob Klinger, Earl Johnson, Mace Brown, and Bill Zuber. Klinger led the league with nine saves while Johnson led the Boston relief corps with five victories. Both played a key role in Boston's game-seven loss to the St. Louis Cardinals in the World Series.

veterans. There were few surprises. Holdovers from the war years were quickly forgotten. Apart from Ferriss no pitcher from the 1945 Sox made the team, and reserve outfielders Catfish Metkovich, Leon Culberson, and Tom McBride were the only returning position players of any consequence.

The Red Sox started fast and took over first place for good on April 28, winning fifteen in a row before losing on May 11. For the next two months they cut a swath through the American League like Patton's army. By June they sported a record of 32-9 and a five-and-a-half-game lead over New York.

The war hadn't hurt Ted Williams. Rather, military life made him physically stronger, and his pilot training aided his concentration, if not his patience with the press. Williams was even more confident, assured, and arrogant than when he left.

"The Kid" had grown up — sort of. The Red Sox were now his team, and for better or for worse, the two became synonymous. They embarked upon similar paths, racking up singular achievements not al-

ways reflected in the final standings, alternately inspiring and frustrating their fans.

Early on, although he was hitting .350, Williams complained, "I haven't been hitting good . . . the pitchers have been lucky so far. I get them in the hole, then they hit the corner for a strike . . . They won't always hit that corner."

He was right. In May and June he cracked nineteen home runs with fifty-three RBIs. No one laughed when the press wrote that Williams might break Ruth's home run record of sixty.

Yet for all Williams's brilliance, the key to Boston's success was pitching. Hughson and Ferriss were the best one-two punch in the game in 1946, while Harris, Dobson, and swing man Jim Bagby kept Boston in the game until the bullpen could take over. Earl Johnson, Clem Dreisewerd, and Bob Klinger, who was grabbed on waivers from Pittsburgh, made up the best relief corps in baseball. They kept games close until Williams, York, or Bobby Doerr weighed in with a home run. The only trouble spot for the team was third base, and the club eventually brought back Pinky Higgins from Detroit to share the job with Rip Russell.

The pennant race was over by mid-June when the Yankees fell back and even the great DiMaggio failed to perform to his pre-war standard. Yawkey rewarded his club early, upping Cronin's salary to forty thousand dollars and giving each player on the team a five-thousand-dollar life insurance policy.

Williams then provided an exclamation point to a season already among the best in team history. On June 9, in the first inning of the second game of a doubleheader against Detroit at Fenway, he hit a fly-ball, not to, but through, right field. It passed over the fence above the bullpen still rising.

Up in row 33, Joe Boucher, a construction engineer from Albany, New York, was caught unaware. Williams's blast hit Boucher on the head, knocking a hole in the stunned man's straw hat. He complained later, "I didn't even get the ball. After it hit my head, I was no longer interested." The longest home run ever hit into the bleachers, it is still marked today by a single red seat in a field of green.

The Red Sox cruised into the All-Star break flirting with a double-digit lead. The game, played in Fenway Park on July 9, corroborated Boston's dominance. Williams, DiMaggio, Pesky, Doerr, York, Ferriss, Harris, and catcher Hal Wagner all made the team.

Before a capacity crowd Williams delivered a signature performance. In his first four at bats he walked, hit a home run into the center-field bleachers, and singled twice as the AL took an 8-0 lead into the eighth inning.

Thirty-nine-year-old junkballer Rip Sewell of Pittsburgh took the mound for the NL. On his way to only eight wins for the season, he was best known for his occasional use of what he called the "eephus" pitch (the term is a phrase from shooting craps). Thrown in a wide arc like a slow-pitch softball, the pitch frustrated sluggers. Only the Cardinal's Stan Musial had ever hit it for a home run.

Williams requested a demonstration before the game and asked, "Would you throw one of those in a ballgame like this?" "Only one," answered Sewell.

Sewell was being shelled when Williams stepped in with runners on second and third. The pitcher admit-

ted later, "I didn't figure it would make much difference how many runs they would score . . . so I thought I'd throw him a couple just to see what he would do with it."

Ted fouled off the first eephus, and then Sewell snuck by a fastball for strike two. A second eephus went wide for a ball.

But a third eephus was over the heart of the plate. According to Williams, "I never swung on a pitch as hard as that one."

The ball reversed course in an exaggerated mirror image of Sewell's toss and sailed into the bullpen as the crowd erupted in cheers. The American League won, 12-0, but after the game all everyone talked about was Williams, who'd finished the day a perfect 4-for-4, what the *Post*'s Jack Malaney called "The most perfect day he has ever had."

Williams stayed hot. Five days later against Cleveland he brought Boston back from an early deficit by smacking three home runs and knocking in eight in an 11-10 win. Between games, he ducked out of Fenway and was spotted cooling off eating a bowl of ice cream in a shop on Lansdowne Street. At the same time, Indian player-manager Lou Boudreau devised his own method to cool Williams.

As Jimmy Dykes had tried five years before, Boudreau decided to use a shift. After Williams doubled down the right-field line in his first at bat, Boudreau ordered his fielders to take what he called the "C formation."

All four infielders lined up to the right-field side of second base, while the right fielder played the line and the center fielder moved into right center. Left fielder George Case was the only player on the left side of the diamond.

The logic of the strategy was twofold. Unless the pull-hitting Williams jerked the ball over the fence, there was no room to hit on the right side. But the shift's psychological effect was equally important, for it challenged Williams's massive ego and provided a distraction.

Williams refused to give in and either bunt or hit the other way. In his first at bat versus the shift he grounded to Boudreau — playing where the second baseman generally stood.

The shift, or variations of it, was employed against

Williams for much of the remainder of his career. But since it was usually used with no runners in scoring position, and Williams eventually began to hit to left field more often, its effectiveness was more limited than most people realize. The shift cost Williams only ten or fifteen hits a year.

With a Boston pennant a foregone conclusion, the press started sniping at Williams. The *Globe* published a ghostwritten column under Williams's byline, which left him wide open in the eyes of the other writers. Then the *Globe* showed its appreciation by reporting that Williams had an eighty-thousand-dollar offer from the fledgling Mexican League. He wanted the Red Sox to match the offer, which even Tom Yawkey found preposterous.

But nothing appeared able to slow the Boston juggernaut. By September 5, Boston led by sixteen and a half games. One more win coupled with a loss by second-place Detroit would clinch the pennant. But as Boston fans have known since birth, the Red Sox are never quite as vulnerable as when success seems certain.

Yawkey promised to throw the players a party to remember. But the Sox suddenly slumped, and the second-place Tigers refused to lose.

Yawkey got impatient. When the club went into Detroit for a two-game series, he ordered ten cases of champagne. But the Tigers belted Boston and the cork stayed on.

The six straight losses unnerved the club, and the press made jokes about the champagne. Finally, on Friday the thirteenth in Cleveland, Tex Hughson spun a three-hitter and Williams lined a ball to left against the shift, his first (and only) inside-the-park home run and first-ever major league home run to left field.

The cork finally came off, but the celebration fell flat. Williams skipped the party, and Yawkey wouldn't let Boston writers in the same room as the players. Still, Boston fans had their best reason to cheer since 1918, and the club received five hundred thousand requests for Series tickets.

Boston limped through the remainder of the season. Cronin didn't panic, but neither did he take command. The Red Sox suddenly appeared vulnerable.

Strong pitching and a healthy offense had masked the team's problem spots — speed, depth, and Cronin's strategic acumen. There was no one on the bench to slam the door defensively or steal a run on the bases. Cronin didn't know what his team could do in a pinch. He had just pushed buttons all year long. That had been plenty.

In the National League the St. Louis Cardinals and the Brooklyn Dodgers ended the season tied and had to play a best-of-three playoff, delaying the start of the Series by four days. To stay sharp and attract a few more paying customers, the Red Sox recruited a team of American League all-stars to play a couple of exhibitions.

Despite the fact that luminaries like Luke Appling, Hank Greenberg, and Joe DiMaggio, wearing a Boston uniform after misplacing his pinstripes, provided the opposition, fewer than two thousand fans turned out to watch.

The game was even more of a disaster on the field than at the gate. Dom DiMaggio jammed a thumb catching a line drive, and in the fifth inning, with Boston leading 2-0, Williams was struck on the right elbow by a pitch from Washington's Mickey Haefner.

It wasn't fractured, but the team announced, "Ted will not be able to play for three or four days." Incredibly, the Sox played the all-stars again the next afternoon, losing 4-2.

The Cardinals swept the Dodgers. On the evening of October 3 the Red Sox boarded a train for St. Louis.

But in an instant, the Series almost became an afterthought. In his column, Dave Egan wrote, "I hate to scoop a brother journalist, particularly one who is laboring bravely under the handicap of an injured writing arm, but this is to inform journalist Ted Williams that left fielder Ted Williams is up for sale." He claimed Williams would be traded after the Series either to New York for Joe DiMaggio and several others, to Detroit for outfielder Dick Wakefield and Hal Newhouser, or to Cleveland for Bob Feller.

Jack Malaney ambushed Eddie Collins at the train station and asked if the report was true. According to Malaney, Collins "almost blew a gasket," blurted out one word — "Nuts!" — then refused further comment. The report spread among the players as the train pulled away, and it was front-page news in every Boston paper the next day.

The Red Sox (*l–r:* Rudy York, Tex Hughson, Bobby Doerr, Ted Williams) celebrate clinching the 1946 American League pennant at Cleveland's League Park on Friday, September 13. Tex Hughson's 1-0 shutout came courtesy of Ted Williams's lone career inside-the-park home run.

A simple denial from Yawkey, Collins, or Cronin would have ended the controversy, but straight talk has never been a strength of the Red Sox front office. Instead, no one denied the report, giving it credibility. Harold Kaese later wrote that the deal was Cronin's idea, but had been vetoed by Yawkey, with Collins left uncomfortably in the middle. While the Sox had the right to trade Williams, to allow the story to leak out on the eve of the club's first appearance in the World Series since 1918 was both inexcusable and one helluva way to run a ballclub.

The Sox were clearly distracted. Williams sat alone for most of the trip and pumped the press for more information, while anonymous teammates told the writers, "We can win without Ted." Meanwhile, Collins, Cronin, and Yawkey kept up their bizarre pact of silence. Kaese finally pigeonholed Yawkey and asked him about the report, to which the owner replied, "No comment," and, when pressed, "Double no comment." The *Post*'s Gerry Hern accurately described

Manager Joe Cronin is carried by *(l–r)* Rudy York, Johnny Pesky, and Earl Johnson as the Red Sox celebrate clinching the 1946 American League pennant, Boston's first in twenty-eight years.

the Red Sox as "the most confused team that has ever gone into . . . the world championship."

Despite Williams's injury, Boston's late-season collapse, and the trade rumor, the Sox were 10-3½ favorites over St. Louis. After their tough battle with the Dodgers, no one gave the Cardinals a chance.

Tex Hughson faced Cardinal lefthander Howie Pollett in the opener at Sportsman's Park. Boston scored a single run in the second, but St. Louis tied the score on Musial's double in the sixth.

The Red Sox had a chance to go ahead in the eighth, but DiMaggio, after leading off with a hit, tried to stretch it into a double and was thrown out. He added to his ignominy in the bottom of the inning, losing catcher Joe Garagiola's flyball in the sun as third baseman Whitey Kurowski scored the go-ahead run.

In the ninth, Higgins was on third and Boston one strike away from defeat when pinch hitter Tom McBride singled to tie the score. St. Louis went down in the ninth and the game entered extra innings.

It was over fast. Rudy York homered to left and war hero Earl Johnson set down the Cardinals. Boston won 3-2, and the club was smugly confident. Tom Yawkey strutted around the clubhouse smoking a big cigar.

But in game two Harry "The Cat" Brecheen, mixing a devastating screwball with curves and fastballs, outpitched Mickey Harris. He scattered four hits and knocked in the only run necessary in the third inning of the 3-0 Cardinal win.

Williams clearly wasn't himself. Although the Cardinals used a shift on him, it really hadn't been needed. They pitched around Williams and held him to only a single. The Series headed to Boston for the next three games, where over the season the Red Sox had accumulated an astounding 61-16 record.

Williams was happy to be home and begged in the press to stay in Boston, saying, "I have never played anywhere else in the majors. They say I don't like my teammates and they say I don't like the Boston fans. Well, if I've ever shown signs of temperament, it's been because I wasn't hitting or because something went wrong somewhere . . . I don't have any control over my future. If Mr. Yawkey wants to trade me, I have to go . . . If he wants to keep me, I stay in Boston, and that's where I want to stay."

Ferriss, whom Cronin had inexplicably passed over for the start in game two, drew the nod in game three opposite Murray Dickson. York homered in the first for Boston, knocking in three runs. Then in the third inning, with two outs, Williams bunted for a hit against the shift to give York another opportunity to hit with a man on base, but he grounded out. Ferriss threw a four-hit shutout and won 4-0 to give the Red Sox a two-to-one edge in the Series.

A Boston victory in game four would have all but ended the Cardinals' chances, but the Red Sox played their worst game of the Series. Cronin pitched Tex Hughson on three days' rest. He and five relievers were shelled, and Pesky, Hughson, Ryba, and Higgins all committed errors as the Cardinals knotted the Series with a 12-3 win. Thus far, apart from Rudy York and Bobby Doerr, the Red Sox simply hadn't been playing very well. Williams was hurt and distracted, Pesky was playing a nervous shortstop, and DiMaggio, as if trying to prove he was his brother's equal, was pressing, running into outs, and making mistakes in the field.

Before game five, Boston got some more bad news. Bobby Doerr, who'd left game four with a migraine, still couldn't see straight. Cronin moved Doerr's replacement, aging Don Gutteridge, into the leadoff slot.

He looked like a genius when Gutteridge singled to start the game. Williams then knocked him in with a hit to collect his only RBI of the Series. Joe Dobson scattered four hits, and Boston put the game away in the seventh on Higgins's run-scoring double. The club left Boston leading in the Series for the third

time and needing only one win to secure their sixth world championship in six tries.

Then Cronin, with Ferriss well rested and Hughson available after his short stint in game four, got cute. He revealed his own lack of confidence in his team and decided to pitch Mickey Harris, announcing he would save his two aces for game seven if needed. St. Louis manager Eddie Dyer was delighted, telling the press, "We got to Harris once and we can get to him again . . . I don't want to have to face Hughson again because he's a great pitcher and due to beat us." With Pollett still out with a sore back, Dyer countered with Brecheen.

Boston jumped out quickly. With one out, Pesky and DiMaggio singled to bring up Williams in the most important at bat of his career.

But Brecheen didn't break. He worked carefully to Williams and walked him. York came up with the bases loaded. So far, Brecheen had been the only Cardinal pitcher to shut the big first baseman down.

He did so again, getting him to ground into a double play. St. Louis went down easily in the bottom of the inning as Harris looked sharp.

In the second, Boston threatened again. Brecheen was only a batter or two away from being pulled as George Munger started warming up for the Cardinals. But in a huge miscalculation, Cronin, coaching third, waved Doerr home after a Higgins single. Left fielder Erv Dusak's short throw was perfect. Brecheen stayed in.

In the fourth, St. Louis catcher Del Rice led off with a single. Four hits, a bunt, and a sacrifice fly later, St. Louis had a 3-0 lead and Harris was in the shower. Hughson came on in relief as Cronin panicked and second-guessed his own gamble.

Hughson stopped the Cardinals cold, but it was too late, and with his history of arm trouble, the stint left him unavailable for game seven. Brecheen gave up only three more hits and St. Louis won 4-1. Hughson's only comment about his relief appearance was revealing. "I wish it had been in a winning game," he said.

Cronin was testy afterward, defending his decision to send Doerr to third and pitch Harris. "I could afford to gamble," he snapped. With a one-game lead, that may have been true, but now the Series was tied

For six decades Fenway Park has literally been my home away from home; an oasis. During that time I have come to know many of the players, several of whom have become my baseball brothers. Wins and losses aside, I cherish my time at the ballpark spent in the company of my nephews and friends in the clergy. The Red Sox are nothing less than my extended family.

For longer than I can remember my front-row seats have been located between the Red Sox dugout and the on-deck circle. Not bad for a teacher proud to have taught in the Boston public schools for five decades. I consider my seats to be the best in the house and they should be, for I have been a season ticket holder without interruption since 1944.

I suppose it hit home this past Opening Day when I overheard fragments of a conversation, dispersed by the chill April wind, between several Red Sox players in which one commented while looking my way, "Can you believe it . . . fifty-five years." I guess I would join them in disbelief as I ponder my many years as a Red Sox season ticket holder. You see, the game of baseball, including my years as a season ticket holder, has been a major part of my life since I was a youngster growing up in Roxbury.

My father, John Dooley, came to Boston from Holyoke nearly a century ago and soon became one of the leaders of the Royal Rooters. The Rooters were a collection of diehard baseball fans who first gathered at the South End Grounds to support the Braves and later allied themselves almost exclusively with the Red Sox. Their number included local businessmen, politicians, and local characters, all of whom were united in their love of the Red Sox, and occasionally the Braves.

My first baseball memories are of being taken to both Fenway Park and Braves Field by my father, who enjoyed the status of one who could place his daughter in the secure con-

For longer than I can remember my front-row seats have been located between the Red Sox dugout and the on-deck circle.

fines of the press box while making the rounds of friends and players prior to games. It wasn't long before he introduced me to players and taught me how to watch the game.

One player who became a fast family friend was Walter "Rabbit" Maranville. The Braves shortstop, a future Hall of Famer, visited us frequently at our summer cottage in Nantasket on weekends and Sundays. This was in the days when many major league teams, including the Braves and Red Sox, were forbidden to play Sunday baseball. It was on such Sundays that my father would see to it that Maranville never touched a drop of alcohol while drying out. My lasting image of him is that of a smiling acrobat playing catch with my brothers in the front

yard. He laughed as he played and later held court on our front porch while regaling my father and his friends with baseball stories.

Because my father rooted for both Boston teams I suppose I could have gone either way regarding my choice of where to purchase season tickets. My decision was made on the basis of the fact that the box seats at Fenway Park had chairbacks and were more comfortable than their counterparts at Braves Field.

It turned out to be a serendipitous choice as my first years at Fenway coincided with the return of those players I call my baseball brothers, namely, Johnny Pesky, Bobby Doerr, Dom DiMaggio, and Ted Williams.

I have lived near the park for many years, and I used to enjoy yelling to Ted Williams as he walked from the Back Bay to Fenway Park. I loved to kid him and yell that he was late and so forth. Before long my cover was blown and Ted went so far as to invite me to dinner with baseball friends such as Herb Score and Rocky Colavito. I still talk to Ted on a regular basis during which time we compare ailments and the like. When I was undergoing radiation treatment Ted knew more about the treatment than anybody — save for my doctors — with whom I had spoken. His intelligence can be as breathtaking as his hitting.

When Ted came back to Fenway for the All-Star Game ceremonies in 1999 I wept as he held court with a collection of the greatest past and present players. When his cart passed my seat I heard him ask Al Forester, who was driving, if he could spot me. As he passed me he smacked his lips in reference to the apricots I send him on a regular basis. Typically, he called me the following Tuesday to say that he loved his apricots and that Al reported to him that I was bawling my eyes out.

I also enjoy keeping up with my other baseball brothers as well as making new friends at Fenway Park. Over the past few season I have collected reams of clippings and the like for players such as Nomar Garciaparra and his family. Not only have I enjoyed their company but I have also enjoyed meeting his college coach. Likewise, I also enjoyed watching a game with Mike Stanley's high school coach. There is never a day at the park when I am not connecting with old and new friends.

Some things never change for me at Fenway Park. During the playing of the national anthem I pray that no player will be hurt during the game. It is a moment that never fails to prompt the memory of having witnessed Tony Conigliaro lying helpless on the ground on that terrible night in August 1967.

I always feel sad for those players at season's end who won't be returning to the team. I also believe that anything is possible, including a new Fenway Park and a world championship.

When she died in the summer of 2000, **Elizabeth Dooley,** a Red Sox season ticket holder for fifty-five seasons, was regarded as the team's guardian angel and most loyal fan. A Boston native, she taught health education for five decades in the city's public schools. She was the first woman to serve on the board of directors of the BoSox Club.

and Boston at a disadvantage. An off-day gave the Red Sox an extra twenty-four hours to worry. Cronin made practice optional.

Murray Dickson started for St. Louis opposite Ferriss, and for the third game in a row Boston nearly broke the game wide open in the first inning. Outfielder Wally Moses and Pesky singled, and Moses scored on DiMaggio's fly to right. Williams then laced a drive to center, but center fielder Terry Moore caught the ball on the run and Dickson escaped trailing only 1-0.

The Cardinals got a run back in the third, then took the lead in the fifth, scoring twice to knock Ferriss from the game. Joe Dobson squelched the rally, but the Cardinals entered the eighth inning needing only six more outs to win the championship.

Rip Russell led off with a pinch-hit single, and Metkovich then hit for Dobson and doubled to left. That was enough for Eddie Dyer. He called again on Brecheen.

Brecheen hadn't let Dyer down or allowed the Red Sox to beat him yet. He appeared up to both tasks, as he fanned Moses and got Pesky to line out to Slaughter in short right as the runners held. Then DiMaggio sliced the ball to the right-field wall. Both runners scored easily to tie the game, but DiMaggio took a bad step rounding first and pulled a muscle. He limped into second, then was replaced by Leon Culberson. With the go-ahead run at second, Williams ended his desultory Series with a popup.

Cronin, ignoring the fact that two of the first four St. Louis hitters were lefthanded, passed over lefty Earl Johnson in favor of righthander Bob Klinger to pitch the eighth. Klinger, teammate Johnny Pesky remembers, was a crafty "sinker, slider pitcher. He was a good pitcher and did a great job for us that year." But only two weeks earlier his son reportedly contracted polio. He'd left the team to be with him and hadn't pitched in almost two weeks.

Lefty Enos Slaughter led off and greeted Klinger with a single to center. Kurowski tried to sacrifice, but he popped a bunt back to the pitcher for the first out. When Rice followed with a fly to Williams, it appeared as if Cronin was off the hook.

Lefthanded outfielder Harry Walker stepped in for the Cardinals. Although Walker would later win a

Ted Williams flinches while taking batting practice prior to the 1946 World Series. Williams's response was due to an elbow injury suffered as the result of being hit by a pitch from Washington Senator pitcher Mickey Haefner. The injury occurred in a pre–World Series exhibition game between the Red Sox and assorted American League all-stars at Fenway Park. It was one reason why Williams batted .200 in the only World Series in which he ever appeared.

batting title, in 1946 he hit only .237. But platooning with Erv Dusak in the Series he'd gone 6-for-16.

Given the events that soon followed, Cronin's decision to stick with Klinger has usually been overlooked. The situation screamed for a pitching change. Walker was hot, and Johnson was warm and ready in the pen. Had Cronin brought him in, Dyer may have pinch-hit Dusak, whom Johnson had already retired in game one. The lefthanded Johnson also would have had an easier time holding the speedy Slaughter close to first base. Cronin's decision — or lack of one — backfired in every way possible.

What happened next was one of the most talked about plays in Red Sox history, known in St. Louis as "Slaughter's mad dash," but in Boston as "Pesky holds the ball." But it is also one of most poorly reported. Fortunately, the play is preserved on film from three angles.

The play began with Klinger, pitching from the stretch, taking the sign from Roy Partee. But he failed to pause and hold the runner. Dyer gave Slaughter the steal sign, and he broke for second off a walking lead.

Pesky, who recalls that "Bobby Doerr was giving the signs, and I was supposed to cover second," broke to cover the bag as Walker reached out and slapped what he later called a "dying seagull" over Pesky's head into left-center field.

Leon Culberson, playing relatively shallow and shaded to right, got a good jump on the ball, but had no chance to catch it. He ran a full fifteen strides — farther than running between home and first — to beat Williams to the ball and catch it on the bounce at his thighs. He then threw quickly but not particularly powerfully to Pesky, stationed on the edge of the infield, his back to the plate. The throw was clearly a rainbow — Pesky recalls that Culberson "kind of lofted the ball."

Stop the film, for the play was already lost. With the ball hit in front of him, Slaughter made his decision to go home as he reached second. Without hesitating he circled well back of third and cut toward home just as Culberson released his throw to Pesky, hitting third base with his right foot and heading directly to the plate. Higgins covered third and tried to deke Slaughter by faking the arrival of a throw.

Pesky remembers that the ball was hit fairly deep, but the film suggests it was somewhat shorter, meaning Culberson probably should have been throwing *home*. But Slaughter's dash surprised him, Williams — who could have alerted Culberson to throw home — and Rudy York, who should have been in position to take the cutoff. York stood like a spectator watching a car accident on the first-base side of the infield, while Bobby Doerr covered second.

The truth is Slaughter's dash surprised *everyone*, including the writers in the press box. The fiction that Pesky held the ball in the first place reveals their stupefaction at the play. In normal circumstances the hit would have been a single, and in normal circumstances it would have moved Slaughter to third. But this wasn't normal — it was the key inning of the World Series. Earlier, St. Louis third base coach Mike Gonzales had taken heat for holding Slaughter at third in a similar situation. Slaughter had complained to Eddie Dyer, and the manager gave him permission to run through a sign if he still thought he had a chance to score, saying, "I'll take the heat."

Red Sox fans have long asked whether DiMaggio would have gotten to the ball sooner or made a better throw. Pesky claims Slaughter told him he'd never have gone home if DiMaggio had been in the outfield. In the list of "what ifs" that haunt longtime Boston fans, this one looms large. But if Cronin had brought in Johnson to pitch, the question might never have come up.

Pesky took Culberson's soft toss just above his waist with his back to the plate. Had the throw been higher, he would have been in a better position to throw. As he caught the ball, Gonzales danced 20 feet down the line trying to stop Slaughter, but Slaughter roared by as Harry Walker slowed between first and second, trying to draw a throw.

As the grainy film shows, Pesky took the throw with his back to the plate, spun toward third, spotted Slaughter, took a quick half windup, and threw home. Catch to throw takes less than a second. He does not pause or freeze with the ball, although his body language exhibits surprise.

Yet it may well have taken him a split second to pick up Slaughter, for he was running a virtual gauntlet on his way to the plate, one of five men in uniform vying for position between third and home. Gonzales was running a parallel track, and Klinger stood frozen in no-man's land halfway between home and third waiting to back up a play at third that never came. And Whitey Kurowski, on deck, raced up and toward the plate while Roy Partee, as he watched the play develop, came out in front of home and took a step down the third-base line.

Pesky released the ball with Slaughter still six strides short of the plate. But the throw drifted a good 8 feet up the third-base line. Partee came out to catch it, and Slaughter slowed before making a pointless slide.

Partee didn't even bother to attempt a tag. Walker pulled into second on the throw. Cronin watched.

The run scored because Slaughter made a great play, and a series of small miscalculations and slight misplays by several Boston players built exponentially, costing the Red Sox the World Series and one

man his reputation. Pesky, who got all the blame, simply made an average play in a situation that was already lost. Had he eyes in the back of his head and an arm like Bob Feller's, *by the time he got the ball Slaughter still would have scored.*

Cronin now ordered Klinger to walk Marty Marion. Then, expecting Dyer to pinch-hit for Brecheen, he called for Johnson. But Eddie Dyer chose to live or die with his pitcher and let him hit. He rolled out for the third out, then trudged back to the mound for his twentieth inning in eight days, three outs away from his third Series victory.

What happened after the legendary play is usually overlooked, but although Boston didn't give up, Cronin made still more mistakes that made defeat certain.

After York singled Cronin sent in backup first baseman Paul Campbell to pinch-run. Campbell wasn't fast, but Culberson, who normally would have been available, was already in the game. And in yet another case of planning for a future that might never arrive, Cronin decided to save the other obvious choice, Tom McBride, in case he was needed to pinch-hit.

With the option to sacrifice available, Cronin had Doerr swing away. It paid off with a single to shallow left, and Campbell pulled up only two bases shy of Slaughter into second.

With Higgins up, a bunt to move both runners into scoring position and take off the double play was mandatory. The Cardinals huddled around the mound and conceded third to Campbell — they could survive a tie but absolutely had to stop the winning run. Kurowski and Musial would charge from the corners, while Marion rotated to cover second and Schoendienst covered first.

Higgins bunted directly at the hard-charging Kurowski. Without hesitation he gunned the ball to Marion at second and Doerr was forced out. Higgins made first. He should have been pulled for a runner — both Gutteridge and McBride were faster — but indecision again paralyzed Cronin.

Partee, hitting .111 in the Series, now came to bat. A squeeze play would tie the game, but Cronin let him hit, and he fouled to Musial for the second out.

Now Cronin pinch-hit Tom McBride for Earl Johnson. He grounded a screwball just past Brecheen to Schoendienst's right. The ball hit the second baseman's glove then bounced up his wrist.

Had a faster runner been on first, Schoendienst would have had to make the longer throw to first, McBride may have beaten the throw, and Campbell may have scored the tying run. But Higgins didn't run well. Schoendienst was able to flip the ball to Marion. Higgins was out by a foot, just enough to make the Cardinals world champions.

The Red Sox were stunned. They knew they had lost a World Series they should have won, blowing a one-game advantage three times, squandering a lead in game seven, and failing to score with two on and no out in the ninth. They had been certain of their superiority all year, but the last forty-eight hours had exposed that as folly. At every critical moment, they had been outplayed and, more significantly, outmanaged.

While the Cardinals carried Brecheen from the mound and celebrated, most Boston players sat disconsolate before their lockers, saying nothing. Only Pesky spoke up, shouldering the blame for a play he couldn't have made and should never have been condemned for. "If I was alert, I'd have had him," he lamented. "When I finally woke up and saw him running for home, I couldn't have gotten him with a .22." No one came to his defense.

Until Bill Buckner's error in the 1986 World Series, Pesky's play had always been considered the most tragic moment in the pantheon of Red Sox postseason tragedies. But had Cronin done a better job with his bench and pitching staff, Yawkey with his front office, or Eddie Collins with his public comments, the play might never have taken place. Cronin offered neither an excuse nor an alibi for the loss, but neither did he take responsibility for putting the Red Sox in position to lose. Pesky was hung out to dry.

In a recent interview, Pesky is remarkably understanding about his historical role in the play. When asked why he accepted the blame, he says, "Well, if they had to blame somebody and wanted to blame me, well, that was fine with me. I could handle it. It didn't bother me. I hit .324 the next year. You know there were two outs, and with two outs you can do

anything. He [Slaughter] made a great play. I couldn't have gotten him."

St. Louis, by the narrowest margin, outplayed Boston, but the gap between the two managers was quite a bit wider. Dyer managed the Cardinals to victory despite a grueling pennant race, a playoff, and the loss of his best pitcher because he turned to the hot hand of Brecheen. Cronin lost because he couldn't get his best players in the game when it mattered most. It should have been no great surprise. As manager of the Senators in the 1933 World Series, Cronin had managed the same way, using his best pitcher, Earl Whitehill, only once in a five-game loss to the Giants.

A teary-eyed Ted Williams was the last man out of the clubhouse. Jubilant Cardinal fans jeered, "Where's Superman?" He returned to Boston as he'd arrived in St. Louis — sitting alone.

Now, when it really didn't matter, Yawkey gave Williams a vote of confidence, releasing a statement that read, "We very definitely will not trade Ted Williams before or during the 1947 season."

But no one was looking forward to 1947. For in Boston, the phrase "Wait 'til next year" has rarely made quite as much sense as the corollary — "What happened last year?"

Yawkey applied the only salve he knew to try to heal the wound. He rewarded each player with bonuses of between one thousand and five thousand dollars. He didn't blanch at the one-hundred-thousand-dollar cost. It was worth it, for although he hadn't bettered the performance of his uncle Bill, by reaching the World Series he now felt he was his equal and confidently predicted a Red Sox world championship in 1947.

More salve was applied a few months later. Williams won the AL's MVP award, one of seven Sox to garner a vote and one of four, with Doerr, Ferriss, and Pesky, to collect a first-place vote.

That was to be the last highlight for a while. The

Leon Culberson poses for a publicity photo at Fenway Park in 1947. Late in game seven of the 1946 World Series Culberson replaced an injured Dom DiMaggio in center field and fielded Harry Walker's game- and Series-winning hit. His weak throw to Johnny Pesky was far more significant than Pesky's alleged delay in allowing Enos Slaughter to score the winning run.

streak of bad luck — or bad decision-making — that had plagued the Red Sox beginning in September of 1946 continued in 1947.

The club never got going. Everyone but Williams and Pesky began the season still in a slump. Then the stalwarts of the 1946 pitching staff — Hughson, Ferriss, and Harris — all came down with arm miseries. Dom DiMaggio hurt his shoulder and it bothered him all year.

The Sox stayed close in April, then fell behind first Detroit and then New York, as the Yankees finally began playing to their pre-war standard again. Boston tried to patch holes through trades, dumping Hal Wagner for catcher Birdie Tebbetts, sending York to Chicago for first baseman Jake Jones, and buying pitcher Denny Galehouse from the Browns, but nothing worked. New York put the pennant away in July. Boston finished third, fourteen games back, winners of twenty-one fewer games than the season before.

But the year was not without its significant events. In early April, Yawkey spent an evening imbibing

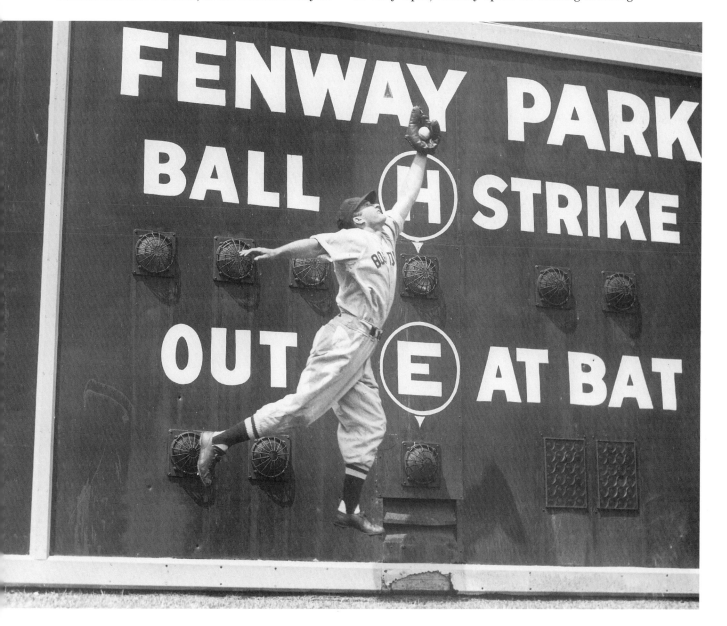

with Yankee co-owner Dan Topping. By the end of the night they had agreed to exchange problems, New York taking the temperamental Williams for Joe DiMaggio, who didn't get along with general manager Larry MacPhail and was still out after surgery on the famous bone spur on his left heel.

The trade was one-sided — in New York's favor. Williams, despite his problematic personality, was in his prime; DiMaggio was damaged goods. But after everyone had their coffee the following morning, Yawkey reportedly came to his senses and tried to tweak the deal, also asking for Yankee catching prospect Larry "Yogi" Berra. The deal quickly fell through.

At about the same time, Brooklyn Dodger owner Branch Rickey pulled baseball kicking and screaming out of the Jim Crow era when he promoted Jackie Robinson to the major leagues. He had informed baseball's sixteen owners of his plan at a secret meeting the previous January. All opposed him, including Yawkey. But baseball commissioner Happy Chandler supported Rickey. Since segregation was in force only through a cowardly and unspoken "gentlemen's agreement," Chandler turned the gutless anonymity of the owners against them, deftly concluding he had no authority to prevent Rickey from promoting Robinson.

With little else to root for, Ted Williams became the

entire story in 1947 — whenever the Sox failed to win, he always was. Although the opposition pitched around him whenever possible, leading to an astounding 162 walks, Williams won his second Triple Crown, finishing the year with thirty-two home runs, 114 RBIs, and a .343 average. He was the favorite to win a second consecutive MVP award.

At the end of the season Eddie Collins retired, and Yawkey convinced Joe Cronin to become general manager, leaving the managerial post vacant.

Cronin knew who he wanted to succeed him. In May of 1946, Yankee manager Joe McCarthy had resigned for what had been described as health reasons. In reality, he was a drunk and had been forced out after going into a drunken tirade on a plane trip from Cleveland to Detroit, turning a diatribe against pitcher Joe Page into an assault on Yankee general manager Larry MacPhail.

Still, McCarthy sported the best winning percentage of any manager in major league history. In a managerial career that began in 1926, he won a pennant with the Cubs in 1929 before joining the Yankees and winning seven more.

Yawkey allowed Cronin to make the decision. He wasn't put off by McCarthy's alcoholism. Men who knew how to take a drink impressed him. Drunken tirades had never disqualified anyone from working Boston's front office. Yawkey was doubly impressed by McCarthy's reputation as the best manager in baseball. He liked collecting the best.

Baseball was McCarthy's life, all he knew and all he cared about. He was singularly responsible for creating the Yankee mystique, changing a team once symbolized by the excesses of Babe Ruth into one known for its discipline and professionalism. A Yankee was expected to be clean, well dressed, and, around McCarthy, well behaved. He expected his players to take their job seriously, protected them from front office interference, and was a fine judge of talent. He didn't take any guff — he was in charge, had the results to prove it, and they knew it. Under

Enos "Country" Slaughter slides across home as he completes his famous "Mad Dash" and scores the eventual winning run in the eighth inning of the seventh game of the 1946 World Series against the Red Sox in St. Louis. Slaughter scored from first on a hit by Harry "the Hat" Walker that was generously scored a double.

his command, his favorite phrase was "You're a Yankee, act like one."

Yet at the same time, he was armed with a peculiar set of prejudices. Among them, he hated Poles, thought all southerners were hotheaded drunks, and pipe smokers too complacent. He divided his own club into those he thought could play and be trusted, and everyone else, whom he considered inferior and kept in the doghouse. His critics, noting the overflow of talent he'd had at his disposal in New York, considered him a "push button" manager who did little more than fill out the lineup card. That had been enough for the Yankees.

Cronin and Yawkey had allegedly approached McCarthy about the Boston job before the 1947 season, but McCarthy turned it down. This time he said yes and received a two-year contract worth one hundred thousand dollars in return.

The move was widely viewed as an attempt to rein in Williams. After all, McCarthy had successfully managed Ruth. The local press salivated at the thought of Williams testing McCarthy, but they also thought he was a huge improvement on Cronin.

Hiring McCarthy was also a sign that Yawkey was ready to spend again. The farm system wasn't producing, and with the heart of his team in their prime, Yawkey didn't want to waste an opportunity to win.

He wanted Cleveland shortstop Lou Boudreau, who reminded him of Cronin. But Cleveland owner Bill Veeck wasn't about to trade him to Boston. So the Sox looked elsewhere.

The St. Louis Browns needed cash. But they'd turned down Detroit's offer of two hundred fifty thousand dollars for All-Star shortstop Vern Stephens and pitcher Jack Kramer. The Browns were rotten, but not stupid. They knew the real money was in Boston. They told Cronin that if Yawkey was willing to cough up the money, Stephens and Kramer could be wearing Red Stockings in 1948.

The two sides started talking, and a simple purchase became more complicated. Finally, over a two-day period in November, Yawkey acquired Stephens, Kramer, and pitcher Ellis Kinder. The Browns received three hundred seventy-five thousand dollars — gulp — and nine marginal players.

Stephens was the key, for he solved two Boston

problems. Boston needed a big bat behind Williams to keep the pitchers honest. And Boston still hadn't found an everyday third baseman. Stephens was a powerful righthanded hitter, a decent if not spectacular fielder, and an annual all-star.

The press assumed McCarthy would move Stephens to third and leave Pesky, who had far better range, at short. But in the spring, McCarthy left Stephens at short and moved Pesky. According to Pesky, McCarthy did so primarily "because the press said Stephens would play third. And McCarthy didn't like the press telling him what to do." He made the move to spite them.

Kramer and Kinder were two solid starters who suffered from lack of support in St. Louis. The hiring of McCarthy and the trade was a shot across the bows at the Yankees.

Dan Topping howled at the news, complaining that the deal threatened to turn the AL into a "seven team league." The Red Sox became an immediate favorite to return to the World Series.

But there were never any certainties in Boston. A week later Joe DiMaggio edged out Williams for the MVP award, 202 points to 201. The Yankees had won the pennant, but DiMaggio hit only .315 with twenty home runs and ninety-seven RBIs. Williams felt robbed and blamed the Boston press.

Three writers from each city picked ten candidates for the award, with points awarded in descending order, from a first-place vote worth ten points to a tenth-place vote worth one. Williams had been named on only twenty-three ballots — one writer completely ignored him. Williams blamed Mel Webb of the *Globe*.

He shouldn't have. Webb didn't vote for the award in 1947. According to a story by Harold Kaese that was published as an insert to the Red Sox program in 1948, the three Boston voters were the *Record*'s Joe Cashman, Burt Whitman of the *Herald*, and Jack Malaney of the *Post*. Kaese claimed they gave Williams the *only* three first-place votes he received and identified the writer who left Williams off his ballot as a midwesterner.

But the twenty-fourth ballot wasn't really to blame either. MVP balloting had been questionable for several seasons. Although DiMaggio received eight first-place votes, *three* writers left him off their ballots.

Yogi Berra, despite playing only eighty-five games, somehow earned two second-place votes, and Philadelphia shortstop Eddie Joost, who hit .206 and led the league in strikeouts, received a total of only three votes, but two were for *first place*.

Two years later, *The Sporting News*'s Dan Daniels revealed that election results were available to the press a week before they became public knowledge. Armed with this inside information some writers had been making a killing betting on the results. In 1949 he estimated that sportswriters in the know had cleared as much as five hundred thousand dollars. Based on Daniels's revelations, the voting procedure was soon changed.

The oddities of the 1947 vote probably resulted from attempts by writers to skew the odds and make their inside information even more valuable. DiMaggio was an accidental beneficiary, while Williams suffered.

Williams began the 1948 season as if determined to prove the electors wrong. McCarthy got off to a good start with his temperamental star on the first day of spring training. Knowing Williams detested wearing ties, for the first time anyone could ever remember McCarthy showed up without a tie himself.

While McCarthy got to know his ballclub, the Sox got off to a horrific start. By the end of May they were 14-23, in seventh place, as the A's, Yankees, and Cleveland all grappled for first. Since September 1, 1946, when they had been anointed as the best in baseball, the Red Sox had gone 113-108 and been mediocre in every way.

Kaese wrote, "The Red Sox, except for Williams, have not been hitting. The Red Sox, except for Williams, have not been fielding." Indeed, entering June, Williams was batting .374 with eleven home runs and forty-two RBIs. Had he been only mortal, the Red Sox would have been in last place.

Then McCarthy started pushing the right buttons. He gave up on Harris and Ferriss and settled on a pitching rotation of Kramer, Joe Dobson, lefty Mel Parnell, and Kinder. Everyone started hitting, and rookie Billy Goodman, a .300 hitter with no power, took over at first base.

Suddenly the Red Sox couldn't lose. Williams hit .460 in June and the Red Sox went 18-6. They briefly nudged into first place in late July and over the next month fought New York, Cleveland, and Philadelphia to stay there. Boston went into first place on August 26 when the A's fell back.

Boston was baseball crazy, for as the Sox surged, the Braves were playing just as well. Sparked by slugging third baseman Bob Elliott and the pitching of Johnny Sain and Warren Spahn, they led the NL by a comfortable margin. An all-Boston World Series looked like a safe bet.

But the Red Sox are never a safe bet. Each time they appeared on the verge of taking over, the Yankees and Indians fought back. By September 24 all three teams had identical records of 91-56. Things started getting strange around Fenway Park. The front office was jumpy. Earlier in the month, Boston had received permission to sell Series tickets. As if expecting to lose, they didn't. Hundreds of thousands of ticket orders sat unprocessed. And in the final week of the season, Yawkey called in every minor league manager and general manager and read them the riot act. On October 1, disgusted with the performance of the farm system, Yawkey unceremoniously fired both assistant general manager Phil Troy and farm system director George Toporcer, odd moves in the last days of a pennant race. Rumors spread that if Boston lost, Joe McCarthy was out.

The Indians pulled ahead, and with three days left in the season, they held a two-game lead over both Boston and New York. They played three games with the Tigers as the Red Sox and Yankees enjoyed an off-day before meeting head-to-head in two games at Fenway Park.

Both challengers were given reasons to believe as Detroit beat Cleveland, cutting the Indians' lead to a single game with only two left to play. But the next day, Cleveland's rookie knuckleballer Gene Bearden threw a shutout, clinching at least a tie for the pennant for Cleveland. The Sox dumped New York out of the race as Ted Williams cracked a two-run homer in the first and Jack Kramer pitched his best game of the year to beat the Yankees 5-1.

Boston needed a victory over New York and another Cleveland loss to force a playoff in Fenway Park on October 3. Entering the final day of the regular season, Sox fans clung to that hope.

Of Ted Williams, Joe Di-Maggio said, "He was the best hitter I ever saw." Williams returned the compliment, remarking, "Joe DiMaggio was the best all around ballplayer I have ever seen." Together, they defined baseball for a generation.

New York could have rolled over, but they reacted like a boxer hopelessly behind on points but refusing to fall. Joe DiMaggio, limping around, in the words of one writer, "like a wounded animal," insisted on playing and keeping the Sox from the postseason. As he drove to Fenway with his brother from Dominic's suburban Boston home, he told his younger brother, "I'll take care of it personally." Dominic responded, "I may have something to do with that." For when DiMaggio and the Yankees played Williams and the Red Sox, reputation, honor, familial bragging rights, and a host of other issues were at stake. The game was just the framework of a larger battle.

DiMaggio fulfilled his promise in the first when he singled in a run as New York jumped out to an early 2-0 lead. But in the second inning Boston fans roared when they learned that Detroit had erupted for four third-inning runs against Bob Feller.

The Red Sox responded with five runs of their own, keyed by a Williams double. Then DiMaggio's fifth-inning double pulled New York back to within one.

But Dominic DiMaggio trumped his older brother with a leadoff home run in the sixth as Boston put the game out of reach by scoring four. Joe DiMaggio singled in another run in the seventh, and in the ninth inning, with the score 10-5 and DiMaggio due to hit, no one yet felt comfortable enough to leave Fenway Park. He singled again, then limped off the field after being replaced by a pinch runner. The entire crowd stood and applauded his effort. As Red Smith wrote afterward of the Sox win, "It wasn't easy. The Yankees have a guy named Joe DiMaggio." But Ted Williams did not go unnoticed. He temporarily silenced his critics by reaching base eight of ten times.

Cleveland lost 7-1, setting up the playoff the next day. The Red Sox didn't celebrate. Williams sat silent before his locker after the game, not wanting to risk a loss of concentration.

Thousands of Sox fans never went home that night, leaving the park only to stand in line for playoff tickets, which quickly sold out the following morning. The Braves had won the NL, and the potential of a streetcar Series had Boston half-mad.

Pre-game speculation focused on the pitching matchup. Most expected the Indians to pitch either Feller or Bob Lemon, while the Sox seemed likely to counter with either rookie Mel Parnell or Kinder.

On the way to Boston Lou Boudreau decided to pitch Gene Bearden on one day's rest, then swore his club to secrecy. Bearden, despite having a metal plate in his skull from head injuries suffered in the war, was hotter than hot. With nineteen wins and the league's lowest ERA, he was 2-1 against the Red Sox and coming off two consecutive shutouts.

Joe McCarthy was cagier, telling the press, "I don't know who I'll pitch. I'll have to have time to think, to check up. We had men working in the bullpen all afternoon. I'll have to find out who did what, who's ready." Joe DiMaggio's heroic performance had forced McCarthy to keep someone warm in the bullpen the whole game.

McCarthy's decision was the most important of his managerial career; it became a defining moment in Red Sox history. More than fifty years later, his choice is still debated among the cognoscenti as if it happened yesterday.

What took place later that day was a complete mystery for some forty years and to some extent remains so. All that is certain is that, in retrospect, McCarthy pitched the wrong man.

The 1948 Red Sox didn't really have an ace. Most assumed Parnell would pitch. He had three days' rest, a 15-8 record, and the staff's lowest Fenway Park ERA. As Parnell recalls, "I assumed I was going to pitch. I went to bed the night before at nine o'clock." Ellis Kinder was also rested and available.

But McCarthy was cautious. In his first-ever interview about the game in 1988, Red Sox pitcher Denny Galehouse, who died in 1998, told Glenn Stout, "Mr. McCarthy sent another player around to ask several players how they felt about pitching . . . I'm not at liberty to say anything and never will about who was asked, but they all had some little reason maybe why they thought they weren't able to do it. They shall remain nameless. I was the only one who said, 'If he wants me to pitch, I'll pitch.' I was the only one who answered that way."

The player McCarthy sent around was catcher Birdie Tebbetts, who confirmed Galehouse's story but, to his death in 1999, refused to speak further about it. "I've never told that story and I don't intend to," he told Stout. "I'm gonna be avoiding it till I write it myself. I've got it on tape. I don't take a chance."

Tebbetts reported back to McCarthy and as he left the park told Galehouse he'd probably be pitching. McCarthy then returned to his hotel room and mulled his choice over a bottle of White Horse scotch.

He balanced his staff's performance against Cleveland over the course of the year against that of their most recent appearances, Tebbetts's comments, and the peculiar wisdom that sometimes flows from a bottle.

McCarthy first dismissed Parnell. In an interview McCarthy gave to Joe Cashman of the *Record* immediately following the playoff, he expressed concern over the fact that Parnell was both a rookie and left-handed. Despite his stellar record in Fenway, Cleveland's power — Boudreau, third baseman Ken Keltner, second baseman Joe Gordon, and catcher Jim Hegan — was from the right side. Besides, said McCarthy, "Mel wasn't too well rested and hadn't looked too good in his last start." He'd given up seven hits, four walks, and a wild pitch in six and two-thirds innings versus the Senators on September 30.

"The choice narrowed down to either Galehouse or Kinder," said McCarthy, both righthanders who he

Former manager Joe Cronin shows Fenway Park to new manager Joe McCarthy on February 3, 1949. In two and a half stormy seasons McCarthy failed to duplicate the success he'd achieved with the Cubs and Yankees as the Red Sox twice lost pennants in heartbreaking fashion.

felt might be able to handle Cleveland's power. He passed over Kinder even though he was well rested and had won four of his last five starts because the Indians had hit him hard earlier in the year.

That left Galehouse, then one of only four active American League pitchers with more than 100 career wins, who McCarthy described as "more experienced . . . an old hand at pressure pitching [with] a better record than Kinder against the Indians." He'd won a World Series game for the Browns in 1944, and on July 30 of 1948 he'd pitched the best game of the year for Boston. In relief of Parnell versus Cleveland he had given up only two hits in eight and two-thirds innings to beat the Indians.

McCarthy ignored the fact that Cleveland had later belted him nine runs in five innings, and that after winning two games in early September he had pitched only twice since September 12 and been shellacked each time.

He also overlooked something far more critical. As

DiMaggio kept New York in the game the day before, Galehouse was told to warm up. As Galehouse recalled in 1988, "I had been in the bullpen Sunday . . . from about the fourth inning on. Mr. McCarthy told me to go down to the bullpen and get loose and stay up when we were at bat and when the Yankees were at bat. So I threw six innings the day before [the playoff]. I don't think people in Boston knew I'd threw for those six innings. That's something that hasn't been brought out at all."

The game ball was in Galehouse's locker when he arrived at Fenway Park the next day, a sure sign he was pitching. But McCarthy wanted to keep his choice secret. "Nobody else knew," says Galehouse. "They just said 'Wander around the outfield.'" He did, shagging flies in the age-old tradition of a pitcher on his day off. When Parnell arrived, McCarthy pulled him aside and said, "Kid, I'm going with the right-hander." When Galehouse started warming up, his teammates learned of McCarthy's decision.

They were shocked. Reserve catcher Matt Batts remembers, "We just couldn't understand it. It wasn't
logical at the time. We had Parnell ready to go, and
Kinder was ready. I would say 100% of the players
were against it."

Lou Boudreau was stunned to disbelief. When
he saw Galehouse throwing, he checked under the
stands to make sure Parnell wasn't warming up in secret, either to start the game himself or take over after Galehouse had faced only a batter or two.

As Galehouse got ready, Boudreau kept the Red

Pitcher Denny Galehouse *(l)* is greeted by catcher Birdie Tebbetts *(r)* who welcomes
the righthanded starter to the Red Sox in this 1947 photograph. In a little over a
season Galehouse would start and lose one of the most controversial games in
team history as he faced the Cleveland Indians in a one-game championship playoff at Fenway Park for the right to face the Boston Braves in the World Series.

Sox waiting. Bearden started throwing only thirteen
minutes before the start of the game. Boudreau also
jockeyed his lineup, inserting two little-used righthanded hitters to take aim at the left-field wall, using
Allie Clark at first base for the only time all season
and right fielder Bob Kennedy. Galehouse didn't concern him.

Galehouse fired his first pitch at 1:30 P.M. Within
minutes, the Red Sox were in trouble.

With two outs, Boudreau stepped to the plate. In

the midst of an MVP season, he jerked a slider high to
left field. Williams drifted back and looked up. The
ball hit the top of the wall and bounced over for a
home run. Cleveland led 1-0. It would not be the last
time a shortstop for the opposition used the wall to
his advantage during a playoff game versus the Red
Sox.

Bearden wiggled out of a jam in the bottom of the
inning. Already exhausted, he took a small shot of
brandy in the dugout, an act he repeated after every
inning.

Both pitchers escaped trouble in the second and
third. Galehouse wasn't sharp, and he was already
getting tired. In the fourth he gave up a leadoff single
to Boudreau, and Joe Gordon followed with another
hit. McCarthy had Kinder start to warm up as Ken
Keltner stepped in.

Boudreau thought about bunting, but the Indians
were hitting Galehouse hard. He let the third baseman swing away.

He did. The ball sailed over the left-field wall for a
three-run home run. Cleveland led 4-0.

The blast deflated Boston. In his private box Tom
Yawkey made an obvious and disgusted exit. Mc-
Carthy came out, took the ball from Galehouse, and
waved for Kinder. The Boston pitcher walked off,
blameless really, accompanied by a chorus of boos
and some scattered applause to await his fate in history.

Kinder gave up another run, then the Indians added
another in the fifth. Bobby Doerr slammed a two-run
homer in the sixth to make the score 6-3, but Bearden drew on whatever reserves he still had while
the Indians continued to chip away at Kinder. Boston
lost 8-3. There would be no streetcar Series.

For the second time in three seasons, the Sox season ended, not just in defeat to a better team, which
is somehow both understandable and explainable,
but in loss, which is often neither. They lost not because of fate or any other kind of fiction, but because
of their own failure and resultant inability — or unwillingness — ever to recognize that fact. Their destiny appeared to be not the glory of a world championship, but the ruin of anticipated triumph. A pattern
began to emerge.

The loss paralyzed the organization, which stood

pat in 1949. They saw the loss as an aberration, a misfortune, a crazy, inexplicable, embarrassing accident not to be spoken of in polite company. The organization didn't blame McCarthy. Yawkey told Harold Kaese, "I'd rather finish second with Joe McCarthy than first with someone else," and that's just what happened. Boston's barrage of base hits continued to mask the lingering problems of depth and pitching.

Instead, just as Pesky was blamed for the failure of 1946, Galehouse took the fall for 1948. Jack Conway of the *Boston Evening American* later claimed to receive over five thousand letters demanding he be traded.

But no deals of any consequence — not even of Galehouse — were made during the off-season. The Sox believed the Indians had played above their heads in 1948 and the Yankees were on the way down. DiMaggio was out after heel surgery, and New York's hiring of Casey Stengel as manager seemed an admission of mediocrity.

In the Baseball Writer's Association of America's (BBWAA) off-season poll, 118 of the 206 writers picked the Red Sox to win the 1949 pennant. The Indians got 79 votes, while only six writers picked the lowly Yankees. Even professorial Harold Kaese confidently predicted a 124-win season — and his tongue wasn't all the way in his cheek when he wrote it.

Spring training was relatively uneventful, apart from the usual attention paid to everything Ted Williams said or did, and he said he would retire in three years, "if I had enough money. I'd retire right *now* if I had enough money."

Right field was up for grabs, and rookie slugger Walt Dropo made an impression on everyone but Joe McCarthy. Although Dropo opened the season in the starting lineup, McCarthy soon sent him back to the minors and returned to incumbent Billy Goodman. Denny Galehouse worked on a knuckleball while the Sox touted young pitchers Chuck Stobbs, Mickey McDermott, and Frank Quinn, none of whom was old enough to vote. But they stuck with a starting rotation of Dobson, Kinder, Parnell, Hughson, and Kramer. For a team coming off the most devastating defeat in franchise history, they were strangely smug.

They played that way to open the season, dropping their first two games and finishing April a desultory

5-6. The DiMaggio-bereft Yankees vaulted into first place.

When Boston continued to underperform, the club did little — releasing Galehouse, who never pitched in the major leagues again, and buying Browns outfielder Al Zarilla for one hundred thousand dollars plus to play right field. He had hit .320 in 1948. Too bad he couldn't pitch, because that's what Boston needed.

Kramer, Dobson, and Hughson, recovering from arm surgery, all got hurt and had to be babied. As each man went down, McCarthy questioned his fortitude.

Williams's bat kept the team afloat early, and they were devastating at home, where Boston's hitters and pitchers knew how to take advantage of Fenway Park. But they were a below-average team on the road. Hits and home runs in Fenway were outs everywhere else.

McCarthy didn't panic, but increasingly depended on the Red Sox starting lineup and their frontline pitchers. He knew that as the weather warmed, so would Boston's vaunted hitting attack. Some would later contend that the 1949 Red Sox were the best club in team history. Considering only their top twelve or thirteen players, that may well be true, for no team in baseball could match the top half of Boston's roster.

But McCarthy's dependence on the same old faces left the team vulnerable when he dipped deeper into his roster. Pesky describes him as "a guy where, if you played every day, you played every day." While Parnell, Kinder, and Dobson all pitched effectively, McCarthy waited until midseason before concluding that Kramer, Hughson, and Harris, who was finally traded, couldn't win. Mickey McDermott was mowing down hitters in Louisville and bonus baby Chuck Stobbs, who McCarthy used all of seven innings in 1948, wasted away. The bench went unused, and McCarthy never really settled on his fourth and fifth starters. Meanwhile Stengel juggled the Yankee roster to perfection as he adapted to a staggering total of seventy-one separate injuries.

When McCarthy finally turned to McDermott and Stobbs in June, Boston won ten of eleven and six in a row to pull to within five games of New York. Bobby

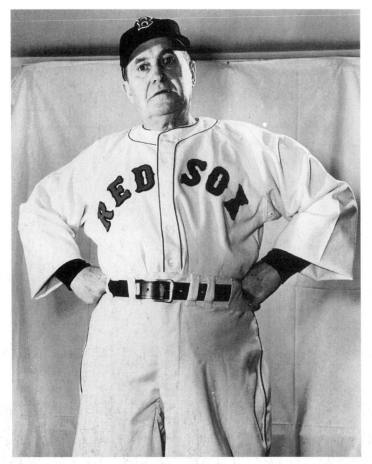

Lured by a two-year one-hundred-thousand-dollar contract, Joe McCarthy arrived in Boston with the expectation of pushing the franchise to the exalted level of the great Yankee teams he led to six world championships in seven World Series appearances. In Boston he finished second.

Doerr, who'd been hobbled by a sore back, started to hit, and Dom DiMaggio ripped off a thirty-three-game hitting streak.

Unfortunately, the Yankees then came into Boston just as the pain in Joe DiMaggio's heel miraculously disappeared. He made his 1949 debut in the series opener on June 28.

He singled to start a three-run rally in the second inning, cracked a two-run homer in the third, took out Junior Stephens at short in the eighth, and caught Ted Williams's flyball with the winning run on third in the ninth in the 5-4 Yankee win. He was Joe DiMaggio again.

The next day, he was even better. After Kinder was staked to a 7-1 lead, DiMaggio's two home runs led the Yankees to a 9-7 comeback victory. He even stopped his brother's hitting streak at thirty-four games with a tough catch.

A plane circled Fenway before the series finale bearing a banner that read "The Great DiMaggio." As one observer noted, "Although there were two DiMaggios present, one was only very good," so the banner must have been referring to Joe. By the end of the game, that was unquestionably true.

He homered off the light tower in left to secure a 6-3 Yankee win as Vic Raschi bettered Parnell, and the Boston crowd, which usually gave Joe polite applause in deference to his brother, finally had enough. They booed loudly as he circled the bases for the fourth time in three days.

The three-game sweep, accounting for almost 20 percent of Boston's sixteen Fenway losses in 1949, dropped the Red Sox to fifth place, eight games behind the Yankees. It sent the club reeling to an eight-game losing streak, culminating in a doubleheader loss to the Yankees in New York on July 4. The Red Sox were a pitiful 35-36, twelve games out of first.

McCarthy was increasingly out of touch. While the regulars liked him because he left them alone and played them every day, the bench players and exiled pitchers groused. They knew that if called on, they'd be stale and likely to fail. According to Harold Kaese's notebooks, McCarthy's continued dependence on the bottle caused him to lose the respect of many players, who second-guessed him. Joe Dobson was so exasperated with McCarthy's moves he told Kaese, "I'd like to hit him upside of the head with a log."

But after the All-Star break a favorable schedule pitted the Sox against the worst teams in the league, and against these lesser foes the Red Sox were almost unbeatable. Everybody who played, played well. On most days, the Red Sox lineup sported a cumulative batting average well over .300.

As Boston surged, the Yankees went from great to simply very good as the injury toll mounted. After winning twenty-four of thirty-two in August, on September 1 the Sox trailed New York by only two games. With eight games still remaining against New York, the Sox were in a pennant race.

They went into the stadium on September 7 for two games trailing by one and a half with a chance to go ahead, but after Yankee starter Allie Reynolds walked or hit the first four men he faced, he settled down and New York beat Kramer, 5-2. But Boston won the finale behind Kinder, 7-1, to keep pace.

The two clubs matched each other for the next week before the Red Sox stumbled, losing a doubleheader to Philadelphia. With fourteen games remaining, Boston trailed by an apparently insurmountable five games.

McCarthy, as if taking a cue from both the 1948 Braves and his mistake in the playoff against Cleveland, knew what had gotten his club close. Since the end of July, Kinder and Parnell together had lost only once. His variation of "Spahn and Sain and two days of rain" meant pitching Kinder and Parnell almost exclusively. They started the bulk of Boston's remaining games and when they didn't were usually the first arms out of the pen. No one could accuse McCarthy of going with the wrong pitcher this time.

Joe DiMaggio had pneumonia and the Yankees slumped. On September 24 in Boston, Kinder shut out New York, and Parnell won his twenty-fifth game the next day on a four-hitter to pull the Red Sox into a tie for first place. The two clubs went to Yankee Stadium the next day to make up an earlier rain-out, and after blowing an early 3-0 lead, Boston rallied and won when Kinder pitched two shutout innings and Pesky scored on a disputed squeeze play.

For the first time all year, Boston was in first place, leading by one with five games to play. But the Sox are never in more danger than when they look like a lock to win. So after beating the Senators sixteen out of nineteen thus far and with a chance to virtually clinch the pennant, the Red Sox promptly went into Washington where pitcher Ray Scarborough baffled Boston with a four-hitter.

But Chuck Stobbs was even better, and Boston nursed a 1-0 lead into the ninth. Then Washington scratched out three singles to tie the game. McCarthy turned to Kinder. He gave up a single to load the bases.

Now it was Parnell's turn. Washington tried to steal a win on a squeeze play, but failed. Parnell then worked the count to 1-2 against pinch hitter Buddy Lewis, but then he bounced a curveball past Tebbetts. Al Kozar scored from third. Ballgame.

With Boston leading the Yankees by a single game, the season came down to two final games in New York. Those looking for bad omens found one, for in the opener the Yankees celebrated Joe DiMaggio Day. And DiMaggio, still weakened by pneumonia, chose to return for this critical season-ending series, telling Stengel he'd take it inning by inning.

Yankee Stadium was packed. Both teams warmed up and then sat for an hour as DiMaggio was feted. With his mother at his side and brother Dominic holding him upright during the extended ceremony,

Ted Williams poses at the throttle of the *Merchants Limited* heading to New York for the final games of the 1949 pennant race. Not only did the Red Sox lose the pennant, but Williams lost the chance for a third Triple Crown when George Kell narrowly beat him out for the league batting title.

the Yankee Clipper received a host of gifts and testimonials. He spoke briefly before concluding, "I'd like to thank the good Lord for making me a Yankee."

Boston was confident, but no one more so than Tom Yawkey. He had a train on standby in Boston to bring the Red Sox wives to New York for a victory celebration. But like the champagne he ordered in 1946, the train would never leave the station.

McCarthy wasn't playing any hunches. Parnell got the ball opposite New York's Allie Reynolds, with Kinder available for the finale.

The Red Sox started off as if the long wait had only served to make them more focused. Dom DiMaggio opened the game with a flare single to right field. Pesky forced him at second, but then Williams pulled a smash down the first-base line. It should have been a double and scored Pesky, but the ball caromed off first baseman Tommy Henrich and umpire Cal Hubbard for another single.

Reynolds wasn't sharp. A wild pitch moved both runners up, and Junior Stephens scored Pesky with a fly to left fielder Johnny Lindell. Reynolds then struck out Doerr to end the threat.

Parnell shut down the Yankees early, and Di Maggio swung like the semi-invalid he was when he struck out in his first at bat. Then, in the third, Reynolds lost it.

With one out, he walked Pesky, Williams, and Stephens to load the bases. Casey Stengel had Yankee relief pitcher Joe Page start throwing.

Now Reynolds tried to aim the ball, and Bobby Doerr hit what was described as "a teasing impossible to handle dunkaroo into short right field" for a single. One run scored as Williams was held at third.

That was enough for Stengel. He waved for Page.

The big lefty was in the midst of perhaps the best season a relief pitcher had ever had in the major leagues to that point, on his way to twenty-seven saves and a 13-8 season. He threw a high-riding, four-seam fastball that exploded over the plate at the letters. Page strode to the mound under orders to save the season, relishing the thought of keeping McCarthy, whom he detested, from winning the pennant.

But Page wasn't quite warm, and he couldn't get the ball down. He walked Zarilla to force in Williams, then walked Goodman to score Pesky.

Birdie Tebbetts came up with a chance to break the game open. Parnell was on deck.

Page still couldn't find the plate, but Tebbetts wanted to end the game. He swung from his heels at Page's tempting four-seamer, striking out on three pitches out of the strike zone. Page then settled down and struck out Parnell, but Boston led 4-0.

With the league's best pitcher on the mound, that should have been enough for Boston. But Parnell had already thrown 291 innings, completing twenty-seven games and pitching in relief six times in the last month. And the Yankees had the best player in the game.

In the fourth, DiMaggio lined the ball into the right-field stands on one hop for a double, then Bauer looped a ball just out of Pesky's reach and DiMaggio scored. Johnny Lindell singled, and then Bauer scored on a sacrifice fly to make it 4-2. Parnell got Jerry Coleman for the second out, so Stengel, who would have pinch-hit had Coleman reached base, left Page in to make the third out.

When Page went back out in the fifth, he was unhittable. In the bottom of the inning the Yankees resumed their hit parade against Parnell. Rizzuto singled through the left side. Then Henrich bounced the ball back through the box, but Parnell, worn down by the long season, couldn't get to the ball. The potential double play rolled in center field. Yogi Berra then drove his next pitch into center to score Rizzuto. It was 4-3.

McCarthy now found himself in unfamiliar territory. Using Parnell and Kinder in relief down the stretch had worked because neither pitcher had required any relief themselves. But now that button wasn't available. Parnell was obviously done, but McCarthy had to save Kinder for the season finale in case Boston lost. So in the 153rd game of the season he turned to a bullpen in which he had absolutely no faith.

He waved Joe Dobson in from his doghouse. He'd hardly pitched and knew he wasn't ready. DiMaggio drilled the ball up the middle. The pitcher knocked it down, but that was all. He then induced Billy Johnson to hit into a double play to end the threat, but Henrich still scored to tie the game.

Page remained untouchable. In the eighth inning, although the situation called for lefty pinch hitter Charley Keller, Stengel stayed with the hot bat of Johnny Lindell against Dobson. Dobson left a pitch up and Lindell jerked it 20 feet fair into the left-field grandstand for a home run. The *Post* reported that, upon reaching the Yankee bench, Lindell "was pounded almost into the semblance of a veal chop" by the exuberant Yankees.

Page held on, and New York won 5-4, setting up a virtual playoff the next day. Both teams had an identical 96-57 record.

Kinder hadn't lost a game he had started since June 6, a remarkable run of fifteen straight wins. Opposite him was New York's Vic Raschi, a quintessential money pitcher who thrived in big games. Both clubs' bullpens were spent. McCarthy and Stengel handed the ball to their pitchers and hoped for the best.

Raschi set down the first two Red Sox hitters, pitched around Williams for a walk, then retired Junior Stephens. That was New York's strategy — pitch around Williams, even walk him, but don't ever let him beat you.

Rizzuto led off for New York, and Kinder left a slider out over the plate. The Yankee shortstop faked a bunt then slapped it down the line over Pesky's head.

Playing Rizzuto to hit the other way, Williams had a long run back toward the bounding ball, which hung along the wall in the corner and got past him. By the time Williams ran it down, Rizzuto was on third.

McCarthy played the infield back, conceding the run. In a normal game, that was sound strategy. But in this game every run counted. Henrich bounced to Doerr and Rizzuto scored to put New York up, 1-0.

Inning by inning that single run grew in importance. Each pitcher worked out of several jams, but neither appeared to weaken. Entering the eighth inning, New York still led 1-0.

Boston was running out of time. Tebbetts went out, and Kinder was due to hit next. In normal circumstances the situation called for a pinch hitter.

But the righthanded Kinder could hit a little and was better than any lefthanded option on the Boston bench. Nevertheless, for the second game in a row McCarthy pushed a button he hadn't used all year.

He called on outfielder Tom Wright, the only lefty bat on the bench, a late-season call-up who had led the American Association in hitting. Kinder was beside himself, as were most of the players on the Boston bench. With all Tom Yawkey's millions, the most important at bat of the season went to a player with a grand total of five major league at bats.

To his credit, Wright worked Raschi for a walk, but Dom DiMaggio grounded into a double play to end the inning. The manager brought in Parnell.

He had nothing left and failed for the third consecutive time. Tommy Henrich led off with a home run, and after Berra singled, McCarthy recognized what was obvious to everyone else. Now, on the final day

A stunned Joe McCarthy ascends the steps to the visitors clubhouse at Yankee Stadium on October 2, 1949, after the Red Sox lost 5-3 to the Yankees on the final day of the season. Needing only to win one of the final two games of the 1949 season to clinch the pennant, the Red Sox lost both games to finish one game behind the Yankees.

of the season for the third year out of four Boston's manager handed the ball in the most dire of circumstances to a pitcher who hadn't thrown in weeks. Tex Hughson, the forgotten star, had last pitched thirty days before.

He got DiMaggio to ground into a double play. But Lindell singled, as did Billy Johnson. Ted Williams bobbled the ball, and Lindell took third. Hughson walked Cliff Mapes to load the bases.

As Jack Malaney later wrote, "The play on which the Yankees won the game was one that very likely will call for second guessing and lengthy debating all through the winter." He was too conservative. At present, the total is fifty winters and still rising.

Yankee second baseman Jerry Coleman fisted a flare to short right. With two outs, everyone started running.

Zarilla — no speed demon and no Dwight Evans in the field — came in and in and in and in as Coleman's bloop dropped. Zarilla could either dive and try for the catch or pull up and concede two runs.

He dove. The ball fell in his glove then bounced out as he landed hard on his knee. Doerr chased it down and all four Yankees kept running. Coleman was thrown out at third, but three more runs had scored.

New York now led 5-0. But the Boston players didn't give up and concede defeat. They never did, although the same could not always be said of their management.

Pesky fouled out to start the inning. Raschi then chose to pitch around Williams once more and walked him, an at bat that cost Williams the batting title and the Triple Crown as the Tigers' George Kell collected two hits that day to edge Williams in the batting race, .3428 to .34275.

Raschi was tired. He threw wild and Williams went to second before Stephens singled. Then Bobby Doerr smashed the ball over DiMaggio's head in center for a triple that scored both. DiMaggio then pulled himself from the game, exhausted and sick, allowing Raschi to take a much-needed breather.

Zarilla, who later had to have knee surgery, limped to the plate and flied out to Mapes in center. Doerr held at third. Goodman then singled through the box to make the score 5-3.

Tebbetts stepped to the plate, the tying run. The Yankee bullpen was still.

Raschi threw and Tebbetts popped up wide of first. Henrich caught the ball and the Red Sox lost again.

The loss hit the club like a punch in the stomach. Tom Yawkey didn't go back to Yankee Stadium for another nineteen years. The dynasty-in-the-making, the team that thought it was better than New York, died without winning a thing.

As the Yankees celebrated, tempers flared in the Red Sox clubhouse as the frustration of the past several seasons burst out. Someone reamed out Williams for botching the eighth-inning single, and whatever reservoir of faith the team had in McCarthy evaporated. Kinder kept looking at McCarthy and giving him the choke sign. He finally exploded and reamed out his manager, who sat and took it without saying a word.

The players' wives gathered at Back Bay Station, not to go to New York for a party, but to pick up their fallen heroes. Williams later described the return trip as "a damn funeral train."

The next day, a subhead in the *Boston Globe* read "No Joy in Mudville."

The Red Sox never really recovered from the three crushing defeats in the final games of 1946, 1948, and 1949. They didn't recover in 1950, and they haven't recovered today.

They became known as a team that didn't just get *beat* in the big games, but somehow and ever more implausibly, actively took part in *losing* them.

Boston fans have always felt deserving of victory. But deep down, they expect only heartbreak and loss.

TEDDY BALLGAME

1950 | 1960

Ted Williams ascends the dugout steps prior to his last
game with the Red Sox on September 28, 1960.

At the end of the 1949 season, most observers still believed the Red Sox were a dynasty-in-waiting, albeit one that increasingly appeared star-crossed. But over the next decade, the character and reputation of the team would undergo a complete turnaround.

By the end of the decade the words of *Boston American* columnist Austen Lake would ring true. In a column written in July of 1959 entitled "For Whom the Bell?" he wrote,

What difference WHO manages the Red Sox, if the player procurement department is as inefficient [as it has been] . . . There's the Real Red Sox cancer spot . . .

Fault with the Red Sox starts at the TOP and travels downward. Much as I dislike saying so, chief fault belongs to Boston's benefactor, rich and sporty Tom Yawkey, who has opened his pecuniary spigots and poured money so lavishly for 26 years of deficit baseball. Tom's overindulgence of his Jersey Street bridesmaids and his ultra patience have been the root of Red Sox failure for twenty-six years. If that be heresy, sue me!

If I were Tom I'd take personal stock and say to me, "Here I've always paid the highest wage scale in baseball. I hire the most expensive intelligences. I've built a model ballyard and sent an army of scouts to bid on the best junior talent available. I've bought the leading big-name players and paid lavish bonus prices. I've tried eight managers and three Gen.-Mgrs. Yet nothing has worked. What's wrong?"

I'll tell you Tom, churlish though it sounds. The trouble is YOU! For unwittingly you have supported 26 Red Sox team years of pampered royalties who got glutted with spiritual fat and grew indolent and apathetic . . .

Lake's stinging rebuke — rare in that it was openly aimed at Yawkey — is an accurate accounting of the failures of the Red Sox throughout the 1950s. One might disagree with Lake's choice of target, but his general assessment was accurate.

As America snoozed through the 1950s, so did the Red Sox. In the end they became both bad and boring. Fans didn't go to Fenway to see the Red Sox win anymore. They went to see Ted Williams, on display in the Fenway museum like a relic of a distant, bygone age. While the Red Sox of this era were not completely impotent, the Yankees, who won the pennant every season but 1954 and 1959, rarely worried about Boston.

The season-ending losses in 1946, 1948, and 1949 provided ample evidence of what was wrong, but the Red Sox refused to recognize it. Although the club lacked depth, in the off-season following 1949 they again made no major trades or gave added attention to player development. In fact, for the second year in a row, they *cut* the farm system, down to eight teams from a 1948 high of fifteen, about half as many as Cleveland or New York.

Neither did they make a serious move to sign the largest pool of talent ever unleashed upon the game at a single time — African-Americans. Although they weren't alone in this regard (only the Indians, Dodgers, Yankees, Giants, Braves, and Cubs had done so, and only the Indians, Dodgers, and Giants had blacks in the majors), Boston's aversion to integration caused them to fall behind both on the field and, eventually, in the eyes of the public.

Boston's Double A farm club in Birmingham, Alabama, shared Rickwood Field with the Negro League Birmingham Black Barons, and the Barons promised Boston first crack at their players, such as young phenom Willie Mays, who had joined the club in 1948 at age seventeen. But in the spring of 1950, when the Sox decided to sign a black player, they passed over Mays, who later told Ted Williams, "I always thought I was supposed to play with you in Boston." Instead, they signed thirty-one-year-old Baron infielder Piper Davis.

The signing didn't represent any landmark change in organizational thinking. It was an empty gesture designed to buy time. Davis played only fifteen games at Single A Scranton, hitting .333, then was released in what Davis was told was a cost-cutting measure.

Such conduct cost Boston dearly and does to this day. Although there were never enough African-American fans in Boston to support a Negro League team, barnstorming black teams often played in and around Boston — even at Fenway Park. Pitcher Will "Cannonball" Jackman's local reputation was on par with that of Satchel Paige, and a number of Bostonians played in the Negro Leagues. But the Red Sox' aversion to signing black players and their unwillingness to ever admit to their error alienated Boston's black fans. Even today many African-American players view the organization and the city as racially backward and refuse to accept trades to the club, handicapping it still.

After the debacle of 1949, McCarthy was viewed with increasing skepticism, yet Cronin and Yawkey chose to retain him. A do-nothing training camp in the spring of 1950 reinforced an already failing status quo. McCarthy didn't make a single change in the starting lineup.

Although the Sox were again favored to win the pennant, there were bad signs from the outset. Boston opened the 1950 season in New York on April 19, jumped out to a quick 9-0 lead, then, as the *Post* described it, "The Red Sox went from the heights of sublimity to the lowest depths of ridicule," and lost 15-10. Those words could serve as an epitaph of the era.

Williams started slowly and so did the Sox. Parnell, Kinder, and Dobson slipped a little, and the rest of the staff was a disaster. By May, Parnell and Kinder were already pitching in relief between starts. The only good news came when Billy Goodman broke his leg, forcing the club to call up Walt Dropo. McCarthy stuck him in the lineup behind Williams and Stephens, and he began hitting better than both men.

Although some veterans, like Williams, considered McCarthy the best manager they'd ever played for, he'd lost the respect of most players. He was increasingly prone to drinking binges that didn't always stop the next morning. He started arriving at the park still drunk from the night before and occasionally missed games while sleeping it off in his hotel. The press usually reported he was down with either the flu or a heavy cold — code words for what really ailed him. Cronin finally warned him that if he showed up drunk again, he'd be fired.

Williams didn't help matters by choosing this time to throw the greatest tantrum of his career. On May 11 in a doubleheader against Detroit at Fenway, he dropped a flyball, then hit a grand slam as Detroit routed Boston, 13-4. After the home run, as those who booed him now cheered, Williams saluted their fickle behavior. As the *Globe* described it, "he raised two fingers skyward to let those fans know . . . how he felt about them." In game two, with the bases loaded and Kinder working on a shutout, Williams misplayed a single and all three runners scored.

As he ran off the field to more boos, he repeated his universally known gesture of disgust three times, to all sections of the ballpark. He was asking for it, and the press gave it to him. Boston lost 5-3 to fall into fourth place.

Dave Egan wrote that baseball had "never wallowed lower in the muck," while Gerry Hern in the *Post* sniffed, "the rules of self-imposed journalistic decency prevented newspapers from explaining the degrading gestures . . . Pictures of the performance he gave were discarded by this newspaper for the sake of the children, ladies and normal persons to whom the actions would have been indecipherable or revolting." The club issued a terse apology on Williams's behalf that Hern accurately described as "somewhat like a mother dragging a reluctant child to a neighbor's house," after breaking a window. It was open season on Williams in the Boston press.

The Sox swooned. They still beat up on the league's bottom feeders, eviscerating the Browns at Fenway on June 7 and 8 by scores of 20-4 and 29-4, but against the better teams, they were hopeless.

After a loss to Detroit on Father's Day dropped the club to 31-28, Joe McCarthy got drunk, stayed drunk, and was still drunk when the club got to Chicago the next day. That was it. Cronin shipped the manager home to Buffalo to recuperate, and coach Steve O'Neill managed the club to two defeats.

Bill Cunningham of the *Herald* delivered McCarthy's Boston epitaph, writing, "McCarthy has had what everybody seems agreed is the most powerful team in the American League for three years. It's died twice in the clutch and he's died with it."

On June 23, the Red Sox announced Joe McCarthy's resignation — for health reasons. Steve O'Neill, who'd been in baseball for over forty years and managed Detroit to a pennant in 1945, took over. Two days later, North Korea invaded the South, marking the beginning of the Korean War.

Of the new Sox manager, Cunningham later wrote, "Steve O'Neill was and is a nice friendly mass of negative protoplasm who went a far piece on the apparent theory that the best way to manage was to stay out of the way. He was simply there, like a school flag unfurled in the gymnasium. He was popular with the players because he gave few orders and practically no criticism." Although O'Neill made no changes, and players laughed when he fell asleep on the bench, they started winning. Boston's sluggers warmed with the weather and soon every man in the starting lineup was flirting with .300.

Dropo, Williams, Stephens, and DiMaggio all made the All-Star team. But in the first inning of the game at Comiskey Park in Chicago, Williams chased after a

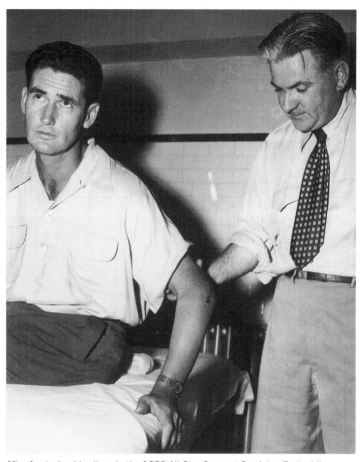

After fracturing his elbow in the 1950 All-Star Game at Comiskey Park while making a catch off Ralph Kiner, Williams subsequently underwent surgery to repair the injury and remove bone chips. Here, Williams is shown with Red Sox team physician Dr. McCarthy, who examines his scar.

ball hit by Ralph Kiner, reached up to catch it over his shoulder, and smashed into the scoreboard. Although he stayed in the game and later singled, he'd broken seven bone chips loose in his left elbow. Two days later, he underwent surgery.

Boston looked finished, but Goodman returned and took over in left. He led the league in hitting, and the emergence of Dropo masked the loss of Williams's power.

In mid-August the Sox won eleven in a row and sixteen of seventeen to get back in the race. By September 12 they were only two games out of first behind Detroit and New York.

Tom Yawkey, who since remarrying only rarely traveled with the team, joined them for an important twelve-game road trip, salivating over the possibilities. Williams was back, and Boston appeared poised to steal a pennant.

The infamous Williams temperament on display in a clubhouse outburst allegedly sparked by a poor at bat.

But they stumbled against the Browns. Yawkey spent one hundred thousand dollars to pry pitcher Harry Taylor from Branch Rickey for help with the final push.

He wasted his money. Beginning on September 20 Boston lost six of eight, and New York put the pennant away. Boston finished third, four games out.

There was no great hue and cry over the team's collapse, just the usual scapegoating. Williams took the brunt of the attack, for Boston's demise coincided with his return. Unnamed teammates said they'd proven "We can win without Ted," and that his self-absorption was a distraction.

The *Globe*'s Harold Kaese summed up the frustration by asking, "If you were Tom Yawkey, what would you do about the Red Sox? . . . Your team bats .303, averages nearly eight runs a game [and] the players receive princely sums . . . Trade Ted Williams? . . . Trade everybody but Williams? . . . Slash salaries? . . . Buy more stars? . . . Alter Fenway Park so the left field fence is not a crutch without which your sluggers limp on the road, when the wind is in the East, or when the air is heavy with wood smoke from Alberta, Canada?"

The real problems were by now so familiar as to be almost invisible: lack of pitching and the inability to win on the road. In the off-season Cronin made a typical knee-jerk trade, overpaying for Red Sox nemesis Ray Scarborough, who always pitched like an all-star against Boston. Against everybody else, he was nothing special.

Cleveland general manager Hank Greenberg then allowed player-manager Lou Boudreau to "take advantage of other options." Cronin and Yawkey thought Boudreau was a wizard and grabbed him, but as a player, he was almost finished. Most viewed him as the manager-in-waiting.

Williams and the Sox got off to their signature slow start in 1951, then both got hot. In late May they won ten in a row to get back in the race.

O'Neill showed no such patience with Walt Dropo. Although the first baseman's 144 RBIs in 1950 had tied him for the league lead and earned him the Rookie of the Year award, in 1951 he slumped and then sat. After forty-seven games he was sent back to the minor leagues. No other Rookie of the Year has ever been treated so abruptly.

In July, twenty-nine-year-old backup outfielder Clyde Vollmer apparently sold his soul. As he imitated Roy Hobbs, Boston surged.

With only twenty-one career home runs to his credit, over the next month the righthanded hitter cracked thirteen more. With nearly every at bat he seemed to win a ballgame.

From a July 6 triple versus New York to a sixteenth-inning grand slam that beat Cleveland on July 28, time and time again Vollmer's late-inning heroics led Boston to victory, a series of clutch performances equal to any in club history.

Vollmer found his performance as mystifying as everyone else did. After one outburst he told the *Herald*, "I honestly don't know what I hit."

But then the clock struck midnight and Vollmer became a borderline player again. New York won two of every three in September and the Sox settled for third place, eleven games behind.

Williams, who hit only .318, was again the people's choice as scapegoat. In the papers anyway, the Sox tried to trade him. But attendance was down, and they wondered who would come to Fenway Park if Williams were gone and the team started to lose.

The one-time dynasty was getting old. Williams, DiMaggio, Doerr, Pesky, Stephens, and Kinder were all over thirty. Bobby Doerr, plagued by a bad back but only thirty-two, retired before the beginning of the 1952 season, marking the beginning of the end.

Bad luck, bad strategy, Father Time, and the New York Yankees had combined to prevent the best Boston team in decades from winning a championship. Yawkey decided to shake things up. After keeping his bankbook closed for most of the previous decade, apart from the occasional late-season pickup, he announced, "I do not want to continue taking New York's dust." His solution was a youth movement.

He released O'Neill and named Lou Boudreau manager, a change not favored by Joe Cronin, just as he had overruled Eddie Collins to hire Bucky Harris nearly two decades earlier.

Instead of buying established players, Yawkey decided the way to win was to buy the best prospects. All of them.

He ordered his scouts not to let anyone outbid them. Over the next year they signed seventeen prospects for the unheard-of sum of nearly eight hundred thousand dollars.

His money was wasted, for the strategy was fatally flawed. Many of the best prospects were young African-Americans, but as yet, no one in the Boston organization, from Yawkey down, felt comfortable with that. All the players they signed were white.

According to Dick O'Connell, then assistant general manager, Yawkey himself would have accepted African-Americans players and occasionally wondered aloud why his Boston scouts hadn't. But the topic didn't really concern him. When Sox scouts gave the lame excuse that they couldn't find any black players, Yawkey and Cronin, both of whom had to know better, simply shrugged, sat comfortably on tradition, and accepted it.

But baseball men like Branch Rickey, Happy Chandler, and Bill Veeck weren't so accepting of the status quo. Their courage changed both their ballclubs and

In 1950 first baseman Walter Dropo enjoyed one of the greatest rookie seasons in Red Sox history as he led the league with 144 RBIs while batting .322 with thirty-four home runs. Within two seasons of his stunning major league debut the former University of Connecticut star was traded to the Tigers.

a way of life in America. Yawkey and Cronin didn't change a thing. And in the end, the Red Sox paid in every way possible — at the gate, in the standings, and in their ongoing legacy.

In January, the organization was rocked when Ted Williams learned he would be recalled into the service on May 1. The Korean War was heating up, and the military was worried that the conflict might escalate. They needed pilots, and Williams, a member of the marine reserves, became one of more than a thousand veteran flyers called back to duty.

Williams was incensed but accepting, writing later, "I was bitter about it, but I made up my mind I wasn't going to bellyache." Had he fought the recall, he likely could have avoided it, but he knew that would endear him to no one.

He went to spring training hoping his broken elbow might medically disqualify him, but Williams was a symbol. Marine doctors never even looked at his x-rays.

At age thirty-three, his baseball career appeared over. Few thought he would return to play. His pending departure hastened Yawkey's youth movement.

Boudreau ushered in a new era for the Sox. Every

position was up for grabs. He seemed eager — a little too eager in the eyes of the team's veteran players — to create a new team from the bottom up.

Veterans like Johnny Pesky and Dom DiMaggio found themselves fighting for jobs as bonus babies, and rookies like Ted Lepcio, Jimmy Piersall, Milt Bolling, Dick Gernert, and Gene Stephens found Boudreau's favor. The vets groused, but Boudreau had Yawkey's backing. For the first time since buying the club, Yawkey seemed willing to concede first place and build for the future.

With few expectations of success, the Red Sox, as if thumbing their collective nose at the pundits, opened the season by winning nine of their first eleven games. On April 30, when the club said good-bye to Williams, the Red Sox were in first place.

In a pre-game ceremony players from both teams linked hands with Williams and a wheelchair-bound war veteran. Ted was given a new Cadillac and numerous other gifts, including a wish book signed by four hundred thousand fans. For one day, anyway, all was forgiven, although Dave Egan churlishly asked, "What are we giving *him* a day for?"

Williams gave a brief speech and thanked the fans.

As his career progressed Ted Williams had to work hard to remain splinter-like. He is shown working out in the shadow of the left-field wall with Red Sox employee John Pohlmeyer.

At the end of the ceremony, he turned to all corners of the park, and while he didn't tip his cap, he did wave it in the air.

Then, with the score tied 3-3, Williams came up in the seventh inning for what many suspected was his last at bat. He drove a Dizzy Trout curveball eight rows deep into the bleachers. Boston won 5-3. Williams left for ground school the next day.

In June the Sox were still tied for first. Winning hadn't been in the plan, but now Boston felt it had to react. The youth movement was put on hold.

Cronin revisited a trade he'd been trying to make for a year with the last-place Detroit Tigers. He sent Dropo, Pesky, and three others to the Tigers for Trout, outfielder Hoot Evers, shortstop Johnny Lipon, and All-Star third baseman George Kell.

The trade shocked Sox fans. Apart from Dom DiMaggio, hardly anyone remained active from the 1946 champions.

Jim Piersall, who'd started the season at shortstop, was shifted to center field to make room for Lipon. Although the Red Sox briefly stayed in contention, they soon slipped back.

Piersall, the most talented and athletic player on

the team, represented the future. Boston needed him both for his skills and for the new era he represented.

Yet his shift to the outfield provided a hint of what was to come. Boudreau, as Bill Cunningham later described, "was like a kid playing with blocks." He constantly shifted players from position to position. While Piersall eventually became the Sox' best defensive outfielder since Tris Speaker, the change of position unnerved him.

The Waterbury, Connecticut, rookie broke down in tears, certain that the Red Sox were planning to get rid of him. Over the next few weeks, his behavior became increasingly erratic. More sensitive observers noted that he hadn't seemed right all year.

He acted strangely, clowning with fans and mocking his teammates, pantomiming the way they threw and ran. On June 12 against the St. Louis Browns, he told pitcher Satchel Paige that he was going to bunt, did so for a hit, then danced off first imitating Paige's motion and snorting like a pig. Paige blew up and the Red Sox won, but no one thought Piersall had acted appropriately. After the game the sage pitcher commented, "That boy's sick."

Piersall was spinning out of control. On June 27, standing in the batter's box against Washington pitcher Connie Marrero, he mocked the pitcher's motion and struck out without swinging. After the game, he snapped at Junior Stephens's son, and the press erroneously reported he'd kicked the boy.

The Sox knew something was wrong, but didn't know what. Exasperated, they sent Piersall down to Birmingham.

The move confirmed Piersall's increasingly paranoid fears and he broke down completely. In New Orleans, he threw a ball at his own pitcher, then ducked when the pitcher threw it back. When the umpire ordered him to retrieve the ball, he did so on all fours like a dog, then played catch with the scoreboard boy. He was thrown from the game and went into the stands and jeered. A few days later the Red Sox had Piersall hospitalized in a Boston area sanitarium.

As later chronicled in the book and movie *Fear Strikes Out*, Piersall was mentally ill. After therapy that included shock treatment, he eventually returned to the club in 1953.

Despite the loss of Piersall, the 1952 Sox hung in

Originally signed as a shortstop, Jimmy Piersall was moved by manager Lou Boudreau to the outfield where he soon developed into the best Red Sox defensive center fielder since Tris Speaker. He was also hospitalized for mental illness during a troubled eight-year stint with the Red Sox.

until September, then collapsed as usual and fell all the way to sixth place, nineteen games behind the Yankees. Meanwhile, Ted Williams completed flight training. He arrived in Korea for combat duty on February 4, 1953.

Boston's disappointing finish led to more changes. On February 9, Stephens was traded to the White Sox for three pitchers. Boudreau confidently announced that the deal "gives us the green light to rebuild our team with young stars."

But the big news during spring training came from the camp of the Braves. Rumors spread that the team was preparing to leave Boston.

Baseball attendance had fallen some 40 percent since 1948, largely because of the growth of television and other leisure-time options. Even the Sox were off nearly a half million fans since 1949.

But the Braves had collapsed completely. Bad luck, bad trades, and bad strategy sent the team tumbling to the second division, and in 1952 only 281,278 fans made their way into cavernous Braves Field. The ballpark, built for the Dead Ball Era, was part of the problem. Hard by the Charles River basin, it was cold and windy and, in comparison to Fenway, had poor sight lines. Braves owner Lou Perini had tried everything to improve the park, even lowering the field, but nothing had worked. Fans were so few, he complained, "I got so I knew all of them personally." Perini was no Yawkey and lost six hundred thousand dollars in 1952.

Jimmy Piersall is shown departing Fenway Park after having been demoted to the minors following a series of incidents during and after a game against the Senators on June 27, 1952. The demotion would lead to Piersall's complete breakdown and subsequent hospitalization.

Help was close by. Rookie third baseman Eddie Mathews had been impressive in 1952, and the Braves, who embraced integration, were loaded. Prospects Bill Bruton and Henry Aaron were ready for the major leagues.

On at least four occasions the Braves had tried to rent Fenway from Yawkey, but had been rebuffed. In 1947 Yawkey turned down Bob Quinn's son John, telling him he'd even refused his sister's request to build a small home eight miles from him on his South Carolina estate. "It was just that strange way I have of wanting everything I have for myself," said Yawkey. "So I said she couldn't do it. I have to say the same thing to you ... I'm a funny person. What's mine is mine and I don't let anybody else have a part of it." Perini asked one more time. Yawkey said no.

In Milwaukee, home of the Braves Triple A franchise, the county had built a new ballpark and was begging for a major league franchise. Browns owner Bill Veeck wanted to move and offered Perini seven hundred fifty thousand dollars for rights to Milwaukee while lobbying the other owners to force Perini's hand. But Perini wanted to give Boston one more year.

In March he tried to put off Veeck. He asked baseball's executive council, which advised the commissioner and enacted rules governing ownership, to make a rule prohibiting the move of a franchise between the first day of spring training and October 1. That would have blocked Veeck and given Perini the one year he wanted. The council was agreeable, but had to vote to make it official.

Therein lay the problem. Tom Yawkey was one of the game's most powerful owners, and he held a spot on the influential council. As Perini waited for a decision, Yawkey was "unavailable," and the council was unable to act. Perini couldn't wait any longer, and on March 13 he announced he would move the Braves to Milwaukee, the first shift of a major league franchise since Baltimore went to New York in 1903.

Boston howled, and several desperate plans to try

Following the Boston Braves' relocation to Milwaukee in 1953, the Red Sox adopted the Jimmy Fund of the Dana-Farber Cancer Research Center as the team's primary charity and have subsequently raised millions of dollars for the internationally recognized organization. During the fifties and sixties the Jimmy Fund billboard was the sole billboard allowed in Fenway Park.

to keep the team were launched. Tom Yawkey suddenly reappeared and now made a grandstand offer to rent Fenway to the Braves after doing his bit of dirty work behind the scenes. Perini did, however, ask Yawkey to take over his Jimmy Fund, the local children's cancer charity Perini had started several years before. Yawkey agreed.

Perini received official approval to move on March 18. The next day, the *Daily Record* appeared edged in funereal black. The Braves became Milwaukee's, where, with rookie Henry Aaron, they became an immediate contender and set attendance records.

Yawkey and the Sox had Boston to themselves, which should have proved beneficial. Instead, there was even less pressure to win. Boudreau continued to play kids.

Hot young prospects like Milt Bolling, Dick Gernert, Ted Lepcio, Gene Stephens, and Tom Umphlett were promoted to the varsity. But Yawkey's spending on prospects backfired. Baseball then decided to curb the inflation caused by Yawkey's profligate spending, ruling that prospects signed for bonuses in excess of thirty thousand dollars had to stay on the major league roster for two years. Boston's eighteen-year-old infielder Billy Consolo, whom Joe Cronin called "another Mickey Mantle," was the first victim. Meanwhile, Boudreau made it clear to veterans like

Dom DiMaggio, who was bothered by eye trouble, that it was time to move on. He retired in 1953 after batting only three times.

In July, after flying thirty-nine missions, crash-landing once, and taking antiaircraft fire on another occasion, Ted Williams was mustered out of the service with ear trouble caused by flying at high altitude. He was thirty-four years old, tired, and sick. He'd done his duty but hadn't liked it, and as soon as he became a civilian, he told the press what he thought about the war. "Do you think we're trying?" he told the press. "We've sat on the 38th parallel for a year and a half or more. Guys are getting killed every day in the line. Don't believe it, buddy, that we're trying."

Baseball wasn't on his mind, but after taking a look at his finances, he signed a contract on July 29 to play the balance of the season.

When Williams returned he went on one of the greatest hitting binges of his career, hitting .407 with thirteen home runs and thirty-four RBIs for the rest of the season. One writer quipped, "Williams has set spring training back ten years."

Paced by Ellis Kinder, who saved twenty-seven games in 1953, Boston's pitching, for once, was the surprise of the league. Unfortunately, their kiddie corps batting order proved anemic. A midseason surge made them a nominal pennant contender, but despite Williams's return the club played .500 baseball the rest of the year. They finished fourth, sixteen games behind the Yankees.

Encouraged, Boudreau confidently announced in the off-season, "At last the Red Sox youth movement

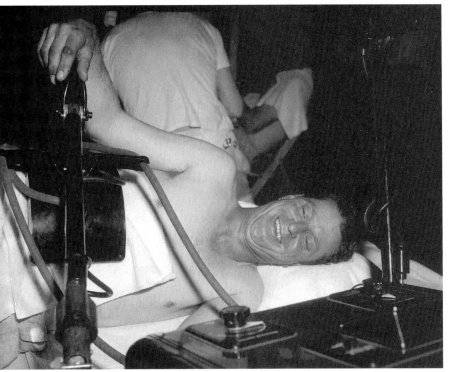

In eight seasons with the Red Sox Ellis Kinder proved one of the most versatile pitchers in club history, equally valuable as both a starter and a reliever. In 1949 his 23-6 won-lost record topped the league in winning percentage (.793) and he twice led the league in saves and relief victories. His off-field exploits, including a love of bourbon, were equally legendary.

has reached maturity." Boston University varsity football sensation Harry Agganis, a superb athlete and local hero who turned down one hundred thousand dollars to play pro football to sign with the Sox, was ready for the majors. A deal with Washington that landed outfielder Jackie Jensen promised to add some punch to the lineup. On paper, it looked good.

On the other hand, Ted Williams, in exchange for twenty-five thousand dollars, gave an exclusive to the *Saturday Evening Post* and announced, "This is my last year . . . I won't wait around for the last gasp."

The Boston press, ticked off that he'd used New York writer Joe Trimble to ghost the story, viewed the announcement as a final chance to get their shots in. Dave Egan wrote, "I think the Red Sox would be well-served by Williams if he should make his retirement retroactive, and start it at once, for he should not be permitted to poison the bassinet brigade. One like him is enough."

Although Cronin didn't believe him, Williams was serious. All his old friends on the Sox were gone, and he disliked Boudreau. On the first day of spring training, Williams brushed off the manager, then slipped and fell in the outfield, breaking his collarbone.

By the time he returned in early May, the Red Sox were already out of it as Cleveland surged toward a remarkable 111-43 record. Mel Parnell broke his arm, and Yawkey gave up on the season. He even *sold* a player for big money, letting George Kell go to Chicago for one hundred thousand dollars.

The Sox were terrible. No amount of shuffling by Boudreau — and he did plenty — helped as the youth movement matured into mediocrity. While the Red Sox finished fourth, their record dropped to 69-85, a staggering forty-two games behind pennant-winning Cleveland, against whom they were 2-20.

The highlight of the season came on September 26, in what most thought would be Williams's last game. There was little fanfare as only the *Boston Globe* bothered to print anything close to a tribute and only 14,175 fans turned out at Fenway Park.

In the seventh inning, in what looked to be his last at bat, he homered into the right-field stands off Washington pitcher Constantine Keriazakos. But the Sox rallied. He came up again in the eighth and popped up. After the game, he reiterated his plans to retire, saying simply, "That's it," and muttering a kind of apologia to the assembled writers, adding, "There was only one of you I really hated."

Soon after joining the Sox in 1937, Pinky Higgins had become a Yawkey favorite and frequent companion in the days when he traveled with the club on the road and went carousing. After Higgins's playing career ended in 1948, Yawkey offered him a job as a coach. He endeared himself to the owner by responding, "I want to start at the bottom and prove I can manage." He'd done so, and in 1953 led Triple A Louisville to the Little World Series. When other clubs showed an interest in Higgins, Yawkey fired Boudreau on October 9 to make room for his friend. He hoped Williams would reconsider his retirement.

Higgins knew many of the younger Sox from the farm system, and he continued the rebuilding job Boudreau had started. Boston broke camp with only four pitchers who had completed a full season in the majors. Faye Throneberry, brother of 1962 Mets cult hero "Marvelous" Marv Throneberry, won Williams's left-field job. The Sox considered Faye a "can't miss" prospect whom they compared to Enos Slaughter.

But Faye and his teammates soon began to hit like Marv. Despite good pitching Boston couldn't score. Only Harry Agganis was hitting. Still, attendance dropped by seventy thousand. Without Williams, Boston fans were about as interested in the Red Sox as they had been in the Braves.

Williams was reconsidering. His wife Doris had filed for divorce in 1954, and the timing of Williams's retirement and eventual return strongly suggests his "retirement" may have been timed to exclude his next contract from his divorce settlement. For once his divorce became final, on May 11, Williams signed with the Red Sox, beating a May 15 procedural deadline that would have precluded his return.

As Williams prepared to return to the Boston lineup, Agganis, hitting over .350 in recent weeks, caught a bad cold. On May 16 he was hospitalized with pleurisy.

A real-life Frank Merriwell, Lynn native Agganis was known as "the Golden Greek" and seemed cut from the realm of legend. One of the most celebrated prep athletes in the history of Massachusetts, he went on to star at quarterback for Boston University and turned down a six-figure offer to quarterback the Cleveland Browns. He signed with the Red Sox instead. In his first year in the minors, he knocked in more than one hundred runs at Louisville and appeared on his way to greatness.

After spending a few days in the hospital, he briefly rejoined the team, but couldn't shake a heavy cough. After complaining of chest pains, he was hospitalized again in Sancta Maria Hospital in Cambridge.

His condition deteriorated into pneumonia. On June 27, with little warning, he lapsed into unconsciousness and died.

Despite Agannis's tragic death, or perhaps because of it, the Red Sox won forty-four of sixty games after Williams's return. In early September, they were part of a four-team pennant race and only three games out of first place.

But too many strong pitching performances had been wasted during the forty-one games Williams missed. The pitching wore out in September, and Boston finished twelve games behind New York at 84-70. Pinky Higgins was named manager of the year.

That performance proved to be an illusion. Although the club matched their record in 1956, they were never in the pennant race. Williams started slowly, then on July 18 earned the enmity of the press and many fans. After cracking his 400th home run against Kansas City at Fenway Park, as he crossed home plate he raised his head toward the "Knights of the Keyboard" in the press box, and like a schoolboy, spat in their direction.

In deference to the occasion, the press let the incident pass without comment, although the *Herald* published a picture of the event. Three days later, as the Sox held "Joe Cronin Night," Williams spit toward the press box a second time. The writers held back again.

But Williams was aching for a fight. On August 7, as the Sox hosted the Yankees before a full house, Boston's Willard Nixon and New York's Don Larsen both pitched shutout ball into the eleventh. Then Williams dropped a flyball, and the boo-birds let Ted have it.

One batter later, he made up for the miscue by snaring Yogi Berra's line drive to the gap. Now the crowd cheered. Fickle praise drove Williams crazy. Before entering the dugout he spit toward the crowd behind first base, then turned and did so toward those behind third, lest anyone feel left out.

In the bottom of the inning, with the bases loaded, Williams walked, driving in the winning run. But he'd wanted to hit, winning or losing be damned, and he tossed his bat 40 feet in the air and stomped to first like a little boy being sent to his room.

Coupled with what the press termed "the Great Ex-

For me, baseball was about taking a beating. It was about being picked last and proving I belonged on the same rocky vacant lot in Dorchester as the older kids who merely needed another body, an "easy out" to even the day's teams. It was about harrowing cheek-high fastballs that tested constantly wavering courage, being overmatched in the batter's box and always questioning how it was possible to love a game that seemed clearly intent on mashing my young psyche into cornmeal. Most days, it succeeded.

Perhaps this early penchant for returning to the baseball diamond each day for new humiliations was the first real proof of a preordained destiny with the Red Sox, where New England gluttons go for their punishment.

My punishment for caring is similar to that of the rest, for believing that a 3-0 lead in the seventh game of 1975, a 2-0 lead in the one-game playoff of 1978, and yet another 3-0 lead in the seventh game of 1986 would produce the high reward of a championship. Or that the Red Sox would do right by the players who made the team interesting in the first place. I know none of this is new ground, for the Red Sox have broken more hearts than a homecoming queen.

Worse is the fact that a cosmic bond exists around the Red Sox. Joe DiMaggio tormented the Red Sox, especially during the last two games of the 1949 season when the Red Sox needed to win one of two games at Yankee Stadium to win the pennant and lost both. Bucky Dent's contribution needs no introduction, just ask Mike Torrez or any New Englander not sleeping under a boulder in 1978.

Both DiMaggio and Dent, two Yankees, were born on my birthday, November 25.

After being driven from the Red Sox by the curiously unimpressed but historically consistent Sox front office, Mo Vaughn signed a six-year, eighty-million-dollar contract with the Ana-

Perhaps this early penchant for new humiliations was the first real proof of a preordained destiny with the Red Sox, where New England gluttons go for their punishment.

heim Angels on — you guessed it — November 25, 1998.

Numerologists could have a field day with that.

But my separate agony is derived from being in the impossible position of being a black Red Sox fan.

I cannot count how many times strangers and new friends — non–New Englanders, of course — return any sounds of excitement, any obvious scoreboard Sox-watching, with a scornful and piteous face. It is a face I know by heart, and the question is always the same: how could you root for these guys?

It is a struggle that has existed since I was a teenager, wondering how it is possible to expend a breath of energy thinking about a baseball team that owns such an infamous history. The Red Sox had a chance to be pioneers. They had Jackie Robinson on a platter in 1945, yet, motivated by nothing more than the pure racism of owner Tom Yawkey and his underlings, they chose not to sign Robinson, thus keeping the color barrier intact.

When the Brooklyn Dodgers finally did integrate the game in 1947, the Red Sox — perhaps thinking integration was a fad — needed twelve more years to sign their first black player. The Boston Bruins — the Bruins! — integrated before the Red Sox.

The Red Sox had a shot to get Willie Mays when he was eighteen years old in 1949, but passed on the man who would become the greatest complete player the game has ever known. The Red Sox have had a problem dealing with race for a century. They could have been the first team to integrate, yet they became the last. The effects of these early blunders can be felt to this day. Black fans and superstar black players alike are hesitant about coming to Fenway.

There is nothing more humiliating for a person than believing he's come of age only to be harshly rebuffed. The hotshot minor league pitcher who takes an unmerciful shelling in the big leagues faces a critical moment of introspection. He will regroup or surely disappear.

Watching the 1982 Cardinals-Brewers World Series with my family in Bos-

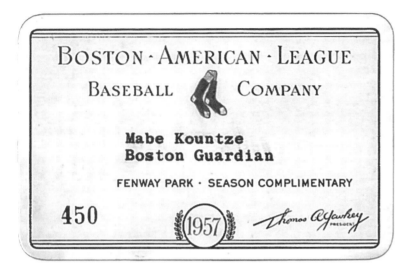

Red Sox season pass issued to Mabrey "Doc" Kountze of the *Boston Guardian*. Kountze was the first African-American writer issued credentials by the team.

ton, I thought I had arrived, not unlike a stud prospect waiting to make a splash against the seasoned veterans.

My uncle Raymond asked me which team I was rooting for and I told him Milwaukee, because the Brewers had Cecil Cooper, who had played for the Red Sox. Also, the Brewers were in the American League and if the Sox couldn't make the Series, I'd just as soon see an AL team win it all. It was pretty sound logic, I thought, and I remember feeling especially proud at that instant for forming a confident opinion.

Everybody laughed.

My uncle Paul dismissed my comment with a quick, abrasive wave of his hand. My grandfather was gruff. Bluntness was his fastball.

"The Red Sox? The Red Sox?" He displayed a tired irritation, his manner suggesting to me that I should know

better. "We don't care about the goddamned Red Sox around here because the Red Sox ain't never had no niggers on the team. Never have, never will. You think about that."

To this day, I cannot remember a moment when I felt more diminished. And I remember soon after that day in my grandparents' living room racing through the gallery of mental images, rewinding a million words of dialogue from a thousand conversations, and I could not remember a single person in my old Dorchester neighborhood actually going to Fenway Park, or even talking about going. The adults in Dorchester talked about ball, but they talked about the Cardinals and the Dodgers, never the Sox.

I felt like an idiot.

I also retrenched and did some homework, lest I be considered a bush leaguer by the adults forever. Watching the Red Sox from a different vantage point now, they were slow, plodding, and colorless. They were a very different

team from the speedy, integrated Cardinals, who boasted black superstars such as Ozzie Smith and Willie McGee. Other teams had numerous black players, while the Red Sox invariably had one, Jim Rice.

The Red Sox were supposed to represent everything that is New England, yet they told Jackie Robinson, Willie Mays, and just about everyone who looked like them to take a hike.

Jilted, I then did the unthinkable. I started rooting for the Yankees.

Part of it was to be contrary. My family had left predominantly black Dorchester for the then-rural, predominantly white environs of Plymouth, about 50 miles south of Boston. But most of my attachment to the Yankees — a team that history shows was once every bit as racist as the Red Sox — was because of Dave Winfield. Here was a player unbowed, confident, and at the top of his game, playing in the biggest city in the country. He was black and lithe, powerful and unafraid,

> *Jilted, I then did the unthinkable. I started rooting for the Yankees.*

which was a welcome sight next to my all-white schooling where black people were always expected to blend, to assimilate. I cannot count how many times white kids would tell me — incredibly, as a way of reaching out — that they didn't mind "black people," but hated "niggers," or that I was "okay for a black kid."

Winfield didn't walk with his head down. His ebullience was a startling contrast to the smoldering distance of Jim Rice, who also happened to be my friend Mike's favorite player. That created an instant rivalry in our world. At that time, Winfield and the Yankees represented what I wanted to be: fearless, polished, and engaging. In later years, Mo Vaughn would represent similar qualities, though I would be past the stage when I needed to glean esteem from a professional athlete.

I could never attach myself to Rice. There was always something foreboding and unfriendly about him. He had power, indeed for a time was the finest player in the game. But while Rice withdrew as his celebrity increased, it was Winfield's charisma that captured me, despite the knowledge that choosing him put me on the wrong side of Athens-Sparta. But more importantly than any Sox-Yankees conflict, Dave Winfield was the first black athlete — quite possibly the first black person I remember — who was not either brooding or broken by the weight of racism. As a teenager, I needed to see that.

As far as I'm concerned, the eternal judgment of the Red Sox is rooted in six words that are yellowed and musty, yet fierce and alive. They are the non-negotiable, unbending truth.

"Get those niggers off the field."

These words were spit forth by a Red Sox official during the farce tryout in 1945 and they not only kept Robinson out of the major leagues for two more years, but also my parents and grand-parents from going to Fenway. Those words represent the prickly, raised scar that serves as a constant reminder of a century of slights, set-ups, and cons. They were the words that would forecast history, that instead of being the first team to field a black player — and quite possibly forever change their team image — the Red Sox became the last.

I only began to inch back toward the Red Sox after the terrifying humiliation

I only began to inch back toward the Red Sox after the terrifying humiliation of 1986, which, for the first time, made me consider the existence of voodoo.

of 1986, which, for the first time, made me consider the existence of voodoo.

Still, the Sox offer occasional, sense-pleasing magic. A walk through the Public Garden reminds me of the night in 1988 when Ellis Burks hit a grand slam in Texas to keep Morgan Magic alive, or when I think about leaving for college in Philadelphia, it's impossible to forget it was the same weekend in '86 when Dave Henderson hit the biggest homer in Sox history to beat the Angels.

But never let it be said that I made it easy on the Red Sox. I didn't, and I still don't. I fought them as hard as Tom Yawkey, Joe Cronin, and his regime fought integration. But you also can't deny what you are and where you're from. A sucker's bet for sure, but true nonetheless.

My dad, once a huge baseball fan, never mentions the Red Sox, unless it is to humor me. He is sixty-one years old, has lived in Boston his whole life, and has never been to Fenway Park. He was a Boston Braves fan, because they integrated Boston professional baseball with Sam Jethroe. When the Braves left at the end of the 1952 season and the Red Sox still refused to integrate, baseball lost its relevance, and he never came back to the game. He was always smarter than I.

At a dinner one night in San Francisco a few years ago, I sat with Willie Mays and talked baseball. Mostly our conversation was about how Mays wanted so badly to play in Boston with Ted Williams and was actually close to playing for the Red Sox, except that Yawkey was still reluctant to break the Red Sox' color barrier. We talked about my father and his idol, Sam Jethroe, and how the Red Sox' refusal to integrate created such a permanent distance between my father and the game that he never came back.

As the conversation eased and I started to walk away, I heard a polite, low whisper summon me back.

"Hey, Howard. Tell your dad it's okay," Willie Mays said to me. "The Red Sox didn't want me, either."

Howard Bryant has been a reporter for the *San Jose Mercury News* since 1995 and has covered the Oakland A's baseball team since 1998. He has written for *USA Today* and *Baseball Weekly,* and his book *Out at Home: The African American Experience in Baseball* will be available in summer 2001.

pectoration," the Sox had to react. They fined Williams five thousand dollars, baseball's largest fine since Ruth broke curfew in 1925.

Many Boston writers, like Harold Kaese, called for Ted to retire "before baseball quits him. He is getting too old for the game — mentally and physically . . . he can't take it at all." Williams was unapologetic, saying, "I'd spit at the same people again."

The next day, before a "Family Night" crowd of thirty thousand, Williams homered to break a 2-2 tie. As he neared home plate, the crowd quieted in anticipation of his next move.

Like a trained performer, he stretched out his arm and in a grand gesture clamped it over his mouth. Thirty thousand fans laughed and were won over.

He had them. For the rest of his playing career, Williams was viewed in a different light. Public opinion sided with him, and he became immune to the withering attacks of the writers, who eventually backed off. Overnight, as if Boston fans realized that Ted Williams was all they had, everything was forgiven, and Williams was greeted and applauded as he had been in his rookie year. A long uncomfortable estrangement was over.

With so much focus on Williams, the performance of the team was almost overlooked. They weren't expected to challenge for the pennant anymore, and they didn't. They repeated their fourth-place finish in 1956 with another in 1957, as the club did a fair imitation of its precursors in the late 1940s, banging the ball all over Fenway Park while the pitching staff tried but failed to keep the opposition at bay.

But the story was always Williams. Surrounded by a potent lineup that included stellar rookie third baseman Frank Malzone, he saw the best pitches he had in years. At age thirty-eight he made a serious run at .400, hitting .388. After the season he accurately quipped, "All the American League's got is me and the Yankees. When I leave this league it's going to be pretty damn dull."

He was right, because even though Jackie Jensen was league MVP and Pete Runnels nearly won a batting title, lack of pitching prevented the club from challenging a so-so Yankee squad that won only ninety-two games. The 1958 Sox finished 79-75, third place once more.

Even their owner seemed to have grown bored with the Red Sox. Tom Yawkey rarely showed his face in Boston. In a way, he was in a position not dissimilar to that of Williams — nearly all Yawkey's favorites were gone, and it was impossible for him to pal around with players thirty years younger than he. His only peers were Williams, Higgins, and Joe Cronin. And in 1959, Cronin would leave the Red Sox

Red Sox outfielder Jackie Jensen at spring training in Scottsdale, Arizona, in March 1957. The 316 likely refers to his .315 batting average from the previous season. The talented Jensen was an extraordinary athlete who not only played in the Rose Bowl as a star for the University of California but also played in the All-Star Game for the Red Sox and the World Series for the Yankees.

to take over as American League president, the first player ever to hold a position of authority in Major League Baseball.

Yawkey appeared to be contemplating selling the club. He'd gotten out of Louisville, bought market rights to San Francisco, sold those to the Giants, transferred the Sox' Triple A franchise to Minneapolis, and moved spring training from Florida to Arizona. High-priced purchases of big-time stars were a thing of the past. While Yawkey, according to *The Sporting News*, had lost a total of more than two million dollars since buying the Sox in 1933 — most of it signing players who never produced — in recent years the club had turned a profit despite their mostly lackluster play. The Red Sox gave up ever

Elijah Jerry "Pumpsie" Green was the first African-American to play for the Red Sox in July 1959. Within a week of his promotion from Minneapolis he was joined in Boston by pitcher and fellow African-American Earl Wilson. With these moves the Red Sox became the last major league team to integrate.

catching the Yankees. The farm system, crippled by its size and the club's continuing reluctance to sign African-Americans, was only nominally productive.

But in 1953 the Red Sox had signed two African-Americans: Earl Wilson and Elijah "Pumpsie" Green. Wilson, a catcher turned pitcher, initially progressed rapidly, but had control problems and in 1957 was

drafted into the marines. Infielder Green, the brother of star NFL defensive back Cornell Green, made slower progress, particularly at the plate. In 1955 Boston offered Brooklyn between one hundred thousand and two hundred fifty thousand dollars for prospect Charlie Neal, but the Dodgers refused.

But apart from these players, Boston's interest in African-American players was minimal — none had been acquired by trade, and Boston's scouting staff included no African-Americans or Latinos. They couldn't sign what they couldn't see, and with the collapse of the Negro Leagues, finding young African-American players meant venturing into the inner city, the black rural South, and the Caribbean, places few Boston scouts went. Locally, Ralph "Stody" Ward, a writer for the *Boston Guardian*, racial activist, and star third baseman on a series of black Boston semi-pro teams, occasionally referred players to the Sox, but none was ever signed.

Attendance was flat, hovering around one million fans per season as the club never took advantage of the absence of the Braves. Yawkey blamed it on the lack of parking. Late in the 1958 season he unveiled a plan to enlarge and modernize Fenway Park. With the construction of the Massachusetts Turnpike beyond the left-field wall, Yawkey wanted to take Lansdowne Street, tear down the wall, push it 30 feet back, and add stands, a new road, and on-site parking.

But civic government was in no mood to underwrite the project. Yawkey could have easily completed the project with his own money, but local government was picking up the tab elsewhere, and Yawkey thought it was his turn. State and city officials disagreed, and when they refused to help the plan died.

At spring training in 1959, it appeared as if the Red Sox, the only team remaining in the major leagues not to field an African-American player, would finally shed that descriptive tag. Shortstop had been a problem for years. Incumbent Don Buddin had the job only because everyone else had played even worse than his mediocre standard.

But Pumpsie Green had a great spring despite being barred from the team's hotel in Scottsdale and commuting from the Giants' hotel in Phoenix. He hit

.400 and Boston writers named him camp Rookie of the Year. But when writers asked Yawkey if Green would make the club, he cryptically responded, "The Red Sox will bring up a Negro when he meets our standards," whatever those were.

When the club broke camp on April 9, Green appeared to have made the team. General manager Bucky Harris announced, "We now have 30 men and can carry that many," at least until early May, when rosters had to be cut to 25.

But as the club barnstormed through Texas, Higgins overruled Harris, presumably with Yawkey's approval. He sent Green back to Triple A, announcing indelicately, "Another season or half-season at Minneapolis is what this boy needs."

Boston writer Al Hirshberg later claimed that Higgins told him, "They'll be no niggers on this ballclub as long as I have anything to say about it." Green's abrupt departure made him a cause célèbre in Boston. The NAACP and other groups called for an investigation by the Massachusetts Commission Against Discrimination (MCAD). On Opening Day, Sox fans showed that they thought Green's time had come. When Don Buddin was introduced, he was booed.

Hearings were held a week later, but neither Yawkey nor Bucky Harris attended. They sent Dick O'Connell to defend the club, which he reported employed eight blacks, one at Fenway Park and seven in the minor leagues. MCAD absolved the Red Sox of charges of racial bias after extracting a promise, in the form of a letter, that the club would make "every effort to end segregation," a tacit admission that up to that time segregation had been club policy.

Green went to Minneapolis, where manager Gene Mauch moved him from short to second. Although he felt more comfortable there, his path to Boston appeared blocked, for Pete Runnels was well entrenched at second base.

With Ted Williams on the disabled list with a pinched nerve in his neck, the Red Sox got off to their customary woeful start. They fell out of the race early as the White Sox and Indians left the rest of the league behind in early May.

When Williams returned he wasn't the same. For the first time in his career he looked overmatched. Harold Kaese asked, "How will the Red Sox get rid

of Ted Williams? . . . Such giants . . . are not easily brushed aside."

The Red Sox were going nowhere. Worse, they didn't seem to care. The players had tuned out Higgins. Like so many other Red Sox managers and front office personnel over the years, part of the reason was alcohol. Higgins was reportedly a binge drinker,

Ted Williams loved to argue with sportswriters almost as much as he enjoyed talking hitting with teammates and opponents alike.

and his example hardly enforced the discipline of his team, which was all swagger and little swat. The Red Sox lost in the worst possible fashion — quietly.

On July 3, with the last-place Red Sox sporting a record of 31-42, Higgins was fired and named a scout. Rudy York was named interim manager, and one day later, Washington coach Billy Jurges took over.

Jurges was delighted and quickly figured out what was wrong with the club. Like the organization, the players had given up. Losing bothered Jurges and he tried to enforce discipline by setting a 1:00 A.M. curfew, but the players responded by sniping at him in the press.

On July 21, the Red Sox finally did something dramatic. Pumpsie Green, hitting .325 and an all-star for the second consecutive year at Minneapolis, was called up to the major leagues. When he got the news, he cried.

The press applauded the move, although most overstated it, as the *Traveler* optimistically reported, "the accusation of discrimination by the Red Sox was silenced last night." Harold Kaese sounded words of caution, calling the promotion "unexpected but meritorious . . . Pumpsie Green can only hope he is given as much opportunity to prove himself as Don Buddin." He was in his third season trying to prove he was a big league shortstop.

Kaese asked precisely the right question, and the answer was "no." Green became a part-timer, and although his playing time increased when Pete Runnels was moved to first base later that season, he never really got an unobstructed shot to win a job outright. Jurges proved as indecisive as Boudreau had been when it came to selecting middle infielders. At the same time, Green lacked confidence, and his skills were probably more suited to a utility role than to a bonafide major league starter.

One week later, Earl Wilson, who was 10-2 with Minneapolis, was also called up. While a sad chapter in Red Sox history had, superficially anyway, drawn to a close, neither player made much difference in 1959. They finished 75-79, nineteen games from first place. Ted Williams hit only .254 with ten home runs.

In the off-season Tom Yawkey told him, "I think you ought to quit." No one wanted to see the Boston hero diminished.

But Williams disagreed. He thought he could still hit. The Red Sox offered him a contract for 1960 at one hundred twenty-five thousand dollars, the same amount he had earned in 1959.

He turned it down and told Dick O'Connell, "I don't deserve what I made last year. I want to take the biggest cut ever given a player." He was still the same Ted, doing things his way. After some reverse negotiations, Williams talked the Red Sox down to ninety thousand dollars.

Beyond shuffling a few warm bodies around, the club made few changes in 1960. They didn't have the material to make trades, and Yawkey no longer had the will to do anything dramatic.

In the final season of his storied career, Williams once again became the entire story. He had a good spring, and on Opening Day in Washington he delivered a 450-foot home run to center field off Camilio Pasqual, tying Lou Gehrig for fourth place on the all-time list. He hit another the next day, but pulled a muscle trotting around the bases and missed nearly a month. Then a virus knocked him out for a few more weeks.

The Sox were already way out of the race and could afford to wait for Williams. Although he hadn't said it, there was little doubt that this was his last season.

He returned to the lineup in late May, playing for nothing more than history and self-respect. The Red Sox used him wisely, giving him plenty of rest, and Williams hit like he had in 1941, banging home runs in bunches, once hitting twelve in eighty at bats. At age forty-one, it was the best-sustained home run streak of his career.

But while Williams was turning back the clock, the organization continued to deteriorate. On May 26 Billy Jurges told the *Globe*'s Clif Keane, "I know what's wrong with this club, but I can't do anything about it. My hands are tied." With those words he essentially fired himself. Harris and Yawkey demanded an apology for his veiled criticism, and ten days later, on June 8, he left the club.

The next day, they exchanged weak-hitting outfielders with Baltimore, trading Gene Stephens for Willie Tasby, the Sox' first trade for an African-American major leaguer, thirteen years after Jackie Robinson broke the color line. One day later, Jurges's departure became public. Yawkey guaranteed more of the same by bringing back old pal Pinky Higgins.

Ted Williams distracted most fans and observers from the disaster on the field. By August, he was among the league batting leaders, although he'd missed too many games early in the season to qualify for the title. *The Sporting News* then sprung a surprise, naming him "Player of the Decade," fully nine years after he had left the game for a second tour of duty in the service, at which time most had considered him too old to ever return. The award was even more impressive considering the competition Williams faced for it, players like eventual Hall of Famers Mickey Mantle, Stan Musial, Hank Aaron, Eddie Mathews, Willie Mays, and Jackie Robinson.

Williams was now the hero of fathers taking their sons to their first game. He even homered off Detroit pitcher Don Lee. Twenty years before he'd homered off his father, Thorton Lee of the White Sox.

In September, as he made his last circuit around the league, he nixed requests to honor him. He simply took his cuts and played the game.

Finally, on September 26, Red Sox publicist Jack Malaney released a statement by Tom Yawkey that announced Williams's pending retirement. The announcement also stated that he'd serve as instructor at spring training in 1961, a compromise after Williams turned down an offer to become general manager.

Williams said nothing. The *Globe* questioned whether the retirement was real. After all, every other time he'd said he was retiring, he had popped up the following spring like the proverbial rubber ball under the rug.

Baltimore came to Boston for the Red Sox' final two home games on September 27 and 28. They battered Boston in the first game, 17-3. Williams walked, popped up, and grounded out in three appearances.

The next day the Sox, strangely enough, blew Williams's retirement out of the headlines, choosing to announce a big front office shakeup. Pinky Higgins finally won the war of wills he'd been engaged in with Bucky Harris ever since the Pumpsie Green episode. Yawkey fired Harris, named Higgins general manager, and promoted Dick O'Connell to business manager. They also announced that Jackie Jensen, who'd recently retired because of his fear of flying, would return in 1961. Williams's retirement was the "and by the way" story of the day.

Fortunately, several chroniclers were in attendance, among them John Updike, who covered the game for the *New Yorker*. But that day Fenway Park

On a count of one and one Ted Williams sends Oriole righthander Jack Fischer's fastball over the Red Sox bullpen for his 521st and last home run in the final at bat of his career.

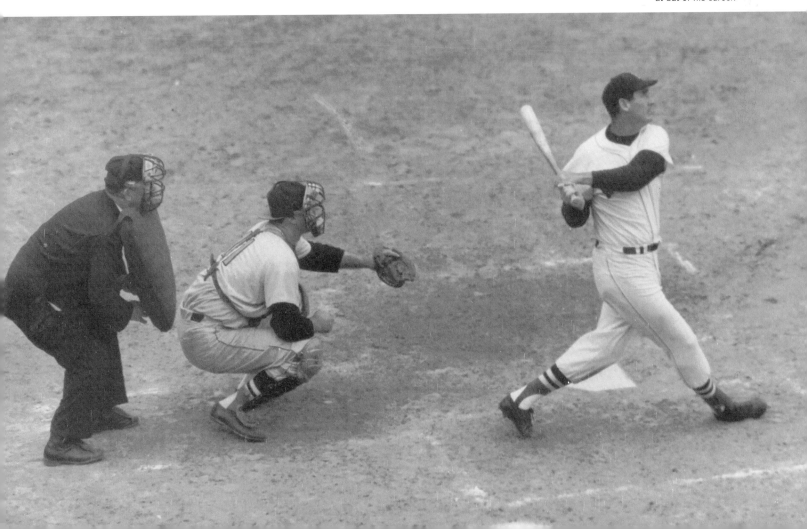

was not anything like the "inside of an old-fashioned peeping type Easter Egg" of Updike's description. The air was cold, the day gray, and the ballpark dressed in glorious urban grit. A few thousand fans spread throughout the grandstand, and a couple of hundred more were scattered throughout the bleachers. That was all.

Williams remained himself to the end. He got to the park early, got a kick out of chasing a few reporters out of the clubhouse who were violating the pregame media ban, and didn't emerge until 12:25, only thirty-five minutes before game time. Then he did a brief TV interview and played catch with Pumpsie Green before awkwardly taking his place on the field.

In a brief ceremony Boston Mayor John Collins proclaimed "Ted Williams Day" and gave several thousand dollars to the Jimmy Fund in Williams's name, but the team itself did nothing. They rarely had for Williams, and besides, he didn't want a big fuss. Broadcaster Curt Gowdy eulogized Williams, ending by saying, "I don't think we'll see another like him."

Williams spoke briefly and to the point.

"Despite the fact of the disagreeable things that have been said about me — and I can't help thinking about it — by the Knights of the Keyboard out there," he said as he jerked his head in the direction of the press box, "baseball has been the most wonderful thing in my life. If I were starting over again and someone asked me where is the one place I would like to play, I would want it to be Boston, with the greatest owner in baseball and the greatest fans in America. Thank you."

As the crowd approximated a roar Williams walked to the dugout, winked, sat down, and prepared to play the last game of his major league career.

Hitless, Williams came up for the final time with one out in the eighth inning. On the cool, overcast day, the lights were turned on as if to illuminate the Splinter on the stage for the final time of his career.

The crowd cheered him for a full two minutes as he stood in the box, swinging the bat, getting ready to hit like he had hundreds of thousands of times before, ever since he was a kid on the sandlots of San Diego.

Finally, the crowd quieted and Baltimore pitcher Jack Fischer threw low for a ball. On the next pitch, Williams swung from the heels and missed.

But Williams knew better than anyone ever has that a batter has three chances. When Fischer threw his second strike, Williams was ready.

He met the buckle-high pitch squarely. Bright with reflected light, the ball soared out toward right field and dropped over the fence in front of the bullpen just off the center-field triangle, caroming off the canvas canopy above the players' bench. It was Williams's 2,654th hit, 1,839th RBI, and 521st — final and most memorable — home run.

The crowd cheered as if suddenly double in size. Williams jogged quickly around the bases and straight into the dugout, never looking up, not even once, as the crowd chanted, "We want Ted, We want Ted!" for several minutes.

He thought he was finished, but at the end of the inning Higgins sent him back on the field. Williams shot him an angry look, then got up and ran hard out to left field as the crowd roared again.

A few steps behind was Carroll Hardy, whom Higgins sent in a moment later to replace him. Williams didn't turn around until he was well into left field. When he spied Hardy he sprinted back hard, head down, stepped on first base, then skipped down the dugout stairs out of view into the corridor that led to the clubhouse, number nine leaving the field for the last time, for all time. The cheers faded a little with each step, and the game of baseball in the city of Boston reluctantly turned a singularly unforgettable, sometimes exasperating, but always fascinating page.

THE COUNTRY CLUB

1961 | 1966

Baseball men in gray flannel suits. Members of the "country club" led by manager Johnny Pesky depart for spring training in 1963. Headed to Scottsdale, Arizona, with Pesky (foreground wearing hat) are (l–r) Mike Fornieles, Chet Nichols, Bob Tillman, Wilbur Wood, and Bill MacLeod.

Without Ted Williams to distract fans from the increasingly sub-par team on the field, seeing the Red Sox play at Fenway Park over the next several seasons was as exciting as watching an accountant at work. Although off the field the players acted like members of the "Rat Pack," on the field they were the proverbial men in gray flannel suits, a dull, nearly faceless collection of players mostly on their way toward baseball oblivion.

The Red Sox had become a "country club," a cushy organization where average players earned All-Star wages. In New York, by comparison, even after winning the World Series, half the roster had to fight to keep their salaries from being cut. But poorly motivated players who cared primarily about only their own statistics found a home with the Red Sox. Befitting the country club reputation, the nineteenth hole was too often irresistible for both players and management.

Expectations were minimal. The front office was usually indifferent, making few trades and apparently satisfied with a group of chronic underachievers.

The team's lack of appeal and charisma mirrored that of the city in which they played. Both the ballclub and the city looked back on a glorious past but faced an uncertain future. People were leaving Boston in droves, and property values plummeted. The Red Sox had also deteriorated since the war from a potential dynasty to a one-man team that could have been named the "Ted Sox." Now, without Williams, no one cared what they were called.

Tom Yawkey now did little more than "act like a rich guy and pretend to work," in the words of one former associate. His familiar old cronies still ran the organization, chief among them Pinky Higgins, protecting the status quo, demanding little from his team, virtually guaranteeing mediocrity. The players took full advantage of him. The Sox didn't even pretend to be capable of challenging the Yankees.

Higgins's ongoing role with the club continued to saddle it with a racist reputation, an ever more anachronistic and embarrassing perception. For while Yawkey felt increasing pressure to sign more African-Americans, when his scouts continued to denigrate African-American prospects and refuse to sign them, Yawkey continued to shrug his shoulders. Over and over again, they signed the same types of players, focusing on schoolboy stars and college hotshots who had already peaked and awkward, lumbering sluggers. They were almost always white, and they usually stalled in Boston's farm system. The few prospects that made it to the big leagues were often rushed and found their youthful enthusiasm greeted with disdain by the team's torpid veterans and entrenched coaching staff.

More and more, Yawkey just wasn't around. In the spring he stayed away from Boston completely because of a chronic sinus condition. By 1961 his suite at the Ritz Carlton Hotel was nothing like the lively place it had been when he'd delighted in inviting star players over to tell stories and drink highballs. Yet he was still a huge fan and looked up to ballplayers; it was said of Yawkey that he never met a big league player he didn't like and never met a Red Sox player he didn't love like a member of his family.

And the Boston players loved him. He was the perfect boss — he paid well and didn't expect much in return. Players on other teams wanted to be traded to Boston because they knew they'd be compensated far above their talents. But as his ballclub spiraled down the league standings, even Yawkey's largesse began to wane. In 1961 the club endured across-the-board pay cuts for the first time in Yawkey's twenty-eight-year reign.

The best hope for the future was a fifteen-year veteran of the organization who never played an inning of organized baseball, but who eventually proved as valuable to the team as any slugger. Executive vice president Dick O'Connell was the highest-ranked member of the front office to achieve his rank through merit rather than by cronyism. Somebody had to do the real work, and O'Connell had risen from assistant general manager by doing the mundane tasks others let slide. Although he would not assume the reins of general manager for four years, O'Connell was already working with minor league director Neil Mahoney to rebuild the team from the bottom up, just as the great Sox teams of the 1940s had been built by former Hall of Fame umpire and minor league director Billy Evans. But unlike Evans, O'Connell didn't have to guard his back against the likes of Eddie Collins and Joe Cronin competing for Tom Yawkey's ear and bank account. In the entrenched Boston bureaucracy, no one else cared enough to view O'Connell as a threat. He did the work of a soldier while the generals told war stories and tossed back scotch.

O'Connell didn't yet have the authority to attack the big issues: an aging ballpark, a disinterested owner, and a dwindling fan base. But player development was another matter. He hired a new generation of scouts primarily because of their qualifications. For the first time, that didn't necessarily require connections to someone in the front office.

Before spring training, the club confirmed that Ted Williams had agreed to stop fishing long enough to serve as a special batting instructor at spring training and take on the do-nothing title of executive assistant to Tom Yawkey. A legion of Boston sportswriters exhaled sighs of relief. They knew that with Williams around, their time in Arizona would be a little less dull. They already missed him.

But one player got the scribes' attention that spring. Carl Yastrzemski was making the jump from the Sox' Triple A affiliate in Minneapolis. The writers were impressed with his bat and confronted with the challenge of spelling his name correctly. Columnist Dick Young in *The Sporting News* referred to him simply as "Yas," which Boston writers corrupted further into "Yaz."

He wasn't the only promising prospect. Infielder Chuck Schilling and pitcher Don Schwall also stood out from the crowd of bored veterans. Yastrzemski later complained that on this club, "The locker room was like a morgue after every game," not because the veterans brooded after a loss, but because they didn't care one way or the other. Yaz and his roommate Schilling were totally ignored, rarely spoken to either on or off the field. Yaz could hardly believe it.

At spring training Yastrzemski, like nearly every big-name Sox rookie of the last decade, was heralded as the successor to Williams, who was supposed to tutor Yaz in the finer points of hitting. Most of Ted's advice went over Yastrzemski's head. He admitted to the press, "I can't understand half of what he says . . . He scares me."

Without a true superstar for the first time since 1933, the press hyped Yastrzemski's arrival all out of proportion, creating an unreachable set of expectations. The *Boston Globe* even ran a series comparing Yastrzemski with Williams. The only difference between the two was about 2,292 games and 7,706 at bats.

That spring also marked the return of one of the team's more troubled prodigal sons. Jackie Jensen was making a comeback.

After voluntarily retiring in 1959 to sort out family difficulties and come to grips with his near-pathological fear of flying, the former MVP and one-time football star had decided to return. In the absence of

Williams, the club hoped Jensen, often referred to as the "Golden Boy" because of his blond hair and prodigious athletic talent, could return to All-Star form.

But not even a top salary could make Jensen like flying. He still wanted to drive or take the train while on the road, sometimes causing him to miss games and undermining team discipline.

At the end of April he decided to retire again, asking a sportswriter to tell manager Pinky Higgins of his decision. He returned to his eighty-thousand-dollar salary a week later, but his days as a major leaguer were numbered.

Carl Yastrzemski played well after a rocky start, and second baseman Chuck Schilling was a fielding wizard. On May 18 twenty-four-year-old pitcher Bill Monbouquette struck out seventeen Detroit Tigers, breaking Smoky Joe Wood's fifty-year-old club strikeout record of fifteen. He missed tying the major league mark of eighteen only when catcher Jim Pagliaroni dropped a two-strike foul tip.

But the major surprise was rookie righthander Don Schwall, who was called up after a 3-1 start with Triple A Seattle. Schwall made his first start three days after Monbouquette's gem and scattered six hits against Chicago to win 2-1.

Boston had signed him purely by chance, for Schwall, who stood 6-foot-6, had originally set his sights on the NBA. While playing for the University of Oklahoma, he had outplayed Kansas star Wilt Chamberlain in several head-to-head battles. But after basketball practice late one winter afternoon, Schwall wandered to the other side of the Oklahoma gym where the baseball team was working out and decided to play catch. Red Sox scout Roderick "Wog" Rice was seated in the stands scouting another player. He later said, "I saw this tall kid in short pants pick up a ball and start warming up. I knew it was Don and I had heard he was a pretty good pitcher. But I was amazed when he started firing the ball. In ten minutes I knew I had a red hot prospect if I could only sign him."

DICK O'CONNELL

Once upon a time, it was possible to get a job in baseball without a degree in sports management or business. In fact, one didn't even need a background in baseball.

Good thing, for if this had not been the case, Dick O'Connell would never have been general manager of the club. And that is a thought at which all Red Sox fans should shudder.

O'Connell was born and raised in Winthrop, Massachusetts. He attended Boston College and worked his way through school as a longshoreman. After graduation, he became a teacher and coach in New Hampshire.

Then World War II interfered. He joined the navy and went to work in naval intelligence in the Pacific.

While stationed in Pearl Harbor, O'Connell had the good fortune to meet fellow officer Jim Britt. In his civilian life, Britt worked as the radio play-by-play announcer for the Red Sox.

As they bid each other farewell — O'Connell thinking he'd probably never see Britt again — Britt told O'Connell that after the war he should look him up at Fenway Park. O'Connell filed the invitation away.

Upon returning stateside, O'Connell recalled Britt's invitation. He gave him a call, was mildly surprised that Britt still remembered who he was, and accepted an invitation to meet him at Fenway Park.

When he arrived in the front office to meet Britt, minor league director George "Specs" Toporcer was in Britt's company.

It just so happened that Toporcer, who lived on Long Island, was looking for an assistant to help him with the thousands of administrative tasks involved in operating the Sox' rapidly expanding network of minor league teams. The three men chatted, and Toporcer was impressed with O'Connell's education and distinguished military background. He offered him the job on the spot.

O'Connell accepted. Over the next two decades he slowly rose through the Red Sox organization. The fact that he didn't have a baseball background probably helped — he had no preconceived notions about what traits a player needed to have or how best to put together a ballclub. He learned by doing, and by the time he became general manager, his philosophy could be distilled into a single phrase, "Just get the best players, that's all, just get the best players." ⟲

Forty thousand dollars convinced Schwall to postpone his education and abandon the hardcourt for the diamond. By the middle of his rookie year he was an all-star, and he appeared at Fenway Park in the second of that season's two All-Star Games, where he gave up the NL's only run in a 1-1 tie halted by rain.

Unfortunately, neither Schwall, who won his first nine decisions at Fenway; Yaz, who hit almost .400 after a slow start; nor Schilling, who Bobby Doerr generously offered was already a better player than he had been in his prime, made much of a difference in the American League standings. While the Yankees and Detroit were on their way to winning more than one hundred games, the Red Sox tried not to lose a similar number.

They shared the same characteristic of so many other Red Sox teams, forging a decent record at Fenway Park while showing no ability whatsoever to win on the road.

On the final day of the season the club played a supporting role in a historic moment in baseball as they faced the Yankees and Roger Maris in the Bronx. Maris broke Babe Ruth's single-season home run mark of sixty with a fourth-inning home run into right field off Red Sox rookie Tracy Stallard. New York's 1-0 victory was their 109th of the year, while Boston finished sixth, 76-86, thirty-three games back.

In their first full season without Ted Williams since 1945, the club had improved by eleven games from the previous season. The main reason was pitching. Schwall won fifteen games and was named Rookie of the Year over Yaz, and Bill Monbouquette and Gene Conley won fourteen and eleven games prior to returning to their respective off-season jobs, Monbouquette as an aide in the Red Sox ticket office and Conley as the Celtics backup center. Schilling set a major league record, making only eight errors for the season, and the press noted he collected more hits than Mickey Mantle. Yastrzemski hit a solid .266 while leading the team in doubles and total bases.

Dick Radatz was nothing less than the best relief pitcher in baseball for four of his five seasons with the Red Sox. Pitching in 286 games for Boston he won 49 games while saving another 104. In one legendary appearance against the Yankees he preserved a victory for Earl Wilson by striking out Mickey Mantle, Roger Maris, and Elston Howard in ten pitches.

But without Williams, attendance dropped nearly 300,000 to 850,589. The club lost money for the twentieth time in Yawkey's twenty-eight years as owner.

And they were still so far behind the Yankees it wasn't funny. They made only one trade in the off-season, exchanging one lousy shortstop for another, getting Houston's Ed Bressoud for Don Buddin. Meanwhile, O'Connell continued to invest in the farm system.

That winter the club sent its top twenty-seven prospects, including several in their first season of professional baseball, to a special three-week pre–spring training camp in Ocala, Florida. Under the tutelage of Johnny Pesky, Ted Williams, and others, the players were put through the paces in two-a-day workouts.

Pitcher Earl Wilson, at age twenty-six already in his tenth season with the organization, returned from a stint in the marines knowing that his time was running out. The African-American rookie, known to teammates as "the King," responded and earned a spot in the rotation. Carl Yastrzemski was visibly more relaxed. When writers asked him about the dreaded "sophomore jinx" he laughed and referred to his rocky rookie season as having been the "freshman jinx." Ted Williams was one year removed, and expectations for Yaz became a bit more human in scale.

The Sox roster was dotted with twenty-one former collegians, a rarity even in the 1960s. Among them were Yastrzemski, Bressoud, Schwall, and a rookie named Dick Radatz. Most had either obtained degrees or continued working toward them in the off-season. Mechanical engineering major Chuck Schilling continued his studies even during the season. Yastrzemski later recalled that when the Sox went on the road, Schilling knew the location of most of the public libraries.

Yaz was the talk of camp as he went 11-for-22 in the final week of training. The Boston press also heaped praise on Schilling, whom they expected to become a star.

But the story of the season became non–roster invitee Dick Radatz. The hulking 6-foot-5, 240-pound plus righthander soon earned the appropriate nickname "the Monster." In his huge hand, a baseball looked like a tennis ball. Radatz didn't just throw fast, he threw a hard, heavy ball that overmatched hitters. The previous year in Seattle Pesky had converted him from a so-so starting pitcher into a reliever. In relief, he didn't have to pace himself, and in his first appearance in the role he had struck out eleven of the first twelve batters he faced.

He made his first major league appearance on Opening Day in Boston striking out Indian rookie Ty Cline and walking one in a scoreless ninth. A few days later in Baltimore he struck out the side, getting the Orioles' Jim Gentile, Jackie Brandt, and Brooks Robinson. Over his first four and two-thirds innings he struck out eight and walked two while yielding only one hit and no runs. He quickly became the most feared relief pitcher in the American League since Ryne Duren.

Good thing, for although Wilson emerged as an effective starter, the sophomore jinx and control problems beset Don Schwall. The words "control woes" served as the standing headline for most of his appearances throughout the season. By midseason he was the subject of trade rumors as Higgins grew impatient.

On May 2, 1962, the Red Sox celebrated the fiftieth anniversary of Fenway Park. Surviving members of Jake Stahl's 1912 world champions were in attendance, including Bill Carrigan, Joe Wood, Hugh Bedient, Larry Gardner, Steve Yerkes, Ray Collins, Olaf Henriksen, and Duffy Lewis. Nine-year-old Buck O'Brien of Dorchester, the grandson of the former Sox Opening Day pitcher of 1912, threw out the first ball.

Unfortunately, the presence of the former champs had no effect on the current edition of the Red Sox, who shared little with their predecessors. After almost reaching .500 in early July, the club soon dropped back.

But the season had its occasional highlights. On June 26 before a crowd of 14,002 Earl Wilson won his sixth game of the season and pitched a no-hitter against the California Angels. He even smashed a third-inning solo home run off Angel starter Bo Belinsky for the game's winning run. In the field he was helped by a superb Yastrzemski catch of a wall-scraping fly by shortstop Joe Koppe in the fifth and a spectacular catch on the dugout steps by Gold Glove third baseman Frank Malzone in the eighth. In a dramatic ninth inning, Ed Bressoud saved the no-hitter by making a great running catch of second baseman Billy Moran's soft liner, and outfielder Gary Geiger ended the game snaring Lee Thomas's 400-foot smash to center.

After the game, the first no-hitter by an African-American in American League history, Wilson humbly remarked, "Honestly, I didn't think I had stuff as good as in other games I haven't finished. This is the first complete game I've had this year. I never had any idea anything like that would ever happen to me. The Good Man was with me tonight."

Yawkey rewarded the pitcher with a one-thousand-dollar bonus and remarked, "I am more excited now than I was during Mel Parnell's no-hitter. Mel was on the way out and Wilson is just beginning to arrive at what could be a brilliant career."

On August 1 Bill Monbouquette duplicated Wilson's feat by hurling a no-hitter against the White Sox at Comiskey Park. The game's greatest drama came in the ninth. After striking out catcher Sherm Lollar to start the inning, Monbouquette had to retire two future Hall of Famers and contact hitters extraordinaire in Nellie Fox and Luis Aparicio to finish his effort. Not since 1916 had two Red Sox pitchers thrown a no-hitter in the same season.

But little else in 1962 resembled 1916. Apart from first baseman Pete Runnels's pursuit of his second American League batting crown and the pitching of Radatz, nothing of note took place on the field. Off the field, however, was another story. One incident epitomized the devil-may-care attitude of the country club.

After starter Gene Conley lost a particularly tough outing at Yankee Stadium, the air conditioning on the team bus broke and it got stuck in traffic as Conley, already hot under the collar because of the loss, cooled off by drinking a few beers.

Conley and Pumpsie Green got off the bus to go to the bathroom, the bus pulled away, and the two players decided to spend the night on the town before catching up with their teammates the next day in Washington.

One drink led to another. And another. Although Green soon came to his senses Conley ended up at Idlewild Airport. He'd bought a plane ticket to Jerusalem and was only stopped because he didn't have a passport.

Two days later Conley sheepishly returned to the team. Tom Yawkey, no stranger to the combination of alcohol and rash behavior, laughed off the incident, fining Conley fifteen hundred dollars but promising to rescind it if Conley pitched well the rest of the year. When Conley ended the season with a career-best 15-14 record, Yawkey handed him a check.

But as the team floundered on the field, they continued to make strides in the scouting and signing of players. Although they still overpaid and overtouted many prospects, dropping one hundred twenty-five thousand dollars for Boston English star Bob Guindon and heralding Pete Jernigan as the second coming of Jimmie Foxx, neither of whom did a thing, the system was beginning to produce.

The final months of the season were dominated by a deathwatch by the press over Higgins's career as manager. The club went backward and finished eighth, 76-84, their worst finish since 1932.

In October, Yawkey fired Higgins only to make him general manager, institutionalizing his stultifying presence. Johnny Pesky, who'd been successful at Seattle, was named manager. However, according to Harold Kaese, the move was made only after Boston had unsuccessfully sought permission from the Yankees to speak to Yogi Berra about the position.

Ignoring the stigma of being the team's second choice, Pesky told the press he planned to clear out the dead wood and remarked that he would command and not demand respect while working to improve the club's woeful performance. Meanwhile, the Sox made several moves to bolster their anemic offense. Unfortunately, Higgins showed the same acumen in the front office that he had on the field. First, he traded bonus babies Don Schwall and Jim Pagliaroni to the Pirates for slugging first baseman Dick Stuart. Then, he shipped Pete Runnels and his .326 average and ten homers to Houston for outfielder Roman Mejias and his twenty-four homers and .286 average. In another apparently minor deal, utilityman Dick Williams was acquired from Houston for Carroll Hardy, best known as the only player to pinch-hit for both Ted Williams and Yastrzemski. Williams, a prod-

uct of the Brooklyn Dodger organization, was eager to latch on to Boston in order to gain more playing and pension time.

The Boston press, bored to death, touted Higgins as the new Frank "Trader" Lane, in reference to the former Indian and White Sox general manager famed for his many deals. Hot Stove League talk also centered around an anticipated move of Yastrzemski to center field, with Roman Mejias taking over in left and veteran Lu Clinton in right.

Attendance had sagged again to only seven hundred fifty thousand. In an attempt to recoup their losses, the club added eight more night games to the 1963 schedule and agreed to lease Fenway Park to the fledgling Boston Patriots of the American Football League.

The Red Sox also expressed their interest in the plans of a stadium commission chaired by Patriots president Billy Sullivan. He wanted the city to build a new sixty-thousand-seat multipurpose stadium with a retractable roof in the South Station area. The fanciful design coincided with the "New Boston" economic development scheme proposed by the city, which was trying to shake itself out of economic doldrums through a series of redevelopment plans, best represented by the Prudential Center.

Tom Yawkey, who was already on record as blaming Fenway Park for his club's lack of success, commented, "I cannot say I will play in any such place until I see the plans for the stadium and know how the stadium will be financed and operated." Like other big league owners, Yawkey was intrigued but wanted the government to foot the bill. But like every other ballpark proposal of the last fifty years, it went nowhere.

The Red Sox weren't going anywhere either, although Pesky was initially successful. In the spring the enthusiastic new manager shook things up by

Earl Wilson made history on June 26, 1962, by becoming the first African-American to pitch an American League no-hitter. He also socked a home run to support his effort. From left he is congratulated by Jim Pagliaroni, catcher Bob Tillman, and Don Gile.

promoting rookie pitchers Dave Morehead and Jerry Stephenson. Both made the Opening Day roster, and Morehead, like Ted Williams a graduate of San Diego's Herbert Hoover High, rewarded Pesky's faith by becoming the first Red Sox rookie pitcher to hurl a shutout in his major league debut since Dave Ferriss in 1945. By June the team was still in contention and playing far better than anyone had expected. The Boston press, starved for a genuine contender, even began comparing them to the great Red Sox teams of the late 1940s. Carl Yastrzemski, after Pesky gave up on the center field experiment, blossomed as a hitter, and Bill Monbouquette led a pitching staff that, backed by Dick Radatz, was finally able to keep the team in the game.

Radatz was the key to the team's success. Teammate and former American League Fireman of the Year Mike Fornieles had helped him complete the transition to reliever. Radatz later said, "When I came up with Boston in 1962, Mike had led the team in saves for the previous two seasons and soon he became my biggest supporter. He gave me all the information I needed on American League hitters and gave me pointers as to how I should pitch to them. He basically set me up to be his successor."

In 1963 Red Sox fans prayed for a late-inning lead, which led to the inevitable entrance of the man they called "Monster." By midseason Radatz was clearly the best reliever in baseball and one of the most dynamic performers in the history of Fenway Park. At times he was simply unhittable.

One memorable performance took place in a 1963 game against the Yankees. Starter Earl Wilson made it into the ninth inning then gave up a hit and two walks to load the bases with no outs. Pesky asked Wilson if he could continue. He said he could, then, as the manager turned back to the dugout, Wilson reconsidered and called out, "Is the big guy ready?" Pesky stopped and waved for Radatz.

Once Radatz reached the mound he quipped to Wilson, "Go crack me open a beer, I'll only be a minute." Then he realized that the next three New York hitters were Mickey Mantle, Roger Maris, and Elston Howard, all of whom had won the MVP award. No big deal. As Radatz remembers, "I struck out Mantle, Maris and Howard on ten pitches. And

that was the day I started my ritual of throwing my hands over my head for a victory or save. I was really thrilled; the crowd came onto the field like it was a World Series. It was my biggest thrill in the majors and you'd better believe Earl was there to greet me at the clubhouse door with my beer."

Before long, Boston viewed a Radatz save as certain as death and taxes. And unlike today's "closer," who usually pitches only the final inning, Radatz was as likely to enter the game in the fifth or sixth inning, with men on base, as he was in the ninth. He thrived in the role and told reporters, "I relish pressure, I live for it."

If Radatz represented the high point of the season, self-centered Dick Stuart represented the opposite. Teammate and future Red Sox manager Dick Williams later said of Stuart, "He was the poorest excuse for a caring baseball player I've ever seen." He often recalled one incident in which Stuart, after being hit with a pitch with the bases loaded, successfully argued to the umpire that he hadn't been struck by the ball so that he could stay at the plate and hit. Stuart then struck out.

The vain and handsome first baseman quickly became something of a Red Sox legend, but did little to help the team win. He cared only about hitting home runs and his own statistics, a common attitude on the country club Red Sox. His atrocious fielding (Stuart made fifty-three errors for Boston in 1963 and 1964) earned him the derisive nickname of "Dr. Strangeglove." Minor league manager Clyde King of the Hollywood Stars once told him, "You're losing more ballgames through the middle of your legs than you're winning with your bat," and Johnny Pesky similarly recalls, "He hit forty-two home runs for me one year, but he let in sixty-two." Yet at the same time he was personally likable, while his outrageous behavior made him popular with fans. He even had his own television program on WBZ.

Stuart's selfishness undermined Pesky's efforts to change the team's attitude. Higgins resented Pesky, and more than a few writers speculated that he'd brought Stuart to Boston simply to aggravate the new manager. And in early summer, after a fine start, the club went into a tailspin that coincided with trouble caused by Stuart. They never recovered.

The arrogant and boorish Stuart constantly chided Pesky, mostly over petty matters. Pesky, ever the gentleman, took it. The team soon grew accustomed to the slugger berating the manager about everything from his wardrobe to game strategy. Once, when Pesky watched Stuart ignore three straight bunt signals and strike out, Pesky pulled him aside in the dugout and lambasted him, "You big son of a bitch, I put the bunt sign on three times and you disregarded it. It's going to cost you."

Stuart's reply, made loud enough for all to hear, was, "I get paid to do one thing for this ball club and I do it very well, and that is to hit the ball out of the ballpark. Don't you ever give me a bunt sign as long as you live." When Pesky benched him, Stuart asked out loud, "What right do you have to bench someone making more than you?"

Although Pesky recalls that he "liked Dick Stuart. I kept playing him every day. He hit a lot of home runs for me," and that the trouble between the two men has since been overstated, Stuart was hard to control. Fines had no effect on him. The press focused on the battle between the manager and the player, turning it into a very public and demeaning battle of will and wit. The front office failed to back Pesky and temper the self-proclaimed star, and over the course of the season Pesky's control of the club eroded. The inmates ran the asylum back into the second division. After July 23 they went 25-43 and tumbled from second to seventh place.

The Red Sox and Twins ended the season at Fenway Park. Minnesota's Harmon Killebrew and Stuart were tied for the league lead with forty home runs. With neither club in contention for the pennant, the battle for the home run title was the focal point of the series.

Killebrew socked five home runs to Stuart's two to win the crown. Afterward, the selfish Red Sox star made the most telling remark of his career, saying, "Hell, Killebrew had a distinct advantage. If I could have hit against our pitching staff, I'd have hit ten."

Although Stuart became the first batter ever to

Little did Red Sox manager Johnny Pesky know that within two seasons his job would be the equivalent of an exploding cigar.

reach the 100 RBI mark in both leagues and led the Sox with 118 RBIs to go along with his forty-two home runs, he also set a team record by striking out 144 times. Yastrzemski won the batting title with an average of .321, Bill Monbouquette won twenty games, and Dick Radatz had a role in forty of the team's seventy-six wins with a sensational 15-6 record to accompany his twenty-five saves and 1.97 ERA.

But help was on the way. Boston fans began reading of the exploits of a promising farmhand named Tony Conigliaro. The East Boston native and graduate of St. Mary's High of Lynn had signed with the Red Sox the previous September, and in 1963 he hit .363 with twenty-four homers and seventy-four RBIs in only eighty-three games in Single A ball. His performance prompted Pesky, a neighbor of the Conigliaro family in suburban Swampscott, to invite the eighteen-year-old phenom to spring training in 1964.

When they opened camp the Red Sox made a con-

The Dead Zone

by Charles P. Pierce

"You can't spend what you ain't got
You can't lose what you never had."

— McKinley Morganfield, American philosopher

Let me explain to you how I first heard the word, which happens to be the gold standard for words that good little Irish-Catholic lads are not supposed to hear from their beloved and respected elders. It is a word equally functional as verb or as noun. It is a word superbly functional in an adjectival way — since 1978, anyway — as Bucky Dent's middle name. Are we clear yet? Good. The editor is immeasurably happy that we are.

Anyway, it was a clear August Sunday in the summer of 1961, which was a good year for neither summit conferences nor the Boston Red Sox, who ended the year at 76-86, a robust thirty-three games behind the New York Yankees, who probably looked upon their erstwhile blood rivals the way that Alan Shepard had looked back at Florida earlier that year.

I was seven, and I was watching the Sox game with my grandfather, a good old Worcester signpainting man named Charlie Gibbons. He was the Sox fan in the family, a staunch Ted Williams supporter who hated most sportswriters for what "that Egan" did to his hero. (He died long before I made my unfortunate career choice. Had he lived, he'd have preferred that I joined the Weather Underground.) The Sunday games were our ritual. I was one

of his two companions. The other was a large green bottle of Narragansett Lager Beer.

(I watched mainly for the Narragansett commercials: wonderfully dry cartoons scripted by Elaine May and Mike Nichols. If you want to test someone's bona fides as a longtime Sox fan, don't ask them about Harry Frazee, or Country Slaughter, or all the rest of it. Ask them if they remember — Hi, Neighbor! — The Parakeet Bar.)

On this particular Sunday, the Sox were losing to some equally incompetent outpost of the American League, and someone hit an easy grounder toward Frank Malzone at third base. Malzone booted the ball, which didn't happen often. (Hey, the man made a couple of All-Star teams.) My grandfather's fist dented the vinyl arm of his recliner.

"MALZONE!" he roared. "You dumb, stupid . . ."

And then, the word.

Now, my grandmother was a stiff and proper sort but, until that moment, I never realized the kind of lateral movement the old girl had. I was quickly hustled out into the mellower precincts of the backyard. I concluded that this was a very important word, indeed. That night, over dinner, my grandfather imparted to me the wisdom he had gleaned from hundreds of moments just like the one that afternoon.

"Charlie," he said to me, "remember this. The Red Sox will always stink. Always."

⊘ ⊘ ⊘

I came of age as a Red Sox fan in the years between 1961 and 1967, when I went from seven to thirteen. This being a baseball book, the essential case must be made with the numbers, so here they are: during those years, the Red Sox were a combined 438-535. They finished, on average, twenty-eight games behind the American League champions, which generally were the New York Yankees, a team that seemed to have the same relationship with the Red Sox as I had with, say, John XXIII, to wit, we did the same things of a Sunday, but there was a great distance between how we did them.

The Red Sox stink. The Red Sox will always stink.

It was a cooler, simpler time. It is said that all things Red Sox changed in 1967, that it was the beginning of an era. It was the dawning of a Golden Age of nonsense, I can tell you that: an age of pseudo-Calvinist baseball apocrypha, trafficked in by slumming Harvard professors, meandering poets, historians with better things to do, and sportswriters trolling for cheap columns. It was a time in which was professed a different and more complex faith:

The Red Sox will blow it. The Red Sox will always blow it.

Consider the difference — the utter, cosmic distinction between "The Red Sox will always stink" and "The Red Sox will always blow it." The former is a purely fatalistic faith, a second cousin to Flannery O'Connor's "Church of Truth Without Christ — where the lame don't walk, the blind don't see, and what's dead, stays that way." It is a peaceful faith, with little expectation beyond the summer sunshine, and no earthly reward save the occasional visiting superstar. It is a faith unshackled from the past and unburdened by the future.

My grandfather's memories stretched warmly all the way back to Bill Carrigan and the only real dynasty that the Red Sox ever had. Yet, in all the time that I watched games with him, on all those Sundays, not once did he mention the events of 1946, or of 1949. No word at all about Pesky holding the ball, or about Joe McCarthy's drunken bungling. I didn't know anything about Denny Galehouse until I was nearly thirty.

There was never any talk about curses, or black clouds, or Nathaniel Hawthorne, no discussion of Athens and Sparta — although I was baffled to hear some of the guys at the signpainting company discussing "Trojans" one afternoon — an earnest disquisition that I quickly realized summoned a rather different reference from classical antiquity. The ballpark was a ballpark was a ballpark. Shrines were in Fatima — or, more prosaically, at the Kelley Square Yacht Club in the Hotel Vernon down at the head of Millbury Street in Kelley Square.

No. The Red Sox stink. The Red Sox will always stink.

And it wasn't as though there wasn't anything to talk about. Pumpsie Green and Gene Conley got drunk and tried to fly to Israel, for pity's sake. (I can

say with some pride that I saw Conley play two of the three sports he was said to be good at. The third one was rather more private, and I'm just as glad for that.) The team hired Mike Higgins and Billy Herman twice each, for pity's sake, which was like handing Captain Joe Hazlewood another boat.

There was "the country club" to argue about. Even in the days before free agency and arbitration, there was a constant drumbeat that Tom Yawkey "coddled" his men to the detriment of his manager. There was the cartoon

---

"The Red Sox will always blow it" is a purely fatalistic faith . . . a peaceful faith, with little expectation beyond the summer sunshine.

---

that was Dick Stuart, comic for a while, but damned eternally for the cardinal crime of being nasty to Johnny Pesky. (I personally would gladly replace, say, Lust as one of the Seven Deadly Sins in favor of Being Nasty To Johnny Pesky.) There was the exploding, pinwheeling promise of Tony Conigliaro.

There was always a great new kid shortstop, somewhere out there in the dim minors. (God love him, but Rico Petrocelli was the first one who actually turned out to be great, and Billy Herman nearly ruined him.) There was always something stirring in Louisville or Toronto. Dick Radatz coming out of the bullpen was a moment for sure

and, one rainy Monday in the cafeteria at Denholm's downtown, I got to shake hands with that promising Yastrzemski kid, whom my grandfather didn't trust, mostly because he wasn't Williams. Compared to my grandfather and Ted, Hemingway's fisherman was Bill on the Car Phone in relation to Joe DiMaggio.

Nevertheless, there were some tough moments. I distinctly remember having to choose to be either Eddie Bressoud or Jim Gosger in a backyard home run derby game. I wondered how the Yankee fans did it. ("Okay, so you be Maris today.") The first game I attended — and, yes, I went with my father — was in 1965, the apotheosis season of my Red Sox youth, in which the team finished a spectacularly bad 62-100 and forty games behind the Minnesota Twins. It was a dank, rainy day. Gosger hit a triple, and the team lost anyway. My father and I bonded that day in our mutual desire to get out of the clammy old place as fast as we could.

Then, there was the day on which I insisted on being Earl Wilson when I pitched, which caused some consternation, because Earl was, you know, a colored player. In fact, the curse of these particular Red Sox years was not the imaginary Curse of the Bambino but, rather, the very real Curse of Tom Yawkey — a.k.a the Curse of Jackie Robinson — which also had very much to do with the continued employment of the horror that was Pinky Higgins, who died in prison after drunkenly plowing his car into a Louisiana chain gang.

Sometimes, the One Great Scorer pays close attention to the work.

☙ ☙ ☙

My grandfather died in the early spring of 1967. He collapsed in his car outside the sign company. He missed the whole damn thing: Yaz's big year, Billy Rohr, Tartabull and Howard and Ken Berry, Lonborg's Cy Young, the two games against the Twins, the wonderful series against the Cardinals, the introduction of all of us to the genius of Bob Gibson, the big loss in the seventh game. All of it, and he wasn't there.

We often said among ourselves what a shame it was, after all those 'Gansetts on all those Sundays in all those Augusts, that he didn't get the chance to watch that utterly riveting drama unfold. As I grew older and less patient with the world, however, I noted how much he would've scoffed at what came later. He was a man who'd made his own business. He would've had no truck with curses or doom or sweetie-pie media posturing for the local yokels. He would not have blamed Pesky for Buckner, or Galehouse for Bucky Dent, or Joe McCarthy for Larry Barnett. Each event would have been stark and primal — existing on its own, floating free, worthy of its own special curse word. What was dead would stay that way.

He never saw '67. I think he died keeping the faith.

Charles P. Pierce is a writer-at-large for *Esquire* magazine, a regular contributor to National Public Radio, and most recently the author of *Hard to Forget: An Alzheimer's Story.*

scious decision to go with younger players, putting four high-priced, first-year pros on their forty-man roster: Conigliaro, Dave Gray, Pete Charton, and Tony Horton. Of the four, only one could be sent back to the minors without clearing waivers. Ted Williams thought Horton was the best hitting prospect he had seen in years. Pesky hoped the teenager could replace Dick Stuart.

But Conigliaro proved to be the best of the bunch, and Pesky agonized over whether to take the teenager north to Boston. On March 22 against Cleveland Conigliaro socked a home run some 450 feet over a 30-foot center-field fence. The Boston press loved him and started calling him simply "Tony C." Even Ted Williams gave the young slugger an understated, rare compliment when, after watching him take batting practice, he told him simply, "Don't change."

In a whirlwind apprenticeship, Sox brass took more than just a passing look at their native son. At one point that spring he played thirty-five innings in twenty-four hours as they pondered his future.

He was rewarded for his efforts with a spot in the starting lineup, the most prominent of a cadre of young players on whom the team was basing its future. Led by the veteran Yastrzemski, the group also included Dalton Jones, Rico Petrocelli, Tony Horton, Dave Morehead, and Russ Gibson.

The Sox were scheduled to open the season on April 15 in New York. It rained. Although the game was canceled, when the weather cleared the Sox scheduled a workout. Conigliaro stayed in bed and slept. He arrived at Yankee Stadium forty-five minutes late.

"I ought to be fined $1000," Conigliaro blurted to the writers. "I ought to be suspended." An understanding Johnny Pesky let him off with a stern warning and a ten-dollar fine. "What a way to start my career," moaned Conigliaro. "I can hear my kids asking me someday, 'What did you do your first day in the big leagues, Daddy?' And I'll say, 'I slept.'" He was just a rookie, but he was already Tony C. — talented, endearing, and a favorite of the fans.

Dick Stuart was the poster child for the country club–era Red Sox. His preoccupation with his statistics was legendary, but in two seasons with the Red Sox he socked seventy-five home runs.

In his first game he singled against future Hall of Famer Whitey Ford, then impetuously accused the Yankee pitcher of throwing a spitter. Upon his return to Boston he was greeted with his photo in the *Boston Herald* above the prophetic headline "Dream Comes True."

Boston's April 17 home opener was a benefit for the newly established John F. Kennedy Memorial Library. Among the 20,123 fans in attendance were most of the Kennedy clan, including Ambassador Joseph P. Kennedy, Bobby Kennedy, Jackie Kennedy, and John F. Kennedy Jr.

Conigliaro, batting in the second inning for the first time ever at Fenway Park, belted White Sox pitcher Joel Horlen's first pitch onto Lansdowne Street. On WHDH-TV Curt Gowdy enthusiastically commented, "Look at that boy. He was in high school a year ago, and has now hit a home run in his first Fenway Park at bat!"

Halfway between first and second, Tony C. broke out in a smile and shook his head in wonder, then bounded home to the embrace of his teammates. Had they been able to reach him the fans would have done much the same.

The remainder of the 1964 season was a dream for Tony C. By June he was receiving two hundred letters a week, mostly from young women. The *Globe*'s Harold Kaese started comparing Tony C.'s rookie year with Ted Williams's and in July wrote a feature story headlined "Will Conig Follow Ruth, Speaker to Hall of Fame?" Of all the current Red Sox, Kaese believed Tony C. was most likely to make it to Cooperstown. It was a heady time for the nineteen-year-old, who lived in a penthouse apartment from which he could look down into Fenway Park.

Usually, Tony C. kept his head, but he was still just a kid. He missed curfew in July and was fined two hundred fifty dollars by Pesky, who commented, "He doesn't do anything wrong — he just wants to stay up all night and sleep all day." Conigliaro proceeded to homer the next day before being hit on the arm by a pitch and being sidelined until September. The injury cost him a shot at several rookie records, but he still made the All-Rookie team.

The rest of the Red Sox also did more than their share at the plate, leading the AL with a .258 batting average and 253 doubles. Their 186 homers set a franchise season record and was second only to the Twins. Yet despite their offensive firepower the team was rife was dissent and once again featured extraordinarily inept pitching, save for the valiant effort of Dick Radatz. Pesky recalls simply, "We just didn't have the pitching. Radatz saved a boatload of games for us." Indeed, the reliever had one of the best seasons a relief pitcher has ever had, leading the league with twenty-nine saves and the Red Sox with sixteen victories while appearing in seventy-nine games and throwing 157 innings.

At one point in midseason Pesky convinced him to

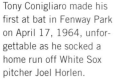

Tony Conigliaro made his first at bat in Fenway Park on April 17, 1964, unforgettable as he socked a home run off White Sox pitcher Joel Horlen.

take a day off. Radatz reluctantly agreed but couldn't resist watching the game on television. As he recently recalled, "Finally I just couldn't stand it. I knew they needed me so I climbed in my car and drove the ten miles to Fenway as fast as I could. Pesky did a double take when he saw me enter the dugout and laughed when he sent me to the bullpen. I ended up saving the game I had started watching on my living room sofa."

He was one of the few bright spots in a season in which Pesky lost all command. Stuart was a continuing problem, but even Carl Yastrzemski grew disenchanted with the manager when Pesky benched

Chuck Schilling. The relationship wasn't helped when Boston writers pointed out that Pesky's .307 lifetime batting average was better than Yaz's.

With two games to go in the season, Pinky Higgins embarrassed Pesky by firing him and replacing him with coach Billy Herman. It was a cruel way to get rid of a Boston baseball legend. The country club had won the day.

Pesky wasn't the problem. The Red Sox were even worse under the laissez faire leadership of Herman. He preferred talking golf to baseball and carried his clubs with him throughout the 1965 season.

In an attempt to shore up the pitching staff, Higgins traded Dick Stuart to the Phillies for starter Den-

nis Bennett. But Higgins was hoodwinked. He didn't know that Bennett had just undergone shoulder surgery. He spent most of the season on the disabled list while Stuart hit twenty-eight home runs in Philadelphia. Conigliaro also proved fragile as he was disabled for the fourth time in three years when he suffered a hairline fracture of the left wrist after being hit by a pitch.

On September 16, with the Red Sox battling Kansas City for last place, pitcher Dave Morehead, before a paying crowd of only 1,247 at Fenway Park, threw a no-hitter against Cleveland. But Boston's front office woes overshadowed his performance. Last place was something even Tom Yawkey couldn't

THE LIMITED MAN

Tony Conigliaro was mod before anyone in Boston knew what mod was, a teen idol in Boston and, for a time, easily the most popular player the Red Sox have ever had. And he was just a teenager equal to any other, with more national acclaim.

After his rookie season in 1964, Tony C. reaped the benefits of being young, handsome, nineteen, and famous in great, grand gulps. "The girls naturally liked him," recalls Rico Petrocelli. "Tony had his pick of beautiful girls."

One night in the off-season at a Framingham nightclub, Conigliaro was recognized and invited on stage. He surprised the crowd by joining the band and singing. He surprised the band by being pretty good. Tony wasn't just a handsome guy who could hit; Tony C. could *croon*.

Talent scouts were scouring the country for such teen idol talent. Word of Tony C.'s vocal capabilities spread, and within a few weeks he had signed with Ed Penney, the agent who also represented Nat King Cole and Burl Ives. Penney had him in the studio within the month.

Tony C.'s first single was released on January 19, 1965. Demonstrating a singing style he described as "the Beatles with a crewcut," the A-side featured a baseball-inspired pop tune aptly entitled "Playing the Field," while on the B-side was the ballad "Why Can't They Understand."

Within a month the record was number fourteen in Boston and had sold fourteen thousand copies. RCA signed him to a four-year contract worth a potential one hundred thousand dollars.

But baseball got in the way. Tony C. wasn't able to release his second single until 1966, the novelty hit "Little Red Scooter," backed by "I Can't Get Over You." When the record came out Tony C. proudly arrived at the Red Sox clubhouse early and placed a copy in each locker.

As Petrocelli recalls, "When he went outside we all got together and put the records back in his locker, like we didn't want them." Tony C. laughed.

Tony C. tried to go national, even appearing on *The Merv Griffin Show* and as an extra in the Otto Preminger film *The Cardinal,* but his talents were more appropriate to the local stage. He was born to play Fenway Park.

One month before he was beaned by Jack Hamilton, on July 17, 1967, Tony C. released his third and final single. The B-side was a Dixieland tune called "Please Play Our Song."

But he was prouder of the A-side, a heartfelt, upbeat tune by Billy Carr that Tony C. told the press was "his song," entitled "Limited Man." The title and refrain of the song would prove strangely prophetic:

> I cannot waste my time that way
> 'Cause life doesn't have a limit.
> I cannot spend my limited life
> Living like a limited man.

But on August 18, 1967, a pitch crashed into his face, changing his life forever. Tony C. would spend the rest of his life a limited man. ⊘

bear, and he had to fire somebody. In what would later prove to be the best decision of his forty-three-year tenure as owner, Yawkey reluctantly fired Higgins and allowed Dick O'Connell to replace him.

Higgins had held the franchise hostage for over a decade as the status quo took root and the team's pennant prospects annually died on the vine. As both manager and general manager Higgins had always taken the path of least resistance. He rarely took chances, was more concerned with protecting his back than with the final standings, and made sure he never did anything to harm his cozy relationship with Tom Yawkey. His reluctance to either sign or trade for African-American players had left the Red Sox at an incredible disadvantage. That fact alone had made their success virtually impossible.

Dick O'Connell was different. As Pesky recalls, "He turned it around. He brought in baseball people." O'Connell would soon prove to be a huge improvement on Higgins and Boston's best general manager since Ed Barrow.

The glow of Morehead's masterpiece quickly faded, and the team limped into the final day of the season needing to win their final game in order to avoid becoming the first team of the Yawkey era to lose 100 games.

Only 487 fans bothered to turn out that day in Fenway Park. During the game, the players could follow conversations in the stands. Yankee ace Whitey Ford won an 11-5 decision over Arnie Early to deliver loss 100. The country club had collapsed, and there was no longer any waiting list for membership. Not even Yawkey's generous salary scale was enough to make Boston attractive anymore.

Although Boston's still-potent offense smacked a league-best 165 home runs, the pitching had been horrendous. Dave Morehead and Bill Monbouquette both lost eighteen games, and Earl Wilson led the staff with a 13-14 mark. Even Dick Radatz slipped to twenty-two saves and a 9-11 record.

Billy Herman earned a stay of execution by keeping on the good side of Carl Yastrzemski and agreeing to continue the youth program that had now been in effect for several seasons. But Herman also fancied himself a general manager. Early in the 1966 season, he talked trade with Yankee manager Ralph Houk and arranged to send Yastrzemski to the Yankees for slumping 1962 Rookie of the Year Tom Tresh and weak-hitting shortstop Phil Linz. When Herman smugly told O'Connell about the deal and told him it was all set, O'Connell called it off.

Under O'Connell, the team moved training camp from Arizona to Winter Haven, Florida. The transfer back to the Eastern time zone allowed writers to meet their deadlines and New England snowbirds a chance to follow the team while vacationing. Herman went along with plans to replace aging Ed Bressoud with Rico Petrocelli at shortstop and promoted overmatched rookie righthander Jim Lonborg to the big leagues. Other rookies included George Scott, Joe Foy, and Jose Santiago.

When spring training began in 1966, Carl Yastrzemski was elected team captain, the club's first since Bobby Doerr had held the post twenty years earlier. The reluctant leader was thus placed in a position in which his close relationship with Tom Yawkey, long rumored to be a factor in several key hirings and firings, was clearly defined. As captain, Yastrzemski was responsible for airing any player gripes or grievances with management. To Yawkey, Yaz filled the role that Ted Williams once had. Yawkey was always available to his resident superstar and when he came to the clubhouse visited his locker before talking with any other player.

Teammates continually pestered their new captain to intercede on their behalf with the owner, particularly in regard to loans against salary. They knew Yawkey was a soft touch and would sometimes simply advance the money and never ask for repayment. Yastrzemski came to hate his role.

Dick O'Connell had nothing to lose by promoting the players developed in Neil Mahoney's farm system, and for the first time in team history a large percentage of the major league roster was made up of African-American ballplayers. Among them were Joe Foy, *The Sporting News* reigning Minor League Player of the Year; George Scott; outfielder Reggie Smith, who had been drafted as a minor leaguer from the Twins organization; George Smith; John Wyatt; Lenny Green; Jose Santiago; Jose Tartabull; and Joe Christopher. O'Connell said, "I don't care what color a player is as long as he can play . . . if he is any good

Righthander Dave Morehead pitched a near-perfect 2-0 no-hitter against the Cleveland Indians on September 16, 1965. On that same day the Red Sox named Dick O'Connell as general manager.

I want to sign him." While those words had long been mouthed by Boston's front office, O'Connell meant it and backed it up with action.

With a roster that averaged only twenty-five years old, O'Connell elected to lose for a season with developing players rather than trot out the same tired, jaded veterans whose selfishness defined the country club. The 1966 Red Sox were more like a minor league club, a team comprised of players who had shared long bus rides in the minors for years prior to arriving in Boston. Their budding talents and camaraderie helped the franchise shed its tired image. The Summer of Love was on the horizon, and America was getting younger. So were the Red Sox.

George Scott, a free-swinging, slick-fielding first baseman electrified the team with ten homers in his first seventy-nine at bats. By mid-June he was tied for the league lead before finishing with twenty-seven. Foy played 151 games at third and hit a respectable .262.

Conigliaro led the league with thirty-two homers despite playing in only 138 games. And Yastrzemski batted .312 and just missed overtaking Tony Oliva for the batting championship despite missing twenty-nine games because of broken ribs and a lacerated kidney suffered in a collision with Jake Wood of the Tigers.

But despite the infusion of young talent, pitching was again the Achilles' heel of the team. Dick Radatz crashed to earth with arm trouble then was traded to Cleveland in June for pitchers Lee Stange and Don McMahon. Dennis Bennett underwent a shoulder operation while Dave Morehead failed to win a game after April. Only Jim Lonborg and Jose Santiago won ten or more games. Under the tutelage of pitching coach Sal "the Barber" Maglie, both were learning the fine art of pitching inside, a most valuable skill at Fenway Park, where righthanded hitters like Tony C. leaned over the plate and tried to jerk the ball over the wall.

On September 8 the team fell into last place. This gave O'Connell, who wanted his own manager anyway, an excuse to fire Herman. Pete Runnels served out the season as interim manager. The club broke even over its last sixteen games, edging out the deteriorating Yankees for ninth place by one-half game. It was a hollow victory, but for the first time since 1948 the team finished ahead of the Yankees.

In late September, after an organizational banquet at Jimmy's Harborside restaurant, O'Connell drove Triple A Toronto manager Dick Williams, fresh off winning the International League postseason playoffs, back to his hotel.

Suddenly, O'Connell pulled his car off the road, turned to Williams, and offered the thirty-five-year-old former player a one-year contract at twenty-five thousand dollars as the Red Sox' new manager. Williams immediately accepted. O'Connell then turned the car around and brought Williams to his Belmont home. Over drinks the two men excitedly discussed their plans for the future, and each discovered he had an ally in the other. By the time Dick Williams left, he'd already received a ten-thousand-dollar raise.

The first thing he did was take out a three-year lease on an expensive furnished apartment he couldn't afford. He did so on purpose, knowing that if he didn't win, he'd be stuck with the debt.

That's just the way he wanted it. The country club Red Sox had never felt any pressure to win, and Williams instinctively knew that that had been a big part of the club's problem. He wasn't about to risk succumbing to their organizational lethargy. By signing the lease, he increased the pressure on himself. Now there was something at stake in every inning of every game he managed. When he later told the press, "I managed each game like it was the World Series because I didn't want my sofa repossessed," he wasn't kidding.

The country club was closed. A ballclub no one had cared about without Ted Williams would soon discover that another man named Williams, in a much shorter time than anyone ever thought possible, could make the Red Sox matter again.

INCREDIBLY BEAUTIFUL PEOPLE

1967

Dick Williams didn't mess around. "This club has become a cruise ship overrun with captains and players thinking they are captain. The cruise is over and you don't need a captain anymore," he told the players. "You have a new boss now — me. Eliminating the club captaincy is my way of letting you know that things will be done one way . . . My way." This was how spring training before the 1967 season began.

Dick Williams stripped Sox captain Carl Yastrzemski of his title and assumed total command. And the Red Sox became a different team.

Although most would later view the rebirth of the Red Sox in 1967 as some kind of miracle, the renaissance of the franchise was more the product of a peculiar set of circumstances that landed the team in the hands of the right man at the right time. The end result was perhaps the most exciting Red Sox season in history, one that started slowly then built before finally exploding like a Roman candle that bathed Sox fans in a lasting glow.

The 1967 season saved the Sox. Had it never happened, it is not inconceivable to think that within a few seasons the Red Sox may well have called some other city home. Instead, fathers started telling sons about Cronin, Foxx, and Grove. Grandfathers recalled Carrigan, Speaker, and Ruth, and a whole new generation of fans discovered the Red Sox. The storied past stirred to life.

It all started with Tom Yawkey. He'd lost interest, stopped drinking, and was resigned to Boston's second-division status. He and Jean spent most of their time in South Carolina living on his estate.

Yawkey's abject neglect left the club almost entirely in Dick O'Connell's hands, leaving him free to hire Williams and make other moves without interference or worrying

Red Sox righthander Jim Lonborg won his twenty-second game on the final day of the season to cap the Impossible Dream by the Red Sox. He is shown engulfed by the mob that descended on the Fenway diamond following the game.

about offending any of Yawkey's cronies. That was the best thing that could have happened. In 1967, Yawkey didn't even speak to Williams until July. And under O'Connell and Neil Mahoney, Boston's increasingly colorblind farm system had never been more productive. With players like Yastrzemski and Lonborg to build around, the Sox were already getting better.

What *was* a miracle was that Williams had been hired in the first place. In 1964 he was going nowhere as player-coach for the Red Sox' Triple A club in Seattle when the club announced the affiliate would move to Toronto in 1965. Manager Edo Vanni didn't want to go.

Williams knew the club and had impressed O'Connell with his no-nonsense style. He accepted the club's offer to become manager at nine thousand dollars a year because he knew it was his only chance to return to the big leagues. He had to win — he needed the money — and the minor league club responded to his urgent, take-charge attitude.

His managerial philosophy was simple and unyielding. "I give 100 percent because I hate losing," he explained later. "And for those players who treat losing and failure lightly I will give them something else to hate — ME. I try to make some players win just to show me up." That approach helped the Maple Leafs win two consecutive IL championships.

Williams cleaned house that spring. Every man on the roster would have to prove he belonged. Yaz was more than willing to give up the captaincy he'd never really wanted. He'd had it with being the only star on a team of losers.

Williams had learned the game in the Dodger organization, and he schooled the Red Sox in the Dodger method, focusing on the incessant repetition of fundamentals. He knew the team had talent. His job was to turn that into wins and losses.

Williams took no one and no thing for granted, and some of what he did was revolutionary. In between throwing and fielding drills, pitchers had traditionally hung around, running sprints and shagging flies. Williams thought that was a waste. To get them in shape and build camaraderie, he had them play volleyball. The pitchers loved it, but old-timers were aghast.

Ted Williams, in camp as a roving batting instructor, kept breaking up the games to regale the pitchers with his complicated theories on hitting. Dick Williams asked Ted to stop several times, but was ignored. Then Dick Williams *ordered* Ted to stop.

No one with the Red Sox had ever *ordered* Ted Williams to do much of anything. Miffed, the greatest hitter who ever lived stomped off, packed his bags, and was overheard sputtering, "Volleyball, what is this game coming to?" He wasn't heard from again for the rest of the season. But Dick Williams had made his point.

As Opening Day approached, veterans fell to the wayside as Williams stuck with the rookies and second-year players he knew from Toronto. With his crewcut and sharp tongue, Williams looked like a marine drill sergeant. He wasn't above reminding his young charges that no matter how hard camp was, it was better than being in Vietnam. But the Vietnam War was merely an irritant to the players. Many avoided combat by joining the reserves.

Although Williams made an impression during training camp, outside observers looked at the Red Sox and saw only more of the same. Oddsmaker Jimmy "the Greek" Snyder made the defending ninth-place club 100-to-1 underdogs.

On the eve of the home opener all Williams would say was, "We'll win more than we'll lose." Most writers covering the club had heard that before and looked forward to reminding the rookie manager of his claim at the end of the season, if he lasted that long.

Opening Day in Boston was more sad than celebratory. The Red Sox had no constituency, and only 8,324 fans turned out at Fenway Park. Fans of the postwar Sox were now middle-aged or older and living in the suburbs, while younger fans and the thousands of students who lived in town knew the club only through their recent reputation as losers.

The 1967 Red Sox were the youngest team in baseball and one of the youngest ever. Except for Jose Tartabull and Yaz, who were twenty-eight and twenty-seven, every player in the lineup was twenty-five or younger. Lonborg beat the White Sox 5-4 as shortstop Rico Petrocelli went 3-for-3 and cracked a three-run homer, but the victory drew a yawn.

Boston lost the next day, 8-5, making three errors and playing more to their accustomed style, then went to New York for the Yankees' home opener on April 14. On a cold and cloudy afternoon rookie southpaw Bill Rohr made his major league debut opposite future Hall of Famer Whitey Ford.

Rohr served notice that this season would be different. With fellow rookie Russ Gibson behind the plate, he dazzled the crowd of 14,375, including Jackie Kennedy and her six-year-old son John. Rookie Reggie Smith hit a leadoff home run — his first — to put Rohr ahead, and he gained confidence with every hitter he retired.

His hat fell off on nearly every pitch, but he kept the Yankees off balance. By midgame the Red Sox bench turned quiet as his teammates realized Rohr was hurling a no-hitter.

In the sixth inning New York's Bill Robinson lined a ball off Rohr's shin, but third baseman Joe Foy picked it up and threw Robinson out. Following a lengthy visit by trainer Buddy LeRoux, Rohr regained his composure and continued to set the Yankees down. Even New York fans started to cheer for him.

Yankee left fielder Tom Tresh nailed the first pitch of the ninth inning, and catcher Russ Gibson cursed as it left the bat. "There was no way that ball was going to be caught," Gibson later recalled. "All I could think was 'There goes the no-hitter.'" But Yaz got a great jump on the ball and made a spectacular diving catch. Then Joe Pepitone lifted a lazy fly to Conigliaro in right for the second out.

With one out to go, Dick Williams hurried to the mound and reminded Rohr that Yankee batter Elston Howard was a notorious first-ball hitter. Rohr worked carefully and with the count 2-2 threw a curve that looked like strike three to everyone but umpire Cal Drummond. The crowd groaned in unison. He threw another curve, and Howard reached out and poked it into right for a clean single. The New York crowd still gave Rohr a standing ovation as Charley Smith flied

Facing Yankee immortal Whitey Ford on Opening Day at Yankee Stadium Red Sox rookie lefthander Billy Rohr pitched a one-hit masterpiece to lead the Red Sox to a 3-0 victory. With two outs in the ninth inning Rohr's no-hit bid was spoiled by Yankee catcher Elston Howard.

out to Conigliaro to end the game. Afterward, Mrs. Kennedy had Rohr autograph a ball for her son.

A week later, Rohr pitched almost as well against New York in Boston, winning 6-1. But then the young pitcher struggled, and the impatient manager sent him back to the minors. Rohr never won another game for Boston and earned just one more major league victory in his career.

Boston players quickly learned that winning was all Williams cared about. He would use any means necessary to motivate his players — benching them,

pulling them from games, and even criticizing them publicly in the press. He proved to be the most quotable personality at Fenway Park since Ted Williams. Although saying things like "Trying to talk to George Scott is like talking to cement" was cruel, the approach usually worked, for as one associate later commented, "He was impartial. He dumped on everybody."

The results soon started speaking for themselves. On April 29 the Sox briefly moved into a tie for first place after Jose Tartabull singled through a drawn-in infield in the fifteenth inning to beat Kansas City at Fenway Park. Afterward, a jubilant Carl Yastrzemski entered the Red Sox clubhouse and yelled to the press, "How do you like our chances now?"

They didn't stay in first, but they didn't fall far back, either. The White Sox and Tigers jumped ahead, while the Red Sox stayed in a six-team pack around .500.

But Williams wasn't satisfied. After a dismal 3-6 road trip that included three one-run losses, Williams benched Yastrzemski. Treating the resident star like just another player both solidified the manager's authority and lit a fire under a player who'd previously been coddled.

Early on the morning of May 14, Yastrzemski met coach Bobby Doerr for an extended session of batting practice. Doerr suggested that Yastrzemski lift his hands and made a minor adjustment in his batting stance.

In the off-season the twenty-seven-year-old Yastrzemski had given baseball his full attention for the first time in his career. He met a Hungarian refugee named Gene Berde, the former trainer for the Hungarian boxing team. Berde worked as a fitness director at a hotel near Yastrzemski's home and, after meeting Yaz for the first time, was unimpressed.

"You think you're in shape? You, the big baseball player, you, the big champion. You can't even run a hundred yards. You no athlete ... I make you an athlete."

Utilityman Jerry Adair, obtained in a trade from the White Sox on June 3 in exchange for Don McMahon and Rob Snow, proved to be a key acquisition for the Red Sox. Among his many key hits in 1967 was his eighth-inning homer on August 20, which helped the Red Sox beat the Angels 9-8 after they had trailed 8-0.

Yaz took the challenge and for the rest of the winter worked out with Berde for several hours each day. He was in the best shape of his life.

After his hitting session with Doerr, the ball began flying off his bat. Later that day in a doubleheader against the Tigers, Yaz led a Red Sox sweep, going 3-for-8 and hitting his third and fourth home runs of the year. He was off to the greatest season of his career.

No one was touting the Red Sox as pennant winners, but the team was obviously improved. Moreover, they were confident. The loss of Tony Conigliaro to a two-week stint in the reserves was hardly noticed, and by the end of May, with the Sox 22-20, Williams even began offering rare words of praise. He told the press that whipping boy George Scott had "found himself . . . He's so strong he can hit it out in any direction, in any park." And after Lonborg beat the Tigers 1-0 in Detroit, Williams called it "the guttiest game I've ever seen pitched in my life."

Among many early-season surprises was veteran reliever John Wyatt. He depended on a Vaseline-aided forkball and a series of reminders written on his glove. On four of the five fingers he wrote the word "think." On the fifth he scrawled, "When in doubt — Use Fork Ball." The former Negro League hurler didn't surrender a run in his first five appearances, and his dependability allowed the club to make a trade.

For the first time since taking over as general manager, O'Connell wasn't building for some distant future. The future was finally the season at hand.

On June 3, at the urging of Williams, O'Connell dealt spare reliever Don McMahon and a minor leaguer to Chicago for veteran Jerry Adair, who could play anywhere. The following day the team obtained starting righthanded pitcher Gary Bell from the Indians for former bonus baby Tony Horton and outfielder Don Demeter.

Although Bell was only 1-5 for the Indians, he'd been an all-star in 1966 and was a bonafide frontline starter. After making the trade O'Connell accurately observed, "This is one of those years when it looks like the pennant is up for grabs. I think we can win it. We've bolstered our starting pitching with experience and ability." No one was running away with the pennant. All ten teams were within ten games of each other.

Both moves paid immediate dividends. Adair got three hits in Bell's Red Sox debut, a 7-3 complete-game victory over the White Sox at Comiskey Park on June 8. Adair soon became the club's equivalent of the Boston Celtics' famed "sixth man," the first player off the bench and able to win a game with either his bat or his glove. Williams, who had been Adair's teammate in Baltimore, called him "the Red Sox secret weapon."

No one should have been surprised by O'Connell's success as general manager, but in Boston, where the front office had always been a haven for Yawkey's cronies, mere competence was a revelation. The club was shedding its losing reputation.

In mid-June, as the Sox played Chicago, White Sox manager Eddie Stanky was asked if Carl Yastrzemski was an all-star. Stanky had little respect for either the Sox or Yaz, both of whom he still considered losers. He called Yastrzemski "an All Star from the neck down." The words stung.

His remarks earned him a generous dose of abuse from Boston fans, who were starting to care again. They bombarded Stanky with boos and everything from cups of beer to batteries. But Yaz got the sweetest revenge. In a doubleheader he went 6-for-9, and the Red Sox split with the mighty first-place White Sox. As Yastrzemski rounded third after hitting his fifteenth homer of the year, he slowed and tipped his cap toward Stanky.

The next night, on June 16, the Red Sox played their best game of the season to date. For nine innings neither Boston's Gary Waslewski nor Chicago's Bruce Howard gave up a run. In the tenth, Williams called on Wyatt, but Chicago went ahead, 1-0.

When Chicago reliever John Buzhardt retired Yastrzemski on a popup and Scott on a line drive, Sox fans gave up and started to file out of Fenway. But Joe Foy stopped them in their tracks with a sharp single to left, setting the stage for Tony Conigliaro.

Since returning from reserve duty, the twenty-two-year-old right fielder had slumped and been dropped to sixth in the batting order. After swinging and missing at the first two pitches, he worked Buzhardt to a full count then drove the next pitch into the left-field

Manager Dick Williams acknowledges a crowd of ten thousand well-wishers at Logan Airport on July 24 as the Red Sox return home from a road trip that saw them extend their winning streak to ten straight games while also winning twelve out of thirteen. The spontaneous demonstration symbolized the rebirth of the franchise in the hearts and minds of New Englanders.

net. Nearly seventeen thousand fans cheered themselves hoarse as the entire Boston bench poured from the dugout to greet Conigliaro at home plate. The next day, for the first time, the phrase "Impossible Dream," the name of a hit song in the musical *Man of La Mancha*, was used to describe the 1967 Sox, appearing in a *Boston Globe* headline. Sox fans soon adopted the phrase.

Stanky got the message. The Red Sox were for real. Before leaving Fenway Park he meekly admitted that Yastrzemski should be the starting All-Star left fielder for the American League. Then, as soon as he was out of town he made an empty threat to sue the Red Sox for not protecting him from their fans. The pennant race was becoming contentious. Boston had the attention of the other teams. Dick Williams loved it.

Even Boston fans were starting to wake up. Last-minute wins were exciting, and the Sox had a knack for coming from behind. Attendance started creeping up as older fans decided to check the team out and young fans came for the first time.

The Sox were tough, too. How tough? When they went to New York in late June, third baseman Joe Foy visited his parents in the Bronx, found their home on fire, and pulled them to safety. The next day, in a scene from a B-movie, he hit a grand slam to beat the Yankees 7-1.

In the following game, Yankee pitcher Thad Tillotson recalled Foy's slam and threw at him.

Jim Lonborg knew what he had to do next. When Tillotson came to bat, Lonborg nailed him on the shoulder. The studious pitcher some called "Gentleman Jim" was learning, and before the end of the season another twenty American League batters would bear bruises from Lonborg pitches.

As Tillotson glared back at Lonborg, Joe Foy shouted at the Yankee pitcher and both benches emptied. It took a dozen New York cops to break it up.

When Lonborg came to bat, everyone in the stadium realized it was payback time, and both benches emptied again. This time cooler heads prevailed, but the two clubs threw at each other for the rest of the game, as Lonborg later brushed back Charley Smith and hit Dick Howser in the lopsided 8-1 Red Sox victory.

Following the game, Lonborg calmly told the press, "I have to protect my players," and explained that he would no longer allow hitters to dig in on him. The victory was already his ninth, only one less than his total in 1966.

Then the Sox caught a series of breaks. On June 27, as Gary Waslewski beat the Twins 3-2, defending AL MVP Frank Robinson of Baltimore suffered a concussion in a baserunning collision, and Detroit right fielder Al Kaline broke his finger slamming his bat into the bat rack. The injuries to the two stars helped Boston's pennant chances dramatically and made an already-tight pennant race even tighter.

At the All-Star break the Red Sox were in fifth place, only two games above .500, but trailed first-place Chicago by only five and a half games. Following the break the Sox split the first two games of a home series against the Orioles, then won four in a row before heading out on a six-game road trip.

Healthy and hot, the Sox went into Baltimore and beat the Orioles twice more behind Lonborg and Jose Santiago. The win pulled the Sox to within one and a half games of first place and was front-page news in Boston.

Pitcher Darrell Brandon pitched a complete-game victory over the Indians on July 21 to give Boston sole possession of second place, and the next day Lee Stange threw a 4-0 masterpiece to lead the team to within a half-game of the top. Then Lonborg struck out eleven and won his fifth in a row, and Bell beat his old teammate Luis Tiant 5-1 as Boston swept a doubleheader.

The ten-game winning streak got everyone's attention and got the club in its first pennant race in more than a decade.

Another generation of Sox fans started falling in love with their team. They were different from the wizened war veterans who had cheered their apparently invincible club in the years immediately following World War II. The old fans were starting to come back, but now young women swooning over Tony C. and hosts of teenagers and college students who identified with Boston's youthful underdogs joined them. It was the 1960s, a time when young people thought they could change the world. The transformation of the Red Sox from also-rans to contenders seemed more proof of their own invincibility.

When the Red Sox returned to Logan Airport fifteen thousand fans were waiting for them. Not even the Beatles, who'd visited Boston a year before, had caused such commotion. The giddy club was stunned by the reception. The players joked that they'd have to sacrifice Tony C. to appease the crowd before fleeing to the team bus behind a flying wedge of state troopers.

Twenty-five years later, Dick Williams wrote, "I will never forget that night we landed at Logan Airport with that wild reception . . . We weren't even in first place and yet we couldn't see out the window of our bus because the fans had pressed themselves around the bus and against the glass. Today Boston is considered the best baseball town in America . . . I felt the franchise was practically reborn that night we arrived at Logan."

Nearly as many people mobbed Fenway Park the

Pitcher Gary Bell (*l*) and catcher Elston Howard (*r*) played key roles in the Impossible Dream after arriving in Boston via trade. Bell won twelve games while Howard provided much-needed experience. His block of home plate at Comiskey Park on August 27 while making a game-ending tag on Chicago outfielder Ken Berry is remembered as one of the key plays of the season.

following day to purchase tickets for the coming homestand, the biggest walk-up sale at Fenway Park since the 1940s. "Go Red Sox" bumper stickers seemed to appear overnight on the bumper of every car in New England and showed up on jeeps and gunboats in Vietnam on the evening news. In the *Globe*, Harold Kaese wrote that with forty-one of their remaining seventy games at home, "The Red Sox should win the pennant easily . . . Maybe I am out of my mind, temporarily deranged, raving in a delirium induced by the ten-game winning streak . . . but nobody could have toured with the Red Sox on that trip . . . without catching the pennant bug."

But the Sox lost to California 6-4 in the first game of the homestand. The next night, they trailed the Angels 5-2 in the bottom of the ninth. The largest baseball crowd in Fenway Park in ten years — 34,193 fans — held its collective breath as Mike Andrews led off the inning with a single to left. Joe Foy then crushed a homer into the left-field screen to bring the Sox to within a run.

Angels manager Bill Rigney pulled pitcher Jim McGlothlin for lefty Clyde Wright, who retired Carl Yastrzemski on a fly to center. Rigney then inserted righthander Bill Kelso to face Tony Conigliaro. Conigliaro jumped on Kelso's first pitch and sent it rocketing into the screen to tie the game.

In the top of the tenth, Yaz redeemed himself. He first speared a drive by Bill Skowron that was ticketed for extra bases, then moments later fielded a hit by Bob Rodgers and gunned out Don Mincher at the plate with the winning run. The plays set the stage for a miracle finish, an impossible dream.

Reggie Smith worked the count to 3-2, then sliced a ball down the right-field line and scooted all the way around to third base for a triple. Russ Gibson then flied out to short left before Jerry Adair stepped in to pinch-hit.

Across town, a Boston cabbie stopped short of the entrance to the Callahan Tunnel so he wouldn't lose the game on the radio, blocking traffic as he waited for Adair to hit. Back in Fenway, as the crowd roared, Adair chopped the ball toward third.

In other Red Sox seasons, such hits had invariably resulted in outs. But not in 1967. The ball took a bad hop that third baseman Paul Schaal couldn't control. Smith scored easily, and the Red Sox poured from the dugout and buried him at home plate in a spontaneous celebration that carried over into the locker room. Tony Conigliaro surveyed his teammates and proclaimed to anyone and everyone over and over again, "We cannot be beat! We cannot be beat!" No one corrected him. For the first time in decades, the Red Sox actually believed those words.

Boston and New England embraced the Red Sox with unbridled enthusiasm that bridged the generation gap and drowned out a summer of dissent. The dominant sound in Boston that summer was neither the Beatles, the Beach Boys, nor chanting protesters, but the voices of radio and television broadcasters Ken Coleman and Ned Martin. Every evening, from

transistor radios on stoops and front porches, car radios on the street, and TVs blaring out apartment windows, they provided the story line of the summer.

By August 1, the Sox were a full twelve games over .500 and only two games behind the White Sox. Then Dick O'Connell made another key acquisition, prying former AL MVP Elston Howard from New York in exchange for minor league pitcher Ron Klimkowski.

Howard initially wanted to retire when he heard about the trade. But former teammate Phil Rizzuto talked him out of it, telling him the Sox were headed to the World Series. The Yankees clinched the deal when they told Howard they'd hire him as a coach at the end of his playing career.

Buoyed by news of the acquisition, the Sox came back from a 3-0 deficit to beat the Kansas City Athletics by a score of 5-3. They flew to Minneapolis for the start of a nine-game road trip still trailing Chicago by two games.

But the Twins were in a pennant race too. They beat Boston 3-0, 2-1, and 2-0, as the Red Sox wasted fine pitching performances by Brandon, Lee Stange, and Lonborg. Although they rebounded to win two of three in Kansas City, they finished the road trip in California just as they had started it in Minnesota, losing three straight one-run games, 1-0, 2-1, and 3-2.

The club returned to Boston to a different reception. Fans were banned from the airport, and the Sox were in fifth place. What was special about the 1967 season seemed about to fade. The pressure seemed to be getting to Dick Williams. He benched George Scott when his weight topped 215 pounds, leading the Angels' Jim Fregosi to quip derisively, "Are the Red Sox being run by a manager or a dietitian?"

Detroit had a chance to bury Boston, but Reggie Smith led off with a home run against Joe Sparma, and Dave Morehead shut out the Tigers in the opener. The team took two of three from Detroit, and attendance at Fenway Park topped the one million mark for the first time since Ted Williams played left field. The California Angels came to Fenway and the Sox hoped to avenge their three-game sweep in Anaheim the previous weekend.

Gary Bell and Jack Hamilton pitched the series opener on August 18. The game was scoreless into the fourth, and then George Scott led off with a drive to left. He tried to stretch the easy single into a double, but was thrown out at second.

The Boston crowd disagreed, and someone threw a smoke bomb onto the field. Police quickly removed it, but the game was delayed ten minutes as the umpires waited for the smoke that hung in the humid air to clear.

Reggie Smith came up next and flied to center. But there was still a tinge of acrid smoke in the air as Tony Conigliaro followed Smith and took his customary stance leaning over the inside of the plate. As Conigliaro wondered if the delay had caused Hamilton's arm to stiffen, the pitcher wound up and his first pitch rode in high and tight.

Tony C. saw it too late. Players later recalled hearing a discernible thud, which they compared to the breaking of a pumpkin, as the pitch struck Conigliaro's left cheekbone just underneath the eye socket. Angel left fielder Rick Reichardt, fully 100 yards away, visibly cringed when he heard the sound. Conigliaro's cheekbone was crushed, his eyeball imploded.

He dropped as if shot and lay motionless. For a split second, no one moved as the scene slowly registered. Then Dick Williams raced from the dugout and Rico Petrocelli dashed from the on-deck circle to Conigliaro's side. He was awake but disoriented. Rico held his friend's hand and told him over and over, "Everything's gonna be okay, everything's gonna be okay," as he watched the side of Conigliaro's face visibly swell. Seconds later, trainer Buddy LeRoux and team physician Dr. Thomas Tierney circled around Conigliaro. Tierney later recalled that he could hear a hissing sound coming from Conigliaro's bruised and swollen head.

They tried to keep the conscious player still as they waited for an ambulance. For ten full minutes Fenway Park was silent as Conigliaro lay kicking his legs before Jim Lonborg, Joe Foy, and Mike Ryan lifted him onto a stretcher and carried him into the clubhouse.

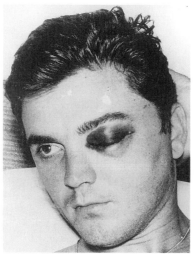

As Conigliaro was carried off the field, the crowd applauded, then turned its attention to Jack Hamilton, who stood next to the mound, head down and arms crossed. They began to boo loudly. Jose Tartabull entered the game to pinch-run as play continued. Petrocelli tripled him home for Boston's first run, and the Sox eventually won 3-2. When Hamilton was lifted after five innings, the crowd booed again, and an angry Carl Yastrzemski exchanged words with the pitcher.

After the game, Hamilton insisted he had not hit Conigliaro intentionally, saying, "I certainly wasn't throwing at him, I was just trying to get the ball over. Tony stands right on top of the plate." Angel catcher Bob Rodgers also disavowed any ill intent, explaining, "The pitch was about eight inches inside and it took off when it got near Tony, it just sailed." Although Tony C. was wearing a helmet, it didn't have the now-common ear flap, a relatively new feature in 1967. The Sox players didn't believe Hamilton. Yaz fumed at his locker and told the press, "All I know is that the kid has a cracked head because of Hamilton."

Conigliaro was rushed to Sancta Maria Hospital in Cambridge, the same hospital where Harry Agganis had died only a dozen years earlier. Later that night, Tom Yawkey went to the hospital and held the young slugger's hand. The next morning, before their nationally televised game later that afternoon, teammates arrived in a steady stream. Jack Hamilton also tried to see Conigliaro. The Conigliaro family turned him away.

The Sox were devastated by the loss of Conigliaro. They were left with a choice — either collapse or play on. That afternoon they took their anger out on the Angels and beat California 12-11.

The two clubs played a doubleheader the next day. In game one switch-hitting Reggie Smith became the first player in Fenway Park and the first Red Sox player ever to sock home runs from both sides of the plate. Boston won 12-2.

Tony Conigliaro shows the effects of his August 18 beaning by Angel pitcher Jack Hamilton. Conigliaro didn't play again until April of 1969.

In game two, the Sox fell behind 8-1. But in the fifth they started to chip away at the lead, and in the eighth inning Jerry Adair capped a 5-for-7 afternoon with a game-winning solo home run into the left-field net. The sweep of the Angels left the Red Sox only a game and a half behind the first-place Twins and a game behind the second-place White Sox. There would be no collapse.

Yet the loss of Conigliaro was significant. At the time he was beaned, he was second on the club to Yastrzemski in most offensive categories. They missed both his power and the protection he afforded Yastrzemski in the lineup. Already, it was obvious he'd be unable to return in 1967, if ever.

For the first time in over a decade fortune smiled on the Red Sox. On August 21, after power-hitting outfielder Ken Harrelson was quoted referring to A's owner Charlie O. Finley as "a menace to baseball," Finley released him. The Red Sox were drawn into the first free-agent bidding war in modern baseball history.

The ability to add a player of Harrelson's ability so late in the season without giving up a player was a unique opportunity. Knowing he could prove the difference in the pennant race, teams in both leagues scrambled after the slugger.

Harrelson quickly learned that patience was a virtue in such negotiations. He'd earned only twelve thousand dollars with the A's in 1967. But as a free agent, his asking price started at eighty thousand dollars. Within two days the Braves had upped the bid to one hundred twelve thousand dollars.

Harrelson was ready to sign, but at the last moment Dick O'Connell called and asked simply, "How much will it take?" Harrelson blurted out, "$150,000." O'Connell replied, "Deal." The player known as "the Hawk" was now a member of the Red Sox.

Many recalled Tom Yawkey's profligate spending decades earlier, and Harrelson's acquisition showed his stamp. After all but ignoring the Sox for several seasons, and even throwing a tantrum in June and threatening to move the team from Boston unless the government built him a stadium, the Sox' surprising appearance in the pennant race invigorated the old owner. Yawkey was not about to let money stand between him and his first shot at a pennant in nearly a generation.

Harrelson arrived in Boston on August 24 just as Conigliaro was being released from the hospital. Tony C. convalesced at his parents' home in Swampscott, his 20/15 vision gone, listening to the Sox on the radio like just another fan. At Fenway Park that afternoon the Red Sox defeated the Senators 7-5 then left for a crucial five-game series in three days with Chicago. They were in a virtual tie with the White Sox for first place.

As the two clubs split the opening doubleheader, Minnesota snuck into first place by half a game. The next day Jerry Stephenson no-hit the White Sox through five innings and led Boston to a 6-2 victory. Meanwhile, the Twins lost to Cleveland, 5-2. For the first time in almost twenty years, the Red Sox were in first place in late August. Sox fans looked at the standings in wonder, and many put the newspaper away for safekeeping.

The first game of the Sunday doubleheader that concluded the series was a microcosm of the entire season, and of all the games Boston played that season, it remains the most memorable. Sox fans could hardly bear to watch on television, but were even more afraid not to. The Sox fell behind, came back, and then almost blew the game twice before emerging with a win. It was that kind of year.

Bell started for Boston and fell behind 1-0, but Carl Yastrzemski ripped two home runs to give him a 3-1 lead. In the seventh, Scott singled home a run to make the score 4-1. But in the bottom of the inning, Mike Andrews blew a tailor-made double-play ball and the White Sox scored twice to make it 4-3.

Boston failed to score off Hoyt Wilhelm in the ninth, and Ken Berry led off with a double for Chicago and was sacrificed to third to chase Gary Bell. John Wyatt came into the game with the tying run 90 feet from home.

He threw one pitch. Duane Josephson hit a soft line drive to right. Weak-armed Jose Tartabull charged in, caught the ball, and came up throwing as Berry tagged.

He made perhaps the best throw of his career, and even then it still wasn't perfect. But now Howard demonstrated why Boston had traded for him.

Following their 6-2 victory over the White Sox at Comiskey Park on August 26 Red Sox players (l–r) Reggie Smith, Carl Yastrzemski, George Scott, and Mike Ryan hold up teammate Joe Foy's number "1" jersey to proclaim the Red Sox' perch atop the American League. The 1967 team was the most integrated and cohesive unit in modern memory.

As the veteran catcher reached up high to catch the ball, he expertly planted his size 12 foot in front of home plate. Berry slid just as he made the catch. As Howard swept back to make a one-handed tag, his foot bounced Berry aside and his glove swept across his leg.

Out. Double play. Game over. Sox in first.

For many fans the play remains the signature moment of the season. Heroics by Yastrzemski and Lonborg were understandable, and even expected. But plays made by role players Tartabull and Howard seemed touched by magic and convinced fans that the Impossible Dream wasn't so impossible. Over the next few weeks, that feeling would grow.

In the final month of the 1967 AL pennant race momentum shifted day by day and sometimes hour by hour as partisans in Chicago, Minnesota, Detroit, and Boston alternately soared and plunged back to earth according to the box score. At various times, each club seemed certain to win. At other times, each

seemed doomed to defeat. Sox fans experienced both extremes during the doubleheader. After their stirring win in game one, Chicago's Gary Peters sent Boston fans back to the depths in game two as he threw an eleven-inning shutout to win 1-0.

The Sox flew to New York and were met by thousands of their fans. The Yankees weren't drawing and correctly assumed that holding Carl Yastrzemski Night at the stadium would attract rabid throngs from across New England. Before the game the Yankees gave Yaz a Chrysler with Massachusetts plates that read "Yaz-8" and fans contributed ten thousand dollars in his name to the Jimmy Fund. Yaz went hitless but Boston won 3-0 behind the pitching of Dave Morehead and Sparky Lyle. They still led Minnesota by .001.

YAZ

Growing up on Long Island, as a teenager Carl Yastrzemski played baseball with his father on a team known as the White Eagles. One scout excitedly reported, "The old man's hitting .450 and the boy's hitting .400."

He should have been a Yankee, but a New York scout offended the elder Yaz when, during contract negotiations, he became exasperated and threw a pencil in the air. The Red Sox were able to sign Yaz because they were the only club willing to pay what the father felt his son was worth.

Yaz had four nearly separate and distinct careers with the Red Sox. From the time he signed as an infielder in 1959 through 1966, he was the future of the team, the guy everyone expected to replace Ted Williams, a notion the Sox reinforced by moving Yaz to left field and bringing him up in 1961, the year after Williams retired. But no matter how well he played, it was rarely good enough, and Yastrzemski played under the shadow of the word "potential."

Beginning in 1967, he reached it, winning the Triple Crown that season, and from 1967 through 1970 Yaz was one of the game's most feared power hitters. Then followed a five-year period when both he and the Red Sox suffered under unrealistic expectations and didn't play up to the expected standard. Everybody's hero in 1967 became the player everyone loved to boo in Fenway Park.

But Yaz was nothing if not resilient. Beginning in the 1975 playoffs, when he hit .455 and then hit over .300 in the World Series, Yaz resurrected his career, driving in runs again and hitting for power. Like Ted Williams in the last stage of his career, Yaz became more than just a player. In the minds of many fans, he was the Red Sox.

Sox fans will never forget his play in the final weeks of the 1967 season. In the season's final twelve games, as the Sox won eight of twelve to win the pennant, Yaz hit .523 with sixteen RBIs, fourteen runs scored, and five home runs. The *Globe*'s Harold Kaese said, "If ever a player in baseball history . . . ever had a two week clutch production to equal Yastrzemski, let the historians bring him forth." None ever has.

Carl Yastrzemski extended himself both literally and figuratively in one of the greatest single-season performances ever in 1967. Not only did he capture the American League Triple Crown, but he also almost single-handedly willed himself to help win every key game of the season. In the final two games of the regular season he went 7-for-8.

On August 29 the team played its third double-header in five days. Jim Lonborg beat Mel Stottle-myre 2-1 in game one. In game two Ken Harrelson socked a home run in his first at bat, but with the score knotted 2-2, the season entered a time warp. Inning after scoreless inning passed as Boston fans sat before their radios and televisions long into the night. Finally, at 1:57 A.M. after over six hours of play, Steve Whitaker homered off Sparky Lyle and the Yankees won 3-2. The next day Boston Edison announced that electric use after midnight had been 40 percent higher than normal.

Both clubs were back on the field the following day. Hitless in his last seventeen at bats, Yastrzemski was exhausted. Williams sat him out.

But with the game tied 1-1 in the eighth, he turned to the best player he had. Yaz entered the game, and in the eleventh he crushed a dramatic home run to deep right center to beat New York 2-1.

The White Sox then came to Boston and Fenway was filled, but the Sox showed signs of exhaustion. They lost three of four. After four glorious days looking down at the competition, Boston fell from first place.

Yaz was still slumping. When he didn't hit the Red Sox were an average team. As his teammates flew to Washington for a Labor Day doubleheader, Yaz remained behind and took several hours of extra batting practice in Fenway with Bobby Doerr before joining his teammates. Tom Yawkey watched him from the stands.

Yawkey, who had kept his distance from the clubhouse for more than a decade, now became a near-constant presence. He wasn't altogether welcome. While some players, like Yaz, basked in the attention of the wealthiest man they'd ever met, Dick Williams, who disliked Yawkey, grated against the intrusion, which he considered "an insult," writing in his autobiography, "You'd have thought he was one of the damn players. He was in the clubhouse, around the batting cage, on the field until the last possible minute, chatting and kibitzing and being about as fake as an owner can be . . . Where had he been when we got our asses kicked earlier in the season? And didn't he know that being friendly with the players would soon make them think they were in good with the owner and didn't have to listen to Williams? Didn't he understand how players worked?"

Yaz broke out on September 5 with two home runs and Boston started winning again, pulling the Sox back into a virtual tie for first place as Boston, Chicago, Minnesota, and Detroit were separated by only a single percentage point. All four received permission to print World Series tickets.

As they jockeyed for position, the Red Sox fulfilled their manager's only pre-season promise on September 10, winning their eighty-second game to assure a finish above .500. But by now that once-lofty goal passed almost without notice.

The pennant was all that mattered. On September 12 Jim Lonborg won his twentieth game, beating the Kansas City Athletics 3-1 at Fenway Park. Boston's sixth win in their last seven games tied the Sox with the Twins for first place.

With only a little more than two weeks remaining in the season, the commissioner's office came up with a scheme to handle the possibility of a first-place tie between anywhere from two to four teams. The solutions ranged from a single-game playoff if two clubs tied for first, to a round-robin double-elimination tournament to account for a three-way tie, to a series of best-of-three semifinals and finals in case four teams knotted at the top. At the beginning of the season the odds of that happening had been calculated at better than thirty million to one. Now, they were considerably less.

But when the Sox dropped three straight to Baltimore, the odds of Boston winning the pennant plummeted. As Boston embarked on an eight-game road trip, the *Globe*'s Ray Fitzgerald put it succinctly, writing, "The Red Sox need a spark."

Carl Yastrzemski must have read the paper. For over the remainder of the season he fashioned perhaps the greatest series of clutch performances one player has ever had, doing it in every way possible, in the field, at bat, and on the bases. Over the course of some 150 games, the four clubs in contention had thus far proven there wasn't a dime's bit of difference between them. But over the final twelve, Carl Yastrzemski proved the difference.

His remarkable streak began in Detroit. After Boston jumped out to an early 3-0 lead, the Tigers came back to tie the game 4-4, then went ahead. But with one out in the ninth, Yaz turned on a Fred Lasher fastball and drove it into the upper deck to tie the game again, and then a Dalton Jones home run won it in the tenth. The win tied Boston with Detroit for the lead.

The next night, Detroit was leading 2-1 when Adair singled and Yaz walked. Scott tied the game with a hit, and Yaz scored the game-winner when he raced home on a wild pitch. The next night in Cleveland, with the game tied 4-4 and two out in the ninth, Yaz singled, Scott walked, and Reggie Smith singled Yastrzemski in with the game-winner again. They stretched their winning streak to four games with a 6-5 win, then got blown out 10-0 in the first game of a doubleheader in Baltimore.

But Yastrzemski wouldn't allow the Sox to stay down. With Boston trailing, Yaz led a comeback, and Boston rolled to a 10-3 win. The following day, his forty-second home run of the season put Boston ahead, but the bullpen failed and the Orioles won 7-5.

Next to Yaz, Jim Lonborg was the most important player on the team. In the last game of the road trip, he proved it, holding Baltimore scoreless through six innings as the Sox built a 7-0 lead. Then Dick Williams, daring to think ahead for the first time all year, gambled and pulled his ace to save his arm in case he was needed in the next few days. The Sox held on to win 11-7 and returned to Boston for two games against Cleveland and two against Minnesota to end the regular season. With only four games remaining, the Red Sox were in a dead heat with the Twins for first place, while Chicago trailed by half a game and the Tigers lurked one and a half behind.

For the first time in ages the Red Sox seemed in control of their own destiny, a prospect Sox fans found both thrilling and absolutely frightening. The up-and-down nature of the pennant race became all the more emotionally exhausting once the pennant seemed theirs to lose. Fenway was only half full that afternoon as Sox fans seemed almost unable to take anymore. Listening on the radio somehow seemed safer.

Gary Bell faced Luis Tiant of Cleveland, and for the first time in weeks the pressure seemed to get to the Red Sox. They played a sloppy game, allowing a popup to fall untouched and making several other errors, falling 6-3 despite Yastrzemski's forty-third home run as the Twins won to move a game ahead. Afterward, even Dick Williams seemed downcast. "This hurts a hell of a lot," he told reporters, "but we played a bad game. This has to be our most damaging loss of the season."

On the following day many Red Sox fans still couldn't bear to watch, and eighteen thousand came to Fenway Park. Desperate, Williams now cashed the ticket he'd punched two days before and brought Lonborg back on two days' rest. It didn't work. In three innings he gave up six hits and four earned runs while Sonny Siebert shut out Boston. The Red Sox pennant chances seemed doomed.

But the pressure affected all four teams. As Boston fell to Cleveland, Minnesota lost to California, and the White Sox dropped two to the lowly Athletics.

"I thought we were gone — dead," said Yaz the next day. "When I heard that Chicago had lost twice to Kansas City I almost couldn't believe it."

Incredibly, with only two games left to play, as if the schedule makers knew each team needed to regroup, both Boston and Minnesota had two days off. As they caught their breath, the White Sox lost to Washington and fell out of the race after 159 games.

Now the Twins had the edge — a split would give them the pennant. The Tigers, while still alive, had a more difficult task. After a rainout, they faced back-to-back doubleheaders versus California to finish the season.

Williams was tempted to bring Lonborg back on two days' rest again, but decided to start Jose Santiago instead. After being used in relief for most of the season, he'd nearly been Lonborg's equal down the stretch. Minnesota manager Cal Ermer opted for ace Jim Kaat.

On this day, Saturday, September 30, Boston fans finally turned out in force for the "now or never" showdown.

Both clubs started out playing nervous baseball. Santiago gave up three hits, a walk, and a run to Minnesota's first four hitters and was in and out of trouble all day. Russ Gibson failed to chase after a popup, and Ken Harrelson misplayed a flyball into a triple.

But the veteran Twins made even more mistakes, and the Red Sox got the breaks, none bigger than when Twins starter Jim Kaat pulled a tendon in his elbow and had to leave in the third inning. Against the Twins bullpen the Sox had a chance.

In the fifth Reggie Smith led off with a double to left center, then Dalton Jones hit a soft groundball to Rod Carew at second. It took a Boston bad hop and everyone was safe. After Santiago and Mike Andrews struck out, Jerry Adair chipped the first pitch he saw into right center to tie the game at 1-1.

That brought up Yaz, and all Boston roared. He rapped a grounder between first and second. Killebrew went for the ball, but missed it. Carew scooped it up, turned to throw to first — and no one was there. Minnesota pitcher Jim Perry had neglected to cover. Jones easily scored the go-ahead run.

Boston put the game away in the seventh when Twin shortstop and former MVP Zoilo Versalles dropped a double-play ball, setting the stage — again — for Yastrzemski, up with men on base and the season on the line.

Minnesota manager Cal Ermer brought in lefthander Jim Merritt as the Fenway crowd chanted for Yaz to get a hit. He worked the count to 3-1, then Yaz cranked the next pitch into the visitors' bullpen, his forty-fourth and biggest home run of the year. Although the Twins' Harmon Killebrew smacked a ninth-inning homer to tie Yaz for the AL home run lead, the Sox hung on to win 6-4.

The victory didn't put Boston into first place — yet. For Detroit won the first game of their doubleheader against the Angels to edge ahead momentarily, but lost the second contest. With one day left in the season, the Sox and Twins remained tied at 91-70. The Tigers were just half a game back at 90-70, but they needed a sweep to tie for the lead and force a playoff.

After the game, Williams's pick to pitch the finale — Jim Lonborg — sat on the trainer's table in the Sox clubhouse and said, "This is the first big game of my life." He had never beaten the Twins, and of his nine losses in 1967, three had been to Minnesota.

For the first time in eighteen years, Boston fans awoke to the opportunity to watch their team win a pennant.

Many lingered over a special Red Sox insert published in the *Globe*'s Sunday edition. Harold Kaese captured the feeling of most fans when he began his Sunday morning column with a homily. "O give us the strength of Hercules, the courage of David, the wisdom of Pericles, the luck that has helped bring us this far, to the edge of paradise, to the golden halyard that raises the pennant," he wrote. "Let the little round ball on the wheel of fortune drop for us and not the Twins."

But when Jim Lonborg got to the park later that day, he wasn't praying. He wrote the figure "$10,000" in the palm of his glove, figuring that was just about what a berth in the World Series would be worth.

Boston fans were ready. Fenway was packed. Fans held up banners that asked "Is Yaz God?" and "Just like '46." Up in Lewiston, Maine, eighty-three-year-old Bill Carrigan sat glued to his television set like millions of other Sox fans. The whole nation was focused on Boston, for the Sox' improbable Impossible Dream of a pennant drive had captured the imagination of the entire country. In an unprecedented move, NBC pre-empted pro football and broadcast the game nationwide.

Lonborg felt great, but then he'd felt great against the Twins before. But in the top of the first, after getting Versalles and Tovar, he walked Killebrew. Tony Oliva then lined a double over Yastrzemski's wild leap in left. Killebrew slowed as he approached third, but Twin third base coach Billy Martin waved him home. Scott took Yaz's throw and had Killebrew by 50 feet, but he tossed the ball over catcher Russ Gibson's head, and the Twins led 1-0.

The Twins' Dean Chance shut Boston down. In the third, Boston hopes started to sink.

With two outs, Lonborg walked Cesar Tovar. Now he had to pitch to Killebrew, and the big first baseman singled. Yastrzemski, who'd done it all, now tried to do too much. Tovar was fast, and Yaz charged the ball to make sure he would stop at second. It went between his legs to the wall and Tovar scored. Minnesota led 2-0.

The score held until the sixth as Sox fans inched

Summary of '67

by Dan Shaughnessy

I was a thirteen-year-old eighth-grader when the Red Sox season began in the spring of 1967. This was before girls, cars, and jobs. Baseball was still the most important thing in my life. It didn't matter that the Red Sox would be bad again. I was accustomed to eighth or ninth place, those low rungs where the Sox jousted with the Kansas City A's and Washington Senators every year.

The Sox had lost 100 games in 1965, finished ninth in '66, and were the usual 100-to-1 shots to win the American League pennant when they opened at home with a 5-4 win over the White Sox in front of 8,234 fans.

We were all a little curious about Dick Williams, the new manager with the flat-top haircut. In spring training he'd predicted that the Sox would win more than they'd lose. This was a startling boast because I had never known of a Red Sox team that played .500 ball. I'd read stories about the great Sox teams of the Babe Ruth era, and I knew Ted Williams took 'em to the World Series in 1946, but the Red Sox of my youth were always terrible. They had managers named Pinky, Billy, and Johnny, and they had an occasional batting champ in Pete Runnels or young Carl Yastrzemski — but they were never in the pennant race, and they never won more than they lost.

Baby boomers are a wildly indulgent lot. We think time started with us, and that's why New England's baby boomer sports fans still celebrate the '67 Red

Sox. Across most of America this is remembered as the Summer of Love, the Summer of Sgt. Pepper's, and the summer of the Vietnam War escalation, but for young Red Sox fans it was the summer of the Impossible Dream baseball season.

Red Sox fans who'll turn fifty early in the new century recite identical stories at the mention of obscure names like Billy Rohr, Thad Tillotson, Jose Tartabull, Rich Rollins, and Dick

---

It didn't matter that the Red Sox would be bad again. I was accustomed to eighth or ninth place.

McAuliffe. None of the above are important baseball players, nor were they the mega-stories of the Sox summer of '67, but each did something that can never be forgotten by the legion of Sox watchers who came of age in the summer of '67.

Yaz, Lonborg, and Williams were the big names, but even the deeds of bit players became folklore when the Red Sox won the closest, most dramatic pennant race of all time. Rohr pitched a one-hitter in his big league debut at Yankee Stadium in April. Tillotson was a Yankee pitcher who sparked a brawl at the stadium when he hit Joe Foy. Tartabull threw out Ken Berry at home plate to win a game at Comiskey in August. Rollins hit the short pop fly that Rico Petrocelli caught to finish the regular season. McAuliffe grounded into a double play in Detroit to clinch the pennant for the Red Sox. Every-

body knows this. Everybody I know, anyway.

The Sox were seven games out and still under .500 in mid-May. They didn't go over .500 for good until a two-game series in New York, which was highlighted by the Tillotson brawl. I remember watching the Yankee Stadium fracas with my dad in our family TV room in Groton, Massachusetts. The TV was black and white and I kept score in an official *Sporting News* scorebook, which I still own. Rico Petrocelli's brother, a stadium cop, was on the field trying to separate combatants.

These Williams Red Sox were exciting. They had bold rookies named Reggie Smith and Mike Andrews. Tony C., Yaz, and Dalton Jones won games with late-inning homers. They reeled off ten straight July wins and flew home to a big reception at Logan after sweeping a doubleheader in Cleveland.

Suddenly, my life had new purpose. I was playing PONY League baseball, but as soon as I got home from games or practice I'd go to the TV or radio to check out the Sox, who were in an actual pennant race. Our family started getting the *Boston Globe* delivered and that made my mornings faster and more fun.

On the night before my sister's wedding, my dad and I drove to Cape Cod to pick up my brother, who was serving as an usher the next day. The Sox were playing the Angels and we were listening to the radio when Jack Hamilton crushed Tony C.'s skull with an inside fastball. It was a wedding weekend for everybody else in my family, but for me it was the weekend that Tony C. got hit. On the day after the wedding, the Sox swept a doubleheader from the Angels, winning game two after trailing 8-0.

The next weekend, Tartabull made his historic throw and I remember being in our dining room, listening to the radio when Darrell "Bucky" Brandon walked four White Sox to blow the second game of the doubleheader.

A week later I was sitting in Bravel Goulart's barber shop on Main Street, looking at the usual stack of magazines, when I saw Yaz on the cover of *Life.* The Sox were national. They were for real.

I lost hope on those last few days before the Twins came to Boston. The Sox lost a pair at home to the Indians (to future Sox Luis Tiant and Sonny

I saw Yaz on the cover of Life. *The Sox were national. They were for real.*

Siebert), and it seemed like the Twins or the Tigers were going to prevail.

But then it was all set: Saturday and Sunday, at home against the Twins and all the Sox had to do was win both to clinch a tie for the American League pennant.

I owned a 20-pound, $50 Grundig reel-to-reel tape recorder which I set up in front of the television for the final two games. It seems silly in this age of video, but I felt a need to record the event for all time. I still have the brittle 7-inch tapes on which Ken Cole-

man, Ned Martin, and Mel Parnell recite the magic of the two-game sweep against the Twins. I was in my bedroom, taping off the radio, when Detroit's Hall of Fame broadcaster Ernie Harwell reported McAuliffe's season-ending double-play grounder.

More than three decades have passed, and the Red Sox of the new century are still beholden to this Impossible Dream crew. Today Sox fans expect competitive teams and capacity crowds, but only fans over forty remember that it wasn't like that in any of the years leading up to 1967.

It's different now. I have made a career writing about baseball and the Red Sox. I have written four books about the team and the ballpark. Many of the gods of my youth are friends and associates. Mike Andrews runs the Jimmy Fund, which saved my daughter's life. I have worked with Rico on the radio and flown in a private jet with Yaz when he was elected to the Hall of Fame. I have dined with Ken Harrelson and skied with Jim Lonborg and his family.

I've tried to tell Jim's kids what he meant to me, what he meant to all of us, when we were thirteen in 1967. There's no way they could understand. You had to be there. I'm glad I was. There'll never be anything like it again.

A card-carrying member of the Red Sox Nation, **Dan Shaughnessy** is a columnist for the *Boston Globe* and the author of numerous books, including the best-selling *Curse of the Bambino, Fenway: A Biography in Words and Pictures, Fenway: Dispatches from Red Sox Nation,* and *Seeing Red: The Red Auerbach Story.*

Rico Petrocelli's catch of Rich Rollins's soft popup to end the final game of the 1967 regular season.

closer to the edge of their seats. Lonborg was scheduled to bat for Boston. Dick Williams wasn't Joe McCarthy and he never moved. The Boston pitcher stepped to the plate.

As Lonborg said later, "I didn't know what I was going to do. But when I got to the plate I saw that [third baseman] Tovar was back a little." Chance threw, and Lonborg pushed a bunt between the mound and third. Chance and Tovar were both surprised, and Lonborg beat it out.

Fans cheered first in surprise and then with delight and finally roared with confidence. *That* was the play, the perfect, impossible, accidental, unexpected virtual act of God they had come to expect all season.

Jerry Adair followed with a single through the infield, moving Lonborg to second. Then Dalton Jones squared to bunt.

The Minnesota infield went into motion to cover the play, but as Chance let the pitch go, Jones pulled the bat back and slapped a line drive to left field.

Lonborg stopped at third. With Yastrzemski coming to bat, there was no sense taking any chances.

Now the roar from Fenway Park could be heard in Kenmore Square and beyond. There wasn't any doubt. Yastrzemski ripped Chance's second pitch to center field for a single. Lonborg and Adair crossed home to tie the score.

Next up was Harrelson. Thus far, in place of Tony C., he'd been something of a disappointment.

He worked the count full, then chopped at a high fastball. The ball bounded to Versalles near second, but rather than take the out in front of him, he threw home and Jones slid in safe. "I saw the man going home for the money," he explained later, "and I always play for the money." Boston led 3-2.

Chance was done. Ermer brought in Al Worthington to face Scott and thirty-five thousand plus screaming lunatics. He threw one wild pitch and then another. Yastrzemski raced to third and then home to put Boston ahead 4-2.

The veteran Twins were playing like scared rookies. Reggie Smith hit a groundball to first, and Harmon Killebrew tried and failed to field it with his knee. Harrelson scored.

Boston led 5-2. The next few innings passed in a blur as all Boston dared to dream of the end and victory. But with two out in the eighth Killebrew and Oliva suddenly singled, and the dream stalled.

Bob Allison then drove a pitch into the left-field corner that the *Globe*'s Clif Keane described as "a double 95 times out of 100." Allison said later, "I just thought I had two [a double] and I looked at Carl." But this was Boston's year to beat the odds and Yaz's year to beat everybody at everything. He gunned the ball to second and Allison was out, although Oliva scored to reduce Boston's lead to 5-3.

In the bottom of the eighth, news of Detroit's 6-4 win in the first game of their doubleheader against the Angels filtered down to the bench. If there was a playoff, Lee Stange would pitch against Detroit the following afternoon. But Boston still had to beat the Twins, and the Tigers had to beat California again for that to happen. For the first time all year, the odds were with Boston.

The early autumn sun sent shadows creeping across the infield as Lonborg took the mound for the ninth. Leadoff hitter Ted Uhlaender sent a grounder to Petrocelli, but it took a bad hop and hit the shortstop just under his right eye for a single. Then future Hall of Famer Rod Carew, representing the potential tying run, stepped in.

Carew grounded the ball at Andrews, who'd come in after Adair had been spiked on a double play in the eighth. Like Adair the inning before, Andrews fielded the ball, tagged the runner, and flipped to first for the double play.

In the on-deck circle Minnesota pinch hitter Rich Rollins was so nervous he mistakenly took one of Zoilo Versalles's bats up to the plate. Boston fans began to relax and started to cheer, a long, slow, deep roar that started soft and then rose and then peaked as Lonborg wound up and released the ball.

Rollins swung. The ball floated in the air to the left side. Petrocelli drifted back to the edge of the outfield and watched the ball settle gently into his glove. Then he threw his arms in the air and started going crazy along with everybody else in Fenway Park.

Thousands upon thousands of fans poured out of the stands and mobbed the Red Sox players. American sport had never before experienced such a scene. As Bud Collins wrote, Lonborg "was sucked into the crowd as though it were a whirlpool, grabbed, mauled, patted, petted, pounded and kissed." The delirious mob lifted him into the air and, as if not believing what had just happened and needing some proof, tore his cap, undershirt, and shoelaces from his body, then tore those into pieces to save and preserve like the relics of a saint. Signs reading "Balt" and "Hous" disappeared from the scoreboard. Kids climbed the backstop. Sod was ripped up from the field. Even the Boston dugout was ransacked, as fans emerged with gloves, helmets, and bats. Others took nothing but memories. Boston hadn't seen such a celebration since the end of World War II. And all the Red Sox had won, so far, was a tie for the pennant.

Carl Yastrzemski was one of the few Red Sox players to escape the mob. When Petrocelli caught the ball, he started in to celebrate, then saw thousands of fans running in his direction and changed his mind. In a 1987 interview he told Glenn Stout that he escaped through the roll-up door along the left-field foul line.

Then Yaz walked beneath the stands alone toward the Boston clubhouse. "There was no one there," he recalled, not a fan or vendor in sight. He was accompanied only by the sound of his own spikes on concrete, the muffled roars of the celebration on the field, and the knowledge that in the two most important games of his career, he had been the best player on the field.

Lonborg escaped with the help of a cordon of Boston police, and the grounds crew cleared the field by turning on the sprinklers. In the clubhouse, the Red Sox doused each other with beer and shaving cream, saving champagne for a pennant celebration.

The party inside the clubhouse and outside Fenway and in a thousand bars and a million living rooms and out was tempered only by the fact that the Tigers were still alive and playing for a trip to Fenway Park for a playoff.

Boston's World Series hopes now lay with Bill

Carl Yastrzemski celebrates in the Fenway Park clubhouse immediately after the Red Sox learn of the Tigers' loss to the Angels on the final day of the season, which results in the Sox championship. Yastrzemski had just capped the greatest individual season ever enjoyed by a Red Sox player in helping lead the Red Sox to their most improbable pennant.

Rigney's California Angels and Tiger pitcher Denny McLain, who hadn't won in a month.

For the next three hours Red Sox players and fans stayed close to the radio. Dick Williams joined Dick O'Connell, Haywood Sullivan, and the Yawkeys in Yawkey's office to listen to the game.

Finally, at 7:43 P.M., with the score 8-5 and the Tigers threatening, Detroit second baseman Dick McAuliffe hit into his first double play of the season, ending the game. The Red Sox were going to the World Series. At midnight, some two thousand fans were still celebrating on the steps of the statehouse.

Before rejoining his team, Williams sent telegrams

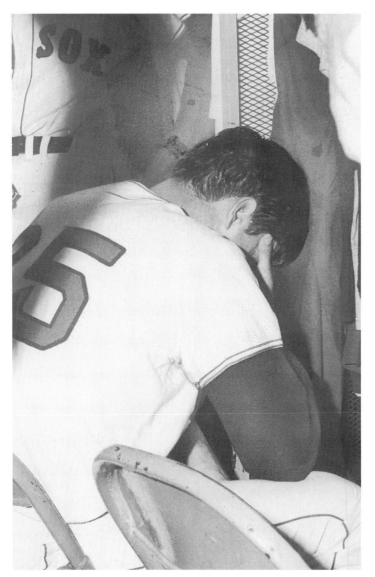

to manager Mayo Smith of the Tigers, complimenting his team on a great season, and to Angel manager Bill Rigney, thanking him for playing the Tigers so tough. Williams added a postscript to Jim Fregosi, reminding him that the "dietitian" had managed the Red Sox to their first pennant since 1946.

The city paused before the World Series as if trying to comprehend what had just happened. Yaz had climaxed his remarkable two-week splurge by going 7-for-8 in the final two games, capturing the Triple Crown as he led the AL with a .326 batting average, 121 RBIs, and tied with Killebrew for the home run title with forty-four. Lonborg's final game win was his twenty-second, tying him with former Sox Earl Wilson of the Tigers for the league high. The 100-to-1 longshots had come in.

Meanwhile, Sox fans went crazy in anticipation. A Jamaica Plain man painted the words "RED SOX THANKS" in letters 4 feet high on the side of his house. Signs saying "GO SOX" and "LOVE YA YAZ" spontaneously appeared in windows and on rooftops all over the city. Army captain Lawrence O'Brien of Somerville, stationed in Vietnam, was willing to do anything to see the Series. When the Sox won the pennant he extended his tour of duty because re-upping gave him an immediate thirty-day leave. He flew home, and the *Boston Globe* provided him with Series tickets.

The pennant came as such a surprise that few Sox fans had given their opponent in the World Series, the St. Louis Cardinals, much thought. The Sox had won with Williams, Yaz, Lonborg, and the Impossible Dream. The Cards had rolled over opponents with the pitching of Bob Gibson, the power of Orlando Cepeda, and the speed of Lou Brock. They didn't need any dream. They were nightmare enough for opponents and entered the Series as prohibitive favorites.

Gibson, who had missed seven weeks of the season with a broken leg after being struck by a line drive hit by Roberto Clemente, returned in September and was fresh and well rested for the Series. St.

Following the Red Sox' season-ending victory over Minnesota, injured outfielder Tony Conigliaro is overcome with emotion as he weeps in front of his locker. His injury denied him the chance to participate in what would have been his only World Series.

Louis manager Red Schoendienst set his rotation to allow Gibson to start three times if the Series went a full seven games.

Williams had no such luxury. Lonborg was already overworked and needed another day. Jose Santiago would have to pitch the opener. Unless there was a rainout or Lonborg came back on two days' rest, he'd be able to pitch only twice. It was the only advantage the Cardinals would need.

The Series opened in Boston on October 4. When Gibson first stepped onto the field he laughed and asked, "Where's the upper deck?" He wasn't intimidated by Fenway's diminutive size. He wasn't intimidated by anything. He'd been to the Series with the Cardinals in 1964, when he'd been named Series MVP.

Santiago and Gibson each pitched two scoreless innings to start game one, but while Santiago was scraping by, Gibson was dominant. None of the Sox, not even Yaz, was getting good wood on his fastball.

In the Cardinal third, Lou Brock lined a single to center, moving to third on Curt Flood's double. He then scored when Roger Maris grounded out to Scott at first.

But Boston came back. With one out, Gibson relaxed and grooved one to Jose Santiago. He hit the second and last home run of his major league career into the left-field screen. Gibson never relaxed again.

For the next three innings both pitchers held the line, but in the seventh, Lou Brock cracked his fourth hit of the game and stole second for the second time. He advanced on a groundout by Flood then scored when Maris grounded to Adair. St. Louis led 2-1.

That's all Gibson needed. He finished with a six-hit, ten-strikeout masterpiece. After the game he dismissed the Red Sox, referring to Yastrzemski as merely a "decent batter." For the first time all season, the magic seemed to have disappeared from Fenway Park, and Sox fans filed out silently. Gibson had everyone thinking. After the stands cleared, Harrel-

Joanne and Judy Fay of Watertown cross their fingers while mailing their World Series ticket application at the Kenmore Station post office just two blocks away from Fenway Park.

son and Petrocelli went back onto the field and took extra hitting.

Boston turned to Jim Lonborg in game two. He stuck with what worked, staying in a hotel the night before and wearing his lucky pair of mismatched spikes that between them had accounted for fifteen wins. Before the game Darrell Brandon gave him a gold paper horseshoe sent by a fan addressed to "the Red Sox pitchers." Lonborg stuck it into his back pocket.

Brock had run wild in game one, and Lonborg delivered an immediate message to start the game, throwing the ball at his chin and sending Brock to the ground. The St. Louis bench howled, and Lonborg looked over and laughed, saying later, "What do they think I'm going to do — give them home plate?" While Yaz cracked a home run off Dick Hughes in the fourth and Boston scored five runs in the seventh, Lonborg was perfect. He ignored intermittent showers and pitched the best game of his career.

He retired the first nineteen Cardinals before walking Curt Flood and took a no-hitter into the eighth. Four outs away from immortality, Julian Javier lined what Lonborg later called "a high slider" into the left-

Boston University student Jane Campbell expressed the feelings of Red Sox fans everywhere when she proclaimed her sentiments while parading with a handmade sign on Jersey Street prior to the seventh game of the World Series on October 12.

The Cardinals were confident and it showed. In game four they battered Santiago with four runs off six hits in just two-thirds of an inning to start the game. Then Gibson continued his mastery of Boston as he scattered five hits and won convincingly, 6-0. St. Louis needed only one more win to become world champions.

But Boston had come back from the brink all season. Lonborg got the ball for game five and pitched his third consecutive masterpiece. He allowed just three hits to beat St. Louis 3-1. His effort established a record for fewest hits allowed in two consecutive World Series starts and had New Englanders praying for rain to give him some rest before game seven — if there was a game seven.

Lonborg's win sent the Series back to Boston, and a reported fifteen hundred fans, "mostly teenage girls" according to the *Globe*, broke through a plate glass door to meet them when they climbed off the plane.

Williams pulled a surprise to start game six. Rookie Gary Waslewski had only been added to the Series roster to replace ailing Darrell Brandon. He'd played for Williams in Toronto the past two seasons and had pitched well in limited duty for the Sox in 1967 and in game three of the Series. The manager passed over Santiago and Bell and gave Waslewski the start.

It was a gutsy move, one that on the surface seemed akin to the decision Joe McCarthy made when he picked Denny Galehouse to pitch the 1948 playoff. But in 1967 there was little moaning about past errors. This was the first Red Sox team in a generation neither intimidated nor inhibited by the past, and maybe the last one as well. McCarthy's mistake in pitching Galehouse was that the decision had been a departure from his usual strategy. Williams had been taking risks and going with the hot hand all year, using no fewer than twelve starting pitchers during the season.

Waslewski kept the Cardinals off balance into the sixth, and for the first time in the Series, Boston's bats exploded. Rico Petrocelli cracked two home runs, and Yaz and Reggie Smith rapped one apiece as the Sox won 8-4. The Series would go to the seventh game.

field corner for a double, but that was all. Lonborg's one-hitter led Boston to a 5-0 win.

In game three St. Louis Cardinal pitcher Nelson Briles answered Lonborg's message with his own, drilling Yaz on the leg with a fastball. Mission accomplished. The umpires warned both clubs to knock it off. Changing speeds brilliantly, Briles mesmerized Boston. Gary Bell got knocked out in the second and the Cardinals won, 5-2.

When Dick Williams was asked who he'd pitch in game seven, he quipped, "Lonborg and champagne." Those three words filled the front page of the *Boston Record American* the next day.

That morning in the *Globe*, Harold Kaese wrote, "This is a story that has to have a happy ending. It has been a fairy tale from April 12 until now." But the fairy tale was already over. The happy ending — winning the pennant — had already happened. Now another generation of Sox fans would learn the essential lesson of the Red Sox' history.

The difference in the Series came down to one day of rest. Gibson had three, but Lonborg had only two days to recover from his last start.

Lonborg started strong and retired St. Louis in the first on nine pitches. But after Joe Foy walked for Boston to open the first against Gibson, the Cardinal hurler just got stronger.

In the third inning, Dal Maxvill, who barely hit his weight, tripled off the centerfield wall, the first sign that Lonborg was tiring, history was starting to repeat itself, and the Impossible Dream was coming to its inevitable end. Lonborg got the next two batters, and then Flood singled to score Maxvill. Maris followed with a hit, and a fatigued Lonborg bounced a pitch to the screen and Flood scored to put St. Louis ahead 2-0.

Gibson himself heralded the dawn in the fifth with a home run, then Brock singled and stole second and third before scoring the Cardinals' fourth run on Maris's flyball. Boston got a run in the bottom of the inning when Scott tripled and scored on a throwing error, but in the sixth the Cardinals hit everything Lonborg threw and scored three more to lead 7-1. He struck

out Curt Flood to end the inning, and the Boston crowd stood and cheered as he walked off the mound, tears streaming down his face. The pitcher, his teammates, and every Boston fan in the world knew it was over.

The 1967 season may have been Boston's, but the Series belonged to Bob Gibson. He scattered three hits and collected his tenth strikeout when George Scott fanned to end the game. The Cardinals won 7-2

The "Lonborg and Champagne" headline gave the Cardinals additional incentive to beat the Red Sox in the deciding seventh game behind the unstoppable pitching of Bob Gibson. Red Sox ace Jim Lonborg pitched on only two days' rest and lasted six innings in a game won by St. Louis 7-2.

CLOUDY, COOLER SEE PAGE 8

Record ★ American

LARGEST DAILY CIRCULATION IN NEW ENGLAND

10 Cents   Thursday, October 12, 1967   44 Pages

COMPLETE

Exclusive! Dick Williams Writes:

Lonborg And Champagne

STORY ON PAGE 36

Red Sox Power Was Turned on by (From Left) Rico Petrocelli, Two Homers, Carl Yastrzemski and Reggie Smith, One Each to capture the title. Afterward, in the cramped visitors' clubhouse, they shouted, "Lonborg and Champagne, Hey! Lonborg and Champagne, Hey!" over and over again while uncorking cases of the stuff. The Red Sox clubhouse was quiet for the first time in weeks.

But for once, although the Red Sox had been defeated, they hadn't lost. One of the more unlikely champions in American League history, they had succeeded merely by reaching the World Series. Extending it to seven games against the Cardinals had been a remarkable achievement. But the 1967 Red Sox had won a larger, more important victory, for they reestablished Major League Baseball in Boston as a viable enterprise. In so doing, they renovated the franchise and simultaneously transformed Fenway Park from a deteriorating, cramped anachronism to a baseball treasure. Tom Yawkey's legacy was saved.

The next morning, fans called the Red Sox ticket office, already looking to buy tickets for 1968. This time, the phrase "Wait 'til next year" was not a symbol of loss, but a sign of optimism again.

"IF IT STAYS FAIR..."

1968 | 1975

Carlton Fisk wills the ball to stay fair as he watches his game-winning home run
sail into the night on the morning of October 22, 1975. Fisk's home run not only
forced a seventh game in one of the greatest World Series ever but came to sym-
bolize the rebirth of the national pastime itself. A nationwide television audience
of over seventy-five million viewers tuned in to the seventh game later that day.

The 1967 season established new levels of expectations for a team that hadn't won anything or even come close in a generation. Sox fans had nearly forgotten what it was like to win; they had completely forgotten what it was like to expect to win. The Impossible Dream made that possible again. After 1967 the relationship between the team, the players, and their fans would never be the same. Everyone wanted more.

Over the course of the 1967 season the Red Sox and their fans rediscovered both their past and their essential character. The challenge would now be both to maintain that posture and to avoid the mistakes and errors that, since 1918, had always marred any kind of success.

They succeeded for all of ten weeks.

On Christmas Eve, the Impossible Dream showed the first signs that the 1968 season would become a potential nightmare. Jim Lonborg enjoyed the spoils of 1967 by cavorting at a Lake Tahoe ski resort with actress Jill St. John. On his last run of the day the Cy Young Award winner caught an edge and tore ligaments in his left knee. Merry Christmas.

Lonborg initially underestimated the injury. He told the *Globe*'s Roger Birtwell, "It didn't hurt appreciably at the time and I slowly side-stepped a mile to the ski lodge. I then drove back to San Francisco on four bad wheels." Once there, he had the leg put into a cast then flew to Boston to have the injury evaluated.

At first, the Sox weren't overly concerned either. Dick Williams said, "I'm not angry with Jim. I'm just relieved it's not as bad as we first thought." Dick O'Connell shrugged his shoulders. "Skiing is a personal thing," he said. "Like playing squash or golf. We can bar a player from participating professionally in another sport like basketball. But this is another thing." But both the *Herald*'s Tim Horgan and *Look* magazine writer William Craig had warned Lonborg that skiing was a risky activity for a Cy Young winner. Lonborg brushed the warnings aside. He was twenty-six years old and he felt indestructible.

The pitcher wasn't the only member of the 1967 Sox who was taking advantage of his sudden fame. Yastrzemski touted all sorts of stuff, most notably "Big Yaz" bread. Sox players were everywhere that off-season signing autographs at car dealerships, speaking at banquets, and doing just about anything they were asked. Ken Harrelson, who was now spending six thousand dollars a year on clothes and flying to California just to have his hair styled, even parlayed his southern charm and eccentric personality into a local one-hour variety show on WHDH-TV entitled *The Hawk*. Doors players never knew existed suddenly flew open. Baseball became a little less important than it had been in 1967. Yastrzemski, despite winning the Triple Crown in 1967, didn't work out with Gene Berde in the off-season. When, years later, Carlton Fisk asked him why, Yaz said simply it was "too hard."

When Lonborg underwent knee surgery at Sancta Maria Hospital, early reports indicated he would return to the pitcher's mound by Opening Day. But in 1968 knee surgery was a much more invasive procedure than it is today and rehabilitation just a word in a medical book. As spring training approached Lonborg could hardly walk. The 1968 Sox hadn't played a game yet and the phrase "Wait 'til next year" was already referring to 1969.

Cy Young Award winner Jim Lonborg stubbornly refused to give up his off-season pursuit of skiing before suffering a severe knee injury on the slopes of Lake Tahoe just prior to Christmas 1967. He is shown here at Killington, Vermont, taking some pointers roughly a month before his injury.

Lonborg's injury came at a critical time, not just in terms of the 1968 season, but for the next several seasons. The Sox planned to build their staff around Lonborg. Dick O'Connell had already engineered several trades to do just that, acquiring veterans Ray Culp from the Cubs and lefthander Dick Ellsworth from the Phillies, both proven winners. Adding their talents to a staff that already included Lonborg, Santiago, Gary Bell, John Wyatt, and Sparky Lyle seemed to make another pennant almost certain.

Lonborg or not, record numbers of fans agreed. They answered the lingering question "Was '67 a fluke?" with their hard-earned cash and purchased a record number of tickets.

The defending champions were now expected to win. Media coverage of the team increased exponentially.

Fans had already learned an essential lesson. In 1967 they had entered into the relationship blindly — rooting for the Sox came without warning labels. But they were learning. Tony C.'s beaning had provided one lesson and Lonborg's injury another. There were reasons why the Red Sox hadn't won a world championship in fifty years.

Dick Williams learned part of the reason in the off-season. He wanted a new contract and agreed with Dick O'Connell on a three-year deal. But Tom Yawkey balked. The richest owner in baseball wanted to give the most successful manager in his tenure only a two-year deal. At length, Williams got his way, but he wondered if Yawkey had what he called "another steambath buddy" in line for his job.

The beginning of spring training was dominated by Tony C.'s attempted comeback. After a season of miracles, one more didn't seem like too much to ask for. At first Tony C. followed the story line. Two batting-practice home runs one day dwarfed reports in the Boston press on both the championship-bound Celtics and Bobby Orr's Bruins.

But hitting home runs off batting-practice pitching was one thing — doing it in a game was another. Conigliaro's eyesight fluctuated and then deteriorated. Teammates winced as he soon started missing even batting-practice pitches by a foot or more. Before long he was plotting his possible comeback as a pitcher.

And if ever there was a year to be a pitcher, it was 1968. Pitching dominated the game like no other time since the Dead Ball Era. That made the loss of Lonborg even more critical.

midmonth to have any chance of catching the Tigers. They dropped all three. Although the club finished 86-76, only six games off their 1967 pace, Detroit won 103 games and the Sox finished fourth, seventeen games back.

Ken Harrelson was virtually the only Red Sox player to have a better year in 1968 than in 1967. He smacked thirty-five home runs with 109 RBIs and a .275 batting average. While that didn't match Yaz's

The Sox started slow and at midseason were stuck at .500. No one was hitting, but then no one in baseball was hitting. The league batted only .230 in 1968. And during a season in which the league ERA was 2.98, Boston's team ERA of 3.33 wasn't good enough.

Lonborg returned in the middle of the year, but as he did Jose Santiago, who was 9-4, hurt his arm and never won another game in the major leagues. Lonborg thought he was fine, but his weakened leg caused him to make a subtle change in his pitching motion. He lost a little off his fastball and started to experience a series of nagging arm injuries. He finished the year 6-10 with a team-high 4.29 ERA.

The club went on a minor tear in August, but needed to sweep a three-game series with Detroit in

numbers in 1967, the Hawk did achieve a dubious triple crown of his own, leading the league in interviews, Nehru jackets, and dune buggies.

Yaz won the batting title with the lowest league-leading average in history, .301. Mike Andrews and Reggie Smith enjoyed superb sophomore seasons as Smith led the league in doubles with thirty-seven and Andrews was third in team batting average at .271, but other highlights were few.

George Scott epitomized the fall. His average tumbled to .171 with only three home runs. Some blamed Williams's browbeating of Scott, but columnist Al Hirshberg pointed out that he tried to pull every pitch, writing, "The Wall embraced Scott like a long lost brother in 1966 and hugged him even more tightly in 1967. The wall was his friend. But when he

Red Sox manager Dick Williams is flanked by Red Sox vice president of player personnel Haywood Sullivan (l) and executive vice president and general manager Dick O'Connell (r) as the Red Sox re-sign Williams to a three-year contract at fifty-five thousand dollars per season following the Impossible Dream season.

tried to get chummy with the wall, it turned its back on him."

To offset the "Year of the Pitcher," baseball initiated some drastic changes in 1969. The pitcher's mound was lowered from 15 to 10 inches and the upper and lower dimensions of the strike zone changed from between the shoulders and the knees to between the armpits and the top of the knees.

Expansion into Seattle, Kansas City, Montreal, and San Diego also led baseball to split each league into eastern and western divisions. Winners of each division would play a best-of-five league championship series (LCS) to decide the pennants prior to playing the World Series. Boston's chance of reaching the postseason doubled.

The AL East Red Sox started the 1969 season with a wave of optimism. Mike Andrews enthusiastically crowed, "Anybody who doesn't like this ballclub has to be out of his mind. If only 90% of our 'ifs' come true, we'll be much better than our '67 team." Everyone appeared healthy, even Tony Conigliaro, whose vision had returned to near normal. His twenty-one-year-old kid brother Billy joined him on the roster.

In Baltimore on Opening Day Tony C. started the game in right field and provided one of the most stirring moments in Red Sox history. In the tenth inning he launched a home run off Dave Leonhard and floated around the bases. When the Sox opened at Fenway, fans gave Conigliaro a two-minute ovation when he came to bat as an airplane soared overhead trailing a large banner that read simply, "Welcome Back." Tony C. then became the happiest player in baseball history to tap back to the pitcher. "I was go-

In 1968 Ken Harrelson led the league in RBIs, Nehru jackets, and shoes. By his own account he spent nearly ten thousand dollars a year on his wardrobe and kept his slacks in the cedar chest pictured in his Brookline apartment.

ing for the downs on that pitch," he admitted later. "I wanted a home run. So what did I do? I hit the ball 15 feet; but I'll take it."

Conigliaro's apparent return made Ken Harrelson expendable. Within a week he was traded with pitchers Dick Ellsworth and Juan Pizarro to Cleveland for pitchers Sonny Siebert and Vicente Romo and catcher Joe Azcue.

But players were beginning to resist being treated like property. Harrelson balked at the deal and said he would rather quit baseball than report to Cleveland. He had too much going on in Boston, including a television production company, a record publishing firm, a book deal, a sub shop, and part-interest in a nightclub called Ken Harrelson's 1800 House.

Harrelson made subs while the Sox and Indians tried to come up with a solution. At length, money talked. Harrelson agreed to go to Cleveland when the Indians doubled his salary.

The *Globe*'s Bud Collins bade the Hawk farewell, writing, "So it's so long to Ken Harrelson, a sports writer's best friend. So long to Italian shoes and no socks, to $500 silk suits and unkempt hair. Goodbye to Hawkmobiles and adhesive tape around the wrists, quotable quotes and tall golf stories. Farewell to the one-handed catch."

Boston contended until midseason but couldn't keep pace with the Orioles, who eventually won 109 games. Despite the fact that the Sox led the league with 197 home runs, as both Yaz and Petrocelli hit 40 and even Tony C. cracked 20, the continuing ineffectiveness of Lonborg and other pitchers led the club to a third-place finish.

There were also problems in the clubhouse. The players started to tune out Williams's constant harping. On August 1 against Oakland, when Yaz failed to leave home plate on a two-out tapper to the pitcher, Williams pulled him from the game, reamed him out in front of his teammates, and fined him five hundred dollars. The tense relationship between the two men led to speculation by the media that Williams's days in Boston were numbered. There was no way the manager could win a war with Yaz, for there was no question with whom Tom Yawkey was aligned.

Earlier in the season the *Globe*'s Clif Keane had asked Yawkey to rank Williams as outstanding, ex-cellent, good, or fair. When Yawkey said he was only "good," Williams demanded to see the owner.

On September 23 Yawkey told Dick O'Connell to fire Williams and his entire staff. Then Yawkey left for South Carolina to escape the heat from the media.

O'Connell disagreed with the move and told the press, "I'm an unwanted speaker; Dick Williams is

Tom Yawkey is shown in the Red Sox press lounge atop Fenway Park in 1970. His firing of Dick Williams at the end of the 1969 season reinforced his complete authority over the team.

not coming back to manage the Red Sox next year. I don't like to have to do this because I like him personally and he did a great job for us in 1967."

The Sox played out the string under caretaker Eddie Popowski. *Globe* columnist Ray Fitzgerald summed up the matter succinctly when he wrote, "The days of wine and roses didn't last long, which should have been predictable. The one thing Thomas A. Yawkey cannot abide, even more than a losing ball team, is an unhappy one, and this year, some players let it be known that they were most unhappy."

It hadn't mattered that the Red Sox had won under Williams after losing for a generation. They hadn't won the way Yawkey wanted them to. He couldn't keep Williams on and still be a buddy to the players. To Yawkey, being a buddy to the players was more important than winning.

Louisville manager Eddie Kasko was named the thirteenth manager in Tom Yawkey's reign. Kasko, a bespectacled former infielder who resembled a college professor, took the opposite approach of Williams.

At spring training in 1970 Kasko eliminated the volleyball games that had led Ted Williams to boycott camp. Instead, the new manager instituted what he termed "Fun Days," which included offbeat baserunning drills that left plenty of time for fishing and golf. All was bliss and contentment with Team Yawkey once more.

But they were also out of contention for a pennant in the first week, opening 3-7. Although Lonborg soon won four straight, just as writers began to herald his comeback, his arm started acting up again. The Sox eventually put him on waivers and sent him to Louisville. Trainer Buddy LeRoux said the pitcher had already been injected with enough cortisone to last the year. "After that," he said, "you need a big assist from Mother Nature."

Fans cast about for a scapegoat. Yastrzemski, despite moving to first base to make room for rookie Billy Conigliaro in left and narrowly missing another batting title, became the people's choice. As Tim Horgan of the *Herald* noted, "Quicker than it takes to say, 'Yaz Sir, That's my Baby,' the fans have turned on the producer, director, and star of The Impossible Dream. And the worse the Red Sox pitching becomes, the more baserunners the Hose leaves stranded, the more games they toss down the drain, the fiercer the fans razz Yaz."

In 1970 the Sox duplicated their 87-75 record but still finished twenty-one games behind Baltimore. Their finish and continuing internal squabbles forced the Sox to make a change.

On October 11 fans reacted in disbelief when they learned that Tony C., fresh off hitting a career-high thirty-six home runs and a team-best 116 RBIs, had been traded to the team that had nearly killed him, the California Angels. The Sox received second baseman Doug Griffin, pitcher Ken Tatum, and outfielder Jarvis Tatum.

The deal was made because attendance had slipped by two hundred fifty thousand and, with Williams gone, the players had split into factions, one led by Tony C. and the other by Yaz. O'Connell was ordered

to do something about it. And as Williams's firing had proved, Yawkey always backed Yaz first.

Yawkey had promised Conigliaro he'd never be traded, and he was devastated, saying, "I am confused by this trade. I don't understand it . . . I'm going to California with one thing in mind, to prove to Boston that it was a mistake. Know anyone who needs an apartment? I just paid next year's rent."

Other trades soon followed as the remnants of the Impossible Dream were cast aside. Mike Andrews went to Chicago for thirty-six-year-old shortstop Luis Aparicio, and Petrocelli moved over to third base.

The trades made little difference on the field. The Sox peaked on May 28 when they beat Oakland rookie sensation Vida Blue to open up a four-game lead in the AL East. More than one writer began to draw comparisons to 1967.

Within a month they were searching for other metaphors as over the next three weeks the Sox lost ten and a half games to Baltimore and the Orioles took over first place. Clubhouse controversies again became the focal point of Boston's season.

Just before the All-Star break Billy Conigliaro exploded. He accused Yaz and Reggie Smith of trying to force him out of the outfield.

Smith responded by saying, "Billy Conigliaro is not a mature player. What he said was not so much an emotional outburst because of his brother. It was malice aforethought. And I don't want to play with him again . . . With his brother Tony it is baseball first, other things second. Not so with Billy, it's the other way around."

Across the continent, Tony C. was announcing his retirement. His eyesight was giving him trouble again. Within hours he boarded a plane to Boston.

Things were so bad that Yaz and the two Conigliaro brothers had to meet at an attorney's office to settle their differences. But the resulting calm in the Boston clubhouse lasted only briefly as players began to openly criticize Kasko. Attendance dropped by another one hundred thousand as no regular hit over .300.

Boston finished third again, 85-77, eighteen games back. Among the few encouraging signs were a 9-2 record by rookie pitcher Bill Lee and sixteen wins from Sonny Siebert.

Lost in a season of turmoil was a minor deal that eventually made headlines. Veteran pitcher Luis Tiant, after breaking his clavicle, had attempted a comeback with Atlanta's Triple A team, the Richmond Braves. Boston scout Lee Stange was impressed. When Atlanta released Tiant O'Connell signed him to a Louisville contract.

It was the best deal O'Connell ever made. Years later he still laughs when he recalls his first meeting with Tiant. The pitcher said simply, "You just give me the ball and I will show you." That he did.

In the off-season O'Connell continued shuffling the deck, sending Lonborg, Billy Conigliaro, George Scott, Ken Brett, Joe Lahoud, and Don Pavletich to the Milwaukee Brewers for outfielders Pat Skrable and Tommy Harper and pitchers Marty Pattin and Lew Krausse. Yaz, Smith, Lyle, and Petrocelli were the only players left from 1967.

The hot stove burned intensely. Many fans were as agitated by the trade as they were by the fact that Kasko, who they booed only slightly less than Yastrzemski, had received a contract extension.

Spring training began under a cloud as the players' union considered a strike. In a preliminary vote on March 12, the Sox were one of the few teams to not support the strike unanimously. Carl Yastrzemski, then the highest-paid player in the majors at one hundred sixty-six thousand dollars per year, was one of four Red Sox players to vote "no."

Yastrzemski commented, "You'd think we've been working in a factory these past five or six years . . . I suppose some sort of boycott would be okay, like not playing on a Saturday if the game is nationally televised." Player rep Gary Peters explained Boston's vote by telling the media it was a result of Tom Yawkey's extraordinary generosity.

On March 22 O'Connell sent reliever Sparky Lyle to the Yankees for first baseman Danny Cater. Cater had always played well against Boston and was considered a more than adequate replacement for George Scott. By the end of the season the trade would be judged as one of the worst in franchise history.

When the strike was finally called the Sox were one of four teams to not give it unanimous support. But after twelve days the two sides reached agreement and baseball resumed.

The first ten days of the season had been lost, and Boston missed seven games. But Detroit missed only six games. The difference would eventually prove critical.

On a belated Opening Day Detroit's Mickey Lolich beat Boston 3-2 when Luis Aparicio tripped over third base trying to score on a Yastrzemski hit and was put out. The manner of the defeat would prove prophetic.

Kasko started the season on the hot seat and stayed there through May as the club played uninspired baseball. The Sox entered June with a record of only 15-19.

But in midseason the club finally shook off a series of small injuries and started winning. Luis Tiant pitched his way out of the bullpen and soon anchored a starting staff that included Marty Pattin, Sonny Siebert, Bill Lee, and rookies John Curtis and Lynn McGlothen.

The Sox turned their season around in August and September, moving into first place. The Boston media began calling Kasko a miracle worker and Tiant a savior. But their highest praise was reserved for rookie catcher Carlton Fisk, a native of New Hampshire, who led the team in hitting. Already the best all-around catcher in team history, he was soon recognized as the new team leader.

On September 29 the Red Sox visited Baltimore for the first game of a season-ending road trip. Yaz struck a two-run tenth-inning home run to eliminate the Orioles from the race as Luis Tiant defeated the Orioles for the fourth time, his fifteenth win since joining the rotation.

After Marty Pattin defeated the Orioles the following night, the Sox lost the finale of the three-game set. That set the stage for a three-game showdown in Detroit against the second-place Tigers, who trailed Boston by only half a game. Another Red Sox season would be decided in its final days.

In game one the Tigers jumped to a quick 1-0 lead over John Curtis when Al Kaline homered. In the third the Red Sox rallied. With one out Tommy Harper and Luis Aparicio singled, then Yastrzemski ripped a Mickey Lolich fastball over center fielder Mickey Stanley's head. The ball hit the top of the fence then bounced back over Stanley toward the infield.

Harper scored easily from third as Aparicio and

Yaz tore around the bases. As Aparicio reached third Sox coach Eddie Popowski waved him home.

He slipped on top of the third-base bag and stumbled awkwardly into foul territory, falling to the ground. As he scrambled to his feet Popowski yelled for him to return to third. As he did, Aparicio stumbled again before making it back. That image — Aparicio on all fours — has since been cast in the Red Sox canon of decisive miscues that cost them championships.

But it was Yastrzemski who made the second out. For as the ball bounded back over Stanley's head, and Aparicio stumbled and fell and stumbled and fell, Yaz tore around second base, head down, thinking triple or home run. He didn't see Aparicio on the ground. If he had, he could easily have stopped and backtracked to second.

One of the cardinal rules of baserunning is to only take third when safe arrival is certain — a runner is already in scoring position at second. Had Yaz noticed his stumbling teammate, Boston would have had two runners in scoring position and still could have scored in a variety of ways.

But when Yaz got to third and finally looked up, Aparicio was still there. Yaz yelled for him to go home, but Aparicio wasn't going anywhere. Yaz started to scramble back to second but was easily put out. Reggie Smith then struck out to end the rally.

While Aparicio's mistake was an unavoidable physical error — the turf was wet at Tiger Stadium because of a backed-up storm sewer — Yastrzemski's mistake was mental. Little Leaguers run with their heads down, not major leaguers. After the game, third base coach Eddie Popowski told Harold Kaese, "I told him [Aparicio] to go back to third and there was no way then to hold Yaz at second."

Aparicio, of course, got all the blame. On the game broadcast, Boston announcer Ned Martin pointed out Aparicio's Opening Day stumble to listeners, underscoring the fall and putting the focus on the uncharacteristic slip rather than the all-too-frequent baserunning miscue by Yaz. Aparicio's slip, like Snodgrass's muff and Pesky's delayed throw, is more the stuff of legend than fact. The Boston loss, like most of the critical defeats in their checkered history, was a team effort all the way.

The following night's game was a must-win for Boston. Tiant, the hottest pitcher in baseball, faced the Tigers' Woody Fryman.

The season ended abruptly in the seventh inning. Dick McAuliffe doubled, then Al Kaline, who did for Detroit what Yaz usually did for Boston, knocked him in with a single. The Tigers clinched the division title, winning 3-1.

Tom Yawkey visited the clubhouse following the game and consoled his players. Many wept openly. Yastrzemski told the press the loss was "the greatest disappointment of my life." Eddie Kasko shook Tiant's hand and in an understatement proclaimed, "Goddamn it, you had one hell of a year."

The game the Red Sox lost to the strike made the finale insignificant, and Boston won a meaningless game that left them half a game shy of a title. The Sox had duplicated their eighty-five wins in 1971 by winning thirty-seven of their last fifty-nine, and finally appeared to be in position again to challenge for the pennant in 1973.

Carlton Fisk was the unanimous selection as AL Rookie of the Year and even placed fourth in MVP balloting, behind Dick Allen, Joe Rudi, and Sparky Lyle, who saved thirty-five games for the Yankees. Danny Cater hit .237 and ended his first season in Boston on the bench.

With the new designated-hitter rule scheduled to go into effect, O'Connell signed former Cardinal Orlando Cepeda as a free agent to fill the role. Cepeda commented, "I have always wanted to play in Boston since Ted Williams was my idol and now I have my chance." The thirty-five-year-old slugger brought 358 career homers and two chronically injured knees to Fenway Park.

But clubhouse troubles for a team some described as "twenty-five players who take twenty-five cabs" sank the club. This time the specter of racial trouble added to the divisive atmosphere.

Reggie Smith was at the center of that dispute. He battled with teammates all year long.

Smith thought there was a double standard in the way black and white players were treated by the Sox and by the Boston media. Earlier that year he complained to *Herald* reporter Fred Ciampa that there was "a code of conduct for white athletes and one for black athletes." Smith went on to charge, "I get it every day from the fans in the stands . . . There are a lot of sick people up there and I'm getting pretty fed up with it." Smith then produced a letter he had received marked by the frequent use of the word "nigger" and splashed with red ink to look like blood.

Smith included the press in his diatribe, saying, "All I ever wanted to do here was my job. I feel there are guys in the press who are racist and won't admit it. I don't mind being knocked for something I do wrong on the field but I can see racism in the form of knocking. For instance, sometimes I've been quoted talking like a hick who never went to school. And that's ridiculous."

With outfielder Tommy Harper on his way to setting the team record for stolen bases with an AL best fifty-four, and Orlando Cepeda rapping .290 with twenty home runs, the Sox stayed close for the first half. They appeared poised to make a move in July after beating the Yankees four out of five as both John Curtis and Roger Moret won 1-0 shutouts. Moret was dazzling for the remainder of the season, winning eleven in a row to finish 13-3.

But on August 10 Smith walked off the field in the

Umpire Bill Kunkel hands Tommy Harper second base after Harper breaks the Red Sox' single-season record for stolen bases with number fifty-three in a game against the Brewers on September 29, 1973.

second inning of a game against the Angels, showered, dressed, and went home without permission. He was fined seven hundred fifty dollars. Smith claimed his knees prevented him from playing and told *Herald* writer Bill Liston, "I have other problems — no one knows what I have gone through this year." By the end of August he was demanding a trade.

Despite enjoying their best won-lost record since the Impossible Dream, the Sox simply couldn't catch Baltimore. During one late-season stretch, the Sox, despite winning eight of nine, actually lost ground as the Orioles were in the midst of a fourteen-game winning streak.

Boston's streak of "close but no cigar" seasons and the changing nature of player relations was wearing on everyone. Even Tom Yawkey sounded weary. He told *The Sporting News*, "I don't know whether I want to stay in baseball much longer. You bet your life I'm disturbed by what's going on. Last year's strike made me stop and think and now here we are again. If this stuff is going to continue every spring I'll have to ask myself if it's all worthwhile."

Kasko paid the price. Despite winning eighty-nine games, the most in his four-year tenure, he was fired on the final day of the season as the era of raised expectations claimed another skipper. Former pitching coach and Pawtucket manager Darrell Johnson was promoted to lead the Red Sox.

On October 23 Reggie Smith got what he wanted and was traded to the St. Louis Cardinals with Ken Tatum for pitcher Rick Wise and outfielder Bernie Carbo. Little did Dick O'Connell know that he had just acquired two charter members of a clique that was soon to be known as the "Buffalo Heads." He did know he had acquired one of the best righthanded starters in the National League.

On December 7 the Sox made another deal with the Cardinals, this time sending pitchers Lynn McGlothen, John Curtis, and Mike Garman to St. Louis for pitchers Reggie Cleveland, Diego Segui, and infielder Terry Hughes.

Darrell Johnson made his mark in spring training, dumping future Hall of Famers Cepeda and Aparicio. Like a latter-day Lou Boudreau, he decided to stake his reputation on youth. Veterans learned that if they didn't keep up, they'd be passed by. Shortstop Rick Burleson, first baseman Cecil Cooper, and outfielders Fred Lynn and Jim Rice were among the players knocking at the door.

Johnson decided to use the designated-hitter slot to give regulars a rest and give youngsters like Cecil Cooper needed at bats. He also announced he would

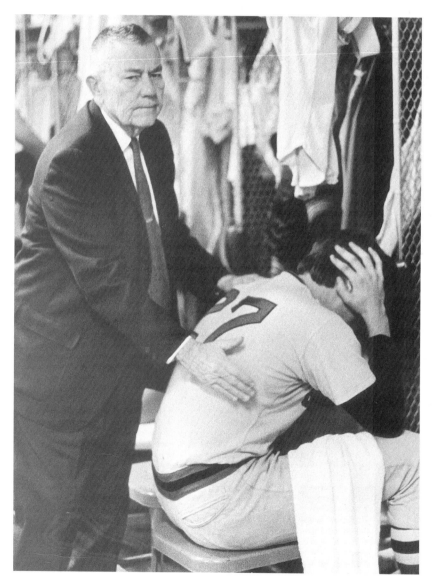

Tom Yawkey consoles Carlton Fisk in the Tiger Stadium clubhouse following the Red Sox' devastating 3-1 loss on October 3 which eliminated them from the pennant race on the next-to-last day of the strike-shortened 1972 season. The Red Sox lost the division by a mere half game. Yawkey would chastise photographer Frank O'Brien shortly after the picture was snapped only to call him the following day to praise him for the superb photograph.

increase the emphasis on defense, telling the *Herald*'s Bill Liston, "I've been saying all along that the best player defensively at three positions — catcher, shortstop, and center field — will get the starting jobs."

The Sox took advantage of a weak AL East in the first half, playing just over .500 baseball but still managing to stay in first place. They lost Rick Wise to arm woes and second baseman Doug Griffin to a Nolan Ryan fastball to the head, but the injuries seemed not to matter.

The coup de grâce, however, was administered at Cleveland's Municipal Stadium on June 28. In a home plate collision Fisk tore ligaments in his knee. He underwent eight hours of surgery and emerged in a full leg cast. Larry Claflin wrote, "Fisk could be the best we have had and now that he is out with him go most of the Red Sox pennant hopes."

Bob Montgomery took over behind the plate. He was no Fisk. Still, Tiant and Bill Lee managed to pitch well enough to keep Boston in first place. With an eight-game lead on August 30 the press started looking ahead to the Sox' first appearance in the LCS against Dick Williams's potent Oakland A's.

But once other teams started playing well, the Sox just couldn't keep pace. They missed Fisk's bat — no regular hit more than fifteen home runs. Boston dropped like a stone.

The beginning of the end came in Baltimore on September 2. The Orioles swept a doubleheader as both Lee and Tiant lost 1-0. That seemed to alert Baltimore to the fact that even after playing .500 baseball for five months, they still had a chance.

The Sox dropped five of their next seven to fall back as the Orioles surged, winning twenty-eight of their last thirty-four.

Reflecting on the collapse, Bill Lee later observed, "The team stopped playing as a unit. Guys tried to win games by swinging for the fences instead of staying within themselves and doing the little things, the

Red Sox catcher Carlton Fisk scuffles with his Yankee counterpart Thurman Munson in this 1973 Fenway Park brawl which also features Carl Yastrzemski, pitcher John Curtis (in glasses), second baseman Doug Griffin (with sideburns), and Fred "Chicken" Stanley (in batting helmet).

fundamentals that had gotten us there in the first place."

Despite the collapse Johnson's team had exceeded expectations as his young players, like Dwight Evans, Rick Burleson, Juan Beniquez, and Cooper, excelled and gained valuable pennant-race experience. And in the final weeks Fred Lynn and Jim Rice served notice that they too were ready for Boston.

To make room in Boston's crowded outfield, O'Connell traded away Tommy Harper, leaving Johnson with the pleasant task of choosing an outfielder from the best crop of young prospects since the days of Tris Speaker. Then in November Tony Conigliaro asked if he could attempt another comeback. O'Connell welcomed him back. After working out with scout Frank Malzone in Winter Haven, Tony C. reported, "My depth perception has never been better, I think I'm going to make it."

When A's pitcher Catfish Hunter was declared a free agent, Boston was the first team to make him an offer and thought they had the inside track — Yawkey had known Hunter for years. But Boston underestimated the market and the Yankees signaled their return by signing Hunter to a five-year deal at 2.85 million dollars.

Training camp had just gotten under way when Carlton Fisk, still hobbled by his knee injury, was hit by a pitch and broke his arm. Veteran Tim McCarver was added while Fisk recovered.

Despite the excellent play of rookies Lynn and Rice, and the apparently successful return of Tony C., who won the DH job, the team left camp to mixed reviews. Pitching was still a problem.

O'Connell tried to get more, offering the Indians five prospects for Gaylord Perry, but the deal died when he refused to include Juan Beniquez. Yet another Red Sox season began with questions about pitching.

Fenway Park had almost a World Series atmosphere on Opening Day as Tony Conigliaro made his triumphant homecoming and Hank Aaron made his American League debut with Milwaukee. Conigliaro received four standing ovations and slashed a single, but within a month his career would end, this time for good, as his vision failed him again.

After a slow start the Sox moved into first place in May. When Yawkey made his first appearance in Boston on June 9 the Sox held a two-game lead.

One reason was center fielder Fred Lynn. He was enjoying the best debut in memory, inspiring comparisons to the greatest players in Boston history.

The Chicago native grew up in El Monte, California, just outside of Los Angeles, and played cornerback as a freshman for John McKay's Trojans at USC and starred for Ron Dedeaux's baseball team. Lynn, who had been drafted by the Yankees in high school, was drafted out of college by the Red Sox with their second pick in 1973. After two seasons in the minors he looked like the best player in baseball.

And in Fenway Park, he may have been just that, a Hall of Fame caliber ballplayer, a combination of Tris Speaker and Ted Williams. His swing was made for Fenway Park, and no player ever took better advantage of Fenway, where from 1974 through 1980 Lynn hit .350 with a .608 slugging percentage, just a tad below the numbers notched by Williams and Jimmie Foxx, made more impressive by the added element of his superb defensive play.

Yet despite his amazing talent, Lynn ran into too many walls in Boston, both real and imagined. Red Sox fans could never quite figure him out and came to the conclusion the laid-back Californian didn't care. They wanted him to have Yastrzemski's grind-it-out personality. So too, eventually, would the front office. But in 1975 the player whose career ended up in Anaheim looked to be a sure bet for Cooperstown.

On June 18 anyone who hadn't already heard about Lynn did. In Detroit he enjoyed a remarkable day,

launching three home runs with a triple and an infield hit, finishing 5-for-5 with sixteen total bases and ten RBIs.

"I've never done anything like this before in my life," he said. "I did hit six homers in six days when I was in college once, and I got five hits in a game once but I don't remember where. It's funny, I hadn't slept. I felt lousy." When asked if he had ever imagined doing something like this, Lynn answered wryly, "Sure, I think the term they used in psychology was 'delusions of grandeur.'"

But he was no illusion. Coach Don Zimmer said, "In all of my 27 years in the game, over 2 1/2 months, I've never seen anyone do everything, hit, hit with power, field, throw — like this kid. Unbelievable." Added *Globe* columnist Leigh Montville, "He has played as if he has been a major league center fielder for years . . . His season has been a total dream walk from beginning to end."

Fisk returned on June 23 and it began to look like Boston's year. O'Connell started plugging holes in anticipation of a pennant run. When pitcher Dick Pole was struck in the face by a line drive, O'Connell immediately replaced him with Cardinal pitcher Jim Willoughby. "Next year" was suddenly "now."

By the All-Star break the Red Sox led by four and a half. They went 38-23 in July and August and extended their lead to six games by Labor Day. Any doubts that Boston couldn't hold their lead were erased on September 16.

Luis Tiant faced Jim Palmer at Fenway Park before a packed house and the national media. His elderly parents had just arrived from Cuba.

Peter Gammons later described the scene as "a frenzied celebration, somewhere between a bullfight and Woodstock. Almost 35,000 crammed into Fenway Park dancing atop the Baltimore dugout and calling for ovations before Luis Tiant even reached the mound. And by the ninth inning, orchestrated by El Tiante's brilliant performance, the old place resounded with a chant of Loo-ie, Loo-ie, Loooo-iee, as the matador finished off his 2-0 victory over the Orioles." It marked the most important victory in a season in which Tiant became Boston's most beloved athlete. Although Boston was torn apart by racial conflicts because of busing, the outpouring of affection toward Tiant from fans of all persuasions was a beacon of hope.

Even more remarkable was Tiant's performance given the circumstances under which he was pitching. According to Dick O'Connell, Tiant was a heavy gambler. He was deeply in debt during the 1975 season and took the mound on more than one occasion after receiving death threats. O'Connell still calls him "the guttiest pitcher I ever saw. He was unbelievable sometimes."

Boston roared to the finish as every starting pitcher won thirteen games or more and rookies Lynn and Rice led a balanced attack made better by the return of Fisk, who hit .331 after returning. But on September 21 Rice was lost when his hand was broken by an errant pitch. At the time Rice was batting .309 with twenty-two homers and 102 RBIs, and he had yet to make an error playing the Wall. In any other season, he was the rookie of the year. In 1975, he wasn't even the best rookie on his team. That honor went to Lynn. The injury sent Carl Yastrzemski back to left field.

On September 27 the Sox clinched their first AL East title, beating the Indians 5-2 while the Orioles lost to New York.

The Oakland A's — even without Catfish Hunter — still had Vida Blue, Ken Holtzman, Reggie Jackson, and Sal Bando. They won the AL West handily and were heavy favorites in the LCS. The best-of-five series opened at Fenway Park on Saturday, October 4. Luis Tiant faced Ken Holtzman in the opener.

Tim Horgan described game one as "both a masterpiece and a mess, a classic and calamity," as the two clubs combined for seven errors and several other miscues. But the Sox had Tiant. He outpitched Holtzman and held the A's to three hits as Boston scored seven runs, most because of a wild throw by Claudell Washington in the first and a dropped flyball by center fielder Billy North in the seventh. Boston won 7-1.

When Rice got hurt, Darrell Johnson had asked Yaz if he could still play left. Yastrzemski replied, "In my sleep." In game two, he proved it.

Yaz turned back the clock. Sal Bando hit two rockets off the wall, but Yaz expertly held him to singles

EL TIANTE

At the height of the Boston school busing crisis in 1974 and 1975 the most beloved man in Boston was black, wore flashy clothes, smoked a big cigar, drove a big car, and worked by night in the Fens. Luis Clemente Tiant was more than a pitcher — he was a performer who captivated Red Sox fans by glancing toward heaven during his inimitable windup and then delivering pitches that hitters didn't have a prayer of hitting. Even today, when Tiant returns to Fenway, chants of "Loo-ie, Loo-ie" still rock Fenway.

His was the most improbable career of any Red Sox superstar. In 1971 the once-unstoppable Indians ace was only three seasons removed from having won twenty-one games with a 1.60 ERA. Arm trouble bounced him first to the Twins and then the Braves organization before Dick O'Connell took a flier on him.

He looked foolish at first, for Tiant struggled in 1971 as he regained arm strength and command, going 1-7. But the Sox stuck with him and he pitched his way into the rotation in 1972, nearly leading the Sox to a division title. In 1973 he blossomed with the first of his three twenty-win seasons with a record of 20-13.

In 1975 Tiant failed to win twenty games but provided Boston's best pitching effort in the World Series. As Tim Horgan described his game one, 6-0 shutout effort, "El Tiante was, in a word, gorgeous as he sketched another of those jobs that belongs more in an art gallery than a ball yard."

He was the quintessential money pitcher, a big-game guy. In 1978, in what would prove to be his last game for Boston, the "caballero," nearing forty, strutted his stuff in the last game of the regular season and won 7-0. As he fired his last pitches the Red Sox learned of their ill-fated playoff date with the Yankees.

But within three months of the playoff loss, the Sox rejected Tiant by offering him only a one-year contract, and Tiant, in turn, rejected the Sox. An era ended when he signed with the Yankees, and the next two years Boston fans with cable TV were appalled to see him shilling Yankee Franks on WPIX, saying, "It's good to pitch for a wee-ner." Only Luis Tiant could ever get away with saying something like that and still remain a Red Sox hero. ⌀

on each. He also made two running catches and threw out Bert Campaneris at the plate. Then he socked a two-run homer off Vida Blue in the fourth to lead a Boston comeback. Cleveland, Moret, and Drago combined for the 6-2 win. As the two clubs left the field the Boston crowd took a page from the Royal Rooters and serenaded A's owner Charlie Finley in his box along third base, singing "Goodbye Charlie, Goodbye Charlie, Goodbye Charlie, we hate to see you go."

In Oakland the A's sent game-one starter Ken Holtzman back out to face the Red Sox on only two days' rest. But his defense let him down once more as Rick Wise and Dick Drago combined to win 5-3. The Red Sox were headed to the World Series.

Since Boston's last appearance in the fall classic, pro football had threatened to supplant baseball as the national pastime. In response, Major League Baseball had initiated dramatic changes, introducing the designated hitter and divisional playoffs. A spate of new multipurpose stadiums had been built, including the Reds' horrific artificially turfed River-

Luis Tiant displays rare batting form in the first game of the 1975 World Series at Fenway Park. Tiant pitched a complete-game five-hitter, stroked a single, and scored the game's first run as the Red Sox won by a score of 6-0.

front Stadium, making Fenway look absolutely antique.

Even the World Series had been modified, as the schedule was altered and games during the week were played at night to accommodate television. As Leonard Koppett wrote in *The Sporting News* on the eve of the Series, "On an absolute scale, baseball attendance is holding its own . . . [But] it is not doing as well as it did a generation ago, nor as well as it could or should."

Baseball's deliberate efforts to "modernize" the game had failed to re-establish the sport in the hearts and minds of America. But baseball had unintentionally set the stage for the game's imminent rebirth. All

the game really needed was a classic Series played in ubertraditional Fenway Park.

The Sox weren't given much of a chance against Cincinnati's "Big Red Machine." The Reds had won 108 games, won their division by 20 games, and blown out the Pirates in the LCS. At virtually every position, save starting pitching, the club of Pete Rose, Joe Morgan, and Johnny Bench appeared better than Boston.

The Sox weren't helped by the fact that they'd be unable to use the designated hitter in the Series, relegating Juan Beniquez and Bernie Carbo to spot duty. Boston's pitchers would have to hit for the first time all year, leading Luis Tiant to joke confidently, "I'm going for the long ball. When I hit the ball, I hit it deep."

A light drizzle coated Boston on Saturday, October 11, for the Series opener. Tiant took the mound for Boston opposite Cincinnati's Don Gullett.

Tiant mesmerized the Reds early, retiring the first ten hitters before Joe Morgan singled with one out in the fourth. He watched him carefully, for the Reds All-Star second baseman had stolen sixty-seven bases in 1975 and had added four more in the playoffs against the Pirates.

Before the Series began Reds manager Sparky Anderson planted a seed with the umpires, complaining that Tiant's pickoff move was illegal. Now, as Tiant threw over to first to hold Morgan, Anderson's power of suggestion paid off. NL ump Nick Colosi called a balk.

But Tiant was never a better pitcher than when he was in trouble. It took him thirteen pitches — no two alike — but he got Johnny Bench to foul out to Fisk before striking out Tony Perez to close the inning.

Don Gullett matched Tiant into the seventh. With the pitcher due to lead off, Johnson never considered a pinch hitter. Tiant responded with a solid single to left.

Dwight Evans tried to sacrifice him to second, but Gullett fielded the bunt and threw the ball into center

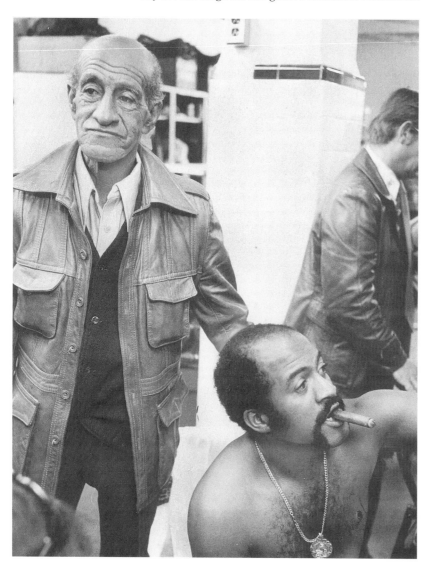

Luis Tiant Sr. shares a quiet moment with his son after the Red Sox' 6-0 victory in the first game of the 1975 World Series. Tiant enjoyed a reunion with his parents after Massachusetts senator Edward Brooke directed a personal request to Cuban president Fidel Castro to have them flown in from Cuba.

field. The miscue rattled him. Denny Doyle followed with a hit to load the bases, bringing up Carl Yastrzemski.

Yastrzemski drilled a single, scoring Tiant, who missed home on his first pass and had to backtrack to find home plate. While his batting skills hadn't deteriorated, his baserunning surely had.

The end came quickly. The Sox went on to score six, and Tiant rocked and spun and rolled to a 6-0 shutout win that Horgan called "The Luis Tiant Show, a rollicking variety hour, a Saturday Afternoon Spectacular that must have entranced some 50 million televiewers better than Sesame Street." On that day a national audience discovered what Boston fans already knew — Tiant was the most entertaining player in the game. Game by game, interest in the Series slowly built.

Tiant even impressed the Reds. Pete Rose, who'd called Catfish Hunter an "average" pitcher, said, "We haven't got anybody in the National League like that . . . those high spinning curve balls take two minutes to come down."

Johnson gambled in game two, turning to seventeen-game winner Bill Lee, who hadn't started since straining an elbow ligament in late August. On another drizzly afternoon at Fenway, Cecil Cooper led off with a double to left, then moved to third on Denny Doyle's third hit of the Series. Yastrzemski then chopped a bouncer to pitcher Jack Billingham, who forced Doyle at second. But Cooper blundered, breaking for home then changing his mind. Caught in a rundown, he was put out, but Yaz made it to second and scored the game's first run on a single by Fisk.

Boston led 2-1 in the seventh when play was stopped for twenty-seven minutes because of rain. Following the delay, Lee gave up a leadoff double to Johnny Bench to start the ninth. Johnson pulled him, and he left to a standing ovation as Dick Drago forced Tony Perez to ground out to Burleson, advancing Bench to third. Foster then flied out to Yastrzemski. Boston was within one out of a 2-0 lead in the Series.

But the Reds had the best blend of power and speed in the game, and while their power could occasionally be checked, their speed never let up. Short-stop Dave Concepcion chopped the ball over Drago's head and beat it out for a hit as Bench scored the tying run. Then he stole second, getting in just ahead of Burleson's tag. Ken Griffey followed with a double off the Wall to score him, and after being held to only one run over their first seventeen innings of Series play, the Reds suddenly led 3-2. Rawley Eastwick closed the door with a perfect ninth inning.

After the game, the glib Lee was unusually terse. Asked his impression of the Series, he answered, "Tied."

The two clubs traveled to Cincinnati for the next three contests, all night games scheduled for prime time.

Rick Wise started for Boston and nursed a 1-0 lead into the fourth. Then the Big Red Machine roared to life, smacking three home runs to go ahead 5-1.

But in this Series no lead was ever safe, not even over the Red Sox. In the seventh inning, DH turned Series pinch hitter Bernie Carbo belted a homer to make the score 5-3. In the ninth with one out and one on, Dwight Evans belted a Rawley Eastwick fastball into the night for a two-run blast that tied the game.

Boston reliever Jim Willoughby had held the Reds scoreless since entering the game in the seventh. In the bottom of the tenth, Cesar Geronimo singled and pinch hitter Ed Armbrister attempted to sacrifice him to second.

As he squared to bunt, Fisk rose from his crouch. Armbrister stepped and leaned over the plate and barely made contact, sending the ball down into the ground then straight back up in the air.

Fisk reached out and over Armbrister to catch the ball and threw to second as the two men briefly became entangled. The throw sailed into center field. Geronimo dashed to third and Armbrister made it to second.

Darrell Johnson sprang from the Boston dugout as Fisk began arguing with home plate umpire Larry Barnett, claiming that Armbrister had interfered with him on the play and caused his throw to go wild.

Johnson made the same argument. So did fifty million fans watching on television, as the play was shown over and over and over again. It was a clear case of interference.

But Barnett never saw it. He insisted loudly that there was no interference on the play. His error may have changed the Series.

Roger Moret was summoned from the bullpen and walked Pete Rose intentionally to set up the double play. After striking out Merv Rettenmund for the first out, Boston's outfield moved in as Joe Morgan came to the plate.

Morgan lofted a flyball to center, deep enough to score Geronimo. The Reds won 3-2.

After the game, the Sox were still incensed by Barnett's call. Carl Yastrzemski fumed and pointed out that none of the umpires in the Series was chosen on merit, saying, "The best [expletive] teams in [expletive] baseball are in the [expletive] Series, but the best [expletive] umpires aren't. They take [expletive] turns, no matter how [expletive] competent they are. Why don't the [expletive] teams take a turn? Next year, how about San Diego and the Angels playing, no matter where they [expletive] finish."

Carlton Fisk was less profane but no less direct, saying, "It's a damn shame losing a ballgame like that. I'm an infielder on a play like that. Well, why isn't the man out? And as far as I'm concerned it's a double play. But there's nobody out and we lose the damn game because this guy is making a joke of umpiring behind the plate."

Barnett tried to explain, saying, "Armbrister did not intentionally interfere with the catcher. It was a collision in process and in my judgement — and it was strictly a judgement play — there was no intentional interference and that's how I called the play."

Barnett was half right. Interference *is* a judgment call, but whether it was intentional or not has no bearing on the call.

Globe columnist Ray Fitzgerald observed, "I have been in many sullen and snarling locker rooms in the last decade, but none as bitter as the one last night. The Grinch had stolen Christmas from the Red Sox."

The firestorm thrust Luis Tiant into the role of both stopper and savior in game four. He delivered a virtuoso performance, tossing 163 pitches at every speed and from every angle. After giving up two first-inning runs he escaped more disasters than Buster Keaton

in a silent feature, rising to the occasion again and again to leave the Reds frustrated short of home. He entered the ninth nursing a 5-4 lead.

Geronimo led off with a single and Armbrister bunted him over, this time managing to leave the box without colliding with Fisk. Rose then walked.

Ken Griffey stepped up and smoked the ball to center field, but in 1975 Fred Lynn was part Tris Speaker. Like his predecessor, Lynn turned and ran at full speed before gracefully pulling down the drive with an over-the-shoulder catch. Joe Morgan then popped up to end the game and the Series was tied. No missed calls, no rain, just the rumble of what the *Herald* called "the Big Tiant Machine."

Following the game Darrell Johnson summed up the feelings of every man on the club. "If a man put a gun to my head and said I'm going to pull the trigger if you lose this game," he said, "I'd want Luis Tiant to pitch that game."

Johnson also announced his rotation for the remainder of the Series. Reggie Cleveland would pitch game five, saving Bill Lee for game six back in Boston. Game seven would be Luis Tiant's, and no one who had watched the Series thus far had any doubt game seven would be needed.

For the first few innings of game five Reggie Cleveland pitched nearly as well as Tiant and Lee had. But with a 1-0 lead in the fourth, Tony Perez — 0-14 in the Series thus far — became a very big 1-for-15, tying the game with a solo home run. His second homer of the game gave the Reds a commanding 5-1 lead.

That was enough. The Reds won 6-2 to draw within one victory of a world championship. As Johnny Bench commented, "We're not the so called Big Red Machine unless all the parts are working. Tonight they were."

The two clubs returned to Boston and rain. Game six was postponed not once but three times, and second-guessing Darrell Johnson became New England's favorite pastime. Some Bill Lee fans argued that it was his right to pitch the must-win sixth game, thereby reserving Tiant for the important game seven. But the rain gave Tiant the rest he needed. Common sense argued that if Boston didn't win game six, game seven would be played only over Darrell Johnson's cold dead body.

JIM RICE AND THE NUMBERS

"I'm paid and should be judged by the numbers." That was all Jim Rice ever asked. Red Sox fans and the Boston media often asked for more, but Rice was resolute. He didn't care if he was liked and he didn't care if he was loved. He refused to tout his own accomplishments. His job was to go out on the field every day and play — not play pattycake with the media, kibitz with fans, or be a cheerleader. He probably should have, because it is undeniable that at times he disrupted the Red Sox clubhouse and that personality has had a long-lasting effect on his reputation. Yet in his terms, the numbers he put on the field provide the most dispassionate way to assess his career.

On another player's résumé, the numbers seem enough to ensure admittance to the Hall of Fame. On the back of Jim Rice's baseball card, they appear to fall just short.

In Rice's rookie year, he hit .309 with twenty-two home runs and 102 RBIs, one of the best rookie seasons in Red Sox history, but was eclipsed by Fred Lynn's even more remarkable season. But he had the bad luck to arrive at the same time as Fred Lynn. Both players had been called up at the end of the 1974 season. Rice did okay, but Lynn hit .419. Entering the 1975 season, Rice was already an afterthought.

Lynn also beat Rice in areas that Rice didn't think should matter but did: Lynn was faster, flashier, more open, sexier in baseball terms, and white — and thereby more celebrated.

Rice played left field, following Williams and Yaz, suffering from the obvious comparisons. Lynn wasn't held to the same standard, for Boston's best center fielders, Tris Speaker and Dom DiMaggio, had already receded from memory. He had the field to himself.

Rice also had the bad timing and misfortune to break his wrist and miss the 1975 World Series, a high point in Red Sox history. With him, they may have won. Instead, he is simply absent from perhaps the most compelling eleven days Boston fans ever experienced.

For the next three seasons, culminating in 1978, Rice had the better numbers, by far, than Lynn. In 1978 he put together one of the best offensive seasons any Red Sox player has ever had. Rice had forty-six home runs with 139 RBIs, a .600 slugging percentage, a .315 batting average, and 406 total bases, the most since Stan Musial in 1948 and more than Ted Williams ever had in a season, an MVP year without question. But bad timing again diminished it, for it came in a year that ended in disappointment so acute that it overshadowed his singular achievement. And in the 1978 playoff game versus New York Rice didn't cap his MVP season with an MVP game.

After 1978 Rice was a victim of expectations. He was never better, although in 1979 and 1983, when he cracked thirty-nine home runs, he was close. But Lynn trumped him in 1979, and in 1983 the Sox were lousy, making each of those seasons appear as something less than what they were. And from 1980 through 1982, he slumped from great to just very good, putting up numbers that chipped away at his reputation.

Like Yaz after 1975, beginning in 1983 Rice rebounded with four nearly spectacular seasons in a row, in all of which he hit twenty or more home runs and knocked in more than one hundred. In 1986, as a thirty-three-year-old veteran, he hit .324, the second highest average of his career, and was again an MVP candidate. But just as Lynn had earlier overshadowed him, now Roger Clemens did the same.

The 1986 World Series could have been his time. Had he come up with a signature performance, like Al Kaline in 1968, Clemente in 1971, Yaz in 1975, or Willie Stargell in 1979, he'd be looked at differently today. But his postseason numbers whisper in comparison to his high-volume marks of the regular season. He hit only .161 with two home runs in the LCS, and although he hit .333 in the World Series, he didn't hit a home run or collect an RBI.

After 1986, bothered by a bad elbow, Rice simply faded. With hallmark career numbers like 400 home runs and a .300 batting average in reach, he fell short of both. The player Hank Aaron once speculated might break his career home run mark ended his career barely halfway there, with 382, with a batting average of .298, numbers that don't quite add up to the Hall of Fame.

But Rice's baseball career wasn't over. Since 1995 Rice has served as Red Sox batting coach, a hiring that most viewed at the time with skepticism. Yet as Dan Duquette has run players through the Red Sox roster, it has been Rice's task to turn them into hitters. He has. Few players have backtracked under his tutelage, youngsters like Mo Vaughn, Nomar Garciaparra, and Trot Nixon have thrived, and he has had some remarkable successes with players plucked off the scrap heap of other organizations, like Troy O'Leary, Jason Varitek, and Brian Daubach. All were failures elsewhere before they reached Boston.

If the man himself won't speak, those numbers do. ⊘

As the deluge continued and with the hypothetical pistol drawn and the trigger cocked at his head, Johnson skipped over Lee and chose Tiant to pitch the sixth game. Lee would pitch game seven.

That didn't make sense in Bill Lee's brain. He whined about being skipped over, telling Peter Gammons while in a damp Fenway Park on Sunday afternoon, "We should have played [last night]. This is my weather. We could have played and no one would have hit a home run . . . Who cares if we lose in six or seven games? The idea is to win and I think we're better off with me pitching in the sixth game. Luis can use that extra day and then you have him matched with Gullett. I'm sure I can beat Nolan. I think I can beat Gullett. The biggest reason Johnson is going with Tiant in Game Six is to satisfy certain elements of the media."

The rain finally stopped and on Monday, October 21, at 8:30 P.M. all Boston settled in for the most anticipated game in club history. Eighty-seven-year-old Duffy Lewis, left fielder on three Red Sox world champion teams and the first player to ascend Duffy's Cliff and patrol the left-field wall, threw out the first ball.

The Sox proved Lee's estimation of Reds pitcher Gary Nolan was correct. With two outs Yastrzemski lined a single to right and was moved to second by a Fisk single to left. Fred Lynn then flexed his MVP muscle by smashing a home run into the right-center bleachers. Boston led 3-0.

Through the first four innings Luis Tiant was at his gyrating best, but in the fifth he showed a crack. After a walk to Armbrister and a hit by Pete Rose, Ken Griffey launched a line drive toward left-center field. Fred Lynn, at full gallop, ran and then jumped for the drive before crashing into the concrete and collapsing as the ball bounded away untouched for a two-run triple. Fenway turned as quiet as a church. As trainer Charlie Moss attended to Lynn everyone worried that Boston would lose yet another promising young outfielder to injury. A ripple of applause then

Rookie center fielder Fred Lynn, shown here in the 1975 World Series, became the first player ever to capture Rookie of the Year and MVP honors in the same season. He and fellow rookie outfielder Jim Rice were known as the "Gold Dust Twins" as they batted .331 and .309 respectively.

turned to full-throated cheers as Lynn first stirred, then stood and remained in the game.

Morgan popped up to Petrocelli, but Tiant still couldn't wiggle loose. Bench lined a single to plate Griffey with the tying run.

Despite four days of rest, Tiant noticeably tired in his 294th inning of the season. In the seventh all he had left was guts and guile and the hopes and dreams of the entire franchise.

That was not enough, and the Reds finally began to decode Tiant's whirling, twirling windup. Griffey and Morgan led off the inning with singles.

Sox fans hoped for one of Tiant's patented escapes, and as he turned his back to sort through his sorcerer's bag of pitches, he found the two he needed, getting Bench on a line drive and Perez on a fly to Evans in right field. That brought up George Foster.

But Tiant's bag was empty. Foster drilled a ball to center field where even Speaker couldn't have caught it, over Lynn's head and off the wall for a two-run double. Concepcion grounded out to end the inning.

Fenway was as still as it had been when Lynn lay injured, only this time the body on the ground was the entire Red Sox team. In the chill night air the crowd watched in silence. The possibility that only nine outs remained in what had been a glorious season was almost too much to bear.

Boston went down quietly in the bottom of the inning. Tiant went back to the mound for the eighth inning, but Cesar Geronimo led off with a home run just inside the Pesky pole. As a yellow metal numeral "6" was placed by hand alongside the "Cin" column in the left-field scoreboard, Luis Tiant trudged off the field, his magic and his right arm exhausted. With him walked all apparent hope for Boston. Roger Moret retired Borbon, Rose, and Griffey in order.

But at an hour in which most Americans were usually in bed, the sixth game was about to provide entertainment unmatched by any dream.

Fred Lynn led off with a drive through the box that caromed off Pedro Borbon's leg for a single. Petrocelli then worked him for a walk. That was enough for the manager some called "Captain Hook." Sparky Anderson called on reliever Rawley Eastwick.

Dwight Evans struck out. Then Burleson lined out to Foster.

Roger Moret was scheduled to hit next, but Johnson had already told Bernie Carbo — a former Red — to get ready to hit. This Red Sox team had some depth.

Eastwick's first pitch fooled Carbo, and he swung with a defensive chop that resembled the closed-eye swing a little leaguer takes when facing the proverbial older kid. Most observers, and Carbo himself, thought it was the worst swing by a major leaguer they had ever seen.

But the swing that followed was as beautiful as the one that had preceded it was ugly. Peter Gammons described what followed as "out came an Implausible Hero to a two out, two on situation against Rawlins J. Eastwick III and Carbo did what he had done in Cincinnati. Pinch hitting, he sent a line drive into the center field bleachers, and the chill of lachrymose had become mad, sensuous Fenway."

Carbo hit the crap out of the ball.

"Funny," he said later, "when I hit the ball, my right hand came off the bat and I didn't think that I had much power behind the ball, but it kept climbing and wound up in the seats. I really didn't think that I had hit it that hard. But it was there."

Fenway Park came back to life. The game was tied 6-6, and as Cooper struck out to end the inning no one cared and most didn't even notice. Hope had returned and the Red Sox felt as if victory was inevitable.

The lights remained on across most of North America as both teams went through the ninth and tenth without scoring. In the eleventh, with a man on, Joe Morgan hit what looked to be a possible Series-winning home run to right.

But Dwight Evans ran back and back to the fence just to the right-field side of the bullpens, following the same track Harry Hooper had followed in a similar situation way back in the Series of 1912. He gauged the distance to the fence perfectly and made a balletlike half-leap while sticking out his glove and catching the ball. Then he wheeled and threw instinctively back toward the infield, where Yastrzemski ranged wide for the ball and relayed it to Burleson, covering first, for an inning-ending double play.

Sparky Anderson called it "the greatest catch I have ever seen."

Night became morning. As the Sox came to bat in the twelfth it began to appear as if the game would never end. They hadn't been able to touch Reds pitcher Pat Darcy. Then Carlton Fisk stepped up to the plate.

Ball one. Moving slowly, Fisk craned his neck, felt his bat, and adjusted his stance before Darcy wound up and released his second pitch of the inning.

Fisk swung. As Peter Gammons wrote a few minutes later for the *Globe*, "And all of a sudden the ball was there, like the Mystic River Bridge, suspended out in the black of the morning," heading to left field as 35,205 fans watched it and prayed.

Inside the scoreboard within the left-field wall, an NBC cameraman kept his camera trained on Fisk, and director Harry Coyle instantaneously sent that image across the country. In Fenway, everyone watched the ball.

Fisk looked up and watched it with everyone else, straining, waving the ball fair, and hoping and praying as if imploring the spirits themselves to deliver his team and New England itself from the cruel clutches of history.

CARLTON FISK

Vermont-born and New Hampshire–raised Carlton Fisk was one of only a handful of New England–born Red Sox stars during the Yawkey era. He was also another in a long line of great New England–born catchers that includes such stars as Mickey Cochrane, Gabby Hartnett, and Jim Hegan, and former Sox Birdie Tebbetts and Bill Carrigan. Like his comrades, Fisk was known for his tough, heady play.

He was selected by the Red Sox as the fourth player in the amateur draft nine months before the Impossible Dream became a reality in 1967.

In 1969 Fisk's natural "local boy makes good" story was the subject of a prime-time documentary produced by WHDH-TV entitled, *How Do You Get to Fenway Park?* For six months in 1969 sportscaster Don Gillis followed Fisk from his home in Charlestown, New Hampshire, through spring training to Eastern League Pittsfield, and eventually all the way to Fenway Park. Sox fans felt as if they knew him already.

Although Fisk had a cup of coffee with the Sox in 1969, he was a late-bloomer and really didn't flourish until making the Sox in 1972 and becoming the unanimous winner of the AL Rookie of the Year Award. Not only did the rookie sock twenty-two home runs, make the All-Star squad, and appear on the cover of *Sports Illustrated,* but he also became a team leader when he took over the Red Sox pitching staff and challenged veterans to defy him.

In one memorable incident recounted by Joe Fitzgerald of the *Herald,* Fisk confronted veteran Sonny Siebert during a sub-par outing, barking, "If you don't feel like doing the job, we'll find someone who does. I'm busting my hump back there and you should be, too. I've got a sister who can pitch better than you." Such confrontations won praise from teammates like Ray Culp, who said, "That kid really assumes control, he's a great leader."

Fisk's Boston career peaked with his game-winning, Series-saving, twelfth-inning home run in game six of the 1975 World Series, since selected by *TV Guide* as the top televised sports moment of the century. After that began a long estrangement from the team by its most popular local product since Tony C.

When the Sox refused to renegotiate his contract in 1979 after doing the same for Jim Rice, the writing was on the wall. His contract arrived too late in 1980, and Fisk took advantage, jumping to the other Sox in Chicago. He left Boston after eleven seasons with a .284 batting average and 162 home runs. Baseball commissioner Bartlett Giamatti later called it "the worst moment for Red Sox fans since the team sold Babe Ruth."

Fisk resurrected his career in Chicago and actually played longer for the White Sox and put up better numbers than he did in Boston, becoming a rare "four-decade" player and a certain Hall of Famer. By the time he retired at age forty-five in 1993, Fisk had apparently burned his bridges to Boston, answering the question of which cap would be engraved on his plaque by saying, "It would have to be the White Sox."

But times change. In 1999 the Sox brought Fisk back as a member of the front office as a special assistant. The player singularly responsible for the most memorable moment in the club's first century may well have an impact in the next. And when he was elected to the Baseball Hall of Fame, the Red Sox' new employee decided the image on his plaque would bear the familiar Red Sox "B." ✍

Then he jumped and danced and jumped and danced and clapped his hands and started running! Sox announcer Ned Martin spoke to the masses and delivered the Word. "He swings, long drive to left field. If it stays fair it's gone . . ." The ball ricocheted off the foul pole.

"Home run! The Red Sox win and the Series is tied."

In their seventy-fourth year the Red Sox had uncovered their most glorious moment, the precise point upon which the past and the future, victory and loss, met and hung in the balance. In seventeen hours, there would be a seventh game. But the sixth game would never end.

Columnist Ray Fitzgerald wrote, "Call it off. Call the seventh game off. Let the World Series stand this way, three games for the Cincinnati Reds and three games for the Boston Red Sox . . . At 12:34 it was over but the people stayed. John Kiley played 'Give Me Some Men Who Are Stout Hearted Men' and the fans sang along. He played the 'Beer Barrel Polka' and 'Seventy-Six Trombones' and they sang some more. Next to me, Peter Gammons began to write. 'What was the final score?' he asked. In such a game, numbers didn't seem to mean much."

Tim Horgan was more to the point, calling the game "the best and worst played, when you consider the myriad chances both teams had to win it easily. It'll take the whole of the long winter to sort out the villains, knights, and knaves that populated this chivaree . . . both teams took and gave their best shots last night in a bitter, glorious, stupid, marvelous, damnable game of rounders."

The seventh game began with the promise of a possible dream. But it ended, as it always seems to, as just another line score in the persistent history of the Red Sox. Bolstered by Bill Lee's flawless pitching Boston took a three-run lead into the sixth. Then the sixth game began to fade and recede, and so too did the Red Sox.

Rose singled, then Morgan flied to Evans in shallow right. Johnny Bench bounced a groundball to Burleson. He flipped to Doyle and as Pete Rose hurtled toward him Doyle threw the relay into the Red Sox dugout. Tony Perez stepped up with two outs and first base open.

Lee, ever the contrarian, ignored the scouting reports that warned him not to throw Perez any off-speed junk. In particular, he was warned not to use his "Lee-phus" pitch, a parabolic arc of a curveball. But Lee was usually playing more than one game at a time. The one on the field always had to compete with the one in his head that was scored according to a discrete set of rules that only Lee himself could account.

He threw the parabolic curve. And Perez hit a parabolic catastrophe over the netting of the left-field wall and into darkness. Now Boston led only 3-2.

In the seventh Lee broke a blister, walked Ken Griffey, and left the game to a standing ovation. But after the events of the previous evening the question for most fans still seemed to be "Who will be tonight's hero?" rather than "In what excruciating manner can the Red Sox break our hearts now?"

No one in Boston ever answered the first question. The solution to the second was soon revealed.

Roger Moret surrendered a game-tying hit to Rose, then turned the game over to Jim Willoughby. He pitched scoreless ball to close out the seventh and eighth innings of the tie game.

But it now became apparent that Darrell Johnson had been born to manage the Red Sox and the moment of his reckoning was at hand. In the bottom of the eighth, after Evans walked and Burleson failed to bunt and then hit into a double play, with the game tied and nobody on and the Reds not close to touching Willoughby, Johnson pulled the trigger and it pierced the heart.

He pulled Willoughby for a pinch hitter.

Until that moment, hardly anyone in Boston believed that it was possible for the Sox to lose the sev-

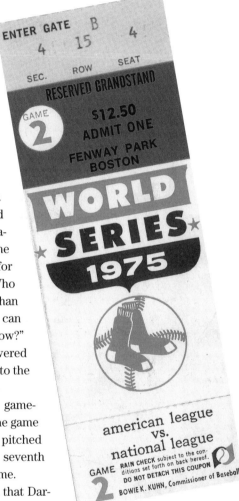

enth game. Now, few thought it would be possible for them to win.

Cecil Cooper struck out. In the ninth, rookie reliever Jim Burton walked to the mound carrying the burden of history.

He walked Griffey to start the inning, and Geronimo sacrificed him to second. Then Dan Driessen grounded out to second and Griffey advanced to third.

Joe Morgan, the 1975 NL MVP, stepped in. With two outs and one ball and two strikes on Morgan, Burton threw a slider low and away. Morgan served it out to right field where it landed clear. Geronimo scored. The Reds led 4-3.

Reds lefty Will McEnany came out to pitch the ninth. Darrell Johnson desperately cast about for someone, anyone, to do what Carbo and Fisk had done the night before.

Juan Beniquez hit for Rick Miller, but he flied out to Ken Griffey. Bob Montgomery hit for Denny Doyle, but he grounded to Concepcion.

No one hit for Carl Yastrzemski. He flied out to Geronimo in left-center. The Reds won the game 4-3 and the Series by the same margin.

In a little under twenty-eight hours the Red Sox and their millions of fans had lived a lifetime of baseball. But their history, at once indescribable and irresistible, had again provided a result that seemed inevitable. In the *Globe* the next day, Ray Fitzgerald wrote, "This was a set of baseball games that almost transcended winning and losing, a string of pearls to be tucked away in a drawer and brought out from time to time to bring back a memory or two." But the key word was "almost."

While Boston confronted loss, elsewhere in America something else had been won. The seventh game drew an amazing seventy-five million television viewers, and over the next several seasons baseball followed the wake of Fisk's sixth-game blast to newfound popularity. Although the Red Sox lost the World Series, they may have helped save baseball.

DEATH, DISAPPOINTMENT, AND DENT

1976 | 1978

The essence of the intense rivalry between the Yankees and Red Sox in the seventies was underscored by the personal rivalry between catchers Thurman Munson and Carlton Fisk. No matchup inspired more of the "Athens v. Sparta" prose common to the era.

After the 1975 World Series few Red Sox fans or even objective observers chose to recall the details of the many small mistakes that cost the club a world championship. Most concurred with pitcher Rick Wise, who said, "They won it. We didn't lose it." Boston was simply beaten by a superb Cincinnati team. In the litany of Red Sox failures, the 1975 Series, like that of 1967, was viewed far more favorably than their 1946 loss to the Cardinals.

In the *New Yorker*, Roger Angell wrote that players would not remember the Series for its result, but for "the honor of having played in it." In the *Globe*, Peter Gammons called 1975 "a season whose life was beautiful and full," and the newspaper gave away stickers that read "Wait'll next year."

It wasn't Joe Morgan's base hit or Tony Perez's towering blast off Bill Lee in game seven that would be the lasting image of the Series, but the parabolic arc of Carlton Fisk's game-ending game-six home run. That moment seemed to herald the impending ascent of the entire Red Sox organization.

Somehow, the glorious defeat left the club and its fans with the belief that this club had somehow earned the right to return to the World Series and win. Baseball's best young outfield would presumably continue to improve, Yaz and Tiant both seemed capable of continuing their Hall of Fame–caliber careers, Fisk and Burleson had yet to peak, and the farm system was still producing promising prospects. This team seemed destined to fulfill the promise of 1967 and erase the past forever.

As the 1977 season approached, that optimism was coupled with urgency. Tom Yawkey was ill with leukemia, but now the world championship he'd almost given up ever winning suddenly seemed within reach. He turned back the clock and gave Dick O'Connell the go-ahead to buy a championship. In November the Sox outbid everyone for Texas pitcher Ferguson Jenkins, at age thirty-one still one of the game's premier players. His acquisition, like that of any number of stars years earlier, seemed to ensure another pennant. In January, the Boston *Herald American* even published a series definitively titled "Why We'll Win in '76."

Everybody should have known better. The 1975 team was actually more the spiritual cousin of the 1946 squad than that of 1967, and the 1976 club would prove kin to the disappointing 1947 Red Sox. All was not quite as "beautiful and full" as it appeared.

Baseball was in turmoil. The Basic Agreement governing player contracts had expired and the Players' Association was lobbying for free agency. In response, the owners voted to lock out the players. March began with spring-training diamonds empty.

Ferguson Jenkins had won twenty or more games in seven of his eleven major league seasons before reaching Boston in 1976. In two seasons with the Red Sox Jenkins was barely a .500 performer with a won-lost record of 12-11 in 1976 and 10-10 in 1977.

Tom Yawkey felt betrayed by the demands of the players and baseball's emerging new order, a situation he had, in fact, helped create. Over decades, his free-spending habits had undercut baseball's argument that the game simply couldn't afford free agency.

Yawkey had paid princely sums and expected blind devotion in return. Instead, his boys were growing up and were beginning to realize that even Yawkey was underpaying them. Fisk, Lynn, and Burleson were clients of Jerry Kapstein, a notoriously shrewd agent known for his ability to extract the highest possible salaries for his clients. Yawkey balked at the notion of paying high salaries to such young, ungrateful stars. When commissioner Bowie Kuhn ended the lockout and ordered the season to start, they briefly held out and started the season with their contract issues unresolved.

Yet at the same time this new age must have seemed eerily familiar to Yawkey. In the past, he'd outspent other owners to such a degree that baseball had changed the rules to stop him. Now, the era of free agency offered him a similar opportunity. De-

spite his illness, this was a game he knew how to play, and he still had the financial resources to do so.

The Red Sox started the season slowly as Jenkins lost 1-0 to Baltimore's Jim Palmer on Opening Day and the club labored through the first few weeks out of sync. The season didn't even seem to begin until late May when the team traveled to New York for a four-game series in Yankee Stadium. The Yankees were already in first place with a 19-10 record, six games ahead of the 13-16 Red Sox.

The rivalry between the two clubs had been reborn, and the series would draw the largest crowds in Yankee Stadium of any four-game set since 1947. Sox fans fully expected Boston's pennant drive to begin in the Bronx. Advance scout Frank Malzone summed up Boston's smugness when he called the Yankees only "an interesting team . . . I'm not sure how far they'll go."

Bill Lee pitched before a raucous crowd in the opener. So far, Lee seemed to be the only Boston player affected by the Series loss to Cincinnati. He was 0-3 with an ERA of almost 10.00.

Although Lee wrapped himself in the trappings of the counterculture, on the mound he was anything but a pacifist. He absolutely *loved* pitching against the Yankees. In his worldview, gritty, urban, stinking New York and their boorish, free-spending owner George Steinbrenner represented all that was evil. To Lee, playing the Yankees was as much a holy war as a baseball game.

Games between the Red Sox and the Yankees mattered again. Both teams stood in the way of what the other wanted. Over the past few seasons the two clubs had engaged in at least one major brawl each year, and those personal conflicts added to the historical and geographic rivalry and turned it into something larger. When Boston played New York the final score rarely decided anything. Other issues remained undecided, to be settled in the next game, the next series, the next year.

Early on, Lee shut down the Yankees. Entering the sixth he trailed only 1-0 and quickly got two outs.

Then he lost it, giving up back-to-back singles to Lou Piniella and Graig Nettles. When Otto Velez followed with a single to Evans in right, Piniella, no sprinter, came home.

The next few moments may well have been the most important of the season. Evans's throw beat Piniella by 20 feet, but Fisk was handcuffed by the throw. Unable to make a swipe tag, he blocked the plate. Piniella, seeing the catcher in an awkward position, half-jumped into Fisk with his knees in an effort to dislodge the ball.

The two collided heavily, and Piniella did a flip as Fisk tagged him out with a combination of his shoulders, chest, and forearms. Both players came up scratching and clawing.

In seconds both dugouts emptied and there were a dozen fights going on all over the field. Players on both sides quickly punched each other out and stood in knots around home plate, grappling with each other.

In the midst of the fray Mickey Rivers suckerpunched Lee, who went down. When he got up Graig Nettles tried to put him in a bear hug. Lee resisted and Nettles threw him to the ground.

Crunch. Lee landed heavily on his left shoulder and both players were thrown from the game.

Lee, the team's only lefthanded starter, tore a ligament in his shoulder and would be out for almost two months. Boston rallied to win 8-2 behind two late Yastrzemski home runs, but the damage had been done. After the game Lee called Yankee manager Billy Martin a "Nazi" and his players "Steinbrenner's Brown Shirts." The Boston press made Lee a hero, but his rash decision to enter the fight had seriously damaged Boston's pennant chances.

The two clubs split the series, but two weeks later New York came to Fenway and took two of three, shaking Boston's confidence. The offense slumped, and Dick Pole failed to make up for the loss of Lee.

Although Darrell Johnson told writers, "Write this down and file it. We will catch the Yankees in six weeks, maybe seven," Yaz cautioned, "We can't let the Yankees get any further in front." By the first week of June, concern turned to panic.

Boston traded Series hero Bernie Carbo to the Milwaukee Brewers for sore-armed relief pitcher Tom Murphy and Bobby Darwin, who in between strikeouts occasionally hit a home run. O'Connell blandly explained, "They wanted him [Carbo] and he wasn't playing here."

Although Murphy eventually helped out in the bullpen, the trade proved unpopular. The magical spell around the team was somehow irrevocably broken.

Darrell Johnson felt it first. He was already starting to crack under the pressure of expectations.

He was ready to quit. After almost every loss, as he reportedly replayed the game over a cocktail or two, he'd call O'Connell and launch into a monologue of self-doubt. O'Connell knew Johnson had lost control of the team, but for the time being more important matters, namely A's owner Charley Finley and Tom Yawkey, distracted him.

Twice before, former A's owner Connie Mack had dumped his high-priced stars on Boston at a premium price, first to Harry Frazee in 1918 and then to Yawkey in the 1930s. Now, current A's owner Charley Finley considered doing the same. No longer able to meet the salary demands of his star players and still turn a profit, he entertained offers for stars like Vida Blue, Rollie Fingers, and Joe Rudi.

Finley and Dick O'Connell dickered for several weeks. Finally, on June 15 — the trading deadline — when Boston was in town to play the A's, Finley decided to do business on virtually a cash-only basis. For one and a half million dollars, he sold the Yankees Vida Blue. For two million dollars and two marginal players — Steve Dillard and Andy Merchant — the Red Sox acquired outfielder Joe Rudi and relief pitcher Rollie Fingers.

The prices were stunning. In the *Herald American*, Tim Horgan called the good news and bad news, writing, "What's good for the Red Sox is not necessarily good for baseball." He also cautioned that "Yawkey has gone this route before and struck out."

Yawkey's role in the transaction is still unclear — O'Connell claims the deals had his approval, while Haywood Sullivan claims they took Yawkey by surprise. But history and the circumstances of Yawkey's illness — he knew he didn't have long to live — suggest he knew what was going on.

Red Sox players were split over the deal. Rudi would cut into the playing time of both Cecil Cooper and Rick Miller. Miller said, "Buy me a cushion for the bench . . . Me and Coop are 'pine brothers.'" Yaz shook his head and said, "I don't know how some franchises can compete," while Petrocelli thought the deal improved Boston's chance to win the pennant by "a thousand percent."

That night, Fingers and Rudi walked from the home to the visitors' clubhouse at the Oakland Coliseum and donned Red Sox uniforms. But Johnson didn't play Rudi that night, saying he needed to rest. Fingers warmed up, but also didn't see action in Boston's 3-2 loss. Had Johnson used either player, it is difficult to imagine the events of the next few days taking place.

On June 16 commissioner Bowie Kuhn barred both the Yankees and the Red Sox from using their new players. Then he voided the deals, claiming they were not "in the best interests of baseball."

Finley howled and promised to sue. Boston players were stunned, and fans went from elation to despair. In his sickbed Tom Yawkey learned that what had been right in 1933 was wrong in 1976. Tired and dying, he decided not to fight the commissioner's decision.

Kuhn's interference scotched any chance Boston had to catch New York. The team deflated afterward, playing .500 baseball and showing signs of coming apart. Former Sox player George Scott, now with Milwaukee, blasted his old teammates, saying, "Too many of them think they're superstars — they're not." The *Herald*'s Larry Claflin offered that the Sox' problem was a "lack of cohesion . . . and playing stupid baseball. With the season nearly past the halfway mark, the Red Sox have still not settled on their best infield."

Indeed, Johnson was being anything but decisive. He second-guessed his own team and, like Lou Boudreau, shuffled the lineup. At various times he benched Burleson, Fisk, and second basemen Doug Griffin and Denny Doyle; moved Rico Petrocelli from third to second; gave Steve Dillard a shot at short; and seemed to be picking his designated hitter out of a hat. No one knew his own role and hardly anyone was happy. As Claflin noted, "Quantity . . . has not made for quality. Quantity has made for confusion."

On July 9, with Boston 39-38 and eight and a half games behind New York, Tom Yawkey died of leukemia in New England Baptist Hospital.

He'd been sick for several years, but since the World Series his condition had deteriorated badly. While the public didn't know the full extent of his illness, those close to the club knew he wasn't getting any better. Chemotherapy had just made him sicker.

All of Boston eulogized him like a native son. There was a deep and genuine outpouring of emotion from most Red Sox fans, players past and present, and those close to the club. Those who knew him personally — or felt they did — experienced an acute sense of loss.

Fans still saw him as the beneficent Mr. Yawkey, a man who employed thousands during the Depression and spent millions trying to bring them a world championship. Watching him peer down on the field from his box at Fenway Park, all they saw was a baseball fan. Since the Impossible Dream season of 1967, his public image had softened. He performed what one observer termed "social penance" through his increased involvement with charities like the Jimmy Fund, which over the years had received more than a million Yawkey dollars in direct contributions, and as the charity's main sponsor, he had facilitated raising millions more. For years, at his insistence, the only sign allowed to be displayed in Fenway Park was for the Jimmy Fund. After Yawkey's death, contributions to the charity increased substantially through the efforts of the Yawkey Foundation.

Players mourned him as a member of the family, a surrogate father. Yastrzemski was visibly shaken. No other Red Sox player ever spent as much time in Yawkey's company as Yaz — the owner and player often met after games and talked long into the night. He shooed reporters away, saying, "I just want time to think."

In recent years, despite his estrangement from his own daughter, Yawkey had become increasingly paternalistic; when Bernie Carbo asked him for an advance on his salary so he could make a down payment on his house, he simply gave him money outright. Former players and other baseball figures down on their luck were often surprised by checks, and Yaz even received personal loans at favorable rates. Yawkey and his wife visited sick players in the hospital, paid medical bills for their families, apologized after trades, offered quiet words of encouragement after losses, and paid the best salaries in baseball.

Many ballpark employees shared a similar relationship. A tearful Fenway usher referred to Yawkey as "the King of Baseball." Local sportswriters, particularly those who'd covered the Sox for years, felt a comparable loss and sense of indebtedness.

The *Herald* called him "baseball's best friend," and Larry Claflin wrote, "Baseball in Boston will never be the same, because no one can possibly love the team, the ball park and the sport the way Tom Yawkey loved it." *Globe* columnist Ray Fitzgerald framed Yawkey's life in terms of his pursuit of a world championship, writing, "He had forty-three years of fun trying."

Yawkey was lauded for his charitable work, which documents filed with his will indicated amounted to approximately one hundred thousand dollars annually in the three years preceding his death, the major beneficiaries being Yale University, the Sidney Farber Cancer Institute (Jimmy Fund), and the Tara Hall Home for Boys in South Carolina. He was also recognized for his conservation work at South Island. But the Red Sox, who won two pennants and had a record of 3,544-3,240 during his years as owner, defined him.

When the team took the field at Fenway that night, organist John Kiley, who usually played "Take Me Out to the Ballgame," remained silent, and the Red Sox trotted out accompanied only by a smattering of restrained applause. The flag in center field hung at half-mast, and the team held a moment of silence in tribute to their owner. Then the Twins drubbed the Red Sox 8-6, despite three-run homers by Yaz and Bobby Darwin, dropping Boston to the .500 mark.

Somehow, that is also the appropriate record for Yawkey, a man whose faults equaled his favors, though in deference to his passing, those faults went all but unmentioned at the time of his death. If the criterion for being a successful owner of a baseball team is leaving behind one of the most beloved franchises in the game, Yawkey was a spectacular success — no team has fans more loyal.

But if that criterion is best measured by world championships, or by other means, Tom Yawkey was a failure, for no other individual has ever owned a major league team for so long without winning a championship. And few owners have had such a

Bill Lee wore this sling for much of the 1976 season after being injured by Graig Nettles and Mickey Rivers in a brawl on May 20 at Yankee Stadium. Lee would later call the Yankees "Steinbrenner's Brown Shirts" and Yankee manager Billy Martin a "Nazi."

spotty record in regard to their overall contribution to the game. His shortcomings saddled his beloved team with a lasting reputation as a losing and perhaps racist organization, hardly a desirable legacy.

The eulogies told only half the story. Despite his forty-three years in the spotlight as Red Sox owner, few people, if any, apart from his wife, really knew him. Dick O'Connell had worked for him for over twenty-five years and never even knew he had a daughter. In many ways Yawkey had remained a cipher, his true motivations a virtual secret.

As noted baseball historian David Q. Voigt once wrote, Yawkey was "the last of a species," a man who "embodied the myth of the gentleman sportsman owner." The myth had long been accepted as the whole truth. In reality, what most people didn't know about Tom Yawkey made him who he was.

Behind the myth, Tom Yawkey usually did things for Tom Yawkey. What was often seen and understood as altruism was at the same time a kind of venal self-indulgence. His admission years earlier to

John Quinn, "What's mine is mine, and I don't let anybody else have a part of it . . . It was just that strange way I have of wanting everything I have for myself," was revealing.

He ran the Red Sox according to that precept — they were his, after all. His method of ownership had more to do with his intense desire to satisfy himself and equal the accomplishments of his adoptive father than any responsibility he felt to please either Sox fans or players — they were only accidental beneficiaries of his personal aspirations. Oh, he wanted to win, but only if winning carried his personal stamp, an attitude embodied in his statement to Harold Kaese in 1948, "I'd rather finish second with Joe McCarthy than first with anyone else." He got his wish.

For forty-three years his need to succeed on his own terms first played a huge role in the failure of the team. Too often he employed front office personnel because of his personal relationship with them, regardless of the team's often disappointing record on the field. What some saw as loyalty left the organization run by sycophants, yes-men, and cronies who botched the job.

Even as a steward of Major League Baseball, Yawkey remained primarily concerned with his own narrow self-interest. Few other owners were in a better position to influence the future of professional baseball — his wealth carried immense weight in baseball's establishment, and he served on the powerful executive committee from 1951 through 1957 and as American League vice president from 1961 through 1973. But time and time again Yawkey took care of Yawkey first or else followed the party line. He escalated salaries, supported baseball's color line, embraced segregation long after every other team in baseball had abandoned it, helped force the Braves out of Boston, fought the formation of the players' union, and argued against free agency only to bust the marketplace as soon as it suited him.

Yawkey's relationship to Fenway Park provides perhaps the best example of his enigmatic approach. After he first purchased the team he saved Fenway by rebuilding it almost completely. But by the 1960s he admitted that Fenway Park was a detriment to his team and expressed little affection for the place. Yet it was his private playground; he loved taking aim at the Wall, so Fenway stayed. He easily could have built a brand-new park with his own money just as Walter O'Malley did in Los Angeles, an act that in the long run would have been immensely profitable and may well have changed the course of the franchise. Yet after the city of Boston rebuffed his request in the late 1950s to take Lansdowne Street for expansion, he stubbornly concluded that a new ballpark was the responsibility of local government. As late as July of 1967, with his club in the middle of its first pennant race in years and attendance skyrocketing, he threatened to move the club if they did not build a new park. Yet today, most hold him solely responsible for preserving one of baseball's gems, albeit one that is increasingly anachronistic. In fact, Yawkey had little to do with that. The success of the 1967 team, which surprised even him, turned the tide of public opinion over both Fenway and the ballclub.

Yawkey's will reflected his sense of possessiveness and self-centeredness. For years, he'd intimated that he'd leave the club to nephew Billy Gardner, who long owned Boston's Triple A team in Louisville, Kentucky. But after Gardner's franchise collapsed, Yawkey stated publicly, "I'll own the team till the day I die. Then I'll decide what I want to do."

His will did just that. As if trying to maintain control from his grave, he left the team to a trust controlled by Jean Yawkey; James Curran, an old friend and business associate; and executor Joseph LaCour. In the long run, that decision led to a decade of uncertainty over the team's future, as various factions struggled for control. Eventually, after Jean Yawkey's death, the team became property of the Yawkey Foundation. Twenty-five years after Tom Yawkey's death, his name and his philosophy still control the franchise.

Over his last few years he'd divested himself of much of his family's legacy to avoid hefty estate taxes, liquidating most of his extensive holdings in timber, oil, coal, iron, and other natural resources, or turning them over to members of his sister's family. That effectively made his own personal worth, at its peak, a mystery even today. At his death the press estimated he'd once been worth in excess of two hundred million dollars.

Yet his total estate was valued at fifty-seven million

dollars, including the ballclub, his South Carolina property, various securities, and a smattering of remaining oil, timber, gas, and mineral interests in some 60,000 acres of land in Texas, Louisiana, West Virginia, and Ontario.

The vast bulk of the estate was left to Jean Yawkey, with considerably lesser sums distributed to charity, a small circle of friends and longtime employees, and his nephews and their children. His daughter Julia received ten thousand dollars.

Significantly, the will ensured that the remaining portion of the estate — represented by the Red Sox and his property in South Carolina — would be maintained as if he had never died. The new owner of the Red Sox would be a trust, a pile of money that guaranteed his legacy would continue. And public access to his South Carolina property would forever be restricted, as if to reserve Yawkey's title and preserve it just as he left it. Even in death, "What's mine is mine" remained his motto.

By 1976 the team he bought for some 1.2 million dollars and on which he lavished another estimated eight to ten million dollars of his personal fortune trying to buy a pennant was worth about twice as much as he'd put into it. Its value has since increased to at least two hundred fifty million dollars, perhaps even more.

Yawkey was cremated and no service marked his passing, although a few days later a helicopter was seen hovering over Fenway Park, leading to speculation that his ashes were strewn across the field. Several weeks later, Boston city councilman Christopher Ianella introduced a resolution to rename Jersey Street "Yawkey Way." It passed unanimously. No name could have been more appropriate. For although Yawkey was gone, Yawkey's way, for better or worse, has remained the way the franchise has been operated in the ensuing decades.

Three days after Yawkey's death, baseball and the players' union agreed to a new Basic Agreement and the club quickly signed Fisk, Burleson, and Lynn, ending at least one distraction. Then, on July 19, Larry Claflin wrote that Johnson's job was in danger, calling him "a confused, worried, unhappy, desperate man" and his team "stupid, careless and indifferent." Two days later, after Boston dropped their fifth game

in six tries in Kansas City, O'Connell fired Johnson, saying, "It is easier to change a manager than the whole club."

Although O'Connell wanted an established manager, none of the names on his short list was available. He hired forty-five-year-old third base coach Don Zimmer as interim manager.

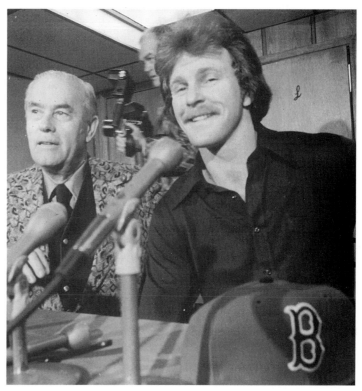

On November 4, 1976, the Red Sox selected Minnesota relief pitcher Bill Campbell in the newly hatched free-agent draft. After signing a five-year contract with the Red Sox for slightly over a million dollars Campbell remarked, "No one's worth that, but if they want to pay me, I'm certainly not going to turn it down."

Zimmer didn't act like an interim anything. He set a curfew and started enforcing club rules that Johnson had let slide.

Boston slowly began playing better baseball. Bill Lee came back at the end of July, and Zimmer benched a fading Rico Petrocelli at third and made Butch Hobson his third baseman. He settled on a lineup and stuck with it. In September, the team surged over .500 by winning fifteen of their last eighteen games to finish half a game ahead of the Indians in third place at 83-79, fifteen and a half games behind first-place New York.

Bob Gibson first saw Fenway Park the day before the opening game of the 1967 World Series. The St. Louis Cardinals Hall of Fame pitcher strolled down the long dank tunnel from the visiting team's clubhouse to the field, climbed the three dugout steps into the golden October sunlight, and stopped to behold a scene that had enthralled millions of people for over thirty years.

And what did the great Gibson think of the fabulous Fens?

"Where's the second deck?" Gibson replied.

The Cardinals' opening game pitcher wasn't the least bit concerned about the left-field wall or the minuscule amount of foul territory or any of Fenway's other hazards. He was too busy counting the house, estimating his cut of the World Series swag, which might have been about twice as much if Fenway had had an upper deck.

Gibson's reaction may or may not have ignited the movement that culminated over thirty years later, this being Boston, in a grandiose, $550 million plan to raze old Fenway and build a larger, kinder, more lucrative facsimile down the street.

The plan was immediately opposed, this being Boston, by a consortium of people who clearly were inspired by the noted author and poet John Updike who, upon visiting Fenway, described it as "a lyric little bandbox of a ball park."

This ignited the literati everywhere, including a few who'd actually been to a ballgame at the Fens.

"Baseball's basilica," intoned Clark Booth, Boston's most eloquent TV commentator.

"The best place in the world to watch baseball," rhapsodized Roger Angell, the *New Yorker* magazine's resident baseball fanatic.

With all due regard and without taking sides, there is nothing either little or lyrical about Fenway's distinguishing feature, the left-field wall, a.k.a. the Green Monster. And there are other parts of the park, notably the right-field grandstand and anything above the second row of the press box, where you can't even see home plate.

Otherwise, after spending forty years covering the Red Sox, I'm certain of this much about their ancestral seat: it is as inscrutable, as controversial, as paradoxical, as maligned, and as beloved as the ballclub it houses.

Inscrutable? For years, Dick O'Connell, the most savvy of all the Red Sox general managers, preached that Fenway's small seating capacity was a financial bonanza because it encouraged the fans to buy their tickets well in advance so they wouldn't get shut out in case the Sox got into a pennant race.

Then, all of a sudden, the Red Sox decided that they absolutely must have a larger park to produce the added revenue they desperately needed to compete with their wealthier rivals for today's multimillionaire players.

Okay, but if the Red Sox don't get into the pennant race some year, will they have to remortgage?

Controversial? Ted Williams, Fenway's most famous inmate and its uncrowned king of controversy, would dump Fenway Park, Wall and all, into Boston harbor, presumably via his own tunnel. Teddy Ballgame told the *Boston Herald*'s Karen Guregian, "You can have a pitcher pitching just a whale of a game and someone gets up and bloops one off the Wall and the whole game changes. I hope they build a completely new park."

Exhibit A here, of course, was Bucky Dent's pop fly that barely toppled into the left-field net and turned the Red Sox' 1978 playoff game around in favor of the New York Yankees.

This was only three years after Carlton Fisk's pop fly off the left-field foul

---

Ted Williams would dump Fenway Park, Wall and all, into Boston harbor, presumably via his own tunnel.

---

pole in the twelfth inning gave the Red Sox a win over the Cincinnati Reds in game six of the 1975 World Series, consequently called "the most thrilling game in World Series history."

How soon people forget that old Biblical saying: "The Wall giveth, and the Wall taketh away."

Do you want paradoxical? Because of the Wall, for too many years, the Red Sox insisted on signing every big, strong, righthanded hitter in captivity: Jimmie

Foxx, Joe Cronin, Vern Stephens, Walt Dropo, Norm Zauchin, Dick Stuart et al. As a result, when the Sox went on the road, they led the league only in long fly-ball outs.

The paradox here is that after Foxx in 1938, all of the Red Sox' American League batting champions save two were lefthanded hitters: Ted Williams, Billy Goodman, Pete Runnels, Carl Yastrzemski, Fred Lynn, Wade Boggs. The exceptions were Carney Lansford in 1981 and Nomar Garciapparra in 1999.

History doesn't record exactly when the Red Sox realized that Fenway was a lefthanded hitter's park, but the Sox were not alone in the dark. When the sainted Casey Stengel managed the Yankees to ten pennants in twelve years, he refused to pitch his Hall of Fame southpaw, Whitey Ford, in Fenway Park. Maybe that's why the Sox' lefthanded hitters fared so well.

Would you like maligned? In his disdain, Ted Williams chose simply to ignore the left-field wall when he was at bat. Even after rival teams shifted all of their players to the right side of the diamond and issued Ted an engraved invitation to hit to left, he refused.

One theory, advanced by one of his teammates, is that the left-field wall made Ted claustrophobic. "Ted loved me," confided Jimmy Piersall, the Red Sox antic center fielder from 1950 to 1958, "because he knew I wouldn't run into him out there. There's so little room in left field because of the

Wall that Ted was terrified the center fielder would collide with him and he'd get hurt." And possibly miss a turn at bat.

Piersall was right at home in Fenway. But the park was beloved by many players, even pitchers. And one

How soon people forget that old Biblical saying: "The Wall giveth, and the Wall taketh away."

of their smartest players scoffs at the theory that the Red Sox will never win a world championship as long as they play in Fenway.

"That's ridiculous," said Dominic DiMaggio, the Little Professor, who also played center field next door to Williams. "The park had nothing to do with it. I loved Fenway. We got along beautifully. And I blessed that left-field wall. It never hurt me. The Red Sox haven't won a World Series since 1918 because they never had a championship pitching staff. Or catcher, until Carlton Fisk came along. And they let him get away."

The few great pitchers the Sox have had weren't bothered by the park.

"Personally, I loved Fenway," said Dick Radatz, arguably the Sox' best relief pitcher, who was also dubbed the Monster as the result of a nickname contest conducted by the late *Boston Traveller*. But Radatz deplored the moniker. "It scares the kids," he explained.

Radatz insists he had no fear of the Green Monster. "I was a fly ball pitcher," he said. "But I never worried about the Wall. And I loved the closeness of the fans. I played off them. They gave me a big, big lift."

Ah, yes. The fans at Fenway. Ted Williams considered them to be one of Fenway's worst hazards, especially those who infested the left-field stands. And the affable Radatz agrees, to a point.

"In my rookie season, 1962," he related, "I didn't allow a run in my first 13 or 14 appearances. I didn't blow a save. Then one day I came in against the Yankees, bases loaded, Moose Skowron at bat. He hit a three-hopper through the right side of the infield and we lose the game and the fans booed the hell out of me. Clete Boyer, the Yankees third baseman, says to me, 'Tough town, kid!' But I still loved Fenway."

That seems to be the prevailing attitude, among players and fans alike. Leave it to Johnny Pesky, who has spent more time at Fenway Park than anyone in its history, as player, coach, manager, broadcaster, whatever, to sum it all up in one slightly inscrutable remark.

"I always loved Fenway," said Pesky, "especially when we had good players."

Tim Horgan is a retired sports columnist for the *Boston Herald*. He is the eight-time winner of the New England Sportswriter of the Year Award as well as the winner of both the John Gilhooly Award for Sportswriting and the National Golf Writers Association Award for Best Story.

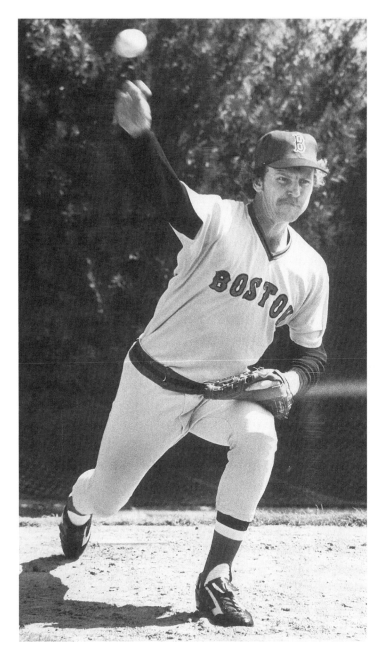

Bill Campbell in action at spring training camp in Winter Haven, Florida. In five seasons with the Red Sox Campbell proved invaluable despite developing arm trouble as the result of being overused by manager Don Zimmer. In 1977 he led the staff in victories with thirteen while leading the league in saves with thirty-one.

Planning for 1977 began immediately. The new Basic Agreement called for a draft of free agents, and on November 4 Boston selected Minnesota relief pitcher Bill Campbell, who declared for free agency after Twins owner Calvin Griffith refused to give him a five-thousand-dollar raise to twenty-seven thousand dollars a year. In 1976 he had pitched 168 innings over seventy-eight games, winning seventeen, saving twenty more, and turning the Twins into a contender.

Boston signed him to a five-year contract worth just over one million dollars, leading Campbell to admit, "No one's worth that, but if they want to pay me, I'm certainly not going to turn it down."

Boston also drafted the Angels' Bobby Grich and Reds pitcher Don Gullett and worked out a trade for Oakland pitcher Mike Torrez, but now Haywood Sullivan had the ear of the Yawkey trustees. The former player turned team vice president had become Mrs. Yawkey's trusted confidant. He thought such sums were outrageous, and the Yawkey estate balked at spending any more money. Instead, they traded youth for experience, reacquiring George Scott and Bernie Carbo from Milwaukee for future star Cecil Cooper. Meanwhile, the Yankees signed Gullett and Reggie Jackson and eventually traded for Bucky Dent and Torrez.

The result was a much stronger Yankee team and a more potent Boston club that lived and died by the home run. Led by Jim Rice's thirty-nine home runs, Boston hit 213 for the season as Scott hit another thirty-three, Hobson hit thirty, Yaz cracked twenty-eight, Fisk chipped in twenty-six, and Lynn, Evans, and Carbo each hit fourteen or more.

When Boston was hitting, they were nearly unbeatable. During one ten-game stretch beginning on June 14, they clubbed thirty-three home runs, including sixteen over a three-game series with New York.

But when they didn't hit it was another story. Not even Campbell, who led the team with thirteen wins and thirty-one saves, could bail out a maddeningly inconsistent pitching staff, which was made even worse by Zimmer's constant tinkering. Only Tiant and Jenkins avoided the bullpen, and as the season progressed the team's veteran pitchers, led by Lee, Jenkins, and Wise, lost all respect for their manager. The Sox were streaky all year, riding a winning streak into first place over Baltimore and New York, then wasting it with the inevitable losing streak that dropped them back.

They led for the last time on August 23 before playing Minnesota. Bill Lee, filling in (as the color man) on Boston's television broadcast, belittled Twins pitcher Dave Goltz while Goltz threw a one-hitter to beat Boston 7-0 and the Yankees defeated Chicago behind Mike Torrez, 8-3. New York ended the misery with a three-game sweep in mid-September and won the division with 100 wins as Boston and Baltimore both finished two and a half games back.

Then came 1978, a season that stuck like a dagger in the hearts of a new generation of Red Sox fans just as 1948 did to their fathers, providing a new definition for the concept of heartbreak. The similarities were uncanny. The 1975 Red Sox had seemed the spiritual cousins of their 1946 forebears, and the 1976 and 1977 clubs were kin to the underachieving 1947 team. The 1978 Red Sox followed suit and became the 1948 Red Sox incarnate. Virtually unbeatable at Fenway Park, they appeared to have everything.

But the 1948 Sox had stumbled early only to come roaring back before falling short, thus providing a glimmer of hope before their eventual demise, something of a franchise trademark. The 1978 team demonstrated a perverse sort of reverse determinism. They elevated expectations to never-before-seen levels before collapsing, yet still arrived at the same place, in a playoff game. Red Sox fans were left with the feeling they'd seen this all before and knew the outcome before the game had even been played.

Everything started innocently enough at the end of the 1977 season. The trust brushed off several offers to buy the team, including one headed by Dom DiMaggio, and decided instead to sell the team to a group led by former team vice president Haywood Sullivan and former trainer Buddy LeRoux, both of whom were close to Mrs. Yawkey. But neither man had enough money to put together a deal. Financing questions held it up until Jean Yawkey agreed to join the new ownership group herself.

There was one immediate consequence: on October 24, Dick O'Connell, whom Mrs. Yawkey disliked, was fired, and Haywood Sullivan became general manager. He wanted to put his personal stamp on the team and demonstrate that O'Connell hadn't been the sole reason for Boston's recent success. While all New England dug out from the "Blizzard of '78," the Red Sox gave everyone reasons to look toward spring. Sullivan first slashed the front office staff to save Mrs. Yawkey some money, a move that would eventually haunt the franchise as much as any trade would. Then he made several controversial transactions that were by turn brilliant, lucky, and short-sighted.

He signed Yankee free-agent pitcher Mike Torrez, simultaneously shoring up Boston's pitching staff while weakening New York's, an outcome that caused many Sox fans to immediately rethink their position on free agency. Relief pitchers Dick Drago and Tom Burgmeier and backup infielder Jack Brohamer were acquired by the same route.

But that was just the beginning. Zimmer, a quintessential no-nonsense conservative baseball man, despised the team's more free-spirited and outspoken players, the self-described Buffalo Heads, who included Jenkins, Carbo, Lee, Wise, Pole, and Willoughby.

They took their moniker from Jenkins's nickname for Zimmer, "buffalohead," so chosen because the pitcher claimed that buffaloes were "the ugliest animals alive," and he held a similar disparaging view of Zimmer (Lee, on the other hand, called him "gerbil"). They were a cliquish, hard-partying, and often bitterly funny group that drove their manager crazy, not so much for what they did and said as for what Zimmer *imagined* they did and said. Boston's younger sportswriters and fans loved them for their glibness and unabashed love of the game. In contrast to more conventional players like Yastrzemski and Fisk, baseball's equivalent of the Dead Heads gave the club some much-needed color.

But Zimmer was Orange County to the Buffalo Heads' Haight-Ashbury. He'd never held a paying job outside baseball and had been raised in the corporate mentality of the Dodger organization. He couldn't handle their iconoclastic approach. Their success drove him even crazier than their failures.

Sullivan shared Zimmer's dim view of the group as well as his desire to rid the club of the perceived troublemakers. In the off-season, Jenkins, Willoughby, and Cleveland were virtually given away.

Then Sullivan handed the California Angels Don Aase and enough money to sign Boston outfielder Rick Miller in exchange for Somerset, Massachusetts, native Jerry Remy. Remy solved Boston's second base situation and provided some much-needed speed at the top of the lineup.

Just before the end of spring training Sullivan engineered another deal, this time giving the Cleveland Indians Rick Wise and Boston's three most promising young players — pitcher Mike Paxton, International League batting champ Ted Cox, and catcher Bo Diaz — for young Dennis Eckersley. The Eck, although only twenty-three, was coming off a season in which he had won fourteen.

The dramatic reshaping made Boston's starting lineup and pitching staff stronger by far, but stripped the club of depth and weakened the farm system. Yet no one noticed, and for three months they were perhaps the best Red Sox team of all time, a terrific blend of power and pitching. Eckersley, Lee, Tiant, and Torrez were all solid starters, and although Campbell's elbow was acting up, Drago, Burgmeier, and Bob Stanley ably manned the bullpen.

On offense, powerful Jim Rice symbolized Boston's dominance. He emerged as the most dangerous slugger in the game, far more potent than his more heralded teammate Fred Lynn, and a more consistent hitter than Carl Yastrzemski had ever been, although he lacked Yaz's defensive ability and dramatic flair. No righthanded hitter since Jimmie Foxx had done so much damage in Fenway Park, and in Fenway Park, that's exactly who Rice was. At home that year he hit .361 and slugged .690. With Burleson and Remy setting the table ahead of Rice, Yaz, Lynn, Fisk, and Evans, they scored runs in bunches.

As usual, it took a while for the club to get going, but in late April they ripped off eight consecutive wins, and Rice got really hot. Boston took over first place on May 13 then hit stride.

On June 15, they beat Oakland 7-3 for their seventh straight win, making them 26-4 at Fenway, 43-19 overall. Torrez had already won ten games and Eckersley and Bill Lee weren't far behind him.

But just before the trading deadline, Buffalo Head Bernie Carbo was sold to Cleveland for less than the waiver price. Bill Lee acted like they'd sold his best friend. They had.

He cleared out his locker and screamed to the press that the sale of the little-used outfielder and DH "just cost us the pennant."

Although Lee returned a day later at Carbo's insistence, he wasn't the same pitcher. For the second time in three seasons his own rash behavior had taken him out of the game. A stretch of poor performances gave Zimmer an excuse to bury him.

Yet outside of Boston, hardly anyone noticed. The Yankees made Boston's problems look silly.

New York had stumbled badly in Boston's wake, and with each loss manager Billy Martin got tighter, owner George Steinbrenner got more impatient, and the defending American League champions became a little more beatable. Reggie Jackson had angered established stars like captain Thurman Munson from the beginning when he'd announced that he was "the straw that stirs the drink," then failed to hit. The addition of relief pitcher Goose Gossage had been a slap in the face to Cy Young Award winner Sparky Lyle, who Graig Nettles said had gone from "Cy Young to sayonara." To make matters worse second baseman Willie Randolph, shortstop Bucky Dent, and center fielder Mickey Rivers were all hurt. Only pitcher Ron Guidry, having the same type of season on the mound that Jim Rice was having at the plate, kept New York close.

The Yankees came to Boston on June 19 trailing the Red Sox by seven games in the standings and a half-dozen more in the blackness of George Steinbrenner's heart. Over the next sixteen days, the two teams were scheduled to play three short series: three games in Boston, two games in New York, then another two in Boston. New York needed to win a majority of the games to get back in the race. If the Sox swept, or came close to doing so, New York's season was over.

In the first series, Eck beat the Yankees for his first time ever, 10-4, before the Yankees won game two, 10-4, when New York's light-hitting shortstop Fred Stanley hit a grand slam. The next night New York called up rookie Jim Beattie from Tacoma to face Boston. He was out of the game in the third inning and on his way back to Tacoma in the seventh as Boston won again, 9-2.

One week later, Eckersley beat New York again, 4-1, before New York won in fourteen innings on a Graig Nettles home run. And in the final series, Eckersley beat New York for the third time in two weeks,

9-5. The second game, mercifully for New York, was rained out and rescheduled in September. Boston had taken four of the six games played. New York was down nine and a half games and the Red Sox had their foot pressed against the Yankees' neck.

At the All-Star break Boston was 57-26, 34-6 at Fenway. The club led second-place Milwaukee by 9 games and was on pace to win 112 games. If they played .500 ball the rest of the season, they would still win 97 games.

Haywood Sullivan gave the *Herald American* a lengthy interview just before the break, detailing the steps he'd taken to create the best club in baseball. His only concern was "injuries . . . That's the only thing that worries me . . . not slumps, injuries." Above the interview ran a cartoon that showed Sullivan astride a shark, à la *Jaws*. In the mouth of the fish, about to be consumed, was a figure wearing a Yankee cap. Significantly, however, the mouth was not yet closed and the cartoonist, in error, neglected to give the bottom jaw a full set of teeth, providing the figure with a route to escape.

After the break, Boston resumed its apparent relentless march toward the postseason. Now Don Zimmer began receiving accolades — the *Herald*'s Joe Fitzgerald absolutely gushed, calling him "bland . . . but beautiful . . . He's done to baseball what Eisenhower did for politics. He's made it so good we can hardly stand it."

It had rarely been better around Fenway Park. After beating Milwaukee 8-2 on July 19 the Sox were 61-28 and still led the Brewers by nine games. Baltimore was twelve and a half games behind. New York was an afterthought at 47-42, fourteen and a half long hard games back. The promise born in 1967 and nearly delivered in 1975 seemed destined to be fulfilled.

The Yankees were at each other's throats, and Boston fans were delighted to watch from afar. Reggie Jackson and Billy Martin had each other in a death-grip and even squared off in the dugout when

Jackson first failed to get a bunt down then kept trying after Martin told him to swing away. Jackson was suspended, and then Martin uttered his famous appraisal of Jackson and Steinbrenner, saying, "The two of them deserve each other. One's a born liar and the other's convicted."

Steinbrenner was not amused at the allusion to his legal trouble (he'd pled guilty in 1972 to making illegal campaign contributions to the Nixon campaign).

(l–r): Carl Yastrzemski, Don Zimmer, and Jerry Remy watch batting practice at Winter Haven, Florida, in 1980. Both Yastrzemski and Remy saw reduced duty because of injury as the team limped to a fourth-place finish. Zimmer was fired with four games left in the season and was eventually replaced by Ralph Houk.

On July 24 he fired Martin and replaced him with low-key Bob Lemon. In the interim, the Yankees quietly won five of six while the Red Sox, for the first time all year, did the opposite.

Don Zimmer wasn't feeling secure. He wanted a new contract, but Sullivan had said he had no intention of extending the contract before the end of the season. Zimmer claimed not to care, but the way he managed told a different story.

Clubhouse manager Vince Orlando displays the helmet worn by Dwight Evans on August 29, 1978, when he was beaned by Seattle pitcher Mike Parrott. Evans's absence from the lineup because of dizziness contributed to the Red Sox slump that eventually cost them what had seemed a sure division title.

He pushed the club to increase their lead, using the same players day after day. He rode the team hard, questioned small injuries, and kept the pressure on. Fisk played with a broken rib, while the bone chips in Butch Hobson's elbow made every throw an adventure.

Cronin and McCarthy had done the same four decades earlier. Now Zimmer got a similar result. He didn't trust his bench, and when he eventually needed it, his players were stale.

By August 1, New York had vaulted past Milwau-kee and Baltimore, and Boston's lead over New York had dwindled to a nervous six and a half games. But on the next two nights, Boston appeared to put the Yankees back in place. They swept two games in New York, winning a seventeen-inning contest played over two days, 7-5, and a rain-shortened finale 8-1.

The two clubs matched each other for the next month, and at the end of August Sullivan's worst fears were realized. On August 26 Jerry Remy was hit by a pitch that cracked a bone in his wrist, knocking him out of the lineup for over two weeks. Frank Duffy filled in, but reminded no one of Remy. And on August 29, Dwight Evans was beaned. Although he continued playing, he was plagued by dizzy spells, slumped, and dropped four flyballs in a week.

At the same time, Hobson's throwing problems got worse — he'd eventually make forty-three errors and become the first regular player in decades to finish with a fielding percentage below .900. But Zimmer loved the hard-nosed young infielder that got the most out of his somewhat limited skills. That was the kind of player Zimmer himself had once been, and he stubbornly kept Hobson in the lineup. Finally, the third baseman, distraught and in tears after another critical error, begged out, admitting, "I'm killing this team." Jack Brohamer played good defense in his stead, but couldn't match Hobson's power, who remained available as DH.

Defense had been an overlooked strength all year, but now the defense let the team down. At the same time, the pitching staff slumped. Bill Lee was in the bullpen after losing seven in a row, Jim Wright didn't win a game after mid-August, and Torrez won only one of his last ten starts. Even Tiant went into a slump. Only Eckersley continued to win.

Still, Boston entered September leading New York by a relatively comfortable six and a half games. The Yankees were scheduled to visit Fenway on September 7 for a four-game series, giving the Sox the opportunity to put the pennant race away and try to get healthy for the World Series.

By then the lead was down to four games. Under Lemon, all that had been wrong with New York had turned right.

For the Red Sox and their fans, the next four days were among the most painful in franchise history, the details of which most would like to forget if they ever could. The Yankees didn't just beat the Red Sox, they beat up on them, doing even more damage to the team psychologically than the significant harm they did in the won-lost column.

Game one was over before many of the capacity crowd in Fenway Park had settled into their seats. Torrez was gone after only two innings while Catfish Hunter was on cruise control. After three innings the Sox trailed 7-0. New York's first twenty-two at bats resulted in thirteen hits. By the fourth, every Yankee starter already had at least one hit.

At the end of that inning, the Sox trailed 12-0 and half the crowd was gone. Boston lost 15-3, and in the *Globe* columnist Ray Fitzgerald was inspired to report "how the touchdowns were scored," calling the contest "a mugging."

The Sox were shell-shocked. "They kicked the crap out of us," said Zimmer. "Maybe we tired the sons-of-bitches out." Dwight Evans offered, "There's nothing demoralizing in that kind of loss," but then again, he was suffering from a head injury.

It got worse. Evans left game two in the second inning with dizziness, leading to a similar evacuation of Fenway Park by Boston fans as New York thumped the Red Sox again, 13-2. On the front page, the *Globe* advised, "If you need directions to home plate at Fenway Park, just stop and ask any New York Yankee."

Game three matched Eckersley's 16-6 record against Ron Guidry's 20-2 mark. Boston opened the first with singles by Burleson and Rice, but failed to score as Guidry retired Yaz and settled down. The Eck pitched well into the fourth, then fell apart with two outs as Chambliss singled, Nettles walked, Piniella blooped a hit into center field, White walked, Dent singled, Rivers singled, etc., etc., etc. New York scored seven two-out runs, and the Yankees made the score hold up as Guidry became the first lefthander since 1974 to shut out the Red Sox in Fenway.

People were running out of words to describe what was happening. NBC announcer Tony Kubek mused, "This is the first time I've seen a first place team chasing a second place team," and *Newsday*'s Joe Gergen quipped, "The Yankees are a game behind and drawing away." An exasperated Fred Lynn observed, "They must be cheating. Those aren't the same Yankees we saw before. I think George Steinbrenner used his clone money. Those were Yankee clones out there from teams of the past."

The final game of the series suddenly became the most important game of the season thus far. Zimmer decided to pitch rookie lefthander Bobby Sprowl, who'd made his first big league start, a 4-1 loss to Bal-

Dennis Eckersley proved to be a major contributor to the 1978 Red Sox as the twenty-three-year-old won twenty games while losing only eight. His colorful vocabulary and effusive nature endeared him to Boston fans in two stints with the team.

timore, only a week before. Before the game, Yaz begged Zimmer to start Lee, but the manager refused to let Lee out of his doghouse, saying Sprowl had "icewater in his veins." Luis Tiant pleaded to pitch on three days' rest, but Zimmer had decided to live or die with Sprowl.

Boston died. The young lefty didn't make it out of the first inning and walked off the field into everlast-

Bill Lee and manager Don Zimmer exchange heated words in the dugout at Fenway Park in 1977. In the stretch drive of the 1978 division race Zimmer refused to start the slumping Lee despite the fact that the lefthander possessed the best won-lost record against the rival Yankees of any pitcher in the league.

ing Red Sox infamy. The Yankees won 7-4 to pull into a tie for the lead. The rivalry between the two clubs was back all right — with the same results as always.

The press in both New York and Boston took a peculiar delight in detailing what they referred to as the Boston Massacre. In four games New York outscored Boston 42-9 and outhit them by a similar margin. The Red Sox made an embarrassing eleven errors. Afterward, Sparky Lyle said simply, "I pity them."

Four days later the Red Sox went to New York for three more games. They lost the first two games 4-0 and 3-2 and now trailed by three and a half with only fifteen games left in the season.

Just when no one expected it, the Red Sox rebounded, winning the series finale as Eckersley defeated New York 7-3. Still, the two clubs looked like they were still heading in opposite directions.

But Boston showed amazing resilience. Over the next week, the Yankees, as if suddenly exhausted by the effort that pulled them back into the race, failed to increase their lead against Milwaukee and Toronto.

With six games left in the season, Boston pulled to within a single game of New York. For the next five days, the two clubs matched each other win by excruciating win as each club watched the scoreboard, waiting for the other to falter.

On the first day of October, still trailing the Yankees by a game, Boston played host to Toronto while New York entertained Cleveland. The Red Sox were riding a seven-game win streak, their best since mid-June, while the Yankees were on a six-game streak of their own. If New York beat the Indians, they won the pennant, no matter what happened in Boston.

But Catfish Hunter pitched his first bad game in nearly two months and Cleveland beat New York 9-2. In the late innings, the Red Sox watched Fenway's scoreboard, which was precisely what Yankees were doing in New York.

Fenway rocked as the crowd saw the Yankees fall further behind Cleveland. Meanwhile, Luis Tiant was spectacular. He threw a two-hitter and Boston won 5-0. After 162 games, Boston and New York were tied with identical 99-63 records. A coin flip a week earlier had determined that if the two clubs ended the season tied, the one-game playoff would be played the next day, October 2, at 1:30 P.M. in Fenway Park.

Boston fans reacted as if they had won a reprieve. Two weeks earlier, the 1978 season had promised to be one of the most painful in Boston history. Now the opportunity to beat New York in a single playoff game to win the pennant held the potential of the most exquisite pleasure Boston fans could possibly imagine. Winning the pennant while simultaneously beating the Yankees was every Sox fan's ultimate dream. Winning the World Series could conceivably be better, but not by much.

But facing the Yankees in a playoff also risked the worst of all possible worlds. Losing a playoff, as the

Red Sox had in 1948, was bad. Losing a playoff to the Yankees was exponentially worse.

They'd have felt more comfortable with Tiant on the mound, or Eckersley, but neither was rested. This time, fortunately, the Boston manager didn't play a hunch and start someone named Galehouse. Instead, Zimmer wisely passed over his other options and gave the start to Mike Torrez, pitching on three days' rest. Those looking for omens took note of the potential symmetry that made it possible for the Yankees' 1977 World Series hero to bump his former club from the postseason.

Both clubs were hot. Boston had won twelve of their last fourteen to offset New York's remarkable 52-21 record since July 19. But the Yankees appeared more confident. They sent their luggage ahead to Kansas City, where the LCS would start. Guidry was pitching, a gaudy 24-3, and besides, the defending world champions already had a Series ring. For them, defeat would be regrettable, but not devastating.

It was different for Boston. It always has been. The consequences of loss loomed even larger than the benefits of victory.

Before the game, both teams were surprisingly respectful of one another, for each had impressed the other with their recent resilience. So far, neither team had lost; each had tried mightily to win. "After all that has happened to both teams," said Carl Yastrzemski, "this is probably the only way this should be settled. But I feel sorry that either team must lose. These are the two best teams in baseball, the greatest rivalry in sports. There should be no loser."

The game started under brilliant sunshine on a perfect early autumn day in New England. In the first inning, both pitchers seemed on their game. Although Jackson flied out deep to left, each retired the opposition in order.

But in the second, Guidry showed signs of fatigue. He'd been devastating all year, but on this day his fastball was a foot or two short, his ungodly slider almost mortal, his control slightly off.

He left a fastball up, and Yastrzemski, at age thirty-nine still one of the best fastball hitters in baseball, pulled a line drive hard down the right-field line and the ball snuck over the fence as if it were trying to hide. Fenway exploded and Boston led 1-0.

The Red Sox threatened again in the third. Scott led off with a booming double. With Brohamer up, Zimmer had him bunt Scott to third. But Burleson failed to bring him home and grounded out, then Remy flied out to end the threat.

New Hampshire native Carlton Fisk handled the Red Sox pitching staff like a latter-day Bill Carrigan. Built like a tight end at 6-foot-3 and 200 pounds, Fisk was an imposing figure to teammates and opponents alike.

New York got the leadoff runner on off Torrez in both the fourth and fifth, but Torrez didn't get rattled. Each time, he set the next three Yankees down in order.

After Torrez struck out Munson for the third time to end the top of the sixth, the score was still 1-0 when Burleson made up for his earlier failure by doubling down the left-field line. Still playing for a single run, Zimmer had Remy sacrifice him to third, then Rice singled for RBI 139 to put Boston up 2-0.

Guidry retired Yaz and intentionally walked Fisk. Fred Lynn stepped into the batter's box.

Although Lynn hadn't quite fulfilled the promise of his rookie season, in Fenway Park he carried a career average of over .350, some seventy points better than his mark on the road, and was still a superstar. He turned on a Guidry slider and jerked it into right field.

Lynn left the batter's box thinking double and hoping for a triple or more, for the ball looked as if it might clear the fence or at least rattle around in the right-field corner, and Yankee outfielder Lou Piniella was no Dwight Evans. But when Lynn reached first base he pulled up.

Lynn and every other fan in Fenway Park had the same thought: What the hell is Piniella doing *there?* He was way, way out of position in front of the right-field belly. So far out of position that Lynn's drive went right to him.

Aware that Guidry didn't have his usual speed, the outfielder had gambled and moved far to his left. Instead of Boston's leading 4-0 with a man in scoring position, the score remained 2-0. Fans looked at one another and dared not mention what they were thinking.

Nine outs separated one team from victory and the other from defeat. Torrez retired Nettles to start the seventh.

Then Chambliss singled. Roy White, the lone member of the Yankees with the team in 1966 when they'd finished last behind Boston, followed with another hit. Lemon pinch-hit Jim Spencer for Brian Doyle, who was filling in for Willie Randolph. Torrez worked carefully and he flied out.

Up came Bucky Dent. An inning later and Dent probably would have been pulled for a pinch hitter. But the game was still close and Lemon felt he needed Dent's defense. Besides, he'd already pinch-hit for Doyle, meaning backup shortstop Fred Stanley had to play second in the eighth. Dent had to bat.

He was no great hitter. His average for the season was only .246, .140 over his last twenty games. If the Red Sox had been able to select the Yankee they most wanted to pitch to in precisely this situation, Dent would have been the overwhelming choice. Lou Boudreau he was not. Zimmer and Torrez were about as worried about Dent as Cronin and Klinger had been about Harry Walker.

A "phantom" ticket to the World Series that never was.

Torrez didn't feel tired and went right after the good field no-hit shortstop. He got ahead with a strike, then jammed Dent badly and fouled the next pitch off his left foot.

Dent jumped out of the box and started hopping around on one leg. He was hurt, and for a few moments it looked as if he would have to leave the game, forcing Lemon to put in a pinch hitter already down two strikes and play someone — Graig Nettles? Paul Blair? — out of position at short.

Torrez stood on the mound watching like a spectator for several minutes as Dent tried to shake the injury off. During the delay, Mickey Rivers noticed Dent's bat was chipped and replaced it.

At length, Dent stepped back in. Then Torrez, perhaps a little cold after the delay, threw a fastball, a little up and a little over the plate.

Dent, choking up a full 2 inches on his bat, took his usual short choppy swing, which usually resulted in short choppy groundballs. This time he hit under the ball on the sweet spot of the bat.

In left field, Yastrzemski drifted back to his right, then slowed and looked up as if noticing for the first time that the left-field wall was so close to home plate. Before anyone else, he *knew.* Dent's bloop fly, which wouldn't have been a home run at any other park in Major League Baseball, dropped from sight into the net.

Dent didn't even see the ball go out. He thought it was off the wall and was running hard around first when he saw the umpire waving him around.

Never, ever, has a home run in Fenway Park been so unexpected, and never, ever has a home run in Fenway Park caused so much damage. The Red Sox lost more than their lead in the game. A generation of Sox fans lost hope as Dent's name stuck in their throats forever.

Fenway Park visibly deflated. New York led 3-2. Torrez was shaken. He walked Rivers, who stole second. With Munson coming up, one of the game's great clutch hitters, Zimmer called time and pulled Torrez for Bob Stanley. Munson lined the ball deep off the Wall for a double to make the score 4-2.

Guidry came back out to start the seventh. George Scott singled and Lemon called for Goose Gossage, the best relief pitcher in baseball in 1978.

Jack Brohamer was the scheduled hitter. Now, in the 163rd game of the season, Boston's lack of depth became obvious. On their bench, apart from a still-dizzy Dwight Evans, sat a grand total of only twenty-six RBIs and *five* pinch hits for the entire season. Zimmer told Bob Bailey to hit for Brohamer. A one-time bonus baby for the Pittsburgh Pirates, Bailey had never fulfilled his promise. He latched on with Boston in the spring primarily to pinch-hit, but thus far was only 1-12 in the role. Thousands of Boston fans and more than a few Boston players thought of Bernie Carbo; he was in Cleveland watching the game on television thinking the same thing they were.

Gossage threw three pitches and Bailey never moved. It was "One, two, three strikes you're out," the oldest song in the game. The threat was over.

In the top of the eighth, Reggie Jackson looked at the calendar, took note of the date, and reminded everyone why he'd earned the nickname "Mr. October." He homered to center field off Stanley to put New York ahead 5-2.

The Sox were in the same position they had been in in their final series against the Yankees in the regular season. No one expected them to come back.

The lingering image of the 1978 season for most Red Sox fans will forever be the sight of Bucky Dent, whose three-run homer off Mike Torrez in the seventh inning of the one-game playoff between the Yankees and Red Sox helped seal Boston's fate. Dent is greeted at home plate by teammates Chris Chambliss (*l*) and Roy White (*r*).

But they did. Jerry Remy led off the eighth with a double. Rice went out, but Yaz, eleven years removed from 1967, singled Remy home, then Fisk and Lynn singled to score Yaz and make the score 5-4.

Fenway awoke. Ultimate peril stood alongside the grandest of all opportunities. In a season in which the Red Sox bolted ahead, then fell behind only to come back in the final days, nothing would be more appropriate than a come-from-behind victory against the best reliever in the game in the last game of the year to win the best pennant ever.

Now Gossage, who had struck out 122 batters in 134 innings in 1978, faced Scott and Hobson, two free-swinging fastball hitters. But Hobson popped up on a high fastball, and Scott struck out on the same.

New York went down easily in the ninth, as if anxious to get back on the field and end the game. Boston had three more chances and Gossage no margin for error.

Desperate, Zimmer sent Evans up to pinch-hit, but he still wasn't right, and Gossage got him easily. But Burleson laid off his high fastballs and walked. Then Jerry Remy hit a line drive to right field.

Late in the afternoon in the fall of the year, the sun hangs low over the grandstand behind third base at Fenway Park. The right fielder, facing almost due west, looks directly into the sun and contrasting shadows of the stands. It is almost impossible to see the ball.

Piniella knew when the ball left the bat it was headed his way, but that was all the information he had. It disappeared amid the sun and shadows. The crowd, already standing, leaned forward. Piniella's body language gave him away. He couldn't see the ball.

Burleson broke for second but had to hold up halfway in case the ball was caught.

Piniella again guessed right. He stepped blindly to his left and the ball miraculously appeared 10 feet in front of him. He stabbed it on one hop with his glove hand. Burleson, the tying run, had to stop at second as Remy made first.

Now Rice flied to deep left-center. Burleson tagged and went to third. Had he been there already, he'd easily have scored on Rice's fly.

Carl Yastrzemski stepped to the plate and was greeted by an almost unbearable roar, not so much a cheer as a gigantic group prayer, deep, pleading, and heartfelt. After fifteen years in a Red Sox uniform, this was by far his most important at bat.

There was little mystery to batting against Gossage. Yaz was a fastball hitter and Gossage a fastball pitcher.

A single would tie the game. With Remy on first and two out, a double could score him and win the game. A home run certainly would.

But Yaz wasn't thinking of a homer. Chambliss held Remy on at first, so if Yaz did double he might not be able to score. But that left a hole on the right side. Yaz was just looking to knock the ball in the hole and tie the game.

Gossage rocked and threw violently — his motion made it seem as if he were trying to detach his arm from his body. Yaz took the pitch low and in for a ball.

Several years ago, Yaz made a rare appearance at a Red Sox fantasy camp, where he gave a hitting clinic to the middle-aged men and women in attendance. Over and over again, as he watched the campers hit, he barked, "Get the head of the bat out. Don't let the pitch beat you!"

Gossage threw his second pitch, about which Munson later asked him, "Where'd that extra foot come from?" in reference to its extra speed. The ball was in, but over the plate, perfect for Yastrzemski. Then, as Yaz later described it, at the last instant, "The ball exploded on me."

He didn't get the bat out. The pitch beat him.

Instead of pulling the ball through the hole, Yaz popped up to the left side. Graig Nettles floated over to the coach's box alongside third and caught it in his glove.

And in the city of Boston, the season of 1978 took its place astride infamy. When Boston fans looked out at the left-field wall, they didn't think of Carlton Fisk anymore.

They thought of Bucky "Bleeping" Dent.

FROM RUIN TO ROCKET AND BACK AGAIN

1979 | 1986

Carl Yastrzemski bids farewell to Boston after twenty-three seasons following a pre-game retirement ceremony on Saturday, October 1, 1983. He retired with seven Red Sox career records, including those for hits (3,419), doubles (646), runs (1,816), and RBIs (1,844). More important, he was an incredible clutch performer who batted .352 in two World Series.

"They killed our fathers and now the sons of bitches are coming after us."
So said an anonymous Red Sox fan moments after the end of the playoff.

That perception was shared by many. Dent's home run and the loss to New York confirmed the Red Sox' inextricable tie to their own past. The loss inspired yet another round of finger pointing that destroyed the one-time dynasty in waiting. Not until it was over did the Red Sox have another opportunity to resume their murderous assault on their fans. They hadn't seen anything yet.

Fans blamed Don Zimmer and Mike Torrez. Zimmer, Sullivan, and LeRoux blamed free agency and players that hadn't even been on the field during Boston's demise. Torrez blamed the Wall. As devastating as the loss was, the fallout would be even worse.

Over the course of Boston's collapse, Zimmer had been vilified by fans who found a forum on Boston's fervent sports talk radio scene. On one station callers weren't even allowed to mention Zimmer by name — the manager had to be referred to by the pseudonym Chiang Kai-shek. After the playoff loss, the volume went up and Zimmer's mistakes were rehashed over and over and over again. Zimmer made the mistake of listening to every word and in 1979 allowed himself to be tortured by the countless anonymous criticisms of Joe from Quincy and Vinnie from Revere.

Reaction to Torrez was more visceral. He never took the mound at Fenway Park again without the accompaniment of a chorus of boos. He won forty-four games over the next four seasons but one pitch and one loss defined him forever.

Sullivan reacted to the defeat as if he could somehow erase its memory by destroying the team that played in the game. He wreaked the most havoc on a Red Sox roster since the reign of John I. Taylor.

His first target was Luis Tiant. From the perspective of the front office, Tiant, who was a free agent, symbolized the economic system they blamed for Boston's demise. He wanted to re-sign with Boston but the front office reminded him of his age and offered only a one-year contract.

The Yankees thought about Tiant's age, too — he was thirty-eight. Then they thought of his crucial role in Boston's clubhouse and his symbolic importance to Red Sox fans. On November 13 they concluded that those two factors alone made it worthwhile to sign Tiant for eight hundred forty thousand dollars over two years. Any games he won on the mound would be a plus.

Tiant meant more to the Sox than ninety-six wins over the last seven seasons. He was the one player in the Boston locker room not confined by the various cliques that made up the team; he made everyone laugh, kept them loose, then went out time after time and won the big game for them. But to the triumvirate of Zimmer, Sullivan, and LeRoux, the bottom line ruled and Tiant wanted too much. And they were just getting started.

Boston fans and players were stunned not only by the loss of Tiant but also by the prospect of El Tiante in pinstripes. On the day of the deal Yaz spoke for both parties, saying, "When they let Luis Tiant go to New York, they tore out our heart and soul."

On December 7 another bomb hit Sox fans. Boston traded Bill Lee to the Montreal Expos. His seventy-five wins in six seasons went to Montreal for backup infielder Stan Papi, a player without distinction and a total of forty-six career hits.

In the wake of Tiant's departure, the loss of Lee was crushing. Although controversial even in his own clubhouse, the lefthander was still valuable. Just as important, Lee enjoyed the media. Every minute he spent shooting his mouth off to writers allowed his teammates some relief from the hordes that circled the club.

The *Globe* correctly observed that the deal was made because "they wanted to get rid of Lee and they did." The graffiti "Who's Stan Papi?" appeared overnight throughout Boston. In less than two years general manager Haywood Sullivan had dumped five starting pitchers: Jenkins, Tiant, Wise, Cleveland, and Lee. All he had to show for it were Dennis Eckersley and free agent Mike Torrez, who was rapidly learning everything he ever cared to know about Denny Galehouse. Only John I. Taylor had ever been more efficient at getting nothing for something.

Sullivan justified his moves by saying, "Three or four years ago we looked at our staff and saw [they] were all getting older . . . We've never had such a large backlog of kid pitchers so close to the majors."

Hobson and Fisk started the season sidelined with bad arms. The starting rotation included Eck, Torrez, Stanley, Steve Renko, and rookie Chuck Rainey. Despite all evidence to the contrary, Sox fans couldn't give up the notion that the Red Sox were still contenders and bought tickets in record numbers.

On Opening Day blind hope masqueraded as cheerful optimism. The *Globe* commissioned John Updike to offer his insights on the day in a front-page story entitled "The First Kiss," and although the Red Sox beat the Indians 7-1 the upcoming season was not the memorable embrace foretold by Updike.

The Red Sox didn't totally collapse in 1979 — they simply began a long slow deflation. Lynn and Rice combined for seventy-eight home runs as the Sox led the league in the category, but Yaz got hurt in the second half, and the pitching staff fell apart. Lee won sixteen games for the Expos, and Tiant won thirteen for a Yankee club thrown off by Thurman Munson's death in a plane crash on August 2. Baltimore won the division title and pennant as the Red Sox sagged to third.

They collapsed in 1980. Injuries decimated the lineup as Remy, Lynn, Rice, Hobson, Yaz, and Eck all missed significant time. Boston's favorite pastime became guessing the day Don Zimmer would be fired. Attendance was down by almost four hundred thousand, and in the underfunded, business-first atmosphere of the Sox under Sullivan and LeRoux, attendance mattered.

Zimmer knew he'd be sacrificed. The man Leigh Montville accurately described as "the public punching bag" finally received the expected news with five games left in the season. Sullivan said, "I'm not blaming Zimmer for anything. A change was needed and we made it. Economics had something to do with it, fan reaction, public relations, on-the-field things — let's be fair about it. Sometimes change creates attitude. I'm looking for a different tone, that's all." He should have been looking for pitching. Johnny Pesky managed the final five games of the year and the Red Sox finished fourth in the division, just over .500.

The only event Boston fans felt good about that season was that Tom Yawkey was picked by the veterans' committee to make Baseball's Hall of Fame, the first owner ever chosen. His selection was a testimony to longevity and connections, for it ignored his failure to win a championship or his star-crossed record as a steward of the game. But Yawkey had been a benefactor of the Hall for years, and his enshrinement was a kind of belated thank-you.

After hiring low-key Ralph Houk as manager, Sullivan continued dismantling the Sox. He decided not to pay anyone more than Jim Rice, who earned seven hundred thousand dollars annually, and blanched when Burleson, Fisk, and Lynn all wanted contracts in the same range. So on December 10 he traded Butch Hobson and the best Boston shortstop since Johnny Pesky to California for Rick Miller, relief pitcher Mark Clear, and young third baseman Carney Lansford.

A few days later Sullivan and LeRoux made the biggest front office error in the history of baseball, no small feat. They misinterpreted a confusing clause in the Basic Agreement and failed to tender a contract to either Fisk or Lynn by a December 20 deadline. The contracts arrived with a postmark of December 22. Both players noticed and filed grievances that promised to make each a free agent. The Sox satisfied Lynn by trading him to California for sore-armed pitcher Frank Tanana and now-aging Joe Rudi, a deal the *Globe*'s Ray Fitzgerald described as "better than nothing," not unlike "the old Irish faculty for making the best out of a bad situation."

But they lost Fisk forever. He was declared a free agent and eventually signed on with the Chicago White Sox, Boston's Opening Day opponent at Fenway.

Outside the ballpark vendors were selling "Haywood and Buddy Are Killing the Sox" bumper stickers. In the eighth inning Fisk came up with two on, and Boston leading 2-0. Stanley threw a sinker that didn't sink and Fisk bounced it off the top of the Wall to make the score 3-2, and Chicago held on to win 5-3. The bumper stickers on cars stalled in traffic became a common sight — and a metaphor for the season.

Ralph Houk's new tone said fifth place on June 12 when the players went on strike. When the strike ended in August, baseball treated the season like a Thursday night bowling league, deciding to crown first- and second-half champions then add another tier of playoffs. Although the Sox played better in the second half, they didn't make the playoffs. Carney Lansford hit .336 to win the batting title, the first righthanded hitter to play in Fenway to do so since Foxx, but Clear and Tanana disappointed.

For the next three years Houk served as caretaker of a team that had no realistic chance of winning any-

thing. For the last time in recent memory, it was possible to go to Fenway Park at the last minute and get a decent seat for almost any game of the season. Most nights, only ten or twelve thousand fans sat scattered throughout Fenway Park, and fans in the bleachers could hear the plate umpire calling balls and strikes. Turnstiles were usually abandoned midgame, and people on the street wandered in for free. The homeless who worked Kenmore Square by day sometimes cruised the bleachers at night, panhandling, a scene that seemed symbolic.

A few singular achievements provided temporary distractions. Just when all had given up hope, Dwight Evans finally fulfilled his promise, displaying offensive skills that matched his defensive prowess.

Since he'd been drafted in the fifth round in 1969 the Red Sox had patiently waited for him to blossom into a superstar. But it had never happened. Although he manned right field for Boston better than anyone since Harry Hooper, at the plate Evans was all promise and little production. But under the tutelage of batting coach Walter Hriniak, a disciple of hitting guru Charlie Lau, Evans put it together in 1981, tying for the league lead with twenty-two home runs and hitting almost .300, standards he'd maintain for much of the next decade.

Unfortunately, Jim Rice ended his spectacular imitation of Jimmie Foxx and started to hit more like Jackie Jensen. Still very good, but no longer great, he missed the protection in the lineup provided by Lynn and a once more-productive Yaz.

Rice and the fans had never embraced each other in the first place, but now they began to look at each other even more warily. All Rice ever wanted was to be judged on his numbers and left alone. Fans wanted him to be someone he wasn't. They never reached an understanding. As Yaz made the transformation into a beloved icon, Rice seemed to play to the level of his team.

Bleacher fans who came to Fenway for little reason beyond the opportunity to drink beer outside turned vicious. Rice, Eckersley, and Clear got blamed for Boston's lousy ballclub and were regularly jeered. The taunts sometimes had an ugly racial tinge; Rice was regularly called "Uncle Ben."

Rice subsequently claimed that he decided to with-

After the death of her husband, Jean R. Yawkey survived legal challenges from fellow partners to emerge as principal owner of the Red Sox. She became a familiar sight, watching every home game from her private suite and making the occasional trip with the team. Here she is shown leaving Boston for the final two games of the 1986 World Series in New York.

draw during his rookie season when certain members of the Boston media threatened to "break him." He never kowtowed to either the media or the fans; as a result, both groups gave him ever more reason to remain remote.

On their way to third place in 1982, the club discovered an overlooked gem in their farm system. For five years, infielder Wade Boggs had hit .300 without impressing anyone in the front office. The organization focused on what he couldn't do, like run, hit for power, and field, while ignoring that he collected base hits like a three-year-old at the beach collects rocks — relentlessly.

But before the 1981 season Boggs got in the best shape of his life, showed some power, and led the International League in hitting. Although the front of-

fice wasn't particularly impressed, Boggs had a good camp in 1982 and made the Opening Day roster because he was cheap. He started the season on the bench, but after Lansford was injured in a collision at home plate he started getting more playing time. Every game he played he seemed to hit a couple of fifteen-hoppers up the middle for a hit.

No one believed it would continue, but it did, and Boggs eventually learned to use the Green Monster to his advantage, slapping pitches off the Wall for doubles. His defense went from poor to adequate, and he set a rookie record by hitting .349 in 1982.

Yet while Boggs became the highest-average hitter of the 1980s, he was never quite celebrated as a genuine superstar. He was bland personally, and his skills were so discreet as to be almost invisible. Not unlike Ted Williams, his obsessive self-absorption — he always referred to himself in the third person — seemed to exclude team accomplishments. His uncanny knack for getting hits and drawing walks was effective, but rarely exciting. Every time he came to bat he seemed to fall behind 0-2, then foul off pitch after pitch until he either walked or bounced the ball deftly through the infield. Watching him hit was like watching a marathoner running alone far ahead of the field. There was nothing compelling about the experience until the end of the race when it was possible to look at the numbers. Year after year he collected well over 200 hits and led the league — again — with a batting average over .350. No Boston player since Tris Speaker — not even Ted Williams — had reached those figures so consistently. At the end of the year, Lansford was traded for outfielder Tony Armas to make room for Boggs in the starting lineup.

As the Sox fell out of contention, younger players like shortstop Glenn Hoffman; infielder Dave Stapleton; pitchers John Tudor, Bobby Ojeda, and Bruce Hurst; outfielder Reid Nichols; and catcher Rich Gedman made it into the lineup. The club took on much the same character it had had in the mid-1950s or early 1960s. They were a boring, faceless collection of players rather than a team of glittering superstars. Cost-cutting caused the farm system to suffer. Most of the remaining prospects had been signed under O'Connell. In a time-honored Red Sox tradition young pitchers were often touted beyond their ability, rushed to the major leagues before they were ready, then given up on prematurely. Players like Allen Ripley, Joel Finch, and Brian Denman took their places as lesser Ken Bretts and Bobby Sprowls.

In 1983 ownership provided the early drama. On June 6, the club was 28-22, optimistic, in first place, and preparing to honor Tony Conigliaro on Tony C. Night. A year before, while in Boston interviewing for a job as color man on the team's baseball broadcast, Conigliaro had suffered a devastating heart attack that left him severely handicapped. The financial burden on his family was tremendous, and proceeds of the game that evening were earmarked for his care.

But at 4:30 P.M. Buddy LeRoux called a press conference and announced that the Yawkey, Sullivan, LeRoux partnership had been reorganized — he'd teamed with minority partners and he was in charge. Sullivan was out and Dick O'Connell was back.

When LeRoux's conference ended, Sullivan's started. He claimed LeRoux's coup was illegal and that he was in charge. With that, all parties proceeded to the courts and a protracted, dirty legal battle for control of the franchise, one that eventually diminished everyone involved.

The Red Sox, naturally, went into an immediate slump and at season's end found their level as a sub-.500 team for the first time since 1966. Carl Yastrzemski provided the only feel-good moment of a smells-bad season on its final day, October 2.

Yaz simply wasn't motivated without a pennant to play for and made the difficult decision to retire. Reaction to the news demonstrated precisely how much he had meant to the new generation of fans he brought to Fenway beginning in 1967. When Ted Williams had retired, few cared enough anymore to come to Fenway to bid him adieu. But Yaz had been a part of the team that had made the Red Sox matter again. His final game was the first that season to sell out.

An hour before the start, Yaz walked onto the field for a long sendoff. He received a six-minute standing ovation, a host of gifts, and words of praise from a variety of luminaries. Then Yaz spoke briefly, thanking everyone, and asked for a moment of silence in memory of his mother and Tom Yawkey.

"New England, I love you," he said, blinking away tears. Then he turned and started a slow jog around the perimeter of the stands, slapping and shaking hands with as many fans as possible as the barrier Yastrzemski had constructed over the years between himself and his fans came tumbling down.

It wasn't a spontaneous act, for Yaz had thought of it several days before, but it was no less effective and moving. "I wanted to show my emotions," he said later. "For 23 years I blocked everything out."

After his victory lap, the game began. He played left field for the last time, and the first time all season. He didn't make a catch, or toss anyone out, but he did grab one ball off the Wall and make a strong throw to second to hold the runner at first for what seemed the thousandth time in his storied career. He came to bat four times and failed to add to his total of 3,419 hits, the most in club history, grounding out each time. The Red Sox lost to Cleveland, 2-1, but no one cared.

When he ran off the field for the last time, recalling Ted Williams's stubborn refusal to tip his cap, Yaz spotted a young boy sitting in the box seats next to the dugout, took off his hat, and gave it to him. He vowed he would never wear a Red Sox cap again. And he never has.

His departure marked the official end of a Red Sox dynasty whose reign never made it through October. Evans and Rice were the only players left from the 1975 team.

Sullivan and Jean Yawkey eventually won their tussle with LeRoux, and when the legal proceedings ended in February of 1984, Judge John Greaney concluded the matter by admonishing both sides "to put aside their differences, get together and do something about the pitching." While Sullivan worked behind the scenes to consolidate his power and eventually buy out LeRoux, he stepped aside as general manager and hired affable New England native Lou Gorman as vice president and general manager. Gorman, who'd served as director of baseball operations for the Mets before joining Boston in a similar capacity, would prove an important hire. The media had long since turned on Sullivan. With Gorman, the franchise appeared to have a chance at a fresh start.

The club's sub-.500 finish gave it license to rebuild,

and in 1984 the Sox underwent wholesale change. A knee injury to Jerry Remy ended his career and handed the second base job to Marty Barrett. Jackie Gutierrez took over for Glenn Hoffman at short and Worcester's Rich Gedman replaced Gary Allenson behind the plate. Dennis Eckersley's long demise allowed Boston to trade him, and the Chicago Cubs gave up the still-valuable Bill Buckner in exchange. John Tudor went to Pittsburgh for power-hitting outfielder and DH Mike Easler, Stanley went back to the pen, and by midseason the Red Sox' starting rotation didn't include a player older than twenty-six.

With their first pick in the 1983 free-agent draft, the Red Sox had selected University of Texas pitcher Roger Clemens. He raced through the organization in 1983, going 7-2 with an ERA under 1.50 in Single and Double A.

Clemens was invited to camp in 1984 and pitched well. Regardless, he was sent down to Pawtucket so that management would be able to push back his eligibility to go to salary arbitration for another season.

On May 11 the Sox sent rookie pitcher Dennis "Oil Can" Boyd and his 0-3 record back to Pawtucket. Clemens was called up a few days later.

No pitcher since Lefty Grove had arrived under a greater set of expectations. At 6-foot-4 and over 200 pounds, Clemens was a prototype power pitcher. From the first time he stepped on the mound in a Boston uniform he was expected to be a star.

That didn't happen right away. He struggled in his first start against Cleveland, giving up five runs and six stolen bases over five and two-thirds innings for a no-decision in a 7-5 Boston loss. But he won his next start against Minnesota and seemed to improve each time out, gaining greater command and becoming ever more aware of what his 95-mile-an-hour fastball allowed him to do to major league hitters. Over twenty starts, he went 9-4.

In contrast to Clemens's blistering efficiency was Boyd, who was recalled a few weeks after Clemens's debut and went 12-9 the rest of the way. Boyd weighed barely 150 pounds and his style of pitching was all attitude. Clemens and Boyd joined mild-mannered lefthanded power pitcher Bruce Hurst, on his way to his second consecutive 12-12 season; Bob Ojeda, also 12-12; and junkballer Al Nipper, an impressive 11-6 in the best young rotation in baseball. In an era of rapidly escalating salaries the fact that they earned a combined salary of five hundred thousand dollars — Clemens made only forty-five thousand dollars — allowed the club to retain veteran position players like Evans and Rice and fill holes without blowing their budget.

Still, the team didn't have a chance to win, and they didn't. Detroit started the season 35-5, and in June the Sox lost nine in a row as Clemens, Boyd, and Nipper adjusted to the major leagues. But by July the future seemed right on time. The Red Sox had one of the best records in baseball in the second half. The addition of slugging center fielder Tony Armas, Easler, and Buckner to a lineup of Rice, Evans, Boggs, and Gedman gave the club one of the most potent lineups in baseball.

The result, of course, was wild optimism in 1985. Houk retired, and veteran manager John McNamara was hired to lead the club on a pennant push. At the beginning of the year Pete Gammons wrote, "The Red Sox are probably better than they've been since October 2, 1978."

But meeting expectations has never been this team's strong suit. After opening the season by beating the Yankees three straight, little went as planned. Clemens hurt his shoulder, Armas pulled a quad muscle, Rice hurt his knee, and much of what had gone right in 1984 went wrong. The team finished an absolutely neutral 81-81, fifth place, eighteen and a half games behind Toronto.

In December, the specter of racism rocked the club again. Former player and minor league instructor Tommy Harper was fired. The previous spring, he'd exposed the fact that the Red Sox had allowed white players to receive passes to an openly segregated Elks Lodge in their spring training home of Winter Haven, Florida. Harper's revelations embarrassed the team and they severed ties with the group.

The Sox claimed Harper was fired for performance-related reasons. Harper believed it was retribution for speaking out. He went to work at a body shop near Fenway. The United States Equal Employment Opportunity Commission agreed with Harper's claim, and the Massachusetts Commission Against Discrimination eventually negotiated a settlement.

The best part of 1985 was that it was over and left expectations for 1986 diminished. Gorman added some depth by trading Ojeda to the Mets for fast-ballers Calvin Schiraldi and Wes Gardner, and the Sox and Yankees made their first trade in years, swapping designated hitters as Boston dealt Easler for Don Baylor.

Yet Roger Clemens was the key. In 1986 he emerged as one of the most dominant pitchers in baseball and demonstrated what he would mean to the club for much of the next decade. Almost by himself, year after year Clemens ensured that the Red Sox would be, at worst, a .500 team.

It didn't really matter if Boggs hit .360 or someone peppered the left-field wall with fifty doubles or hit forty home runs. What mattered was Clemens. When he won, so did Boston. He stopped losing streaks, filled Fenway Park, and ensured a certain level of respectability. Whenever another Boston pitcher approached his level and the remainder of the division was relatively weak, Clemens made otherwise flawed Boston teams contenders. When more than one pitcher stepped up, they were much better than that.

That's what happened in 1986, a season in which most expected the Red Sox to finish in the middle of the division race, for Clemens was coming off shoulder trouble and the rest of the staff was still unproven. But from game one, Boston's pitching was better than expected and the Eastern Division, as a whole, weaker.

Clemens ripped off three straight wins and became the pitcher Sox fans had been waiting for. But on April 29 before 13,414 fans against the Seattle Mariners at Fenway Park, Clemens went national. He struck out twenty hitters, something no major league pitcher had ever done before.

Clemens became a national figure overnight. The Red Sox surged, winning thirteen of seventeen to pull into first place on May 15, then winning six of seven to open up a lead.

On June 30 they solidified the pitching staff, trading the popular Steve Lyons to the White Sox for forty-one-year-old future Hall of Famer Tom Seaver. Although Seaver was only 2-6 with Chicago, he'd won thirty-one games over the previous two seasons.

Clemens remained nearly unhittable, and through June, unbeatable, going 14-0 before losing two tough decisions to Toronto and Oakland in the first week of July. As the All-Star break neared, Boston's lead in the division race approached ten games.

Clemens wasn't the only Boston player putting together a good first half. Jim Rice, although his power numbers were down, was hitting over .330, while Don Baylor had crushed fifteen home runs.

But pitching was still the difference. To back Clemens, Oil Can Boyd was a stellar 11-6, and Bruce Hurst was rounding into shape after being sidelined.

Clemens was a lock for the All-Star team and was selected to the squad on July 10 by Kansas City manager Dick Howser. But when Oil Can Boyd learned his 11-6 mark hadn't been enough to impress Howser, he exploded, storming out of the clubhouse. He sat in his car, too upset to drive, telling reporters, "I want my reward and I want it today . . . I've got a good

In pressure situations pitcher Dennis "Oil Can" Boyd made the pitching mound his personal stage. Boston never knew quite what to do with the Can, who professed to feeling "old-timey" on the mound, wore his socks in a traditional mode, and aspired to pitch as well as his hero Satchel Paige.

CLEMENS'S TWENTY K'S

Roger Clemens was born in Ohio and moved to Texas at age fourteen. An older brother took command of his athletic career and steered Clemens to the rich baseball tradition at Spring Hills High School and then the University of Texas under coaching legend Clif Gustafson. On the same team with later major leaguers Spike Owen, Mike Capel, and Calvin Schiraldi, Clemens earned All-American honors and led Texas to the Collegiate World Series.

From the moment the Red Sox signed him with their first-round pick in 1983, they expected him to be a star. He soared through the farm system and reached the major leagues in the middle of the 1984 season after only seventeen minor league starts.

But Clemens was still growing, and arm trouble cut short both his 1984 and 1985 seasons. By 1986, some were beginning to question whether he'd ever reach the level of greatness the Red Sox had so confidently predicted. But his arm healed, and in 1986 he got off to a good start and began striking out hitters in increasing numbers. His teammates took note and during his windup started counting down "One, two, three, blast-off!" hence the nickname "Rocket."

Before he took the mound on April 29 against Seattle, Bill Buckner turned to Al Nipper and said of Clemens, "He's going to strike out eighteen tonight," one short of the existing major league record.

In the first inning, Clemens, who hadn't pitched in six days because of a rainout, struggled with his control, going to a full count against all three hitters before blowing away Spike Owen, Phil Bradley, and Ken Phelps on fastballs that exploded through the strike zone.

In the second, Gorman Thomas became the first hitter to get the bat on the ball, lining out to left, and then Clemens struck out Dave Henderson and Ivan Calderon. Meanwhile, Seattle's Mike Moore was shutting out the Red Sox.

In the fourth inning, Spike Owen, Clemens's former teammate at the University of Texas, led off. On one of about only twenty curveballs Clemens threw all night, Owen swung at a pitch almost in the dirt and punched the ball though the left side for a single to break up Clemens's no-hitter. He ran to first base laughing at his good fortune.

The hit seemed to motivate Clemens, and he punched out the next two hitters before Gorman Thomas floated a foul ball off first base. Don Baylor, making a rare start at first base as Buckner DH'd, dropped it. Given a reprieve, Thomas struck out looking. After four innings, Clemens had nine strikeouts, and fans started doing the math — he was on a record pace.

He struck out the side in the fifth and the first two men in the sixth to set an AL record with his eighth consecutive strike-out.

Owen then came up for the third time and lined out deep to center. The streak was over, but Clemens had fourteen strike-outs through six innings.

He struck out Bradley and Phelps to start the seventh, bringing up Thomas. The two-time American League home run champion pulled a ball into the net to give Seattle a 1-0 lead. After Jim Presley grounded out to end the inning, Clemens fired his glove into the dugout. He knew the mistake to Thomas could cost him the ballgame.

But Boston went ahead in the bottom of the inning on Dwight Evans's three-run homer. In suburban Boston, a young fan who

had earlier started pasting large letter "K's" on the back wall of the bleachers whenever Clemens pitched was watching this game on television. He convinced his mother to drive him to Fenway Park for the finish.

Clemens had already thrown over a hundred pitches. But with seventeen strikeouts already, he was on pace to shatter the record.

He struck out Calderon to lead off the eighth, tying the Red Sox record of seventeen held by Bill Monbouquette. After Tartabull singled, he notched Dave Henderson for number eighteen before pinch hitter Al Cowens flied out to end the inning.

When Clemens took the mound in the ninth, all thirteen thousand fans rose, and the back wall of the bleachers was decorated with eighteen K's. Clemens knew he was one strikeout shy of tying the major league record held jointly by Steve Carlton, Tom Seaver, and Nolan Ryan. In between innings, he'd been watching the game on television in the Red Sox club-house.

Spike Owen led off and struck out swinging. Nineteen.

With two outs remaining, Clemens had a chance to make history. The Mariners' Phil Bradley didn't have a chance. When Clemens's third pitch passed for a strike, Fenway exploded.

Clemens had a chance for strikeout number twenty-one, but Ken Phelps ended the drama and the game by grounding out.

It was one of the most dominating pitching performances in baseball history. Of the 138 pitches Clemens threw that night, 97 were strikes. Of those, only 10 were put in play and only 2 — Spike Owen's single and Gorman Thomas's home run — were pulled. ⚾

On April 29, 1986, Roger Clemens became the first major league pitcher to record twenty strikeouts in a nine-inning game as he defeated the Seattle Mariners. It was a feat he duplicated in Detroit on September 19, 1996.

mind to go back [home] to Mississippi. I have had it with this town . . . I'm an angry young man."

He was in between agents and nearly broke; his telephone had even been disconnected. Making the All-Star team would have earned him a much-needed twenty-five-thousand-dollar bonus.

And he should have made the club. Howser selected only eight pitchers. The Rangers' Charlie Hough and Brent Strom of Cleveland were clearly chosen only because a player from each team had to be on the squad. But none of that excused putting a personal goal before that of the team.

He was hardly the first Red Sox pitcher to jump the team — Babe Ruth, Carl Mays, Wes Ferrell, Gene

Following his suspension in July 1986 Dennis Boyd shouts at a photographer as he attempts to get into his car parked underneath the stands at Fenway Park. He had just been informed that his suspension had been continued.

Conley, and Bill Lee had done so in the past. Boyd had even gone on a similar tirade when snubbed in 1985 and been fined. This time he was suspended for three days.

The situation quickly became awkward and uncomfortable for all involved parties, made worse by Boston's mixed record in regard to African-American players. Boyd was clearly troubled, but he had the second-most wins on the team, and the Sox needed him.

The club intimated he was on drugs, welcomed Boyd back after an apology, but suspended him again when on the night of the All-Star Game he was rousted by some undercover police. He agreed to be hospitalized for evaluation.

Boyd's departure briefly precipitated a now-expected Boston collapse. Boston won only three of ten while he was out of the rotation.

The Red Sox clearly needed him. Seaver was struggling, and Clemens was pitching like a mere mortal. Boyd returned on August 5, and although he lost to Chicago 3-1 in his debut, the Sox won their next four and were back on track.

On August 17, Gorman worked a trade with Seattle to shore up the club's defense and depth. Rookie shortstop Rey Quinones had been inconsistent and was tainted by his friendship with Boyd. He was dealt with a package of prospects to Seattle for shortstop Spike Owen and outfielder Dave Henderson.

Owen solidified the infield, and the Sox staved off challenges by the Yankees, Orioles, and Tigers. On August 30, Clemens won game number twenty, beating Cleveland 7-3 while notching his 200th strikeout of the season.

Boston appeared to have weathered their slump, and fans started getting giddy at the prospect of a Boston pennant. A local fanzine, the *Sox Fan News*, speculated on a dream matchup between the Mets and Red Sox in the World Series. The same issue even ran a story called "How the Red Sox Won the 1975 World Series." Boston ached for deliverance from their history. On September 4 the *Globe*'s Dan Shaughnessy observed, "The Sox and their fans are haunted by a history of autumnal collapse, but there is ample evidence to suggest this unit can prevail," citing their superior pitching and a favorable schedule. With twenty-nine games remaining, Boston led by four and a half games over Toronto.

Shaughnessy was right. The Sox ran off a twelve-game winning streak at Fenway, and on September 28 Oil Can Boyd pitched an eight-hitter and Boston beat Toronto 12-3 to clinch the division title and earn the right to play California for the pennant. Meanwhile, the Mets and Astros would play for the National League title.

The league championship series matched two clubs increasingly obsessed by the past. Angel manager Gene Mauch, who'd felt slighted after not being named Boston manager back in 1961, was still haunted by his experience as Philadelphia manager in 1964. His Phillies had led the NL by six and a half games with only two weeks to go before losing ten straight to blow the pennant. In 1982 his Angels won the first two games of the AL LCS over Milwaukee before collapsing. Mauch was perhaps the only man on the planet of baseball who looked at Boston's ill-starred past with envy. How he ever avoided managing the Red Sox is a wonder.

Despite the loss of Seaver to a knee injury, Clemens made Boston the favorite. Yet those who looked for signs of trouble started finding them in the last week of the regular season.

History refused to be passed by. The major events of the Sox' improbable past began to recur and coil around the present. The 1986 Red Sox started to reenact the roles of their ancestors in some strange public ritual. The entire history of the Red Sox was destined to be replayed and repeated with triumph and despair the only conceivable outcomes.

It all started in the second inning of Roger Clemens's final, meaningless regular-season start on October 1 when the pitcher was hit on the elbow by a line drive off the bat of Baltimore catcher John Stefaro. Clemens's arm went numb and hearts sank throughout New England.

X-rays were negative, just as they'd been when Ted Williams had been hit by a pitch prior to the 1946 World Series. Then the Yankees came into Boston. Reminding the club what they were up against, the Yankees beat the Red Sox four straight. Don Mattingly went 8-19 in a futile attempt to wrest the batting title from Wade Boggs, who reminded no one

of Ted Williams in 1941. He sat out the final four games with a small injury to preserve his crown.

Then the front office took a page from 1946. In a radio interview on the eve of the championship series, Gorman defended the club's standing policy of limiting pitchers to two-year contracts by saying Clemens was a "question mark" because of concerns over his arm. That wasn't quite as disruptive as announcing he'd be traded to the Yankees, but it ticked off the odds-on favorite to win the Cy Young.

In the opening game of the LCS on October 7,

Dwight Evans enjoyed a career renaissance after the age of thirty as he employed the perfect Fenway Park swing while socking the majority of his 385 career home runs and leading the team to a pennant in 1986 and division titles in 1988 and 1990. His Gold Glove skills made him the finest Red Sox right fielder since Hall of Famer Harry Hooper.

"... fools pray only that the Beast depart"
("Dragon Country," Robert Penn Warren)

My most memorable post–Red Sox game moment occurred during the '86 American League Championship Series. I'd stayed around for the end of the press conference under the stands at Fenway Park and recorded my story at WBUR, which used to be just around the corner from the ballpark. It was about 2:30 in the morning. I was hiking up Commonwealth Avenue toward the Brookline side street where I'd left my car. Approaching a subterranean bar called the Dugout, which was, of course, closed, I noticed the movement of something — a cat, I first thought — on the concrete steps leading up from the club to the sidewalk.

It wasn't a cat. It was a cat-sized and confident rat. With a sidelong glance and lip raised for snarling, he indicated that I, not he, was the interloper. I walked briskly in a semicircle away from him. I may have been whistling. I was hoping he'd be too stuffed with whatever he'd been eating to come after me.

But that is a short, unpleasant story, so I'll fall back on my second most memorable post–Red Sox game moment. That occurred ten days or so later, well after I'd managed to get by the rat and the Sox had managed to get by the Angels. Boston looked as if it might also be about to get by the Mets to win the World Series. On this

particular night, Bruce Hurst had thrown a complete game to beat New York 4-2, giving the Sox a three games to two edge. Once again I'd stayed late at the ballpark for the press conference. Hurst, a devout and pleasant man who especially enjoyed bringing his children into the clubhouse, inadvertently provided the most surprising early-morning moment of that event. When a writer remarked that it must be tough for opposing hitters to face the high fastballs of Clemens and the off-speed curves and sinkers of Hurst on successive nights, Hurst replied, "It's not how hard it is. It's where you put it." His delivery was as flawless as it was innocent. He didn't even smile.

Early on that October morning, ugly, old Kenmore Square seemed less discouraging than usual. All the Sox had to do was win one of the next two in New York, and Boston would be champion. Already our guys had beaten the Mets at Shea in games one and two, foiling Ron Darling's best efforts and making Dwight Gooden look like a chump. Clemens was due for a gem. How hard could it be?

At that chilly, early-morning hour outside the empty ballpark, it was easy to see it that way. Many of us thought it could happen. As it turned out, many of us were fooled. But as I zipped up my jacket and walked away from the square, out toward the street where I hoped my car would still be parked, another possibility occurred to me. Blame the imp of the perverse, but I wondered if maybe the Sox, who'd beaten the Angels against the odds and

led the Mets by a game, could still find a way to sidestep success . . . and if maybe it would be better that way.

A couple of days earlier, the producer who'd employed me as National Public Radio's postseason game guy in Boston had called to say that no matter how it came out, he wanted me to write a wrap-up story for the day after the final game of the Series. On that early-morning walk up Commonwealth Avenue after game five, I realized that I'd already begun composing leads for the piece that would tell of the first Red Sox championship since 1918:

"Last night the curse was foiled."

"As a New York crowd one part disappointment and two parts disbelief watched unhappily or wandered disconsolately out of Shea Stadium, the Red Sox beat the Mets and several generations of stubborn ghosts."

"The Red Sox win the World Series! The Red Sox win the World Series! The Red Sox win the World Series!"

I didn't like any of them. The problem was and is that some team is always breaking a losing streak, winning a first championship in however many years, and rewarding its long-suffering fans with the whole whatever. Though the fan in me rooted for Boston to accomplish that result, the responsibility of transcribing it didn't appeal to the writer in me.

But what if the Boston team, ahead three to two in the Serious after being waved on through the ALCS by a team even more determined to self-destruct than the Red Sox had been, could trump the Angels and re-establish itself as the more creative and dependable loser? It would be a terrible moment for Boston fans, sure. But Boston fans had been building their lives around terrible moments for generations, and the story of defeat, especially a defeat which, despite the weight of accumulated tragedy, managed to seem as new and strange as it felt inevitable . . . that would be the story more fraught with possibilities. That would be a story a writer could embrace. I hadn't been writing about sports for very long when that traitorous thought crept, ratlike, into my tired mind. No more than eight or nine years, and only part-time. As more years went by and chronicling games and players became my livelihood, I would stop rooting for one particular team. That didn't mean I never pulled for members of the Red Sox. I'd been a Dennis Eckersley fan well before he came back to Boston in 1998. His return to Fenway was fun. He'd been sober for a long time then, and he talked thoughtfully and compellingly about maintaining his sobriety and a claim on the balanced life he'd established for himself and with his family.

But by that time I was a huge Felipe Alou fan, too. He brought to the task of managing his baseball team an exceptional level of dignity and responsibility. Well past sixty, he stood straight and bounced on the balls of his feet when he walked, and when he talked about the low-budget, patched-together club with which he banged away at the iron of the National League East each season, he could be simultaneously

proud, resigned, and very funny. Year after year his clubs were defined more by the departure of the accomplished and promising players the front office had peddled to contenders than by the Hispanic hopefuls and career spare parts who happened to be wearing the Expo uniform for the summer, but Felipe Alou never complained, and no manager ever inspired more respect or a better effort.

I also became an admirer of Dwight Gooden, the very same pitcher who, in October of 1986, seemed to be the guy

---

Clemens was due for a gem. How hard could it be?

---

the Red Sox would have to beat once more if they were going to spit in history's eye. As a fastballer in his twenties, Gooden could be nasty and self-absorbed. Listening to him was a necessary chore. But by the time he came back into baseball following all sorts of personal difficulties, including drug and alcohol addiction, he'd developed not only a sense of perspective, but also a sense of humor. Once during his tour with the Cleveland Indians, Gooden arrived late in the visiting clubhouse at Fenway Park — an entrance I'm sure he'd timed — wearing a forest green suit that appeared to be made of velvet. He looked as if he'd just come from a costume party where he'd certainly have won first prize as an exceptionally large black Robin Hood. The pro sports clubhouse is not a place where sartorial choices go

unremarked upon, and Gooden's teammates hooted and pointed and laughed. When they'd returned to adjusting their socks and wristbands, I asked Dwight Gooden if the reception he'd received had met the expectations he must have had when he picked out the ridiculous suit.

"You gotta keep 'em loose," he said with a laugh. But in the same conversation, he talked about the humility and serenity that were driving his ongoing recovery and the quiet delight with which he welcomed each succeeding day of the career that he thought he'd tossed away.

Over the years I've found lots of other players on the third-base side of "the lyrical little bandbox" easy to cheer for. I liked Matt Merullo when he was trying to establish himself as a catcher with the White Sox, not only because he was an open and articulate guy who swung from his heels, but because his grandfather, former Cub shortstop Lennie Merullo, is one of the most delightful human beings God ever put on the planet. How could I root against Lennie Merullo's grandson just because he happened to be hitting for the visitors at Fenway Park? Especially when he was facing a Red Sox pitcher who'd beaten up his wife in a motel room and then been delighted to learn almost immediately that as far as the Sox were concerned, what the pitcher did on his own time, including assault, needn't interrupt his pitching career?

But I don't want to let the chronology of this story scuttle any further afield than it already has, and I have to be honest. In October of 1986, with the Red Sox ahead of the Mets three games to two, I didn't know anybody on the opposing team that well. There was no excuse for treachery against the home side. The idea that a truly original Sox loss — a failure worthy not just of inclusion in the catalog of bad decisions, bad breaks, and bad players characterizing Boston over the decades, but a failure so stunning that it would assume a place at the *top* of the dark list — would be a writer's dream . . . this was an idea as spooky and unexpected as that rat on the steps of the bar had been.

But once acknowledged, the thought, unlike the rat, was not unwelcome. I didn't walk around it. Its novelty was seductive and its implications were heady. I'd been a baseball fan since before I could remember, and always that meant being the fan of a team. In fact, under the same geographical imperative that explains most sports loyalties, I'd only rooted for two teams. The first was the New York Giants of Willie Mays, who became the San Francisco Giants of Willie Mays, Juan Marichal, Orlando Cepeda, and Willie McCovey. I may have been the only kid in the suburbs of New York whose loyalty was not affected by the team's flight across the continent. For years I pretended that it hadn't happened. The second was the Red Sox of Luis Tiant, Bill Lee, Ned Martin, and Jim Woods. (I know, I know. Neither Martin nor Woods ever threw a pitch or swung a bat for those Sox, but if

you don't regard them as parts of the Sox experience of those days, may the play-by-play in your personal purgatory be all broadcast school graduates who'd rather sell you beer, fruit juice, and insurance than tell you a baseball story.)

In any case, here, surprising as bright, beady eyes and a lip set to snarl in the dark, was a new take on baseball altogether. Here was the notion, forming at that most awful and wonderful time when just nine unhittable innings from Clemens or Boyd or Hurst and one measly run for the home side would change everything, that I didn't want everything changed as much as I wanted fodder for a better story. If that meant Boston had to find still another way to lose, I wanted that.

Of course the Red Sox found a way. Maybe that made me a rat. Or maybe it just made me a fellow who could acknowledge the place of the rat in a story that would grow much larger. Consider Bill Buckner, who ran past me on his way up the dugout steps on Opening Day at Fenway Park in 1986 mumbling, "I'd rather be lucky than good," and eventually moved to Idaho and went into real estate development. According to Red Sox chronicler Dan Shaughnessy, Buckner's first project was a subdivision of starter homes, which he insisted on calling Fenway Park. Even if you don't respect him for his long productive career and his exemplary work ethic, you have to love his survivor's sense of irony.

Or think on Bob Stanley, who told me years ago that of course he'd had

dreams of being on the mound when the Red Sox won the World Series. He smiled and said he knew exactly how wonderful that would have felt. Then he told me the story of how his son had recovered from cancer some years after the '86 debacle. If it is a man's lot to enjoy a ration of blessings and to endure a ration of pain, what rat would be so low as to say it has gone badly for Bob Stanley? Not Stanley himself, who thanks God and does not brood.

Maybe it's age that's inclined me to prefer those stories to the victory tales peppered with self-congratulatory clichés ("focus," "nobody gave us any respect") and punctuated by the popping of champagne corks. In any case, I wouldn't object now if the Red Sox were once again to find themselves just one unhittable strike from a championship. I'd smile if that last, necessary pitch slipped past the opposing hitter and caught the corner for strike three. But while lots of Sox fans regard the fall of 1986 as painful, shameful, even unmentionable, the writer who would turn away from the last cold mornings of that improbably extended summer would be a fool.

Bill Littlefield is the host of WBUR and National Public Radio's *Only a Game.* He served as guest editor for the 1998 edition of *Best American Sports Writing* and is the author of a baseball novel, *Prospect,* as well as several books of sports essays, including *Champions: Stories of Ten Remarkable Athletes* and *Keepers: Radio Stories from "Only a Game" and Elsewhere.* A professor of humanities and writer-in-residence at Curry College, he has taught writing and literature there since 1976.

Clemens responded with his worst performance of the season, and California won behind pitcher Mike Witt's five-hitter, 8-1. Although the Red Sox came back to win game two 9-2 behind Bruce Hurst, Boston lost game three, 5-3.

In game four, Clemens was Clemens for eight innings, carrying a 3-0 shutout into the ninth. Then, after giving up a leadoff home run and two singles, McNamara turned to Calvin Schiraldi. Since taking over for Bob Stanley as Boston's closer he had been almost untouchable.

He was touched by the Angels. Rice lost Gary Pettis's flyball in the lights for a double, and after an intentional walk loaded the bases, Schiraldi hit Brian Downing to plate the tying run, then gave up the game-winning hit in the eleventh to Bobby Grich. After holding the past at bay for much of the season, the dam had finally broken.

Schiraldi seemed destined to take his place with Galehouse and Torrez as a premier Boston goat. He seemed fatalistic in defeat. "I blew it," he said. "I screwed up. No question about it."

Mauch's team was now one win away from giving their manager his first pennant. But Mauch's personal destiny wouldn't allow Boston's epic saga to unfold without resistance.

With Hurst pitching, the Sox nursed a 2-1 lead into the sixth. Then Dave Henderson, who'd entered the game as a defensive replacement when Tony Armas sprained an ankle, lost a flyball in the sun and the Angels tied the game. Bobby Grich followed with a long fly to center. Henderson tracked it to the fence and left his feet with a chance to join Harry Hooper and Dwight Evans in the Red Sox postseason-catch Hall of Fame.

He came down joining Al Zarilla, for the ball landed in his glove but was knocked loose when his wrist hit the fence, falling on the other side for a home run. California led 3-2.

Entering the ninth, California led 5-2 and Witt was cruising. Buckner singled, then Rice struck out. Two outs to go.

Don Baylor then homered to make the score 5-4, but Witt got Dwight Evans to pop out. One out to go.

Police encircled the field to protect it from the impending celebration. The crowd of sixty-four thousand stood as one in anticipation of the Angels' first pennant.

Then, with Gedman coming up, Mauch made a change. He brought in lefthander Gary Lucas. The move made sense. Lucas had always owned Gedman.

But the Angel pitcher's body was suddenly taken over by the spirit of Jack Chesbro. He threw the ball

A star-crossed Calvin Schiraldi enjoys the fruits of victory following the Red Sox' clinching of the 1986 division title. Within a month he would ride a roller coaster that saw him on the mound when the Red Sox defeated the Angels for the pennant and also saw him allow three straight tenth-inning singles (with two outs) in game six of the World Series at Shea Stadium.

wild and hit Gedman with the first pitch, his first hit batsman of the season.

With Dave Henderson due up Mauch called for reliever Donnie Moore. Despite a sore arm, he'd saved twenty-one games that season. Henderson worked the count to 2-2 on a series of fastballs. The Angels were one strike away from the World Series.

Catcher Bob Boone called for a split-fingered fastball. Moore threw it, but the ball hung over the plate.

Henderson jerked it into the air toward left, then danced and jumped down the line on his tiptoes. The ball sailed eight rows deep into the left-field stands as Gene Mauch stared fate in the face and cringed. Boston sculptors began carving out Henderson's statue. Boston led 6-5. As Clemens said later, "We were on our deathbeds at 5-2. The heartbeat meter was a straight line. Then Hendu goes deep, and it starts beeping again." They were alive.

But no team in baseball has ever been better at snatching defeat from the jaws of victory. In the bottom of the ninth, first Bob Stanley and then Joe Sambito failed to put the game away. The Angels tied it

before Steve Crawford got the final out to send the game into extra innings.

In the eleventh, the pendulum of fate swung back Boston's way. Moore tired and Boston loaded the bases with no outs. Henderson hit a fly to center that scored Don Baylor and seemed to secure his place in Red Sox history. Schiraldi got through the eleventh and Boston won 7-6.

The Angels couldn't handle it. They careened through the final two games of the series in Boston like a drunk in a hurry to get home. Boyd won game six 10-4, and Clemens won game seven 8-1. The Red Sox won the pennant. Mauch and the Angels never recovered.

As Boston looked forward to the World Series it was hard to look at the unlikely events of the league championship series without concluding that the Red Sox were a team of destiny. They had taken everything history could possibly throw at them and survived. The unlikely, the unfortunate, and the unbelievable had already happened, and the Red Sox had beaten all three.

The Mets had won the National League championship just as the *Sox Fan News* had earlier predicted. The Mets weren't the Yankees, but they were the next best thing. For Boston fans a World Series win over the New York *anythings* was the sweetest of all possible thoughts. New York was favored, but no one cared. That would make it even better.

Boston fell over itself blathering over the Sox. The *Globe* even published a postseason special in which literary luminaries like Stephen King, George V. Higgins, Doris Kearns Goodwin, and David Halberstam waxed poetic about the Olde Towne team. Wade Boggs called his club "a team of magic." Calvin Schiraldi, on the mound in relief of Clemens in the finale and ecstatic at having the goat horns ripped out of his head, described his journey as "highest high, lowest low. And now I'm drinking champagne."

Boston players tried to stay focused, deflecting any

Jim Rice *(l)* greets Don Baylor *(r)* following the latter's 1986 home run at Fenway Park. Baylor, a former American League MVP with the Angels, was acquired in that rarest of deals, namely via a trade from the Yankees in exchange for Mike Easler. Baylor and Rice would both enjoy superb seasons in helping the Red Sox get to the World Series.

talk about fate, and most pleaded total ignorance of their own infamous history. But all that had happened in the previous ten days, in the preceding year, and in the entire life of the franchise was slowly but inexorably building toward the most improbable climax of all.

In the opener in New York, Hurst and Schiraldi combined on a 1-0 shutout as Boston scored the only run it needed when Rich Gedman hit a groundball through the legs of Met second baseman Tim Teufel. Gooden and Clemens faced each other in a dream matchup in game two, but neither made it past the sixth inning. Clemens, however, was backed by the support of eighteen hits and the Sox won, 9-3, to go ahead in the Series 2-0. The victory was Boston's fifth consecutive postseason win.

But back in Boston for game three, former Sox pitcher Bob Ojeda beat Boyd 7-1 to keep the Mets alive. With a chance to bring back Hurst on three days' rest, McNamara went with Nipper, and Massachusetts native Ron Darling beat him to tie the Series. Then Hurst went the distance to beat Dwight Gooden 4-2 and put the Red Sox only one game away from their first world championship since 1918.

As both clubs traveled to New York for the conclusion, Dan Shaughnessy asked rhetorically in the *Globe*, "Is this the threshold of a dream, or the eve of destruction? Are baseball's heartbreak kids finally going to keep a promise, or are they just setting you up for one final apocalyptic, cataclysmic fall?" *Sports Illustrated* headlined its story on the Series to date "Poised for Another El Foldo?"

The Red Sox didn't want to hear it. Dwight Evans even said he was happy to leave Boston and end the Series in New York because of the fatalism that accompanied every Boston achievement. "Some people call this Beantown," he said. "I might call it Panictown."

Everything seemed to be lining up Boston's way. Clemens was ready to pitch. The heroic Henderson was playing better than Armas ever had. Hurst's complete game left the Boston bullpen well rested. Even Bill Buckner's balky ankles, which caused him to run like he was stepping on marbles, had held up. Boston had ex-Mets Schiraldi, Seaver, and Lou Gorman on board ready to wreak revenge. All the Mets had was

Bruce Hurst, here shown in front of his locker following the Red Sox' clinching of the American League Eastern Division on September 28, 1986, had a superb postseason in 1986. He not only won the critical fifth game of the league championship series against California but also went on to win games one and five against the Mets in the World Series. Before the Red Sox lost game six in heartbreaking fashion it had been announced that Hurst was to be named Series MVP had the Red Sox won.

former Boston manager Darrell Johnson on the payroll as a scout.

Confident, the Red Sox seemed to say all the right things before the game. But those bland statements would later read like cruel jokes. "It's at hand, but it's not over," said Dwight Evans. "We're not going to celebrate until the last out and the *last pitch.*" Asked if he'd given any thought to playing Baylor at first instead of a slumping Buckner, John McNamara quipped, "It'll be Buckner. He's *hobbling at 100 percent.*" Not even the press was immune. *Globe* reporter Leigh Montville wrote, "Every day I say I will do the Buckner story and every day something or someone interferes ... I have to do the *Buckner story* sometime before this World Series ends." His story about Buckner's sore ankles appeared before game six under the unintentionally clairvoyant headline "Buckner's Story Is Painfully Familiar." That it would certainly be.

All across the country, in groups that cut across gender and generations, Red Sox fans gathered on the evening of October 25 for game six. Boston fans never before looked forward to a game with such anticipation.

History was head down and sleeping in the corner of the dugout, the last man on the roster, whom nearly everyone had forgotten. Sox fans, who'd learned the hard way to enjoy the ride but to never, ever hazard to imagine arriving at their desired destination, began to dream — for a while.

Game six started and the Sox easily and efficiently took command. At first everything went according to some great plan that seemed designed to spare their fans any undue worry on this most splendid of nights. Boggs singled off third baseman Ray Knight's glove to start the game. After Barrett and Buckner went out, Rice walked and Evans doubled off the wall in left center, missing a home run by a couple of feet. Boggs scored to put Boston ahead 1-0, but Rice cautiously stopped at third and was stranded. In the second, Owen and Boggs and Barrett singled, and wide smiles greeted Owen when he crossed home plate to make the score 2-0. Boston looked confident and loose while the Mets seemed tight and nervous. Ojeda was one pitch away from the off-season.

Then Bill Buckner flied out to the warning track in right. The Sox had missed a chance to put the game away, but at the time that seemed a fair trade for another run. Ojeda then settled down.

It didn't matter; Clemens was unhittable. He struck out six of the first nine hitters and was perfect through four innings.

But in the fifth, he walked Darryl Strawberry, who immediately stole second. Ray Knight singled to score him.

Laughter in living rooms turned nervous.

Then Mookie Wilson singled to right. Dwight Evans charged the ball, but it bounced off his chest for an error and Knight took third. Eyebrows raised.

With runners on the corners, a one-run lead, and no outs, McNamara conceded the run in favor of a potential double play. Throats tightened.

Now Evans's error proved critical. Danny Heep, pinch-hitting for shortstop Rafael Santana, hit into the double play, but Knight scored to tie the game.

Teeth clenched.

The 2-2 score held through the sixth, but the Mets had to play to win. Afraid Ojeda was tiring, Met manager Davey Johnson put in reliever Roger McDowell to start the seventh inning. McDowell walked Marty Barrett, then Buckner grounded in the hole to second. He was out easily, but Barrett, breaking with the pitch, advanced.

Next, Jim Rice bounced the ball toward Ray Knight at third. He fielded it clean, but threw high off first baseman Keith Hernandez's glove. Rice was safe and Barrett went to third.

Now Dwight Evans hit a groundball to short. Rice was running on the play and beat the flip to second, although Evans was out at first. Barrett scored to give Boston the lead again, 3-2.

New England allowed itself to breath again.

Gedman followed with a hit to left and hearts leapt. Third-base coach Rene Lachemann waved Rice around third, a move that seemed to surprise the slugger. He reminded no one of Enos Slaughter and ran almost straight to third, then circled for home far, far into foul territory. Out. History stirred and started to stretch.

Clemens got through the seventh easily but broke a blister on the middle finger of his left hand.

He was scheduled to hit third in the eighth. Dave Henderson led off with a single through short, and Spike Owen bunted him to second. High-fives were at the ready.

McNamara was now faced with a decision not dissimilar to that which Joe McCarthy had faced at the end of the 1949 season with Ellis Kinder. He could leave his pitcher in, have him bat and probably not score, or go to a pinch hitter and try for an extra run.

McNamara decided the run outweighed the value of having Clemens on the mound and made the same decision as McCarthy; he'd pinch-hit for his pitcher. Besides, he'd been burned in game four against the Angels by calling on Schiraldi too late. Later, McNa-

After rescuing the Red Sox with his ninth-inning two-run home run in game five of the American League Championship Series against the Angels, Dave Henderson seemingly did it again in game six of the World Series when he led off the tenth inning with his tie-breaking home run. Henderson is shown just as he realizes the ball is leaving Shea Stadium.

mara reportedly said Clemens asked out because of the injury to his finger. Clemens has always claimed the decision was the manager's alone.

It didn't matter. After 135 pitches, Clemens was out of the game. History picked up a bat and started swinging.

So did Don Baylor. With thirty-one home runs and ninety-four RBIs batting primarily against right-handed pitching, he was the obvious choice to hit. But McNamara made a mistake similar to McCarthy's. Instead of hitting Baylor and his 1,982 career hits, he tabbed rookie lefthander Mike Greenwell, with eleven big league hits. Baylor went to the clubhouse to take some swings and watch the game on television.

Greenwell almost beat him there. McDowell punched

him out on three pitches. But then Boggs and Barrett walked to load the bases.

With the lefthanded Buckner due up next, Davey Johnson pulled McDowell for lefthander Jesse Orosco.

Perfect. Perhaps McNamara had been right to save Baylor after all. He could hit for Buckner, who was 11-for-55 in the postseason, 4-for-27 in the Series, and had hit only .218 against lefties all year. Then after Baylor hit, Dave Stapleton could take over at first, shoring up Boston's defense in the late innings. In games one, two, and five of the Series, all Boston wins, Stapleton had been playing first at the end of the game.

Baylor saw Orosco strolling in from the pen and went to the dugout, ready to hit. History brushed him

aside and whispered in McNamara's ear. McNamara said nothing as Buckner, "hobbling at 100 percent," minced to the plate. He flied out on the first pitch to end the inning, then went back on the field to start the eighth.

Now Schiraldi took the mound for Boston. The Mets had soured on him because they didn't think he had enough pitches to start, or enough composure to relieve. He soon proved them correct.

Pinch hitter Lee Mazzilli greeted him with a single, then Lenny Dykstra bunted back to Schiraldi. He tried for the out at second, but threw into the dirt.

Johnson decided to try another bunt with Wally Backman. This time Schiraldi threw to first for an out, but the runners moved up.

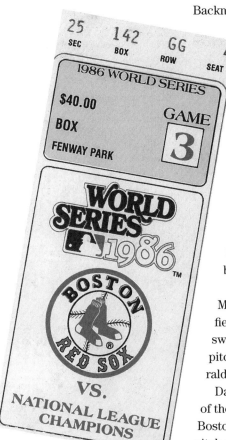

The crowd at Shea could smell it. Schiraldi looked like he wanted to crawl under the rubber. He walked Keith Hernandez, then went 3-0 on Gary Carter.

Carter got the green light. He hit a liner to left, right at Jim Rice, but Mazzilli scored, and Sox fans looked out windows and considered jumping. Strawberry flied out to end the inning, but the score was tied, 3-3.

Neither club scored in the ninth. Mazzilli replaced Strawberry in the field as Johnson pulled a double switch, bringing in Rick Aguilera to pitch. McNamara stayed with Schiraldi.

Dave Henderson became the hero of the moment. He led off the tenth for Boston and smashed Aguilera's second pitch off the *Newsday* billboard in deep left, then danced and hopped around the bases. Boston led, 4-3, and in living rooms and barrooms all over New England popcorn and beer spilled to the floor amid unimagined, unchecked, backslapping, foot-stomping, yell-until-hoarse glee. That Henderson had done it seemed perfect, absolutely perfect. Of all the Red Sox players none had

seemed more oblivious of their past than he, their latest arrival. He had no idea that the last time the Red Sox had won a World Series the big hero had been the team's fourth outfielder playing in place of their leading home run hitter.

Owen and then Schiraldi struck out, but Boggs — Boggs! — slapped a double to left. Steady Marty Barrett grounded a single up the middle that even Boggs could score on for the insurance run. 5-3. A Boston world championship was now virtually certain. Shea was silent apart from pockets of Boston fans that cheered and shook their fists in the collective face of New York, saying, "Take that!" History? Who cares?

Unglued, Aguilera hit Buckner. Rice flied out to end the inning. So what? That just made the celebration even closer.

The Red Sox were three outs away from a world championship.

After sixty-eight seasons of scapegoating and blame, finger-pointing and reproach, sixty-eight seasons of denial followed always by destruction and doom, sixty-eight seasons of having the wrong man on the mound, the wrong guy at the plate, and the wrong manager at the wheel, in the name of Galehouse and Cronin, McCarthy and Torrez, Zimmer and Lee, and goddamn Bucky "Bleeping" Dent, the seasons 1946, 1948, 1949, 1967, 1975, and 1978 were about to be rendered over and done and gone for all time.

Red Sox. World champions.

Those words waited to be paired together in the throats of every Sox fan in the world. But unnoticed, the only one on the field for the last sixty-eight seasons stood and sighed, then stepped forth and chose sides. History does not wear a "B" on his cap.

Schiraldi came on to get the final three outs. Sweet. Being on the mound for the final three outs to beat the Mets in the World Series offered him the opportunity to erase the memory of what had been a shattering experience pitching for New York.

Wally Backman flied out to left. One out and cries of delight.

Then Keith Hernandez hit the ball deep to center field. Henderson drifted back and made the catch on the warning track. Two outs and tears of joy.

The message "Congratulations Red Sox" prematurely flashed on the scoreboard before the embarrassed operator switched it off. In the Boston locker room, attendants draped plastic over the players' lockers in anticipation of the celebration. The press box nearly emptied as reporters raced to the clubhouses, forming questions as they ran, anticipating postgame interviews with the victorious Red Sox and losing Mets. Once there, they huddled around television monitors to watch the end of the game like most of America. Jean Yawkey and Haywood Sullivan stood side by side beaming at one another. Champagne cooled in buckets of ice.

Gary Carter, known by Ted Williams's old nickname, "the Kid," stepped in for the Mets. Schiraldi just tried to throw strikes. Carter just tried to make contact. The end was as close as a single pitch.

Both men succeeded. Schiraldi threw a strike and Carter slapped the nothing fastball down the middle softly to left for a single.

Aguilera was scheduled to hit in Strawberry's place. Johnson called for Kevin Mitchell. He was reportedly on the phone in the clubhouse making airline reservations to fly back to his home in San Diego.

Mitchell rushed out, stepped in, lined to center. Base hit. Carter stopped at second.

Ray Knight came up. Schiraldi threw a fastball for a strike, and Knight fouled off his second pitch. 0-2. The world championship was still close enough to touch, close enough to taste, precisely one strike, 60 feet and 6 inches away.

Schiraldi threw. Great pitch, hard and in. Knight was jammed. He pulled off the ball and hit it on the trademark, breaking his bat.

Plunk. The ball floated and floated and landed in shallow center field and Boston hearts sank. Carter scored and Mitchell alertly went to third. The score was 5-4.

Mookie Wilson was due up. McNamara went to the mound and waved for Bob Stanley.

New England groaned. Although he hadn't been scored on in the Series, Stanley had been the whipping boy all year. As he struggled through the season, he'd dreamed of this precise moment, for all baseball players are really little boys, and baseball-playing little boys dream of only two things — throwing the last pitch of the World Series or hitting it to win the

Bill Buckner realizes the nightmare of being one strike shy of a world championship and losing. Mookie Wilson's grounder has just skipped under his glove, giving the Mets an improbable win in game six of the 1986 World Series.

game. Stanley was from Maine and had been with the Red Sox in 1978. Hell, he'd even given up the winning run in the playoff against the Yankees. It was his turn to win. He knew what his dream was.

So did Mookie Wilson. Wilson went down 0-1, then took two balls, then fouled off a pitch. 2-2. One strike away. Again.

Another foul ball. Then another. Then, for the fifth time, the Red Sox were still one strike away from victory. The sinkerballer's next pitch was down and away from Wilson. He didn't swing.

But pitchers don't dream of wild pitches and catchers don't dream of passed balls. Those are nightmares. All Red Sox fans know for sure is that the pitch bounced off Gedman's glove to the backstop. Mitchell scored from third and Knight went to second. 5-5.

In Shea, Met fans started roaring and Boston fans shut up and tried to disappear. They did other things other places, much of it unspeakable. Wilson fouled off two more pitches, and then, on Stanley's tenth pitch, then . . .

. . . Wilson topped the ball toward Bill Buckner at first.

The first baseman stepped in gingerly, bent down, and reached to field the ball.

The moment froze.

Baseball is a game of repetition. The simplest move becomes automatic. But the simplest game becomes something that can still break your heart.

Buckner reached down. And as Buckner reached down, the ball bounced on the ground between his legs, and as it bounced he lifted his glove slightly for the expected hop.

The ball stayed down and scooted untouched beneath his glove, then bounced and rolled and bounced to where none could catch it, though millions tried, straight into the unerring arms of History.

And nothing has ever been the same, because when Buckner missed the ball, nothing changed.

Knight wheeled around third waving his arms and jumping and the Mets poured from the dugout as he landed on the plate with both feet and disappeared.

The Mets didn't win — History did. And the Red Sox lost. Again.

Hangovers were instantaneous and severe. Mike Torrez screamed, "I'm off the hook!" Darrell Johnson was sprayed with champagne in the Met clubhouse. Buckner pushed Pesky aside, his career distilled into a single moment, the lead of his obituary already written. Stanley and Schiraldi elbowed past Galehouse and Willoughby. Don Zimmer, Joe McCarthy, and Joe Cronin welcomed John McNamara to the brotherhood. Mookie joined Bucky as an improbable villain and regional epithet. The dark corner deep in the heart of all Red Sox fans everywhere got a little darker and a lot more crowded.

The Red Sox had made the impossible plausible. In retrospect, it almost seemed unavoidable.

More than one Boston fan woke Sunday morning and turned on the television or looked at the morning paper to confirm that the ultimate nightmare had indeed taken place.

They read of Bob Stanley saying, "Seventy-eight was bad, but this is the worst," of Bill Buckner saying, "If God wanted it to be the other way around, that's how it would have been." They heard John McNamara say, "I don't know nothing about history."

Boston fans walked around the next day with the dazed look of the survivors of an airline crash. Then, as if to extend New England's agony, it rained that night in New York. Game seven was postponed to Monday.

Sox fans sleepwalked through work Monday, and nobody talked baseball. The overwhelmingly foregone conclusion only seemed cruelly postponed. While watching game six had been akin to a drunken public wake celebrating the apparent death of the hated past, watching game seven would be a private funeral for close friends and family only.

It hardly mattered that the rain gave Bruce Hurst an extra day of rest and McNamara an excuse to skip over Oil Can Boyd to start game seven, although in the end, Boyd might have been the better choice. Hurst thought his season was over after game five and had to shift gears, while Oil Can may have been the only Boston player self-absorbed enough to be unaffected by the loss. He was upbeat and excited after game six, looking forward to a chance at redemption, the only player on the team who really wanted to keep playing. When game seven was postponed and McNamara told him he wasn't pitching, he cried.

No matter. And it didn't matter that Hurst pitched well in game seven. And it didn't matter that Boston took a 3-0 lead in the second when Evans and Gedman homered, or that McNamara turned to Schiraldi again when Hurst faltered, and then Nipper. Or that the Red Sox clawed back from a 6-3 deficit in the eighth to make the score 6-5 before the Mets scored two eighth-inning runs to go ahead 8-5, or that Boston went down meekly, without a hit or baserunner in the ninth.

The Mets were world champions. The Red Sox lost. History drank champagne.

Again.

THE PUBLIC TRUST

1987 | 2000

Red Sox manager John McNamara watches as Red Sox
captain Jim Rice unfurls the banner honoring the 1986
American League championship on Opening Day 1987.

Not a player on the field and not a Sox fan watching on television emerged unscathed from the devastating loss to the Mets. None would ever escape the feeling of watching the ball bounce between Bill Buckner's legs.

For eighty-five seasons of occasionally good and often bad baseball, Boston fans had nevertheless knit their dreams and aspirations to the Red Sox. But over much of the next decade that singular moment caused that unique bond between the Red Sox and their fans to begin to weaken and unravel.

After 1967, Sox fans spent the next two decades believing not only that the Sox could win, but that they should. After 1986, that changed. Not that Sox fans abandoned their team, for they still turned out at Fenway Park in record numbers, but a trust was somehow broken. For many, blind faith was replaced by cynicism.

Many fans just didn't expect anything from them anymore, except, perhaps, disappointment. Although it would take several seasons for all the rifts to appear, the complete mending of that relationship has yet to take place. Even today, the emotional scars still show through the Red Sox. Beneath the surface enthusiasm, nothing but a world championship will ever, ever suffice again; a City Hall Plaza rally in support of the 1999 Red Sox held two days after their loss to the Yankees in the 1999 LCS drew two hundred fifty people. Ever since 1986, division championships and wild-card berths have almost become euphemisms for loss as much as reasons to celebrate. Those ersatz titles may be sufficient elsewhere, but not in ever-skeptical Boston. Red Sox fans have learned to take pleasure from individual accomplishments and the temporal pleasures of being in Fenway Park rather than from the team's ultimate finish in the standings.

The 1986 World Series loss cut so deeply into the psyche of Boston's front office that in the off-season they were virtually paralyzed. The Mets exposed weakness in the bullpen and at first base, but the shell-shocked club was in denial. Apart from allowing free agents Tony Armas, Sammy Stewart, Dave Stapleton, and Tom Seaver to walk away, the club made few moves. All the guilty parties — Buckner, Stanley, Schiraldi, and McNamara — remained as if staked out in the open under the glare of an unrelenting sun. Sox fans, as much as they wanted to, would never forget this loss, or forgive it.

After the season, Clemens was named American League MVP and won the first of his eventual five Cy Young awards. John McNamara was named AL Manager of the Year, but everyone connected with the team knew the only legacy of the 1986 season that mattered was game six.

In January the first casualties began to surface. The Sox allowed Rich Gedman to file for free agency. Gedman didn't know it yet, but he was among the first players to be victimized by a policy of collusion among the owners. That winter they conspired to ignore free agents and to keep salaries artificially low, a strategy that eventually cost them millions in legal damages. Gedman received no serious offers and had no choice but to return to Boston. According to the rules of free agency, he wasn't allowed to re-sign with Boston until mid-May. He then got hurt and Haywood Sullivan's weak-hitting son Mark became starting catcher by default.

Spring training delivered more problems. Roger Clemens turned down a five-hundred-thousand-dollar contract offer and walked out, then Oil Can Boyd got a sore shoulder. Boston opened the season without their two winningest pitchers in 1986 and their starting catcher.

Bob Stanley was Boston's starting pitcher on Opening Day. 'Nuf 'Ced. Boston lost to Milwaukee 5-1.

Clemens finally signed for two million dollars over two seasons, but started the season 4-6. Rookies Mike Greenwell and Ellis Burks pushed their way into the lineup as Rice faded and Dave Henderson, his shot at lasting fame past, resumed his otherwise undistinguished career. Buckner, unable to escape his fate, was released in July.

Boggs hit twenty-four home runs and led the league with a .363 batting average. Clemens finally turned his season around and won his twentieth game on the final day of the season, but other than Bruce Hurst, no other Boston starter finished the year with an ERA under 5.00. Boyd won one game. Bob Stanley was 4-15. The Red Sox tumbled to fifth place behind Detroit, finishing 78-84.

Thump.

The team's poor finish forced the Sox to make some changes, not all of which were their idea. The Chicago Cubs experienced brain lock and offered Lou Gorman premier closer Lee Smith in exchange for Calvin Schiraldi and Al Nipper.

Gorman quickly announced the deal before the Cubs came to their senses. Smith gave Boston the closer they desperately needed and rid the club of another reminder of 1986. The Sox shed more dead weight during spring training and broke camp with four rookies on the roster — most notably outfielder Brady Anderson — and six others with less than a year of major league experience. Boyd's arm felt better, and the Red Sox appeared to have enough pitching to remain competitive, while Boggs, Evans, Rice, Burks, and Greenwell promised enough offense that many picked the Sox to win the Eastern Division. John McNamara, in the final year of his contract, was told he had to produce to get another.

But the Red Sox started slow. Boyd's arm started acting up again and Rice got off to a poor start. McNamara started fiddling with his lineup, running players in and out almost at random. The team played .500 baseball and split into opposite camps, one of fading veterans loyal to McNamara and the other of rookies and young players politicking to play.

The ownership situation didn't help. Haywood Sullivan fell out of favor as Jean Yawkey put her trust into longtime aide John Harrington. He'd first joined the team in 1973 as comptroller and now became team president and the power behind the throne. Caught in the middle was general manager Lou Gorman. The lines of authority blurred.

In June, everything hit the fan. Wade Boggs was slapped with a palimony suit by longtime girlfriend Margo Adams, whom he had taken on road trips and led some to believe was his wife. The uncomfortable situation quickly got worse. Adams publicly implicated other players for similar indiscretions. Mrs. Yawkey was mortified. The clubhouse got ugly. The Sox turned into Team Turmoil.

They apparently fell out of the race in mid-June in a three-game series against first-place New York. McNamara started pressing for a new contract. Sullivan wanted to give him one. Mrs. Yawkey didn't.

On July 12, Margo Adams went on a talk show and claimed Boggs had taken photos of teammates in compromising positions — what Boggs termed operation "Delta Force" — to protect himself in case they ever threatened to reveal his own improprieties. Everything exploded.

At the All-Star break McNamara said of the 43-42 Sox, "I'm very happy to be one game over .500." He was the only person who felt that way.

Roger Clemens emerged from the University of Texas via the 1983 amateur draft to become the best Red Sox pitcher since Luis Tiant. His fastball invited comparisons to that of Nolan Ryan, and in twelve seasons with the Red Sox he tied Cy Young's career victory record with 192 while capturing three Cy Young Awards.

Jean Yawkey had had enough. "Delta Force" was the last straw. She was embarrassed by the Margo Adams situation and blamed McNamara for failing to keep control of his team and failing to win. Just two hours before the Sox were scheduled to play Kansas City in a doubleheader at Fenway on July 14, Sullivan asked Yawkey to clarify McNamara's status. She did, and fired him over the objection of both Sullivan and Gorman.

Boston had two hours to get a manager. Purely by default, fifty-seven-year-old third-base coach Joe Morgan was asked to fill in until Boston could hire a permanent replacement.

Morgan, who lived and grew up in nearby Walpole, was 100 percent New Englander, a regular guy who knew in his bones what the Red Sox meant to the region. He'd played semipro ball in the old Blackstone Valley League, played baseball and hockey at Boston College, signed with the Braves, and played eighty-eight games in the major leagues, none for the Red Sox. He was managing in the minors in 1974 when he heard there was an opening in Pawtucket. He called Dick O'Connell at home and asked for the job. O'Connell told him, "A lot of people have been talking about wanting it and making a lot of calls, but you're the only one who called *me.*" He was hired on the spot and had served the organization ever since, becoming a major league coach in 1985.

He became the first local guy to manage the Sox since Shano Collins in 1931 and 1932. Simple and unassuming, Morgan was a quintessential baseball guy. Until winning a World Series share in 1986 he had still worked in the off-season, driving a snowplow on the Mass Pike. He had nothing to lose and he knew it.

Lou Gorman announced he had a list of twenty-four candidates for the job and expected to interview at least ten, saying, "We'll consider every possibility, including minorities." The top candidate was Cardinal pitching coach Mike Roarke, a friend of both Gorman and Harrington.

Morgan didn't make the list. The only person who considered Morgan a candidate was Morgan. The press thought he was a buffoon and the players laughed at him. His favorite phrase was the non sequitur "Six, two and even" (which also appears as a line spoken by Humphrey Bogart in *The Maltese Falcon*). But he didn't suffer fools and his plain-speaking hid a shrewd but occasionally impenetrable baseball mind that played hunches and wasn't afraid to go against the mythical "book" of baseball strategy.

"Interim means nothing to me," he told the press after finding out he was piloting the club. He had waited for this moment for years and wasn't intimidated by the job.

He proved it that evening, putting Red Sox captain Jim Rice in his place. For as the slugger's skills had diminished he hadn't provided leadership. He had reportedly become a disruptive force in the clubhouse, where his surly presence cast a pall over everyone. There were no stars in Morgan's eyes, and he dropped Rice to seventh in the batting order. He also benched Spike Owen and made Jody Reed his shortstop. Then he used every available man on the roster as the Sox swept the Royals in a doubleheader.

Then they won the next day. And the next day. And the next.

Boston's sixth straight win forced the Sox to remove the adjective "interim" from Morgan's title. Secure, his signature moment came in the club's seventh consecutive victory. In the eighth inning, Morgan pinch-hit light-hitting Spike Owen for Jim Rice.

Enraged, Rice slammed his bat into the rack and pulled his manager out of view into the runway leading to the Red Sox clubhouse.

Three pitches later a flushed and furious Morgan returned to the bench alone and announced, "I'm the manager of this nine!" Rice was suspended for three games.

For three weeks Morgan managed like Carl Yastrzemski had played in 1967. The press called it "Morgan Magic," and the Sox won nineteen of twenty to catch the Yankees and then kept going. After Boyd went down again Gorman packaged prospects Brady Anderson and Curt Schilling and sent them to Baltimore for Mike Boddicker to give the Sox a third starter. In mid-September, as all New England anticipated a collapse, they faced down the Yankees in a three-game set and swept to the division title.

The magic didn't end until October. But against the Western Division champion Oakland A's, the Sox were overmatched. Hurst and Clemens lost two heartbreakers and the A's rolled to a four-game sweep behind rejuvenated closer Dennis Eckersley.

Naturally, the team started to implode before they even left the clubhouse. Dwight Evans whined about not being used as a pinch hitter in the last game, and the charter flight back to Boston turned into a drunken round of recrimination. Bruce Hurst, a devout Mormon, left the plane during a layover when he felt his teammates got out of hand.

In an interview with a Boston television station in December, Roger Clemens complained that he had to carry his own luggage and, "There are a lot of things that are a disadvantage to family" in Boston. Sox fans howled.

A month later he trumped himself, complaining in another TV interview that if reporters didn't stop writing about his family (which they had never done), "Somebody's gonna get hurt." Boston's best pitcher since Joe Wood managed to alienate everyone.

Bruce Hurst turned down a better offer from Boston to go to San Diego and wasn't replaced. L'affaire Margo then raised its head again. In a magazine interview she repeated some pillow talk. Among other revelations, she claimed Boggs told her Jim Rice "thinks he's white."

By spring training, the defending division champs were defensive and divided. On Opening Day in Baltimore Wade Boggs was greeted with chants of "Margo, Mar-go!" Clemens blew a lead, Lee Smith pulled a groin muscle warming up, and Morgan's use of a five-man infield in the final inning backfired as Boston lost, 5-4. The magic faded fast as the club started off 0-4.

Reproach and reproof became the favorite pastime in Boston's clubhouse. Everything bad that could happen did.

Morgan criticized players in print, and in turn they sniped to the press behind his back, questioning his contrarian game strategy and use of relief pitchers. Morgan buried Bob Stanley. Oil Can Boyd got a blood clot in his shoulder. Rice didn't hit and hurt his elbow. Pitcher Wes Gardner was arrested for assaulting his wife. Ellis Burks, who had seemed on the precipice of superstardom after hitting .294 with eighteen home runs and twenty-five stolen bases in 1988, got off to a slow start, then got hurt and got blamed for not being Willie Mays. He was supposed to be Boston's Great Black Hope but was uncomfortable in the spotlight.

But the big problem, as usual, was pitching. Hurst hadn't been replaced. He won fifteen games in San Diego. Had he done that for Boston they may well have won the division. Instead, they had to win thirteen of their last sixteen to finish respectably at 83-79, only six games behind Toronto in an increasingly mediocre Eastern Division. In the final week of the season, Bob Stanley retired and Jim Rice was released. Dan Shaughnessy accurately noted that both were "usually cited for what they were not rather than for what they were." Rice hit 382 home runs and hit .298, but it hadn't been enough to win a championship. Stanley became the only Boston pitcher to both win and save over one hundred games, but he'd been on the mound in game six. Neither got the sendoff they expected and, despite their problems, probably deserved. They were simply shown the door.

Expectations were low in 1990. The team continued to shed reminders of the 1986 World Series by signing free-agent catcher Tony Peña and sending Rich Gedman to Houston in a minor trade. First baseman Nick Esasky left for Atlanta as a free agent, which allowed the club to sign closer Jeff Reardon, making Lee Smith expendable. He was sent to St. Louis for outfielder Tom Brunansky.

Then, as if trying to prove something, the team gave Bill Buckner a tryout. He made the club.

The 1990 Red Sox intimidated no one. Apart from Clemens, hardly a man on the team played to his expected level.

Dwight Evans showed his age and left fielder Mike Greenwell, who once appeared ready to fulfill the tradition of Yaz and Rice in left, was exposed for what he was, a good Fenway hitter but a defensive liability. First baseman Carlos Quintana provided little power. Boggs slumped to .302, his lowest average since reaching the big leagues. Burks continued to plateau as a very good, but not great, player. Right fielder Tom Brunansky helped Boston's outfield but continued a premature decline.

But Roger Clemens was fabulous. He went 21-6 with an ERA of 1.93, second starter Mike Boddicker won seventeen, and the other starters all had career years. Boston's pitching kept them in the race.

They even weathered the temporary loss of Jeff Reardon to back surgery and appeared to put the division away with a ten-game winning streak that gave

(l–r): Debbie Boggs, Wade Boggs, and Barbara Walters pose on the set of the ABC news magazine *20/20* on which Boggs revealed to Walters details of his highly publicized affair with Margo Adams.

them a six-and-a-half-game lead in early September. Reliever Larry Andersen was acquired for the stretch run at the apparent cost of a nonprospect, a minor leaguer named Jeff Bagwell. Then Clemens went down with an inflamed tendon in his shoulder and the Sox were exposed.

From September 12 to September 24 they lost ten of twelve and the Blue Jays nudged ahead in the division race. But the Jays were even more flawed than Boston. The two clubs fought a war of attrition as each tried to hand the other the title. Fortunately, the two clubs faced each other in a three-game series in Boston in late September. Somebody had to win.

In the first game Boston DH Jeff Stone got his only hit of the year to knock in the winning run. Clemens returned to action the next night, Brunansky cranked three home runs, and Boston won again before dropping the last game of the series.

The Sox then won and lost to Chicago. With one day remaining in the season, Boston held a one-game lead over the Blue Jays. If the Sox lost to Chicago and the Jays beat Baltimore, the two clubs would have to play a one-game playoff to decide the title.

Boston scored three second-inning runs and Mike Boddicker shut down the White Sox into the seventh, when he allowed a single run before turning the game over to Reardon.

He cruised. But with two outs in the ninth, no one on base, and Boston fans poised to rush the field, the fates gave Boston a flashback.

Reardon got two strikes on the White Sox' Sammy Sosa. As soon as the fact that the Red Sox were one strike away from winning registered, Sosa roped a single to center field. Then the White Sox' Scott Fletcher stepped in. Reardon hit him. Suddenly, light-hitting shortstop Ozzie Guillen was up representing the winning run.

As Reardon prepared to pitch to Guillen, right fielder Tom Brunansky later admitted, "I told myself that if Guillen hit the ball in front of me, I was going to let it bounce and play it. But if it was to my left, toward the wall, I was going to dive."

Reardon threw and Guillen pulled a bending line drive down the right-field line. Brunansky ran and ran and ran toward the Pesky pole as the ball dropped down, then half-dove and half-slid for the base of the wall as the ball descended toward the same spot.

That corner of the ballpark is invisible from most of Fenway Park and often impenetrable even by the all-seeing eye of television. The season hung in the balance of an obstructed view as Sosa and Fletcher kept running.

Not a dozen people in the ballpark saw Brunansky make the catch, but one of them, fortunately, was umpire Tim McClelland. As Brunansky sprinted toward him yelling, "Timmy, I've got the ball, I've got the ball!" McClelland signaled "out" and the Red Sox won a most unlikely division championship in spectacular fashion.

Those who read the Red Sox like tea leaves tried to find signs in the victory that vindicated the club for 1986 and pointed toward another world championship, but sober observers knew that was a stretch. Boston still had to beat Western Division champion Oakland, and in 1990 even Roger Clemens's 20-6

record wasn't enough. Oakland pitcher Bob Welch was 27-6, Dave Stewart 22-11.

The Sox went quietly, losing three in a row, 9-1, 4-1, and 4-1. They didn't even bother to wait for loss number four before ripping Morgan. Boston's relief staff, tired of warming up then not pitching, held a sophomoric protest, sitting in front of their lockers covered with ice packs. One anonymously charged that Morgan was "managing scared," and another whined, "When we won the division he didn't even come in and congratulate us." But it was the Boston lineup, not Morgan, that was hitting .198 versus Oakland, and Boston's bullpen that had given up eleven runs in six innings of relief.

The Red Sox played game four as if they couldn't wait to lose. After a scoreless first, with one out in the second the A's Carney Lansford singled. Terry Steinbach followed with a single to left, went to second on Greenwell's error, then Lansford scored on Mark McGwire's groundout.

Willie Randolph stepped in and walked on four pitches. As Mike Gallego came up, Clemens jawed at home plate umpire Terry Cooney. Cooney yelled at Clemens to throw the ball.

As captured on television, Clemens looked up at Cooney and mouthed, "Put your [bleeping] mask on and get your [bleeping] ass back behind the plate."

Cooney tossed Clemens. Joe Morgan roared out from the dugout, Marty Barrett threw a tub of Gatorade, and Sox coach Dick Berardino tried to restrain him and got shoved down the dugout steps. The whole season went sour in thirty seconds.

Morgan and Barrett were also thrown from the game. Tom Bolton came on in relief. They needed Ernie Shore. Gallego doubled to make the score 3-0. Oakland won 3-1. Series over. Six, two and not very even. Not even close.

Mrs. Yawkey, like her late husband, tried to solve the Sox' myriad problems by throwing money their direction. Salaries were rising and the Sox seemed determined to help their escalation.

But few free agents of real ability were available that winter, and when Mike Boddicker went over the wall and signed with Kansas City, Boston was desperate. Gorman signed what was left. In rapid succession he acquired pitcher Matt Young, slugger Jack

Clark, reliever Larry Andersen, and pitcher Danny Darwin for a total of twelve years and more than thirty million dollars. Darwin became the highest-paid player in Red Sox history.

Had those players been Hall of Famers, the expense may have been justified. But they weren't even all-stars. The Sox overpaid for mediocrity, which in turn forced them to overpay even more to sign players like Tom Brunansky and Mike Greenwell to new contracts.

Part of the problem was the club's convoluted ownership situation. Mrs. Yawkey and John Harrington consistently outflanked and outvoted Haywood Sullivan, who had a contractual right of first refusal if Mrs. Yawkey ever decided to sell the team. He stayed on and refused to be bought out. Gorman was caught in between. No one was in charge and everyone was in charge.

In January Roger Clemens added to his increasingly erratic reputation by assaulting a cop, but the Sox still signed him to a five-year deal worth twenty-one and a half million dollars. Evans, Boyd, Marty Barrett, and hitting coach Walt Hriniak were let go. On paper the Sox looked strong — for a while they had the highest payroll in baseball. The *Globe* even called them "the most highly touted Red Sox team since 1978."

On Opening Day, Jack Clark hit a grand-slam home run and the Sox beat Toronto 6-2. The front office congratulated itself on its wisdom.

But Boston peaked 162 games too soon. All the money spent was wasted, as Clark's bat noticeably slowed, Danny Darwin got hurt, and Matt Young couldn't throw strikes and refused, all season, to throw to first base to hold runners on.

The Sox were soon in disarray again, although in a division sportswriters were calling the "AL Least," they remained nominally competitive. Then the club found itself on the defensive again in regard to its racial issues.

Ellis Burks was the only African-American on the team. The club didn't think that meant anything, but

Dwight Evans acknowledges one of the many standing ovations he received at Fenway Park during a nineteen-year stint in Boston which saw the graceful right fielder win eight Gold Gloves. Evans also hit twenty or more home runs in each of eleven seasons.

it looked suspicious, and in this case, perception was everything. With a host of African-American stars poised to become free agents, Boston was at a tremendous disadvantage.

Black faces at Fenway Park were rare. Few African-American fans identified with the team. The *Globe* reported that in one Fenway crowd of more than thirty-four thousand, only seventy-one could be identified as African-American.

The club pointed to Pawtucket, where slugging first baseman and former first-round pick Mo Vaughn appeared on the precipice of stardom. He'd almost

Center fielder Ellis Burks provided one of the few bright spots in the 1987 season as the rookie batted .272 with twenty homers.

made the club in the spring and at midseason was wearing out Triple A pitching.

Vaughn was a precious commodity to the Red Sox, a player whose symbolic importance matched his talent. For Vaughn was both African-American and a New Englander — he'd grown up in Norwalk, Connecticut.

He was called up on June 26, just in time for an important series with the Yankees. Morgan announced, "He'll bat sixth. He'll be in there against right-handers until further notice."

Vaughn was well aware of his importance to the team. His mother had done volunteer work with Rachel Robinson, and Vaughn wore number "42" in honor of Jackie Robinson.

When his name was called out in the pre-game announcement of the starting lineup, a capacity Fenway crowd stood and cheered like they had for no rookie since Ted Williams.

Vaughn went hitless in his debut, and Boston lost to New York 7-0, their fourth loss in a row to drop three and a half games behind Toronto. Although Vaughn played relatively well, he had trouble adjusting to big league pitching and displayed little of his vaunted power.

Nothing could disguise Boston's mediocrity or continuing problems in the clubhouse. In late August, Mike Greenwell and Vaughn scuffled around the batting cage. Veterans griped as Morgan gave youngsters playing time, then they circumnavigated the manager to complain to either Gorman or Boston's ownership troika. Clemens kept Boston close once again but they finished second to Toronto.

Somebody had to pay for the failure and waste of nearly thirty million dollars. In this, Boston's ownership was unified. They couldn't fire each other, so they fired Joe Morgan, replacing him with Pawtucket manager and former player Butch Hobson.

Lou Gorman said the move had less to do with any failure on Morgan's part than with the fear that someone else would hire Hobson. "We couldn't risk losing such a talent in our organization at this time," he said. Observers wished he'd shown the same concern over Jeff Bagwell, who led Houston in home runs, RBIs, and batting average and would soon be named NL Rookie of the Year.

While Morgan was not perfect, of Boston's forty-one managers at the time only Morgan and Bill Carrigan had led the Red Sox into the postseason twice. That fact of history seemed lost on Yawkey Way.

Morgan took the news hard. He knew he'd been fired because he managed without regard to the size of players' contracts, and it had cost him. In the free-agent era, the manager was not necessarily the most powerful man in the clubhouse.

"If you notice a guy nagging you because you took him out last night, it's not much fun," he said about his experience. "And there's plenty of that to be had today . . . They [the players] can't handle it [being taken out of a game]. It's sad but true. It's unbelievable." Later, he proved he knew his ballclub better than anyone else in the organization did when he warned, "This team isn't as good as people think they are."

The front office loved Hobson's perceived toughness. He had been a hard-nosed player and had played football at the University of Alabama for legendary coach Bear Bryant, with whom he was compared. He talked like a football coach, but in five seasons as a minor league manager he'd finished over .500 only twice. The Sox hoped he was the new Dick Williams.

But Hobson looked scared and awkward from day one. He proved he wasn't prepared for the scrutiny of the job on his first day, contradicting Gorman by admitting he'd had no other offers from other teams.

The Sox signed Minnesota lefthander Frank Viola for three years and 13.9 million dollars to pair with Clemens, and the annual payroll surged to forty-two million dollars, but they did little else of consequence. Then, on February 20, Jean Yawkey suffered a stroke. She died six days later.

She was no more willing to give up control of the Red Sox than her late husband had been. Apart from her two-thirds interest in the Red Sox, she left the bulk of the remaining Yawkey fortune to charity. The team, two-thirds of which was owned by her JRY Corporation, was left under the control of the Jean R. Yawkey Trust, managed by John Harrington, who now controlled two votes to Haywood Sullivan's one. Although many believed the trust would soon sell the team, they underestimated the tenacity of Harrington

and the foresight of Yawkey. The trust — and whoever serves as trustee — could keep the Sox forever as long as it met its charitable obligations.

The Red Sox were rather awful in the spring, and Hobson seemed tighter and more ill at ease every day. First baseman Carlos Quintana was injured in a car accident in Venezuela, and Hobson seemed to be tempting the fates when he brought back his old manager Don Zimmer as third-base coach.

Although Vaughn and Plantier homered on Opening Day, the Yankees beat Boston and Clemens 4-3, hardly an auspicious debut for Hobson. A few days later the Sox played a game that could sum up the Sox during Hobson's tenure, in which appearances were always deceiving, players were overpaid to underperform, and nothing was ever quite what it seemed to be. In Cleveland on April 12, maligned pitcher Matt Young pitched a complete game and didn't give up a hit. But he still lost and didn't even get credit for the no-hitter.

The Sox were similarly out of sync all year long. Matt Young never won a game, and although Viola and Jeff Reardon pitched relatively well, Boston couldn't hit or stay healthy. This time Clemens wasn't enough to ensure respectability. Mo Vaughn was back in Pawtucket by June, and Burks, Greenwell, and Jack Clark, who couldn't hit anymore anyway, all spent extended periods on the disabled list. Harrington seemed anxious not to send any more good money after bad and let the team go.

Boston finished last in the division, 73-89, their worst finish since 1966. In response Harrington pared payroll and shed players he thought were problems. The Sox dropped nearly ten million dollars in salary. Ellis Burks, the one-time superstar in waiting, wasn't tendered a contract when the Sox determined he was an injury risk. He signed with the Cubs (in 1999 he was one of only four players from the team still active).

The club washed its hands of Wade Boggs, who'd been a lame duck ever since the Adams affair and had hit only .259 in 1992. He signed with the Yankees, but Sox fans didn't take offense. His stock had dropped so low that most thought Boggs and New York deserved each other.

The Sox made a lot of noise about making trades

For a decade and a half since '67 carried the Red Sox from the Dick Stuart Dark Age to their renaissance, their preferred persona had been as the Harvard of baseball. In the halcyon days of their rivalry with the Yankees in the seventies, they liked to think of themselves as Athens, the Yankees as Sparta.

Then came June 5, 1983, when people came to realize that the tawdry, personal ownership infighting that had devalued the team since the death of Tom Yawkey in 1976 not only cost them a chance to take that '75 team and build a champion, but, in reality, had reduced the Olde Towne Teame to the status of Building 19. If we thought it couldn't get any lower than (WBZ sportscaster) Bob Lobel playing and replaying Haywood Sullivan saying, "Open the bar" in response to Carlton Fisk being declared a free agent, well, that night twenty-nine months later was the nadir.

It was the Night of the Living Buddy, the infamous Coup LeRoux. It was supposed to be Tony C. Night, a fundraiser to help the Conigliaro family defray the costs of keeping the then-thirty-eight-year-old former star alive, with most of the other members of the 1967 Impossible Dream team in town for the event. Several members of the team were already in the pressroom atop Fenway Park late that afternoon, with tables of hors d'ouevres, two open bars, and a chorus line of television cameras set for interviews with Dr. Jim Lonborg, Carl Yastrzemski, Rico Petrocelli et al. Conigliaro, whose career was snuffed out when he was hit by a pitch in the eye at the age of twenty-two, had been in a coma for two years, and while everyone anticipated that this would be a weepy, gushy evening, it was special for Tony's teammates and fellow winners of the 1967 pennant.

Billy Rohr was there. Billy Rohr was 1967, even if he won only two games and was outta town by June. He was as memorable as Gary Bell, or Lee Stange. As they stood around the pressroom, players recounted their stories. Darrell Brandon remembered Jose Tartabull's throw to Elston Howard that cut down Ken Berry, and Howard's unforgettable leg block of home

The tawdry, personal ownership infighting that had devalued the team since 1976 had reduced the Olde Towne Teame to the status of Building 19.

plate. Dalton Jones remembered Eddie Stanky calling Yaz "an all-star from the neck down." Mike Andrews recalled that famous doubleheader against the Angels when they came back from 8-0. Rico recalled how they knew they could win the night Tony C. hit the fifteenth-inning homer off nemesis John Buzhardt. They all lingered and were talking about how their role in baseball and New England lore was not just about finishing first and taking the Cardinals to the seventh game of the World Series, but about romance. "We shared something few athletes ever will," Andrews said. "Our season wasn't quite like anything else in sports. We weren't the best team that ever played, but in the context of New England and history and how a region gives its heart to one team, we experienced the best."

It was nearly 4 P.M. when Dave O'Hara, the esteemed Boston sports editor of the Associated Press, poked his head into the pressroom and announced, "The Red Sox have called a major press conference for 4:30." Sure enough, thirty minutes later in walked Buddy LeRoux — the former trainer turned owner — with former general manager Dick O'Connell and attorney Al Curran, LeRoux's business partner and a Red Sox limited partner. Dick O'Connell? He had been fired by Tom Yawkey's widow Jean when she engineered the sale to Sullivan and LeRoux and was well known to be a bitter rival of Sullivan's group.

As Petrocelli, Jerry Stephenson, Dave Morehead, Lonborg, George Thomas, and other members looked on in disbelief, LeRoux announced that he, Curran, and Kentucky coal miner Rogers Badgett were taking over the team. LeRoux announced that they had pooled their limited partnerships, that they added up to 18 of the 30 said blocks, and that they thus were reorganizing the general partnership. LeRoux said that Haywood Sullivan was thus fired as general manager, and, effective at 4:30 P.M.,

EDT, O'Connell was the general manager.

For more than half an hour, LeRoux, O'Connell, and Curran answered questions, the players remaining in the back of the room, watching. When LeRoux began heading for the door, in walked Red Sox publicity director Dick Bresciani. "The Red Sox," Bresciani announced, "have a major news conference in twenty-five minutes."

"How many Red Sox are there?" asked Stephenson. "Is this like a stock split?" asked Rohr.

In the twenty-five minutes, LeRoux called all the Red Sox office employees together and told them that he had taken over and Sullivan had been fired. "From here on," LeRoux told them, "accept only orders from me and from Dick O'Connell."

LeRoux left the meeting room. Sullivan stood up. "Ignore everything you just heard," Haywood told the stunned employees. "Accept orders from me, and not from LeRoux or O'Connell."

Sullivan then gathered his attorneys, John Harrington of the Yawkey Foundation, and his lawyers from Bingham, Dana and Gould, and made his way to the press room. "What you were told is a phony," said Sullivan. "There is no takeover. I am still the general manager and one of three general partners. We will be in court tomorrow morning to obtain an injunction to prove our side."

LeRoux later told the media that Sullivan, Jean Yawkey, and Harrington had precipitated the mess by firing Curran as team counsel. LeRoux said there was an automatic buyout trigger

mechanism. Sullivan told the media that this was typical Buddy — crass.

Whatever, the effect was that the focus of the franchise turned from the team that Ralph Houk was trying to hold together to the chaos upstairs; from June 6, 1983, to June 6, 1984, the club was 76-89, and starting with Coup LeRoux, the 50-62 record the rest of the season resulted in Boston's first losing season since 1966. In the ensuing year, ownership spent its time preparing briefs, walking in and out of Suffolk Superior Court. Then when they got to court, all the dirty laundry was aired, of how LeRoux accused Jean Yawkey of wackiness and Harrington of being a self-promoting opportunist. LeRoux was accused of sitting in his Fenway office and making calls trying to buy the Indians, and it was testified that LeRoux called infielder Jerry Remy when Remy was under anesthesia (following knee surgery) to try to talk contract.

After a long public trial, Ms. Yawkey, Sullivan, and Harrington won. Superior Court Judge James Lynch wrote that it was "a high stakes, 'commercial case,' pure and simple. That it happens to involve conflict for control of a professional baseball franchise — considered by many to be a community asset — is almost coincidental. As we have seen, the issues involve business documents and financial strategy, with the emphasis on profit after taxes rather than pennants after playoffs." Eventually, LeRoux, Badgett, and associates were bought out. Mrs. Yawkey then had two of the three controlling

general partner shares, and that, too, created another civil war. When Roger Clemens came off a historic MVP Cy Young season in 1986 and the Red Sox held to their rights to keep him under their fiscal thumb until he had arbitration rights, Sullivan and his GM Lou Gorman let him walk out of camp; between commissioner Peter Ueberroth and Harrington, Clemens got a special deal. Eventually, it became Haywood's people against Harrington and Yawkey's people, a situation so bad that it was suggested that each side wear identification badges. Train-

Trainers, clubhouse men, and grounds crew workers were part of the us-vs.-them spy system.

ers, clubhouse men, and grounds crew workers were part of the us-vs.-them spy system, until Sullivan was bought out for thirty-three million dollars. Dumb? Haywood took his buyout and turned them into more millions in the Naples, Florida, development market.

There were those who felt that Yawkey himself was one of the biggest reasons that the Red Sox never won for him. Cartoons in the 1950s referred to the Townies as "The L'il Rich Kids," and three years after his death Tom Burgmeier and Steve Renko dubbed the Sox motto as, "25 guys, 25 cabs." The chaos his death left cost the Red Sox their shot at winning in 1977, because O'Connell's assistant John Claiborne had a free-agent deal with Bobby Grich killed and a deal for Dave

Kingman quashed. When the Sullivan vs. Harrington/Yawkey thing got ugly, Gorman was in the middle, and the team stagnated. Free-agent signings were disasters. Harrington fired local hero Joe Morgan believ-

There were those who felt that Yawkey himself was one of the biggest reasons that the Red Sox never won for him.

ing that he had Whitey Herzog in line, but Herzog backed out and they were forced to promote Butch Hobson. In 1979, Herzog was fired in Kansas City; Sullivan had a deal with Whitey and Ms. Yawkey refused to allow Haywood to fire Don Zimmer. But, remember, the original sale was to a partnership run by the trainer LeRoux and the bullpen catcher Sullivan and was denied by other owners, forcing Ms. Yawkey to step in for fear that it would be opened to bids.

Legitimate bids, of course, would have gone to the estate, but they were not allowed, and into the twenty-first century the Red Sox moved with an estate as owner.

Peter Gammons serves as a studio analyst on ESPN's *Baseball Tonight* and has served as a Major League Baseball correspondent on ESPN since 1988. He also writes a weekly baseball column for the *Boston Globe*, where he began his career as a reporter in 1969, and is a regular contributor to *Baseball America.*

Jamaica Plain native John Harrington was handpicked by the late Jean Yawkey to oversee the management of the Red Sox and Yawkey Foundation after her death in 1992. Harrington, a Boston College graduate and former faculty member at his alma mater, helped orchestrate the expansion and revised playoff format introduced in the nineties.

and signing players of "character," but it was mostly meaningless chatter. They turned down a chance to deal for Mark McGwire because of concerns over his health, and Boston's reputation in regard to African-American players made it impossible to attract top players like Joe Carter, Barry Bonds, or Kirby Puckett.

"Anywhere but Boston" — or words to that effect — became a common part of the trade clause in the contracts of many of the best African-American players, often forcing the Sox to overpay for the few African-Americans who did agree to come to Boston. The desperate Sox threw a two-year contract worth 9.3 million dollars at free agent Andre Dawson, a once-great player whose bad knees left him a near-cripple. Another three million dollars landed problematic outfielder Ivan Calderon. Neither would have gotten similar money from any other club in baseball.

Dawson and Calderon didn't change anything for the Red Sox, either on or off the field. The Sox lost two of every three in spring training. Although Mo Vaughn emerged as a bonafide power hitter, the club was little changed from 1992.

On June 20, with the team 30-38 and already thirteen games out of first, Hobson appeared on his way out, but when the Sox won fifteen of nineteen, Hobson was given a contract extension.

By August 10 the Sox were 63-49 and pennant fever was sweeping the Hub. Then the competition began sweeping the Sox. Boston finished fifth, 80-82, as even Clemens pitched poorly, ending the season 11-14, his first season under .500.

General manager Lou Gorman was bumped upstairs and made executive vice president, and on November 23, Haywood Sullivan threw in the towel and agreed to a buyout. Harrington became the club's virtual owner.

Although he'd served the Sox for over two decades, his rise to the top following Jean Yawkey's death was even more improbable than that of Sullivan and LeRoux after Tom Yawkey's death. But his background was in business, not baseball. To some, it seemed as if the hired help had won the inheritance.

His first task was to replace Gorman. Thirty-five-year-old Montreal general manager Dan Duquette was the only candidate.

Duquette was a lifelong Red Sox fan, a native of Dalton, Massachusetts, where he caught Jeff Reardon in Little League. He played baseball and football at Amherst College, then joined the Milwaukee Brewers in scouting and player development, where he quickly rose to become director of player development. He then moved on to Montreal, where in 1991 he became the youngest GM in baseball.

He was a new breed of baseball executive, schooled in the use of computer analysis and a new generation of baseball statistics. He wasn't part of baseball's well-entrenched old-boy network. In Montreal he earned a reputation as a savvy judge of talent and creative administrator who did a lot with a little. Montreal was one of the poorest teams in Major League Baseball, yet under Duquette the farm system kept producing players, particularly from overseas, and Duquette had been adept at picking up valuable players from the scrap heap. The Expos, although they never made the playoffs, won more than expected. With Boston's budget, Duquette was expected to thrive.

But Duquette soon learned that Boston wasn't Montreal. With the Expos, he had the luxury of laboring in virtual anonymity. In Boston, the general manager's public role was at least as important as his other skills. Apart from a few favored reporters, Harrington didn't appear to trust the press and rarely spoke out. The general manager was the face of the franchise. And as Lou Gorman had learned, that added responsibility made for a much more complicated job.

Duquette was given free rein to rebuild a deteriorating club, reconfiguring the minor league system and scouting department and ridding the front office of holdovers and perceived dead wood. More significantly, he was expected to change the Red Sox' image.

Duquette believed an organization was built through scouting and a successful team constructed around speed, defense, and pitching — hitting the ball over the left-field wall wasn't enough. Harrington was disenchanted with spending millions on players he considered unworthy. Duquette was expected to get better results while spending more efficiently. The subtle message appeared to be that under Duquette,

while the club would still use "the Yawkey tradition" as a public relations tool, the Yawkey era would come to an end.

One era certainly did end in 1994. In the wake of the strike, Major League Baseball realigned into three divisions in each league and added another tier of playoffs to accommodate two additional division winners and two "wild card" teams with the next-best record. Traditionalists howled.

The scheme helped out so-called small-market teams, which Harrington claimed the Red Sox were. He quickly became one of baseball's most powerful executives and, in consort with acting commissioner and Milwaukee owner Bud Selig, was one of the architects of the new system. No team would better benefit from realignment than Boston.

Its effect on baseball was substantial and profound. By doubling the number of teams in the postseason, the new system was designed to maintain fan interest in franchises that would otherwise be out of the pennant race. It did that, allowing otherwise mediocre teams to masquerade as contenders, creating a sometimes specious championship for also-rans.

In comparison, had such a system been in effect from 1968 to 1993, Boston would have reached postseason play seven additional times. Instead, managers were fired and players traded away for their failures.

But other effects were even less desirable. By doubling the number of contenders, more teams felt pressure to make late-season deals to stay competitive, risking long-term success for short-term gain. The overall result of the new system was that wealth had an even greater impact on the final standings, and the gap between baseball's "haves" and "have-nots" increased. Both salaries and ticket prices continued to escalate unchecked. This helped Boston, which after masquerading as a small-market club in reality still had the financial resources to compete with anyone.

Duquette received a pass during his first season at the helm, and he needed it. The Sox were still awful, and the few moves he made had no effect. Any pretensions the Sox had for a winning season ended on May 3 when Frank Viola blew out his elbow.

But Sox fans did get a sense of how Duquette liked

to operate. As he picked through baseball's pile of discards, he ran players in and out of Boston almost every week. To his supporters, he was a genius. To others it appeared he was throwing so much up against the wall that some of it inevitably had to stick. By August forty-six players, including twenty-three pitchers, had worn a Boston uniform. The expression "You can't tell the players without a scorecard" was nowhere more true than in Boston.

It didn't really matter in 1994 because the season ended on August 11 when the men who own baseball continued their legacy of labor miscalculations. They played hardball with the players, who went on strike. Neither side budged, and the season was canceled. The game suffered as fans threw their hands up in disgust and wished a pox on both houses.

The 1994 Red Sox were a team even realignment couldn't help. They finished fourth, next to last in the new five-team AL East, 54-61.

As soon as it became clear that the season was over, Butch Hobson, Boston's least successful manager since Billy Herman, was fired. Duquette wanted his own guy, an experienced manager who would also serve as the organization's spokesperson.

He hoped to hire a big name like Oakland manager Tony LaRussa, baseball's reigning managerial genius, but LaRussa had little interest in Boston. Duquette finally settled on the glib Kevin Kennedy, who had managed in Texas for two years before the players tuned him out and revolted.

As the strike lingered on, Duquette got going. The Sox seemed to be willing to lose for a while to allow Duquette to implement his new order. They shed more salaries and traded for problematic, high-priced slugger Jose Canseco. He had the potential to hit fifty home runs in Fenway and provide some needed protection for Vaughn in the lineup.

The Players' Association called a moratorium on free-agent signings during the strike, but Duquette kept trying. He acted aggressively, and under the new system ownership tried to unilaterally impose, he worked out deals to acquire Montreal reliever John Wetteland, Kansas City starting pitcher Kevin Appier, and Cub outfielder Sammy Sosa.

But when the courts ruled the owners' action was illegal the deals evaporated. With John Harrington serving as ownership's lead negotiator, the player strike lingered into the spring, and the men who owned baseball decided to open spring training and start the season with replacement players — amateurs, free agents, and minor leaguers willing to cross the picket line. Of all the stupid moves Major League Baseball has ever made, this was the dumbest.

No one was fooled. The obvious sub-par product further offended fans and made Major League Baseball look foolish. Finally, on April 2, both sides came to their senses and resumed business as usual. The strike had been for nothing. Baseball's twenty-eight teams lost nearly one billion dollars and gained nothing. Belt-tightening became the rule, particularly in Boston.

Harrington cut Boston's budget to twenty-five million dollars. Instead of Wetteland, Sosa, and Appier, the Sox settled for Erik Hanson, Mark Whiten, and Stan Belinda, supplemented by scrap-heap gambles like knuckleballer Tim Wakefield and outfielder Troy O'Leary.

Only the most optimistic observers picked the Red Sox to finish higher than third in the AL East. Clemens was out with shoulder woes when an abridged 144-game season started on April 26. On Opening Day in Boston, Sox fans booed when the players were introduced, but Aaron Sele combined with four relievers to shut out the Twins 9-0.

Duquette had a better run of luck than Joe Morgan. Every button he pushed and every player he acquired came through. Career years became the norm. John Valentin started hitting home runs, and Mo Vaughn started hitting a lot of home runs. Tim Wakefield pitched like he did down the stretch for Pittsburgh in 1992. The Sox won ten of eleven in May, then surged into June. When Clemens made his first start on June 7 and defeated California 5-1, the Sox led by nine.

Mo Vaughn led the charge as the club showed a propensity for last-minute heroics not seen in Boston since 1967. He learned to hit the outside pitch to left and take advantage of the Wall. He was more popular than Jim Rice had ever been, a better hitter than Lynn, and the Sox' most consistent lefthanded power hitter since Ted Williams. On July 2, his two home runs keyed a 12-11 Red Sox win over Detroit. One day later he battered the Royals and their ace Kevin

Appier, hitting two long home runs and a triple to knock in six runs in Boston's 12-5 win. Of Vaughn, Kevin Kennedy said, "I've never seen anyone so strong."

Boston's surprising showing forced the organization to change course. In the diluted divisional set-up, the future was now. Duquette made a move.

On July 6 he traded prospect Frankie Rodriguez to the Twins for closer Rick Aguilera. The move paid immediate dividends as Aguilera faced his old teammates in his first appearance for Boston and struck out Kirby Puckett to save a 4-3 Boston win.

Then Vaughn proved he had more in common with Williams than his bat. Controversy dogged the player Boston fans called "the Hit Dog."

One night in a Boston nightclub a notorious gang member, his girlfriend's former boyfriend, confronted him. The two fought and Vaughn was knocked to the ground and then kicked by his opponent's entourage. The next day, his eye was swollen shut.

Vaughn wasn't seriously hurt and apologized, saying, "I'm upset about this. I wasn't looking for trouble." But the incident marked the end of Vaughn's honeymoon with the front office. Although fans gave

Mo Vaughn connects for a first-inning home run in a nationally televised game against the Atlanta Braves on August 31, 1997. Vaughn left Boston via free agency following the 1998 season after socking 230 career homers for the Red Sox in eight seasons.

him a pass, the front office never seemed to look at him quite the same way again. Vaughn, who was heavily involved in various charity endeavors in Boston's African-American community, eventually came to resent what he saw as a lack of trust and respect from Boston's front office, intimating that he was being treated differently because of his race. The relationship slowly deteriorated.

Boston romped to the division title, winning fourteen of fifteen and twenty-two of twenty-five after August 1 to open up a fifteen-and-a-half-game lead over New York. In the stands at Fenway Park fans sported signs that read "Duquette for President." Every player he touched seemed to start playing like an all-star, and he was heralded as Boston's best GM since Dick O'Connell and perhaps the best ever. Fifty-three different players wore Boston uniforms in 1995, and most helped win at least one game.

The Sox clinched the title on September 20, beating Milwaukee 3-2. After the game exuberant players, including MVP candidate Mo Vaughn, jumped on Boston police horses brought in to control the crowd and paraded around the field. When John Harrington was asked if he was worried seeing Vaughn in the saddle, he quipped, "I was worried about the horse."

They finished 86-58, seven games ahead of the Yankees, who naturally edged out California to win the first wild-card berth. Cleveland won the Central Division with a stellar 100-44 record, while Seattle won the West.

But in the postseason, reality struck. Boston drew the Cleveland Indians in the first round of the playoffs. Compared to Boston's Salvation Army squad, the Indians were Nordstrom's.

Clemens started for Boston in the opener, lasted seven innings, and left trailing 3-2. The Sox tied the score, went ahead in the eleventh, but Cleveland won in the thirteenth, 5-4. Then in game two Orel Hershiser mesmerized Boston on three hits to win 4-0.

The series returned to Boston for game three, but that didn't help the Red Sox. The confident Indians checked out of their hotel before going to Fenway Park. The clock had struck twelve for streaky Tim Wakefield in mid-September. He'd lost his final three regular-season starts, and the Indians knocked him senseless with a five-run sixth and won 8-2 to sweep the series.

The loss exposed Boston. Against the Indians, the club's patchwork lineup came undone. Players like Lee Tinsley, Mike Greenwell, and Dwayne Hosey just didn't match up with Kenny Lofton, Albert Belle, and Manny Ramirez. The Indians had pitched around Vaughn and Canseco, the only two players they feared, throwing fastballs in and off-speed pitches away. Both were too anxious and went a combined 0-for-27 in the series, stranding seventeen runners and striking out nine times.

Mo Vaughn and Jose Canseco engage in an animated discussion during a Fenway Park workout in 1995. Both sluggers helped the team to their first division title in five seasons as Vaughn captured American League MVP honors. Both combined for an abysmal 0-for-27 performance in the three-game Cleveland sweep of the first round of the 1995 divisional playoffs.

Once again, apparent victory and a winning season caused the Sox and their fans to confront loss. The tag line of the season became not the club's quite remarkable achievement, but their 0-13 record in the postseason since game five of the 1986 World Series.

In the off-season it became clear that a team put together on the fly created some problems. Rebuilding was swept aside as the club went giddy over their surprise finish. Players like Wakefield, Canseco, and Hosey had to be retained and rewarded. But the problem with catching lightning in a bottle was that it didn't last.

The club appeared to be better than it was, and to maintain their lofty position in the standings, they had to ratchet up spending. Pitchers Tom Gordon and Jamie Moyer were signed as free agents, and when Rick Aguilera returned to Minnesota, the Sox acquired Heathcliff Slocumb from the Phillies in a trade. Infielder Wil Cordero, a Duquette favorite and former all-star whom Montreal could no longer afford, was brought over in another deal. And 1995 AL MVP Mo Vaughn was signed to a three-year deal.

In the end the 1996 Sox were a club with plenty of power, but little speed, no defense, and a pitching staff that, apart from Clemens, intimidated no one. They were a typical Red Sox club, not a team of the future but one that looked an awful lot like Boston's losing clubs of the past. They planned to play Jose Canseco, the '90s version of Dick Stuart, in right field. The Yawkey era wasn't over after all, but had been extended ad infinitum.

On May 1 Boston's 6-19 record was the worst in baseball. In response, pitching coach Al Nipper was fired.

By midseason, injuries and the utter failure of players like Dwayne Hosey forced Boston to change course. Now defense and speed became a priority. Jeff Frye took over at second, and Darren Bragg, acquired from Seattle when Boston dumped Moyer, finally gave the Sox an outfielder who could catch the ball. Vaughn and Greenwell started to hit, and Clemens rebounded from a poor first half to resume his place as one of baseball's premier starters. The ballclub went from, as Kennedy described it, "a team that just went from station to station [on the bases],

just waiting for a three-run homer," to a younger, more aggressive club.

They began August 22-6 and made a nominal run for the wild card. In September, rookie Nomar Garciaparra was recalled from Pawtucket and became the club's best-fielding shortstop since Rick Burleson.

But Boston had lost too many games in April and May. Even though Clemens matched his twenty-strikeout record against Detroit on September 19, winning his 192nd game in a Boston uniform to tie Cy Young for the club record, Boston fell short. They were eliminated from the race for anything on September 27.

True to form, as soon as the Sox were mathematically eliminated, the diatribes of defeat began. Mike Greenwell wanted a new contract, but when Duquette told him he'd only be a part-time player because Wil Cordero would play left field, the Gator shot his mouth off, calling Duquette's offer "degrading," and said he was leaving. Roger Clemens, disappointed that the Red Sox questioned his health and his desire for a four-year deal, intimated that he was leaving as well.

Duquette and Harrington addressed the problems only obliquely, Harrington saying, "During the season is not really the time to be conducting off-season business and contract negotiations." But a week later, Kevin Kennedy was fired. He got the blame for the broadsides leveled by Greenwell and Clemens at the end of the season. Duquette cited a lack of "cohesiveness" in the organization, explaining, "We supplemented a division champion," and that the players he'd added to the club in 1996 had all produced, conveniently ignoring the holdovers from 1995 who failed miserably. Canseco demanded a trade.

The usual noise was made about signing a big-name manager, with Pittsburgh's Jim Leyland at the top of the list this time. But Leyland turned the Sox down in favor of Florida, and other candidates were unwilling to cede control of the roster to Duquette. On November 6, Roger Clemens severed his ties with Boston by filing for free agency.

On November 19, the Sox finally selected Braves coach Jimy Williams as their manager. Williams was a solid, stolid "baseball guy" best known for blowing a division race as Toronto manager in 1987 and effectively being fired by his players after they revolted in 1989. The choice excited no one. At his initial press conference, he came off as a cross between John McNamara and Joe Morgan, exhibiting the suspicious nature of the former combined with the verbal creativity of the latter. When asked about Jose Canseco's potential contribution to the club he responded, "If a frog had wings he wouldn't bump his booty." The press laughed at him. It would take Williams an extended period of time before he was able to convince observers that, like Morgan, the way he talked didn't have a whole lot to do with the way he managed.

A month later Roger Clemens signed a four-year contract with Toronto that made him the highest-paid player in the game. The player singularly responsible for making the Red Sox competitive for more than a decade was gone.

Both parties had gotten tired of each other. Clemens was accustomed to being the big star and having the front office cater to him. He thought all he had done for the club was worth the biggest contract in baseball.

Duquette was less romantic. He thought Clemens was "in the twilight of his career" and not worthy of a long-term deal. It would not be the last time Duquette would have trouble with a veteran who preceded him in Boston.

The Sox seemed to recognize that Clemens's departure changed the dynamic of the ballclub. In their 1997 media guide, they included, for the first time, "The Boston Red Sox Mission Statement." It reads,

The Boston Red Sox organization is dedicated to maintaining a perennial, championship-caliber baseball team and providing our fans high quality Friendly Fenway experiences at the ballpark, throughout our community and through broadcast services.

The statement is telling, for it appears to admit that the goal of the Boston Red Sox is not to win a championship, but merely to create a "championship-caliber" team. In baseball's new age, in which eight teams qualify for postseason play and usually another six or eight enter September with some kind of chance to earn a wild-card spot, "championship-caliber" can mean a .500 record.

Duquette continued to sign players on the fringe, getting outfielder Shane Mack, lately of Japan, and adding sore-armed pitchers Steve Avery and Bret Saberhagen to the mix, while trading Canseco to Oakland for John Wasdin and adding others soon to be forgotten.

John Valentin walked out in spring training when he was moved from short to second to accommodate Garciaparra, but Nomar was clearly the better player. That was just the first of a series of troubles and snafus that Jimy Williams would face in his inaugural season at the helm.

The Sox opened the 1997 season against the Angels. Entering the ninth, Boston trailed 5-2, and Bragg and Garciaparra struck out against closer Troy Percival. The Angels were one strike away for the next twenty minutes.

John Valentin started a rally with a double. Then Vaughn walked on a 3-2 pitch, Reggie Jefferson got an infield hit, Naehring walked on a 3-2 pitch, Cordero walked on a 3-2 pitch, Rudy Pemberton was hit by a pitch, and pinch hitter Troy O'Leary beat out yet another infield hit to put Boston ahead 6-5. Heathcliff Slocumb survived a scary final inning, and the Red Sox won. It was Boston's best Opening Day comeback since 1902. Unfortunately, it was also just about the highlight of the season.

By mid-May the Sox were in last place and few players other than Vaughn and Garciaparra were playing well. Vaughn had perhaps his best day ever in a Boston uniform on May 30. In five plate appearances against the Yankees, he was perfect. In order, he singled off the Wall, homered into the Sox bullpen, homered to left-center, walked, and homered into the Sox bullpen again as the Sox beat the Yankees 10-4. But Boston was still in last place.

The Sox trailed by nineteen games when the season turned tabloid. Wil Cordero, uncomfortable in the outfield and not hitting, was arrested for assaulting his wife. The Sox reluctantly bowed to community pressure and kept him out of the lineup for nearly two weeks, brought him back, then benched him again when his wife made more allegations and Cordero laughed his way through an ESPN interview. Vaughn had arthroscopic knee surgery and was likewise absent from the lineup.

The Sox quickly went from bad to worse. Roger Clemens made his Fenway debut in a Toronto uniform on July 12 and struck out sixteen. Then Vaughn made the news again when he was accused of punching a patron in a Rhode Island strip club.

But Nomar Garciaparra saved the season. His emergence as one of baseball's premier shortstops may well have saved Jimy Williams's and Dan Duquette's jobs. No shortstop in club history had ever offered the combination of offense and defense provided by Garciaparra.

Quiet, unassuming, and apparently allergic to touting his own accomplishments, Garciaparra was the perfect antidote to a season marked by scandal. He combined the best qualities of every Red Sox shortstop in history, displaying Pesky's bat and demeanor, Burleson's arm, Junior Stephens's and Rico Petrocelli's power, and Luis Aparicio's range and speed. He was the rarest of players, particularly for the Red Sox, a five-tool guy who demonstrated the sixth sense to know when to keep his mouth shut.

But Vaughn's inability to stay quiet dominated the last half of the season. His contract was due to expire, and in June the Sox made a multiyear offer for eight and a half million dollars annually. Vaughn and his agent never responded, and in September Duquette and Vaughn clashed as Duquette reportedly told Vaughn, "If you ever want to leave Boston, just let me know."

After losing Clemens Duquette vowed he'd never again allow another frontline player to walk away and receive nothing in return; he'd trade them first. He claimed the club's offer to Vaughn was "a fair market offer."

But Vaughn was equally stubborn. He thought his stature in the community, not to mention his ability, counted for something despite his recent troubles. "I don't want to stay," he said. "They're playing games." He charged that the Sox were lying to the press about their previous offers, bad-mouthing him in private, and having him followed by detectives. To Vaughn, the issue was one of respect.

The standoff continued through the end of the season. A discernible chill could be felt on Yawkey Way whenever Vaughn's name was mentioned. The Sox fi-nally released Cordero on September 28. Boston finished in fourth place, 78-84.

The Cordero debacle and Vaughn's contract situation left the team desperate to make a positive move. Clemens hadn't been replaced and Boston's pitching was awful.

Like Lou Gorman before him, Duquette felt comfortable dealing with the club he'd worked for most

On September 9, 1996, Mo Vaughn donned a top hat and tails to accept a check from Fleet Bank in support of his Mo Vaughn Youth Development Program. With Vaughn are program participants (l–r) Travis Davis, Naimah Rashid, and Patricia Nurse.

recently. Twenty-six-year-old Montreal pitcher Pedro Martinez had emerged as one of the game's best pitchers in 1997 and Duquette knew that, like Cordero, the Expos couldn't afford to keep him. On November 18 he traded pitching prospects Carl Pavano and Tony Armas Jr. to Montreal for Martinez.

But Martinez was signed only through 1998. Boston needed to sign him. Otherwise they'd have given up a top prospect for the privilege of having Martinez for a single season.

The player had all the leverage. Martinez and the Sox immediately began negotiating a new deal.

The Sox were under some pressure to move quickly. Thomas Sneed, the club's African-American former manager of the 600 Club, had been harassed — his white girlfriend's photograph on his desk had been defaced. He'd tried to resolve the problem through channels, but felt the Red Sox had failed to address the issue. He was preparing to file a complaint with MCAD.

Before the charges were made public the Sox signed Martinez to a six-year seventy-five-million-

JASON AND MO

Say what one will about Mo Vaughn's controversial six seasons as a Boston Red Sox, one fact is undeniable. While Vaughn played for the Red Sox, kids loved him.

Kids were attracted to Vaughn on several levels, not the least of which was his intimidating physical presence. Up close, Vaughn is oversized in the same way a pro wrestler is oversized, with the legs, arms, and torso of a man who should be much taller. He is, literally, a person one cannot walk past, but must walk around. To kids, he was huge, literally and figuratively.

But Vaughn also reached out to kids, both on the field and off, setting up his own youth development program, visiting schools in the inner city, even taking groups of kids to the Boston Ballet. In the company of kids, the suspicion and hostility that sometimes marked his final years in Boston was never on display.

Cynics always see angles whenever a ballplayer does anything for charity, and maybe Vaughn had an angle when he did things for kids. A lot of professional athletes do. But when it comes to kids, it almost doesn't matter. The thing is, the kids don't care. There's no angle when they choose their heroes.

Vaughn's relationship with one particular child stands out. In April of 1993, Vaughn received a request to call a patient at the Dana-Farber Cancer Institute in Boston on his birthday. Through the Jimmy Fund, Dana-Farber enjoys a close relationship with the Red Sox. Sox players make regular visits to the facility, usually without publicity, and over the years a number have made significant financial contributions as well.

There was nothing unique about the request that came to Vaughn. What was unique was the patient, an eleven-year-old boy from Albany, New York, named Jason Leader, who was ill with blastoma.

When Vaughn called on April 23, Leader couldn't believe it, but he soon got over his shyness. He peppered Vaughn with questions and, despite his illness, impressed Vaughn with his cheerfulness and optimism. By the end of their conversation, Vaughn, who'd been distracted and slumping, felt his own mood change. Leader had cheered up Vaughn rather than the other way around.

As the two said their goodbyes, Vaughn blurted out, "You know what, man? I'm going to hit a home run for you."

He knew he shouldn't have said that. Players only hit home runs on demand in Hollywood. Vaughn quickly forgot his promise as he prepared for that night's game against the Angels.

But Leader didn't forget. He told his doctor. He told his nurses. He told his family. He told everyone he met, and the media found out. It wasn't a set-up. Mo Vaughn was going to hit a home run for him that night. It was that simple. He'd promised.

Leader wasn't allowed to stay awake for the game, but went to sleep that night with the belief that only children have. Mo Vaughn was going to hit a home run. It was something for a sick child to look forward to for one more day.

The first two times Vaughn came up that night, he failed to make good on the promise he'd forgotten about. But in his third at bat, Mo Vaughn hit a ball over the center-field fence.

After the game, a reporter asked Vaughn about the promise. Embarrassed, he admitted, "I'd completely forgotten about that. But I'm happy for him. I hope he gets strength from that. I hope he learns dreams can come true."

The next morning Leader woke up and asked if Vaughn had hit a home run. He was answered with smiles.

The media made the story even bigger. When the Red Sox returned to Boston, Leader was invited to a game. He got to meet Vaughn, sit in the dugout, and throw out the first pitch. Vaughn even gave him the home run ball, which had been returned to him after the story got out.

It's just a story, but a sweet one. For the sixteen additional months that Jason Leader lived, it was the only story about Mo Vaughn that really mattered. ⌀

dollar deal, with a club option for a seventh year. At twelve and a half million dollars annually it was more than a million dollars more per season than that of any other pitcher in baseball and the biggest contract in baseball. Sneed's charges became public a week later.

Signing Martinez to such a long-term deal was a risk. Although he had been 17-8 with a 1.90 ERA in 1997 for Montreal, at only 5-foot-11 and less than 170 pounds he was small for a starting pitcher, and 1997 had been his first truly outstanding season in the majors. Longevity was a genuine question.

But Boston needed him. Like Clemens, if he stayed healthy and continued to produce he was the kind of pitcher that could ensure that the Red Sox would remain "championship caliber."

But the deal also exposed the club's financial state. Harrington had been claiming the Sox were a small-market club with a ballpark that didn't bring in enough revenue for the club to compete. As Dan Shaughnessy noted in the *Globe*, Martinez's contract "flies in the face of the rhetoric that's been spilling out of Yawkey Way." At one time the same money could have locked up both Clemens and Vaughn.

Vaughn wondered where Martinez's deal left him. He found out when Duquette told a television reporter, "We're not going to wait. If we're not able to sign him, we're not going to let him walk away."

Vaughn didn't help his position when he flipped his car on the freeway outside Boston and was charged with driving under the influence of alcohol when he refused to take a Breathalyzer. But the Sox weren't in a position of power either — Vaughn's salary demands and the club's alleged whisper campaign that raised questions about his character made him hard to deal. Then the Sox signed John Valentin to another sizable contract and extended the contracts of Williams and Duquette, further alienating Vaughn. Yet he stayed on.

The best move Duquette ever made was trading closer-wannabe Heathcliff Slocumb to pitching-des-perate Seattle for pitcher Derek Lowe and catcher Jason Varitek. In the waning days of the 1997 season, the Sox had tried Tom Gordon in the role, and he appeared to be the solution. Just in case, they signed fading free agent and Boston favorite Dennis Eckersley as well. Fleet outfielders Damon Buford and Darren Lewis were added to provide some defense in the outfield.

On Opening Day in Oakland Martinez performed

In 1998 Tom "Flash" Gordon established a new Red Sox single-season save record with forty-six and set a major league record with forty-three consecutive saves. While converting forty-six of forty-seven save opportunities Gordon won his only blown save against Oakland with an 8-6 victory on April 14.

as promised, striking out eleven in a 2-0 win. But the Sox went on to lose six of their next eight before playing their home opener on April 10. Entering the ninth, the Sox trailed Seattle 7-2.

Troy O'Leary opened the ninth with a broken-bat single off Heathcliff Slocumb. Two hits, two walks, and a hit batsman later, Mo Vaughn ended it with a grand slam to right field. As he crossed the plate, the chant "Sign Mo Now!" resonated through the ballpark.

The victory keyed the best stretch of baseball the club played all year, as they won twenty of twenty-six from April 10 through May 10, coming from behind nine different times, including seven times in the last inning. In many ways, the season resembled 1995, Duquette's first year. He was a genius again — sort of.

Gordon thrived as the closer, Pedro won nineteen, the careful handling of Bret Saberhagen resulted in fifteen wins, Lewis and Buford hit in Fenway like they rarely had elsewhere, and a platoon of Varitek and Scott Hatteberg gave Boston its best catching since Tony Pena. Williams proved more adept as manager than many expected. With Garciaparra continuing to improve and Vaughn putting on a yearlong salary drive, the Sox were "championship caliber."

But the Yankees rendered any dream of winning a divisional title moot. New York took over first place on the last day of April and by June led Boston by nine and a half games to effectively clinch the division title.

But in baseball's new order, Boston didn't have to compete with New York. All they needed to win the wild card was one hot month and the ability to play .500 baseball the rest of the season. That's about what happened. After May 10, the Sox were a rather ordinary 72-64. But they won the wild-card spot on September 24 with a 9-6 win over Baltimore and broke out the champagne.

They finished 92-70, the second-best record in the American League to New York's 114-48. Western and Central champions Texas and Cleveland glided to divisional titles, and Bernie Williams just nosed out Mo Vaughn for the AL batting title.

Boston was brimming with optimism again. An absolutely effervescent John Harrington touted his own foresight in the *Globe*, happily observing, "In the old system, we would have been out of it." In the new system, they could be out of it and still be in it.

The club's postseason strategy was no secret. In a chance meeting in July, Duquette said, "In a short series with Pedro, I like our chances. Anything can happen."

The Red Sox and Vaughn opened the series against Cleveland eager to erase the memory of 1995. They bombed the Indians in the opener behind Martinez 11-3 as Vaughn made up for his 0-for-17 in 1995 by going 3-for-5 with a double, two home runs, and seven RBIs. True believers pronounced, "This is the year."

Four batters into game two everyone was checking the shuttle schedule to New York as the Sox jumped ahead 2-0. When Dwight Gooden imitated Clemens and was ejected, everything seemed to be going Boston's way. But Dave Burba shut down Boston in relief and Tim Wakefield soon followed Gooden from the game, not because of something he said, but for the stuff he threw that the Indians hit back. Cleveland won 9-5.

Back in Boston for game three, Cleveland hit four solo home runs, three off Saberhagen, to push Boston to the brink. But in a short series, with Pedro, anything can happen, right?

Wrong, at least in 1998. Facing elimination, the Sox chose to forgo their chances of advancing in the playoffs to protect their seventy-five-million-dollar investment. Martinez reportedly begged to pitch game four on three days' rest — this is why the Red Sox had acquired him, after all — but Boston's vaunted brain trust decided to save him for a game they never played. Late-season pickup and Houston castoff Pete Schourek started.

Schourek, to his credit, avoided the infamy of Galehouse by pitching shutout ball, but Boston bats went limp in the finale. Still, they led 1-0 when closer Tom Gordon, who hadn't blown a save since April 14, imploded. Cleveland won 2-1. The Sox walked off the field at Fenway Park to the same sound they'd heard on Opening Day, "Sign Mo Now!"

But pride got in the way on both sides. To assuage the public, the Sox made a last-ditch, half-hearted offer to retain Vaughn, but in mid-November, Vaughn, his 230 home runs, 752 RBIs, and .304 career batting average walked. He signed with the Angels for eighty-five million dollars.

Suddenly money was no object to the Red Sox. They overpaid for good-hit, no-field infielder Jose Offerman of the Royals, then wooed Albert Belle, who actually was the bad apple the club imagined Vaughn to be, and who wanted even more money. The club then turned toward Yankees center fielder Bernie Williams.

But like every other big-name free agent since Bill Campbell, he simply used Boston's interest to give him leverage with the Yankees, with whom he re-signed. Unable to replace Vaughn, the Sox shored up their pitching staff with the affordable arms of Pat Rapp and Mark Portugal, and Duquette invited the usual suspects to spring training, such as veteran minor league sensation Brian Daubach.

By Opening Day the Sox seemed more interested in the 1999 All-Star Game at Fenway Park and plans for a new ballpark than in winning a world championship. The organization seemed eager to relegate their first century to the past and get on to the next as soon as possible.

But no one told Jimy Williams. For the 1999 Red Sox closed the century by taking their fans on a farewell tour of franchise history. Although most observers picked the apparently punchless Sox to finish third or fourth in the division and collect somewhere around eighty-five wins, the Sox performed above expectations all year long, raising hopes of longtime fans who should have known better while simultaneously recruiting another generation of true believers. Yet the season still ended in classic Red Sox fashion as Boston watched New York take their twenty-fifth world championship since 1918 as winter prematurely chased October away once more.

The 1999 season demonstrated that in baseball's new order the line between mediocrity and respectability is deceptively thin. They seemed to take a little from each of several overachieving predecessors — the clubs of 1988, 1967, and 1912 in particular — and won more than they had any right to. Manager Jimy Williams decided on a strategy of going with the hot hand, platooning, and hoping for the best.

In 1999 the best was Pedro Martinez, who pitched like Joe Wood in 1912 and Roger Clemens in 1986, al-

beit a bit less often than either. When Martinez pitched the Sox were the best team in baseball. But that would have been true even if he'd pitched for the 1962 Mets. Martinez was that good.

Keyed by Martinez, the lesser Sox played over their heads and rendered injuries to players like Tom Gordon and Garciaparra irrelevant. Brian Daubach spent five months playing like Walt Dropo before becoming Norm Zauchin in mid-August, Bret Saberhagen pitched like Lefty Grove in twilight, Ramón Martinez returned from shoulder surgery, and even

George "the Peanut Guy" hawks his assortment of "peanuts, cashews, and pistachios" on Yawkey Way, where he was a fixture for over fifty seasons. Following the 1998 season the Red Sox attempted to remove vendors from the choice street locations they had occupied next to Fenway Park for generations.

Jose Offerman made the All-Star team. Jimy Williams seemed more like Joe Morgan every day — in a good way.

The Sox took over first place and on May 15 took advantage of their good favor by unveiling their latest plan for a new ballpark. Scheduled to open in 2004, the new Fenway Park would be constructed some 600 feet south of old Fenway, retaining the same footprint and other precious quirks while adding all the desired modern amenities like luxury boxes, preferred seating, and expanded concessions.

Unfortunately it also included a number of undesirable features, such as a cantilevered upper deck with thousands of new seats far more remote than any in old Fenway, the virtual banishment of outside vendors, and the same precise field dimensions that have made it almost impossible for the team to attract topnotch free-agent pitchers. They dismissed out of hand any notion that old Fenway's dimensions might have had something to do with the team's failure to win a championship since 1918. All this on land the Sox don't own for a half billion dollars they don't have.

The plan was predictably controversial, for the Sox virtually ignored the people on the street, those who lived nearby, and their own players during the design process. Pedro Martinez, for one, hated the new plan. When *Globe* reporter Gordon Edes asked him if he was looking forward to pitching the first game in the new Fenway, he said, "Who says I'm pitching the first game? Five years from now, who knows where I'll be? I don't agree with the same dimensions. Three [hundred] fifteen in the [left-field] corner? Come on. They need a regular park, a normal park. The dimensions have got to be like Atlanta or Colorado. Leave Fenway Park there. Let it be a relic."

But the Sox loaded up on high-priced consultants to sidestep local preservationists and grease the political skids. A surprisingly cooperative local press kowtowed to the party line and touted the proposed new park as the best of all possible worlds.

By the All-Star break the Sox were 49-39, four games behind New York but three games ahead in the wild-card race. Martinez was a stellar 15-3 and the Sox jockeyed their rotation so he could start the All-Star Game, giving fuel to those who thought that even the Sox themselves didn't believe their own performance.

Martinez was, in a word, magnificent. But his exuberance blew out his shoulder and landed him on the disabled list. The paranoid waited for the inevitable collapse.

But the Sox hung together, and Martinez returned to form several weeks later. The front office then reacted to pressure from both Toronto and Oakland for the wild-card spot by retooling.

Although their greatest need was starting pitching, they ignored the available arms of Kevin Appier, Scott Erickson, and Chuck Finley. Instead they blew their budget and committed nearly ten million extra dollars to acquire DH Butch Huskey from Seattle and two pitchers coming off arm trouble, Cardinal Kent Mercker and Cub reliever Rod Beck.

Righthander Pedro Martinez arrived in Boston in November 1997 via a trade with the Montreal Expos for minor leaguers Carl Pavano and Tony Armas Jr. He soon electrified Fenway Park while winning nineteen and twenty-three games in his first two seasons with the Red Sox. In 1999 he became only the third Red Sox pitcher to win the Cy Young Award.

Those moves gave the Sox the fourth-biggest payroll in baseball. But they were designed to win a wild-card berth, not a World Series. Huskey won two games with his bat in his first week, Mercker proved better than the alternatives, and Rod Beck was almost perfect in his first half-dozen times on the mound.

But the Sox paid dearly for the privilege of finishing second. Harrington later said, "I never wanted to use the bank's money to pay our bills, yet that happened," admitting the team lost money and would probably have to spend another ten million dollars just to retain the players they already had in 2000. Observers then noted that the Sox signed only twenty of their fifty picks in the amateur draft, presumably because they couldn't afford to sign more, a dismal record for an organization that still claimed to be building the farm system.

The last season of the century couldn't pass without controversy. On August 14 Martinez showed up late for work. When teammates complained, Jimy Williams started reliever Bryce Florie in his place. Although Pedro got the win in relief, he was miffed, and over the next few days he challenged his manager and Dan Duquette in obscenity-laced tirades, making it clear that if the team wanted to get rid of him, he was ready to go. But when his teammates didn't back him Martinez came back into the fold.

With three weeks remaining in the season the Sox embarked on a make-or-break twelve-game road trip to Seattle, Oakland, New York, and Cleveland. They responded by playing their best baseball of the season, virtually clinching the wild-card berth with a three-game sweep of the Yankees and drawing to within three and a half games of New York for the division title.

Yet public enthusiasm was tempered. When the Sox concluded the sweep by beating Roger Clemens and New York 5-1, television ratings for the New England Patriots home opener were more than double that of the Red Sox game. Suspended judgment was running rampant as "Won't be fooled again" remained the Sox fans' motto.

The road trip ended on September 15 as the Sox took two of three from Cleveland, their likely opponent in the playoffs, and excitement finally began to build. The Sox had won twenty-one of twenty-six and the division title appeared within reach.

But the ballclub's everlasting problem has always been the way they react to pressure, both on and off the field. The shortcomings of both were revealed during the season's final days.

While mouthing the claim that they were still trying to catch the Yankees, the Sox turned to a six-man pitching rotation to save arms for the playoffs, tacitly delivering the division title to New York and settling for the wild card. All momentum was suddenly lost as baseball's best team over the preceding month finally started playing to their predicted standard.

Conditions quickly deteriorated. Some veterans were angered and team chemistry shaken when Mark Portugal — second on the team in innings pitched to Martinez — was released. Then Nomar Garciaparra went down after being hit on the wrist on September 24 in Baltimore as the two clubs waged a stupid beanball war. It would prove to be the most inconvenient HBP for Boston since Williams was drilled by Mickey Haefner on the precipice of the 1946 World Series.

But the presence of Pedro Martinez made it chic to pick the Sox over the Indians, even in Boston. Those who should have known better bought the argument Duquette and Harrington had been promoting since 1998 — aim for the wild card, pray Martinez wins every postseason start, and if the club steals an additional game or two, "Ladies and gentlemen, presenting your world champion Boston Red Sox." The strategy is based on the achievements of Bob Gibson in the 1967 Series and Mickey Lolich in 1968, each of whom started and won three games to lead their team to the title.

The approach has been an extraordinarily easy sell, but in the new, extended playoff system, no single pitcher, not even Pedro Martinez, can pitch enough to win a title.

Boston's dependence on Martinez increased on the precipice of the playoffs as Pat Rapp, third on the team in innings and with a stellar ERA since the All-Star break, was left off the playoff roster. Lame-duck DH Reggie Jefferson, the Sox' only lefthanded bat off the bench, was also dropped when Boston decided to carry an extra infielder to back up Garciaparra. Jefferson went home.

Boston opened the playoffs in Cleveland on October 6. But Martinez had a history of late-season fatigue, and in the fourth inning he pulled a muscle in his back. He finished the inning, then left the game, taking with him all apparent hope for Boston. All the fears that had been held at bay all year rushed in, and every decision the Sox had made since September 15 suddenly appeared wrong. Another Red Sox season seemed certain to end in disappointment. The only question that remained was one of precisely how.

Boston answered with one final tease. After dropping the first two games 3-2 and 11-1 to fall behind two games to none, the Sox stormed back, winning game three 9-3 after Cleveland pitcher Dave Burba got hurt, then returning to Boston and winning game four by the extraordinary score of 23-7.

Game five was a fine wreck of a ballgame, a beautiful mess as each team desperately tried to lose for the first three innings. The Indians came up to bat in the fourth with the score tied 8-8.

Pedro Martinez shocked everyone by taking the mound, leaving the question of why he didn't start the game hanging. But he got the organization off the hook by ripping off Boston's best-ever individual postseason pitching performance, mesmerizing the Indians for six hitless innings. Boston scored four late runs to win the game 12-8, the series 3-2, and get Indian manager Mike Hargrove fired.

But the Yankees, as always, stood between the Red Sox and the World Series, while the Mets had won the right to play Atlanta for the National League pennant. Sox fans salivated at the myriad possibilities of redemption, dreaming of beating both New York teams in succession to win the World Series, turn the page on their past, and render the year 1918 irrelevant forever.

It was a nice dream, but way too much to ask for. For while the Sox played the Yankees better than anyone else in the playoffs, that wasn't saying much. For they still played the way they always have against the Yankees whenever it has mattered. And the twenty-five-time world champions still played the way they always have against the Red Sox.

THE BEST YEAR EVER? PEDRO IN '99

In 1999 Red Sox pitcher Pedro Martinez fashioned one of the greatest seasons ever by a pitcher in a Red Sox uniform. That's a short list to begin with that on the traditionally pitching-poor Sox, and with apologies to Jim Lonborg and Luis Tiant, includes only Cy Young in 1901, 1902, 1903, and 1904, Joe Wood in 1912, Dutch Leonard in 1914, and Roger Clemens in 1986. But that doesn't diminish what Martinez accomplished. Any starting pitcher whose ERA for the season is nearly three runs better than the league average has certainly achieved something extraordinary.

For most of 1999 Martinez was remarkable, mixing one of the game's best fastballs with *the best* changeup and a devastating curve, all thrown with impeccable control and at any time in the count. He demonstrated an unmatched feel for pitching that often made it appear as if he was able to read the hitter's mind and throw precisely the pitch he was least prepared for in the exact place he was least expecting it. Sometimes, it was like watching an older kid mow down Little Leaguers, never more so than on September 10 versus the Yankees when he struck out seventeen and gave up only a single hit — a line drive home run by Chili Davis. If not for that one pitch, the game may well have been considered the best pitched game in major league history.

Numbers rarely tell the story of a player or a season, but in regard to Pedro Martinez, they bear repeating. For it may well be another century before another pitcher manages to do what Martinez did in 1999. ⊘

PEDRO MARTINEZ GAME BY GAME IN 1999

DATE	OPPONENT	W-L	REC	ERA	IP	H	R	ER	HR	BB	SO	HB	WP	BK
04/05	@KANSAS CITY	W	1-0	3.00	6.00	6	2	2	1	1	9	0	0	0
04/10	@TAMPA	W	2-0	3.46	7.00	7	3	3	0	1	9	0	0	0
04/15	CHICAGO (A)	L	2-1	3.15	7.00	6	3	2	0	1	10	0	0	0
04/20	@DETROIT	W	3-1	2.28	7.67	3	0	0	0	3	10	0	0	0
04/25	CLEVELAND	W	4-1	2.21	9.00	7	2	2	0	1	10	1	0	0
05/01	@OAKLAND	W	5-1	2.06	7.00	5	1	1	0	3	13	1	0	0
05/07	ANAHEIM	W	6-1	1.74	8.00	6	0	0	0	0	15	0	0	0
05/12	SEATTLE	W	7-1	1.81	8.00	4	2	2	1	1	15	0	0	0
05/18	NEW YORK (A)	W	8-1	1.89	7.00	10	2	2	0	4	11	0	2	0
05/23	TORONTO	W	9-1	1.98	6.00	8	3	2	0	1	6	0	1	0
05/29	@CLEVELAND	W	10-1	2.01	8.00	5	2	2	0	0	9	0	0	0
06/04	ATLANTA	W	11-1	1.91	9.00	3	1	1	1	2	16	0	1	0
06/09	@MONTREAL	L	11-2	2.16	6.00	6	4	4	0	2	10	0	0	0
06/15	MINNESOTA	W	12-2	2.17	8.00	5	2	2	0	1	8	1	0	0
06/20	TEXAS	W	13-2	2.10	8.00	6	1	1	0	0	10	0	0	0
06/26	CHICAGO (A)	W	14-2	2.08	5.00	3	1	1	1	1	4	0	0	0
07/02	@CHICAGO (A)	W	15-2	2.02	8.00	7	1	1	1	0	5	0	0	0
07/07	@TAMPA	L	15-3	2.10	8.00	7	3	3	0	2	14	1	0	0
07/18	FLORIDA			2.51	3.67	12	9	7	0	0	3	1	0	0
08/03	CLEVELAND			2.48	5.00	3	1	1	1	1	7	0	0	0
08/08	@ANAHEIM	W	16-3	2.46	5.00	3	2	1	0	3	5	0	0	0
08/14	SEATTLE	W	17-3	2.45	4.00	3	1	1	1	1	6	0	0	0
08/19	OAKLAND	L	17-4	2.52	7.00	7	3	3	1	0	11	0	0	0
08/24	@MINNESOTA	W	18-4	2.40	8.00	4	1	0	0	1	15	0	0	0
08/30	KANSAS CITY	W	19-4	2.36	6.00	4	1	1	0	1	11	0	1	0
09/04	@SEATTLE	W	20-4	2.26	8.00	2	0	0	0	3	15	0	0	0
09/10	@NEW YORK (A)	W	21-4	2.20	9.00	1	1	1	1	0	17	1	0	0
09/15	@CLEVELAND			2.21	7.00	8	2	2	0	1	14	0	1	0
09/21	TORONTO	W	22-4	2.11	9.00	3	0	0	0	2	12	1	0	0
09/27	BALTIMORE	W	23-4	2.08	8.00	6	2	1	0	0	12	1	0	0
10/02	@BALTIMORE			2.07	1.00	0	0	0	0	0	1	1	0	0

1999 TOTAL

W-L	S	ERA	GS	CG	SHO	IP	H	R	ER	HR	BB	SO	HB	WP	BK
23-4	0	2.07	29	5	1	213.33	160	56	49	9	37	313	9	6	0

The details were excruciating. If any Sox fan had forgotten the pain their club could cause, they were reminded as October quickly came and went. In both games one and two Boston led early only to lose late, as their defense, relief pitching, clutch hitting, and the umpires all let them down.

Then the series came to Fenway. Hyperbole and rhetoric ruled as game three's pitching matchup between Martinez and Roger Clemens was touted like a championship bout in the World Wrestling Federation.

Clemens was greeted with the pent-up frustration and anger of generations. Martinez and the Sox gave their fans one glorious day of retribution as they battered the one-time local hero into submission and rolled and romped to a one-sided 13-1 win.

But it was a hollow and, in the end, meaningless victory. For while the Sox rollicked, the Yankees reacted just as they had after Martinez had struck out seventeen Yanks on September 12. As New York outfielder Paul O'Neil observed, "We didn't get beat by the Red Sox; we got beat by Pedro Martinez."

And the Yankees went back to playing the Red Sox in game four. Saberhagen pitched well, but the Sox threw the game away in the eighth inning, albeit with help from umpire Tim Tschida, who on a key play called a phantom tag by Chuck Knoblauch on Jose Offerman.

Then, in the ninth inning with the game lost, Jimy Williams blew his cool at another bad call and got tossed. Drunken fans at Fenway threw plastic bottles on the field, briefly stopping play and embarrassing everyone. The Yankees then slapped the Sox down in the finale as Boston again left men on base, again failed to catch the ball, again ran out of pitching, and again failed at every critical moment as the most crucial at bats of the series were given to guys like Scott Hatteberg, Trot Nixon, and Damon Buford. Two rotten errors by the umpires hurt, but they were the kind of mistakes good teams render unimportant.

And the kind of mistakes that make the Red Sox the Red Sox.

Before the start of the 2000 season, the Red Sox made their plans clear. Their desperation for a new ballpark went into overdrive. In 2000 they would completely ignore the marketing possibilities of their own 100th season of play while embarking on a relentless public relations push for the new park. The season was almost an afterthought, and that's the way it played out.

After the usual lopping off of players who only a few months earlier had been key performers, such as number-two starting pitcher Pat Rapp, Duquette worked a trade with the Astros, sending a couple of minor leaguers, including shortstop prospect Adam Everett, to Houston for outfielder Carl Everett, whom Duquette called "a genuine five-tool player."

That may have been true, but Everett also acted at times as if amid those tools a couple of screws had worked their way loose. Although he filled a need and was coming off the best season of his career, with 25 home runs and 108 RBIs, the trade did raise a few eyebrows. The Astros had payroll problems, but if Everett was so good, how come he'd been so cheap to acquire? The Red Sox would find that out.

But they really, really, really, *really* needed pitching. Winning as many games as they had with the pitching staff that Jimy Williams had to work with in 1999 was enough to earn him "Manager of the Year" honors. While Pedro Martinez had been magnificent and Derek Lowe had emerged as a top-shelf relief pitcher, that was it. Saberhagen was held together with bailing wire, and no one else could get anyone out.

Duquette, after spouting that what the Red Sox really needed was a left-hander to match up against the Yankees, then went out and signed washed-up left-hander Jeff Fassero on December 22. Merry Christmas, Sox fans.

The 2000 season was a year to cash out and rake in the profits of optimism that always followed a season of surprising performance. That was the attitude from the start. Even though the Red Sox were picked by *Sports Illustrated* to win everything, the front office didn't seem to make that much of a priority.

Boston got off to a pretty good start against a bunch of really bad teams, as Nomar Garciaparra raked the ball all year, Everett had a tremendous first half, and Pedro was Pedro. On May 28 the Sox and Yankees met in New York with first place on the line and Pedro against Clemens.

For the first time since Clemens had joined the

Yankees, he pitched against the Red Sox like the pitcher who had once won 192 games for them. But Pedro was just as effective, and the game entered the ninth scoreless. Then Clemens failed to pick up Jeff Frye's ground ball and Trot Nixon came up. Earlier in the game, Clemens had caught Nixon looking, and when the outfielder started to argue, Clemens threw his weight around and barked, "That's a strike." Now Nixon got his revenge, clubbing a home run to deep right field to beat Clemens, 2-0.

A few weeks later, Clemens went down with a groin pull, and the Yankees suddenly looked very beatable. Now was the time for the Red Sox to make their move.

But this is one of the reasons the Red Sox are the Red Sox. Duquette kept spouting the fiction that Bret Saberhagen, on rehab, was going to come back in the second half. Meanwhile, the Yankees went out and got David Justice, and the Red Sox rotation, after Pedro, consisted of only a bunch of guys, usually brother Ramón Martinez, Fassero, Brian Rose, and Peter Schourek.

But don't forget New Fenway Park. The Sox unveiled their plans for the inventively named "New Fenway Park" in detail on May 19 in a splashy presentation that included an interactive website and a splashy brochure in local newspapers. They planned to retain Fenway Park's footprint and quirky on-field features and surround it with a park that looked a great deal like Baltimore's Camden Yards. It would cost only $627 million or so, and "all" the Sox wanted local government to provide was about 44 percent — some $275 million.

Put it this way. In the artist's rendering of the park that the Red Sox put in the brochure and on their website, there were five Red Sox infielders scattered across the diamond. The Red Sox had about as much of a chance getting their ballpark as getting away with playing with five infielders.

By July they were fighting to stay above .500 as the Yankees couldn't quite pull away. It was one of those seasons that begged for a bold move — for the acquisition of a player who could put them over the top, a pitcher who could pair with Martinez and give the Sox a top-of-the-rotation one-two punch that could take a team playing win-one-lose-one baseball and

help it put together the three- and four-game winning streaks that deliver a pennant.

But these were the Red Sox, and it was hard to ask the city and state for a couple of hundred million and then spend big for some players. And as Duquette fiddled, the Red Sox got burned. Oh, he made moves, acquiring pitcher Rolando Arrojo, infielder Mike Lansing, outfielder Dante Bichette, and a few others, the same kind of retreads he usually acquired in the spring. And Carl Everett, after a first half that sent him to the All-Star game, began a second half that seemed destined to send him to the doghouse as he was suspended for ten days after going off and headbutting umpire Ron Kulpa.

All that combined to make the Red Sox worse in a season in which the Yankees and the division title were up for grabs. And over three days in early September, the Yankees beat the Sox three in a row as Tomo Ohka, Martinez, and Schourek fell to Clemens,

Shortstop Nomar Garciaparra captured the imagination of Red Sox fans with a succession of outstanding seasons following his Rookie of the Year effort in 1997. Here he leaves the dugout following Boston's loss to New York in the 1999 ALCS.

Pettitte, and the immortal Randy Keisler. Boston trailed by 9 games with 22 to play, and even when Arrojo beat Orlando Hernandez in the series finale, it was clear to the Red Sox that the season was over.

There was only one problem. The Yankees would finish the season in horrible fashion, losing 16 of 19. But the Red Sox were ill prepared to do anything about it. Duquette declared the season was over and in the waning days, Carl Everett chose to show up late before a game with Cleveland and when Jimy Williams tried to bench him, Everett pulled a nutty, only to be bailed out by Duquette. He backed Everett, leaving his manager hanging, and "dysfunc-

tional" became the favorite adjective of every Boston sportswriter.

New York won the division with a so-so 87-74 mark as the Sox finished only two and a half games back. But it was the biggest two-and-a-half-game margin in baseball history. The Yankees went on to win the World Series.

But despite all this, the season ended on a high note anyway. On October 6, John Harrington spoke the words that few thought they would ever hear in their lifetime — the Boston Red Sox were for sale. The Yawkey Trust was cashing in.

Finally, some good news.

O glorious day.

THE FIX

2001 | 2003

Eight days before he and his partners took control of the Red Sox for the highest price ever paid for a major league baseball franchise, John Henry watches Pedro Martinez throw heat in the Florida sun of Fort Myers in February 2002.

At the press conference announcing the sale of the team, John Harrington was both maudlin and reflective. He bemoaned the end of the Yawkey legacy, got teary-eyed when he mentioned Tom and Jean, and said, "God willing, my last act will be to turn this incredible team over to a diehard Red Sox fan from New England." Although he cautioned that the sale process would be laborious, he said he hoped that a new owner would be in place "by the beginning of next season."

The ballpark plan was dead — a new ownership group was certain to have its own plan in regard to the ballpark issue. Speculation immediately swirled about who would get involved in the bidding, from local pooh-bahs like broadcasting mogul and grocer David Mugar, banker Terry Murray, real estate developer Frank McCourt, concession king Joe O'Donnell, and shopping mall czar Steve Karp, to New York cable maven Charles Dolan or even some unknown dot-com zillionaire. The Sox, including both Fenway Park and a portion of the lucrative cable channel NESN, were a prize. Most observers expected the Red Sox to stand pat in the off-season while the sale went through.

Yet over the next year and a half it would become clear that God and guesses would have little to do with the sale of the Sox. The sale process would not just be protracted; its agonizing pace would be nearly proctological. And the resulting new ownership would receive a lasting lesson about the franchise that would prove just as painful.

It soon became obvious that although the team was for sale, Harrington's hands were still welded to the wheel. The Yawkey Trust was slow to provide needed information to buyers and even slower in assessing the offers. Or perhaps the sale was already a done deal anyway and they were just dragging their feet until everything lined up.

It seemed likely that the Red Sox would avoid bold or costly moves during the process. Jimy Williams, with another year left on his contract, would stay, as would Carl Everett. But in November the notion of lame-duck ownership was blown out in an orgy of spending not seen since Tom Yawkey first received his birthright. The "Yawkey tradition" would end the way it began, with a frenzy of misplaced spending, only this time the next tenant would be left to foot the bill, as Harrington and company acted as if they'd been given a stolen credit card.

In the off-season, three notable free agents were on the market, the top player, by far, being Seattle shortstop Alex Rodriguez. But there were also Baltimore pitcher Mike Mussina and Cleveland outfielder Manny Ramirez.

Rodriguez was out of reach, even for the Monopoly money the Sox were playing with,

On April 9, 2001, Hideo Nomo became the first Red Sox pitcher to throw a no-hitter since Dave Morehead performed the feat at Fenway Park in 1965. Nomo's gem was also the first no-hitter ever pitched at Baltimore's Camden Yards.

contract worth $160 million, then added pitcher Hideo Nomo for one year at $4.5 million and spent nearly another $20 million on a host of others — David Cone, Tim Wakefield, Frank Castillo, and so on.

That was, in the old Eddie Collins phrase, "a whale of a lot of the coin of the realm." And the best part was that the Yawkey Trust, which had to approve the expenditures, wouldn't have to foot the bill. After years of crying poor mouth, it was suddenly no problem to push the payroll to $110 million — Steinbrenner territory — which made one wonder if they'd had the money before and simply chosen not to spend it. Messrs. Harrington and Duquette were clearly trying to buy themselves a going-away present to create a legacy to justify over five decades of the Yawkey tradition, and Duquette undoubtedly was looking to simultaneously secure a job in a new administration. Harrington and Duquette left the impression that each had already picked out his favorite police horse to ride around Fenway Park after winning it all.

There were still a lot of ifs, but the acquisitions were intriguing. While neither Nomo nor Cone were Mussina, in combination they did have the potential to buck up the starting rotation, and the prospect of Ramirez batting behind Garciaparra, who had just won his second consecutive batting title with a .372 average, and in front of a presumably calmer Carl Everett had Sox fans drooling. They began to dream those dreams again.

Then came spring training, and before the Red Sox even left Fort Myers, Carl Everett had been suspended for skipping a bus trip and Nomar Garciaparra had undergone surgery for a split tendon in his wrist, an injury that had bothered him since that ill-timed bean-ball war with Baltimore. The season hadn't even started and David Cone had already come up with the line of the year when he said, "I thought the Bronx Zoo was something, but this place takes the [expletive] cake."

The 2001 season would play out in rough imitation of 2000, but minus the same optimism. In May, Jason Varitek dove for a foul ball and fractured his elbow. Everett was either hurt or complaining for most of the year, Derek Lowe fell apart, Dante Bichette, Jose Offerman, and Mike Lansing led a group of disgrun-

but Mussina was precisely the kind of player the Red Sox needed. Paired with Martinez, a pitcher like Mussina could finally give the Red Sox a semblance of a rotation to compete with the Yankees. But after Mussina teased the Mets and Red Sox, and pushed up his price, he signed with — who else? — the Yankees. That left Ramirez.

He was not a great player, for Ramirez is neither fast nor particularly interested in running the bases or fielding. But at the plate he is a hitting savant. Duquette signed Ramirez to an enormous eight-year tled veterans who thought their bloated contracts made them stars, and Jimy Williams, to the consternation of almost everyone, seemed to pick lineups out of a hat. But Nomo tossed a no-hitter, David Cone was Saberhagen in somewhat less pain, and Ramirez was, well, Ramirez. He hit well, but first balked at moving from right field to left, and then after he did he professed a preference to just serving as designated hitter.

Whatever. As the saying around Boston went, it was just "Manny being Manny" — and just another overpaid Red Sox superstar who had his own set of rules.

Nevertheless, in 2001 the Red Sox again rode an easy early schedule into first place. But on June 27, Pedro Martinez, with a 7-2 record and a sore shoulder since beating the Yankees at the end of May, went on the disabled list with right-shoulder tendonitis. The Yankees soon began to pull away.

That hadn't been in the plan. The Yawkey Trust was supposed to win on the way out, and so was Du-

quette. Although trailing the Yankees, the Sox were very much alive in the wild-card race, and when Garciaparra returned on July 27, and with Martinez also soon scheduled to give it a try, the Sox still felt they had a shot. At the trading deadline on July 31, they made a last-ditch effort to save the season by dealing Tomo Ohka for Montreal closer Ugueth Urbina.

But Jimy Williams was managing this nine, and he wasn't going along with the plan. Saberhagen blasted him on a national radio show, and despite the presence of Urbina, Williams kept using Derek Lowe and Rod Beck as closers. Dan Duquette reacted like someone had stolen the strawberries. On August 16, with the Sox five games behind New York and two games behind Oakland for a wild-card berth, he fired Williams. After a brief flirtation with Felipe Alou, he hired stat-oriented pitching coach Joe Kerrigan to a two-year contract. "Joe knows our players, he knows our team, and he knows our market," said Duquette. Then Kerrigan set out to prove all that was true. In a matter of weeks things went from bad to worse to beyond belief.

On August 31, on the heels of a five-game losing streak, the Sox had one last opportunity to salvage the season, a three-game series with the Yankees in Fenway Park. When they were swept, the organization was left exposed and the franchise, from the top down, left teetering. Duquette found somebody else to blame and fired new pitching coach John Cumberland. Now the clubhouse erupted, and even these self-absorbed Sox had had enough. Garciaparra yelled out, "This is why no one wants to [expletive] play here," and was miffed when his words appeared in print. The Sox then went into New York and, just before 9/11, lost three in a row.

But even that horrific event didn't stop these Sox from continuing their embarrassing spiral. Over the final weeks the Red Sox yawned and spit tobacco juice when "God Bless America" was sung, Everett

The rocky relationship of general manager Dan Duquette and manager Jimy Williams came to an abrupt end on August 16, 2001, when Williams was fired and replaced by pitching coach Joe Kerrigan. Within weeks the club dropped out of contention, and before the end of spring training in 2002, within days of taking over the team, the team's new owners replaced Duquette.

charged that Kerrigan was a bigot, and Pedro Martinez balked when Kerrigan wanted him to keep pitching in a season already lost and in a fit of pique reportedly ripped off his jersey and threw it onto the field. If the Red Sox wanted to honor the Yawkey tradition in its final season of ownership, they had done so in spades, because everything that had gone wrong during that era went wrong in 2001.

And then, incredibly, in the off-season Dan Duquette remained at the helm, steering the ship toward a distant horizon only he could see, apparently oblivious to the fact that the anchor was down and he was never, ever leaving port. By December he'd added more than $30 million of contracts, picking up DH/first baseman Tony Clark on waivers from the Tigers and signing free agent center fielder Johnny Damon, although he did manage to deal Carl Everett to Texas. He even sent out a bizarre letter to club season ticket holders that made the 2001 season sound like one of the most successful in club history and embarked on a public relations campaign to try to rehabilitate his robotic reputation, making sure everyone knew that in 2001 the "Red Sox spent more time in first place than the Yankees." It was by turns laughable and a little pathetic. The sale couldn't come fast enough.

Someday someone should write a book detailing the process of the Red Sox sale, but that probably won't happen until certain parties are given immunity, others are placed in the witness protection program, and there are more than a few deathbed confessions. The whole thing reeked.

At the start the smart money said the club would go to a local guy, that the fix was in to steer the club to one of the guys who'd long paid tribute to Harrington in case the opportunity to buy the Sox ever arose. This was Boston, after all, where who you know is more important than anything else. At first it appeared this would be concessionaire Joe O'Donnell and shopping mall developer Steve Karp, both of whom had spent more than a decade and many millions positioning themselves as local favorites and cozying up to Harrington.

But there were plenty of other local guys, or guys with local ties, trying to weasel their way into a deal, even if their chances of doing so were mostly imaginary, from Ted Williams's insufferable son John-Henry Williams to certain well-heeled members of the local media who were simultaneously reporting on the sale. Everybody who wanted to be an insider or thought they already were was jockeying for position at the trough.

Finally, in November 2001, the Sox announced that they'd winnowed down the myriad number of bids to six. All had passed initial scrutiny by MLB and were prepared to pay upward of $600 million for the team, the most ever paid for a franchise. O'Donnell headed one group, and another was put together by real estate developer Frank McCourt, who owned waterfront land that could serve as a site for a new park. Then there were bids by cable tycoon Charles Dolan, by attorney-financier Miles Prentice, and by Boston Bruins owner Jeremy Jacobs. A sixth group had originally been headed up by the onetime ski mogul Les Otten, who was a buddy of Duquette's — Duquette had served on the board of directors for Otten's American Ski Company before Otten cashed in and the company went south. Otten was now bucked up by the addition of TV producer and former San Diego Padres owner Tom Werner. But at the last minute another name emerged atop that group, one John Henry, chairman and founder of an "alternative investment firm" specializing in commodities and derivatives. He already owned the Florida Marlins, and in a stunning coincidence MLB *just happened* to approve his sale of the Marlins to Montreal owner Jeffrey Loria in time for Henry to jump into the Sox sweepstakes. The transaction also just so happened to be part of baseball commissioner Bud Selig's scheme to "contract" baseball as MLB took over Montreal and discussed lopping off franchises in Minnesota and elsewhere. The Otten group rapidly morphed into the Werner-Otten group, and finally into the Henry-Werner group as they all compared bank accounts.

Now the lengthy sale process made sense. Ever since Harrington had taken command of the Sox, he'd served as one of Selig's favorite toadies, so eager to be a big player that he'd done the commissioner's bidding in any number of ownership committees that during Selig's tenure had steered baseball's bloated boat up against the rocks and pilings over and over

Part of the Duquette legacy was the talented but troubled Carl Everett, whose on-field antics veered from temper tantrums to his heavenly home run trots complete with finger-pointing finales in which he claimed to be pointing toward God.

again. And now, it appeared, all MLB wanted was just one little favor in return. After all, John Henry was still playing ball and Tom Werner already had. They were known to support a financial "realignment" of baseball in favor of revenue sharing between franchises — a cause dear to Selig's heart, for his Milwaukee Brewers, the team he once owned, were perhaps the most pathetic franchise in baseball, terminally underfunded and mismanaged.

That's when things got really strange, because once the final bidders were selected, the other three groups smelled a rat and thought the fix was in. The month of December unfolded like a gigantic game of liars' poker, a final frenzy of changing alliances as bankers and high-profile hangers-on good for window dressing were injected into the mix. Bluffs, backstabbing, and bullshit were measured out in equal portions. McCourt and Jacobs dropped out, although McCourt tried to forge an alliance with Miles Prentice.

In the end, Prentice and Dolan stayed at the table and at the eleventh hour O'Donnell tried to stay in the mix. Desperate, but rich, he tried to forge an alliance with Henry, but each wanted to be named chairman and have the other sit in the second row. O'Donnell didn't like the view from there and dropped out of the bidding altogether. On December 20, Harrington and the various limited partners who owned a piece of the legacy announced that they had finally accepted an offer. By now the Henry-Werner group — officially known as New England Sports Ventures — also included a heady backlist of major players. These ranged from the New York Times Company — which by extension also included its triple-A franchise, the *Boston Globe* — to onetime Padres and Orioles executive Larry Lucchino, to former Maine senator George Mitchell. Mitchell had long been rumored to be interested in succeeding Selig as the next commissioner of baseball. His addition to the group conveniently nixed that possibility, and he led up the group of small-print partners, a bunch of other guys who either had money or a name needed to assuage the Trust and pacify MLB.

Surprise, surprise. The bid from New England Sports Ventures was accepted by the Trust.

Dolan and Prentice cried foul, claiming their bids had been even higher but had been rejected. That was probably true, but now there was no turning back, although their complaints would result in some unwelcome scrutiny of the Trust by Massachusetts attorney general Tom O'Reilly. Eventually, after Charles Dolan stomped his feet and raised his bid, O'Reilly forced another $30 million into the coffers of the Trust, upping its take from the sale to $420 million and creating a super-charity with almost $1 billion in the bank. The Red Sox limited partners, who saw a 20 to 1 return on their initial investment, shared the other $300 million or so.

On March 1, 2002, the new owners of the Red Sox, who included (l–r) John Henry, Tom Werner, and Larry Lucchino, were finally introduced to Red Sox fans at an on-field reception prior to an exhibition game at City of Palms Park in Fort Myers, Florida.

But none of that meant much yet, really, because the keys had not yet been handed over to the new owners. Until every *t* was crossed and every *i* dotted, Harrington and Duquette, whom Harrington had strongly recommended be retained by the new group, were still atop Yawkey Way. Denial — appropriately enough — would be the final act of the Yawkey tradition.

Meanwhile, the new group, while privately miffed, was publicly cautious and deferential, praising John Harrington and saying the right things. In their initial statement to fans, they said, "The Boston Red Sox represent the spirit and passion of New England. We will become active and visible members of this great community and always remember that the team belongs not to us, but to all of you." Right.

As spring training approached, the Sox were still in limbo, and Dan Duquette was still walking around saying he was in charge and expected to remain on, even though there were absolutely no indications of that from the Henry group. In his comments, Larry Lucchino, who would serve as the new club president, made it clear that Duquette was history, comments that were lost on Duquette. Spring training was already under way, but finally, late in the afternoon of February 27, 2002, only 510 days after the team was put up for sale, John Henry and Larry Lucchino gave the thumbs-up sign from their box at City of Palms Park in Fort Myers.

Thus ended the 69 years of the failed Yawkey tradition. There was little mourning. In the next months even the windfall of dollars the Trust was due to distribute in the Yawkey name ended up tarnished as the Trust focused on well-heeled benefactors to such a degree — dropping $15 million on Boston College for an athletic center, for example, and another $25 million on Mass. General Hospital — that O'Reilly had to step in and remind them that they weren't allowed to spend like "drunken sailors" and that concepts like "conflict of interest" were not to be trifled with. Although the Yawkey dollars will eventually, surely, do a great deal of good, there are aspects of that reign that no amount of money can ever, or should, erase.

The new guys didn't wait around — there was a lot to fix. On the last day of February they fired Dan Duquette, naming assistant general manager Mike Port interim GM. And in a final bizarre chapter, Duquette, in a tearful good-bye, seemed genuinely shocked that he had been let go. "I had been looking forward to working with the Henry group, but they didn't see me fitting in," he said. No Red Sox GM had ever faced greater expectations than Duquette, and perhaps no Red Sox GM ever squandered more of an opportunity. For while Duquette finally shed the bigoted reputation that had hung around the organization for years, was open to the new ideas afloat in baseball, in the end he'd been given the combination to the vault and still failed. Despite stocking his team with stars — and letting more than a few slip away for nothing — his impersonal approach seemed to mirror the institutionalized arrogance of the organization. The end result had been schizophrenic — the organization acting as if no one would notice that the team they put on the field couldn't win and never had.

But like many other employees during the Trust's final days, Duquette may have had the last laugh. Over the last 510 days, dozens of employees were reportedly given long-term contracts complete with confidentiality clauses, golden parachutes that guaranteed future silence. Duquette would leave in tears but spend the next two years laughing all the way to the bank as he pulled down a salary much larger than his replacements were earning.

Joe Kerrigan was canned five days later and replaced for a few days by third-base coach Mike Cubbage, and then by former bench coach Grady Little, a player favorite.

A great fog lifted from the organization over the next weeks as the new owners, represented most often by Henry and Lucchino, got high marks just for being comparatively normal. They were generally nice — to media and to the fans — as were their first hires, many of whom had worked with Lucchino in either San Diego or Baltimore. Since the protracted sale process had left them with a ballclub already built by someone else, in their inaugural season public relations was job number one. They received, and deserved, a mulligan for 2002.

But there was also some disquiet over the makeup of the group, for their alliance with the *Boston Globe*, through the parent Times company and NESN, made it uncertain whether hard questions were ever going to be asked and pursued, particularly after puff piece after puff piece about the team began appearing in the papers. Before long *Globe* writers were making required soft-core contractual appearances on NESN.

There also appeared to be an inherent flaw in the way the organization was set up. With three titular heads — Lucchino as president and CEO, Henry as principal owner, and Tom Werner as chairman — it wasn't clear who was really in charge. Three people had shared power once before in Red Sox history, when Jean Yawkey, Haywood Sullivan, and Buddy LeRoux served as co-owners, and the result had been disastrous. It would remain to be seen whether the Henry group's public smiles reflected similar camaraderie behind closed doors, when tough decisions have to be made and egos are at stake. For now, however, they were still very much in the spring of their reign and basking in the glow.

The 2002 season would give the new group a quick lesson in all things Red Sox, for just in case they hadn't been paying attention, the entire season, at least in terms of wins and losses, would be played out as a rerun of the past two seasons. It was uncanny.

First came early success — including a spate of wins against the Yankees before the games meant anything, spiced by the traditional early-season injury to the franchise player, in this case Manny Ramirez, who broke his finger when sent home in a questionable decision by Mike Cubbage against Seattle on May 12. The Sox, who still led the division by four games, soon peaked.

Next came the midseason swoon, sparked by their usual desultory play against the National League in interleague play as Manny Ramirez took a liking to Pawtucket and stayed there for more than a week on injury-rehab. Atlanta then bounced the Red Sox out of first place for good on June 28. And while the Yankees grabbed their needed replacement parts in midsummer, the Red Sox, true to form, waited until the last minute, snatching Cliff Floyd and Bobby Howry at the trading deadline on July 31.

Then came the rest of the season, when the Yankees stretched out their lead and the Red Sox slowly, inexorably, fell further behind. Boston somehow managed to finish out of the money again despite seven players on the All-Star team, 20 wins from both Martinez and a rejuvenated Derek Lowe, 40 saves from Ugueth Urbina, a batting title from Manny Ramirez, and 120 RBI from Nomar Garciaparra. After starting the season 40-17, they were only 53-52 thereafter. But for the first time in a while, there was a minimum of controversy.

Well, not entirely. Although the Red Sox organization bore no responsibility for it, the circumstances surrounding the death of Ted Williams on July 5 nevertheless must be included as one of the more bizarre chapters in Red Sox history.

In a season that also saw the deaths of former GMs Dick O'Connell and Haywood Sullivan, as well as former broadcaster Ned Martin, Williams's death caused every Sox fan everywhere to pause and reflect. Few players have ever meant so much to an organization. For better and worse, and sometimes at the same time, Ted Williams was the Red Sox. When he passed, all New England mourned.

And then, only a few days later, it seemed like a morbid joke. His daughter Claudia and son John-Henry, who as a favor the Sox had actually signed to a minor league contract, placed Williams's body in an Arizona cryonics facility known as Alcor. Although Claudia and John-Henry produced an oil-stained scrap of paper with Ted's signature on which Williams apparently indicated that was where he wanted to go, longtime friends found the notion untenable. In an instant, Ted Williams went from being an icon to the butt of Jay Leno jokes.

Although Claudia and John-Henry asked that no memorial be held, the Red Sox did so anyway on July 22, in a dignified celebration of Williams's life at Fenway Park that featured many of his teammates and other Red Sox players. It was the first time in a long time that the organization had gotten something right.

But the primary role of the new group in 2002 was to make friends and influence people. They were visible, responsive, and even a little creative as they quieted the talk of a new ballpark and did some tweaking to Fenway, sticking in a few more rows of field boxes. They talked the place up, made players give out autographs, let kids run the bases, and generally made nice to everyone. They didn't win, but then again, it hadn't been their team. They knew, however, that they would be held to a different standard in 2003.

As soon as the season ended, it was time for them to act again. They adhered to the notion that the GM is more important than either the players or the manager. The farm system was barren, and out in Oakland Billy Beane was the GM of the moment, valued for his embrace of baseball's new statistics, "sabermetrics" (which in reality was new only to the media and the owners, for most of the statistical insights had been well established long before), and his ability to use that information to glean diamonds from coal. He had made Oakland an annual contender despite a payroll of less than $40 million. With the debt service many expected after the purchase of the Red Sox, the notion of doing more with less was pretty attractive to the new owners. After paying $700 million for the team, they would soon have to either increase revenues or reduce payroll or else they weren't going to make much on their investment. John Henry, whose arithmetic wizardry was the backbone of his fortune, could certainly do the math.

And Beane wanted to come to Boston. He had been saying so publicly for years and even had a clause in his Oakland contract that allowed him to entertain an offer from the Red Sox. The only other candidate had been his assistant, Massachusetts native J. P. Ricciardi, but he'd grown tired of waiting and earlier in the year had taken an offer too good to refuse to be the GM of Toronto.

In early November, the Red Sox received permission to talk to Beane, and Larry Lucchino started negotiating. It was time for the new regime to learn lesson number one — the only one needed — about what it's like to own the Red Sox. For this franchise, there are no sure things, no safe bets, and no done deals. Ever. New hires ought to have words to that effect tattooed on their foreheads as a requirement of their employment.

On November 10, Lucchino thought he had a deal, and Beane even spent a few hours in the surreal position of negotiating on behalf of the A's for the compensation the club would receive for his own release. Beane had agreed to a four-year contract worth $2.5 million a year, the most lucrative ever given to a general manager. The Sox had been willing to do anything. They agreed that Beane would be allowed to split his time between California and Boston to stay close to his teenage daughter from his first marriage. Tom Werner's gal pal Katie Couric had even called Beane's current wife and sung "Happy Birthday" to her.

But that night Beane couldn't sleep, saying later, "I sort of wasn't doing cartwheels. I knew something wasn't right." According to Beane, that something was his daughter. Joining Boston in any capacity cost him time with her. He was also made uncomfortable by the fact that doing the job on a bicoastal basis might not work. After consulting with old friend J. P. Ricciardi, the next day he backed out.

The Sox were stunned, but accommodated Beane and let him go. They went back to the pile of contenders, but none were nearly as attractive as Beane. They had to move fast — it was already mid-November, and there were free agents to be signed and trades to be made, moves for which Port and his assistant, Theo Epstein, had already laid much of the groundwork. So the Sox decided to take a chance, not on Port, who had had a rough time as Angels GM a decade earlier and lacked cachet, but on Epstein, a Lucchino protégé and designated wunderkind.

The twenty-eight-year-old had had a meteoric rise in baseball, parlaying the connections that come to a well-off young Yale graduate from Brookline whose novelist-father teaches at BU. He'd interned with the Orioles and served as director of baseball operations for the San Diego Padres before joining the Red Sox in March 2003 as assistant GM under Mike Port.

Like Duquette, Epstein had always dreamed of working for the Red Sox. The Sox already knew him and liked the fact that he had Boston roots, a law degree, and, in an organization obsessed with class-consciousness, an Ivy League background. More-over, on the way up Epstein had made himself invalu-able to certain segments of the media, for whom he's been a valuable background source for several years. He also knew baseball's other young-gun GMs, like Beane and Ricciardi, and knew his way around sa-bermetrics. At his suggestion, the team had already hired stat guru Bill James as a senior adviser. Al-though Epstein lacked much of the experience the Sox claimed to be looking for when they started their search, they surrounded him with a support group of ex-GMs like Port, Bill Lajoie, and Lee Thomas. It was essentially a GM-by-committee concept, with Ep-stein in the big chair and Lucchino looking over his shoulder and a lot of guys hovering around. Besides, they wouldn't have to pay him $2.5 million a year, and of all the members of the front office, only Epstein could talk about growing up a Red Sox fan and make it sound plausible — he'd been one of those kids left in tears after game six of the 1986 World Series.

Now the organization got busy. They cut loose guys like Urbina, claimed guys on waivers, signed free agents, and made a few trades, like the one that delivered second baseman Todd Walker from Cincin-nati, dealing a few nonprospects but taking on a big-ger contract the Reds didn't want.

They didn't sign a big free agent but did grab a lot of little ones, role players and hitters they thought might thrive in Fenway, most notably Yankee pitcher Ramiro Mendoza, Minnesota first baseman David Or-tiz, Marlin first baseman Kevin Millar, and Cub in-

fielder Bill Mueller. Like the Sox in Duquette's first few years, most of these acquisitions — which also included guys like Jeremy Giambi — would end up thrown up against the wall to see who would stick.

Yet the nature of the acquisitions was telling. The club focused on relief pitchers and hitters. Defense and starting pitchers weren't quite as important, and

Manny Ramirez was touted by Dan Duquette as the second coming of Jimmie Foxx and came close to duplicating the Hall-of-Famer's offensive glory with three seasons (2001 to 2003) in which he averaged 37 home runs, 112 RBI, and a .325 batting average.

On August 7, 2003, David Ortiz *(r)* socked two home runs to help lead Boston to a 9-3 win and a three-game sweep of the defending world champion Anaheim Angels at Fenway Park. Center fielder Johnny Damon congratulates Ortiz following the victory that left Boston only two and a half games behind the Yankees.

in the spring the organization shared at least part of the logic behind its acquisitions.

Bill James had written at length about how better to use the bullpen. Suggesting that the standard approach of bringing a closer into the game for the final inning was flawed, James touted instead an "optimal usage pattern": after the seventh inning the relief ace would be used for two innings in a tie game, for two innings with a one-run lead, and for one inning in other situations or when he needed the work. The idea was to use the best reliever in what were, statistically, the more important innings rather than in the final inning as a standard closer.

The concept morphed into something the media dubbed "closer by committee," since the choice of reliever would no longer be obvious based on the in-

ning of the game. "Setup" men, long relievers, and closers would be fluid, based on situational parameters. The closer might pitch the final inning one day, the seventh inning of a tie game the next time out, or the eighth inning while trailing in the game after that. And thus began a season-long search for the Supermen who could fill that role.

By Opening Day it was clear that while the 2003 Red Sox had some obvious strengths — such as offensive firepower and, with Martinez, Lowe, and Wakefield, top-of-the-rotation starting pitching — defense and the bullpen remained question marks.

In a sense, everything that would happen during 2003 was played out in the first two games of the season when the Red Sox opened in Tampa Bay. On Opening Day the Red Sox and Pedro Martinez carried a 4-1 lead into the ninth inning. Enter the bullpen. Alan Embree failed to retire a single hitter, even giving up a home run to Terry Shumpert, before giving way to Chad Fox.

Again, victory seemed assured. Fox induced a double-play ground ball to Nomar Garciaparra. But Garciaparra hesitated, and the Red Sox never got that double play. Light-hitting Tampa Bay outfielder Carl Crawford, who would end the season with far more infield hits than home runs, pulled a ball just over the wall to give the Devil Rays a remarkable 6-4 win. Welcome to the big leagues, Theo.

The next day Tim Wakefield carried a lead into the late innings. This time Bobby Howry blew it, giving up a tying two-run homer to Rey Ordonez in the eighth. But these Red Sox would show remarkable resiliency and the ability to come back with the best of them. In the sixteenth inning Kevin Millar homered to give the Red Sox a 9-8 win.

That's how it went for the Red Sox for the next six and a half months — Goofus one day, Gallant the next. No lead was safe — by either team. Boston's bullpen blew lead after lead after lead, assisted by shoddy defense and poor baserunning, only to be bailed out by a relentless offense. When they hit a lot, they usually won. When they didn't, they lost.

It was exciting, aggravating, thrilling, impossible-to-watch-and-impossible-not-to baseball. The Red Sox scared the hell out of the opposition and their own fans in equal measure. Players from whom little was expected, like David Ortiz and Bill Mueller, began to come through in big ways, and at least as far as most could see, this club seemed to get along.

The PR-conscious new organization knew how to play to its strength, to tout the new and happy Red Sox as a bunch of runny-nosed kids just playing for the love of the game, with every win and every positive move a sign of pluck and organizational genius, every loss and failure just a sign of something that needed to be tweaked later, and would be.

As Larry Lucchino had said months earlier, the impression the Sox wanted to leave was that "these are not your father's Red Sox." Off the field that was certainly true, and a suddenly boosterish and compliant local press corps, freed from decades of ill treatment, ate up all the free shrimp and almost everything else the club wanted them to. Fans and media alike were thrilled when the Red Sox elevated their battles with the Yankees to a fever pitch. After the Red Sox lost to New York in their bid to sign Cuban refugee pitcher Jose Contreras, Lucchino called New York "the evil empire," and the Red Sox seemed more obsessed with beating the Yankees than anything else, leaving the impression that if the club could just beat the Yankees a world championship was some kind of fait accompli.

And for the first time — well, almost — the Red Sox apparently beat the Yankees to the punch, making an early trade designed to put them over the top instead of waiting until the last minute. Infielder Shea Hillenbrand was traded to the Diamondbacks for pitcher Byung-Hyun Kim.

For any other team in baseball, the trade made a lot of sense. But for a team competing against the Yankees, it was whacko, and fraught with psychological peril. After suffering the ultimate pitching collapse against the Yankees in the 2001 World Series, Kim had been emotionally fragile ever since. What stat ever made the Sox think he could pitch effectively against them now?

Still, at times the brassy, brawny, increasingly confident Red Sox seemed capable of greatness. After they battered the Yankees in New York on July 4 and 5, outscoring the Yankees 20-5 and beating Wells and Clemens, they were ready to skip the rest of the season. Owner John Henry gushed, "I wish the playoffs started right now." Never had a Red Sox team been more eager to win. Or so far ahead of itself.

Because as the season progressed, underneath the veneer of a team that adopted the unlikely trademarked rodeo phrase "Cowboy up!" as its motto, there were a number of disquieting signs. Manager Grady Little infuriated the front office time and time again in his strategy, eschewing numbers for his own gut feelings. On several occasions John Henry wanted him fired as the Sox owner, publicly reticent and mild mannered, proved prone to private explosions — after all, you don't make a billion dollars whispering all the time. The first time he wanted Little fired was after the manager left Mike Timlin in to pitch to slugger Jim Thome in an interleague game against the Phillies. Thome homered, and the Sox eventually lost. Lucchino and Epstein managed to talk Henry out of sacking the manager, something they'd do repeatedly every time Henry thought — or read on the Internet — that Little had misused his pitching staff.

And although the Sox seemed capable of beating New York, every single time they had a chance to make a statement against the Yankees, they failed to — that win on July 5 had put the Sox two games out of first place and in position to draw into a tie with a sweep. But in the end Boston gained nothing as Byung-Hyun Kim spit the bit in the finale, effectively ending any thoughts the Red Sox had of ever using him in a meaningful contest against the Yankees for eternity. It soon became clear that, stripped of all the spin and stats, this Red Sox team was really not a whole lot different from a lot of Red Sox teams over the years. They were built around offense, with a lot of one-dimensional, slow-footed hitters who could neither field nor run the bases, and had little depth and not enough pitching. There was nothing new about that.

And each time they tried to make a move to solve those problems, it backfired. Epstein was like the rookie phenom who hits .450 his first time around the league and then everyone starts throwing curveballs. Byung-Hyun Kim was a complete nonfactor, and over the summer the Red Sox tried to buck up their pitching with everyone from virtual freebies like retreads Rudy Seanez and Bruce Chen to costly trades for

Scott Sauerbeck, Scott Williamson, and Jeff Suppan. These deals were as disastrous as the acquisitions of Ortiz and Mueller and Millar had been successful.

The Yankees won the division, but the Sox were helped out when the Mariners collapsed in September. Oakland won the West, and Boston, with only two more wins than in 2002, won the wild-card slot to make the playoffs for the first time in three years.

To hear the Red Sox talk, one would have thought the playoffs were just a pesky little diversion. They got *way way way* ahead of themselves and after beating Baltimore to clinch the wild card celebrated like they'd won the World Series. The game wasn't even over and John Henry was on TV counting his chickens. After the game the players spilled gallons of champagne, ten thousand fans paraded through

the streets chanting, "Cowboy up!" and several Sox continued the party by serving up drinks in a local bar. The phrase "Act like you've been there before" got repeated a lot over the next few days. You could smell a giant setup in the works.

Throughout baseball the Red Sox were quickly gaining a not very savory reputation. On the field and off, the Sox were viewed as increasingly arrogant, prone to gloating, and rubbing success in their opponents' faces. A great many people in the baseball world began to hope this team would get theirs in the end.

In the playoffs that followed, the Sox played some of the most exciting baseball in club history, as comebacks and collapses and comebacks followed each other with dizzying rapidity. Someday it may be possible for Sox fans to recall the ballclub's stirring performance against the Oakland A's, coming back from a two-game deficit to take the divisional series. And someday they may even be able to do the same with the first six games of the ALCS versus the Yankees, for the two historic rivals played a series for the ages, full of turns and counterturns, spiced by the game-three debacle in Fenway Park. That one began with a Martinez pitch to Karim Garcia's head in the first round, continued with an enraged Don Zimmer being taken down to the canvas by Martinez in the middle rounds, and ended with a ninth-inning TKO in the bullpen between Garcia, Yankee reliever Jeff Nelson, and a member of the Fenway Park grounds crew. The series had it all and more — Pedro and Roger and Jeter and Nomar and a generation of arguments and taunts and myths condensed into one excruciating week and finally distilled into a single finale, a game seven to decide it all. Someday it may be possible for Sox fans to recall these games fondly.

But not in this life.

Because when seasons end the way 2003 did, they have a way of erasing *everything* that came before and sending shock waves that wreak havoc through the organization for *years*. Was the game-seven loss the worst in franchise history? That's like asking

After a convoluted series of deals on two continents, free-spirited first baseman Kevin Millar, shown here sharing a laugh with Nomar Garciaparra, finally arrived in Boston in the off-season prior to the 2003 season.

which eye you want poked out. Bucky Dent, Buckner, or Boone? Pick your poison.

There was one huge enormous omen before game seven — the 26th time the two teams would play each other, more than any two teams had ever before played in a season. Before the game the Red Sox made an embarrassing rookie mistake, the kind made by an organization too eager to pat itself on its back, too ignorant of its own history, and way too quick to celebrate. On the afternoon of game seven, the grounds crew painted the 2003 World Series logo onto the infield grass in foul ground behind home plate at Fenway Park. Worse, they allowed photographers to take pictures of it. And incredibly, unbelievably, they even allowed a crew to shoot a video of the scene. Before game seven, every single New York Yankee had seen it. And Sox fans who were old enough remembered rumors of champagne bottles being opened in the Red Sox clubhouse in the final inning of game six of the 1986 World Series and lockers draped with plastic hurriedly removed. This wasn't the World Series, but it was the Yankees, and by now, in this season, everybody believed that winning this game also meant winning the Series. As Jeff Horrigan would write in the *Boston Herald* a day later, that logo would "lay beneath a blue tarp . . . like a corpse covered with a sheet."

The Sox, despite not hitting, had won game one in New York 5-2 when Mike Mussina kept throwing gopher balls and Tim Wakefield mesmerized the Yankees. And after the battle royal of game three, they had bounced back after a rainout and won game four as Wakefield came back and did it again. And then they had won game six when the Boston bats, quiet for the last two weeks, finally awoke and the Sox stormed from behind and belted the Yankees 9-6.

Entering game seven, for the first time the Red Sox seemed to have momentum, and Pedro Martinez was finally, finally scheduled to pitch the game he'd been acquired to pitch and been paid millions for, game seven against the Yankees with everything at stake.

There was poetry in that, for the Yankees would counter with turncoat Roger Clemens. For a Red Sox fan, what could possibly be sweeter than sending Clemens into retirement, with his ridiculous insistence that he was a Yankee and would only enter the

Theo Epstein was hired as only the eleventh general manager in Red Sox history on November 25, 2002. In his first season, Epstein nearly steered his team to the top of the American League, only to lose a heartbreaker to the Yankees in an excruciating seventh game at Yankee Stadium.

Hall of Fame in a Yankee hat, to an inglorious defeat in his final game, to leave the sour taste in *his* mouth finally and forever? In a sense, everything it had ever meant to be a Red Sox fan was at stake, an ultimate, final, glorious vindication, with the Red Sox piling atop one another rolling on the field at Yankee Stadium.

And it started perfectly. In the second inning, Clemens collapsed, gave up a single to Kevin Millar, and then a home run, deep, to — who else? — nemesis Trot Nixon. One out later, Varitek doubled and Yankee third baseman Enrique Wilson threw a ground ball away. The Red Sox were ahead 3-0, and Clemens had already thrown more than 40 pitches.

Then Pedro cruised. There had been speculation after game three that he was hurt, and he probably was, but he looked strong, in command. Millar led off the fourth with a home run, and now it was 4-0 and Clemens was on his way out.

Trot Nixon was in Clemens's head and worked a six-pitch walk. Then AL batting champion Bill Mueller singled, and the Sox had men on first and third and a sour-looking Joe Torre walked out and took the ball from Clemens.

The Yankees were desperate. They brought in, not one of their relievers, but Mike Mussina in the first relief appearance of his career. The Sox had done that against Oakland with Lowe, and it worked, but now Boston's bullpen was hot and it was the Yankees who were afraid to use the pen — a lovely turnabout. Perfect.

But Mussina struck out Varitek, and then Jeter took Damon's ground ball and kept it himself and threw to first for a double play, a throw that the guys with the radar guns later said was the hardest-thrown ball all night — 98 mph — faster than any pitch thrown by Pedro or Roger or anyone else. But it still was 4-0.

Jason Giambi led off the Yankee fifth with a home run. So what? Pedro was staying ahead, throwing strikes, and the Red Sox were ahead 4-1. And it was still 4-1 after six. In the seventh, Giambi took Pedro deep again, but in the top of the eighth, off David Wells, Ortiz had answered with a home run of his own in "take that" fashion and the Sox led 5-2 and needed only six more outs to make history not matter anymore.

Just six more outs. The cocky Red Sox were all smiles and hugs on the bench. The *Washington Post*'s Tom Boswell had already written, "Nothing makes up for 85 years of tasting bile. But the feast of Red Sox revenge, served cold last night in Yankee Stadium, certainly constitutes a delicious start . . . . The team with Boston on its chest finally left the Bronx with a pennant in its arms rather than egg on its face." Manny Ramirez had already been on his cell phone in the clubhouse, calling his friends and relatives, telling them to go ahead and make their arrangements; the Red Sox were going to the World Series. It was as certain as that logo on the field.

Pedro was done. When he left the mound after the seventh, he'd given that little kiss and point to God, the sign that he knew his work was done, and a bunch of Red Sox had come over and wrapped him in their arms and given him a hug.

It sounded crazy now, but after the Oakland series Grady Little had quipped, "After 167 games I still don't know who my closer is." Since the playoffs had started, though, the relief staff had been automatic. Mike Timlin hadn't given up a run, Embree was the lefty specialist, and Scott Williamson, finally, began to close games out. In over 16 innings of pitching, those three had given up only seven baserunners. At the precise time the Sox needed a bullpen, it had finally arrived. And all they needed were six more outs.

Then, in the bottom of the eighth, Martinez walked back out to the mound. Most Sox fans started scratching their heads and checking their pulse. Uh, Grady — Pedro was *done*. He had kissed the sky, accepted the congratulations of teammates, and passed the threshold of his effectiveness, having thrown his 100th pitch to strike out Soriano to end the seventh. Yet there was Martinez throwing his warm-up pitches and Nick Johnson stepping in.

Martinez said later that, after the seventh inning, "I thought I was coming out until they told me the other way," and that even then he told Grady Little to "get the lefty ready, and Tim Wakefield." But he went back out in the eighth and got Johnson to pop up, even though he had to throw seven pitches to do so.

And that brought up Derek Jeter, a player some Sox fans insult by wearing foul T-shirts, by chanting "Nomar's better," and by derisively calling him "Captain Intangibles." He got ahead with two strikes, but then, with Varitek standing and holding his glove over his head, Martinez's next pitch, number 110, wasn't up enough. It was at the top of the strike zone, out and over the plate, and Jeter, playing with a ruptured ligament in his thumb, shut everyone up by rifling the pitch into right field. Trot Nixon looked surprised as the ball took off over his head and Jeter pulled into second with a double. There were way too many people who had seen that picture of the World Series logo who remembered it now and started thinking about 1986.

After Jeter's hit, every Red Sox fan screamed for Little to remove Martinez — most could cite opponent batting averages off Martinez after 100 pitches, and after 105 it was a not very pretty .370 in 2003. "GET HIM OUT" was spoken through clenched teeth in a million throats.

These were the Yankees, after all, and the playoffs. This wasn't Tampa Bay. Just a few weeks before, in a meaningless contest on September 16, Little had left Martinez in against the Devil Rays for 122 pitches. John Henry had a nutty after that one and screamed that it would cost the Red Sox the whole season. Martinez had won the game, and Little had defended the strategy as part of a plan to "stretch Martinez out" before the playoffs, but ever since Martinez had seemed a little off, a little weak. And getting Martinez weak was, as everyone knew, New York's game plan, the one they had developed to give themselves a chance against the greatest pitcher in the game after that 17-strikeout one-hitter he'd thrown against them in 1999. They just tried to keep the game close and get Martinez to throw a lot of pitches. Then, either Pedro faltered or the Yankees got to the bullpen, and everyone knew what happened then. In the past few seasons the plan had worked to perfection. In more than 20 regular-season starts against the Yankees since then, Martinez was 7-8. They either hit him or got him out of the game, and as often as not, the Boston bullpen had caved in before expectations and the Yankees' stranglehold on history.

But this bullpen, at least right now, was different. Timlin, Embree, and Williamson were sound, and the matchups favored Boston. But Little sat on his hands as Bernie Williams stepped in, worked the count to 2-2, and rocketed pitch number 115 up the middle for a single. Jeter scored, 5-3.

Pedro was done, clearly. He couldn't finish hitters off now. His location was off. He was done.

Grady Little finally stood up, walked to the mound, started talking. Martinez nodded, nodded again. Embree stopped throwing in the pen and looked in. And then Grady patted Pedro on the shoulder and walked back to the dugout.

WHAAAT?

That brought up Hideki Matsui, and the screams from Red Sox followers rose in intensity as Yankee fans nudged each other and smiled. Embree was ready. The left-handed Matsui had been hitting the

ball hard, doubling off Martinez in the fourth. Martinez was gassed; you could see it on his face and feel it in your bones. He had that look that only Red Sox fans know, the one they'd seen before on Bob Stanley, Calvin Schiraldi, and Mike Torrez. And Martinez had told Little to "get the lefty ready." But Little had asked him if he could get Matsui out and Pedro had nodded.

Two strikes again, but Martinez couldn't finish. Matsui turned on the ball and ripped a nothing fastball not too far up and not too far in down the left-field line. A ground-rule double that sent Williams to third and Matsui, the tying run, to second. And now Martinez had thrown 118 pitches and wasn't Pedro Martinez anymore but one of those pitchers the Red Sox were afraid to use.

And Little still sat there. After the Ortiz home run in the top of the inning, Theo Epstein had started smiling and accepting handshakes from the people he was sitting with. Now he sat stone-faced. He hadn't lived this before, not really. He was one year old in 1975, only four in 1978, and twelve in 1986, too young to have his heart *really* ripped out by its roots. Like many others in a whole new generation of fans who had fallen in love with this team, Red Sox history was only something he'd read about.

Now he would live it.

Todd Walker came to Boston in November 2002 in Theo Epstein's first trade as Red Sox general manager. Walker blossomed at the plate while leading Boston with clutch hits during a memorable 2003 playoff run against the Athletics and Yankees.

Little stayed on the bench. Embree stayed in the pen. . . . And nothing changed.

Posada watched three pitches, swung through a strike, and then, at 2-2, stayed with a pitch that should have beat him, a fastball in, and number 123 of the night. But he fought it off, lofted it into center, where Damon, playing deep, and Nomar and Todd Walker all converged and watched it land in the center of a perfect triangle where pennants are lost.

Williams scored. Matsui scored.

The game was tied. Yankee Stadium was going crazy. And in bars across New England fans fell to their knees as if shot.

Every Red Sox fan in the world knew, absolutely knew, what was going to happen next, even after the inning was over, even after Little finally brought in Embree and Timlin and particularly after they both pitched fine, and even after Wakefield, who'd been mighty for the last month, came in to pitch the tenth and then came back out to pitch the eleventh. And especially after the Yankees turned to Mariano Rivera, and he pitched three tough innings, making tough pitches, working out of jams.

You knew it would end this way.

For when a knuckleball pitcher throws the ball, he has no idea where it is going or what it is going to do. If he releases it right, the ball spins maybe once or twice on its way home, dancing and diving, missing the bat.

Or else it doesn't. And on Wakefield's first pitch of the eleventh inning, to Aaron Boone, it did not. It spun more than twice, much more, rolling over again and again and then dropping into the heart of the plate, pulled down only by gravity and the weight of history, and Boone swept his bat through the ball and sent it soaring up and out and into this book, another tragic chapter of this story, sending people into the street numb and shaken.

Yankees 6, Red Sox 5. Season done.

Cowboy oops.

It was unspeakable, unbelievable, and thoroughly predictable. In a way it was like every other agonizing loss in Red Sox history. Yet in some ways it was like none that had ever come before, for not only did it come against the Yankees, in a season that had seemed different, but it happened all at once—

boom, game over — and it happened because of a mental, and not a physical, error. No one blamed Wakefield or Martinez. And no one blamed Aaron "Bleeping" Boone.

They blamed only Grady "Bleeping" Little.

And like every other excruciating loss in Red Sox history, this one rapidly shook the organization to the core. Little was surprised, even shocked, at the reaction of fans, and he immediately became the most disliked Red Sox manager this side of Don Zimmer. He didn't help himself when he defended leaving Martinez in by saying, "We've been doing it that way all season." But he hadn't, and everyone knew that. And this wasn't the season, this was the *end* of the season, and there's a big, big difference.

He couldn't survive his decision, and didn't deserve to, but he probably deserved better treatment on the way out. The organization distanced itself from Little just about as fast as Boone's home run had left the park, strung him up, and left him hanging behind pursed lips and "no comments." No one in the front office brought up the fact that most of Epstein's deals once the season started had backfired, that Scott Sauerbeck and Jeff Suppan had been abysmal failures and Byung-Hyun Kim was such a psychological mess that they'd left him off the roster, that Little and the Red Sox had gone into the postseason with only about 20 players they had any intention of using, or any faith in, and that, in the end, that was what had cost them the pennant. And they didn't mention that they'd milked this gloriously flawed team that could hit but do little else for all it was worth, that they hadn't beat the Yankees in any game they really had to all year long, that if the Mariners hadn't collapsed in September they wouldn't even have made the playoffs, that if the A's had just bothered to touch home plate the Red Sox wouldn't have made it to the ALCS at all, and that if it hadn't rained after game three the Yankees probably would have won the ALCS in five games. They didn't take any blame, not a bit of it. They were geniuses, and don't you forget it.

Over the next few days, when no one in the front office stepped up to defend Little, the deathwatch began. His contract was up, and now Little made it easy by saying that since he'd been hung out he really wasn't sure he wanted to come back anyway. All the

In the "What were they thinking?" department, the Fenway Park grounds crew worked overtime to install a World Series logo prior to the start of Boston's seventh-game league championship showdown with the Yankees. Within hours of its installation, the grounds crew knew they'd be pulling a double shift to remove it.

"Cowboy up" crap fell to the floor in the wake of the loss.

But it didn't stop there. For two years the fiction that the Red Sox under the Henry-Werner ownership group was just one big smiley happy family had been an easy sell. Over the next few weeks it was shattered as we learned about a clubhouse fractured by its stars and "Cowboy up" heroes were cut loose without a contract offer. Suddenly John Henry didn't seem so different from those who had run this outfit before.

Little was sacrificed in a weird press conference. Epstein looked like he was telling the school principal he hadn't thrown that spitball, and you could almost see Henry's hand making Larry Lucchino's lips move. They stuck to the script but looked like they didn't believe a word they said. Grady Little was a living saint, but — uh — by the way — uh — he's — uh, uh (sotto voce) — *notcomingback*. Even Dan Duquette had never looked so uncomfortable, or less credible. According to reports, Lucchino and Epstein had been inclined to keep Little, at least for another year, only to be vetoed by the only vote that mattered, John Henry's.

Well, at least now everyone knew the era of ownership by committee was over. Over the course of the season John Henry had become ever more enamored of fan websites where every one of Grady Little's decisions had been pored over like Lee's battle plan at Gettysburg. And he'd fallen for Internet columnists who managed with hindsight games they never played and only watched on TV. They told Henry what he wanted to hear, particularly after they found out he was listening to them. And over the course of the year Henry, just a fan himself with a pile of money, had found himself thinking the same way they did.

He'd been close to pulling the trigger on Little a half-dozen times, but these Red Sox kept bouncing back and never going into the tailspin that would have given him a chance, and when they finally fell behind the Yankees in September, it was too late to let Little go. The only way Little was ever going to keep his job was to win the whole thing, and even if he had, the Red Sox probably would have lowballed a contract offer and then acted surprised when Little walked away.

John Henry wanted him gone and that was that — the rest was spin. Oh, and by the way, every single employee in the organization got the message not to forget whose ball and bat it was.

Three days later the Sox released a letter to season ticket holders signed by Lucchino. Amid the usual pap designed to massage season ticket holders back into the fold were some telling comments and omissions. The letter mentioned the Red Sox commitment to fielding an "entertaining and competitive team," which seemed a lot like the "championship-

Less than an hour after Aaron Boone's home run beat the Red Sox in game seven of the 2003 ALCS, award-winning columnist Thomas Boswell of the Washington Post filed this story capturing the bleak mood of Red Sox nation.

What Johnny Pesky did for relay throws and Bill Buckner did for routine ground balls, Grady Little did for managing Thursday night at Yankee Stadium.

Pesky hesitated and a World Series was lost. Buckner lifted his glove an instant too soon and another world title evaporated. Now, add Little to the Boston Red Sox litany of infamy. The second-year manager froze at the switch, leaving his exhausted ace Pedro Martinez on the mound in the eighth inning before a howling Yankees throng Thursday night. With a 5-2 lead and only five outs left to grab the American League pennant, Little ignored a bullpen that had allowed only one run in 16 1/3 innings in this postseason.

Instead, as the baseball world watched in disbelief, Little sat glued to his seat as Derek Jeter doubled, Bernie Williams singled, Hideki Matsui doubled and, finally, Jorge Posada doubled to tie the score at 5.

By the time Little finally waved to his bullpen — which performed perfectly for the next 2 2/3 innings — the lead and the flag were gone. Baseball always ensures that such monumental gaffes have their appropriate punishment, no matter how cruel they seem. On the first pitch of the 11th inning, the Yankees' Aaron Boone blasted a Tim Wakefield knuckleball deep into the left-field seats for a 6-5 New York victory.

"Derek Jeter told me that if we just waited the [Yankee] ghosts would

---

For years, Red Sox fans will have the same bitter thought: "Somebody pass the dynamite. Put it under poor Grady's rear end."

---

show up," yelled a jubilant Boone after his pennant-winning home run.

Now, the Yankees will attempt to beat the Florida Marlins in the World Series and claim their 27th world title since the last Series triumph by a Red Sox team in 1918. For Red Sox fans — hello, out there, are there any Red Sox fans left or did this finally kill off the last of the breed? — only anger and regret will be left. And, as always seems to be the case in Boston, one indisputable goat. Or, in New England's case, scapegoat.

For years, Red Sox fans will have the same bitter thought: "Somebody pass the dynamite. Put it under poor Grady's rear end. Light the shortest fuse you can find. Please, blow that man out of his seat and send him to the mound to get a new pitcher."

But Little never budged as this game — and a role as a clear favorite in the World Series over the Marlins — escaped. And now New England will have another installment of sorrow to regurgitate endlessly. Will this one-night saga be analyzed for another 85 years, the length of time since the last Red Sox world title? Why not? After this defeat, the Curse of the Bambino, or whatever you choose to call the psychological shackles that imprison the Red Sox, has risen in credibility to the level of a Euclidian postulate. If no man can disprove it, and every succeeding piece of evidence supports the theory, then it must be true, right?

Curses, foiled again. That's "curses" plural.

The same disastrous, seemingly preordained fate that befell the disbelieving Chicago Cubs earlier this week has now fallen like a ton of rocks on top of a Red Sox team that seemed even more certain of its pennant than the Cubs had been. At least the Cubs could, to a degree, blame one of their own fans. It's not fair, of course. The Cubs themselves allowed every one of the Florida Marlins eight eighth-inning runs in game six of the NLCS.

But where can the Red Sox point? Every serious fan understands that even the greatest pitchers run out of gas. Martinez has, in particular, been a six- or seven-inning pitcher for the last two years. Twice in this postseason he has thrown 130-pitch games — well past his usual limit. In this game seven of the American League Championship Series, Martinez did everything that should have been asked of him.

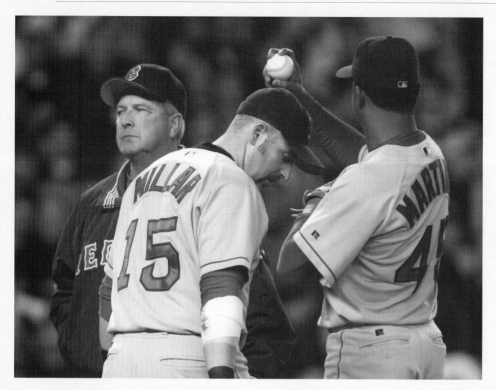

Grady Little contemplates what turned out to be his final game in a Boston uniform as he removes Pedro Martinez after the Yankees' miracle comeback to tie game seven of the 2003 American League Championship Series.

Through seven innings, he had allowed only two solo home runs to Jason Giambi. That three-run Red Sox lead — the same margin held by the Cubs in the eighth inning of their potential pennant-clinching game six — would probably have been enough if Little had used his bullpen as he has in all 173 of the Red Sox' previous games this season.

But, when the greatest stakes are on the table, managers seem to become fixated with their superstar pitchers. "I'll lose with my best," is the dugout saying. And, year after year, the managers who fall for this mantra actually do end up losing.

Perhaps Alan Embree, Mike Timlin, and Scott Williamson, none headed to the Hall of Fame, would have met the same fate as Martinez. But there is

another saying in baseball — one used by the best managers, not the worst: "Lose the right way."

Little, as much as any manager in many years, lost the wrong way. The last nine New York hitters to face Martinez had three singles, three doubles, and a home run. That's a .777 batting average and a 1.444 slugging percentage. Think maybe Pedro was losing it? Out in the bullpen were Embree, Timlin, and Williamson, who have had one of the most spectacular relief Octobers in many years. They'd allowed four hits, three walks and one run in 16 1/3 innings while striking out 24 men.

As if to substantiate the theory that Little was a true heir to the dismal Red Sox tradition of finding exotic ways to lose game sevens in October,

Embree and Timlin did, in fact, enter the game and pitch perfectly. With Posada on second base, Embree got Giambi to fly out to center field. Timlin then entered and escaped the eighth without further damage and worked a 1-2-3 ninth. Would they have pitched as well with a lead as in a tie game? Why not? The season was on the line either way.

For Yankees fans, this Red Sox defeat went far beyond glee on the Joy Meter. Every hit that Martinez allowed in that eighth inning was a blow struck on behalf of Yankees coach Don Zimmer, outfielder Garcia, and catcher Posada — the three most offended Yankees in Saturday's Fenway Fights. Those blows, the fates seemed to say to Martinez, are what you get if you throw a fastball behind Garcia's head or make a threatening bean-ball gesture toward Posada (who got the final game-tying hit off Martinez) or, in the case of Zimmer, sling an angry 72-year-old man to the ground during a bench-clearing dust-up.

Karma counts in baseball. Sammy Sosa corked his bat. Is he in the Series? Now, Martinez will watch as well.

Thomas Boswell has covered baseball and other sports for the *Washington Post* for more than three decades. An award-winning writer, his books include *How Life Imitates the World Series* and *Why Time Begins on Opening Day.*

caliber team" in the old mission statement of the Yawkey Trust. Although the letter extolled the play of guys like Johnny Damon, Derek Lowe (whom it referred to as the fan-familiar "D-Lo"), Kevin Millar, and Trot Nixon and even tossed a bon mot to Red Sox uber-fan Ben Affleck and his main squeeze Jennifer Lopez, the names of those *not* mentioned cast an ominous and unmistakable shadow.

Nomar. Manny. Pedro.

The next day the Red Sox put Ramirez on irrevocable waivers. His agent confirmed that playing for the Yankees had always been his childhood dream. The Yankees didn't claim him, though, and neither did anyone else. Now, apparently, he is going to remain with the Red Sox.

But they had to do something — there was just too much doom and gloom to smile through. And John Henry, finally in command, made it so. The last Red Sox owner with enough of his own money to play out the fantasy had gone about buying his favorite players: Tom Yawkey had bought Joe Cronin, Jimmie Foxx, and Lefty Grove. Henry, knowing that a host of contracts expire at the end of 2004, decided now was the time to shoot the works. The Sox went after Texas shortstop Alex Rodriguez and tried to dump Ramirez on the Rangers. After being rebuffed, they then went after Arizona pitcher and former farmhand Curt Schilling.

It cost only a few prospects, for this was essentially a money deal and a favor to — surprise — Milwaukee, which would quickly send slugger Richie Sexson to Arizona for one of Boston's prospects in what was essentially a three-way deal. The D-Backs finally had to pay for their excesses and didn't want the last year of Schilling's contract. After the Sox agreed to give him a two-year extension plus an option year worth about $13 million per season, tying him up until 2007, Schilling agreed to the deal. The glib right-hander, who won one game in the 2001 World Series when the Diamondbacks beat the Yankees, was smart enough to court the Boston Internet crowd in an online chat that was certain to be leaked and to say all the right things. "I like the thought of playing in the biggest rivalry in front of some incredible fans," he said. Sox followers swooned at the prospect of a Martinez-Schilling combo at the start of the rotation, and the Sox spoke with smug certainty about their chances in 2004.

All the while the manager question hung in the air, but no one cared anymore. After all, as the Grady Little experience demonstrated, in this organization the manager is way down on the organizational chart, far behind the owner, the president, the GM, about a half-dozen players, and the groundskeeper. The Red Sox made sure they hired someone compliant who promised he would reflect the philosophy of the front office and read the minds of those in charge and do things the way they want, for the reasons they hold dear — or at least someone who told them that at his interview. To this end, on December 4 they hired former A's bench coach and Philadelphia manager Terry Francona, whom Theo Epstein referred to as "a dynamic partner to the front office" with an "absolute commitment to preparation." A Schilling favorite from their time together in Philadelphia, from 1997 through 2000 Francona led the Phillies to an unremarkable 285-363 record.

"The one thing you die for is a chance to win," he said. "To have a chance to win and to be expected to win is what you coach for."

Good luck. History suggests he might need it. But be careful what you wish for, and rent, don't buy.

After the end of the season, the front office made several telling comments. Spokesperson Dr. Charles Steinberg asked reporter Howard Bryant if he thought Red Sox fans would view the 2003 season as a success. Bryant was incredulous and told Steinberg that by ending the way it ended, "it was a *disaster*."

"Fascinating," answered Steinberg.

Fascinating?

And a defensive Theo Epstein told a reporter, "They'll be wrong about this team in the history. What this team was truly will never be reflected on the paper."

Wrong, Mr. Epstein. Read on.

Wanting to win and thinking you should have is a dangerous attitude. Just because the Red Sox haven't won a World Series since 1918 doesn't mean they're entitled to now. That's a fact, not a stat. And that reality has just been drilled into the skulls of an entire new generation of Sox fans. But world championship teams don't have a manager they don't believe in or

leave that manager undermanned entering the play-offs, they don't get stuck with Tim Wakefield on the mound when the closer sits in the pen, they don't push a fading starting pitcher past the point of effectiveness, and they don't go all season without a bullpen. And they also don't draw a line between the playing field and the front office, blaming the manager for everything bad while holding themselves blameless.

The loss to the Yankees and the fallout that has already taken place and is destined to be felt over the next several seasons makes it clear that despite a long overdue and welcome change in ownership, the essential truth of this franchise remains unchanged. In most of their 100-plus seasons, the Red Sox have not been the better team.

Can the Red Sox win a world championship? Of course — if the Marlins can, then surely the Red Sox can too. Will they? Not yet, because while the names have changed and continue to change, the results so far have been all too familiar.

And that's been the case in every season since 1918 — not with Ban Johnson pulling the strings and not with Tom Yawkey as owner. And not with Cronin playing short and Denny Galehouse pitching or Jackie Robinson walking away. Not with McCarthy managing and Ted Williams pouting, not with Dick Stuart at first or the Monster on the mound, not with Tony C. rolling on the ground or Yaz playing the wall or Aparicio scrambling back to third. Not with Luis chomping cigars, Fisk waving the ball fair, or Lee throwing the eephus. Not with Zimmer pitching Sprowl or Haywood mailing contracts, Buckner playing first or Pedro throwing the change and Nomar tapping his toes. Not in 1946, 1948, 1949, 1967, 1975, 1978, 1986, 1988, 1990, 1995, 1998, and 1999.

And, most certainly, definitely, not in 2003.

Maybe next year.

The Red Sox have advantages that other teams lust after, but some significant handicaps remain. Their loyal and rabid fan base is the most resilient in the game. They have supported the Red Sox with an ardor that has evolved into blind devotion, a passion that makes others envious. And Fenway Park, beautiful, glorious Fenway, continues to be filled to capacity. They have been tested — God, how these fans have been tested — but as yet their faith has not been shaken, and they have not abandoned their allegiance. Nevertheless, as another generation of Red Sox fans absorbs their own painful loss and earlier generations add another to the list, one can't help but wonder just how much more they can take.

To win, the Red Sox must overcome more than any team in baseball — the historic expectation of loss, a feeling that filters its way down to each and every player. In recent years the Red Sox have finally shed some of the more onerous traits of their history, such as the abject racism that kept them down, so needlessly, for so long. And thankfully the notion that the

Red Sox are doomed to lose because of anything that has anything to do with either Babe Ruth or Harry Frazee is now about as stale as that loaf of Yaz bread in the freezer. But none of this has finally, truly and forever, released the club from the grip of its past, and the events of 2003 have only added to that burden.

When the Henry-Werner group purchased the team, the institutionalized failure of the Yawkey tradition finally ended. Yawkey and his failed reign is rarely recalled by the Werner-Henry group, and the club has been wise to distance itself from that era. But for that end to truly be significant, the new owners must continue to learn from the past and move in other directions, for if the end result is simply a change in the name at the top and not in approach, the legacy of that tradition may well continue. There are lessons in their errors, and the Red Sox would do well to heed them, for they face a far wiser and more sophisticated group of fans now than ever before. Now fans know when they are being lied to, or when ownership is disingenuous. The Yawkey tradition lasted as long as it did because over the years it pacified fans under kindly old myths. That won't work now — or at least not for very long.

One thing about this franchise hasn't changed, at least not in ways that really matter — Fenway Park.

Oh, they've tweaked the edges, put those wonderful seats on the wall, and taken over the streets, turning a trip to the ballpark into a squeaky clean suburban experience. But if Fenway Park ever becomes the sole focus of this franchise — as Chicago has done with Wrigley Field — then the future risks looking an awful lot like the past.

Listen, since 1992 Fenway Park has been the model upon which a generation of ballparks have been built, from Baltimore's Camden Yards to Philadelphia's new ballpark. To date there are no less than seven ersatz Fenways, with more destined to come.

And what do they have in common, apart from their nooks and crannies and cozy dimensions? *No team playing in one of them has ever won a championship* — and only the Indians have even made it as far as the World Series. But since the building of Camden Yards, every team that has won a world championship has done so in other ballparks, all of which share similar traits. In comparison, their playing fields are oversized. Arizona, Anaheim, Florida, New York, Toronto, and Atlanta have all won championships while playing in one of the larger parks, and that may be no coincidence. While Fenway Park offers the promise of always-full stands, a wonderful atmosphere, and a chance to make a profit, ample evidence has accrued since the expiration of the Dead Ball Era that, like Wrigley Field, the unique configuration of the Fenway Park playing field makes the task of winning a world championship even more difficult. If that is to change for the Red Sox, then so too may their home address eventually have to change from Yawkey Way. The franchise — and their fans — may someday have to choose a chance to win a championship over Fenway Park.

For many of the last 100 years and more, the commitment of this franchise to the goal of winning a world championship has not matched the devotion of the team's fans. The Henry-Werner group must recognize that their ultimate responsibility is to win

Former Phillies manager Terry Francona was hired to manage the Red Sox after the Yankee Stadium seventh-game debacle led to Grady Little's firing. Known as a player's manager, Francona enjoyed a strong relationship with Curt Schilling in their time together in Philadelphia.

and not just come close. At this point no season can otherwise be considered a "success," and it is futile and stupid to argue that history has somehow gotten it wrong — that was the excuse for generations and it doesn't work anymore. Their challenge will be to accomplish this goal before squandering the faith and goodwill with which they have been welcomed in Boston.

Maybe that's what the Schilling signing and a host of other moves after the 2003 season are really about. Just as Tom Yawkey always had the *ability* to outspend the Yankees but never the will, so too does John Henry. He's far richer than Steinbrenner, and he had to be galled to see his old club, the Marlins, win a world championship. He may have decided to break the bank to win now and worry later about the contractual mess it may leave behind, or else just sell out while the price is high and walk away a hero. At this point Boston fans will gladly take any kind of Faustian bargain he makes, as long as the Sox win it all.

But their patience is not inexhaustible, and this team would do well to act sooner rather than later. Curt Schilling guarantees nothing more than a chance at victory, and he's not the first savior this club has acquired — Foxx, Grove, Cronin, Junior Stephens, Ken Harrelson, Don Baylor, Pedro Martinez, and a cast of thousands have all carried that mantle before, and none have had anything to show for it. If the Red Sox have made the choice to spend their way to the top, they better not stop halfway — too many have passed without a championship in their lifetime.

And that is the one area in which the Red Sox have achieved success beyond that of any other team in the game. The Red Sox matter to their fans, not just now, or from April to October, but from October to April, all year, every year, not just in Boston and not just right now, but from the beginning of their history and into the future.

If one ever questions that, then sit down with Boston fans anywhere in the world and start talking baseball. Over more than a century, the Red Sox have always been worth talking about.

APPENDIX A
RED SOX CENTURY TEAM PRE- AND POST-WORLD WAR II

RED SOX CENTURY TEAMS

Comparing players across eras is notoriously difficult, as is selecting a team of nine players to represent the best players in Red Sox history. For that reason the authors have selected two Red Sox Century rosters to honor Sox stars of both the pre–World War II and post–World War II eras. The pre-war team honors a manager, club executive, and twenty-two players, reflecting an era before the relief pitcher was prominent and a time when major league rosters were smaller. The post-war team honors a manager, executive, and twenty-five players, the current size of the major league roster.

Years with the Red Sox and significant career statistics for those years are presented for each player through 1999.

PRE-WORLD WAR II

MANAGER Bill Carrigan (1913–1916, 1927–1929) 489-500
Managed back-to-back world champions in 1915 and 1916 and nurtured the young Babe Ruth.

EXECUTIVE Owner Joe Lannin (1913–1916)
Kept the Sox on top despite the Federal League threat.

INFIELD

1B Jimmie Foxx (1936–1942) .320, 222 HR, 788 RBI
Perhaps the greatest righthanded hitter of them all. Fifty home runs in 1938 is still a Red Sox record.

2B Bobby Doerr (1937–1944, 1946–1951) .288, 233 HR, 1247 RBI
Still the best-fielding and best-hitting second baseman in club history, Doerr is still in the top ten in most Red Sox career offensive categories.

SS Heinie Wagner (1906–1913, 1915–1916, 1918) .251, 396 runs, 141 SB
Only Wagner and Harry Hooper played for four Red Sox world champions. Also served as coach and managed the Sox in 1930.

SS Everett Scott (1914–1921) .246, 355 runs, 344 RBI
Anchored the infield of three world champions and was the best-fielding Red Sox shortstop until Johnny Pesky.

SS Joe Cronin (1935–1945) .300, 119 HR, 737 RBI
Eight-time Boston all-star and the best-hitting shortstop of his generation. Also managed the club from 1933–1947.

3B Jimmy Collins (1901–1907) .296, 448 runs, 385 RBI
Acknowledged as the greatest third baseman of his era and architect of the Sox' first championship team.

3B Larry Gardner (1908–1917) .283, 496 runs, 481 RBI
Vermont native was a steady performer for a decade.

OUTFIELD

LF Duffy Lewis (1910–1917) .289, 500 runs, 629 RBI
World Series star who played the incline in left field like it was his backyard. Hit .433 in 1915 World Series.

LF Ted Williams (1939–1942, 1946–1960) .344, 521 HR, 1798 runs, 1839 RBI
Arguably the greatest hitter who ever lived, and certainly the greatest Red Sox hitter ever.

CF Chick Stahl (1901–1907) .292, 470 runs, 339 RBI, 105 SB
Had he lived longer, he'd be in the Hall of Fame. At the time of his suicide in 1907 he was the American League career leader in most important offensive categories.

CF Tris Speaker (1907–1915) .336, 703 runs, 570 RBI, 266 SB
The best all-around player in club history, able to win with his bat, his glove, his arm, and his speed. Regularly collected thirty or more outfield assists per season.

RF Harry Hooper (1909–1920) .272, 988 runs, 497 RBI, 300 SB
With Speaker and Lewis he made up the greatest defensive outfield of the era. Hit two home runs in the 1915 World Series.

Heinie Wagner

Harry Hooper

Bobby Doerr

Joe Cronin and
Jimmie Foxx

Mel Parnell and
Ellis Kinder

RF Buck Freeman (1901–1907) .286, 82 HR, 713 RBI
This slugger held the club career home run record until
Jimmie Foxx.

CATCHERS

C Lou Criger (1901–1908) .231
A defensive specialist, in the first open balloting for the
Hall of Fame, Criger collected more votes than many
eventual enshrinees.

C Rick Ferrell (1934–1937) .302
Highest career batting average of any Red Sox catcher
and brother of Sox pitcher Wes Ferrell.

PITCHERS

RHP Cy Young (1901–1908) 192-112, 2.00 ERA,
39 shutouts, 1355 K
From 1901 through 1904 he won 119 games. In only one
season with Boston his ERA was above 2.15. And that
doesn't even begin to tell his story.

RHP Bill Dinneen (1902–1907) 85-86, 2.81 ERA,
156 CG
"Big-game" pitcher paired with Young to form the
club's best-ever pitching combo. Was 3-1 in 1903 World
Series with 2.03 ERA. Later became an umpire.

RHP Joe Wood (1908–1915) 116-56, 1.99 ERA, 986 K
Thirty-four wins in 1912 is still a club record. Even
after hurting his arm, from 1913 to 1915 he went
35-13 and led the AL with a 1.49 ERA in 1915.

RHP Carl Mays (1915–1919) 72-51, 2.21 ERA,
14 shutouts
If not for one pitch, he'd be in the Hall of Fame. From
1916 to 1918, he outpitched Ruth. Also a boyhood
coach of Johnny Pesky.

LHP Dutch Leonard (1913–1918) 90-63, 2.14 ERA,
769 K
1914 ERA of 0.96 is still the major league record. Won
every game he pitched in the World Series.

LHP Babe Ruth (1914–1919) 89-46, 2.19 ERA
The best lefty in the league from 1915 to 1917. World
Series record 3-0 with 0.87 ERA.

LHP Lefty Grove (1934–1941) 105-62, 3.06 ERA
Rebounded after poor 1934 season to lead Sox in ERA
four of the next five seasons.

POST–WORLD WAR II

MANAGER Dick Williams (1967–69) 260-217
He led the team to the most important pennant in club
history as one hundred to one odds were surmounted
to capture the "Impossible Dream" pennant of 1967.

EXECUTIVE Dick O'Connell, General Manager
(1965–1977)
He remade the Sox in the mid-sixties and signed such
players as American League MVPs Fred Lynn and Jim
Rice as well as Hall of Famer Carlton Fisk.

INFIELD

1B Mo Vaughn (1991–1998) .304, .542 slg%, 230 HR,
752 RBI
The 1995 American League MVP was the first New
England–born superstar for the Red Sox since Carlton
Fisk.

2B Jerry Remy (1978–1984) .281, 802 hits,
.978 fielding%
The Fall River native arrived in Boston at age twenty-
two after having served as captain of the California
Angels. He led American League second basemen with
double plays with 114 in 1978.

SS Johnny Pesky (1942, 1946–1952) .313, 1277 hits,
776 runs
The slick-fielding SS led the league in hits in his first
three seasons and has worked in many capacities for
the team for six decades.

SS Junior Stephens (1948–1952) .283, 122 HR,
721 hits, .492 slg%
Stephens averaged more than twenty-eight homers per
season for the Red Sox and was a key member of the
strongest teams in franchise history.

SS Nomar Garciaparra (1996–present) .323, 1231 hits,
173 HR, 669 RBI
One of three shortstops currently in the American
League (Derek Jeter and Alex Rodriguez are the others) establishing Hall of Fame credentials.

3B Frank Malzone (1955–1965) .276, 1454 hits,
131 HR, 716 RBI
The three-time winner of the Gold Glove, Malzone was
a consistent batter, hitting twenty or more doubles for
seven consecutive seasons.

3B Wade Boggs (1982–1992) .338, 2098 hits, 422 Db,
1067 runs
During his decade in Boston Boggs compiled a career
batting average second only to Ted Williams in franchise history while making himself into a Gold Glove–
caliber third baseman.

OUTFIELD

LF Ted Williams (1939–1942, 1946–1960) .344,
521 HR, 2654 hits
Regarded with Babe Ruth as the greatest hitter ever,
Williams dominated Boston sports for three decades.

LF Carl Yastrzemski (1961–1983) .285, 3419 hits, 452 HR, 1844 RBI

In his twenty-three-year career Yastrzemski captured three American League batting championships and the 1967 MVP Award while leading the team to two World Series. In fourteen World Series games he batted .352.

LF Jim Rice (1974–1989) .298, 2452 hits, 382 HR, 1451 RBI

The eight-time all-star hit twenty or more homers for eleven consecutive seasons while helping to lead Boston to World Series appearances in 1975 and 1986.

CF Dom DiMaggio (1940–1953) .298, 1680 hits, 1046 runs

The best-fielding Red Sox center fielder since Tris Speaker was also a superb hitter who invited comparisons with his brother Joe.

CF Fred Lynn (1974–1980) .308, 828 hits, 124 HR, .520 slg%

In 1975 Lynn was the first player to ever capture MVP and Rookie of the Year honors in the same season.

RF Dwight Evans (1972–1990) .272, 2373 hits, 379 HR, 1435 runs

A superb fielder with a rifle arm, Evans was the master of the toughest sun field in Major League Baseball for nearly twenty seasons.

RF Tony Conigliaro (1964–1970, 1975) .267, 162 HR, .488 slg%

Boston-born Conigliaro was the second-youngest player after Mel Ott to reach the 100 homer plateau in a star-crossed career that saw him suffer a near-fatal beaning in 1967.

CATCHERS

C Carlton Fisk (1969, 1971–1980) .284, 162 HR, .481 slg%

New Hampshire native Fisk first made his mark as a unanimous selection as Rookie of the Year in 1972. He later hit one of baseball's most memorable homers to win game six of the 1975 World Series.

C Rich Gedman (1980–1990) .255, 741 hits, 83 HR, 356 RBI

Worcester, Massachusetts, native Gedman assumed the tough role of replacing Carlton Fisk while helping lead Boston to the 1986 World Series. In eleven league championship series games Gedman batted a solid .357.

PITCHERS

LHP Mel Parnell (1947–1956) 123-75, 113 CG, 20 shutouts

The best lefthanded pitcher in Red Sox history amassed a stellar 71-30 record at Fenway Park. In 1949 he was 25-7 with a 2.77 ERA and on July 14, 1956, he pitched a no-hitter against the White Sox.

RHP Jim Lonborg (1965–1971) 68-65, 3.94 ERA, 784 K

In 1967 Lonborg became the first Red Sox pitcher to win the Cy Young Award as he led the team to the pennant with a record of 22-9 and a league-leading 246 strikeouts.

LHP Bill Lee (1969–1978) 94-68, 3.64 ERA, 321 games

During the seventies the outspoken lefty won seventeen games in three straight seasons (1973–75) while mastering the New York Yankees.

RHP Luis Tiant (1971–1978) 122-81, 3.36 ERA, 1075 strikeouts

Tiant enjoyed a career revival in Boston during which time he won twenty or more games in three seasons. In 1975 he helped lead the team to the World Series in which he won two games against the Reds.

RHP Roger Clemens (1984–1996) 192-111, 3.06 ERA, 2590 strikeouts

Not only did Roger Clemens win three Cy Young Awards while with Boston but he also set and then tied a major league record of twenty strikeouts in one game in 1986 and 1996.

RHP Pedro Martinez (1997–present) 84-27, 2.26 ERA, 1456 strikeouts

Acquired from Montreal in November 1997 Pedro Martinez has electrified Boston with two spectacular seasons in which he led his team to wild-card titles. In 1999 he won the Cy Young Award while becoming the first Red Sox pitcher since Cy Young to lead the league in wins, ERA, and strikeouts.

RELIEVERS

RHP Ellis Kinder (1948–1955) 86-52 (39 victories in relief), 3.28 ERA, 91 saves

The colorful righty was as durable as he was versatile, winning twenty-three games in 1949 while twice leading the league in saves during his eight seasons with the Red Sox.

RHP Dick Radatz (1962–1966) 49-34, 2.65 ERA, 104 saves

In four of his five seasons with Boston Dick Radatz was the best reliever in baseball. He twice led the American League in saves and relief victories.

RHP Bob Stanley (1977–1989) 115-97, 1707 inn, 637 games, 132 saves

The versatile Stanley was at different stages of his career a spot starter and long relief specialist who sometimes was called upon as a closer. His 637 games are the career record for Red Sox pitchers.

Jim Rice

Tony Conigliaro

Carlton Fisk

APPENDIX B
THE RED SOX RECORD

YEAR	RECORD		GA/GB	WINNER	MANAGER	OWNER
1901	79-57	(2)	-4	Chi	Collins	Somers
1902	77-60	(3)	-6.5	Phil	Collins	Somers
1903	**91-47**	**(1)**	**+14.5**	**Bos**	**Collins**	**Killilea**
1904*	95-59	(1)	+1.5	Bos	Collins	Taylor
1905	78-74	(4)	-16	Phil	Collins	Taylor
1906	49-105	(8)	-45.5	Chi	Collins (136) C. Stahl (18)	Taylor
1907	59-90	(7)	-32.5	Det	Young (7) Huff (8) Unglaub (28) McGuire (106)	Taylor
1908	75-79	(5)	-15.5	Det	McGuire (115) Lake (39)	Taylor
1909	88-63	(3)	-9.5	Det	Lake	Taylor
1910	81-72	(4)	-22.5	Phil	Donovan	Taylor
1911	78-75	(5)	-24	Phil	Donovan	Taylor
1912	**105-47**	**(1)**	**+14**	**Bos**	**J. Stahl**	**McAleer**
1913	79-71	(4)	-15.5	Phil	J. Stahl (80) Carrigan (70)	McAleer
1914	91-62	(2)	-8.5	Phil	Carrigan	Lannin
1915	**101-50**	**(1)**	**+2.5**	**Bos**	**Carrigan**	**Lannin**
1916	**91-63**	**(1)**	**+2**	**Bos**	**Carrigan**	**Lannin**
1917	90-62	(2)	-9	Chi	Barry	Frazee
1918	**75-51**	**(1)**	**+2.5**	**Bos**	**Barrow**	**Frazee**
1919	66-71	(6)	-20.5	Chi	Barrow	Frazee
1920	72-81	(5)	-25.5	Cleve	Barrow	Frazee
1921	75-79	(5)	-23.5	NY	Duffy	Frazee
1922	61-93	(8)	-50	NY	Duffy	Frazee
1923	61-91	(8)	-37	NY	Chance	Frazee Quinn
1924	67-87	(7)	-25	Wash	Fohl	Quinn

Note: Bold denotes won World Series. Asterisk (*) denotes won pennant and division title, (**) denotes wild card champion. From 1969 onward place standings and winner refers to American League Eastern Division.

YEAR	RECORD		GA/GB	WINNER	MANAGER	OWNER
1925	47-105	(8)	-49.5	Wash	Fohl	Quinn
1926	46-107	(8)	-44.5	NY	Fohl	Quinn
1927	51-103	(8)	-59	NY	Carrigan	Quinn
1928	57-96	(8)	-43.5	NY	Carrigan	Quinn
1929	58-96	(8)	-48	Phil	Carrigan	Quinn
1930	52-102	(8)	-50	Phil	Wagner	Quinn
1931	62-90	(6)	-45	Phil	S. Collins	Quinn
1932	43-111	(8)	-64	NY	S. Collins (57) McManus (97)	Quinn
1933	63-86	(7)	-34.5	Wash	McManus	T. Yawkey
1934	76-76	(4)	-24	Det	Harris	T. Yawkey
1935	78-75	(4)	-16	Det	Cronin	T. Yawkey
1936	74-80	(6)	-28.5	NY	Cronin	T. Yawkey
1937	80-72	(5)	-21	NY	Cronin	T. Yawkey
1938	88-61	(2)	-9.5	NY	Cronin	T. Yawkey
1939	89-62	(2)	-17	NY	Cronin	T. Yawkey
1940	82-72	(4)	-8	Det	Cronin	T. Yawkey
1941	84-70	(2)	-17	NY	Cronin	T. Yawkey
1942	93-59	(2)	-9	NY	Cronin	T. Yawkey
1943	68-84	(7)	-29	NY	Cronin	T. Yawkey
1944	77-77	(4)	-12	St. L	Cronin	T. Yawkey
1945	71-83	(7)	-17.5	Det	Cronin	T. Yawkey
1946	104-50	(1)	+12	Bos	Cronin	T. Yawkey
1947	83-71	(3)	-14	NY	Cronin	T. Yawkey
1948	96-59	(2)	-1	Cleve	McCarthy	T. Yawkey
1949	96-58	(2)	-1	NY	McCarthy	T. Yawkey
1950	94-60	(3)	-4	NY	McCarthy (62) O'Neill (92)	T. Yawkey
1951	87-67	(3)	-11	NY	O'Neill	T. Yawkey
1952	76-78	(6)	-19	NY	Boudreau	T. Yawkey
1953	84-69	(4)	-16	NY	Boudreau	T. Yawkey
1954	69-85	(4)	-42	Cleve	Boudreau	T. Yawkey
1955	84-70	(4)	-12	NY	Higgins	T. Yawkey
1956	84-70	(4)	-13	NY	Higgins	T. Yawkey
1957	82-72	(3)	-16	NY	Higgins	T. Yawkey
1958	79-75	(3)	-13	NY	Higgins	T. Yawkey

YEAR	RECORD		GA/GB	WINNER	MANAGER	OWNER
1959	75-79	(5)	-19	Chi	Higgins (72) York (1) Jurges (80)	T. Yawkey
1960	65-89	(7)	-32	NY	Jurges (81) Higgins (73)	T. Yawkey
1961	76-86	(6)	-33	NY	Higgins	T. Yawkey
1962	76-84	(8)	-19	NY	Higgins	T. Yawkey
1963	76-85	(7)	-28	NY	Pesky	T. Yawkey
1964	72-90	(8)	-27	NY	Pesky (160) Herman (2)	T. Yawkey
1965	62-100	(9)	-40	Minn	Herman	T. Yawkey
1966	72-90	(9)	-26	Balt	Herman (141) Runnels (16)	T. Yawkey
1967	92-70	(1)	+1	Bos	Williams	T. Yawkey
1968	86-76	(4)	-17	Det	Williams	T. Yawkey
1969	87-75	(3)	-22	Balt	Williams (153) Popowski (9)	T. Yawkey
1970	87-75	(3)	-21	Balt	Kasko	T. Yawkey
1971	85-77	(3)	-18	Balt	Kasko	T. Yawkey
1972	85-70	(2)	-0.5	Det	Kasko	T. Yawkey
1973	89-73	(2)	-8	Balt	Kasko	T. Yawkey
1974	84-78	(3)	-7	Balt	Johnson	T. Yawkey
1975	95-65*	(1)	+4.5	Bos	Johnson	T. Yawkey
1976	83-79	(3)	-15.5	NY	Johnson (85) Zimmer (76)	J. Yawkey
1977	97-64	(3)	-2.5	NY	Zimmer	J. Yawkey
1978	99-64	(2)	-1	NY	Zimmer	JRY Corp.
1979	91-69	(3)	-11.5	Balt	Zimmer	JRY Corp.
1980	83-77	(4)	-19	NY	Zimmer (155) Pesky (5)	JRY Corp.
1981	30-26 29-23	(5) (2)	-4 -1.5	NY Mil	Houk	Yawkey Trust/Sullivan/LeRoux
1982	89-73	(3)	-6	Mil	Houk	Yawkey Trust/Sullivan/LeRoux
1983	78-84	(6)	-20	Balt	Houk	Yawkey Trust/Sullivan/LeRoux
1984	86-76	(4)	-18	Det	Houk	Yawkey Trust/Sullivan/LeRoux
1985	81-81	(5)	-18.5	Tor	McNamara	Yawkey Trust/Sullivan/LeRoux
1986	95-66*	(1)	+5.5	Bos	McNamara	Yawkey Trust/Sullivan/LeRoux
1987	78-84	(5)	-20	Det	McNamara	Yawkey Trust/Sullivan
1988	89-73	(1)	+1	Bos	McNamara (85) Morgan (77)	Yawkey Trust/Sullivan

YEAR	RECORD		GA/GB	WINNER	MANAGER	OWNER
1989	83-79	(3)	-6	Tor	Morgan	Yawkey Trust/Sullivan
1990	88-74	(1)	+2	Tor	Morgan	Yawkey Trust/Sullivan
1991	84-78	(2)	-7	Tor	Morgan	Yawkey Trust/Sullivan
1992	73-89	(7)	-23	Tor	Hobson	Yawkey Trust/Sullivan
1993	80-82	(5)	-15	Tor	Hobson	Yawkey Trust/Sullivan
1994	54-61	(4)	-17	NY	Hobson	Yawkey Trust
1995	86-56	(1)	+7	Bos	Kennedy	Yawkey Trust
1996	85-77	(3)	-7	NY	Kennedy	Yawkey Trust
1997	78-84	(4)	-20	Balt	Williams	Yawkey Trust
1998	92-70	(2)**	-22	NY	Williams	Yawkey Trust
1999	94-68	(2)**	-4	NY	Williams	Yawkey Trust
2000	85-77	(2)	-2.5	NY	Williams	Yawkey Trust
2001	82-79	(2)	-13.5	NY	Williams/Kerrigan	Yawkey Trust
2002	93-69	(2)	-10.5	NY	Little	Henry-Werner Group
2003	95-67	(2)**	-6	NY	Little	Henry-Werner Group

MOST VALUABLE PLAYERS

YEAR	PLAYER	AVG.	HR	RBIs
1912	Tris Speaker	.383	10	98
1938	Jimmie Foxx	.349	50	175
1946	Ted Williams	.342	38	123
1949	Ted Williams	.343	43	159
1958	Jackie Jensen	.286	35	122
1967	Carl Yastrzemski	.326	44	121
1975	Fred Lynn	.331	21	105
1978	Jim Rice	.315	46	139
1995	Mo Vaughn	.300	39	126
		W-L	ERA	
1986	Roger Clemens	24-4	2.48	

TRIPLE CROWN WINNERS

YEAR	PLAYER	AVG.	HR	RBIs
1942	Ted Williams	.356	36	137
1947	Ted Williams	.343	32	114
1967	Carl Yastrzemski	.326	44	121

CY YOUNG AWARD WINNERS

YEAR	PLAYER	W	L	ERA	K
1967	Jim Lonborg	22	9	3.16	246
1986	Roger Clemens	24	4	2.48	238
1987	Roger Clemens	20	9	2.97	256
1991	Roger Clemens	18	10	2.62	241
1999	Pedro Martinez	23	4	2.07	313
2000	Pedro Martinez	18	6	1.74	284

ROOKIES OF THE YEAR

YEAR	PLAYER	POSITION
1950	Walt Dropo	First base
1961	Don Schwall	Pitcher
1972	Carlton Fisk	Catcher
1975	Fred Lynn	Outfielder
1997	Nomar Garciaparra	Shortstop

SELECTED BIBLIOGRAPHY

BOOKS

Alexander, Charles. *John McGraw*. New York: Viking Press, 1988.

———. *Our Game: An American Baseball History*. New York: MJF Books, 1991.

Allen, Lee, and Tom Meany. *Kings of the Diamond*. New York: Putnam, 1965.

Angell, Roger. *Season Ticket*. Boston: Houghton Mifflin, 1988.

Asinof, Eliot. *Eight Men Out*. New York: Holt, Rinehart and Winston, 1963.

Atkinson, Brooks. *Broadway*. New York: Macmillan, 1970.

Barrow, Ed. *My 50 Years in Baseball*. New York: Coward and McCann, 1951.

Berry, Henry, and Harold Berry. *The Boston Red Sox: The Complete Record of Red Sox Baseball*. New York: Macmillan, 1984.

The Boston Red Sox. *Official Media Guides*, various editions.

———. *Official Scorebook Magazine*, various editions.

———. *Official Yearbook*, various editions.

Brown, Warren. *The Chicago White Sox*. New York: G.P. Putnam's Sons, 1952.

Cataneo, David. *Tony C.* Nashville, Tennessee: Rutledge Hill Press, 1997.

Christopher, Matt. *At the Plate with . . . Mo Vaughn*. Boston: Little, Brown, 1997.

Clemens, Roger, and Peter Gammons. *Rocket Man*. Lexington, Massachusetts: Stephen Greene Press, 1987.

Coleman, Ken, and Dan Valenti. *The Impossible Dream Remembered*. Lexington, Massachusetts: Stephen Greene Press, 1987.

Creamer, Robert. *Babe: The Legend Comes to Life*. New York: Simon and Schuster, 1974.

Crehen, Herbert F., and James W. Ryan. *Lightning in a Bottle, The Sox of '67*. Boston: Branden Publishing Company, 1992.

Engel, Lehman. *American Musical Theater*. New York: Collier Books, 1967.

Ewen, David. *A Journey to Greatness*. New York: Henry Holt, 1956.

Fischler, Stan, and Richard Friedman. *The Comeback Yankees*. New York: Grosset & Dunlap, 1979.

Fitzgerald, Ed, editor. *The American League*. New York: A. S. Barnes, 1955.

Gammons, Peter. *Beyond the Sixth Game*. Boston: Houghton Mifflin, 1985.

Gilbert, Bil. *They Also Served*. New York: Crown Publishers, 1992.

Ginsburg, Daniel E. *The Fix Is In: A History of Baseball Gambling and Game Fixing Scandals*. Jefferson, North Carolina: McFarland Publishing, 1995.

Goldstein, Richard. *Spartan Seasons*. New York: Macmillan, 1980.

Golenbock, Peter. *Fenway*. New York: G.P. Putnam's Sons, 1992.

Green, Stanley. *The World of Musical Comedy*. New York: 1962.

Halberstam, David. *Summer of '49*. New York: William Morrow and Company, 1989.

Helyar, John. *Lords of the Realm*. New York: Ballantine Books, 1994.

Hirshberg, Al. *The Red Sox, the Bean and the Cod*. Boston: Waverley House, 1947.

———. *What's the Matter with the Red Sox?* Cornwall, New York: Dodd, Mead and Co., 1973.

Holtzman, Jerome. *The Commissioners*. New York: Total Sports, 1998.

Johnson, Dick, editor, text by Glenn Stout. *Ted Williams: A Portrait in Words and Pictures*. New York: Walker and Company, 1991.

Kaese, Harold. *The Boston Braves*. New York: G.P. Putnam and Sons, 1948.

Keene, Kerry et al. *The Babe in Red Stockings*. Champaign, Illinois: Sagamore Publishing, 1997.

Kountze, Mabrey "Doc." *50 Sports Years Along Memory Lane*. Medford, Massachusetts: Mystic Valley Press, 1979.

Lee, William F., and Dick Lally. *The Wrong Stuff*. New York: Viking Press, 1984.

Lieb, Frederick. *The Boston Red Sox*. New York: G.P. Putnam and Sons, 1947.

———. *Connie Mack: Grand Old Man of Baseball*. New York: G.P. Putnam and Sons, 1945.

———. *The Detroit Tigers*. New York: G.P. Putnam and Sons, 1946.

———. *The Philadelphia Phillies*. G.P. Putnam and Sons, 1953.

Linn, Ed. *The Great Rivalry*. New York: Ticknor & Fields, 1992.

Lowry, Philip. *Green Cathedrals*. Reading, Massachusetts: Addison Wesley, 1992.

Mack, Connie. *My 66 Years in the Big Leagues*. Philadelphia: John C. Winston, 1950.

McGarigle, Bob. *The Story of Carl Mays, Submarine Pitcher*. Jericho, New York: Exposition Press, 1972.

Meany, Tom. *The Yankee Story*. New York: E.P. Dutton, 1960.

Miller, Jeff. *Down to the Wire*. Dallas: Taylor Publishing Company, 1992.

Murdock, Eugene. *Ban Johnson: Czar of Baseball*. Westport, Connecticut: Greenwood Press, 1982.

Neft, David S., and Richard Cohen. *The Sports Encyclopedia: Baseball*. 1997 edition. New York: St. Martin's Press, 1997.

A. J. Reach and Company. *The Reach Official American League Baseball Guide*. Philadelphia: A. J. Reach Company, 1902, 1904.

Reynolds, Bill. *Lost Summer: The '67 Red Sox and the Impossible Dream*. New York: Warner Books, 1997.

Ritter, Lawrence. *The Glory of Their Times*. New York: Macmillan, 1984.

Seymour, Harold. *Baseball: The Early Years*. New York: Oxford University Press, 1960.

———. *Baseball: The Golden Years*. New York: Oxford University Press, 1971.

Shaughnessy, Dan. *The Curse of the Bambino*. New York: Dutton, 1990.

———. *One Strike Away*. New York: Beaufort Books, 1987.

Smelser, Martin. *The Life That Ruth Built*. New York: Quadrangle/New York Times Books, 1975.

Sowell, Mike. *One Pitch Away*. New York: Macmillan, 1995.

The Sporting News. *Daguerrotypes*. St.

Louis, Missouri: The Sporting News, 1968.

———. *The Sporting News Official Baseball Guides*, various editions.

———. *The Sporting News Official Baseball Register*, various editions.

Stark, Benton. *The Year They Called Off the World Series*. New York: Avery Books, 1991.

Story, Ronald, editor. *Sports in Massachusetts: Historical Essays*. Westfield, Massachusetts: Westfield State College Institute for Massachusetts Studies, 1992.

Stout, Glenn, and Dick Johnson, editors. *Jackie Robinson: Between the Baselines*. San Francisco: Woodford, 1997.

———. *Joe DiMaggio: An Illustrated Life*. New York: Walker and Company, 1995.

Stump, Al. *Cobb*. Chapel Hill, North Carolina: Algonquin Books, 1994.

Thorn, John, and Pete Palmer, editors. *Total Baseball*, various editions.

Tuohey, George. *Boston Base Ball Club 1871–1897*. Boston: Miller Press, 1897.

Tygiel, Jules. *Baseball's Great Experiment*. New York: Oxford University Press, 1983.

Voigt, David Q. *American Baseball Volumes I, II and III*. Norman: University of Oklahoma Press, 1983.

Walton, Ed. *Red Sox Triumphs and Tragedies*. New York: Stein and Day, 1980.

Williams, Dick, and Bill Plaschke. *No More Mr. Nice Guy*. New York: Harcourt, Brace and Jovanovich, 1990.

Williams, Ted, and John Underwood. *My Turn at Bat*. New York: Simon and Schuster, 1969.

Yastrzemski, Carl, with Gerald Eskenazi. *Yaz: Baseball, the Wall and Me*. New York: Doubleday, 1990.

Yastrzemski, Carl, and Al Hirshberg. *Yaz*. New York: Viking Press, 1968.

Zingg, Paul. *Harry Hooper, An American Baseball Life*. Urbana: University of Illinois Press, 1993.

SERIALS

Baseball Magazine
Boston Baseball
Buffalo Head Society: A Red Sox Journal
Diehard
The Fan
Sox Fan News

The Sporting News
— various years for all

NEWSPAPERS

The Boston American
The Boston Daily Record
The Boston Globe
The Boston Herald
The Boston Herald American
The Boston Morning Journal
The Boston Post
The Boston Record American
The Boston Times
The Boston Transcript
The Boston Traveller
The New York Herald-Tribune
The New York Times
— various years for all

SELECTED ARTICLES BY THE AUTHORS

"1918 Sidebars," by Glenn Stout. *The Official 1993 Red Sox Yearbook*.

"The 1903 World Series," by Glenn Stout. *1993 Red Sox Official Scorebook Magazine*.

"The Ayes Had It," by Dick Johnson. *The Official 1997 Red Sox Yearbook*.

"Birth of a Legend: Babe Ruth as a Red Sox Rookie," by Dick Johnson. *1994 Red Sox Official Scorebook Magazine*.

"Bye-Bye Ballgame," by Glenn Stout. *SportBoston*, April 1990.

"The Case of the 1947 MVP Ballot," by Glenn Stout. *The Sporting News*, December 20, 1993.

"Casey and the Bat," by Glenn Stout. *Sox Fan News*, September 1986.

"The Crazy Eights," by Glenn Stout. *The Official 1988 Red Sox Yearbook*.

"Diamonds Aren't Forever," by Glenn Stout. *Boston Magazine*, September 1986.

"Doc's Cause: Curing Baseball of Bigotry," by Glenn Stout. *The Middlesex News*, July 28, 1987.

"A Farewell to Arms," by Glenn Stout. *The Boston Globe FOCUS*, August 20, 1989.

"Forever Fenway," by Glenn Stout. *The Official 1987 Red Sox Yearbook*.

"The Grand Exalted Ruler of Rooters' Row," by Glenn Stout. *Sox Fan News*, August 1986.

"The Last Champions," by Glenn Stout. *New England Sport*, July 1993.

"The Manager's Endgame," by Glenn Stout. *Boston Magazine*, May 1986.

"Pitching Puzzle," by Glenn Stout. *Boston Magazine*, October 1989.

"Royal Rooter," by Glenn Stout. *Boston Herald Sunday People*, October 3, 1993.

"Summer of Love," by Glenn Stout. *SportBoston*, May 1990.

"The Wall," by Dick Johnson. *1999 All-Star Game Official Program*.

"The World Champion 1916 Red Sox: Bill, Babe and Back-to-Back Champs," by Dick Johnson. *1996 Red Sox Official Scorebook Magazine*.

"World Championship Album, 1915 Red Sox," by Dick Johnson. *1990 Red Sox Official Scorebook Magazine*.

"Yaz Looks Back: A Conversation," by Glenn Stout. *The Fan*, November 1987.

SPECIAL COLLECTIONS

The Boston Tradition in Sports Collection: The Harold Kaese Collection. Boston Public Library.

The Michael T. "Nuf 'Ced" McGreevey Photographic Collection. Print Department, Boston Public Library.

The Sports Museum of New England: Bill Carrigan Archives.

The Sports Museum of New England: Dick Thompson Photographic Archive.

The Sports Museum of New England: Vera Vaughn Memorial Archive.

ON-LINE RESOURCES

Bosbaseball.com
RedSox.com

INDEX

ILLUSTRATION CREDITS

Michael Andersen: 47, 49, 58, 121, 128, 183, 191, 199, 205, 219, 225, 357, 358

Associated Press: 135, 141, 271, 295, 296, 362

Baseball Antiquities: ii left, 85, 94, 102, 105, 109, 111

Boston Globe/Frank O'Brien: 352

Boston Herald: iv left, iv right, v left, xviii bottom left, 20, 173, 181, 186, 195, 201, 202, 206, 243, 248, 252, 265, 266, 290, 303, 308, 313, 315, 316-317, 319, 320, 322, 323, 327, 333, 336, 337, 338, 344, 345, 346, 347, 351, 370, 373, 375, 378, 382, 383, 384, 390, 394, 397, 400, 406, 411, 413, 414, 417, 419, 421, 422, 426, 429, 430, 433, 435, 437, 438, 443, 445, 446, 448, 449, 451, 452, 455, 456, 458, 459, 461, 463, 465, 467, 468

Courtesy of the Print Department, Boston Public Library: 81, 119, 161, 171, 216, 234, 280

Courtesy of the Print Department, McGreevey Collection, Boston Public Library: 1, 2, 5, 7, 9, 12, 15, 16, 18, 19, 21, 23, 24, 27, 28, 35, 36, 39, 41, 42, 45, 46, 53, 55, 57, 63, 65, 68, 71, 76

Boston Red Sox: 335, 341, 342

The Brearley Collection of Rare Negatives: vi-vii, 212, 223, 228, 231, 232, 237, 277, 291, 293

Joe Hickey: 399 top

The Brian Interland Collection: 215, 227, 278

Richard A. Johnson Collection: xvi top, 31, 368, 386, 389, 398-399, 445

Richard A. Johnson/photograph by Richard A. Johnson: 401, 405, 407

National Baseball Hall of Fame: ii second from left, ii third from left, xviii top, 17, 50, 59, 62, 69, 73, 74, 83, 101, 124, 131, 145, 148, 153, 162, 177, 185, 193, 196, 226, 268, 445 bottom

Greg Rahal: 410

The Sports Museum of New England: endpapers, ii right, iii left, iii middle, iii right, iv middle, v right, viii, x (both), xi, xii, xiii, xiv-xv, xvi bottom, xvii, xviii bottom middle, xviii bottom right, xix (all), 61, 66, 77 top, 77 bottom, 78, 86, 89, 91, 93, 97, 98, 104, 107, 113, 114, 127, 133, 136, 157, 161, 163, 168, 169, 170, 174, 187, 188, 189, 190, 192, 198, 204, 209, 211, 217, 218, 220, 221, 229, 238, 240, 245, 246, 251, 256, 259, 263, 269, 273, 274, 279, 281, 282, 283, 284, 287, 289, 300, 305, 310, 325, 328, 339, 353, 354, 365, 367, 381, 387, 409, 446 (all), 447 (all), 453